RENAISSANCE LETTERS

Revelations of a World Reborn

The publication of this work has been aided by a grant
from the Andrew W. Mellon Foundation

Other Books on Renaissance and Mediaeval Subjects by
R. J. Clements:

Critical Theory and Practice of the Pléiade (Cambridge, Harvard Press, 1942; New York, Octagon Books, 1970)

Platonism in French Renaissance Literature, with Robert Valentine Merrill (New York, N. Y. U. Press, 1957)

The Peregrine Muse: Studies in Comparative Renaissance Literature (Chapel Hill, University of North Carolina Press, 1959)

Picta Poesis: Humanistic and Literary Theory in Renaissance Emblem Books (Rome, Edizioni di Storia e Letteratura, 1960)

Michelangelo's Theory of Art (Zurich, Buehler Buchdruck, 1961; New York, N. Y. U. Press, 1961; London Routledge and Kegan Paul, 1962; New York, Gramercy Press, 1963)

La teorica di Michelangelo (Milan, Alberto Mondadori, 1964)

Michelangelo scultore, co-author (Rome, Curcio, 1963)

Michelangelo: A Self-Portrait (New York, Prentice Hall, 1963; New York, N. Y. U. Press, 1968)

The Poetry of Michelangelo (New York, N. Y. U. Press, 1965; London, Peter Owen, 1966; Italian edition forthcoming with Alberto Mondadori, Milan)

American Critical Essays on the Divine Comedy, editor-author (New York, N. Y. U. Press, 1967; London, University of London Press, 1967)

RENAISSANCE LETTERS

Revelations of a World Reborn

Edited with Introductions,
Commentary and Translation by

Robert J. Clements
New York University
and
Lorna Levant
The Juilliard School

NEW YORK UNIVERSITY PRESS

Copyright © 1976 by New York University
Library of Congress Catalog Card Number: 75-21806

ISBN: 0-8147-1362-9 (cloth)
0-8147-1363-7 (paperback)

Library of Congress Cataloging in Publication Data
Main entry under title:

Renaissance letters.

Includes index.
1. Renaissance—Sources.   I. Clements, Robert
John, 1912-   II.   Levant, Lorna.
CB361.G74   940.2′1   75-21806
ISBN 0-8147-1362-9
ISBN 0-8147-1363-7 pbk.

Manufactured in the United States of America

In Memoriam
Oscar Levant

PREFACE

To edit an anthology of Renaissance correspondence, some letters from our own century became necessary. For assurance that we were not overlooking conspicuously significant letters, we addressed ourselves to specialists in various national literatures of the Renaissance. Several important items thus came to light, and we express gratitude to Professors Richard Fabrizio (Pace College), Joseph Gibaldi (University of Georgia), Richard Harrier (New York University), Fred Nichols (City University of New York), Abraham Keller (University of Washington), Isidore Silver (Washington University), and Terence Spencer (University of Birmingham). For a modest grant toward preparation of the bookscript we thank the New York University Graduate Council on Research. A grant-in-aid from the Rockefeller Foundation guaranteed publication of this volume.

Cross-references among letters in this anthology are common. Such *renvois* reveal the unity of opinion and interest in the Renaissance. They remind the reader that certain well-known figures are more fully represented. They serve to fill in details and enrich the background as notable events or dramas evolve: the heightening rivalry and enmity of Elizabeth Regina and Mary, Queen of Scots; the increasing pressures turned upon Galileo and even Copernicus; the slow, frightening *Drang nach Westen* of the Turkish armies and navy, and many others.

We decided to be sparing of footnotes except for items not conveniently identified in dictionaries or common reference books, and referred much exegetical material to the Chapter Introductions. Letters have been dated as specifically as possible. Birth and death dates of almost all correspondents are included with their first appearance in any given chapter. In the few cases where these dates have been impossible to establish, as with the unfortunate Mr. Pery in the Inquisitional prison of Seville, the date of the letter itself will place the writer more or less within his generation. Letters are presented chronologically within chapters.

In view of the addiction of the letter-writers of Humanism to Latin quotations, often thoughtfully summarized or paraphrased, we have only rarely supplied Englishings. Where we have chosen to include a translation with extremely useful footnotes, those notes of the translator have sometimes been retained. Some notes from definitive editions have also been reprinted. Translations undertaken by ourselves are initialed.

After culling through thousands of informative and appealing Renaissance letters, the editors optimistically prepared a corpus of over 600, every one of which seemed indispensable for our purposes. The ten chapter-introductions utilized and distilled the contents of these 600 texts, acknowledging their constant presence by many cross-references. After editors had given us a more prudent appraisal of the desirable and adequate length for such an anthology, the volume was reduced to its present economy of size. The contents of the excised letters still inform the general introduction and chapter-introductions, without tell-tale cross-references, enriching and broadening these summaries.

R. J. C.
L. L.

INTRODUCTION

The Renaissance Epistle

The men and women of the Renaissance, busy as they were in every endeavor, were a communicative lot. Whenever they could get together, they exchanged their ideas in courts, salons, cénacles, homes, taverns, and the newly-founded academies. Like the talkative Greeks of Plato's symposium, they could, as one observes from Castiglione's *procès-verbal*, *The Book of the Courtier*, converse until daybreak. They bought manuals like Guazzo's handbook of "civil conversation," found that they really did not need them, and the tide of interpersonal communication, as speech professors call it, continued unabated.

When they could not get together, however, they availed themselves of the personal letter. The mails were slowly becoming dependable again, as they had been in Ancient Rome. Taking into account the uncertainties and varieties of postal transmittal, the total of Renaissance letters which have come down to us is a staggering one. In the Middle Ages the courts, guilds, and universities had maintained makeshift postal services. Mail charges had been collected from either mailer or addressee. For roughly two centuries, the span encompassed by the present anthology, the services sponsored by the European governments became increasingly more satisfactory. There was even a regular postal service (via Calais) between England and the Continent, mentioned in Letter X-8. The "pony" express or relay was the usual carrier. International mail services were maintained by bankers (the Fuggers, Medici, Bardi, for example) and merchants, until ordered curtailed in the seventeenth century. Just as governments kept an eye on what was being published, so did they keep a power of surveillance on what was being mailed, especially the exchange of letters between Catholic and Reformational areas. Without post office departments until the mid-nineteenth century, governments encouraged, subsidized, controlled, and took revenue from the postal routes. When the service deteriorated, as we learn in Sir Bryan Tuke's letter to Lord Cromwell (1533), the King ordered the situation corrected—or else. It must be admitted, however, that despite the many complaints about the dangers and inefficiency of travel, complaints about the mail service are rare in the letters to follow.

Apparently the *cacoethes scribendi* mocked by Juvenal was a characteristic of the Revival of Antiquity. Erasmists have traced 2500 letters from the Dutch Humanist to friends and correspondents all over Europe, along with the many answers received. Erasmus usually wrote in the international language of Latin, the vehicle of the replies from Thomas More, Rabelais, Ulrich von Hutten, and others. Latin was by no means an exclusivity of the Humanists and Churchmen, however, and when Ferdinand of Austria spread to the West the news that the Turks had annihilated the army of Hungary and continued unimpeded marching up the Danube Valley, his letters were in Latin (VII-6). Aretino, the most communicative of all, left 3300 letters—the best known, unfortunately, being those intended to cajole, bribe, threaten, or blackmail. Most of the letters chosen for this volume are the ingratiating ones intended to entertain or instruct. Michelangelo, target of several of Aretino's letters (see III-13), stole time from his burdened schedule to pen 495 known letters to patrons, friends, family, and assistants. These, with the corresponding *carteggio* of answers, constitute an accurate week-by-week record of his life and art until his final, eighty-eighth year. Emperors, kings, and queens were always writing or dictating letters, each one a footnote to history. This latter remark need not apply to the many love letters of Henri IV and his retinue of mistresses (IX-20), usually ending with the Catullian thousand kisses. Churchmen found ample time to write. Fray Antonio de Guevara (*passim*), with his pithy personal letters rich in quotations from Greek, Latin, and patristic authorities, was actually inventing the literary form—perhaps we are the first to posit this thesis—which Montaigne was to practise under the title of "essay." Saint Teresa of Avila (V-21) busily promoted her new order of barefoot nuns through 437 letters (Aguilar edition) to king and adolescent novitiate alike.

Of the great Renaissance figures, only Shakespeare, born the year Michelangelo died, denied posterity a single personal letter, leaving only dedicatory missives like the one to the Earl of Southampton on presentation of his *Venus and Adonis* (II-10). Nor do we have letters to Shakespeare, except the one in which Richard Quiney of Stratford duns him for money (X-20).

Just as manuals of conversation were inevitable in a Renaissance committed to many-sided didacticism, so also were manuals on letter-writing, or *segretari*, of which twenty had appeared in Italy by 1600. Typical is Angell Day's derivative *The English Secretorie* (London, 1599), bogged down in its stilted rhetorical tradition. Day teaches that a successful letter should contain a variety of standard rhetorical devices (emphasis, suasion, etc.) and fills his manual with sample letters invented for every kind of occasion, including consolation to a friend for the loss of a relative. It is obvious that such contemporaries as Roger Ascham or Montaigne writing to a wife on the death of a child hardly required Day's advice on the exercise of solace. About the only letter Angell Day does not envision is one written by a rejected wife asking her husband not to have her beheaded. For that delicate and uncommon occasion the present volume will provide a model (IX-8). The general purposes of letter-writing are listed by Day as "to require, counsel, exhort, command, informe, commend, entreat, advertise, gratulate, or whatever other purpose." If the model-letters composed by Day are often wooden and empty, one can only conclude that an Elizabethan who required their assistance to court a maiden or console a bereaved relative deserved no better. Erasmus, too, wrote a treatise in the rhetorical tradition on letter-writing, proposing as models Cicero, Pliny, and Politian. Yet his own creative letters carried more influence among his contemporaries than did his tract.

The Humanistic Renaissance left letter-writers, fortunately, other options than this Scholastic or rhetorical tradition. Horace's twenty-two verse epistles had been known through the Middle Ages, and the verse-epistle was widely practised.

By the Cinquecento the models afforded by Ovid, Claudian, and Ausonius were also available. The sprightliest verse-epistles of the time were written by Clément Marot, usually on his personal predicaments and addressed to the King of France. Examples from England especially worthy of mention are Samuel Daniel's verse epistle to the Countess of Bedford (II-12) and Wyatt's farewell to court life addressed to John Poins (VI-8). Other contemporary examples were Ben Jonson's *Forests* (1616) and Donne's *Letters to Several Persons of Honour*. Often the writer of verse-epistles became self-conscious and pedantic, illuminating less well the potential of this genre. A demonstration of the verse-epistle at its spontaneous natural best is the *caudato* sonnet of Michelangelo to his jocular friend Giovanni da Pistoia (III-5).

After the easily-classifiable letters in the rhetorical, Horatian, or "familiar" traditions, letters could overlap other recognized genres. It was possible to convert a letter to a friend into a sermon, as we remember from John Donne's prose epistle to Sir Robert Carre, Knight (1624), with its admission: "Sir, I took up this Paper to write a Letter, but my Imaginations were full of a Sermon before, for I write but a few hours before I am to preach, and so instead of a Letter I send you a Homily. Let it have this much of a Letter."

One is reminded of certain letters by Saint Teresa or other preachers which are little more than devotions or homilies. Citing the letters of Fray Antonio de Guevara, we have already alleged that a letter may be a personal essay in disguise, just as two or three of Montaigne's essays were written for individual friends.

Other letters in this anthology assume the added character of political tract, imprecation, eulogy, bills for service rendered, travel log, and so on. The letters reporting geographical discoveries and exploration are a very special category, and those in Chapter VIII by Columbus, Vespucci, Balboa, Magellan, Cortés, Verrazzano, and Raleigh contain revelations of interest. The aforementioned Fugger letters, written to the Augsburg bankers by their representatives in all parts of the known world, constitute a fascinating corpus of information. Up to 1525 the canny internationalist Jacob Fugger (see VI-5) read these reports most attentively. The Fugger correspondents reported and interpreted news from near and far before the advent of the newspaper, informing recipients of such historical events as the Saint Bartholomew's Day massacre (V-19), the defeat of the Spanish Armada (VII-19), the Battle of Lepanto (VII-14), and the beheading of Mary Stuart (VI-16).

The bulk of the letters in this collection, however, are of the type known in antiquity, the Middle Ages, and the Renaissance as *familiares*. They avoid a book-learned style of composition, presenting rather a spontaneity which permits them more easily to shed light upon not only the man of the Renaissance, but the phenomenon of the Renaissance itself (Chapter I). Recalling Christopher Morley's justification of such projects ("letters make the best anthologies"), we have selected letters which (Morley's words) exhibit the mother-of-pearly shimmer inside the oyster of fact. Beyond their literary values, our letters shed light on the interests, concerns, prejudices, hopes, and general preoccupations which distinguished Renaissance man from his predecessors and—to a lesser extent—from those who followed him. A massive reading of these letters (all anthologies are inevitably too brief) reveals aspects of Renaissance thought and concern less directly apparent from other sources. To appreciate the extent of terror over Turkish expansionism shown in these letters (Chapter VII) one would otherwise have to be an historian of the Renaissance. To appreciate the shattering impact of Luther's gradual break with Rome (V-4 and V-7), the same would have to be true. Mindful of the vilifications aimed at Copernicus (IX-12), Galileo (IV-22), and the new astronomers one appreciates more fully their final vindication. The servility imposed by patrons on their greatest Humanists, writers, artists, and musicians emerges in a disturbing dimension, with Monteverdi revealing the lengths to which a great composer must go to protect his integrity. Michelangelo wins our pity as he documents how the tomb of a pope could impede his entire career (III-11). As for further perceptions and conclusions provided by the letters in this volume, these will receive comment in the individual brief introductions to the ten chapters.

That the Renaissance letter was to be viewed as an important literary genre or even art form is obvious from the great numbers of letters which, although addressed to a single recipient, were patently intended to be widely read. This was an integral part of the Revival of Antiquity, for the letters of Horace and Cicero—and even Petrarch well before the invention of printing—were composed for wide circulation. Thus, when Michelangelo penned a letter to King Francis I, tone and style become unusually self-conscious, for he knew that the French court would share it. The same was true when Jonson enlivened his request to the Earl of Newcastle for resumption of his pension (II-16), or when Clément Marot addressed his ingratiating verse-epistles to the King of France, requesting such favors as release from jail. Before his death in 1536 Erasmus had reworked for printing many of his letters, acknowledging in effect that they were really intended not for individuals, but for posterity. Sometimes this depersonalized a letter, leaving Sperone Speroni, the philologist, to fight in vain against the tendency of ambitious letter-writers in the Renaissance to "don courtly, royal clothes" when setting out to compose an epistle.

The greatest proof of the seriousness with which the Renaissance took the personal letter—beyond publishing or buying a vast number of "secretarial" manuals discussed above—is the number of available anthologies or *epistolari* available then. Paulus Manutius, son of the great Humanist-printer of Venice (I-4) brought out a popular anthology in 1542, and it had to be reprinted fifteen times by 1567. The late Miss K. T. Butler has left us much information on this plethora of epistolaries, finding that Aretino's florilegium of 1537 was the first and that within a half-century later Montaigne was to write in his *Essays* (1580): "Ce sont grands imprimeurs de lettres que les Italiens. J'en ay, ce croy-je, plus de cent volumes." This would represent an "average of two or three collections annually over a period of forty-two or forty-three years." Miss Butler further records that the first epistolaries to appear in France and England were largely translations and adaptations of the Italians. The best-known of these would include De Tronchet's *Lettres missives et familières* (1567), Fulwood's *Enemie of Idleness* (1568), Fenton's *Golden Epistles* (1576), Fleming's *Panoplie of Epistles* (1576), and Étienne Pasquier's *Lettres*.

So well did Italians serve as exemplars that by 1756 the author of a manual on letter-writing, Milani, decried the paucity of Renaissance letter-collections on the peninsula, because "the Ultramontanes have carted them all away from Italy."

In case the reader has been wondering how publishers were able to accumulate such large numbers of personal letters for their anthologies, the answer is that they bombarded leading figures and Humanists for copies the latter had written or received. Thus, when the printer Paulus Manutius writes to Alfonso Importuni for interesting epistles received from friends, he receives in return a bonanza of letters by Vittoria Colonna, Annibal Caro, Paulus Jovius, and others. Yet Importuni holds back in two regards. Certain of his friends would be embarrassed to have certain letters appear in print. Moreover, he will send only copies of letters he is unwilling to relinquish and will not be responsible for errors of the copyist.

In view of this venerable tradition of anthologizing letters, and in view of the fact that Renaissance editions of letters are as unavailable now as Milani found them to be in the eighteenth century, it comes as a surprise that no anthology of Renaissance letters in the English language or in any other translation is today available. This regrettable absence accounts for the present volume. For while the collected letters of Erasmus, Aretino, Machiavelli, Wyatt, Henry VIII, Queen Elizabeth, Henri IV, and Charles V and others are now available in English (see Acknowledgements), collections summarizing the Renaissance productivity in this fascinating broad field are not to be found. Several of the translations into English of other letter-writers not yet available in English have been undertaken by the author-editors as indicated.

We have treated poor Angell Day and his *Secretorie* rather cavalierly. With this on our conscience we turn back to quote him in a parting thought, admitting to an *esprit d'escalier*. For was it not this English gentleman who defined the letter as "the Messenger of the Absent"? An indisputable definition, when applied as he intended to those absent in space, and doubly meaningful when applied to the many Renaissance gentlemen and ladies absent in time as well as space whose words await our pleasure in the following pages. Words like those of Rabelais's Arismapians and Nephelibates accumulated for many years in the cold air, only to be thawed out and heard anew.

CONTENTS

CHAPTER II: LITERATURE. THEATER.   51

CHAPTER III: THE FINE ARTS. MUSIC.   93

CHAPTER V: RELIGION. REFORMATION AND COUNTER-REFORMATION. THE NEW BIBLES. CENSORSHIP. THE INQUISITION.

185

CHAPTER VI: GOVERNMENT AND POLITICS. LIFE AT COURT. THE NOBILITY.

CHAPTER VII: WARFARE.   295

CHAPTER VIII: TRAVEL. EXPLORATION. COLONIES. 343
FOREIGN PEOPLES AND TRADE.

CHAPTER IX: LOVE SACRED AND PROFANE. 381
MARRIAGE AND FAMILY. STATUS OF WOMEN.

CHAPTER X: DAILY LIFE. DOMESTIC CONCERNS. TOWN VS. COUNTRY. PASTIMES. MONEY.

LIST OF PLATES

Credits: Jacket Portrait: Alinari, Florence. Plate I: Copyright, The Frick Collection, N. Y. II: Alinari, Florence. III: Alinari, Florence. V: Bruckmann-Art Reference Bureau. VII: Alinari-Art Reference Bureau. IX: New York University Art Institute. X. Alinari, Art Reference Bureau. XI: National Portrait Gallery, London. XII: Alinari, Florence. XIII: Alinari, Florence. XIV: Alinari, Florence. XV: Metropolitan Museum of Art. Gift of J. P. Morgan, 1900. XVII: National Portrait Gallery, London. XVIII: Alinari, Florence. XIX: Alinari, Florence. XX: Alinari-Art Reference Bureau. VI: Metropolitan Museum of Art, New York City, Rogers Fund, 1952.

CHAPTER 1

RENAISSANCE. HUMANISM. THE GENTLEMAN-SCHOLAR.

I. *Sir Thomas More* by Holbein

II. *The School of Athens* by Raphael

The nature, limits, and even validity of the term Renaissance to describe the world reborn after 1450 have stimulated debate since Michelet used the term in 1855. He did not invent the concept, for the word "rebirth" in several variant forms was known to the sixteenth century. Vasari, Lomazzo, and Armenini used respectively the words for rebirth, resurgence, and reflowering for the sixteenth-century culture. In France Amyot and LeRoy hailed the new restitution or rebirth. Shortly after Michelet's history appeared the Swiss historian Jacob Burckhardt used "Renaissance" to present posterity with the concept of a sustained and uniform movement of the human spirit effecting a radical break with life and thought of the Middle Ages. Burdach, Thode, Huizinga, and other historians have seen the Renaissance as merely a logical projection of tendencies already incubating in the Middle Ages. Such leading American historians point out that such early scholars as Petrarch or even John of Garland represented attitudes widespread during Humanism. To us these early scholars could best be labeled proto-Humanists. The evident saltations of Renaissance culture and science have supported Burckhardt's and John Addington Symonds' view of the Cinquecento as something far more radical than a continuum. These saltations the reader will find documented in the symptomatic letters of the present anthology.*

A valid reason for favoring this latter interpretation is the self-consciousness of

* Some recent historians, especially American, reject the term Renaissance and feel more at ease with the protean term Early Modern Period. This would seem to place an unnecessary burden of proof on the Renaissance Society of America and other academic bodies and journals which find the traditional term valid if conceivably elastic. Other historians accept a middle position of the British historian G. M. Trevelyan, who finds the Dark Ages followed by the "twilight" glimmerings of the Late Middle Ages, preceding in turn the sunlight of the Renaissance. Pushing the Renaissance back to the twelfth or thirteenth century challenges the position of the Mediaeval Academy, which the senior editor of this anthology served for seven years as Secretary of Publication. For the Mediaeval Academy for decades has set the terminal date of the Middle Ages at 31 December, 1500, thus reclaiming John of Garland, Petrarch, and Boccaccio as its own. If we are more conciliatory by mentioning 1450 above, it is because the great spurt of discoveries by and about man—astronomical, geographical, physiological, sociological, philological, and other—recorded in this anthology coincided just in time to be made known to the world through the printed book. Indeed, the replacement of the manuscript by the book (remember that MS of Homer coveted by Boccaccio and Petrarch which they could not between them afford to buy) was in itself a saltation meriting a special historical nomenclature.

If, in several volumes on Renaissance themes (see list in the front matter above), the senior editor

Renaissance man, persuaded as he was that he lived in a new Golden or Saturnian Age. Indeed, the Spaniards were quick to call their own phase of the Renaissance the Golden Age. Deprecation of the thought, literature, and institutions of the Middle Ages became contagious, with Rabelais characterizing the Mediaeval period as that "thick Gothic night" and Du Bellay dismissing all forms of Mediaeval literature as "groceries." To Erasmus (I-5) a world in which the rulers of states and the Church seek peace and encourage learning cannot be other than an Age of Gold. In a letter to Cardinal Wolsey he sees the Golden Age developing in England, Germany, and Italy—even in such lesser areas as Denmark, Scotland, and Ireland—despite those Schoolmen still about "too old to hope" or "too stupid to learn."

The world that is reborn is of course that of Periclean Athens and Augustan Rome. The centers of Europe were to rival these venerable cities. Individual writers were to become "new swans" rivaling those of antiquity, with Rabelais hailed as the new Aristophanes and Ronsard as the new Pindar, or later the new Anacreon, and so on, with almost every woman poet of the period saluted as "the new Sappho." All of this underlines how very conscious the Renaissance Humanists were of being "reborn."

The Renaissance Humanists never got to Greece, even though they struggled to master the Greek language. Many of them got to Rome, however, and found to their dismay that it was only a shadow of its former self. Of the many who reflected their disappointment that the archetypal center of Greco-Roman culture was falling into neglect, none expressed this concern more urgently than the authors of the report to Pope Leo X (I-6)—apparently Castiglione in collaboration with his friend Raphael—appealing to that pontiff to save the last vestiges of ancient Rome before it was too late.

The study of Greek was of course frowned upon by the Church of Rome, since it would encourage translations of the New Testament at variance with the official readings. When Rabelais and Pierre Lamy were studying in the Franciscan monastery at Fontenay, they started covertly to learn ancient Greek. When Greek manuals were discovered in their quarters, they fled in panic. As we learn from a

---

has felt that 1600-1625 might serve as a terminal point, the Renaissance drifted with the Western Heritage thrust, starting in Italy and lingering longer in England, Spain, and Portugal. Its late phase was complicated by many intellectual currents: Counter-Reformation, Baroque, Mannerism, etc. Influenced by the very content of our letters, we have found a few epistles creeping into the anthology from as late as the reigns of Charles I and Felipe IV.

In any case, we invite you to read the letters for pleasure and for their inherent interest and charm, unconcerned about academic controversies condemned by Alciati. At the end you will sense the coherence of a great period of history, whatever and whenever its antecedents, and be warmed by Mr. Trevelyan's brilliant noontide sun.

letter to them from Guillaume Budé, one of the three great Hellenists of Renaissance France—with Lefèvre and Muret (I-15)—they were pardoned through intervention of the King himself (I-10). The study of Greek was finally sanctified by King Francis's creation of the Ecole Trilingue—in defiance of the Catholic Sorbonne—in which Latin, Greek, and Hebrew were taught. The Renaissance zest for languages is evident in the famous letter of Father Gargantua to his schoolboy son Pantagruel, spurring the lad to learn "perfectly" Greek, Latin, Hebrew, Chaldean, and Arabic. Finding competent professors of Greek was not easy, as Renaissance epistles testify. In Bembo's letter to Martin Giorgio of the University of Padua (1527), Bembo urges that in view of the lack of such teachers, Padua should recall Bernardin Donato at a much higher salary. When the city of Louvain also founded its *école trilingue,* professors of Hebrew and Latin were quickly found. Remembering the exiled Greeks from Constantinople who had fled the fall of that city to the Ottoman Turks (VII-1), bringing Greek language and culture with them, Erasmus contacted one of them, the eminent John Lascaris, to help find the right teacher for Louvain at a "handsome salary of about seventy ducats, which may be augmented having regard for his personality" (I-9), so that students "may at once imbibe the genuine pronunciation of the language."

Thus, Greek language and thought were studied with equal avidity. The news that the great Venetian printer Aldus Manutius was to print the works of Plato in Greek, "awaited with the greatest interest by the learned world," excited Erasmus and his colleagues (I-2). Yet the revival of Greek or Hebrew was not achieved at the expense of Latin. The *lingua franca* of Latin, the "Esperanto of the Middle Ages," was by no means abandoned by the Humanists or other educated men. When Rabelais wrote to Erasmus or Tiraqueau, or Scaliger to his enemy Dolet, it was of course in Latin. Youngsters began learning Latin as early as their first masses.

The activities—indeed, duties—of the Humanists were many. Their obligations included locating ancient or neglected manuscripts which deserved wide circulation, selecting them, "restoring and correcting them" (I-4), editing, translating, printing, interpreting or footnoting them. An excited early letter of Poggio Bracciolini (29 May, 1416) to Guarino of Verona announces triumphantly the locating at the San Gall Monastery of a dusty lost manuscript of Quintilian. Of necessity the Humanists worked closely with the printers. Indeed, some great printers like Aldus Manutius or Henri Estienne were full-fledged Humanists. Greek manuscripts which came to light were usually translated first into Latin—as was the case with the rediscovered *Poetics* of Aristotle—and then quickly into the vernacular. Thus, the two Greek tragedies which Erasmus submitted to Manutius for publication in October, 1507, he had translated into Latin (I-2). So great was his interest in bringing out ancient wisdom that he was willing to bear the printing costs himself. The same zeal inspired the translation of the Greek epistles of Theophylactus Simocatta, "not so much epistles as rules and precepts for a useful arrangement of human life," which Copernicus in 1509 translated into Latin (I-3). It was then the turn of a less learned man to make them universally available in Polish.

Since all these ancient works being revived were not Christian in character, a distinction evolved between "humane" and "divine" (that is, Christian) letters. The dedication of Hellenic letters after Socrates to man the microcosm gave impetus to the collective term Humanism. The Humanists quoted the claim of the Roman Terence: "Nothing concerning man do I deem alien to myself." Aldus Manutius recalls to Navagero, Humanist, poet, and Ciceronian scholar, the Socratic "Know thyself," a famous phrase rightly used "not to lessen arrogance, but also that we may be aware of our blessings" (I-4). This letter shows how integral a part of Humanism was the contribution of the printers. So successful was Aldus Manutius in commissioning and publishing the works of pagan antiquity that the papal court engaged his son Paulus to become the official printer of the Roman curia.

The ideal Humanist of the Renaissance was Erasmus, by character, learning, and activity. Yet to Erasmus that title belonged to another, Thomas More, to whom he dedicated his masterpiece, *Praise of Folly* (II-1). If we wish a close, detailed view of Thomas More—probing depths which even Holbein was unable to suggest in his half-length portrait of More—we must read the lengthy reply of Erasmus to the German scholar Ulrich von Hutten (I-7) who had requested such a description of More. It is a memorable portrait, comparable to Castiglione's blueprint of the ideal courtier (II-4), Navagero's letter on Charles V as an ideal monarch, or Guevara's projection of the ideal Captain (VII-4).

The Humanists, by the way, founded many important literary and scientific academies, especially in Italy: the Crusca in Florence, the Arcadi in Rome, the Lincei in Rome, and a lesser-known society founded at Brescia, then a small town on the Lombard plain, dedicated especially to Italian literature and language (II-5). They also engaged in strident literary feuds, awarded honors, and even encouraged the staging of ancient tragedies and comedies (II-8).

The Humanists, interested in education and the spread of learning, gave their inevitable advice to the young. Erasmus wrote to his young friend Christian to live up to Pliny's motto, "All your time is lost which you do not impart to study" (I-1). Remembering the advice about *mens sana in corpore sano,* he also counseled exercise of the body. Similarly, Sir Henry Sidney urged young Philip Sidney to enrich his tongue with words and his wit with matter, and to be a gentleman, "courteous of gesture, affable to all men, with diversity of reverence, according to the dignity of the person" (I-13). Nor did he forget the counsel, "use exercise of body." Advising in turn his younger brother Robert, Philip Sidney—surely aware of Gargantua's advice to his giant son Pantagruel—recommended a vast number of disciplines, including music, but did not forget the noble exercise of arms, including both sword and dagger, although dueling was being banned in England (X-21). Thus the ideal of the Humanist is extended to that of the gentleman-scholar preached by Bacon and his generation and incorporated literally into the statutes of Harvard College in 1636. It is echoed of course in Castiglione's *Courtier* and faintly suggested in the "few precepts" of Polonius to his departing son Laertes.

Education then spurted far ahead of the rote learning of the Mediaeval schools, limited to the trivium and quadrivium and dominated by "the whole rabblement of Schoolmen pledged to Duns Scotus and Thomas Aquinas," as Gabriel Harvey stipulates in his letter (I-14). Education, extricating itself from the direction of the Churchmen, proceeded to evolve from the program derided in Rabelais's *Gargantua* (the first phase of the young giant's schooling) toward the goal of Montaigne, the formation of "a head well made and not a head well filled." All the goals of Humanism were slowly built into the curricula of the schools, even though the leading schools would embark on their own fashions, dadas, and tangents (I-14).

All in all, the universities carried the burden of consolidating the gains of Humanism, becoming a happy refuge for the intellectuals. Roger Ascham rejected both life at court and life abroad to return to Cambridge, where he would live "most gladlie" (I-12). As the universities developed, the new availability of the printed book spurred their library holdings, especially as wealthy gentlemen-scholars like Thomas Bodley bequeathed to them fine collections of volumes.

Lest we over-idealize the schools of the Renaissance, we must remember that the independence of the student body led to considerable campus "contestation." Even in the Middle Ages student power was great. At Bologna, for example, the disapproval of a dozen students had sufficed to have a professor dismissed. Bologna had not changed. Giuseppe Pallavicino's letter from there (I-11) testified to student attacks on professors so violent that he feared for his life. The great classicist at University of Rome, Marc-Antoine Muret, found students so unruly, uncouth, and threatening that he resigned abruptly from his teaching post (I-15).

If students thus maintained their freedom of behavior, academic freedom was not always guaranteed by the powerful Renaissance monarchs or bishops. A sad breach of such freedom at Cambridge University is described in Joseph Mead's letter to Sir Martin Stuteville (I-17). The misguided new monarch Charles I, despite opposition from the teaching faculty, appointed as Chancellor the authoritarian Duke of Buckingham. Another unexpected intrusion of a monarch upon academic freedom was Queen Elizabeth's campaign to forbid young students to study in the continental universities, especially those in Catholic countries, to further their education (I-16). Yet Bacon and others continued to recommend travel as a final educative experience, and in 1593, when Elizabeth got her brainstorm against study abroad, she was bitter and distressed about King Henri IV of France having just become a Catholic, as she took pains to write him that same year (VI-20).

I-1   Desiderius Erasmus to Christian [Noorthon]

In a letter of advice to his student, Desiderius Erasmus (1466?-1536) outlines a daily plan for productive study and optimum health.

Paris (1496)

Avoid nocturnal lucubrations and studies at unseasonable times. They exhaust the mind and seriously affect the health. The dawn, beloved of the Muses, is the fit time for study. After dinner either play, or walk, or take part in cheerful conversation. Possibly even among these amusements some room may be found for improvement. Take as much food as is required, not for your pleasure, but for your health. Before supper take a short walk, and after supper do the same. Before going to bed read something exquisite and worth remembering, of which you will be thinking when overcome by sleep, and for which you will ask yourself again when you wake. Let this maxim of Pliny rest always in your mind: All your time is lost which you do not impart to study. Remember that nothing is more fugitive than youth, which, when once it has flown away, never returns. But I am beginning to preach, after promising to be nothing but a guide. Follow, sweetest Christian, the plan I have traced, or any better that you can. Farewell.

1-2   Desiderius Erasmus to Aldus Manutius

Erasmus commends the Venetian printer Aldus Manutius for promoting the classical revival by publishing the writers of antiquity, and offers to the Aldine press two tragedies he has translated.

28 October, 1507

There is a wish, most learned Manutius, which has many times occurred to my mind. As not only by your skill and the unrivalled beauty of your typography, but also by intelligence and learning of no common order, you have thrown a vast light upon the literature of Greece and Rome, I should be glad if those merits had brought you in return an adequate profit. For as to fame, there is no doubt that to the furthest posterity the name of Aldus Manutius will fly from mouth to mouth among all that are initiated in the religion of letters. Your memory then, as your character now, will deserve not only admiration but love, because you devote yourself to the restoration and publication of good authors, with the greatest solicitude, but, as I hear, with no proportionate gain. Like Hercules you are employed in labours of the noblest kind, which are of more advantage to others than to yourself. I am told that you are editing Plato in Greek, a book expected with the greatest interest by the learned world. I should like to know what authors you have printed on the subject of Medicine. I want you to give us Paulus Aegineta.[1] I wonder what has so long prevented you from publishing the New Testament,[2] a work, which if I guess aright, will be exceedingly welcome even to the great majority of our class, I mean the class of theologians.

I send you two tragedies, which I have translated boldly enough, but whether with corresponding success you will judge for yourself. . . .

I should not be afraid of undertaking the work at my own expense and risk, were it not that I shall have to leave Italy in a few months. For the same reason I am anxious to get the thing done as soon as possible. It is scarcely a ten days' business. If you insist on my taking a hundred or two hundred copies for myself,

1. An Alexandrine botanist
2. Erasmus was to translate the New Testament into Latin (see V-2).

although Mercury (as patron of commerce) is not apt to be very propitious to me, and it will be inconvenient to have a parcel to carry, still I will not refuse to take them, provided you fix a favorable price.

Farewell, most learned Aldus, and pray rank Erasmus among those who heartily wish you well. You will do me a favour by letting me know whether you have in your warehouse any authors not in common use; as those learned Englishmen have charged me to make the inquiry. If on the whole you are not inclined to print the Tragedies, please return the copy to the bearer, to be brought back to me.

I-3   Nicolaus Copernicus to Bishop Lucas Watzelrode

The Polish astronomer Nicolaus Copernicus (1473-1543) whose name has become synonymous with the heliocentric theory of the universe, was also a cultivated Humanist who in 1509 published his Latin translation of the Greek epistles of Theophylactus Simocatta "to make them more generally accessible." The Byzantine Theophylactus lived in the 7th century A.D.

In dedicating the work to his uncle (and patron) Bishop Lucas Watzelrode of Ermland, Copernicus explains the value and appeal of the epistles.

1509

Most Reverend Lord and Father of this Country.

It seems to me that Theophylactus, the scholastic, has quite excellently compiled moral, pastoral and amorous epistles. Surely he was guided by the consideration that variety delights us above all. The inclinations of men are very dissimilar and they are pleased by very dissimilar things. Some like weighty thoughts, others those which lure by levity; some love the serious, while others are attracted by the play of fancy. Because the multitude takes pleasure in so very different things, Theophylactus let light subjects alternate with heavy ones, frivolity with seriousness, so that the reader can choose what he likes best from the rich mass of flowers, just as in a garden, as it were. All that he offers, however, is of such great utility that his poems appear to be not so much epistles as rules and precepts for a useful arrangement of human life. The proof of this is their comprehensive brevity. Theophylactus has taken his subject matter from various authors and most edifyingly presented it in a compressed form.

Hardly any one will deny an inner value to the moral and pastoral poems. A different judgment might perhaps be passed on the love letters which from their title might seem wanton and frivolous. But as the physician customarily softens bitter medicine by the addition of sweet ingredients, to make it more agreeable to the patient, so the more frivolous poems have been added here; besides, they are kept so pure that they might as well bear the name of moral epistles. Under such circumstances I deemed it inequitable for the epistles of Theophylactus to be read only in the Greek language. To make them more generally accessible, I have tried to translate them into Latin, to the best of my ability.

To you, Most Reverend Sir, I now dedicate this small gift which is in no relation, to be sure, to the favors I received from you. Whatever I use and create by my intellectual powers I rightly deem your property; for it is indubitably true what Ovid once wrote to Caesar Germanicus: "It is your glance that makes my spirit fall and rise."

I-4   Aldus Manutius to Andrea Navagero

Aldus Manutius (1450-1515), who published the first printed editions of Greek and Roman classics, was the author of prefaces to these publications (as well as a few books of his own). One such preface, revealing some of the scholar-printer's ideals, is addressed to the Venetian Humanist Andrea Navagero, who edited classical texts for the Aldine press.

1514-15

To Andrea Navagero

All those who devote themselves to the composition of new works, or the restoration and correction of ancient ones, not only for their own benefit but for that of others (for, as Plato has wisely said, we are not born for ourselves alone, but partly for our native land, partly for our parents, and partly for our friends), all those, I say, need peace and quiet, and betake themselves from the concourse and company of men into solitude, as into harbour. For the sacred studies of letters and the Muses themselves always require leisure and solitude, and especially when one would write works which he wishes to be "worthy of being smeared with cedar oil and preserved in smooth cypress." This indeed you, my Navagero, have done frequently and happily; for, leaving the city and the company of men, you take yourself off to the country, to places ruled by peace and tranquility, as in former years to the laurel and olive groves of Lake Garda, "when the gates of war, grim with iron and close-fitting bars, have been closed." There, free of all those cares and troubles which hinder the excellent studies of letters, "such music makest thou as the Cynthian god modulates with fingers pressed upon his well-skilled lyre."

But as for me, there are two things especially, not to mention some six hundred others, which interrupt and hinder my zealous studies: first of all, the numerous letters of learned men which are sent to me from all over. If I were to answer them, I would spend all my days and nights writing letters. Then there are those who visit me, some to greet me, some to find out what is new, and others (and this is by far the largest number) for lack of anything else to do—for then they say, "Let's go to see Aldus." They come in droves and sit around idly, "like a leech that will not let go the skin, till gorged with blood." I pass over those who come to recite their poetry, or some prose composition they want published by our press, and this very often clumsy and unpolished, since they "cannot brook the toil and tedium of the file," and they put off giving their attention to the poem which should be corrected, which "many a day and many a blot has not restrained and refined ten times over to meet the test of perfection."

I have begun at last to protect myself from those who pester and interrupt me. For to those who write to me I either reply not at all, when the letter is not very interesting, or, if it is important, I answer very briefly. Since I do this not from pride or rudeness, but simply so that I may use whatever time I have in publishing good books, I ask that no one should take it too hard, but accept it in the spirit in which I do it. And so that those who come to say "hello," or for any other reason, may not continue to interrupt my work and serious study, I have taken care to warn them, by putting up a notice, like an edict, on the door of my office to this effect:

WHOEVER YOU ARE, ALDUS BEGS YOU ONCE AND FOR ALL TO STATE BRIEFLY WHAT YOU WANT, AND THEN LEAVE QUICKLY, UNLESS YOU HAVE COME, LIKE HERCULES, TO SUPPORT THE WEARY ATLAS ON YOUR SHOULDERS, FOR THAT IS WHAT YOU WILL DO WHEN YOU ENTER THIS WORKSHOP

But, on the other hand, there are men who are learned in both Greek and Latin, who by frequent and diligent visits to my office render Herculean service to me.

Of these you, most excellent Navagero, have enabled me to rest as Atlas did, by your most accurate collation of these very books of Cicero, *On Precepts for Orators,* and *On Fullness of Expression,* and *On the Study of Eloquence,* with those ancient manuscripts which have been discovered. And now you are zealously performing the same task with his orations and his divine books on philosophy, and so felicitously that soon some of these, which for a long time were only to be found here and there, may go out into the hands of scholars in a more correct form. I do not say how diligently, how skilfully, how learnedly you have been untiring in correcting, by the good exemplars which you possess, not only certain prose works, but especially the best works of the poets, which you have most kindly promised to give to me, such is your generosity and your love of good letters, because, when they are finished, I want to publish them from my press.

Indeed, you have often urged me, even saying: "Aldus, what are you thinking of? Why don't you ask me for Vergil, Horace, Tibullus, Ovid, and others? You can hardly believe how carefully I have emended them from ancient manuscripts!" Thus you have so bound me to you that I love you not less than myself, and I greatly desire a very long life for both of us. For, since as a young man you have become so accomplished in both prose and poetry that you are almost the equal of those ancients who won the highest praise for their work in both forms, I do not doubt that you will be the greatest ornament of our age, and, with our Bembo,* "another hope of great Rome."

Although it does not escape me that you, in your modesty, will not listen to this willingly, yet because I know that I speak the truth and because you know from your own experience how very rightly that famous phrase "Know thyself" is used not only to lessen arrogance, but also that we may become aware of our blessings, I wish to speak thus to you about yourself, following the example of many and learned men. And not to mention others, both Greek and Roman, who were wont to do this very thing, Pliny the Younger—in that most skilful and divine panegyric which, when he was about to begin his consulship under the Emperor Trajan, he delivered to the assembled Senate—thought it most honourable and appropriate to utter the highest praises of that emperor in his presence, because he knew both that these were certainly very true and that this ruler was fully aware of his own virtues. For Trajan was not only an emperor but the best of men. Whence it is that now, when an emperor is being crowned, they say this to him first of all: "May you be happier than Augustus and better than Trajan." It may be added that our epistles or prefaces are of such a kind that it seems to us proper, for the same reason, that although we seem to write privately to one man, we nevertheless write publicly for all who read our words in friendly fashion. For this reason also,

* See Letter II-5.

we consider it permissible to say something to him to whom we are writing, by way of introduction concerning those works to which we add epistles or prefaces of this kind—not in order to instruct him (for this would be arrogant), but so that he may examine our words, and may be their judge, and so that those who do not know these things (for we want always to make them known) may learn them from us. We have resolved, therefore, that this should be done here. And we have chosen you, most learned Navagero, as judge, both for other reasons and because you know, as well as you know your own fingers and fingernails, the matters which are treated in these books on the knowledge of speaking. For those works that at great pains we have prepared for publication we ought to recite or submit in writing to those who are qualified to praise them if they are good, and to criticize them if they are bad, as Quintilian used to have poems recited to him, and would say, when he did not approve of something, "Pray correct this and that.". . .

You then, my Navagero, will readily allow us to say these things to you, since you are at once very learned and very kind, and also because when they are said to you they are spoken to all those into whose hands these books of ours may come. You will, therefore, read the brief introductory discussions we have written for these books of Cicero, and not reproachfully, as Hannibal did Phormio (as a barbarian indeed), but you will let me off kindly, as you usually do, when you have read them. . . .

I regard what I have said about these works as written casually. For I have been even more pressed and harassed by business than perhaps anyone else. May God help me and deliver me from these wicked and most grievous vexations by which I am pursued, and may He ordain that, when my lands have been lost and I thus lament:

Behold to what a pass strife has brought our unhappy citizens! For these have we sown our fields!

or thus:

We have lived to see the day—an evil never dreamed—when a stranger, holder of our little farm, could say, "This is mine, begone, ye old tenants!"

you, who are also a divine poet (for you are another like Vergil), will sing these lines, or others like them, to console me, your compatriot:

Happy old man, so these lands will still be yours . . . and you will be allowed to quit your long slavery, and elsewhere find the gods ready to aid you.

For after I have finally reached the point when like Sisyphus I have at last brought to the summit of the mountain the rock which I have untiringly rolled for so many years, "lying under the spreading beech's shade," I myself may be able to say, "It is a god who wrought for us this peace."

I-5   Desiderius Erasmus to Wolfgang Fabritius Capito

In a letter to the Chaplain Preacher of Basel, Erasmus hails the new tide of greatness in human achievement and foresees an era of enlightenment and peace. It is somewhat ironic that on the eve of the Reformation, he is apprehensive that a possible revival of Paganism or Judaism, spawned by interest in the ancients, will threaten Christendom.

Antwerp, 26 February, 1517

It is no part of my nature, most learned Wolfgang, to be excessively fond of life; whether it is that I have, to my own mind, lived nearly long enough, having entered my fifty-first year, or that I see nothing in this life so splendid or delightful that it should be desired by one who is convinced by the Christian faith that a happier life awaits those who in this world earnestly attach themselves to piety. But at the present moment I could almost wish to be young again, for no other reason but this, that I anticipate the near approach of a golden age, so clearly do we see the minds of princes, as if changed by inspiration, devoting all their energies to the pursuit of peace. The chief movers in this matter are Pope Leo and Francis, King of France.[1]

There is nothing this king does not do or does not suffer in his desire to avert war and consolidate peace; submitting, of his own accord, to conditions which might be deemed unfair, if he preferred to have regard to his own greatness and dignity rather than to the general advantage of the world; and exhibiting in this, as in everything else, a magnanimous and truly royal character. Therefore, when I see that the highest sovereigns of Europe—Francis of France, Charles the King Catholic, Henry of England, and the Emperor Maximilian—have set all their

1. See Letter VI-7.

warlike preparations aside and established peace upon solid and, as I trust, adamantine foundations, I am led to a confident hope that not only morality and Christian piety, but also a genuine and purer literature, may come to renewed life or greater splendour; especially as this object is pursued with equal zeal in various regions of the world—at Rome by Pope Leo, in Spain by the Cardinal of Toledo, in England by Henry, eighth of the name, himself not unskilled in letters, and among ourselves by our young King Charles. In France, King Francis, who seems as it were born for this object, invites and entices from all countries men that excel in merit or in learning. Among the Germans the same object is pursued by many of their excellent princes and bishops, and especially by Maximilian Caesar, whose old age, weary of so many wars, has determined to seek rest in the employments of peace, a resolution more becoming to his own years, while it is fortunate for the Christian world. To the piety of these princes it is due, that we see everywhere, as if upon a given signal, men of genius are arising and conspiring together to restore the best literature.

Polite letters, which were almost extinct, are now cultivated and embraced by Scots, by Danes, and by Irishmen. Medicine has a host of champions; at Rome, Nicolas of Leonice; at Venice, Ambrosius Leo of Nola; in France, William Cop and John Ruelle; and in England, Thomas Linacre. The Imperial Law is restored at Paris by William Budé, in Germany by Udalric Zasy; and mathematics at Basel by Henry of Glaris. In the theological sphere there was no little to be done, because this science has been hitherto mainly professed by those who are most pertinacious in their abhorrence of the better literature, and are the more successful in defending their own ignorance as they do it under pretext of piety, the unlearned vulgar being induced to believe that violence is offered to religion if anyone begins an assault upon their barbarism. For in the presence of an ignorant mob they are always ready to scream and excite their followers to stone-throwing, if they see any risk of not being thought omniscient. But even here I am confident of success if the knowledge of the three languages [2] continues to be received in schools, as it has now begun. For the most learned and least churlish men of the profession do in some measure assist and favour the new system; and in this matter we are especially indebted to the vigorous exertions of James Lefèvre of Etaples, whom you resemble not only in name but in a number of accomplishments.

The humblest part of the work has naturally fallen to my lot. Whether my contribution has been worth anything I cannot say; at any rate, those who object to the world regaining its senses are as angry with me as if my small industry had had some influence; although the work was not undertaken by me with any confidence that I could myself teach anything magnificent, but I wanted to construct a road

2. i.e., Hebrew, Greek, and Latin.

for other persons of higher aims, so that they might be less impeded by pools and stumbling blocks in carrying home those fair and glorious treasures.

Why should I say more? Everything promises me the happiest success. But one doubt still possesses my mind. I am afraid that, under cover of a revival of ancient literature, paganism may attempt to rear its head—as there are some among Christians that acknowledge Christ in name but breathe inwardly a heathen spirit—or, on the other hand, that the restoration of Hebrew learning may give occasion to a revival of Judaism.[3] This would be a plague as much opposed to the doctrine of Christ as anything that could happen. . . . Some books have lately come out with a strong flavour of Judaism. I see how Paul exerted himself to defend Christ against Judaism, and I am aware that some persons are secretly sliding in that direction. I hear also that some are intent upon other schemes, which do nothing for the knowledge of Christ, but only cloud men's eyes with smoke. So much the more do I wish you to undertake this province; I know that your sincere piety will have regard to nothing but Christ, to whom all your studies are devoted. Take pains to commend me to the Reverend Father, Christopher, Bishop of Basel . . .

I-6   Baldassare Castiglione (with Raphael da Sanzio) to Pope Leo X

The author of this letter to Pope Leo X, probably Castiglione in collaboration with Raphael, decries the decay of ancient Roman architecture and calls upon His Holiness to preserve the antique ruins of the Eternal City. To this end he has agreed to plot out on a map of Rome the ancient structures to be saved. Regarding Castiglione, see Letter II-2.

(1513-1521)
There are many men, Most Holy Father, who, since they measure with their own feeble judgement the great things written of the Romans—of their arms, their city of Rome with its wonderful art, riches, ornament and the grandeur of its buildings—believe these things to be more fable than truth.

3. For a contrary view, read Zwingli (Letter V-8).

But to me it has seemed, and does still seem, otherwise.

For, if one considers what may still be seen amid the ruins of Rome, and what divine gifts there dwelt in the hearts of the men of ancient times, it does not seem unreasonable to believe that many things which to us would appear to be impossible were simple for them. Now I have given much study to these ancient edifices: I have taken no small effort to look them over with care and to measure them with diligence. I have read the best authors of that age and compared what they had written with the works which they described, and I can therefore say that I have acquired at least some knowledge of the ancient architecture.

On the one hand, this knowledge of so many excellent things has given me the greatest pleasure: on the other hand the greatest grief. For I behold this noble city, which was the queen of the world, so wretchedly wounded as to be almost a corpse. Therefore I feel, as every man must feel, pity for his kindred and for his country. I feel constrained to use every part of my poor strength to bring to life some likeness, or even a shade of that which once was the true and universal fatherland of all Christians. For Rome was so noble and so powerful that men believed her to be, alone under the heavens, above all fortune and beyond nature, exempt from death and destined to endure forever. It seemed that time, jealous of the glories of men and not wholly trusting to her own powers for their destruction, allied herself with the fortunes of the heathen and iniquitous barbarians who added sword and fire to the sharp file and the poisonous teeth of the chisel. So the famous works which now more than ever should appear in the flower of their beauty, were burned and destroyed by the brutal rage and savage passions of men wicked as the wild beasts. Yet not completely so, for there still remains to us the skeleton of those things, though without their ornament—the bones of the body without the flesh, one might say. And why should we bewail the Goths, the Vandals, and other perfidious enemies of the Latin name, when those who above all others should be fathers and guardians in the defence of the poor relics of Rome, have even given themselves over to the study—long study—of how these might be destroyed and disappear. How many Pontiffs, Holy Father, who held the same office as yourself, though without the same knowledge, the same valour or greatness of soul—how many, I say, of these Pontiffs have permitted the ruin and defacement of the ancient temples, of statues and arches and other edifices that were the glory of their builders? How many allowed the very foundations to be undermined that pozzolana might be dug from them, so that, in but a little time, the buildings fell to the ground? How much lime has been burned from the statues and ornaments of ancient time? I am bold to ask how much of all this new Rome that we see today, however great, however beautiful, however adorned with palaces and churches and other buildings has been built with lime made from ancient marbles? * Nor

* a complaint at the time voiced by many, including Michelangelo.

can I remember without grief that during the time I have spent in Rome—not yet twelve years—so many beautiful things have been ruined: as, for example, the Meta that was in the Via Alexandrina; the arch at the entrance to the Baths of Diocletian; the Temple of Ceres on the Sacred Way; a part of the Forum Transitorium burned and destroyed only a few days ago and lime made from its marbles; and the greater part of the Basilica of the Forum, ruined. Besides all these, how many columns have been broken and cracked in two, how many architraves and beautiful friezes shattered? It is the infamy of our time that we have suffered these things, of which it can truly be said that by comparison with what has been done today Hannibal would appear to have been a pious man. Therefore, O Holy Father, let it not be last in the thought of Your Holiness to have a care that the little which remains of the ancient mother of glory and of the Italian name, witness of the divine spirits whose memory even today creates and moves us to virtue—spirits still alive among us—should not be altogether wiped out by the depredations of the evil and the ignorant. These, unhappily, do hurt to those souls who of their own blood brought forth so much glory for the world, for our country and for ourselves. May Your Holiness, while keeping the example of the ancient world still alive among us, hasten to equal and to surpass the men of ancient days, as you even now do, by setting up magnificent buildings, by sustaining and encouraging the virtuous, by fostering talent, by rewarding all noble effort—thus sowing the fruitful seeds among the Christian princes. For, as by the calamities of war are brought to birth the destruction and the ruin of the arts and sciences, so from peace and concord are born the happiness of men and that highly-prized serenity of spirit that may imbue us with strength to accomplish work reaching to the heights of achievement. Because of the divine wisdom and authority of Your Holiness this has become the hope of every man of our century. And this is truly to be the merciful Shepherd, yes, the greatest Father of the world.

But to go back to what I have already said: Your Holiness has commanded me to make a drawing of ancient Rome—as much as may be known from what can be seen today—with those buildings showing so much of what remains that, with careful study, you may know exactly what they were. Those that are completely ruined and no longer visible may be understood by the study of those that still stand and can be seen. To this end I have tried to use every skill of mine, so that the mind of Your Holiness and those others who shall profit by our effort shall no longer be left in ignorance, but enjoy the fruits of our work. . . .

If, wishing in every way to obey, I have been fortunate enough to serve Your Holiness, first and Supreme Prince of all Christian lands, I may call myself the most happy of all Your devoted servants. So I pray rightly to value this opportunity of placing my work in the holy hands of Your Holiness, whose most sacred feet I humbly kiss.

(See also Letter III-6, in which Raphael comments to Castiglione on the beautiful forms of ancient architecture.)

I-7   Desiderius Erasmus to Ulrich von Hutten

In complying with a request from the German writer Ulrich von Hutten for a full-length word portrait of Thomas More, Erasmus provides subsequent generations with an unforgettable characterization of one of the greatest of Renaissance Humanists.

Antwerp, 23 July, 1517

Most illustrious Hutten, your love, I had almost said your passion for the genius of Thomas More,—kindled as it is by his writings, which, as you truly say, are as learned and witty as anything can possibly be,—is, I assure you, shared by many others; and moreover the feeling in this case is mutual; since More is so delighted with what you have written, that I am myself almost jealous of you. It is an example of what Plato says of that sweetest wisdom, which excites much more ardent love among men than the most admirable beauty of form. It is not discerned by the eye of sense, but the mind has eyes of its own, so that even here the Greek saying holds true, that out of Looking grows Liking; and so it comes to pass that people are sometimes united in the warmest affection, who have never seen or spoken to each other. And, as it is a common experience, that for some unexplained reason different people are attracted by different kinds of beauty, so between one mind and another, there seems to be a sort of latent kindred, which causes us to be specially delighted with some minds, and not with others.

As to your asking me to paint you a full-length portrait of More, I only wish my power of satisfying your request were equal to your earnestness in pressing it. For to me too, it will be no unpleasant task to linger awhile in the contemplation of a friend, who is the most delightful character in the world. But, in the first place, it is not given to every man to be aware of all More's accomplishments; and in the next place, I know not whether he will himself like to have his portrait painted by any artist that chooses to do so. For indeed I do not think it more easy to make a likeness of More than of Alexander the Great, or of Achilles; neither were those heroes more worthy of immortality. The hand of an Apelles is required for such a subject, and I am afraid I am more like a Fulvius or a Rutuba than an Apelles. Nevertheless I will try to draw you a sketch, rather than a portrait, of the entire man, so far as daily and domestic intercourse has enabled me to observe his likeness and retain it in my memory. But if some diplomatic employment should ever bring you together, you will find out, how poor an artist you have chosen for this commission; and I am afraid you will think me guilty of envy or of wilful blindness in taking note of so few out the many good points of his character.

To begin with that part of him which is least known to you,—in shape and stature More is not a tall man, but not remarkably short, all his limbs being so symmetrical, that no deficiency is observed in this respect. His complexion is fair, his face being rather blonde than pale, but with no approach to redness, except a very delicate flush, which lights up the whole. His hair is auburn inclining to black, or if you like it better, black inclining to auburn; his beard thin, his eyes a bluish grey with some sort of tinting upon them. This kind of eye is thought to be a sign of the happiest character, and is regarded with favour in England, whereas with us black eyes are rather preferred. It is said, that no kind of eye is so free from defects of sight. His countenance answers to his character, having an expression of kind and friendly cheerfulness with a little air of raillery. To speak candidly, it is a face more expressive of pleasantry than of gravity or dignity, though very far removed from folly or buffoonery. His right shoulder seems a little higher than his left, especially when he is walking, a peculiarity that is not innate, but the result of habit, like many tricks of the kind. In the rest of his body there is nothing displeasing,—only his hands are a little coarse, or appear so, as compared with the rest of his figure. He has always from his boyhood been very negligent of his toilet, so as not to give much attention even to the things which, according to Ovid, are all that men need care about. What a charm there was in his looks when young, may even now be inferred from what remains; although I knew him myself when he was not more than three and-twenty years old; for he has not yet passed much beyond his fortieth year. His health is sound rather than robust, but sufficient for any labours suitable to an honourable citizen; and we may fairly hope, that his life may be long, as he has a father living of a great age, but an age full of freshness and vigour. . . .

He seems to be born and made for friendship, of which he is the sincerest and most persistent devotee. Neither is he afraid of that multiplicity of friends, of which Hesiod disapproves. Accessible to every tender of intimacy, he is by no means fastidious in choosing his acquaintance, while he is most accommodating in keeping it on foot, and constant in retaining it. If he has fallen in with anyone whose faults he cannot cure, he finds some opportunity of parting with him, untying the knot of intimacy without tearing it; but when he has found any sincere

friends, whose characters are suited to his own, he is so delighted with their society
and conversation, that he seems to find in these the chief pleasure of life, having an
absolute distaste for tennis and dice and cards, and the other games with which the
mass of gentlemen beguile the tediousness of Time. It should be added that, while
he is somewhat neglectful of his own interest, no one takes more pains in attending
to the concerns of his friends. What more need I say? If anyone requires a perfect
example of true friendship, it is in More that he will best find it.

In company his extraordinary kindness and sweetness of temper are such as to
cheer the dullest spirit, and alleviate the annoyance of the most trying
circumstances. From boyhood he was always so pleased with a joke, that it might
seem that jesting was the main object of his life; but with all that, he did not go so
far as buffoonery, nor had ever any inclination to bitterness. When quite a youth,
he wrote farces and acted them. If a thing was facetiously said, even though it was
aimed at himself, he was charmed with it, so much did he enjoy any witticism that
had a flavour of subtlety or genius. This led to his amusing himself as a young man
with epigrams, and taking great delight in Lucian. Indeed, it was he that suggested
my writing the *Moria,* or Praise of Folly, which was much the same thing as
setting a camel to dance.

There is nothing that occurs in human life, from which he does not seek to
extract some pleasure, although the matter may be serious in itself. If he has to do
with the learned and intelligent, he is delighted with their cleverness, if with
unlearned or stupid people, he finds amusement in their folly. He is not offended
even by professed clowns,[1] as he adapts himself with marvellous dexterity to the
tastes of all; while with ladies generally, and even with his wife, his conversation is
made up of humour and playfulness. You would say it was a second Democritus, or
rather that Pythagorean philosopher, who strolls in leisurely mood through the
market-place, contemplating the turmoil of those who buy and sell. There is no
one less guided by the opinion of the multitude, but on the other hand no one
sticks more closely to common sense. . . .

When of a sentimental age, he was not a stranger to the emotions of love, but
without loss of character, having no inclination to press his advantage, and being
more attracted by a mutual liking than by any licentious object.

He had drunk deep of Good Letters from his earliest years; and when a young
man, he applied himself to the study of Greek and of philosophy; but his father was
so far from encouraging him in this pursuit, that he withdrew his allowance and
almost disowned him, because he thought he was deserting his hereditary study,
being himself an expert professor of English Law. For remote as that profession is
from true learning, those who become masters of it have the highest rank and

---

1. Holbein's painting of More and his family, executed about 1527, includes More's jester.

reputation among their countrymen; and it is difficult to find any readier way to acquire fortune and honour. Indeed a considerable part of the nobility of that island has had its origin in this profession, in which it is said that no one can be perfect, unless he has toiled at it for many years. It was natural, that in his younger days our friend's genius, born for better things, should shrink from this study; nevertheless, after he had had a taste of the learning of the Schools, he became so conversant with it, that there was no one more eagerly consulted by suitors; and the income that he made by it was not surpassed by any of those who did nothing else; such was the power and quickness of his intellect.

He also expended considerable labour in perusing the volumes of the orthodox Fathers; [2] and when scarcely more than a youth, he lectured publicly on the *De Civitate Dei* of Augustine before a numerous audience, old men and priests not being ashamed to take a lesson in divinity from a young layman, and not at all sorry to have done so. Meantime he applied his whole mind to religion, having some thought of taking orders, for which he prepared himself by watchings and fastings and prayers and such like exercises; wherein he showed much more wisdom than the generality of people, who rashly engage in so arduous a profession without testing themselves beforehand. And indeed there was no obstacle to his adopting this kind of life, except the fact, that he could not shake off his wish to marry. Accordingly he resolved to be a chaste husband rather than a licentious priest.

When he married, he chose a very young girl, a lady by birth, with her character still unformed, having been always kept in the country with her parents and sisters,—so that he was all the better able to fashion her according to his own habits. Under his direction she was instructed in learning and in every kind of Music, and had almost completely become just such a person as would have been a delightful companion for his whole life, if an early death had not carried her away. She had however borne him several children, of whom three girls, Margaret, Alice and Cecily, and one boy, John, are still living.

More did not however long remain single, but contrary to his friends' advice, a few months after his wife's death, he married a widow, more for the sake of the management of his household, than to please his own fancy, as she is no great beauty, nor yet young, *nec bella admodum nec puella,* as he sometimes laughingly says, but a sharp and watchful housewife; with whom nevertheless he lives, on as sweet and pleasant terms as if she were as young and lovely as any one could desire; and scarcely any husband obtains from his wife by masterfulness and severity as much compliance as he does by blandishments and jests. Indeed, what more compliance could he have, when he has induced a woman who is already elderly,

2. More indentifies these (Letter I-8) as Augustine, Jerome, Ambrose and Cyprian, Chrysostom, Gregory, and Basil.

who is not naturally of a yielding character, and whose mind is occupied with business, to learn to play on the harp, the viol, the spinet and the flute, and to give up every day a prescribed time to practice. With similar kindness he rules his whole household, in which there are no tragic incidents, and no quarrels. If anything of the kind should be likely, he either calms it down, or applies a remedy at once. And in parting with any member of his household he has never acted in a hostile spirit, or treated him as an enemy. Indeed his house seems to have a sort of fatal felicity, no one having lived in it without being advanced to higher fortune, no inmate having ever had a stain upon his character.

It would be difficult to find any one living on such terms with a mother as he does with his step-mother. For his father had brought in one stepmother after another; and he has been as affectionate with each of them as with a mother. He has lately introduced a third, and More swears that he never saw anything better. His affection for his parents, children and sisters is such, that he neither wearies them with his love, nor ever fails in any kindly attention. . . .

He has been thrust more than once into an embassy, in the conduct of which he has shown great ability; and King Henry in consequence would never rest until he dragged him into his Court. "Dragged him," I say, and with reason; for no one was ever more ambitious of being admitted into a Court, than he was anxious to escape it. But as this excellent monarch [3] was resolved to pack his household with learned, serious, intelligent and honest men, he especially insisted upon having More among them,—with whom he is on such terms of intimacy that he cannot bear to let him go. If serious affairs are in hand, no one gives wiser counsel; if it pleases the King to relax his mind with agreeable conversation, no man is better company. Difficult questions are often arising, which require a grave and prudent judge; and these questions are resolved by More in such a way, that both sides are satisfied. And yet no one has ever induced him to accept a present. What a blessing it would be for the world, if magistrates like More were everywhere put in office by sovereigns! . . .

He published his *Utopia* for the purpose of showing, what are the things that occasion mischief in commonwealths; having the English constitution especially in view, which he so thoroughly knows and understands. He had written the second book at his leisure, and afterwards, when he found it was required, added the first off-hand. Hence there is some inequality in the style. . . .

However averse he may be from all superstition, he is a steady adherent of true piety; having regular hours for his prayers, which are not uttered by rote, but from the heart. He talks with his friends about a future life in such a way as to make you feel that he believes what he says, and does not speak without the best

3. On Erasmus's early admiration for Henry VIII, set Letter VI-4.

hope. Such is More, even at Court; and there are still people who think that Christians are only to be found in monasteries! Such are the persons, whom a wise King admits into his household, and into his chamber; and not only admits, but invites, nay, compels them to come in. These he has by him as the constant witnesses and judges of his life,—as his advisers and travelling companions. By these he rejoices to be accompanied, rather than by dissolute young men or by fops, or even by decorated grandees, or by crafty ministers, of whom one would lure him to silly amusements, another would incite him to tyranny, and a third would suggest some fresh schemes for plundering his people. . . .

You have now before you an ill-drawn portrait, by a poor artist, of an excellent original! . . .

(See also Letter V-9, in which Thomas More's words to his daughter Margaret exhibit his unusual strength of character.)

I-8　　Sir Thomas More to the Professors and Masters of the University of Oxford

As the most important Humanist of England, Thomas More (1478-1535) knew that the study of Ancient Greek was the key discipline distinguishing the New Learning from the preceding Scholastic education dominated by the Churchmen. He was of course aware of the opposition of Rome to the study of Greek, but he was taken aback on discovering that such an opposition still could exist within the faculty of his own beloved University of Oxford. He remonstrates, but with his usual good humor.

Abingdon
29 March (1518)

Thomas More to the Reverend Fathers, the commissary,* proctors, and others of the guild of masters of the University of Oxford, greeting.

I have been wondering, gentlemen, whether I might be permitted to communicate to scholars of your distinction certain conclusions to which I have

---

* i.e., the Vice-Chancellor.

recently come. Yet I have hesitated in approaching so brilliant a group, not so much on the ground of my style as on that of seeming to give an exhibition of pride and arrogance. Who am I, the possessor of little prudence and less practice, a scholar of mediocre proportions, to arrogate to myself the right to advise you in anything? And how can I dare to offer advice in the field of letters especially, when any one of you is fitted by his wisdom and erudition to give advice in that field to thousands?

At first sight, Venerable Fathers, I was therefore deterred by your unique wisdom. But, on second thought, I was encouraged; for it occurred to me that only ignorant and arrogant fools would disdain to give a man a hearing, and that the wiser and more learned you were, the less likely you would be to think highly of yourselves or to scorn the advice of others. I was further emboldened by the thought that no one was ever harmed by just judges, such as you are above all, simply on the ground that he offered advice without thinking of the consequences. On the contrary, loyal and affectionate advice, even if imprudent, has always deserved praise and thanks.

Finally, when I consider that, with God's help, I ought to offer you whatever slight learning I have acquired, since it was at your University that my education began, it seems the duty of a loyal friend not to pass over in silence what I deem it serviceable to bring to your attention. Since, then, the only danger in putting my pen to paper seemed to lie in the fact that a few might deem me too audacious, while I know that my silence would be condemned by many as ingratitude, I have preferred that the whole world should condemn my audacity rather than that anyone should have the chance to say that I showed myself ungrateful to your University, the honor of which I feel myself bound to defend to the uttermost. Moreover, no situation has, I believe, arisen in recent years, which, if you desire to maintain the honor of that institution, more urgently requires your serious attention.

The matter is as follows: when I was in London recently, I rather frequently heard that some members of your teaching body, either because they despised Greek or were simply devoted to other disciplines, or most likely because they possessed a perverse sense of humor, had proceeded to form a society named after the Trojans. The senior sage christened himself Priam; others called themselves Hector, Paris, and so forth; the idea, whether as a joke or a piece of anti-Greek academic politics, being to pour ridicule on those devoted to the study of Greek. And I hear that things have come to such a pass that no one can admit in public or private that he enjoys Greek, without being subjected to the jeers of these ludicrous "Trojans," who think Greek is a joke for the simple reason that they don't know what good literature is. To these modern "Trojans" applies the old saw, "Trojans always learn too late."

The affair aroused much comment, all very critical; and I myself felt somewhat bitter that even a few academics among you had nothing better to do in their spare time than to cast slurs on their colleagues' subjects. But I kept in mind that one could not expect the whole crowd of academics to possess wisdom, temperance, and humility; and so I began to dismiss the matter as a triviality. However, since I have been here in Abingdon in attendance at the court of His Victorious Majesty (Henry VIII), I have found that the silliness is developing into a form of insanity. For one of the "Trojans," a scholar in his own estimation, a wit of the first water in that of his friends, though slightly deranged in that of anyone observing his actions, has chosen during Lent to babble in a sermon against not only Greek but Roman literature, and finally against all polite learning, liberally berating all the liberal arts.

His whole performance was of a piece. Perhaps such a body of nonsense could not be preached on the basis of any sensible text; in any case, he followed neither the old custom of elucidating a whole passage of Scripture, nor the recent one of expounding some few words of Scripture; instead he elaborated on some stupid British proverbs. So I have no doubt that his frivolous sermon very deeply disturbed those who heard it; since I see that all who have heard fragmentary reports of it are unfavorably impressed.

What man in the audience, in whose breast burned even a spark of Christianity, would not groan at the degradation of the royal office of sacred preaching, which gained the world for Christ—above all at the hands of those whose supreme duty it was to protect it with the authority of their office? Who could possibly have devised a more outrageous insult than for an avowed preacher, during the most solemn season of the Church's year, in the presence of a large Christian congregation, in the sanctuary itself, from the elevation of the pulpit (as it were from the throne of Christ), and in view of the Sacred Body of Christ, to turn a Lenten sermon into Bacchanalian ravings? What a look must have been on the faces of the audience, who had come to hear spiritual wisdom, and saw the laughable pantomime he put on in the pulpit! They had expected to listen in reverence to the Word of Life; when they departed, all they could record they had heard was an attack on humane letters and a defamation of the preaching office by a fatuous preacher.

It would have been no reproach to secular learning if some good man, who had retired from the world to monastic life, suddenly returned and used this speaker's phrases: "much in watchings, much in prayer" or "the path to be trod by those who seek for heaven" or "other matters like humanistic education, trivial if not a positive hindrance to the spiritual life," or "simple country folk, and the unlettered, flying quicker to heaven," etc., etc. All this could have been borne from such a man. His simplicity would have been pardoned by his audience. They would have generously admitted his saintliness, and given serious consideration to his piety, devotion, and righteousness. But when they saw a man with the academic ermine over his shoulders, step on to the platform in the midst of a gathering composed solely of academics, and calmly proceed to rant against all humane learning, one would have had to be stone blind not to notice a signal pride and wickedness, a positive hatred of the higher arts. Many must have wondered indeed how such a man could get the idea that he had to preach either about Latin, of which he did not know much, or about the liberal arts, of which he knew less, or about Greek—in which he could not even grunt that it was "all Greek" to him!

If such an abundance of material had been supplied by the seven deadly sins, an altogether suitable theme for sermons, who would have believed him totally inexperienced therein! Though, as a matter of fact, what is it but sloth, when one is in the habit of denouncing rather than of learning that of which one is ignorant? And what is it but hatred, when one defames those who know what one deprecates but does not comprehend? And what is it but supreme pride, when he wishes no kind of knowledge to be prized save what he has falsely persuaded himself that he knows, and when he even—not from modesty, as might be the case with other people—arrogates more praise to himself for his ignorance than for his knowledge?

Now as to the question of humanistic education being secular. No one has ever claimed that a man needed Greek and Latin, or indeed any education in order to be saved. Still, this education which he calls secular does train the soul in virtue. In any event, few will question that humanistic education is the chief, almost the sole reason why men come to Oxford; children can receive a good education at home from their mothers, all except cultivation and book learning. Moreover, even if men come to Oxford to study theology, they do not start with that discipline. They must first study the laws of human nature and conduct, a thing not useless to theologians; without such study they might possibly preach a sermon acceptable to an academic group, without it they would certainly fail to reach the common man. And from whom could they acquire such skill better than from the poets, orators, and historians?

Moreover, there are some who through knowledge of things natural (i.e. rational) construct a ladder by which to rise to the contemplation of things supernatural; they build a path to theology through philosophy and the liberal arts, which this man condemns as secular; they adorn the queen of heaven with the spoils of the Egyptians! This fellow declares that only theology should be studied; but if he admits even that, I don't see how he can accomplish his aim without some knowledge of languages, whether Hebrew or Greek or Latin; unless, of course, the elegant gentleman has convinced himself that there is enough theology written in English or that all theology can be squeezed into the limits of those (late scholastic) "questions" which he likes to pose and answer, for which a modicum of Latin would, I admit, suffice.

But really, I cannot admit that theology, that august queen of heaven, can be thus confined. Does she not dwell and abide in Holy Scripture? Does she not pursue her pilgrim way through the cells of the holy Fathers: Augustine and Jerome; Ambrose and Cyprian; Chrysostom, Gregory, Basil, and their like? The study of theology has been solidly based on these now despised expositors of fundamental truth during all the Christian centuries until the invention of these petty and meretricious "questions" which alone are today glibly tossed back and forth. Anyone who boasts that he can understand the works of the Fathers without an uncommon acquaintance with the languages of each and all of them will in his ignorance boast for a long time before the learned trust his judgment.

But if this foolish preacher pretends that he was not condemning humanistic education in general but only an immoderate thirst for it, I can't see that this desire was such a sin that he had to deal with it in a public assembly, as if it were causing society to rush headlong to ruin. I haven't heard that many have gone so far in such studies that they will soon be overstepping the golden mean. Further, this fellow, just to show how immoderate *he* could be in a sermon, specifically called students of Greek "heretics," teachers of Greek "chief devils," and pupils in Greek "lesser devils" or, more modestly and facetiously as he thought, "little *devils"*; and the zeal of this holy man drove him to call by the name of devil one whom everybody knows the Devil himself could hardly bear to see occupy a pulpit. He did everything but name that one (D. Erasmus), as everybody realized just as clearly as they realized the folly of the speaker.

Joking aside—I have no desire to pose as the sole defender of Greek learning; for I know how obvious it must be to scholars of your eminence that the study of Greek is tried and true. To whom is it *not* obvious that to the Greeks we owe all our precision in the liberal arts generally and in theology particularly; for the Greeks either made the great discoveries themselves or passed them on as part of their heritage. Take philosophy, for example. If you leave out Cicero and Seneca, the Romans wrote their philosophy in Greek or translated it from Greek.

I need hardly mention that the New Testament is in Greek, or that the best New Testament scholars were Greeks and wrote in Greek. I am but repeating the consensus of scholarship when I say: however much was translated of old from Greek, and however much more has been recently and better translated, not half of Greek learning has yet been made available to the West; and, however good the translations have been, the text of the original still remains a surer and more convincing presentation. For that very reason all the Doctors of the Latin Church—Jerome, Augustine, Bede, and a host of others—assiduously gave themselves to learning Greek; and even though many works had already been translated, they were much more accustomed to reading them in the original than are many of our contemporaries who claim to be erudite; nor did they merely learn it themselves, but counseled those among their successors who wanted to be theologians above all to do the same.

So it is not as if I were just giving your Worships good advice about preserving the study of Greek. I am rather exhorting you to do your duty. You should not allow anyone in your university to be frightened away from the study of Greek, either by public assemblies or private inanities, since Greek is a subject required in every place of learning by the Church Universal. Common sense is surely enough to convince you that not all of your number who give themselves to the study of Greek can be blockheads; in fact, it is in part from these studies that your university had acquired its pedagogical prestige both at home and abroad.

There seems to be an increasing number of cases where Oxford has benefited from the presence of men nominally studying Greek only, but really taking the whole liberal arts course. It will be a wonder if their enthusiasm for you does not evaporate when they realize that so serious an enterprise is held in such contempt. Just think, too, what they are doing at Cambridge, which you have always outshone; those who are *not* studying Greek are so moved by common interest in their university that they are actually making large individual contributions to the salary of the Greek professor!

You see what I mean; and much more could be said to the point by men with better minds than mine. All I am doing is warning you of what others are saying and thinking, not telling you what it behooves you to do. You see much better than I that, if wicked factions are not suppressed at birth, a contagious disease will spread, and the better half be slowly absorbed by the worse, and that outsiders will be forced to take a hand in helping the good and wise among you. Any former student of the university takes its welfare as much to heart as you who are its living members. And I am sure that the Reverend Father in Christ who occupies the See of Canterbury (William Warham), who is the Primate of all our Clergy, and who is also the Chancellor of your university will not fail to do his part. Whether for the clergy's sake or yours, he rightly feels interested in preventing the decay of learning; and learning will perish if the university continues to suffer from the contentions of lazy idiots, and the liberal arts are allowed to be made sport of with impunity. And what about the Reverend Father in Christ, the Cardinal of York (Thomas Wolsey), who is both a patron of learning and himself the most learned of the episcopate? Would he endure patiently if aspersions were cast in your university on the liberal arts and the study of languages? Will he not rather aim the shafts of his learning, virtue, and authority at these witless detractors from the arts?

Last but not least: what of our Most Christian King? His Sacred Majesty has cultivated all the liberal arts as much as ever a king did; indeed, he possesses greater erudition and judgment than any previous monarch. Will his wisdom and piety suffer him to allow the liberal arts to fail—through the interests of evil and lazy men—in a place where his most illustrious ancestors wished that there be an illustrious seat of letters, a place which is an ancient nursery of learning, whose products have been an ornament not only to England but to the whole Church, a place which possesses so many colleges that have perpetual endowments specially designated for the support of students (in which respect there is no university outside the kingdom that can compare with Oxford), a place in which the aim of all its colleges and the purpose of all its endowments is none other than that a great body of academics, delivered from the necessity of earning their daily bread, might there pursue the liberal arts?

I have no doubt that you yourselves will easily in your wisdom find a way to end this dispute and quiet these stupid factions; that you will see to it not only that all the liberal arts may be free from derision and contempt but that they shall be held in dignity and honor. By such diligence in intellectual pursuits you will reap benefit for yourselves; and it can hardly be said how much you will gain favor with our Illustrious Prince and with the above-mentioned Reverend Fathers in Christ. You will forge an almost miraculous bond between yourselves and myself, who have thought that all this had to be written now in my own hand out of my deep personal affection for you. You know that my services are at the disposal of each and all of you. May God preserve your glorious seat of learning unharmed; and may He grant that it flourish continually in virtue and in all the liberal arts.

Thomas More

I-9   Desiderius Erasmus to John Lascaris

The Renaissance interest in classical languages is reflected in the following letter of Erasmus to John Lascaris, soliciting a recommendation for the chair of Greek professor at Louvain. A scholar as well as a diplomat, Lascaris had as a young man benefited from Cardinal Bessarion's plan to educate Greek youths in Italy following the capture of Constantinople by the Turks (see Letter VII-1). Among his many accomplishments were his contributions to Aldus Manutius' edition of the *Rhetores Graeci*.

Louvain, 26 April, 1518

Most illustrious Sir, Jerome Busleiden, a learned and influential man, and an incomparable ornament of this kingdom, having died in his journey to Spain, has bequeathed several thousand ducats to found at Louvain,—where is now a most flourishing University,—a new College, in which the three tongues, Hebrew, Greek and Latin, are to be publicly and gratuitously taught, with a handsome salary of about seventy ducats for the Professor, which may be augmented having regard to his personality. The Hebrew professor is already on the spot, and the Latin professor too. For the Greek chair there are several candidates; but my advice has always been, that a Greek by birth should be sent for, so that the pupils may at once imbibe the genuine pronunciation of the language. My opinion has been approved by all those who are taking part in the business, and they have given me authority to send,—in their names,—for any person whom I might judge to be fit for the work. I beg you therefore, for the sake of your usual kindness to me, or of your interest in Good Letters, if you know any one, who you think would do credit to your recommendation and mine, to get him to fly hither as soon as possible. The cost of his journey will be found for him; a salary and also a lodging will be provided. He will have the most honourable and most courteous persons to deal with, and he may trust this letter of mine as well as if the matter were transacted by means of a hundred indentures; between honest men there is no need of signing and sealing. Do take care and find me a suitable man, and I will take care, that he shall not regret his coming hither.

I-10   Guillaume Budé to Pierre Lamy

As young friars in the Franciscan monastery at Fontenay, François Rabelais and Pierre Lamy were placed in confinement after books in Greek were found in their possession, but managed to flee. Knowledge of Greek (which would permit free examination of the New Testament in the original language) was condemned by the Church at the time. The great Hellenist of France, Guillaume Budé (1468-1540), after intervening on their behalf, wrote to reassure Pierre Lamy as follows:

1523

O immortal God, Thou who presidest over their holy congregation and over our friendship, what news has reached me? I learn that you and Rabelais, your Pylades,* because of your zeal in the study of the Greek tongue, are harassed and vexed in a thousand ways by your brothers, those sworn enemies of all literature and all refinement. O fatal madness! O incredible error! Thus the gross and stupid monks have been so carried away by their blindness as to pursue with their calumnies those whose learning, acquired in so short a time, should be an honour to the entire community. . . . We had already learned and seen with our own eyes some marks of their insensate fury; we knew that they attacked ourselves as the chief of those who had been seized, as they say, by the fury of Hellenism, and that they had sworn to annihilate the cult of Greek letters, recently restored, to the eternal honour of our epoch. . . .

All friends of learning were ready, each in the measure of his power, to succour you in this extremity, you and the small number of brothers who share your aspirations towards universal knowledge . . . but I have learned that these tribulations ceased since your persecutors discovered that they were placing themselves in hostility to people of credit and to the King himself. Thus you have honourably emerged from this trial and will, I hope, resume your work with renewed ardour.

(See also Letter IV-7, in which the physician Rabelais exhibits his Hellenism and calls for a return to the "legitimate" medical science of the ancients.)

I-11   Giuseppe Pallavicino to Cardinal Morone

In fear for his life, the Rector of the University of Bologna appeals to the cardinal in authority to take measures to curb the student violence.

Parma, January 1, 1545

It may be that your Reverend Lordship is clearly informed about that student from Lucca, who, when I was with two gentlemen and accompanied by my

* closest friend, as Pylades was to Orestes.

servants, came up behind my back and without reason struck a blow against my head in order to kill me. Suddenly there appeared on his behalf more than thirty scoundrels from Lucca and Florence, as well as Bologna, armed with poles and lances which they took into that house where they managed to hide him. Upon learning of this your Reverend Lordship took those measures which were possible at the time, ordering the gates of the city closed for three days. Nonetheless, the not very vigorous show of authority in that other student riot (when the professor was struck down among the factions), rather out of respect for someone's hidden feelings than for the righteous will of your Reverend Lordship, emboldened the students to commit an even greater disturbance if the school's authority had not intervened. The world may judge the worth of such a man who might in this way assassinate every great man.

Unless some appropriate measures are taken as such a situation requires, it is my judgment that some of these students from Bologna will try to demolish the University. I have, to avoid grave trouble, left the city temporarily. But meanwhile I beg as Rector, which I still am, that your Reverend Holiness with prudence and authority make an example of all reckless students in future cases of villainy.

You may remember that his Excellency, Duke Francesco of Milan, ordered Rizzo, one of the principals of University of Pavia, to have his head cut off for trying to slap the Rector. Even if this punishment cannot be meted out in the case of this man who fled, you can by other means find some remedy for this situation. For the rest then, while I as Giuseppe Pallavicino shall continue to have my conscience aggravated by the nature of these too familiar assassinations, you will take such appropriate measures as God may will. Herewith falling silent, I shall humbly kiss the hands of your Most Reverend Lordship.

Your Humble Servitor,
Giuseppe Pallavicino
(trans. R. J. C.)

I-12   Roger Ascham to Sir William Cecil

Having served at court as tutor to Princess Elizabeth and abroad as secretary to England's ambassador to Charles V, the English scholar Roger Ascham (1516-1568) seeks Sir William Cecil's help in returning to a quiet academic life at Cambridge.

Brussels, 24 March, 1553

Sir,

if I shold write oft ye might think me to bold, and if I dyd leave of, ye might judge me eyther to forget your jentlenesse or to mistrust your good will, who hath allreadye so bownd me unto yow as I shall rather forget myself, and wisshe God also to forget me, than not labor with all diligence and service to applie myself holie to your will and purpose. And that ye shall well know how moch I assure my self on your goodnesse, I will passe a peece of good manners, and be bold to borow a litle of your smaull leysor from your weightie affaires in the comon welth. Therfore, if my letters shall find yow at any leysor, thei wol troble yow a litle in telling yow at lenght, as I promised in my last letters deliverd unto yow by Mr. Francis Yaxeley, whi I am more desirous to have your help for my staye at Cambridge styll, than for any other kynde of living else where. I having now som experience of liffe led at home and abrode, and knowing what I can do most fitlie, and how I wold live most gladlie, do wel perceyve their is no soch quietnesse in England, nor pleasur in strange contres, as even in S. Jons Colledg to kepe company with the Bible, Plato, Aristotle, Demosthenes, and Tullie. Whiche my choise of quietnes is not purposed to lye in idlenes, nor constrayned by a wilfull natur bicause I wol not or can not serve else where, whan I trust I cold applie my self to mo kyndes of liffe than I hope any need shall ever drive me to seeke, but onlie bicause, in chosing aptlye for myself, I might bring som proffet to many others. And in this myne opinion I stand the more gladlie, bicause it is grownded upon the judgement of worthie Mr. Dennye. For the Somer twelvemonth before he departed, dynnor and supper he had me comonlie with him, whose excellent wisdom, mingled with so pleasant mirth, I can never forget; emonges many other taulks he wold saie oft unto me, if two dewties did not comaund him to serve, th'on his prince, th'other his wiffe, he wold surelie becum a student in S. Johns, sayng, "The Corte, Mr. Ascam, is a place so slipperie, that dewtie never so well done, iss not a staffe stiffe enough to stand by alwaise very surelie; where ye shall many tymes repe most unkyndnesse where ye have sown greatest pleasurs, and those also readye to do yow moch hurt, to whom yow never intended to think any harme": which sentences I hard very gladlie than, and felt them sone after my self to be trewe.* Thus I, first by myn own natur, than moved by good cownsell, after driven by ill fortun, lastly caulled by quietnesse, thought it good to couche myself in Cambridge ageyn. And in very deed to many be pluckt from thens before thei be ripe, though I myself am witherd before I be gatherd; and yet not so, for that I have stand to long, but rather because the frute which I beare is so very smaull. Yet seyng the goodlye croppe of Mr. Cheeke is almost cleen carryed from thens,

---

* Chapter VI below will contain a barrage of letters attacking life at court, by Cornelius Agrippa, Thomas Wyatt, and Aretino.

and I in a manner alone of that tyme left a standing straggler, peradventur, though my frute be very smaul, yet, bicause the grownd from whens it sprong was so good, I may yet be thought somwhat fitt for seede, whan all yow the rest ar taken up for better store, wherewith the king and his realme is now so noblie served. . . .

Therfor, sir, to be shorte, ye bind me to serve yow for ever, if by your sute the kynges majestie wol graunt me this privilege, that, reeding the Greek tong in S. John's, I shold be bownd to no other statutes within that universitie and colledge. And som reason I have, to be made free and jorneyman in lernyng, whan I have allready served out three prentyships at Cambrige. This sute also, I trust, is not made out of season, whan thinges ar rather yet to be ordred by the grace of our Visitors, than by the law of any statute, but I heare saie the Visitors have taken this ordre, that every man shall professe the studie eyther of divinitie, law, or physick, and in remembring thus well England abrode, thei have in myn opinion forgotten Cambrig it self. For if som be not sufferd in Cambrige to make the fourth ordre, that is surelie as thei list, to studie the tonges and sciences, th'other three shall nayther be so many as thei shold, nor yet so good and perfitte as thei might. For law, physick, and divinitie need so the help of tonges and sciences as thei can not want them, and yet thei require so a hole man's studie, as he may parte with no tyme to other lerning except it be at certayn tymes to fetch it at other men's labor. I know Universities be instituted onelie that the realme may be served with preachers, lawyers, and physicions, and so I know likewise all woodes be planted onelie eyther for building or burnyng; and yet good husbandes, in serving, use not to cut down all for tymbre and fuell, but leave alwaise standing som good big ons, to be the defense for the newe springe. Therfore if som were so planted in Cambrige, as thei shold neyther be carryed awaye to other placese, nor decaye there for lack of living, nor be bownd to professe no one of the three, but bond them self holie to help forward all, I belive, preachers, lawyers and physicions shold spring in nombre, and grow in bignes, more than comonlie thei do. And though your Mastership get me the priviledge, yet, God is my judge, Scripture shold be my cheefe studie, where in I wold trust, eyther by wryting or preaching to show to others the way, both of truth in doctrin, and trew dealing in living; yea, if I do not obteyn this sute of libertie in lerning, where I am sure I cold do moch good, than I besiche your Mastership help to bestowe some litle benefice on me, where I might in a corner occupie the smaull talent which God hath lent me. And if I shall be neyther so luckye as to injoye the first, nor judged fitte to be cauld to the second, than there is a third kynd of living, wherin I cold find in myn harte to leede my liffe for a while, if your wisdom will me, not otherwise, and that is in leyng abrode in som strange contrye for a yeare or two. This last daye as I taulked with a Sig^or Marco Antonia Damula, the ambassador of Venice, to whom I am exceding moch beholden, he said unto me, if I had desire to live for a yeare or two in Constantinople, Damasco, or Cayro, he wold provide I shold be in place where I should be partaker of weightye affaires. I said, my desire was bent moch that waye save onelie I wold not be in place to receyve any wagese, more than the benefit of a table, mary in reading with some great man, whan leisor shold give leave, the course of the grek stories or other parte of lerning, I cold indevour myself, but I wold live surelie by the benefit of my prince and contrye. He said if he had known my purpose before Navagerius went last Ambass. to the Turke, he cold so have placed me, as I shold hereafter have cand him moch thank. Therfor, sir, if I do not obteyn neyther of my requestes at home, I trust, I cold do the kynges majestie good service, and your mastership moch pleasur abrode, by diligent advertisementes of affaires from thens, if by your means the kynges majestie for a yeare or two wold bestow som honest stipend on me, that myn interteynment from home might so give me credite abrode as I might have both libertie to lern, and leysor to wryte, soche thinges as were worthie to cum to your knowledge. . . . I have made my lotes, and set them in ordre, as I wisshe them to chance, and if it please your wisdom to draw for me, even as I know ye can discerne the fittest so shall I esteem it to be the luckiest, whatsoever shall cum first to your hand. And think not that your jentlenes doth more bolden me now to make this sute, than it doth bind me for ever to be at your comaundment, as God knoweth, who have yow and all yours in his keeping. I wold be glad to here that ye have receyved thies letters.

Your Masterships
to comaunde
R. Ascham.

I-13   Sir Henry Sidney to Philip Sidney

The inspiring letter which Sir Philip Sidney's father sent him is a model of advice on how to become a gentleman-scholar in the best tradition of Humanism, anticipating the pages of Peacham or Francis Bacon. Unlike so many such letters, it was not apparently composed for wide circulation or eventual publication. Henry Sidney (1529-1586) was a courtier under Elizabeth and counselor for Irish affairs.

Ireland, 1566

Son Philip:

I have received two letters from you, one written in Latin, the other in French; which I take in good part, and will you to exercise that practice of learning often; for that will stand you in most stead in that profession of life that you are born to live in. And now, since this is my first letter that ever I did write to you, I will not that it be all empty of some advices which my natural care of you provoketh me to wish you to follow, as documents to you in this your tender age.

Let your first action be the lifting up of your mind to Almighty God by hearty prayer; and feelingly digest the words you speak in prayer, with continual meditation and thinking of Him to whom you pray, and of the matter for which you pray. And use this as an ordinary act, and at an ordinary hour; whereby the time itself shall put you in remembrance to do that you are accustomed to do in that time.

Apply your study to such hours as your discreet master doth assign you, earnestly; and the time I know he will so limit as shall be both sufficient for your learning and safe for your health. And mark the sense and the matter of that you do read, as well as the words; so shall you both enrich your tongue with words and your wit with matter, and judgment will grow as years grow in you.

Be humble and obedient to your masters, for, unless you frame yourself to obey others—yea, and feel in yourself what obedience is, you shall never be able to teach others how to obey you.

Be courteous of gesture and affable to all men, with diversity of reverence according to the dignity of the person. There is nothing that winneth so much with so little cost.

Use moderate diet so as, after your meal, you may find your wit fresher and not duller and your body more lively and not more heavy. Seldom drink wine, and yet sometimes do, lest, being enforced to drink upon the sudden, you should find yourself enflamed. Use exercise of body, yet such as is without peril to your bones or joints it will increase your force and enlarge your breath. Delight to be cleanly as well in all parts of your body as in your garments; it shall make you graceful in each company—and otherwise loathsome.

Give yourself to be merry; for you degenerate from your father if you find not yourself most able in wit and body to do anything when you are most merry. But let your mirth be ever void of all scurrility and biting words to any man; for a wound given by a word is oftentimes harder to be cured than that which is given by the sword.

Be you rather a hearer and bearer away of other men's talk than a beginner and procurer of speech; otherwise you shall be accounted to delight to hear yourself speak. If you hear a wise sentence or an apt phrase, commit it to your memory with respect of the circumstances when you shall speak it. Let never oath be heard to come out of your mouth, nor word of ribaldry; so shall custom make to yourself a law against it in yourself. Be modest in each assembly and rather be rebuked of light fellows for maidenlike shamefastness than of your sad friends for pert boldness. Think upon every word that you will speak before you utter it, and remember how nature hath ramparted up, as it were, the tongue with teeth, lips—yea, and hair without the lips, and all betokening reins and bridles for the loose use of that member.

Above all things tell no untruth; no, not in trifles. The custom of it is naughty. And let it not satisfy you that for a time the hearers take it for a truth; for after it will be known as it is to your shame. For there cannot be a greater reproach to a gentleman than to be accounted a liar.

Study and endeavour yourself to be virtuously occupied. So shall you make such a habit of well-doing in you as you shall not know how to do evil, though you would. Remember, my son, the noble blood you are descended of by your mother's side; and think that only by virtuous life and good action you may be an ornament to that illustrious family. Otherwise, through vice and sloth, you may be counted *labes generis*,[1] one of the greatest curses that can happen to man.

Well, my little Philip, this is enough for me, and too much, I fear, for you. But if I find that this light meal of digestion nourish in anything the weak stomach of your capacity, I will, as I find the same grow stronger, feed it with other food.

Commend me most heartily unto Master Justice Corbet, old Master Onslow, and my cousin, his son.[2] Farewell! Your mother and I send you our blessings, and Almighty God grant you His, nourish you with His fear, govern you with His grace, and make you a good servant to your prince and country!

Your loving father, so long as you live in the fear of God,

H. Sidney.

1. a blot on the family escutcheon.
2. "Old Master Onslow" was Sheriff of Salop and "Master Justice Corbet," a Justice of the King's Bench, was Recorder of Shrewsbury.

I-14   Gabriel Harvey to Edmund Spenser

Radical changes in education are illuminated in this letter of Gabriel Harvey
(1550?-1630) to Edmund Spenser describing new reading tastes at
Cambridge, their common alma mater.

After 1576

But I beseech you, what News all this while at Cambridge? That was wont to be
ever one great Question. What? *Det mihi Mater ipsa bonam veniam, eius ut aliqua
mihi liceat Secreta, uni cuidam de eodem gremio obsequentissimo filio, revelare: et sic
paucis habeto. Nam alias fortasse pluribus: nunc non placet, non vacat, molestum esset.*
Tully and Demosthenes nothing so much studied, as they were wont: Livy, and
Salust possibly rather more, than less: Lucian never so much: Aristotle much
named, but little read: Xenophon and Plato, reckoned amongst Discoursers, and
conceited Superficial fellows: much verbal and sophistical jangling: little subtle
and effectual disputing; noble and royal Eloquence, the best and persuasiblest
Eloquence: no such Orators again, as red-headed Angels: an exceeding great
difference between the countenances, and ports of those, that are brave and
gallant, and of those, that are basely, or meanly apparelled: between the learned
and unlearned, Tully, and Tom Tooly, in effect none at all.

Machiavelli a great man: Castiglione of no small reputation: Petrarch, and
Boccaccio in every man's mouth: Galateo and Guazzo never so happy: over many
acquainted with Unico Aretino: the French and Italian when so highly regarded of
Scholars? the Latin and Greek, when so lightly? the Queen Mother at the
beginning, or end of every conference: many bargains of Monsieur: Shymeirs a
noble gallant fellow: all inquisitive after News, new Books, new Fashions, new
Laws, new Officers, and some after new Elements, and some after new Heavens
and Hells too. Turkish affairs familiarly known: castles buried in the Air: much
ado, and little help: Jack would fain be a Gentleman: in no age so little so much
made of, everyone highly in his own favor, thinking no man's penny, so good silver
as his own: Something made of Nothing, in spite of Nature: Numbers made of

Ciphers, in spite of Art: Geometrical Proportion seldom, or never used, Arithmetical over much abused: Oxen and Asses (notwithstanding the absurdity it seemed to Plautus) draw both together in one and the same Yoke: *conclusio fere sequitur deteriorem partem.*

The Gospel taught, not learned: Charity key cold: nothing good, but by Imputation: the Ceremonial Law, in word abrogated: the Judicial in effect disannulled: the Moral indeed abandoned: the Light, the Light in every man's Lips, but mark me their eyes, and tell me, if they look not liker Owlets, or Bats, than Eagles: as of old Books, so of ancient Virtue, Honesty, Fidelity, Equity, new Abridgements: every day fresh span new Opinions: Heresy in Divinity, in Philosophy, in Humanity, in Manners, grounded much upon hearsay: Doctors contemned: the Text known of most, understood of few: magnified of all, practiced of none: the Devil not so hated, as the Pope: many Invectives, small amendment: Skill they say controlled of Will: and Goodness mastered of Goods: but Agent, and Patient much alike, neither Barrel greatly better Herring.

No more ado about Caps and Surplices: Master Cartwright nigh forgotten: the man you wot of, conformable, with his square Cap on his round head: and Non-resident at pleasure: and yet Non-residents never better baited, but not one the fewer, either I believe in Act, or I believe in Purpose. A number of our preachers fib to French Soldiers, at the first, more than Men, in the end less than Women. Some of our pregnantest and soonest ripe Wits, of Hermogenes' metal for all the world: Old men and Counsellors amongst Children: Children amongst Counsellors, and old men: Not a few double sacred Tani, and Changeable chameleons: over many Claw-backs and Pick-thanks: Reeds shaken of every Wind: Jacks of both sides: Aspen leaves: painted Sheaths, and Sepulchres: Asses in Lions' skins. . . .

Concerning the chiefest general point of your Mastership's letter, yourself are not ignorant that scholars in our age are rather now Aristippi than Diogenes: and rather active than contemplative philosophers: coveting above all things under heaven to appear somewhat more than scholars if themselves wist how; and of all things in the world most detesting that spiteful malicious proverb, of greatest Clerks, and not wisest men. The date whereof they defend was expired when Duns Scotus and Thomas Aquinas with the whole rabblement of Schoolmen were abandoned our schools and expelled the University.

And now of late forsooth to help countenance out the matter they have gotten Philbertes Philosopher of the Court, the Italian Archbishop's brave Galatro, Castiglione's fine *Cortegiano,* Bengalasso's Civil Instructions to his Nephew Seignor Princisca Ganzar: Guazzo's new Discourses of courteous behavior, Jovio's and Rasseli's *Emblems* in Italian, Paradine's in French, Plutarch in French,

Frontine's *Stratagems,* Polyene's *Stratagems,* Polonica, Apodemica, Guigiandine, Philip de Comines, and I know not how many outlandish braveries besides of the same stamp.

Shall I hazard a little farther: and make you privy to all our privities indeed. Thou knowest *non omnibus dormio et tibi habeo non huic.* Aristotle's *Organon* is nigh-hand as little read as Duns's *Quodlibet.* His economics and politics everyone oweth by rote. You can not step into a scholar's study but (ten to one) you shall lightly find open either Bodin's *De Republica* or LeRoy's *Exposition* upon Aristotle's *Politics* or some other like French or Italian Politic Discourses.

And I warrant you some good fellows amongst us begin now to be prettily well acquainted with a certain parlous book called, as I remember me, *Il Principe* di Niccolo Machiavelli, and I can peradventure name you an odd crew or two that are as cunning in his *Discorsi sopra la prima Deca di Livio,* in his *Historia Fiorentina,* and in his Dialogues *della Arte della Guerra* too, and in certain gallant Turkish Discourses too, as University men were wont to be in their *parva Logicalia* and *Magna Moralia* and *Physicalia* of both sorts; *verbum intelligenti sat;* you may easily conjecture the rest yourself; especially being one that can as soon as another spy light at a little hole.

But, howsoever, most of us have expired the setting down, or rather setting up of this conclusion touching the expiring of the foresaid date as a most necessary University principle and main foundation of all our credit abroad; methinks still for some special commonwealth affairs and many particular matters of counsel and policy, besides daily fresh news and a thousand both ordinary and extraordinary occurrences and accidents in the world, we are yet (notwithstanding all and singular the premises) to take instructions and advertisements at your lawyers' and courtiers' hands, that are continually better trained and more lively experienced therein, than we University men are or possibly can be, or else peradventure when we shall stand most in our own conceits we may haply deceive and disgrace ourselves most, and in some by-matters when we least think of it, commit greater errors, and more foully overshoot ourselves than we be yet aware of or can conjecturally imagine.

I-15   Marc-Antoine Muret to Cardinal Sirleto

Wearied by a disorderly and threatening student body, the eminent professor of rhetoric of the University of Rome begs permission to resign and retire to some quiet spot outside the capital. Muret (1526-1585) was widely considered the equal of Lefévre d'Etaples and Budé as Hellenist.

(1584?)

Most Illustrious and Reverend my esteemed Monsignore,

I beg your illustrious and reverend Holiness that to the many other favors you have extended to me on other occasions, you add one more which I shall hold as the greatest of all, and to communicate on the earliest possible occasion to His Holiness the following articles.

First, it is now twenty years that I have been lecturing at the University of Rome with great effort and incredible diligence. For the grace of God, I believe that I have carried out this charge reasonably well.

Now at last at sixty years of age I need a bit of rest, especially since, over and beyond a few other physical handicaps, I have lost all of my upper and two lower teeth, which makes it difficult for me to speak and from day to day reduces my health.

I have supported infinite indignities from the perpetual insolence of the students, who when a man goes to great pains to say something good and useful, respond with such cries, whistling, rackets, villainies and other dishonest acts, that I know not sometimes where my brain has fled.

That the walls of the schools are usually seen full of such abominable mottoes and pictures of such ilk that many prelates, religious men, and other honorable people who come to hear me are overcome with horror on noticing them, it seeming to them, and rightly, to be entering not a school but the most infamous and dishonest of those which cannot even decently be named.

That I wishing to punish these ugly acts, have been many times during the past years hooted, threatened, as much as if to announce publicly that if I did not shut up, they would smash in my face.

That it is an obvious thing that many come into the University with daggers.

That this very year, having been forced several times without being able to lecture, one Saturday—it was the 10th of December—in the middle of my lecture there was thrown mightily against me a melon with the manifest peril of putting out an eye. At which point I withdrew without saying another word, fearing even worse, to the great scandal of some prelates who happened to be present at the time.

That the professorial chairs of the doctors have long since become pillories or worse, such is the insolence of these youngsters.

That I, having been by nature perhaps too sensitive, now appreciate these things to such a point that I now am aware of what harm they could do me, if I have to undergo them further.

That I, in these respects, can no longer lecture with a good mind, and although to content your Holiness I should be willing to put a thousand lives out to risk, if I had a thousand lives, nevertheless throwing myself to your holy feet, I beg and entreat you, for the love of God, that you deign to permit me to leave my professorship, and with good grace. Nor do I wish as compensation anything else as the price of the troubles I have endured than that I may pass these few last years, spared from being exposed to perpetual scorn, vilification, and dissatisfaction.

And if the lengthy servitude of twenty years or more will seem to Your Holiness worthy of some sort of compensation to sustain my old age and bring up my poor young grandson, of whom I have great hopes for his goodness and learning, you will bring into play that infinite charity which Your Holiness has displayed toward so many others. In any case, I shall not fail in this matter to feel obliged to you, whom I could never sufficiently repay with my very life. Withdrawing to some place near Rome, where I can live peacefully with less expense, I shall continually pray to God, as I must, for Your Holiness. Nor, so long as I shall live, shall I desist preaching by voice and by writing the incredible goodness of Gregory XIII Pontifex most deserving of Glory, to whom let God grant a most long and felicitous life in this world, and Paradise in the other.

I pray your most excellent and Reverend Holiness that you make every effort to obtain this favor and I most humbly kiss Your hands.

Your most humble and devoted Servitor,
Marcantonio Mureto
(trans. R. J. C.)

I-16　　The Lords of the Council to the Lords Lieutenants of Sussex

Foreign study was recommended to young gentlemen by Francis Bacon and other Humanists as part of their philosophy of education. The universities of Paris, Bologna, Padua, Alcalá, and Wittenberg accepted young Englishmen. Realizing that many of these universities were in papist countries, Elizabeth Regina took measures as ruthless as those of the Inquisition itself to get the scholars back and check the loyalty of their families or patrons.

31 December 1593

To our verie good Lords the Lord Admirall and the Lord Buckhurst, the Lieutenants of the County of Sussex, and in theire absence to the Deputie Lieutenants of that County.

After our verie hartie commendacions, the Queenes Majestie finding noe small inconvenience to growe unto the Realme by sending out of the same the Children of many Gentlemen under coulour of learning the Languages, wherby they are for the most parte bredd and brought uppe in the Popish religion and corruptnes of manners, to the manifest prejudice of the State heere; which her Majesty, desirous to reforme as a disorder of no small importance, hath geven order that Inquisition be made throughout the Realme what sonns of Gentlemen are at this present beyonde the Seas conveyed over at any tyme within seaven yeares last passed, and by what lycence they are gone. And for such as are departed out of the Realme, if they be sonnes of anye Recusants or of such as doe conforme themselves in shewe onelie to avoide the danger and penalties of the Lawes, it is not to be doubted but that the intention of their parents hath bene to have them brought upp and instructed in Poperie: and of those, many doe become Seminarie Priests, Jhesuits, and unsounde subjects, and sent hither to pervert such as are dutiefull and well inclyned, and to practice thereby to disturbe the quiett and happie governement of her Majestie. Wee therefore for the better execution of her Majesties direccion in this behalf, have made speciall choice of you as of persons in our opinions meete for your loyallties and affection to her Majestie and the good of the Contrye, to be ymploied in this service, and doe hereby require and auctorize you and every of you, joyntlie and severallie, by all good meanes to enquire and examine what Gentlemen within that Countye have at this present any sonnes, kinsemen, or other persons, whose education hath bene committed to their chardge, or whome they doe relieve or any way mayntaine out of the Realme, being sent over under colour to learn Languages or for any other respectes, not being notoriouslie imployed in her Majesties martiall services, or trade of merchandize, as apprentices or factors to knowne Marchaunts, and to sende us a cathologue of the names as well of the fathers and parents or of theire tutors and patrons, as of the sonns and other parties so sent over or mayntayned, in what parts they are, and how long they have been absent. And of those fathers, parents, and other frends by whome any such have bene sent out of the Realme, yf any of them be founde to be Recusants, or have bene evill affected, and in your knowledge are but faynedlie refourmed, you shall cause bonds to be taken in good sommes of money to her Majesties' use for their personall appearance before us by a certen day, by you to be prefixed; and before the bonds so taken, you shall by auctoritie hereof enter and make search in theire howses, for Jhesuits, Seminarie Priests, and other suspected persons, and apprehende and committe them to prison yf any suche shall be founde; as allso to open and make search in their closetts, chests, desks, and coffers, (onelie for books, lettres, and wrytings that may anie way concerne matter against the State or the Religion here established) which you seaze and send hither unto us forthwith; signifying the manner of your proceedings, and your oppinions of the men and the matters appearing by your search against them, that wee uppon their appearance may take order with them aswell for the revocation of their sonns and kinsmen as for any matter that by your endevours may be discovered against them. And if the residence of anie of theis shall happen to be farre distant from you, or any one of you, then may you by vertue of theis our Lettres make choice of such one or twoo honest gentlemen, being Justices of the Peace and not partiallie affected towarde them, inhabiting neare unto them, to whom you may give direction for the performance of the search, &c. And for your particular Warrant therein you may sende unto them a coppie of this our Lettre under your hand (which shalbe unto them as sufficient as the originall unto you). Herein wee require you to use your best and uttermost endevours, and with as much convenient dilligence as you may, to retourne us your orderlie Certificat, answering the severall poynts of theis our Lettres and Direccions. Soe fare you well. From Hampton Court the last of December 1593.

We leave to your LL. to appoint your Deputie Lieutenaunts and such of the

Justices of the Peace for th'execucion of this service within your charge as you shall thinck to be fitte.

Your very loving ffrends
Jo. Puckering C. S.   W. Burghley.   Essex.
C. Howard.   W. Cobham.   T. Buckhurst.
Ro. Cecyll.   Jo. Fortescue.

I-17   Joseph Mead to Sir Martin Stuteville

When the faculty of Cambridge University started deliberations to fill the vacant post of University Chancellor, replacing the deceased Lord Suffolk, the King violated academic freedom, brutally imposing on them the arrogant Duke of Buckingham (assassinated not long afterward). Mead's sarcastic letter shows how an angry and rebellious faculty ends up by eating crow. Joseph Mead (1586-1638) was a theologian and Biblical scholar born in Essex.

Christ Coll., 3 June, 1626

Worthie Sir

That you might not altogether want news this Week through your abundance the last, *We* have bred some; that the Age being so fruitful of wonders we Academians might not be wanting to produce something for the world to wonder at. To tell you plainly we have chosen the Duke of Buckingham our Chancellor and that with more than ordinary triumph. I will tell as much as my time will let me.

Our Chancellor my Lord of Suffolk died on Sunday about two a Clock in the morning: which no sooner came to our ears on Monday, but about dinner time arrives Dr. Wilson (my Lord of Londons chaplain) without Letters, but with a message from his Lord that we should chuse the Duke; such being his Majesty's desire and pleasure. Our Heads meet after Sermon, when by Dr. Wren, Beale, Maw, Pask, this motion was urged with that vehemency and as it were confidence of authority, that the rest were either awed or perswaded; and those that would not yet durst not adventure to make further opposition, though they inclined, (if it be lawful to say so) to more advised counsel. It was in vain to say that Dr. Wilson's bare word from his Lord was no sufficient testimony of his Majesty's pleasure; nor such as might be a ground of an act of such consequence, that we should by this Act prejudge the Parliament: that instead of Patronage we sought for, we might bring a lasting scandal and draw a general contempt and hatred upon the University as men of most prostitute flattery: that it would not be safe for us to engage ourselves in publick differences: that at least to avoid the imputation of folly and temerity in the doing, it would be wisdom to wait our full time of fourteen days, and not to precipitate the Election. To this was answered, "The sooner the better, and more acceptable." If we stayed to expect the event in Parliament, it would not be worth "God-ha-mercy!"

Upon the news of this Consultation and Resolution of the Heads, we of the Body murmur, we run one to another to complain. We say the Heads in this Election have no more to do than any of us; wherefore we advise what to do and who to set up. Some are for my Lord Keeper, others for my Lord Andover (Berkshire); but lest we might be found over weak, being distracted, we agree that he that shall find most voices of these or any other set up, the rest should all come to him. Hereupon on Tuesday morning (notwithstanding every Head sent for his Fellows to perswade them for the Duke) some durst be so bold as to visitt for the contrary in publick. Others more privily inquired how their friends and others were affected. But the same day about dinner time the Bishop of London arrived unexpected, yet found his own Colledge (Queen's) most bent and resolved another way to his no small discontentment. At the same time comes to town Mr. Mason (my Lord Duke's Secretary) and Mr. Cosens, and Letters from my Lord of Durham expressly signifying in his Majesty's name (as they told and would make us believe) that his Majesty would be well pleased if we chose the Duke. My Lord Bishop labours, Mr. Mason visits for his Lord, Mr. Cosens for the most true Patron of the Clergy and of Scholars. Masters belabour their Fellows. Dr. Maw sends for his, one by one, to perswade them, some twise over. On Thursday morning (the Day appointed for the Election) he makes a large speech in the Colledge Chapel that they would come off unanimously; when the School Bell rung he caused the Colledge Bell also to ring as to an Act, and all the Fellows to come into the Hall and to attend him to the Schools for the Duke, that so they might win the honour to have it accounted their Colledge act. Divers in Town got hacknies, and fled to avoid importunity. Very many, some whole Colledges were gotten by their fearful Masters, the Bishop, and others, to suspend, who otherwise were resolved against the Duke, and kept away with much indignation: and yet for all this stirre the Duke carried it but by three Votes from My Lord Andover whom we voluntarily set up against him, without any motion on his behalf, yea without his knowledge. You will not believe how they triumphed (I mean the Masters above-named) when they had got it. Dr. Pask made his Colledge exceed that night, &c. Some since had a good mind to have questioned the Election for some reason: but I think they will be better advised for their owne ease. We had but one Doctor in the whole Towne durst (for so I dare speak) give with us against the Duke, and that was Dr. Porter of Queen's. What will the Parliament say to us? * Did not our Burgesses condemn the Duke in their charge given up to the Lords? I pray God we hear well of it: but the actors are as bold as lions, and I half believe would faine suffer that they might be advanced.

Thus, with my best respect, I rest and am
Yours most ready to be commanded
Joseph Mead

---

* This body, as Mead later reported, "was wonderfully exasperated by our Election, aggravating it as an act of Rebellion" on the part of the professors.

CHAPTER 2

LITERATURE. THEATER.

III. *Baldassare Castiglione* by Raphael

IV. *Actor and Actress* by Olivier Gatti

As it does in every century, literature displayed the new spirit of the era as well as any other medium, and with greater wit. At the same time it demonstrated how the break with the past and with a dominating Greco-Roman heritage was accomplished only with difficulty. Aristotle, for example, had clearly indicated that the three genres best justifying the existence of creative literature were epic, tragedy, and comedy. Thus, certain Humanistic writers like Trissino, Ronsard, and Lope de Vega felt duty-bound to write epics—of lesser quality than one might have expected—in order to turn to the other genres they preferred. However, the Greco-Roman influence on the Humanistic authors was a much happier and productive one than the relatively poor legacy left by the Middle Ages. Mediaeval literature had been composed under, or despite, the heavy-handed authority of the Church, empire, monarchy, or feudalism itself. Of the manuscripts which survived into the Renaissance, few pleased the sixteenth-century authors. Even so, it comes as a shock to learn that the erudite John Donne could be so angry as to "fling away" Dante, the most typical and meaningful of Mediaeval poets (II-11).

We have observed in Chapter I the veneration of Renaissance writers for the Greco-Roman classics. Erasmus, in a letter on Terence, found even the comedies of Terence of "a marvelous purity, propriety, and elegance of diction." At the end of his incidental remarks on his epic poem, *La Franciade,* Pierre de Ronsard writes, "To your knees, *Franciade,* adore the *Iliad.*" In a poem to his valet Corydon (a Greekish renaming of Jacques or whatever the fellow's name was) Ronsard states that he is retiring to his study to read in three days the *Iliad* of Homer and will brook no interruption, even if the King himself should happen by. (If his mistress should come by, he adds, send her up.) Ronsard, Erasmus, Rabelais, and the other Humanist writers knew Greek as well as Latin, well enough to write in it. Nothing pleased Erasmus so much as to be told by Sixtinus that his verses have an Attic quality, a light touch or seemingly unconscious art. This seeming effortlessness, by the way, was considered the most characteristic quality of a true gentleman, as Count Canossa observed in Castiglione's *Book of the Courtier.* Even though Manuel Chrysoloras had first started teaching Greek in Florence in 1397, the opposition of the Church, mentioned in Chapter I, made teachers hard to find.

After the Greek epic poets, dramatists, lyricists, and satirists had been translated, first into Latin and then into the vernaculars, the high quality of their works inspired the Renaissance writers to imitate and emulate them. It took a while for the Renaissance dramatists, as dedicated to Medea, Eurydice, Cleopatra, Sophonisba, and to Agamemnon, Oedipus, and Hector, to realize that heroes and heroines of their own time (Mary Stuart, Inez de Castro, Wilhelm Tell, Don Carlos) had lived tragedies capable of eliciting pity, fear, and wonderment equally well. Late to feel the effects of the Renaissance, the English turned quickly to the old myths and histories. The only letter we possess of Shakespeare is the epistle to the Earl of Southampton dedicating his *Venus and Adonis* (II-10), a myth equally popular in art (III-16). So meaningful and even allegorical were some Greek themes that Samuel Daniel's borrowing of the story of Philotas for a tragedy was unfortunate. For once his generation of playgoers decided that the conspirator Philotas was really the Earl of Essex in ancient disguise, the playwright had vehemently to deny it (II-13). Even Edmund Spenser admitted to Raleigh in 1589 that in his *Faerie Queene* he followed the example of "all the antique poets historicall: first Homer, who in the persons of Agamemnon and Ulysses hath ensampled a good governour and a vertuous man, the one in his *Ilias,* the other in his *Odysseis"* (II-9).

The most practised forms of Renaissance literature were epic, tragedy, comedy, and lyric poetry (sonnet, elegy, madrigal, canzone, ballad). Yet this period, with its increasing freedom for the writer, saw a revival of satire which rivaled that of Aristophanes and Archilochus or of Horace and Lucian. Not only was there a lengthy series of satires by Brant, Murner, Barclay, Berni, Aretino, Pulci, Erasmus, Rabelais, and Cervantes. There was moreover an epidemic of prose and poetry lampooning judges, lawyers, physicians (IV-6, IV-9), alchemists (IV-1), churchmen, pedants, and a multitude of social and moral types. The three most successful satirists of the sixteenth century were surely Erasmus, Rabelais, and Cervantes. Erasmus was almost as gentle as Horace, heightening his satire only with theologians (and Pope Julius): "I have never blackened any man's character, while I have tilted in a playful way at the common and most notorious vices of mankind," wrote Erasmus to John of Louvain. Erasmus wrote his satire praising folly while waiting out a lumbago attack with Thomas More (II-1), whose *Utopia* showed that he too could have become a fine satirist. As for Cervantes, taxing by his *Quixote* both the chivalric romances of his time and the idealism and optimism of many compatriots, his book became so popular that, like Rabelais, he was kept busy trying to prevent unauthorized or spurious versions of his masterpiece (II-14).

To the mind-blown authors of the Renaissance—and the satirists were the best exemplars—literature could and should have a social purpose. That literature should strive to form gentlemen is attested by the large number of courtesy books at the time starting with Castiglione's *Courtier* (1528) and appearing continually until Henry Peacham's manual on gentility (1622). Since Vittoria Colonna was the widow of the famous Marquis of Pescara (VII-4), Castiglione submitted his manuscript before publication to this great lady and rejoiced in her enthusiastic praise (II-4). His satisfaction turned to irritation, however, when he learned three years later that she was still showing the unreturned manuscript around to her friends. Another writer conscious of the *engagement* of literature was Niccolò Machiavelli, whose bawdy comedy *The Mandrake* is nowadays considered to be an allegory of the rape of the Florentine Republic by the Medici. His concern for politics and warfare, which impelled him to compose his patriotic tract of *Realpolitik, The Prince,* permeates his personal letters, such as his missive to Bartolomeo Cavalcanti on the losing military strategies of Pope Clement VII (VII-7). A well-known and appealing letter of Machiavelli chronicles his rural way of life in exile composing *The Prince* (II-3).

The opposition or control of the Church, with its formidable weapons of the *Index of Forbidden Books,* the Inquisition, the *obstat,* and excommunication, is dealt with in Chapters I, III, and V of this anthology. Even the Christian Humanist Erasmus loses his temper when Churchmen "pronounce it wicked for Christians to be readers of Terence's plays." The writer most conspicuously trapped between the twin authorities of the Reformation and the Counter-Reformation was the epic poet Tasso, whose spirit was broken by persecutions real and imaginary until he found himself "fit neither for writing nor work" (II-6).

So sensitive were the writers of the late Cinquecento to Church criticism that upon arriving in Rome in 1580, Montaigne went immediately to the censors of the curia and sought their judgment on his brand-new book of *Essays.* Despite a few objections (reliance on pagan authorities, preference for fate over providence, etc.), the Vatican did not blacklist the book. The blacklisting took place in the following century, long after Montaigne's death. The bookstores had to be cautious about marketing controversial materials, whether literary or scientific—such as the works of Kepler or Galileo (Chapter IV).

To form a solidarity against critics and antagonists of church or state (the Calvinists had established their own list of banned books, including poetic romances), authors of common tastes and ideas grouped together in cénacles, clubs, pleiads, salons, and—like the other Humanists—in academies, like the literary academy at Brescia which so pleased Cardinal Bembo (II-5).

One historian of Renaissance literature did a book on the "gladiators of the republic of letters." There were indeed many feuds in this republic: Rabelais vs. Scaliger, Harvey vs. Nashe, Ronsard vs. Saint-Gelays, Gosson vs. Sidney, Lope vs. Cervantes, and so on. Scaliger tried to pick a fight with Erasmus, who disregarded his provocative letter. Feuds were often based on opposing literary judgments, and Erasmus was only too aware of the fickleness of such opinions, the more so when his *Praise of Folly* (II-1) was being praised and damned at the same time. A feud between a poet and his mistress to whom he devoted two books of *amores* is a strange one, but such a *différend* developed between Ronsard and his skittish young girl friend Hélène de Surgères (II-7). Ronsard was just as offended as Ariosto had been when Cardinal Ippolito d'Este leafed through his dedication copy of the *Orlando Furioso* and asked, "How on earth did you think up all this nonsense?"

Mention of Cardinal Ippolito poses the question of the Maecenate system and how it affected art and letters. The matter will receive considerable attention in Chapter III, where we shall find artists and musicians having a sea of troubles with their patrons. Of the poets and prose-writers mentioned in the present chapter, Erasmus was a protégé of Henry VIII and others, Machiavelli of the Medici, Tasso of the Este family of Ferrara, Ronsard of Francis I and Marguerite de Navarre and later monarchs, Shakespeare of the Earl of Southampton, Daniel of the Countess of Bedford, Spenser of Lord Grey, while Lope de Vega leaned on the Duke of Sessa for most of his adult life, drafting love letters for Sessa, humoring him, and giving him constant advice about his health and his conquests. Quevedo had as his patron King Philip IV of Spain, but another powerful favorite of Philip, the Count-Duke of Olivares, had Quevedo banished from court overnight and imprisoned without trial in a sordid cell described below by Quevedo (II-17). By the time Ben Jonson was obliged to think up an ingratiating manner to coax the Earl of Newcastle to send him his pension, there seemed to be no new and arresting way to phrase such an appeal. One must agree, however, that Jonson rose magnificently to the occasion (II-16).

Theater had a splendid resurgence in the Renaissance, given the excellent translations of ancient comedy and tragedy as well as the proliferation of new plays, especially comedies, either farcical or learned, and often leaning on Plautus, Terence, and Menander. The rigid Aristotelian distinctions between comedy and tragedy persisted in the plays performed in schools and courts, but Shakespeare and Lope de Vega mixed comic and tragic elements to the applause of the general public. Lope, called by Cervantes a monster of nature for his prolixity, penned some 1800 plays, of which about 500 survive. He was so widely enjoyed that when he found that two plays in a row met a luke-warm response, he decided to abandon the theater (II-15). Machiavelli's *Mandrake* and Bibbiena's *La Calandria* (II-2) influenced English comedies of the Elizabethan period, and Jonson's *Volpone* owed its best traits to the Italian comedy.

Two letters have come down to us offering splendid descriptions of the staging, one of a tragedy and one of a comedy. The *Oedipus Tyrannus* of Sophocles, so obviously known to the author of *Hamlet,* was universally accepted as the greatest tragedy of antiquity. The *Follies of Calandro* of Bibbiena, less famous than *The*

Mandrake, received a widely heralded premiere at the Court of Urbino, while *Oedipus* had an impressive performance in the famous theater of Palladio at Vicenza (II-8). Each letter on these events shows the great pains taken at the time to perfect the acting, staging, libretto, incidental music of interludes, etc. Furthermore, these two letters are evidence of what an important intellectual, artistic, and social phenomenon the theater had become in the Renaissance, surpassing even its lofty status in ancient Athens.

In enumerating the conspicuous literary genres in which the Renaissance excelled, we have limited them to the forms conventionally presented in histories of literature. Returning now to our claim in the General Introduction, it is obvious that the verse or prose epistle was as important a genre as it had been in Roman times. We remember Copernicus's belief that the Greek epistles of Theophylactus, which he had translated into Latin, were such an important genre as to be "not so much epistles as rules or precepts" for human conduct (I-3). Other ancient letters even more influential are listed in our General Introduction. Aldus Manutius, also mentioned there for his anthologies, was so busy a printer that when he paused to pen a letter himself, it was to be read by many or even to be used as a preface to some book (I-4). Forms of the verse-epistle by Michelangelo, Wyatt, and Daniel are included in this anthology (III-5, VI-8, II-12). Just as there were scores of *artes poeticae* in the Renaissance to teach our ancestors to write poetry, so were there "secretaries" or manuals to help them elevate their letters to the status of literature. Perhaps no correspondent, dipping his quill into an inkwell, was more certain of writing *sub specie aeternitatis* than was Erasmus, who went so far as to consign to a printer in Louvain a copy of his letter to Wolfgang Capito (I-5) before it was even received by its addressee.

II-1   Desiderius Erasmus to Sir Thomas More

In an epistle to Thomas More to whom the *Praise of Folly* is dedicated, Erasmus (1466?-1536) explains how he came to write his famous satirical monologue and offers an apologia for the choice of subject matter.

9 June (1510)

When of late days I was returning from Italy to England, being unwilling to
waste the whole time that I had to spend on horseback in illiterate talk, I
sometimes preferred either to think over some of our common studies, or to enjoy
the recollection of the friends, no less amiable than learned, that I had left here. Of
these, my More, you were among the first I called to mind, being wont to enjoy
the remembrance of you in your absence, as I had, when you were present,
enjoyed your company, than which I protest I have never met with anything more
delightful in my life. Therefore, since at any rate something had to be done, and
the occasion did not seem suited for serious meditation, I chose to amuse myself
with the *Praise of Folly*. What Pallas, you will say, put that idea into your head?
Well, the first thing that struck me was your surname of More, which is just as
near the name of *Moria* or Folly, as you are far from the thing, from which by
general acclamation you are remote indeed. In the next place I surmised, that this
playful production of our genius would find special favour with you, disposed as
you are to take pleasure in jests of this kind—jests, which, I trust, are neither
ignorant nor quite insipid—and generally in society, to play the part of a sort of
Democritus; although for that matter, while from the unusual clearness of your
mind you differ widely from the vulgar, still such is your incredible sweetness and
good nature, that you are able to be on terms of fellowship with all mankind, and
are delighted at all hours to be so. You will therefore not only willingly receive this
little declamation, as a memento of your comrade, but will adopt and protect it, as
dedicated to you and become not mine, but yours. For censors will perhaps be
found who may complain, that these trifles are in some parts more frivolous than
becomes a theologian, and in others more aggressive than consists with Christian
modesty, and will exclaim that we are bringing back the old Comedy, or the Satire
of Lucian, and seizing everything by the teeth. But those who are offended by the
levity and drollery of the subject should consider, that this is no new precedent of
mine, the same thing having been done over and over again by great authors; that
many ages ago Homer made sport with the Batrachomyomachia, Maro with his
Gnat and Salad, Ovid with his Nut; that Polycrates and his corrector Isocrates
eulogized Busiris, Glauco injustice, Favorinus lauded Thersites and the ague,
Synesius baldness, Lucian the fly and the parasitic art; that Seneca wrote a
ludicrous apotheosis of the emperor Claudius, Plutarch the dialogue of Gryllus
with Ulysses, Lucian and Apuleius both chose the Ass for a subject, and an author
mentioned by Jerome the testament of the pig, Grunnius Corocotta.

Therefore these gentlemen, if they please, may suppose me to have been
playing a rubber of bowls for my own recreation, or, if they like it better, to have
been riding a hobby horse. For when we allow every department of life to have its
own amusements, how unfair would it be to deny to study any relaxation at all;

especially if the proposed pastime may lead to something serious, and ridiculous subjects be so treated, that a reader not altogether thickheaded may derive more profit from them than from some solemn or brilliant arguments found elsewhere; as when one author in a studied oration eulogizes Rhetoric or Philosophy, another writes the praises of some prince, advocates a war against the Turks, predicts future events, or invents fresh quibbles about things of no importance at all. For as nothing is more trifling than to treat serious questions frivolously, so nothing is more amusing than to treat trifles in such a way as to show yourself anything but a trifler. Of my work it is for others to judge, but unless I am altogether deceived by self-esteem, we have praised Folly not quite foolishly.

To reply to the imputation of mordacity, I would observe that genius has always enjoyed the liberty of ridiculing in witty terms the common life of mankind, provided only the licence did not pass into fury. And this makes me more surprised at the nicety of people's ears in the present day, which can scarcely bear anything but solemn titles. Indeed you may find some so perversely religious, that they will rather tolerate the gravest insults directed against Christ, than suffer a Pope or Prince to be aspersed with the slightest jest,—especially if the matter affects the loaves and fishes.

But when a writer censures the lives of men without reflecting on anyone by name, I would ask whether he does not appear as a teacher and adviser rather than a detractor. And pray, how many names can I accuse myself of mentioning? Besides he who passes over no class of mankind is evidently angry with no individual, but with every vice; and therefore if any one shall be found to cry out that he is hit, he will either betray his consciousness, or at any rate his fear. St. Jerome used this kind of writing with much more freedom and bitterness, sometimes not sparing to mention names; while we altogether avoid names, and so temper our pen, that the intelligent reader may easily see that we have sought rather to amuse than to wound. For we have not followed Juvenal's example, nor made acquaintance anywhere with the hidden sink of wickedness, but have endeavoured to pass under review not so much what is shocking as what is ridiculous. Finally, if there is anyone not appeased by these arguments, he may at any rate recollect that it is an honour to be blamed by Folly, and as we have made her the speaker, we were bound to preserve the consistency of the character. But what need have I to suggest such arguments to an accomplished advocate like you, who are able to plead with the greatest skill even causes that are not the best. Farewell, most eloquent More, and defend your *Moria* with all your might.

NOTE: An epistle of a later date, addressed by the author to Martinus Dorpius in defence of the *Moria,* the publication of which had been regretted by his correspondent, contains further details on its composition and publication.

I was staying with More after my return from Italy, when I was kept several days in the house by lumbago. My library had not yet arrived; and if it had, my illness forbade exertion in more serious studies. So, for want of employment, I began to amuse myself with the *Praise of Folly*, not with any intention of publishing the result, but to relieve the discomfort of sickness by this sort of distraction. I showed a specimen of the unfinished work to some friends in order to heighten the enjoyment of the ridiculous by sharing it. They were mightily pleased, and insisted on my going on. I complied, and spent some seven days upon the work; an expenditure of time, which I thought out of proportion to the importance of the subject. Afterwards the same persons who had encouraged me to write contrived to have the book taken to France and printed, but from a copy not only faulty but incomplete. The failure of the work to please the public was sufficiently shown by its being propagated in type more than seven times in a few months, and that in different places; I wondered myself, what people found to like in it.

II-2   Baldassare Castiglione to Ludovico Canossa

Castiglione (1478–1529) arranged for the premiere of Bernardo da Bibbiena's lusty comedy, known as *The Follies of Calandro* or *La Calandria*, even writing the play's prologue himself when the author's failed to arrive on time. Its performance at the Court of Urbino on 6 February, 1513, included all the musical interludes or *intermezzi* (allegorical spectacles having nothing to do with the main plot), and proved a great social and artistic success. Compare the premiere of this comedy with that of the tragedy of Oedipus at Vicenza described later in this chapter.

1513

To Ludovico Canossa

It is some time since I received a letter from your Excellency, to which I did not reply at first, out of curiosity to see if you would become my debtor for more than one letter! At length I must confess that you have won the day, and in reply I will tell you that I cannot recollect the precise date on which I gave you those hundred ducats to send to Naples. But I know this, that it was when our two lady duchesses left Rome and I stayed behind for ten or twelve days, intending to go to Naples, and then changed my mind and gave you the money, and returned to Urbino with the Cardinal of Pavia. Now you will remember the whole thing!

I send you my Marine Elegy, which please pass on to M. Pietro Bembo. I beg you to read it and give me your opinion on the poem. I know not if it is worth your perusal, but I know well that it cannot possibly equal your expectations or be worthy of your praise. As for my delays, you are aware how many reasons I have to excuse them. Our comedies have gone off well, most of all the *Calandria,* which was represented in a truly magnificent style, which I need not describe, since you will have heard full accounts from many who were present. But I will tell you this much. The scene represented was an outer street of the town, between the city wall and its last houses. The wall with its two towers was represented in the most natural way possible, rising from the floor of the stage to the top of the hall. One tower was occupied by the pipers, the other by the trumpeters, and between the two there was another finely constructed rampart. The hall itself, where the audience sat, occupied the place of the moat, and was crossed as it were by two aqueducts. The back of the wall above the tiers of seats was hung with the tapestries of the Trojan War. Above these was a large cornice in high relief, bearing the following inscription in large white letters on a blue ground, running the whole length of the hall:

Both in wars abroad and in games at home, Caesar displays his strength, for both alike are fit work for great minds.

From the roof of the hall hung great bunches of foliage, almost hiding the ceiling, and from the rosettes of the vault wire threads were suspended, to which two rows of candelabra in the shape of letters were fastened, from one end of the hall to the other. These thirteen rosettes made thirteen letters, spelling the words *Deliciae Populi,* and these letters were so large that they held seven or ten torches, which lighted the hall brilliantly.

The scene was laid in a very fine city, with streets, palaces, churches, and towers, all in relief, and looking as if they were real, the effect being completed by admirable paintings in scientific perspective. Among other objects there was an octagon temple in low relief, so well finished that, even if all the workmen in the duchy of Urbino had been employed, it seemed hardly possible to think that all this had been done in four months! This temple was completely covered with beautiful stucco reliefs, the windows were made to imitate alabaster, the architraves and cornices were of fine gold and ultramarine blue, with glass jewels here and there, looking exactly like real gems; there were roundels of marble containing figures, carved pillars, and much more that would take me too long to describe. This temple stood in the centre of the stage. At one end there was a triumphal arch about two yards from the wall, marvellously executed. Between the architrave and the vault an admirable representation of the story of the Horatii had been painted to imitate marble. The two niches above the pillars supporting the arch were filled with little Victories bearing trophies in their hands made of stucco. On the top of the arch stood a most beautiful equestrian statue of a figure in armour, striking a vanquished man at his feet with his spear. To right and left of this rider were two little altars with vases of burning flame that lasted to the end of the comedy.

I will not describe everything, as I feel sure you will have heard a good deal already; nor will I tell how one of the plays was composed by a child and recited by children, who perhaps put their elders to shame. They certainly acted marvellously, and it was a new thing to see little old men, not a foot high, preserving a gravity and severity of manner worthy of Menander. Nor will I attempt to describe the strange music of these comedies, played by minstrels who were all out of sight, and placed in different corners; but I will come at once to our Bernardo's *Calandro,* which gave the greatest pleasure. And since the prologue arrived very late, and the actor who had to recite it could not learn it by heart in time, another which I had written was recited in its place, and met with general approval. Otherwise little was changed, only a few scenes which, perhaps, were not fit for recitation, but little or nothing else, and it was performed exactly as it is written.

These were the *intermezzi.* First a *moresca* by Jason, who appeared on one side of the stage, dancing in antique armour, looking very fine, with a splendid sword and shield. On the other came two bulls, so lifelike that several of the spectators took them for real animals, breathing fire through their nostrils. The good Jason yoked them to the plough and made them draw it, and then sowed dragon's teeth in the furrows. Presently ancient warriors sprang upon the stage in a way that was, I think, excellently managed, and danced a fiery *moresca,* trying to kill Jason all the while. As they were leaving the stage, they fell upon each other and were slain, without being actually seen to die. Then Jason appeared again, dancing exquisitely with the golden fleece on his shoulders; and this was the first interlude, or *moresca.* The second was a very beautiful chariot of Venus, with the goddess seated and holding a lighted taper in her hand. The car was drawn by two doves, who certainly seemed to be alive, and who were ridden by two Amorini with lighted tapers in their hands and bows and quivers on their shoulders. Four Amorini went before the car, four followed after, all bearing lighted tapers in the same manner, dancing a *moresca* and flourishing their burning torches. Having reached the end of the stage, they set fire to a door, from which nine gallants issued all ablaze with light, and danced another most beautiful *moresca.* The third *intermezzo* was a chariot of Neptune drawn by two sea-horses with fish scales and fins, wonderfully well imitated. Neptune himself rode in the car with his trident, attended by eight monsters, four before and four behind, all as well done as it is possible to imagine, and dancing a sword dance with the chariot all aflame. These beasts were the strangest creatures in the world, but no one who did not see them can have an idea what they were like. The fourth was a car of Juno, also ablaze with light. The goddess, wearing a crown on her brow and a sceptre in her hand, appeared seated on a cloud which encircled the chariot, and surrounded by numberless heads blowing the winds of heaven. This car was drawn by two peacocks so beautiful and lifelike that I could not believe my eyes, and yet I had seen them before, and had myself given directions how they were to be made. In front were two eagles and ostriches, behind two sea-birds and two large parrots, with gaily coloured plumage. All of these were so well done, my dear Monsignore, that I am quite sure no imitation ever came so near to reality, and they all danced a sword dance with a grace that it is impossible to describe or imagine.

When the comedy was ended, one of the Amorini, whom we had already seen, appeared suddenly on the stage, in the same habit, and explained in a few verses the meaning of these *intermezzi,* which was a separate thing from the comedy itself.

First of all there was the battle between earth-born brothers, when, as we see today, there is war between those nearest of kin, who ought to live at peace, as set forth in the fable of Jason. Then comes Love, who kindles first mankind and earth, then the sea and air, with his sacred flame, and seeks to drive away war and discord and join the whole world in blessed concord. This indeed, you will say, is rather a hope and devout aspiration, but the vision of war, alas! is all too real for our misfortune! I did not mean to show you the verses that Love sang, but yet I send them, and you can do what you like with them. They were written in great haste, by one who was struggling all the while with painters and carpenters, with actors and musicians and dancers. When the verses were ended Love disappeared. The sound of hidden music, proceeding from four viols, was heard, and then four voices singing a verse to the strains of a beautiful melody, as it were an invocation to Love. So the *festa* ended, after giving the greatest satisfaction and pleasure to the spectators. If I had not praised the whole thing so much, I would have told you what share I had in it; but I will not do this, for fear your Excellency should think that I flatter myself!

II-3   Niccolò Machiavelli to Francesco Vettori

After the fall of the Florentine Republic and the restoration of the Medici in 1512, Machiavelli (1469-1527) withdrew to a nearby farm to write *The Prince,* a book calling for a ruler to unite Italy, and dedicated to the Duke of Nemours, son of Lorenzo the Magnificent. The following letter, describing his twofold life—rustic by day and writer by night—is widely known.

Cascine, 10 December 1513

Magnificent Ambassador:

"Never late were favors divine." [1] I say this because I seemed to have lost—no, rather mislaid—your good will; you had not written to me for a long time, and I was wondering what the reason could be. And of all those that came into my mind I took little account, except of one only, when I feared that you had stopped writing because somebody had written to you that I was not a good guardian of your letters, and I knew that, except Filippo and Pagolo, [2] nobody by my doing had seen them. I have found it again through your last letter of the twenty-third of the past month, from which I learn with pleasure how regularly and quietly you carry on this public office, and I encourage you to continue so, because he who gives up his own convenience for the convenience of others, only loses his own and from them gets no gratitude. And since Fortune wants to do everything, she wishes us to let her do it, to be quiet, and not to give her trouble, and to wait for a time when she will allow something to be done by men; and then will be the time for you to work harder, to stir things up more, and for me to leave my farm and say: "Here I am." I cannot however, wishing to return equal favors, tell you in this letter anything else than what my life is; and if you judge that you would like to swap with me, I shall be glad to.

I am living on my farm, and since I had my last bad luck, I have not spent twenty days, putting them all together, in Florence. I have until now been snaring

---

1. Petrarch, *Triumph of Eternity* 13. Notes to this letter are the translator's.
2. Filippo Casavecchia and Pagolo Vettori, brother of the recipient of the letter.

thrushes with my own hands. I got up before day, prepared birdlime, went out with a bundle of cages on my back, so that I looked like Geta when he was returning from the harbor with Amphitryon's books.[3] I caught at least two thrushes and at most six. And so I did all September. Then this pastime, pitiful and strange as it is, gave out, to my displeasure. And of what sort my life is, I shall tell you.

I get up in the morning with the sun and go into a grove I am having cut down, where I remain two hours to look over the work of the past day and kill some time with the cutters, who have always some bad-luck story ready, about either themselves or their neighbors. And as to this grove I could tell you a thousand fine things that have happened to me, in dealing with Frosino da Panzano and others who wanted some of this firewood. And Frosino especially sent for a number of cords without saying a thing to me, and on payment he wanted to keep back from me ten lire, which he says he should have had from me four years ago, when he beat me at *cricca* at Antonio Guicciardini's. I raised the devil, and was going to prosecute as a thief the waggoner who came for the wood, but Giovanni Machiavelli came between us and got us to agree. Batista Guicciardini, Filippo Ginori, Tommaso del Bene and some other citizens, when that north wind was blowing, each ordered a cord from me. I made promises to all and sent one to Tommaso, which at Florence changed to half a cord, because it was piled up again by himself, his wife, his servant, his children, so that he looked like Gabburra when on Thursday with all his servants he cudgels an ox.[4] Hence, having seen for whom there was profit, I told the others I had no more wood, and all of them were angry about it, and especially Batista, who counts this along with his misfortunes at Prato.[5]

Leaving the grove, I go to a spring, and thence to my aviary. I have a book in my pocket, either Dante or Petrarch, or one of the lesser poets, such as Tibullus, Ovid, and the like. I read of their tender passions and their loves, remember mine, enjoy myself a while in that sort of dreaming. Then I move along the road to the inn; I speak with those who pass, ask news of their villages, learn various things, and note the various tastes and different fancies of men. In the course of these things comes the hour for dinner, where with my family I eat such food as this poor farm of mine and my tiny property allow. Having eaten, I go back to the inn; there is the host, usually a butcher, a miller, two furnace tenders. With these I sink

3. A reference to a story founded on the *Amphitruo* of Plautus.

4. Gabburra, apparently a butcher, is unknown.

5. Batista Guicciardini was podestà of Prato when it was taken by the Spanish forces in 1512; as an immediate result the Medici were restored to Florence. It is remarkable that Machiavelli could jest about the fall of Prato and its attendant atrocities. For the public reaction to the sack of Prato, see Michelangelo's comment (Letter VI-3).

into vulgarity for the whole day, playing at *cricca* and at trich-trach, and then these games bring on a thousand disputes and countless insults with offensive words, and usually we are fighting over a penny, and nevertheless we are heard shouting as far as San Casciano. So, involved in these trifles, I keep my brain from growing mouldy, and satisfy the malice of this fate of mine, being glad to have her drive me along this road, to see if she will be ashamed of it.

On the coming of evening, I return to my house and enter my study; and at the door I take off the day's clothing, covered with mud and dust, and put on garments regal and courtly; and reclothed appropriately, I enter the ancient courts of ancient men, where, received by them with affection, I feed on that food which only is mine and which I was born for, where I am not ashamed to speak with them and to ask them the reason for their actions; and they in their kindness answer me; and for four hours of time I do not feel boredom, I forget every trouble, I do not dread poverty, I am not frightened by death; entirely I give myself over to them.

And because Dante says it does not produce knowledge when we hear but do not remember, I have noted everything in their conversation which has profited me,[6] and have composed a little work *On Princedoms,* where I go as deeply as I can into considerations on this subject, debating what a princedom is, of what kinds they are, how they are gained, how they are kept, why they are lost. And if ever you can find any of my fantasies pleasing, this one should not displease you; and by a prince, and especially by a new prince, it ought to be welcomed. Hence I am dedicating it to His Magnificence Giuliano.[7] Filippo Casavecchia has seen it; he can give you some account in part of the thing in itself and of the discussions I have had with him, though I am still enlarging and revising it.

You wish, Magnificent Ambassador, that I leave this life and come to enjoy yours with you. I shall do it in any case, but what tempts me now are certain affairs that within six weeks I shall finish. What makes me doubtful is that the Soderini we know so well are in the city, whom I should be obliged, on coming there, to visit and talk with. I should fear that on my return I could not hope to dismount at my house but should dismount at the prison, because though this government has mighty foundations and great security, yet it is new and therefore suspicious, and there is no lack of wiseacres who, to make a figure, like Pagolo Bertini, would place others at the dinner table and leave the reckoning to me.[8] I beg you to rid me of this fear, and then I shall come within the time mentioned to visit you in any case.

6. This seems to be Machiavelli making notes on Livy's *History* for his own *Discourses,* out of which rose *The Prince.*

7. Giuliano de'Medici, Duke of Nemours, son of Lorenzo the Magnificent. He resided in Florence after the restoration of the Medici in 1512, but in 1513 withdrew to Rome.

8. Pagolo Bertini is unknown and the meaning of the sentence is uncertain.

I have talked with Filippo about this little work of mine that I have spoken of, whether it is good to give it or not to give it; and if it is good to give it, whether it would be good to take it myself, or whether I should send it there. Not giving it would make me fear that at the least Giuliano will not read it and that this rascal Ardinghelli will get himself honor from this latest work of mine.[9] The giving of it is forced on me by the necessity that drives me, because I am using up my money, and I cannot remain as I am a long time without becoming despised through poverty. In addition, there is my wish that our present Medici lords will make use of me, even if they begin by making me roll a stone; because then if I could not gain their favor, I should complain of myself; and through this thing, if it were read, they would see that for the fifteen years while I have been studying the art of the state, I have not slept or been playing; and well may anybody be glad to get the services of one who at the expense of others has become full of experience. And of my honesty there should be no doubt, because having always preserved my honesty, I shall hardly now learn to break it; and he who has been honest and good for forty-three years, as I have, cannot change his nature; and as a witness to my honesty and goodness I have my poverty.

I should like, then, to have you also write me what you think best on this matter, and I give you my regards. Be happy.

Niccolò Machiavelli, in Florence

II-4   Vittoria Colonna, Marchioness of Pescara, to Baldassare Castiglione

Castiglione was delighted to learn of the high opinion Vittoria Colonna (1492-1547) held of the manuscript copy of the *Book of the Courtier* he submitted to her. Later his feelings turned to bitterness when the aristocratic poetess kept it for over two years, allowing sections from it to be copied as far away as Naples. Vittoria was the widow of the gallant Marquis of Pescara, mentioned in several letters of this anthology (especially VII-4).

---

9. Piero Ardinghelli was secretary to Pope Leo X. Machiavelli seems to have feared that, if Giuliano had not read *The Prince,* Ardinghelli would steal ideas from it and offer them as his own.

20 September, 1524

Excellent Lord,

I had not forgotten that I must keep my promise to you. I was so painfully conscious of it that it kept preventing me from the sheer enjoyment of reading it, worrying that I must get your book back to you without rereading it as often as I wished. But at least it would be useful to me to keep it for good in a fine, printed version. Since you are doing me a disservice in demanding its return, and because I am already in the middle of my second reading of it, I beg Your Lordship to let me finish it. I promise to get it back to you soon, since I take it from your letter that you are about to depart from Rome. It will not be necessary for you to send for it, since I'll return it safe and sound. I need not go on and on about what I think of your book, for the same reason you tell me that it would be superfluous to belabor the beauties of the Duchess. Even though I have promised you an opinion, I'll not send you an ornamental letter giving you to understand what you already know better than I. I shall adhere to the unadorned truth, swearing by an oath on the life of my dead husband, the Lord Marquis, that I have never seen nor expect to see another better or equal work in prose approaching its merits.

Beyond the beautiful and novel subject, the stylistic excellence is such that with an unprecedented suavity, it leads you up a gentle and fruitful slope without your ever noticing that you are gradually ascending or realizing that you are on a different level than before. The upward path is so cultivated and adorned that it is hard to ascertain who labored to embellish it: art or nature. Let us not even mention the witty conceits, the profound maxims, that shine no less than gems in a simple gold setting, in no way diminishing their light. No other gems equal these, nor could their mounting be better. But what can I say of the exactly-right words which demonstrate that Lombard words can convey the clarity of Tuscan. It is fortunate that this demonstration has come late, so that the fame of the writer who has proved this point may be widely acknowledged now. I observe that when you use an unusual term, it is not because you abandon Tuscan deliberately, but that the Lombard comes naturally.

The jests and anecdotes in the book are appropriate and well-told. Although many of those who invented them are dead, I could not help envying them their wit. Of that section which most pleases and obliges me, which concerns the perhaps well-deserved theme of the continence of ladies, I intend to say naught. But I shall not be silent on what impressed me most: the proof that he who can write Latin is as different from other writers as goldsmiths from bronze-workers. However simple the goldsmith's work, its shining excellence betokens its beauty. But bronze works, even executed with genius and subtlety, cannot win in comparison. And your new vernacular language bears such majesty that it concedes naught to any Latin work. I do not marvel that you have formed a perfect Courtier, for by merely holding a mirror before you and looking into it, you could describe him as you did. Yet our greatest difficulty being to know ourselves, I claim it more difficult to form oneself than another. For yourself or your mirrored creation you deserve such praise that I entrust it to Signore Datari, whom alone I judge equal to the task of saying it for me.

(trans. R. J. C.)

II-5   Cardinal Bembo to Giulio Porcelago

Pietro Bembo (1470-1547) expresses enthusiasm upon hearing of the establishment of a society at Brescia devoted to the study of literature in the vulgar tongue. Five years earlier Cardinal Bembo had written an influential book on the vernacular language, *Prose della volgar lingua*.

6 July 1530

I have read with much pleasure your letters, honored and kind Messer Giulio, by which you inform me of the new society founded there in the city by many youths who are devoting themselves to the vulgar tongue and getting together on all the feast days to their common benefit and pleasure; where our Messer Emilio reads Petrarch to them and also my own prose writings, which discuss the language problem. And truly, I feel much satisfaction and rejoice greatly upon hearing that Italian men are taking care to learn to speak well with the speech of their birth and to understand well the notable writings in the vernacular, above all Petrarch, master and leader of Italian poetry; in this way they too will write and will know how to do it in the correct manner: and thus, this language will grow rich, which is still wanting in fine and distinguished poets and prose writers when compared with Latin and Greek which have such an abundance of them. And even sweeter and dearer to me is hearing this about your citizens, inasmuch as they, through their spoken language, might perchance appear to many people as being necessarily more removed from this care and concern than are others: this will make your praise and reward still greater. Then, since you are off to such a good start on this fine endeavor, as you write me, may it follow that all of you boldly proceed from good to better, continually progressing, each on his own, as befits gentlemen and enterprising spirits. For in this manner approaching the worthy and desired goal, one attains everlasting fame and glory. Give my regards to Messer Emilio and greet all that noble and virtuous society together, thanking them for the affection that you say they bear me, and offering my services to them. Stay well.

(trans. L. L.)

II-6   Torquato Tasso to Scipione Gonzaga

Imprisoned by the Duke of Ferrara in the Ospedale di Sant'Anna where he was to remain for seven years, Torquato Tasso (1544-1595) reveals to Scipione Gonzaga the persistent dread that his creative yearnings will go unfulfilled. His epic poem *Jerusalem Delivered* had been widely censured by Churchmen, and Tasso had suffered fits of paranoia and melancholy.

May 1579

. . . Ah me! Wretched me! I had planned to write two epic poems on the most noble and worthy theme, four tragedies for which I had already shaped the story, and many works in prose, and of substance so beautiful and useful to men's lives; and to couple philosophy with eloquence in such a way as would leave my imprint upon posterity; and I had resolved to end my days in glory and highest honor. But now, oppressed by the weight of so many misfortunes, I have abandoned every thought of glory and honor; and I would deem it a great happiness if without suspicion I could slake the thirst which continually torments me and if, like one of these ordinary men, I could lead my life in freedom in some humble lodging; if not healthy, which I can no longer be, at least not so painfully sick; if not honored, at least not loathed; if not by the laws of men, by those of brutes at least, who in rivers and springs freely quench the thirst which (and it helps me to repeat it) inflames my whole being. Nor do I indeed fear the extent of my illness as much as the horrible thought that continually rises to the surface of my mind: knowing at most that in such a condition I am fit neither for writing nor work. And the fear of continual imprisonment greatly increases my despondency as well as the disgrace which I had best get used to; and the foulness of my beard and hair and clothes, and the sordidness and filth weary me painfully; and above all, loneliness afflicts me, my cruel and natural enemy, which even in more favorable circumstances was sometimes so trying that at untimely hours I went out seeking or meeting company. And I am sure that if she * who has reciprocated in such small measure my love should see me in such a state, she would have some compassion for me. . . .

(trans. L.L.)

* probably Tasso's longtime friend and patroness, Leonora d'Este.

II-7   Pierre de Ronsard to Scévole de Sainte-Marthe

France's "Prince of Poets," Pierre de Ronsard (1524-1585) immortalized three beloved women, as he reminded them, in his odes and sonnets: Marie Dupin, Cassandre Salviati, and Hélène de Surgères. Although he published two books of *Sonnets pour Hélène*—a "September Song" to a very young girl he never possessed—she objected to some of these being included by him in the final 1584 edition of his complete works. She worried about her reputation at court. Such ingratitude prompted the following outburst to his friend Scévole de Sainte-Marthe.

Le Vendômois, 5 July, 1583

Sir my very old friend,

It is, as Aristophanes said, an unbearable load to serve a master in his dotage. To make a parody of this saying, it is a great misfortune to serve a mistress who has no judgment or reason in the area of poetry, who does not know that poets, principally in petty and minute stuff like elegies, epigrams, and sonnets, respect neither order nor time. That's the business of historians who develop everything bit by bit. I beg you, Sir, not to consent to heed Mademoiselle de Surgères' demands in this matter and not to add or remove anything in my sonnets, if you please. If she doesn't find them good, let her leave them alone. This is the only worry I have on my mind. They say that the King is coming to Blois and to Tours, and for that reason I'm fleeing to Paris and shall stay there briefly, for I hate the court like death. If she wants to design some marble over the fountain,* let her go

* Ronsard had celebrated in verse a fountain near Croixval, naming it after Hélène. She apparently wished to have this fact commemorated in a marble tablet.

ahead. These are the impulsive ideas of women, which last only a day, and for which they wouldn't consent to spend a penny to have them come off well. Show her this letter if you find it a good idea. I kiss your hands affectionately. From your Croixval, this fifth of July (1583). Your humble friend and servant,

Ronsard

(trans. R. J. C.)

II-8 Filippo Pegafetta to an "Illustrious Lord and Patron"

When the great architect Palladio had completed the sumptuous Olympic Theater at Vicenza, it was decided by the local Academy that only the greatest tragedy known, *Oedipus Tyrannus* of Sophocles, was worthy of first gracing its boards, Sunday, 3 March, 1585. The enthusiastic description of the theater, capable, Pegafetta writes, of accommodating 3000, and of the tragedy itself, with the varied musical accompaniment, illustrates the self-consciousness of the man of the Renaissance. We gather further from the letter that this production of *Oedipus* was for modest Vicenza the social event of the year.

Vicenza, 4 March, 1585

Most illustrious Lord and most honored Master!

If my hand would be obedient to my mind, as Michel Agnolo Buonarroti, the eminent painter, sculptor, and architect used to say, and if the social activities, the flow of wine, and the bustle of the carnival permit me, I would like to please Your Highness and Your friends by describing the theatrical pomp and the magnificence of the tragedy which yesterday was recited in this city. But the aforementioned circumstances will excuse me if I only mention the highlights of this marvellous spectacle, leaving a fuller report to the time when I shall speak to you. Palladio, wanting to leave behind him a perfect work of art, convinced the Academicians of Vicenza, called the Olimpici, that, in view of the fact that their noble institution many times recited eclogues, pastorals, comedies, tragedies, and other such pleasures for the enjoyment of the people, they should build a theater according to the ancient custom of the Greeks and Romans. . . . Little by little they have brought to an end the masterly and admirable work of art. The theater can easily accommodate 3,000 spectators. It is such a charming sight that everybody is usually pleased by it due to the exquisite beauty of its proportions. The eyes of the laymen receive the overall impression of an incredible loveliness, which arises from the friezes, architraves, cornices, festoons, columns with very beautiful capitals, and bases with many metopes sculptured in low stucco relief. And there are perhaps eighty stucco statues, made by the best masters, representing the likenesses of the Academicians, and each one of these statues was done more than once until it had assumed the proper resemblance. I leave aside the balustrades, the doors, and the windows, which it would take too long to enumerate in a brief letter. But I shall say that even the smallest detail seems to have been executed by Mercury and adorned by the Graces themselves. The stage perspective is likewise admirable, very well understood and seen, with its five principal sections, or rather entrances, which represent the seven streets of Thebes. The city is an exhibition of beautiful houses, palaces, temples, and altars in the style of antiquity, and of the finest architecture. It is made of strong wood so that it may last for ages to come. It cost 1,500 ducats. Just think, Your most illustrious Lordship, a complete building designed by Palladio in the last years of his life and in the full mastery of his knowledge. Palladio had asked the Olimpici to have his name inscribed in it, for he was so proud of his achievement and thought that he would never design anything better. In this theater, which cost 18,000 ducats with all its appurtenances, the Academicians produced—in tune with the edifice—the noblest tragedy ever written, *Oedipus the King* . . . by the Athenian poet Sophocles, exalted above all others by Aristotle. Thus in the most famous theater of the world, the world's most excellent tragedy was given. The translation from the Greek into the vernacular was done by the celebrated Orsato Giustiniani. Angelo Ingegneri, capable of such things, has directed this tragic business. The choral music was composed by Andrea Gabrieli,[1] organist of St. Mark's. The settings were designed by Vincenzo Scamozzi, architect of Vicenza. The costumes were by [Alessandro?] Maganza. The president of the Academy is the Illustrious Leonardo Valmarana, who has the soul of Caesar and was born for generous enterprises. This explains why he made the Empress [Maria of Austria] reside in his house, and in the true spirit of chivalry he did not overlook any opportunity to please and invite the strangers who passed through the city, and, for their delight, to offer his gardens, which can almost stand comparison with the Sallustian Gardens of ancient Rome. The president and the other Academicians were all lavishly dressed, and all of them did not spare any efforts or money to make this

1. The first composer whose motets and Masses exploited fully the architectural resources of St. Mark's, Gabrieli has been called the "master composer of Venice's grandeur."

event perfect in every respect. There were eighty stage costumes. The tragedy has nine speaking parts, and the cast had been doubled by understudies to provide for any emergency. Two of the players, the King and the Queen, were magnificently dressed in gold cloth. Accommodations had been courteously provided for about 2,000 gentlemen from Venice and the State as well as from other countries, not counting the others, so that on the streets of Vicenza one could see nothing but noblemen and noblewomen, carriages, horses, and strangers who had come to attend the performance, and all quartered at the inns, without being known in other ways than that they were strangers. There was an incredible display of kindness on the part of the Academicians toward all the guests, when the latter reached the entrance, where quite a crowd had assembled, and when they were shown their seats inside, receiving, upon request, refreshing wines and fruits; and everything had been personally supervised by the members of the Academy, especially the accommodation of the ladies down in the orchestra, where four hundred chairs had been placed for them, strangers and natives. Among the ladies was the wife of the illustrious French ambassador and one of his nieces. There were more than 3,000 spectators. People came early, that is, between sixteen and twenty o'clock. The performance began at one-thirty at night [i.e.; 7:30 p.m.] and was over by five o'clock [11 p.m.]. Some, for instance, I and some of my friends, stayed there perhaps eleven hours, not getting tired at all. Because of seeing one new face after the other, watching the ladies being seated, and the assembly as a whole, the time passed very fast. In different places of the thirteen tiers there were some exits, so that nothing in the way of comfort for the spectators was overlooked. The illustrious Captain and several Senators were present. The Mayor remained outside. For security reasons and as a sort of guard of honor, soldiers were posted at the gates. When the time had come to lower the curtain, a very sweet smell of perfume made itself felt to indicate that in the city of Thebes, according to the ancient legend, incense was burned to placate the wrath of the gods. Then there was a sound of trumpets and drums, and four squibs exploded. In a twinkle of an eye the curtain fell before the stage. I can hardly express in words, nor can it be imagined, how great the joy was, and the infinite pleasure felt by the spectators when they, after a moment of stunned surprise, watched the prologue, and when the sound of harmonized voices and divers instruments could be heard from a distance behind the scenic façade—hymns sung in the city, and prayers and incense offered to the gods to obtain from them health, the alleviation of hunger and pestilence, which harassed that city for so long. Then began the tragedy proper, and not one point was missed throughout the entire action. The actors are of the best sort, and they are dressed neatly and lavishly according to each one's station. The King had a guard of twenty-four archers dressed in Turkish fashion, pages, and courtiers. The Queen was surrounded by matrons, ladies in waiting, and pages. Her brother, Creon, was likewise accompanied by an appropriate entourage. The chorus consisted of 15 persons, seven on each side, and their leader in the center. The chorus spoke, as is required, in pleasing unison, so that almost all the words could be clearly understood, an effect which is very difficult to achieve in tragedies. The story of Oedipus is full of pity and terror. . . . As it is the task of tragedy, by representing an illustrious and stormy deed, to arouse in the hearts of the spectators pity and terror and to soften the callous souls, purging them, according to Aristotle,[2] or freeing them from such passions as hatred, constant anger, and the desire for revenge, one should think that this tragedy, so perfectly conceived, and composed with so much art, and, above all, so exquisitely performed, should produce its effects and eradicate the afflictions with which part of this our most courteous, courageous, and ingenious city is befallen.

II-9   Edmund Spenser to Sir Walter Raleigh

In a letter to Sir Walter Raleigh, who was for a time his neighbor in Ireland, Edmund Spenser (1552?-1599) sets forth his purpose in writing *The Faery Queene*. In doing so, he obligingly furnishes a plot summary of this famous work.

Januarie 23, 1589.

Sir,—

Knowing how doubtfully all Allegories may be construed, and the booke of mine, which I have entituled *The Faery Queene*, being a continued Allegorie, or darke conceit, I have thought good, as well for avoyding of jealous opinions and misconstructions, as also for your better light in reading thereof, (being so by you commanded) to discover unto you the generall intention and meaning, which in the whole course thereof I have fashioned, without expressing of any particular purposes, or by-accidents therein occasioned. The generall end therefore of all the booke, is to fashion a gentleman or noble person in vertuous and gentle discipline. Which for that I conceived shoulde be most plausible and pleasing, beeing

2. The Greek scientist's *Poetics* had justified tragic dramas as purging the spectators through pity, fear, and awe.

coloured with an historicall fiction, the which the most part of men delight to read, rather for varietie of matter than for profit of the ensample: I chose the historie of king Arthure, as most fit for the excellencie of his person, beeing made famous by many men's former workes, and also furthest from the danger of envie, and suspicion of present time. In which I have followed all the antique poets historicall: first Homer, who in the persons of Agamemnon and Ulysses hath ensampled a good governour and a vertuous man, the one in his Ilias, the other in his Odysseis: then Virgil, whose like intention was to doe in the person of Aeneas: after him Ariosto comprised them both in his Orlando: and lately Tasso dissevered them againe, and formed both parts in two persons, namely, that part which they in philosophy call *Ethice,* or vertues of a private man, coloured in his Rinaldo; the other named *Politice,* in his Godfredo. By ensample of which excellent Poets, I labour to pourtraict in Arthure, before he was king, the image of a brave knight, perfected in the twelve private morall vertues, as Aristotle hath devised; the which is the purpose of these first twelve bookes: which if I finde to be well accepted, I may be perhaps encoraged to frame the other part of the pollitike vertues in his person, after he came to bee king.

To some, I know this Methode will seem displeasant, which had rather have good discipline delivered plainly in way of precepts, or sermoned at large, as they use, then thus clowidly enwrapped in Allegoricall devises. But such, mee seeme, should be satisfied with the use of these dayes, seeing all things accounted by their showes, and nothing esteemed of, that is not delightfull and pleasing to common sense. For this cause is Xenophon preferred before Plato, for that the one, in the exquisite depth of his judgment, formed a Communewealth such as it should be; but the other, in the person of Cyrus and the Persians, fashioned a government, such as might best be. So much profitable and gracious is doctrine by ensample then by rule. So have I laboured to doe in the person of Arthure: whom I conceive, after his long education by Timon (to whom he was by Merlin delivered to be brought up, so soone as he was borne of the Lady Igrayne) to have seene in a dreame or vision the Faery Queene, with whose excellent beautie ravished, hee awaking, resolved to seeke her out: and so, being by Merlin armed, and by Timon thoroughly instructed, he went to seeke her forth in Faery land. In that Faery Queene I mean Glory in my generall intention: but in my particular I conceive the most excellent and glorious person of our soveraine the Queene, and her Kingdome in Faery land. And yet, in some places else, I doe otherwise shadow her. For considering shee beareth two persons, the one of a most royall Queene or Empresse, the other of a most vertuous and beautifull lady, this latter part in some places I doe expresse in Belphoebe, fashioning her name according to your owne excellent conceipt of Cynthia (Phoebe and Cynthia being both names of Diana).

So in the person of Prince Arthure I sette forth Magnificence in particular, which vertue, for that (according to Aristotle, and the rest) it is the perfection of all the rest, and containeth in it them all, therefore in the whole course I mention the deeds of Arthure appliable to that vertue, which I write of in that booke. But of the twelve other vertues I make xii. other knights the patrons, for the more varietie of the historie: Of which these three bookes containe three. The first, of the Knight of the Redcrosse, in whom I expresse Holinesse; the second of Sir Guyon, in whome I set foorth Temperance; the third of Britomartis, a Lady knight, in whom I picture Chastitie. But because the beginning of the whole worke seemeth abrupt and as depending upon other antecedents it need that yee know the occasion of these three knights severall adventures. For the Methode of a Poet historicall is not such as of an Historiographer. For an Historiographer discourseth of affaires orderly as they were done, accounting as well the times as the actions; but a Poet thrusteth into the middest, even where it most concerneth him, and there recouring to the things forepast, and divining of things to come, maketh a pleasing analysis of all. The beginning therefore of my historie, if it were to be told by an Historiographer, should be the twelfth booke, which is the last; where I devise that the Faery Queene kept her annuall feast twelve daies; uppon which twelve severall daies, the occasions of the twelve severall adventures hapned, which being undertaken by xii. severall knights, are in these twelve books severally handled and discoursed.

The first was this. In the beginning of the feast, there presented him selfe a tall, clownish younge man, who falling before the Queene of Faeries desired a boone (as the manner then was) which during that feast she might not refuse: which was that hee might have the atchievement of any adventure, which during that feast should happen; that being granted he rested him selfe on the floore, unfit through his rustisite for a better place. Soone after entred a faire Ladie in mourning weedes, riding on a white Asse, with a dwarfe behind her leading a warlike steed, that bore the Armes of a knight, and his speare in the dwarfes hand. She, falling before the Queene of Faeries, complayned that her father and mother, an ancient King and Queene, had bene by an huge dragon many yeers shut up in an brazen Castle, who thence suffered them not to issew: and therefore besought the Faery Queene to assigne her some one of the knights to take on him that exployt. Presently that Clownish person upstarting, desired that adventure; whereat the Queene much wondering, and the Lady much gaine-saying, yet he earnestly importuned his desire. In the end the Lady told him that unlesse that armour which she brought would serve him (that is, the armour of a Christian man specified by Saint Paul, v. *Ephes.*), that he could not succeed in that enterprise: which being forthwith put upon him with due furnitures thereunto, he seemed the goodliest man in al that company, and was well liked of the Lady. And eftesoones taking on him knighthood, and mounting on that strange Courser, he went forth with her on that adventure: where beginneth the first booke, viz.

A gentle knight was pricking on the playne, etc.

The second day there came in a Palmer bearing an Infant with bloody hands, whose Parents, he complained to have bene slaine by an enchauntresse called Acrasia: and therefore craved of the Faery Queene, to appoint him some knight to performe that adventure, which being assigned to Sir Guyon, he presently went foorth with the same Palmer: which is the beginning of the second booke and the subject thereof. The third day there came in a Groome, who complained before the Faery Queene, that a vile Enchaunter, called Busirane, had in hand a most faire Lady, called Amoretta, whom he kept in most grievous torment. Whereupon Sir Scudamour, the lover of that Lady, presently tooke on him that adventure. But beeing unable to performe it by reason of the hard Enchauntments, after long sorrow, in the end met with Britomartis, who succoured him, and reskewed his love. . . .

This much, Sir, I have briefly over-run to direct your understanding to the wel-head of the History, that from thence gathering the whole intention of the conceit, ye may as in a handfull gripe all the discourse, which otherwise may happely seem tedious and confused. So humbly craving the continuance of your honourable favour towards me, and th' eternall establishment of your happiness, I humbly take leave.

Yours most humbly affectionate,

Edm. Spenser.

II-10   William Shakespeare to the Earl of Southampton

On the dedicatory page of *Venus and Adonis,* William Shakespeare (1564-1616) pays homage to the Earl of Southampton, whom biographers have recorded as his sole patron.

1593

Right Honourable,—

I know not how I shall offend in dedicating my unpolished lines to your lordship, nor how the world will censure me for choosing so strong a prop to support so weak a burden: only, if your honour seem but pleased, I account myself highly praised, and vow to take advantage of all idle hours, till I have honoured you with some graver labour. But if the first heir of my invention prove deformed, I shall be sorry it had so noble a godfather, and never after ear so barren a land, for fear it yield me still so bad a harvest. I leave it to your honourable survey, and your honour to your heart's content; which I wish may always answer your own wish and the world's hopeful expectation.

Your honour's in all duty,
William Shakespeare.

II-11   John Donne to Henry Wotton

In sharing his thoughts on reading with his lifelong friend Henry Wotton, John Donne (1573-1631) expresses sharp annoyance with Dante for a verdict rendered in *The Divine Comedy.*

(1599?)

Sir,

I am no great voyager in other men's works: no swallower nor devourer of volumes, nor pursuant of authors. Perchance it is because I find born in myself knowledge or apprehension enough for (without forfeiture or impeachment of modesty I think I am bound to God thankfully to acknowledge it) to consider him and myself: as when I have at home a convenient garden I covet not to walk in others' broad meadows or woods, especially because it falls not within that short reach which my foresight embraceth to see how I should employ that which I already know to travail for inquiry of—more were to labour to get a stomach and then find no meat at home. To know how to live by the book is a pedantry, and to do it is a bondage. For both hearers and players are more delighted with voluntary than with set music. And he that will live by precept shall be long without the habit of honesty: as he that would every day gather one or two feathers might become brawn with hard lying before he make a feather bed of his gettings.

That Earl of Arundel [1] that last died (that tennis ball whom fortune after tossing and bandying brickwalled [2] into the hazard) in his imprisonment used more than much reading, and to him that asked him why he did so he answered he read so much lest he should remember something. I am as far from following his counsel as he was from Petruccio's: but I find it true that after long reading I can only tell you how many leaves I have read. I do therefore more willingly blow and keep awake that small coal which God hath pleased to kindle in me than far off to gather a faggot of green sticks which consume without flame or heat in a black smother: yet I read something. But indeed not so much to avoid as to enjoy idleness. Even when I began to write these, I flung away Dante the Italian—a man pert enough to be beloved and too much to be believed. It angered me that Celestine, [3] a Pope so far from the manners of other Popes that he left even their seat, should by the Court of Dante's wit be attacked and by him thrown into his purgatory. And it angered me as much that in the life of a Pope he should spy no greater fault, than that in the affectation of a cowardly security he slipped from the great burden laid upon him. Alas, what would Dante have him do? Thus we find the story related: he that thought himself next in succession by a trunk through a wall whispered in Celestine's ear counsel to remove the papacy: why should not Dante be content to think that Celestine took this for as immediate a salutation and discourse of the Holy Ghost as Abraham did the commandment of killing his son? If he will needs punish retiredness thus what hell can his wit devise for ambition? And if white integrity merit this what shall Male or Malum which Seneca condemns most, deserve? But as the Chancellor Hatton being told after a decree made that his predecessor was of another opinion he answered "he had his genius and I had mine": so say I of authors that they think and I think both reasonably yet possibly both erroneously. That is manly. For I am so far from persuading—yea, counselling—you to believe others that I care not that you believe not me when I say that others are not to be believed. Only believe that I love you, and I have enough.

I have studied philosophy therefore marvel not if I make such account of arguments *quae trahuntur ab effectibus.*

1. Died in 1595 after ten years' imprisonment.

2. Corruption of *bricole,* tennis term for the rebounding of the ball from the wall of the court; hazards are the winning openings.

3. Celestine, entering the papacy at 79, wearied of the office in five months and resigned (December, 1294), permitting the ill-famed Boniface VIII to succeed him. Donne is incorrect in saying that Dante placed Celestine in Purgatory. Worse, Dante placed him in the Inferno (III, 59-60).

II-12   Samuel Daniel to the Countess of Bedford

In this justly admired verse epistle published in the year of James I's accession, Samuel Daniel (1562-1619) praises devotion to studies as the way to self-fulfillment. The Countess of Bedford, also the patroness of Jonson, Donne and Drayton, had charge of the Queen's masque for the first Christmas of the new reign, and upon her recommendation Daniel's work, *The Vision of the Twelve Goddesses,* was presented at Hampton Court in January 1604.

To the Lady Lucy, Countess of Bedford

1603

Though virtue be the same when low she stands
  in th' humble shadows of obscurity,
    As when she either sweats in martial bands
Or sits in court clad with authority,
    Yet, madame, doth the strictness of her room
    Greatly detract from her ability;
For, as in-wall'd within a living tomb
    Her hands and arms of action labor not,
    Her thoughts, as if abortive from the womb,
    Come never born, though happily begot.   10
But where she hath, mounted in open sight,
    An eminent and spacious dwelling got
    Where she may stir at will and use her might,
There is she more herself and more her own;
    There in the fair attire of honor dight
    She sits at ease and makes her glory known;
Applause attends her hands, her deeds have grace;
    Her worth, new-born, is straight as if full grown.
    With such a goodly and respected face
Doth virtue look, that's set to look from high,   20

And such a fair advantage by her place
   Hath state and greatness to do worthily.
And therefore well did your high fortunes meet
   With her, that gracing you, comes grac'd thereby;
   And well was let into a house so sweet,
So good, so fair, so fair, so good a guest,
   Who now remains as blessed in her seat,
   As you are with her residency bless'd.
And this fair course of knowledge whereunto
   Your studies, learned lady, are address'd   30
   Is th' only certain way that you can go
Unto true glory, to true happiness;
   All passages on earth besides are so
   Incumb'red with such vain disturbances
As still we loose our rest in seeking it,
   Being but deluded with apparances;
   And no key had you else that was so fit
T' unlock that prison of your sex as this,
   To let you out of weakness, and admit
   Your powers into the freedom of that bliss   40
That sets you there where you may oversee
   This rolling world, and view it as it is,
   And apprehend how th' outsides do agree
With th' inward, being of the things we deem
   And hold in our ill-cast accounts to be
   Of highest value and of best esteem;
Since all the good we have rests in the mind,
   By whose proportions only we redeem
   Our thoughts from out confusion, and do find
The measure of ourselves and of our pow'rs;   50
   And that all happiness remains confin'd
   Within the kingdom of this breast of ours,
Without whose bounds all that we look on lies
   In others' jurisdictions, others' pow'rs,
   Out of the circuit of our liberties.
All glory, honor, fame, applause, renown,
   Are not belonging to our royalties,
   But t' others' wills, wherein th' are only grown;
And that unless we find us all within,
   We never can without us be our own,   60

Nor call it right our life that we live in,
But a possession held for others' use,
  That seem to have most int'rest therein;
  Which we do so dissever, part, traduce,
Let out to custom, fashion, and to shew,
  As we enjoy but only the abuse
  And have no other deed at all to shew.
How oft are we constrained to appear
  With other countenance then that we owe,
  And be ourselves far off, when we are near!   70
How oft are we forc'd on a cloudy heart
  To set a shining face and make it clear,
  Seeming content to put ourselves apart
To bear a part of others' weaknesses!
  As if we only were compos'd by art,
  Not nature, and did all our deeds address
'T"opinion, not t' a conscience what is right;
  As fram'd b' example, not advisedness,
  Into those forms that intertain our sight.
And though books, madame, cannot make this mind   80
  Which we must bring apt to be set aright,
  Yet do they rectify it in that kind,
And touch it so as that it turns that way
  Where judgment lies; and though we cannot find
  The certain place of truth, yet do they stay
And intertain us near about the same,
  And give the soul the best delight that may
  Encheer it most, and most our spirits inflame
To thoughts of glory, and to worthy ends;
  And therefore in a course that best became   90
  The clearness of your heart, and best commends
Your worthy pow'rs, you run the rightest way
  That is on earth, that can true glory give,
  By which, when all consumes, your fame shall live.

II-13 Samuel Daniel to the Earl of Devonshire

An unpleasant episode in Daniel's life occurred when his tragedy *Philotas* was misinterpreted by some as a sympathetic commentary on the Essex rebellion, but he pointed out that three acts had been shown to both Lord Mountjoy and the Master of the Revels as early as 1600 (before the Essex affair). In the following letter, Daniel tries to appease Mountjoy, recently created Earl of Devonshire, angry that his name had been used in clearing the poet of blame.

(1605)

My Lord,

    Understanding your lordship is displeased with me, it hath more shaken my heart than I did think any fortune could have done, in respect I have not deserved it, nor done or spoken anything in this matter of *Philotas* unworthy of you or me. And now having fully satisfied my Lord of Cranborne, I crave to unburden me of this imputation with your honour: and it is the last suit I will ever make. And therefore I beseech you to understand all this great error I have committed.

    First I told the Lords I had written three Acts of this tragedy the Christmas before my Lord of Essex' troubles, as divers in the city could witness. I said the Master of the Revels had perused it. I said I had read some part of it to your honour and this I said having none else of power to grace me now in Court and hoping that you out of your knowledge of books, and favour of letters and me, might answer that there is nothing in it disagreeing nor anything, as I protest there is not, but out of the universal notions of ambition and envy, the perpetual arguments of books and tragedies. I did not say you encouraged me unto the presenting of it; if I should I had been a villain, for that when I showed it to your honour I was not resolved to have had it acted, nor should it have been had not my necessities overmastered me. And therefore I beseech you let not now an Earl of Devonshire overthrow what a Lord Mountjoy hath done, who hath done me good and I have done him honour: the world must, or shall know mine innocency whilst I have a pen to show it, and for that I know I shall live *inter historiam temporis* as well as greater men, I must not be such an abject unto myself as to neglect my reputation, and having been known throughout all England for my virtue, I will not leave a stain of villainy upon my name whatsoever error else might scape me unfortunately thorough my indiscretion, and misunderstanding the time: wherein, good my Lord, mistake not my heart that hath been and is a sincere honourer of you and seeks you now for no other end but to clear itself, and to be held as I am (though I never more come near you)

Your honour's
poor follower and faithful servant,
Samuel Daniel

(Fortunately, a reconciliation followed, and when Devonshire died, Daniel wrote a panegyric on him.)

II-14   Miguel de Cervantes to Francisco de Robles, Diego de Alfaya, and Francisco de Mar

Very few writers in the Renaissance could make a living on their works and had thus to depend on the patronage system or a remunerative profession or trade. Two of the most popular novelists, Cervantes and Rabelais, did earn large sums for their masterpieces, but both suffered financial loss from the plethora of unauthorized or pirated editions and variants of their works. In the following letter, rich in legal formulas, Cervantes (1547-1616) tries through his notaries to prevent a spurious edition of *Don Quixote* from appearing in Lisbon.

Valladolid, 12 April, 1605
Let all those who see this letter granting power of attorney know that I, Miguel de Cervantes Saavedra, resident of this court, do declare as follows: having composed a book entitled *The Ingenious Knight Don Quijote de la Mancha,* our lord king has given and granted his privilege and licence, duly transmitted, that I or anyone whom I empower to do so may print and sell the work in the Kingdoms of Castille and the monarchy of Portugal for a period of ten years, forbidding under penalty that any other individual without my authorization or permission may

print or sell it, as the aforementioned licence states and makes clear. It has come to my notice that a few persons in the monarchy of Portugal have printed or intend to print the aforesaid book without my authorization or permission, contravening the royal licence mentioned above. Thus, in the best legal manner and form, I authorize and recognize by this letter that I am conferring all my full and free power, as is due and fit, on Francisco de Robles, royal bookseller, the lawyer Diego de Alfaya, and Francisco de Mar, residents in the city of Lisbon, each singly or as a group *in solidum*, to initiate criminal action in the proper way and form against the person or persons who have, without my permission, printed the aforesaid book in any region or the Kingdoms of Castile or Portugal. Let them seek punishment and sentencing of those persons under the royal law, submitting in my name petitions, plaints, demands, citations, protests, subpoenaing of witnesses, documents and proofs. Let them request embargoes, surrenderings, imprisonments, selling or selling back of goods, and let them take possession of them and let them put the accused under oath and submit them to all other judicial or extrajudicious rigors of inquiry as may be necessary, which I by virtue of my holding the royal privilege would submit were I present.

At the same time, in view of the printing and sale of the aforesaid book, let them negotiate concerning powers and permissions as may seem appropriate with those in a position to print or sell the book in the Kingdoms of Castile or Portugal for the period during which I hold the rights. Let them charge and receive in my name the agreed sum of *maravedís* or goods for the licence to have printed or to print henceforth, establishing by legal documents the authorities and agreements corresponding to the order and consent of Francisco de Robles, the true executor of my royal permission according to a written agreement drawn up and attested by the present letter. Any and all authority to carry out this letter's instructions I confer on the aforesaid three names, placing under obligation my present or future wealth as a legal bond in the presence of the five undersigned witnesses.*

Miguel de Saavedra Cervantes
(trans. R. J. C.)

---

* A few repetitious legal formulas have been omitted or simplified in this translation.

II-15   Lope de Vega to the Duke of Sessa

The most prolific playwright of the Renaissance, the "monster of nature," as Cervantes called him, claimed the authorship of 1500 plays of various kinds and wrote in 1609 a famous rhymed essay, *The New Art of Writing Plays*, which condemned the so-called rules of Aristotle and announced that the playwright (like Shakespeare) should cater to the taste of the theatergoers. At the pinnacle of his career, Lope de Vega (1562-1635) suddenly announced to his longtime patron and friend, the Duke of Sessa, that he had decided to abandon the theater. His being an ordained priest is a factor in the decision and his being depressed over the fatal illness of his mistress Marta de Nevares.

Madrid, late 1630

This thought will appear as news to Your Excellency, although actually it is not, merely having been not entirely resolved. I have for some days desired to stop writing for the theater, partly because of my age, which befits more serious things, and partly because of the weariness and mental depression it brings me. I decided this during my illness, if I were to survive that storm and arrive safely in port. But, as it happens with everyone, once I had kissed the shore I forgot the storm at sea. Now, Lord Excellency, I have learned that two plays I submitted, well written but badly listened to, displeased the public, either because they want young playwrights or because heaven doesn't want a clergyman meeting his death while writing a string of comedies. In any case, it is only right to abandon them, to avoid being like beautiful women whom everyone jokes about in their old age.

I therefore entreat Your Excellency to acknowledge openly one of Your henchmen who has for more than twenty-five years served You in secret. For without Your favor I shall not succeed in this design, and request some modest salary, which, added to the pension I receive, will help me get through the little of life that is left to me.

My services as chaplain will be of use to You. I shall say masses for Your

Excellency every day, and I shall likewise assist You in writing or soliciting whatever Your service or taste requires.* There's no difficulty about it, any problem being resolved by switching from *merced* to *vos* and inscribing it that way in Your records. The favors You did me over the years are too many to count, so that it is fitting that You reduce them to a set number, and that people should know, if they don't already, that You are my Lord and that the Sessa household has acquired a white Juan Latino more slavish than a black. One chaplain more doesn't add much to Your Excellency's budget, nor does it actually change our present status, and I with free time shall serve You better. Without servants coming and going, I shall be always in sight.

This is not a sudden decision. As I said above, I considered it a long time before taking up my pen. But if, for reasons I do not anticipate, this proposition should displease Your Excellency (as my misfortunes allow me to fear), I shall have had the honor to make this offer, due more to necessity than obligation, begging Your Excellency's pardon for my boldness, which is not necessarily repudiated even when it is not granted what it requests.

May God keep Your Excellency many years, as I desire and is necessary.

Your Excellency's chaplain and slave,
Bro. Lope de Vega Carpio
(trans. R. J. C.)

(The Duke declined the services of this priest who had sired fourteen children from ten women. Lope regained his spirits and wrote in 1632 his greatest prose work, *La Dorotea*.)

II-16   Ben Jonson to the Earl of Newcastle

In desperate straits, Ben Jonson (1572?-1637) invents a fabulous dream as a stratagem to plead for funds from his patron, the Earl of Newcastle. The pension referred to in the postscript, incidentally, was resumed in 1634, with arrears, through the intercession of Jonson's friend the Earl of Dorset.

20 December, 1631

My Noble and most honor'd Lord.

I my selfe beeing no substance, am faine to trouble You with shaddowes; or

---

* For many years Lope had written love letters for the Duke to send his many mistresses.

(what is less) an Apologue, or Fable in a dreame. I being strucken with the Palsey in the Yeare 1628. had by Sir Thomas Badger some few monthes synce, a Foxe sent mee for a present; which Creature, by handling, I endeavored to make time, as well for the abateing of my disease, as the delight I tooke in speculation of his Nature. It happen'd this present year 1631, and this verie weeke, being the weeke Ushering Christmas, and this Tuesday morneing in a dreame, (and morneing dreames are truest) to have one of my servants come up to my Bed-side, and tell mee, Master, Master the Foxe speakes: Whereat, (mee thought) I started, and troubled, went downe into the Yard, to witnes the wonder; There I found my Reynard, in his Tenement the Tubb, I had hyr'd for him, cynically expressing his owne lott, to be condemn'd to the house of Poett, where nothing was to bee seen but the bare walls, and not any thing heard but the noise of a Sawe, dividing billatts all the weeke long, more to keepe the family in exercise, then to comfort any person there with fire, save the Paralytick master; and went on in this way as the Foxe seem'd the better Fabler, of the two. I, his Master, began to give him good words, and stroake him: but Reynard barking, told mee; those would not doe, I must give him meate; I angry, call'd him stinking Vermine. Hee reply'd, looke into your Cellar, which is your Larder too, You'le find a worse vermin there. When presently called for a light, mee thought, I went downe, & found all the floore turn'd up, as if a Colony of Moles had beene there, or an army of Salt-Peter men; Whereupon I sent presently into Tuttle-street, for the Kings most Excellent Mole-chatcher to relieve mee, & hunt them: But hee when hee came and veiw'd the Place; and had well marked the Earth turn'd up, tooke a handfull, smelt to it, And said, Master it is not in my power to distroy this vermine; the K: or some good Man of a Noble Nature must helpe you. This kind of Mole is call'd a *Want*,* which will distroy you, and your family, if you prevent not the workeing of it in tyme, And therefore god keepe you and send you health.

The interpretation both of the Fable, and Dreame is, that I wakeing doe find Want the worst, and most workeing Vermine in a house, and therefore my Noble lord, and next the King, my best Patron: I am necessitated to tell it you. I am not so impudent to borrow any sume of your Lordship, for I have no faculty to pay: but my needs are such, and so urging, as I doe beg, what your bounty can give mee, in the name of good Letters, and the bond of an evergratefull and acknowledging servant

To your honour
B. Ionson

Yesterday the barbarous Court of Aldermen
have withdrawne their Chander-ly Pension,
for Verjuice, & Mustard. 33^{11}—6^s—8^d.

---

* a pun: want = mole.

II-17   Francisco de Quevedo to the Duke of Olivares

Scholar, poet, and satirist as well as diplomat, Francisco de Quevedo (1580-1645) was one of the most honored writers under Philip IV of Spain until accused of writing a "memorial" against the King's favorite, the Duke of Olivares, which Philip found lying under his napkin at a banquet. Very soon thereafter Quevedo was hustled off to a wretched imprisonment at San Marcos in Léon without trial. After four years of debilitating suffering, during which he wrote pious, Christian works, he was released "more dead than alive" to spend his last months at the Torre de Juan Abad in Ciudad Real. In 1641 he wrote another "memorial," this one to the author of his misfortunes, the Duke of Olivares.

León, 7 October, 1641

Excellent Lord,

May God give your Majesty many fortunate years of life, and to your arms the successes which Your Excellency desires, so that Your Excellency, remembering His greatness and forgetting my person may read this memorial.

MEMORIAL

Sir: My imprisonment occurred one year and ten months ago, 7 December, on the Eve of the Conception of Our Lady, at half-past ten at night. In the rigorous climate of winter, I was dragged without cape or shirt, 61 years of age, to this royal convent of San Marcos of León, where I have been all this time in harsh detention, suffering of three wounds, which with the chills and the nearness of a gutter at the head of my cot have left me with ulcers. Without a surgeon, I have tried to cauterize them with my own hands as others watch with pity. So wretched am I that they have sustained me and kept me alive by charity. The horror of my travails make them all shudder.

I have only one attendant, a nun of the Barefoot Carmelites, of whom I can say only that she commends me to God. Aware of my sins, I recognize the piety of suffering. I myself am the voice of my conscience and acknowledge my life as it is. If Your Excellence found me worthy, mine would be the praise. If you found me evil and made me worthy, the praise would be yours. Although I may be unworthy of pity, Your Excellency is most worthy to possess it, a virtue befitting a great lord and minister. "Nothing," says Seneca, consoling Marcia, "do I deem so worthy of those of lofty station than to pardon many things and never ask for pardon themselves." What greater fault could I commit than persuade myself that my misfortunes are to measure the extent of your magnanimity! I beg of Your Excellency time to vindicate myself. People have heard my enemies talk about me. What I ask is that you hear me talk about myself. My accusation will be more authentic, being exempt of hatred.

I protest in God's name that of everything that has been said about me, my only fault is to have lived in such an unexemplary way that my foolish actions may be interpreted as abominations. I am not claiming that I am the victim of defamatory envy, although it could be, since there are wretches invidious of the more wretched, like fortunate men of the less fortunate—the ultimate accomplishment of human malice. As I must pardon in those who abhor me that they solicit my ruin, the greatness and generous nature of Your Excellency must not pardon their soliciting You not to pardon me. Those who see me do not consider me a prisoner, but one condemned to a rigorous death. For this reason I am not waiting for death but consulting with it. I am living the tediousness of death. All I need to be dead is the sepulcher, the resting place of the dead.

I have lost everything. My property, which never was much, is now nothing—between the high cost of my imprisonment and those who have made off with it. As for my friends, my adversity terrifies them. The only thing remaining is my faith in Your Excellency. Can it not offer me some clemency, or reduce this harshness for several years? My Lord, I do not request this inevitably short period of time to live longer, but rather to live well—even if briefly—that I may be no small parcel of the glory of Your Excellency's name. Your Lordship's majesty, authority, and greatness should intercede together. I am not asking that my punishment cease, but that its prosecution be entrusted to my penance. For another's harshness is a far milder source of torments than one's own shame.

If anyone is to be found possessing Your Excellency's worth, virtues, eminency, style, and learning, it is Pliny the Younger. Let Your Excellency listen to a passage favorable to me in Book VIII of his *Epistles to Geminius:* "Notwithstanding I judge as best and outstanding that man who pardons others in such a way as though he himself sinned every day, even though that man abstains from sinning as though incapable of pardoning others." Let Your Excellency be that most worthy and outstanding gentleman, as the deeds of your clemency and the examples of Your forbearance all attest, You having had to bear the weight of so many ingrates and the martyrdom of so many traitors now that France keeps plotting against this monarchy.

This will be the last outcry to reach the ears of Your Excellency, an outcry my memory has helped to frame. Permit me to be more concerned about my gratitude for your beneficence than about the rigors of my peril. For Your enlightened fame will always gain more glory from awarding mercy to me than from my downfall. As the Emperor Trajan said when being consulted by Pliny the Younger (Book X of his *Epistles)*: "You could have no doubts, my beloved Pliny, about deciding to come and consult me, since you know very well that my intention is not to acquire men's reverence through fear and terror." These words of Trajan, who will doubt that they are from Your Excellency's mouth, revealing your own thought and intention? The times, more than his merits, advanced this worthy emperor to become such a majestic monarch, like Yourself in private life so unambitious and disinterested.

May Our Lord keep Your Excellency, whom we need. From the Royal Convent of San Marcos in León, of the Order of the glorious apostle Saint James.

He who from Your Excellency hopes for new life,

Don Francisco de Quevedo
(trans. R. J. C.)

(The Duke of Olivares fell from royal favor in January, 1643, and the great poet left his prison a broken man the following June.)

CHAPTER 3

THE FINE ARTS. MUSIC.

V. *Albrecht Dürer* (self-portrait)

VI. *Musicians* by Caravaggio

If all the fine arts represented a rebirth of antiquity through subject matter, genre, or style, nothing acknowledged that debt so explicitly as the revival of the three ancient orders of Ionic, Doric, and Corinthian. If the ancients were the masters whom the Renaissance architects sought to rival, it was rare for a sixteenth-century master to be judged the equal of the ancients, as Michelangelo thought Bramante to be (III-17). The reigning arbiters of architecture, Palladio (1518-80) and Serlio (1475-1554) were steeped in classicism. Like them, Michelangelo was much influenced by the architectural manual of the Roman Vitruvius, who lived in the first century before Christ, a work which circulated in many editions during the sixteenth century. The Gothic style which governed churches and civic buildings during the Middle Ages gave way to classical designs. Castles and country homes gave up their thick walls and moats and fortress-like appearance. The campaign to restore and rival the buildings of antiquity, expressed by Castiglione and Raphael (I-6), was a dual enthusiasm of artists and architects. When Pope Julius II decided to build a mausoleum which would be the eighth wonder of the world and cast in shade the mausoleums of the past, Michelangelo was chosen for what he was eventually to call "the tragedy of the tomb" on which he wasted his "youth and manhood." His experience was a painful illustration of what artistic servitude could be under the Maecenate system (III-11), so severely indicted by Tolstóy in *What is Art?*

Kings, noblemen, Churchmen, and the new wealthy merchants sought the role of art patron. Many letters reflect, with less passion than Michelangelo's, the uneasiness of artists and musicians under the Maecenate system. Dürer found Jacob Heller a very demanding master, pinching pennies, complaining about details of execution, and setting up such impossible goals as a painting to include a hundred faces (III-3). Dürer was able to handle another patron, Wilibald Pirkheimer, more easily, admonishing him when necessary, "Now be lenient with me and don't get into a passion so easily. Be gentle like me" (III-2). Peter Paul Rubens, in a letter to Annibale Chieppio, exhibits a badly-bruised ego inflicted by a powerful patron. His several complaints included time pressures, false attribution of his works, the imposition of ignorant collaborators, and even careless damaging of some paintings (III-20).

Yet it was the jeremiads of Michelangelo about the artist's hardships which resounded longest and loudest, starting from his first arrival in Rome. Even as he was presented with the contract to undertake the painting of the Sistine Ceiling, he signed it "sculptor" to indicate his dissatisfaction. Later he wrote a verse-epistle in the form of an extended sonnet to his friend Giovanni da Pistoia; complaining of the egregious demands of this commission, he concludes: "the place is wrong, and no painter I" (III-5). Michelangelo often resorted to sarcasm with patrons, answering Pope Julius's complaint that the disciples on the first version of the Sistine Ceiling were not sumptuous enough with the rejoinder that disciples, unlike pontiffs, were poor. Equally sarcastic was his covertly obscene letter destroying the papal project of erecting a colossus in Florence's San Lorenzo Square (III-7). Yet another sarcastic and destructive letter was written by Michelangelo to demolish totally young Sangallo's plan for rebuilding the dome of Saint Peter's permitting the counterfeiting of money and the rape of nuns (III-17). Nor was Michelangelo's rival and antagonist Da Vinci reticent about upbraiding patrons. His "angry" letter to Piacenza's Commissioners of Buildings concludes, "Open your eyes and try to ensure that your money is not so spent as to purchase your own shame" (III-1). To show that he could be gracious and courtly, even with a patron, Michelangelo penned to King Francis I a charming letter refusing a commission. Letters of Michelangelo showed him as angry at assistants and apprentices as he could be at patrons, especially the "dry turd of a boy" he took on as apprentice in 1510 (III-4).

Letters exchanged between the artists and friends or clients eminent in the field of letters show a harmonious relationship. Such are Annibal Caro's letter to Vasari ordering a *Venus and Adonis* (III-16), generous in tone, or that of Cellini explaining to Varchi that he cannot undertake the portrait medal of Cardinal Bembo until the latter's beard is full-grown (III-9). Michelangelo enjoyed a cordial relationship with Benedetto Varchi, who "discovered" his poems and explicated two of them before the Florentine Academy. It was Varchi who drew Michelangelo out of his reticence to theorize about art by eliciting a famous letter, albeit a somewhat impatient one, on the essential unity of the arts (III-15). Other friendships between literary men and painters emerge from their letters: Aretino and his fellow townsman Titian, to whom he characterized a Venetian sunset as a work of art painted by "the errant fancy of nature, the master of all great masters" (III-12); Castiglione's exchange of letters with Raphael, that gracious and pampered artist who had so few quarrels with patrons, but who complained that beautiful female models were so rare that he had to paint from Platonic concepts set up in his own mind (III-6).

The relations between Michelangelo and Aretino worsened with time. After the literate "blackmailer" sought without success to coax the gift of a painting out of Michelangelo, he became increasingly hostile, making allusions to

Michelangelo's friendships with his male models and friends, including Gherardo Perini and Tommaso Cavalieri (IX-5), and condemning the mural of the *Last Judgment* as more worthy of a brothel than a chapel (III-13)—a curious accusation from the man who defended the bronzeworker Marcantonio of Bologna, who had engraved on copper sixteen ways of making love, and persuaded Pope Clement to free Marcantonio from prison (III-10) with a jibe at "dirty-minded laws which forbid the eyes to see the very things which delight them most."

In the Renaissance poets and artists, both of whom enjoyed a new and heightened status in the Humanistic environment, generally arrived—despite Aretino and Michelangelo—at a mutual respect, and indeed inspiration, with poets inspiring artists. Politian's stanzas for the joust of Giuliano dei Medici inspired Botticelli's *Birth of Venus* (mentioned in III-16). Artists often inspired poets, as Velásquez's *Breda* was inspired by Calderón and inspired in turn Manuel Faria y Sousa's poem on the canvas. Often the artist himself was capable of impressive poetry, with Michelangelo, Leonardo, and Raphael among early Renaissance exemplars of the Apollo-Apelles.

The Burckhardt view of the Renaissance as a saltation is supported in that period by music as well as the fine arts. The invention of printing did much for the spread of music. Starting in 1501 the printer Petrucci was publishing hunting songs, quickly followed by a variety of compositions. By 1525 Pierre Haultin had mastered the printing of notes and staff together. The *Miserere* of Josquin des Prez (1445-1521) is accepted as the finest early example of counterpoint. Another Flemish composer of distinction, contemporary of the famous Orlando di Lasso (Lassus), Jan Sweelinck (1562-1621) not only created music, but with that professional self-consciousness one associates with Renaissance artists, theorized on the origins and nature of music (III-19), designed principally "to move and moderate the emotions of the soul." Sweelinck was an organist, the organ gaining prominence during this time. Another organist and composer, William Byrd, left us an interesting letter enumerating the many benefits one derives from singing (III-18). The intensive training demanded by music and the rigors of the profession made all musicians of importance dependent on patrons, including Church patronage. The Church's greatest protégé was Giovanni Pierluigi da Palestrina (1525-94), musical director of the Lateran and of Santa Maria Maggiore who finally became choirmaster of St. Peter's. His masses and liturgical music won him the inevitable title of "the Homer of music."

So essential was the role of patron to music that even though there was little love lost between Martin Luther and the Dukes of Bavaria, patrons of the composer Ludwig Senfl among others, Luther could forgive all grievances against the Dukes because they "cultivate and honor music in this manner" (III-8).

Indeed, Luther will "praise and venerate them mightily." Several composers, by the way, endeared Luther to music by composing settings for the *Passion* as translated by Luther.

The difficulty of musicians, as easily exploited as were artists, in dealing with hard-thinking patrons is clearly illustrated in a letter of Heinrich Schütz to Wilhelm Ludwig Moser, each of the two serving as intermediaries for the actual patron and protégé. Schütz represented the composer Samuel Scheidt of Halle and Moser the Elector of Saxony, who had not yet paid for some pleasant compositions in the Flemish style dedicated to His Grace (III-22).

Corresponding to the affinity between Renaissance poets and artists, there was obviously a close working relationship between composers and the poets who wrote the words of their madrigals, odes, canzoni, etc. It was such composers as Tromboncino, Concilione, and the great Jacob Arcadelt who discovered the lyrical qualities of Michelangelo's madrigals and sonnets, almost never published during his lifetime except with musical settings. When Arcadelt set one of Michelangelo's sonnets to music about 1542, the artist was humble and grateful, insisting in a letter that the words were not worthy of the music. Such collaboration extended to street-singers and Aretino, who liked to hear the words of his verses "on the lips of your street-singers" (III-14). Another important collaboration between poets and musicians were the songs and musical interludes which were part of most Renaissance plays, whether comedy (II-2) or tragedy (II-8).

New musical forms were appearing, such as the oratorio and chorale (introduced into the service by Luther), but the most predictable form was opera. Opera owes its origins to a group of Florentine Humanist writers who met regularly at the home of the Bardi and became known as "the Chamber of the Bards." In their effort to write "regular" tragedy conforming to the "rules" of Aristotle's *Poetics,* they noted that Aristotle listed *melopoeia* (melody) as one of the six elements of tragedy. They began writing tragedies to be sung and called them *opere per musica* (works for music). Their first themes reflected their interest in classical Greek and Roman theater and myth. In 1594 Jacopo Peri set to music Rinuccini's drama on Daphne. Peri and Caccini composed the opera *Euridice* in 1600. One of the enthusiastic group of the Camerata dei Bardi, Vincenzo Galilei (father of the astronomer) shows in a letter to the Duke of Mantua how they sought to recreate musical recitation rather than polyphony, thus adhering to "the use of the ancient Greeks," even though opera turned out to be more versatile than the Greek dramas they thought they were recreating.

The greatest composer of opera was Claudio Monteverdi (1567-1643), whose *Orfeo* (1607) was a landmark of the new genre. To the librettist of the *Orfeo,* Alessandro Striggio, councillor of the Duke of Mantua, Monteverdi voiced a gentle protest at being requested to waste his talents on libretti of inferior quality (III-21). In a surprising burst of literary criticism, Monteverdi makes it clear that he wishes to create settings for libretti only by such poet-playwrights as Striggio and Rinuccini.

Many letters from Renaissance artists and musicians complain that the wars of the period were detrimental to the advance of their professions. Michelangelo articulates this in letters and in his dialogues with Francisco de Hollanda. The theme developed in Ambrogio Lorenzetti's murals in the City Hall of Siena was unanimously subscribed to: Concord is the guardian of arts and progress. Even when Leonardo da Vinci has extolled to Duke Lodovico of Milan his diverse talents as military engineer and architect, he hastens to add: "In time of peace, I believe I can give you as complete satisfaction as anyone else" (VII-2).

III-1 Leonardo da Vinci to the Commissioners of Piacenza

Leonardo (1452-1519) had indeed achieved a fine reputation when he was commissioned to do a bronze equestrian statue of Duke Sforza of Milan. However, this project was never completed and he was chided for his failure by Michelangelo. Yet he knew metallurgical chemistry and felt competent to give advice on projects in bronze.

c. 1484

Illustrious Commissioners of Buildings! hearing that your Excellencies have resolved upon the construction of certain great works in bronze, I propose to offer you certain counsels on the subject. First, then, take care not to act so swiftly and hastily in awarding the commission that by your speed you put it out of your power to make a good choice both of subject and of a master, as Italy has a number of men of capacity. Some fellow, that is, who by his incompetence may afterwards afford occasion to your successors to cast blame on yourselves and your generation, judging that this age was poorly equipped either with men of good judgment or good masters, seeing that other cities and especially the city of the Florentines were almost at this very same time enriched with such beautiful and great works in bronze, among these being the gates of their baptistery. Florence indeed, like

Piacenza, is a place of resort, where many visitors congregate, and these when they see its beautiful and stately works of art form the impression that the city must have worthy inhabitants, seeing that these works serve as evidence of this; but they form quite a different impression if they see a great expenditure in metal wrought so poorly that it would be less of a reproach to the city if the doors were of plain wood, for then the material would have cost little and, therefore, would not seem to require a great degree of skill.

Now, the parts principally sought for in cities are their cathedrals, and, as one approaches these, the first objects which meet the eye are their doors by which one enters into the churches.

Beware, gentlemen of the Commission, lest the too great speed, whereby you desire, with such swiftness as I perceive you use, to allot the commission for so important a work may become the reason why what was intended for the honor of God and of men may prove a great dishonor to your judgment and to your city, where, as it is a place of distinction and of resort, there is an innumerable concourse of visitors. This disgrace would befall you if by your negligence you put your trust in some braggart who, by his subterfuges or by the favor here shown him, were to be awarded such a commission by you as should bring great and lasting shame both to him and to you.

I cannot help feeling angry when I reflect upon the sort of men who have made me a confidant of their desire to embark upon such an undertaking, without giving a thought to their capacity for it—not to say more.

One is a maker of pots, another of cuirasses, a third makes bells and another collars for them, another even is a bombardier; yet another is in the Duke's household and boasts that he is by way of being an intimate acquaintance of Messer Ambrogio Ferrere, and that he has some influence and has made certain promises to him, and if this does not satisfy you he will get on his horse and ride off to the Duke and will get such letters from him that you will never be able to refuse him the work.

But consider to what straits the poor masters who by study have made themselves competent to execute such works are reduced, when they have to contend against fellows like these! What hope have they of being able to look for reward for their talent!

Open your eyes and try to ensure that your money is not so spent as to purchase your own shame. I can assure you that from this district you will get nothing except the work of hard, mean or clumsy masters. There is not a man who is capable—and you may believe me—except Leonardo the Florentine, who is making the bronze horse of the Duke Francesco;* and you can leave him out of

* Duke Francesco Sforza (1401-1466), father of Duke Lodovico il Moro of Milan (see Letter VII-2).

your calculations altogether, for he has a work to do which will last him the whole of his life, and indeed I doubt whether he will ever finish it, so great it is.

III-2   Albrecht Dürer to Wilibald Pirkheimer

In an amiable letter to his patron Wilibald Pirkheimer, Albrecht Dürer (1471-1528), the famous German painter, engraver and woodcut designer, gives news of his stay in Venice and his impressions of some Italian painters, particularly the old Giovanni Bellini whose influence is apparent in Dürer's works from this Venetian period.

Venice, 7 Feb. 1506.

First my willing service to you, dear Master! If things are going well with you I am as glad with my whole heart for you as I should be for myself. I recently wrote to you and hope that the letter reached you. In the meantime my mother has written to me, scolding me for not writing to you; and she has given me to understand that you hold me in displeasure because I do not write to you. She said I must duly excuse myself to you, and she takes it very much to heart, as her way is.

Now I don't know what excuse to make except that I am lazy about writing, and that you have not been at home. But as soon as I heard that you were either at home or coming home, I sat down at once and wrote to you; I also very specially charged Castel (Fugger) to convey my service to you. So I humbly pray you to forgive me, for I have no other friend on earth but you. I don't believe, however, that you are angry with me, for I regard you in no other light than as a father.

How I wish you were here at Venice! There are so many nice men among the Italians who seek my company more and more every day—which is very pleasing to one—men of sense and knowledge, good lute-players and pipers, judges of painting, men of much noble sentiment and honest virtue, and they show me much honour and friendship. On the other hand there are also amongst them some of the most false, lying, thievish rascals; I should never have believed that such were living in the world. If one did not know them, one would think them the nicest men the earth could show. For my own part I cannot help laughing at them whenever they talk to me. They know that their knavery is no secret but they don't mind.

Amongst the Italians I have many good friends who warn me not to eat and drink with their painters. Many of them are my enemies and they copy my work in the churches and wherever they can find it; and then they revile it and say that the style is not *antique* and so not good. But Giovanni Bellini has highly praised me before many nobles. He wanted to have something of mine, and himself came to me and asked me to paint him something and he would pay well for it. And all men tell me what an upright man he is, so that I am really friendly with him. He is very old, but is still the best painter of them all. And that which so well pleased me eleven years ago pleases me no longer; if I had not seen it for myself I should not have believed any one who told me. You must know too that there are many better painters here than Master Jacob (Jacopo de' Barbari) is abroad *(wider dawsen Meister J.)*, yet Anton Kolb would swear an oath that no better painter lives than Jacob. Others sneer at him, saying if he were good he would stay here, and so forth.

I have only to-day begun to sketch in my picture, for my hands were so scabby *(grindig)* that I could do no work with them, but I have got them cured.

Now be lenient with me and don't get in a passion so easily but be gentle like me. I don't know why you will not learn from me. My friend! I should like to know if any one of your loves is dead—that one close by the water for instance, or the one so that you might supply her place by another.

Given at Venice at the 9th. hour of the night, on Saturday after Candlemass in the year 1506.

Give my service to Stephan Paumgartner and to Masters Hans Harsdorfer and Volkamer.

Albrecht Dürer.

III-3   Albrecht Dürer to Jacob Heller

Exasperated by an exceedingly difficult commission, that of the Heller altarpiece, Dürer doggedly refutes the slanders of his exacting patron, Jacob Heller.

Nürnberg, 4 Nov. 1508.

Dear Herr Jacob Heller, in my last letter I wrote you my candid and sincere opinion and you have angrily complained of it to my cousin, declaring that I twist my words. I have likewise since received your letter from Hans Imhof. I am justly surprised at what you say in it about my last letter: seeing that you can accuse me of not holding to my promises to you. From such a slander each and everyone exempts me, for I bear myself, I trust, so as to take my stand amongst other straightforward men. Besides I know well what I have written and promised to you, and you know that in my cousin's house I refused to promise you to make a good thing, because I cannot. But to this I did pledge myself, that I would make something for you that not many men can. Now I have given such exceeding pains to your picture, that I was led to send you the aforesaid letter. I know that when the picture is finished all artists will be well pleased with it. It will not be valued at less than 300 florins. I would not paint another like it for three times the price agreed, for I neglect myself for it, suffer loss, and earn anything but thanks from you.

I am using, let me tell you, quite the finest colours I can get. Of ultramarine I shall want 20 ducats' worth alone, not counting the other expenses. When the picture is once finished, I am quite sure that you yourself will say that anything more beautiful you have never seen; but I dare not expect from beginning to end to finish the painting of the middle panel in less than thirteen months. I shall not begin any other work till it is finished, though it will be much to my hurt. Then what do you suppose my expenses will be while I am working at it? You would not undertake to keep me for that time for 200 florins. Only think what you have repeatedly written about the materials. If you wanted to buy a pound of

Ultramarine you would hardly get it for 100 florins, for I cannot buy an ounce of it good for less than 10 or 12 ducats.

And so, dear Herr Jacob Heller, my writing is not so utterly crooked as you think, and I have not broken my promise in this matter.

You further reproach me with having promised you, that I would paint your picture with the greatest possible care that ever I could. That I certainly never said or if I did I was out of my senses, for in my whole life-time I should scarcely finish it. With such extraordinary care I can hardly finish a face in half a year; now your picture contains fully 100 faces, not reckoning the drapery and landscape and other things in it. Besides who ever heard of making such a work for an altar-piece? no one could see it. But I think it was thus that I wrote to you—that I would paint the picture with great or more than ordinary pains because of the time which you waited for me.

Besides, knowing you as I do, I feel sure that if I had promised you to do something, which you saw yourself would be to my loss, you would not desire its fulfilment. Nevertheless—act in the matter as you will—I will still hold to what I have promised you; for as far as ever I can I will live honestly with everyone. If, however, I had not made you a promise I know what I would do. But I have felt obliged to answer you that you may not think I have not read your letter. I hope when once you see the finished picture, all will come better. So be patient, for the days are short, and this affair as you know admits of no haste, for there is much work in it and I will not make it less. I rest my hopes on the promise which you made to my brother-in-law at Frankfurt.

You need not look about for a purchaser for my Madonna, for the Bishop of Breslau has given me 72 florins for it, so I have sold it well. I commend myself to you. Given at Nürnberg in the year 1508 on the Sunday after All Saints' Day.

Albrecht Dürer.

III-4   Michelangelo Buonarroti to his father Lodovico

The short temper of Michelangelo (1475-1564) was something his friends and family had to learn to cope with. Witness his reaction when a boy, engaged to look after his housekeeping, is interested only in being taught sculpture.

January, 1510

Most Revered Father, . . . I shall not have any work done until this agreement is drawn up. Please tell him [Bernardino] how the matter stands. About the boy that came—that scoundrel of a muleteer swindled me out of a ducat, and swore that he had agreed for two broad ducats of gold: and all the other boys who come here with muleteers receive no more than ten *carlini.* I was more angry about it than if I had lost twenty-five ducats, for I see that it was the father's fault, who wanted to send him on muleback in state. Oh, I never had such luck, not I! And more than that, both the father and the lad assured me that he would do anything, look after the mule and sleep on the ground if necessary; and now I have to look after him instead. As if I wanted other vexations besides those I have had since I came back! I have had the boy I left here ill ever since my return. He is getting better now, it is true, but he has been at death's door and was given up by the doctors for about a month, and during all that time I have not been to bed, to say nothing of other troubles. Then there comes this dry-turd of a boy, who says that he does not want to lose time and that he wants to learn. When he was in Florence he said that two or three hours a day would be sufficient: now the whole day is not enough and he wants to be drawing all night as well. His father has put him up to this. If I were to say anything to him he would declare that I did not wish him to learn. I wanted somebody to look after the house; and if he was not prepared to do this they ought not to have put me to this expense. But they are schemers, and working for their own ends: but enough. I beg you to have him fetched away, for he annoys me to such an extent that I can bear him no longer. The muleteer has received so much money that he can very well afford to take him back again: he is a friend of his father's. Tell the father to send for him. I shall not give him another *quattrino,* for I have no money. I will put up with him until he is sent for, but if they do not send for him I shall dismiss him although I told him to go away the second day he was with me, as well as afterward on several occasions, and he does not realize it. . . .

. . . If you should meet the boy's father, explain the matter to him gently: tell him he is a good lad but too refined, and not suited for my work, and that he must send for him.

III-5   Michelangelo Buonarroti to Giovanni da Pistoia

The attrition involved in painting the vast expanse of the Sistine Ceiling in
the unfamiliar medium of fresco so exhausted Michelangelo that he shared
the humor of the situation with his friend Giovanni da Pistoia in an extended
sonnet.

June/July 1510

I' ho gia fatto un gozzo. . . .
In this hard toil I've such a goiter grown,
Like cats that water drink in Lombardy,
(Or wheresoever else the place may be)
That chin and belly meet perforce in one.
My beard doth point to heaven, my scalp its place
Upon my shoulder finds; my chest, you'll say,
A harpy's is, my paint-brush all the day
Doth drop a rich mosaic on my face.
My loins have entered my paunch within,
My nether end my balance doth supply,
My feet unseen move to and fro in vain.
In front to utmost length is stretched my skin
And wrinkled up in folds behind, while I
Am bent as bowmen bend a bow in Spain.
No longer true or sane,
The judgment now doth from the mind proceed,
For 'tis ill shooting through a twisted reed.
Then thou, my picture dead,
Defend it, Giovan, and my honour—why?
The place is wrong, and no painter I.

(A small accompanying sketch of himself standing and painting the Ceiling, as well as the text of the sonnet itself, belies the widespread fiction that Michelangelo painted the vault while lying on his back.)

III-6   Raphael da Sanzio to Baldassare Castiglione

By the time he succeeded Bramante as chief architect of St. Peter's, Raphael da Sanzio (1483-1520), who had been summoned to Rome when comparatively unknown, was one of the most celebrated of living artists, famous as a scholar as well. In addition to Castiglione, whose portrait he painted in 1516, he numbered among his intimate friends Andrea Navagero and other poets, as well as Cardinals Bembo and Bibbiena.

What does the painter do when faced with a paucity of suitable models? Raphael confronts the problem, below.

Rome, n.d. (c. 1514)

Sire. I have done drawings in several styles based on the concept of Your Lordship. And everyone is pleased, unless they are all flattering me; but I fail to succeed in my own estimation because I fear I shan't succeed in yours. I send them to you. May Your Lordship choose a few, if you deem any of them worthy.

Our Lord, while doing me honor, has placed a heavy burden on my shoulders. This is the care of constructing St. Peter's. Indeed I hope I won't crumble beneath it, all the more so because the model I have made pleases your Lordship and is praised by many fine talents. But I rise with an even loftier thought. I should like to discover the beautiful forms of ancient architecture; nor do I know if this pursuit shall be the flight of Icarus. Vitruvius has given me great enlightenment, but not so much as I need. About the *Galatea,** I would consider myself a great master if I were half the many things that Your Lordship claims. But in your words I recognize the love you bear me; and I tell you that in order to depict a beautiful woman I would have to see divers beauties, provided that Your Lordship might join me to choose the best one. But lacking in wise verdicts and beautiful

* Raphael's fresco, *The Triumph of Galatea*, in the Farnesina, Rome.

women, I avail myself of certain Ideas that are born to my intellect. Whether this in itself has any artistic merit, I know not: indeed I am weary of it. I wait upon Your Lordship.

(trans. L.L.)

(See also Letter I-6, which develops Raphael's enthusiasm for the beauties of ancient architecture.)

III-7   Michelangelo to Giovan Francesco Fattucci

The following ironical and audacious letter was instrumental in destroying a pet project of the Pope to erect a colossal statue in San Lorenzo Square, Florence.

October/December 1525

Messer Giovan Francesco: If I took as much strength as I took delight from your last letter, I should believe myself able to execute—and soon—all the things about which you write me; but since I haven't so much strength, I shall do what I can. . . .

About the colossus forty spans high which you tell me is to go, or be placed, at the corner of the loggia of the Medici Garden where it meets the angle of Messer Luigi della Stufa's place, I have given this thought and not a little, as you ask me. It strikes me that on the aforesaid corner it wouldn't go so well, since it would occupy too much space on the road. But it would turn out much better on the other side, in my opinion, there where the barber shop is, for it would have the square before it and would not encumber the street. And since there might be objections to carrying off said barber shop out of love for the income [*entrate*] it affords, I have thought that said figure might be made to sit down. The behind would be placed so high that, making the work empty on the inside, as befits something constructed of pieces, the barber shop could stay underneath and would not lose income. And that this shop may have, as it has now, a place for the smoke to disappear through, it seems to me that I could put in the statue's hand a cornucopia which would serve as chimney. Then since I should leave the head of such a statue empty, the same as the members, of this too I think we might make some practical use. There is here on the square a huckster, a very good friend of mine, who has told me in confidence that one could put a fine dovecote in it. Another fanciful thought occurs to me which would be much better, but it would require making the figure much larger. This could of course be done, since you can build a tower out of sections. This thought is that the head might serve as a bell tower for San Lorenzo, which badly needs one. With bells inserted up there and sound issuing from the mouth, it would appear that the colossus were crying mercy and especially on feast days, when the bells ring most often and with the heaviest peals.

III-8   Martin Luther to Ludwig Senfl

In a letter to Ludwig Senfl, considered to be the finest German composer of Catholic church music of his day, Martin Luther (1483-1546) declares his belief in the supremacy of music.

Coburg, 4 October 1530

Grace and peace in Christ. Although my name is so hated that I must fear the letter I am sending will not be received and read by you, excellent Ludwig, in sufficient safety: nevertheless [my] love for music, with which I see you adorned and gifted by my God, conquers this fear. Which love also awakens the hope that my letter may not be the bearer of any danger to you; for who, even in Turkey, would scold, if one should love art and praise the artificer? Although your Dukes of Bavaria themselves are extremely ill-disposed toward me, I nevertheless praise and venerate them mightily above all others, for they cultivate and honor music in this manner. Nor is there any doubt that there are many seeds of good virtue in these souls who like music; indeed, I deem those who do not like it as the tree-trunks and stones. For we know that music is also hateful and intolerable to the evil spirits. And I plainly judge, nor am I ashamed to assert, that there is no art, after theology, that can match music; for it alone, after theology, lends that which otherwise only theology lends, to wit, quiet and a contented mind; a manifest token that the devil, author of baleful cares and of the restlessness of the multitudes, flies from the voice of music almost as he flies from the word of theology. Hence it is that the prophets used no art as they did music, assigning their theology not to geometry, nor to arithmetic, nor to astronomy but to music, for they held theology and music in close proximity, and spoke the truth by means of psalms and canticles. But why am I now praising music, endeavoring in such a meager letter to paint, or rather disfigure, so great a thing? But that is how abundantly and zealously I love it; it has often refreshed me and freed me from great distress. I return to you, praying that if you have a copy of this canticle: "In pace in id ipsum" * you will have it transcribed and sent to me. For that tenor has delighted me from my youth and now much more, since I also understand the words. I have not seen that antiphon set for several voices. I do not wish to burden you, however, with the task of setting [it], but presume you have it from another quarter. I hope indeed that the end of my life may be near. And the world hates me, nor can it endure me; I, again, loathe and detest it. And so may the very good and faithful shepherd take my soul. Wherefore I have already begun to chant this antiphon and desire to hear it set. Lest you should not have it, or not know it, I herewith send [it to you], pictured with its notes; if you wish, you can set it also after I die. The Lord Jesus be with you for ever. Amen. Forgive my boldness and wordiness. Greet all of your musical choir with reverence on my behalf.

Martinus Luther

III-9   Benvenuto Cellini to Benedetto Varchi

The lively goldsmith Cellini (1500-1571) assures the Humanist Varchi that his failure to move ahead with a medallion of Cardinal Pietro Bembo is not due to indolence, but to Bembo's decision to grow a beard. Only when the beard is several inches long, around Lent, should he undertake to finish the commission.

Rome, 9 September 1536

I understand from your most courteous letter that it would give you pleasure if we were to meet in Venice in order to be a little more accessible to you; and I assure

---

* I will both lay me down in peace, and sleep.

you that all your pleasures are no less desirable to me than to you; and at a time mutually agreed upon I shall come to Venice; but I am very sorry that our dear Luca cannot come, according to what he writes me. He is staying because of his lawsuit. . . .

My dear Messer Benedetto, you tell me that our Messer Pietro Bembo is letting his beard grow. This certainly pleases me a great deal because we shall do a work of a much more graceful form. Now, to tell you how the situation stands, with this whim of his to let the beard continue to grow, I would have you understand that in two months it will not be as long as one would wish, because it won't be more than two inches in length and will be imperfect. Therefore, should his head be engraved on the medal in this state, when the beard finally reaches its full growth my medal will not be a good likeness; and if he shaves it, even less will he resemble this medal with the short beard. Now it seems to me that, desiring to create something which truly endures, we must let the beard achieve its full growth, which won't be until Lent. Then we can produce a work of greater merit. Don't think I'm saying this to procrastinate because I swear to you that any time at a moment's notice from you I should immediately mount my horse as willingly as anything I've ever done, and thus I give you my word. If this seems satisfactory and you deem it fitting that His Lordship be notified of it, and if you think I might humbly proffer my opinion to His Lordship, inform me and I shall do it; and have no doubt that I shall come, in all things I stand ready to do your bidding. . . . Stay well, and God protect you.

(trans. L.L.)

III-10   Pietro Aretino to Battista Zatti

In a candid discussion of censorship, Pietro Aretino (1492-1556) argues that the human phallus deserves to be freely represented in painting and sculpture.

Venice, 19 December, 1537

No sooner had I persuaded Pope Clement to set free Messer Marcantonio of Bologna who had been imprisoned for having engraved on copper the sixteen methods, etc., than I had a sudden desire to see those pictures which had caused tattle-tale Giberti * to insist that the worthy artist ought to be hung and drawn.

When I saw them I had the same kind of impulse which made Giulio Romano do the original paintings, and inasmuch as the poets and the sculptors, both ancient and modern, have often written or carved—for their own amusement only—such trifles as the marble satyr in the Chigi Palace who is trying to assault a boy, I scribbled off the sonnets which you find underneath each one. The sensual thoughts which they call to mind I dedicate to you, saying a fig for hypocrites. I am all out of patience with their scurvy strictures and their dirty-minded laws which forbid the eyes to see the very things which delight them most.

What wrong is there in beholding a man possess a woman? It would seem to me that the thing which is given to us by nature to preserve the race, should be worn around the neck as a pendant, or pinned onto the cap like a broach, for it is the spring which feeds all the rivers of the people, and the ambrosia in which the world delights in its happiest days.

It is what made you, who are one of the greatest living physicians. It is what has produced all the Bembos, Molzas, Fortunios, Varchis, Ugolin Martellis, Lorenzos, Lenzis, Dolces, Fra Sebastianos, Titians and Michelangelos, and after them all the popes and emperors and kings. It has begotten the loveliest of children, the most beautiful of women, and the holiest of saints.

Hence one should order holidays and vigils and feasts in its honor, and not shut it up in a bit of serge or silk. The hands indeed might be hidden since they gamble away money, sign false testimony, make lewd gestures, snatch, tug, rain down fisticuffs, wound and slay. As for the mouth, it spits in the face, gluttonizes, makes you drunk and vomits.

To sum up, lawyers would do themselves honor if they added a clause about it in their fat volumes with something too about my verses and his attitudes.

When you write to Frosinone, greet him in my name.

III-11   Michelangelo Buonarroti to Cardinal Alessandro Farnese

John Addington Symonds rightly calls the following letter, concerning the "tragedy of the tomb" of Julius II, "one of the most weighty autobiographical documents from the hand of Michelangelo in our possession."

* Giovanmatteo Giberti, enemy of Aretino, later Bishop of Verona.

October, 1542

Monsignore. Your Lordship has word sent to me that I am to paint and not have doubts about anything. I reply that one paints with the brain and not with the hands; and that he who cannot have his brain about him does himself a disservice; so until my affairs are arranged, I shall not do anything good. The rectification of the last contract has not come; so long as the previous agreement is operative, drawn up under Clement, I am stoned every day as though I had crucified Christ. I tell you that it was not my understanding that the aforesaid contract had the approval of Pope Clement. I say that the contract which I heard read before Pope Clement was not like the copy I afterward received, and the reason was as follows: I was sent off the very same day by Clement to Florence: Gianmaria of Modena, the agent, was with the notary, and made him draw it up in his own way, so that when I returned home and verified it I found a thousand more ducats had been put down as paid to me than was really the case; I found the house in which I live had been put down against me, and several other things which would nearly ruin me; Clement would never have allowed it, and Fra Sebastiano [del Piombo] begs me to let the Pope know of this and have the notary hanged, but I do not wish it, because I do not consider myself bound by a contract which I should not have agreed to had I been consulted. I pledge my word that I am not aware of ever having had the money of which the said contract speaks, and which Gianmaria says he finds I have received.

But let us suppose I have received them because I have acknowledged it, and cannot get out of the contract; and not only that sum, but other money as well, if other can be found, and total it and see all I have done for Pope Julius in Bologna, Florence, and Rome, in bronze, marble, and on canvas, and see what I deserve. I say, with a clear conscience and according to what Pope Paul allows me, that I ought to receive 5000 *scudi* from the heirs of Pope Julius.

I also say that I have had such paltry rewards for my labors from Pope Julius, partly through my own fault for not being able to manage myself. If it had not been for what Pope Paul has done for me, I should today be dying of hunger; but, according to the agent, it appears as if I have become a rich man, and even gone so far as to rob the church; they make a great ruckus over it, and I might, I daresay, find means to hush them, but I am not equal to it. After the contract before Clement was made, and I had returned from Florence and commenced work on the sepulcher of Julius, Gianmaria, agent to the old Duke [of Urbino] told me that if I wished to give the Duke great pleasure I should go about my business, that he did not care anything about the tomb, but my serving Pope Paul vexed him sorely. Then I began to see why my house had been put into the contract, to make me go away, and let them lay hold of it with all their strength; one can easily see what they are wishing for, and even those who are not friends of their master's would be ashamed of them. . . .

I find myself having lost my youth and manhood, tied down to this tomb, which I defended as much as possible with Popes Leo and Clement; and my excessive loyalty which no one consented to acknowledge has ruined me. Thus my destiny wishes it! I see many men with incomes of 2000 or 3000 crowns lying in bed, while I with my very great efforts manage to grow poorer.

But to return to painting, I do not wish to deny anything to Pope Paul: I shall paint unhappy and shall paint unhappy things. I have written this to your lordship, for whatever happens you can explain the truth better to the Pope. And I should even be grateful if the Pope should hear my story, to know just how this war is made up which is being waged against me. Let him understand who should understand. . . .

There still occurs to me something else to be said. This ambassador stated that I have lent at usury monies of Pope Julius, and that I became rich from them: as if Pope Julius had ever advanced me 8000 ducats. The monies which I received for the sepulcher means the monies I paid out at that time on the tomb; it will be seen that they were close to the total specified in the contract made out in Clement's time. In his first year in office, Pope Julius commissioned me to make his tomb,* and I stayed eight months at Carrara excavating marbles and sending them to the Piazza of St. Peter's where I had my lodgings behind Santa Caterina; then Pope Julius decided not to build his tomb during his lifetime, and set me to painting. Then he kept me in Bologna for two years doing his statue in bronze that was melted down later; then I returned to Rome and I stayed with him until his death, keeping my house always open, without provision or payment, continually living on the money for the tomb, since I had no other income. After the aforementioned death of Julius, Aginensis wanted me to keep on with the tomb, on an even grander scale; so I brought the marbles to the Macello de' Corvi [Michelangelo's later studio] and had that part of the project done which is walled in at San Pietro in Vincoli, and I completed the figures which I have at home. At that time, Pope Leo, not wanting me to work on that tomb, pretended that he wished to complete the Façade of San Lorenzo in Florence and asked Aginensis for me. He therefore permitted me nevertheless to work on the sepulcher of Pope Julius at Florence. . . .

I beg your Lordship, when you have time, to read this account, and to use it to my benefit, and to know that there are still witnesses to many of the things herein written. I should even be gratified if the Pope were to see it and if everyone were to see it, because I write the truth and indeed understate, and I am neither usurer nor thief, but a Florentine citizen, noble and son of a gentleman, and not a nobody. . . .

---

* The cost of building this colossal tomb was widely viewed by contemporaries as the reason for Pope Julius's and Pope Leo's intensified sale of indulgences. See Letter V-6 on the Lutheran revolt.

To continue my history of the tomb of Julius, let me say that when he changed his mind about having it built during his lifetime, certain shiploads of marble arrived at the Ripa [dock] which I had meanwhile ordered at Carrara. Unable to get the cost of lading from the Pope, he having repented of the enterprise, I had to borrow to defray the cost of either 150 or 200 ducats, lent me by Baldassare Balducci, that is, by the bank of Messer Jacopo Gallo. At that time workmen came from Florence, some of whom are living today, and I furnished with beds and furniture the house which Julius gave me behind Santa Caterina, and with other things for the aforementioned tomb. All of this being accomplished without receiving money, I was greatly embarrassed. And as I was pressing the Pope as hard as I could to get on with the project, one morning when I was there to talk to him about finances, he had me dismissed by a lackey. As a bishop from Lucca who was witness to the incident said to the lackey:

"Don't you recognize this man?"

The lackey said to me,

"Pardon me, sire, but I am ordered to act thus."

I returned home and wrote as follows to the Pope:

"Most Blessed Father, I have this morning been expelled from the Palace on orders from your Holiness; therefore I am advising you that from now on, if you wish me, you will seek for me elsewhere than in Rome."

I sent this letter to Messer Agostino, the steward, to be given to the Pope; and at home I called in Cosimo the carpenter, who was staying with me furnishing my home, and a stone mason, still alive today, who was staying with me and I said to them:

"Go to a Jew's, and sell what's in this house, and then come up to Florence."

I went off and took a seat in the post carriage and went off toward Florence. The Pope having received my note, sent five horsemen in pursuit, who caught up with me at Poggi Bonsi at about three hours after dark and handed me a letter from the Pope which read, "Once you have seen this letter, under pain of our displeasure, return to Rome." The horsemen wanted me to answer, to prove that they had found me. I replied to the Pope that whenever he observed those courtesies which were his obligation, I should return. Otherwise, he should not expect ever to have me again. And during my stay afterward in Florence, Julius sent three briefs to the Signory. At the last one, Soderini the chief councilor, summoned me and said, "We don't wish to go to war with Pope Julius because of you. You must return, and if you consent, we shall write you letters of such authority that if he harms you, he will be harming the Signory." So I took the letters and went back to the Pope. What happened afterward would take a long time to tell. Suffice it to say that this business cost me more than a thousand crowns, because when I had fled from Rome, there was a lot of talk to the disparagement of the Pope; and almost all the marbles which I had on St. Peter's Square were sacked, especially small ones. I had therefore to start over anew. So that I say and claim that I ought to receive as damages or interest from the heirs of Julius II 5000 ducats; and he who took from me my youth and honor and possessions now calls me a thief. . . .

I beg your Lordship, for the love of God and Truth, when you have time, straighten up these matters, so that whatever happens I may defend myself to the Pope against those who speak ill of me, without any of the true facts, and who have with false information given the Duke a picture of me as a great scoundrel. All the discords between Pope Julius and me grew out of the envy of Bramante and Raffaello da Urbino; and that was the reason for his not finishing the tomb in his lifetime. By this they hoped to ruin me, and Raffaello had indeed good reason to, for all that he had of art he got from me.

III-12   Pietro Aretino to Titian

In a missive to his friend Titian, leader of the Venetian school of painting, Pietro Aretino (1492-1556) describes in vivid detail the fleeting splendor of a sunset in Venice.

Venice, May, 1544

Having eaten alone, my good friend, although it is not my usual habit, or to put it better, having eaten in the company of an unpleasant quartan fever which did not even permit me to enjoy my food, I arose from the table consumed by the same despondency with which I had sat down, and in this mood I leaned my arm against the window sill, and my arm on my chest, and indeed almost my whole body. Then I began to look upon the marvelous scene outside.

Infinite boats, some laden with foreigners and others with the people of our own city, were moving about on the water. They diverted not only the onlookers, but the Grand Canal itself which diverts all those who plough its waves. In front of my eyes, two gondolas were having a race. Each was guided by a famous boatman and their contest gave great sport to a crowd of spectators, which thronged the Rialto Bridge, the fish markets, the Santa Sofia ferry landing, and the Casa da Mosto to see the regatta.

But while this group and that one seethed here and there applauding joyously, I, who was almost a man who was so revolting to himself that he does not know what to do either with his mind or with his thoughts, suddenly turned my eyes toward the sky. Since God created it, it had never been so beautiful with its subtle pattern of lights and shades. Indeed, anyone who had wished to record it would have been consumed with envy because he was not you. You will see this when I try to tell you about it.

To begin with, although the houses were of real stone, they seemed to be some unreal fabric. Next you must visualize the atmosphere. In some places, it was transparent and living, in other places turgid and dead. Think, too, of how I marvelled at the clouds, although in reality they were nothing but condensed humidity. In the center of the scene, half of them seemed to touch the very roofs of the houses, while the other receded into distance. On the right hand, they were like a poised mass of gray-black smoke.

Certainly, I was astonished at the various colors which they showed. Those near at hand burned with the flames of the sun's fire, while those in the distance had the dull glow of half-molten lead. Oh, with what clever strokes the paint brushes of nature gave perspective to the very air, withdrawing it skillfully from the palaces just as you, Titian, make it draw backward in your landscapes. In certain places, there appeared a green-blue, and in other a blue-green, which were truly composed by the errant fancy of nature, the master of all great masters. With lights and shadows, she brought forth or subdued in manner that which she thought ought to be brought forth or subdued.

And so I, who know that your brushes are the very soul of her soul, cried out three or four times: "O Titian, where are you now?" *

By my faith, if you had painted what I describe to you, you would have turned men stock-still with the same astonishment that confounded me when I looked upon the scene that I am telling about, and realized that its wonder would not last.

(See also Letter X-10, in which Aretino further develops the eye-filling delights of the "most jocund view in all the world" offered by Venice.)

* Is Aretino (who lectured artists on their choice of subjects, as in III-13) reproaching Titian for consistently rejecting Venetian scenes in favor of allegories and portraits? Titian's "landscapes" are few.

III-13   Pietro Aretino to Michelangelo Buonarroti

Furious that the great Michelangelo has dared to deny him some requested
paintings, Aretino informs him that his *Last Judgment* is a salacious work fit
for a brothel. It is interesting to note how sharply his views on human
anatomy in art contradict those expressed in letter III-10, above.

                                              Venice, November, 1545
My lord, now that I have seen the final sketch of the whole of your *Last
Judgment,* I acknowledge that I recognize the distinguished charm of Raphael in
its agreeable beauty of invention. However, as a baptized Christian, I blush at the
license so unbecoming to a man of genius, which you have used in expressing your
concept of that final day which our true faith makes us long for with all our heart
and soul.

So, then, that Michelangelo, so great in fame—that Michelangelo, renowned
for his wisdom—that Michelangelo, whom all admire—has chosen to demonstrate
to the whole world that he is no less impious in matters of religion, than he is
perfect as a painter! How can it be possible that you, who, since you are divine, do
not deign even to associate with your fellow human beings, have dared to do this in
the highest temple of God—yes, even upon the highest altar raised to Jesus, in the
most sacred chapel in the world, in the place where the great cardinals of the
church, its venerable priests, indeed the Vicar of Christ himself, contemplate and
adore His body, His blood and His flesh, with Catholic rites, and with solemn
ceremonies and holy prayers?

If it were not sacrilege to make the comparison, I would congratulate myself
upon my virtue when I wrote my book about Nanna, [1] and would measure my wise
restraint against your talented outspokenness. I would point out that although I
dealt with lewd and shameless matters, I used comely and decorous language, and
spoke in chaste and blameless words, whereas you, on the contrary, although you
paint upon so lofty theme, show us saints and angels, the former without earthly
decency, the latter without heavenly honor.

1. Also known as *Sei Giornate,* these dialogues depict the life of libertines and prostitutes.

For, look you, the very heathen not merely clothed Diana when they modelled her, but even when they made a naked Venus, had her cover, with her hands, those parts which should not be shown. But here comes a Christian, who, because he values art more than religion, deems it a royal show, not merely to paint martyrs and virgins in improper attitudes, but to show men dragged off by their genitals, something which even those in a house of ill repute would close their eyes rather than see.

Yes, it is in a brothel rather than this holy choir that your work belongs, and it would be better if you had denied Christ Himself than that you believed in Him and destroy the faith of others. Yet, at that, do not believe that your excellent and audacious masterpiece will go unpunished. Its very marvel makes it certain that your good name will be destroyed.

But you can restore it again if you will only change the indecent parts of the damned into flames of fire, and those of the blessed into sunbeams, or at least imitate the modesty of the Florentine, who have covered up those of your handsome David with gilded fig leaves. And yet David stands upon a public square, and not in a sacred chapel.

Now as God may pardon you, I want you to know that I do not write all this out of annoyance that you never sent me the things I asked for. Yet the truth is that if you had sent me what you had promised, you would have done only what it was in your own interest to do, since by so doing, you would have silenced all those spiteful tongues, who say that only certain Gherardos and Tommasos can obtain them.[2]

Yet what right have I to hope for anything, when not even the king's ransom paid over to you by Pope Julius so that his descendants would be able to put his ashes in a tomb carved by your hand, was enough to make you keep your plighted word? But know this, mighty painter, it is not your ingratitude and greed but the merits and enlightenment of the high Shepherd that will decide his fame, for God wills it that he should live forever even though he is in a simple tomb, and not because your genius built for him some mighty monument. In the meantime, your failure to fulfill your contract is but common thievery.[3]

The damned spirits that you have painted are beautifully designed but they lack any kind of religious meaning, and for that reason I pray only that God may inspire His Holiness Paul to the same action He once inspired blessed Gregory. That Pope chose to tear down all the proud statues of pagan gods in Rome rather than to let their beauty turn the people's reverence from the humbler images of the saints.

2. Gherardo Perini was apparently a young model intimate with Michelangelo. By contrast, Michelangelo's relations with the young nobleman Tommaso Cavalieri were of a chaste, Platonic nature (see Letter IX-5).

3. A totally false charge. See above, III-11.

Finally, if when you had set about creating your picture of the universe and hell and heaven, you had steeped your soul in those concepts of glory, honor and terror sketched out for you by the teaching, example and learning of my letter which the whole world now reads, I do not hesitate to assert that not only would Nature never regret the distinguished genius that her benign influences had bestowed on you—and even as it is, your artistic skill makes you the symbol of all art's wonder—but Heaven itself, which sees all things, would continue to stand guard over your masterpiece as long as the hemispheres moved under her ordered rule.

Postscript. Now that I have blown off some of my anger at the unkind way in which you rewarded my devotion, and have taught you that while you are divine, I am not of water, I bid you tear up this letter. I have done so myself. But do not forget that I am one to whom kings and emperors reply.

III-14   Pietro Aretino to Modanese

Pietro Aretino extolls the art of street singers, those eloquent vendors of nostrums capable of duping even skeptics through the power of song. Modanese was such a figure in the streets of Venice.

Venice (1545)

Messer Francesco degli Albizzi [1] of Mirandola tells me that he and Titian were compelled by the reports given birth to by your eloquence to stop and listen and so find out with what manner of reciting you lifted me up to the heavens when you sang my praises from a stand in the piazza at Ferrara. That you did this, I congratulate myself no less than I would have congratulated myself, if Apollo had said the same of me in one of the cloisters of Parnassus, improvising poetically. I am also under an obligation to you for dedicating my works to Sansovino, since that which I inadvertently did not take care to do, you have thoughtfully brought about by inscribing them to this outstanding man from your lofty platform.

But even as I write this to you, some intellectual snobs who see me writing it,

1. Francesco degli Albizzi was a courtier attached to Giovanni and later Cosimo dei Medici.

heap scorn on me by saying that they have little respect for me because I not only allow myself to be, but rejoice at being, on the lips of your street singers. Poor fellows! They do not know that your profession entertains all the dead-beats of the world, and that it is the truth that there is no one who has no possessions, no one who is needy, no one even who is miserly, who, at the first note from your lyre, at the first verse that you speak, at the first rattling off about your wares, does not stop, pawn all he has, and then shell it out so as to buy the recipes, the bandboxes and the legends that you give, by selling them, even to those who are certain that you are worth nothing, that you are of no importance.

Street singers, ah? Street singers, eh? They alone are the ones who, possessing nothing, obtain all, and what is more important, while they posture before the crowd as buffoons, the crowd, making itself the ape of their endeavors, chatters back at them, goes into contortions and splits its jaws laughing with the same kind of unrestraint with which these fellows tie themselves into just the knots that you would expect from the kind of folk, who to catch the ear of the people, gives them a deluge from their tongues.

But if the clumsiest practitioners of trade of which you are the light, the altar, and the idol, can do this, what marvel that your high-sounding harmonies can captivate Chieti friars, and the little brothers of poverty, and even Lutherans? These fellows are not quite buffalos, donkeys and stupid oxen.

"I would like," said a mad fellow the other day, "to change all my limbs into a left and right hand, if only to do nothing else but wash them in the cakes of soap sold by Modanese. Like him, it is so fragrant, so smooth and so precious."

And what do you think they pay this or that preacher for accomplishing from the pulpit what you do from your bench?

Certainly the fellow—I don't know who he was—who rushing forth from his native land stark naked, said: "I carry all my worldly goods with me" was a street singer and not a philosopher, for it is only this band of brigands who, without burdening themselves with anything, end up with everything on their back.

The street singers I say, set forth with their saddlebags filled with jests, chatter, presumption, persuasive talk, lies, madnesses, intrigues, ballads, and curses. The latter they hurl at themselves when, wounded and slashed, they find the oil that they advertised as the best in the world, absolutely worthless to heal the dagger strokes they get for their jests. They go where their legs take them, and they find money, credit, friendships, harlotries, relatives, offices, together with griefs and woes enough to satisfy anyone who does not realize that to mountebank it, you do not have to be a great rogue like Morgante or even an imitation one like Margutte.[2] It is enough to be like one of that galley crew of servants who diddles

2. Morgante and Margutte were comic heroes of Luigi Pulci's mock epic poem.

his master by swearing that he will serve him well, or like the other kind who murders the poor fellow who serves him with lies about taking good care of him.

But I don't want to go into the subject any further for then I would have to take up princes, captains, merchants, poets, lawyers, patricians, pedagogues and friars and then they would say I was a whole regiment of Pasquinos.[3]

Let it be enough then—after I have thanked you for the reputation you have gotten me in the eyes of all—to proffer you prayers in abundance that you, with your natural eloquence, will clang forth my name as loudly as you can, for I count it more glory to be shouted about by the first charlatan of the world than I am angry at the fables which are made up about me by the hundred most mediocre learned men of the universe.

III-15   Michelangelo Buonarroti to Benedetto Varchi

Asked to join a referendum on the relative merits of painting and sculpture, Michelangelo impatiently decrees that each is part of the same artistic process.

March/April 1547

So that it may be clear that I have received your little book, which duly reached me, I will make such a reply as I can to what you ask, although I am very ignorant on the subject. In my opinion painting should be considered excellent in proportion as it approaches the effect of relief, while relief should be considered bad in proportion as it approaches the effect of painting. I used to consider that sculpture was the lantern of painting and that between the two things there was the same difference as that between the sun and the moon. But now that I have read your book, in which, speaking as a philosopher, you say that things which have the same end are themselves the same, I have changed my opinion; and I now consider that painting and sculpture are one and the same thing, unless greater nobility be imparted by the necessity for a keener judgment, greater difficulties of

3. *Pasquino,* a mutilated statue near Rome's Braschi Palace, to which humorous and scurrilous little satires were affixed by usually anonymous poets.

execution, stricter limitations and harder work. And if this be the case no painter ought to think less of sculpture than of painting and no sculptor less of painting than sculpture. By sculpture I mean the sort that is executed by cutting away from the block: the sort that is executed by building up resembles painting. This is enough, for as one and the other, that is to say both painting and sculpture proceed from the same faculty, it would be an easy matter to establish harmony between them and to let such disputes alone, for they occupy more time than the execution of the figures themselves. As to that man who wrote saying that painting was more noble than sculpture, as though he knew as much about it as he did of the other subjects on which he has written, why, my serving-maid would have written better! An infinite number of things still remain unsaid which might be urged in favour of these arts, but, as I have already said, they would take up too much time and I have very little to spare seeing that I am old and almost fitted to be numbered among the dead. For this reason I beg of you to excuse me. I commend myself unto you and I thank you from the bottom of my heart for the too great honour you do me—an honour not suited to such as I am.

III-16   Annibal Caro to Giorgio Vasari

The question of the Renaissance artist's freedom of choice of topic and of the "invention" or detailing of the work has been much discussed. Respecting the learned Annibal Caro (1507-1561), Vasari obviously did not resent his customer's specific suggestions on how best to paint the *Venus and Adonis* he was ordering.

Rome, 10 May 1548

My desire to possess an important work from your hand is incited by both my esteem for you and a desire for self-gratification, because I should like to set it before certain critics who know you more as a rapid painter than an excellent one. I talked about this with Botto not with the purpose of adding to your burdens, but for when you had finished off some of your major projects. But since you yourself offer to execute it right away, think of how much more precious it will be to me. As for quickness or slowness I defer to you, because I judge it possible to do something quickly and well, where the creative fury rushes in as in painting, which in this respect as in all others is very similar to poetry. It is quite true that people believe that in creating less rapidly, you do better. But this is more probable than necessarily true, because one might say that works that are distended out and not resolved, and not accomplished with that fervor of the beginning, turn out worse. In fact, I should not wish you to think that I want something done by you in such a temperate way that I was not waiting for it with impatience. And so I wish you to know that I say slowly, that is thoughtfully and with diligence—not too much diligence—as people say of that apprentice of yours, who never got around to taking his hand from the canvas. But in this matter I take comfort, since the slowest motion that you make arrives before the swiftest motion of other painters. And I am sure that you will serve me well in every way, not only because you are you, but because I know that you are fond of me, and I see with what enthusiasm you set yourself to this commission. And from this rapid technique of yours I have already sensed the great perfection of the completed work. So do it, I pray, when and how it appears best to you; for the invention I leave everything in your hands, remembering another resemblance of poetry and painting, and since you are moreover as much poet as painter. Since in poetry and painting alike concepts and ideas are expressed with more affection and more zeal when original with the artist than when suggested by others.

Provided that there are two nude figures, male and female (which are the two greatest subjects of your art), do that myth in the manner which appears best to you. Beyond these two principal figures I am loath there should be many others, unless they were to be small and distant, for it appears to me that the rather broad background will give them greater grace and set them in greater relief. If you ask me my own inclinations, Venus and Adonis appear to me a composition of two of the most beautiful bodies that you could make or that anyone has ever made. Keeping this in mind, it would be a good thing if you imitated as far as possible the description of them in Theocritus. But since putting all the figures of the myth on the canvas would make a too intricate grouping, which as I said before would not please me, I should do simply Adonis embraced and admired by Venus with that affection with which one sees dying the things most dear to one, decked out in a purple cloak, with a wound in his thigh, and with a few streaks of blood about his person, with his hunter's gear lying on the ground—if that wouldn't take up too much space—and with a fine hound. And I should leave out the nymphs, the graces, and the Parcae that Theocritus includes, and those cupids which administer to him, watching him and casting him in the shade by their wings. I should make room for only those other cupids in the distance who are pulling a swine from out the forest, of whom one strikes it with his bow, another pierces it with an arrow, and the third ties it up with a cord to bring it to Venus. And I should indicate, if possible, that roses are born out of the blood and poppies from the tears. This or some similar invention captures my fancy since, beyond sheer charm, I should like there to be the appeal of sentiment, without which figures have no spirit. If you don't wish to do more than one figure, the Leda, especially that of Michelangelo, delights me immensely. And that Venus which [Botticelli] did, issuing forth from the sea, would make, I imagine, a fine sight. Yet, as I have said, I shall be satisfied with whatever you yourself select. As for the canvas, I am resolved that it should be five palms in length and three in height. As for that other work of yours, it is inappropriate for me to say anything about it, since you have resolved that we should have a look at it together. In this way, you will be able to conclude the whole business to your own advantage, for I'm certain that I shall have little other than praise for it. Stay well.

(trans. R.J.C.)

III-17   Michelangelo Buonarroti to Bartolomeo [Ferratini]

Michelangelo's outrageous wit, conjecturing the counterfeiting of money and the impregnating of nuns within the Vatican itself, did much to discredit and rule out Antonio da Sangallo's plans for remodeling Saint Peter's.

Rome, 1555

Messer Bartolomeo, Dear Friend.—It cannot be denied that Bramante was a skilful architect and the equal of any one from the time of the ancients till now. It was he who drew up the original plan of St. Peter's, not full of confusion but clear and straightforward, with ample light and detached from the surrounding buildings so that it did not in any way interfere with the Palace. It was considered to be a fine design, and there is still evidence that it was so; indeed, every architect who has departed from Bramante's plan, as Sangallo has done, has departed from the right way, and that this is true may be seen by anyone who looks at his model with unprejudiced eyes.

In the first place, the outer ring of chapels he shows will exclude all the light provided by Bramante in his plan; and not only this, but he has not provided any fresh means of lighting, while there are so many gloomy lurking-holes both above and below that any sort of knavery could easily be practised, such as the hiding of banished persons, the counterfeiting of money, the rape of nuns, and other shenanigans: and when at night the time comes for shutting up the church it would require twenty-five men to make sure that no person remained there in hiding, and it would be sufficiently difficult to find them. Furthermore, there would be this other drawback, that in adding this circular work to the outside of Bramante's plan it would be necessary to pull down the Pauline Chapel, the Offices of the Seal, the Ruota, and many other buildings. I do not think that even the Sistine Chapel would remain intact. . . .

III-18   William Byrd to The Reader

The year the Spanish Armada was defeated, 1588, also ushered in a period of glorious music in England with the publication of two collections of madrigals: Nicholas Yonge's *Musica Transalpina* and *Psalms, Sonnets, and Songs of Sadness and Piety* by William Byrd (1543-1623), the greatest figure in sixteenth century English music. It is in this volume, dedicated to Sir Christopher Hatton, that Byrd sets down the following "open letter" to the reader, with its amusing plea to take up singing.

1588

The Epistle to the Reader

Benign reader, here is offered unto thy courteous acceptation music of sundry sorts and to content divers humors. If thou be disposed to pray, here are psalms; if to be merry, here are sonnets; if to lament for thy sins, here are songs of sadness and piety. If thou delight in music of great compass, here are divers songs which, being originally made for instruments to express the harmony and one voice to pronounce the ditty, are now framed in all parts for voices to sing the same. If thou desire songs of small compass and fit for the reach of most voices, here are most in number of that sort. Whatsoever pains I have taken herein I shall think to be well imployed if the same be well accepted, music thereby the better loved and the more exercised.

In the expressing of these songs, either by voices or instruments, if there happen to be any jar or dissonance, blame not the printer, who, I do assure thee, through his great pains and diligence, doth here deliver to thee a perfect and true copy. If in the composition of these songs there be any fault by me committed, I desire the skilful either with courtesy to let the same be concealed or in friendly sort to be thereof admonished, and at the next impression he shall find the error reformed, rememb'ring always that it is more easy to find a fault then to amend it.

If thou find anything here worthy of liking and commendation, give praise unto God, from whom, as from a most pure and plentiful fountain, all good gifts of science do flow, whose name be glorified forever.

The most assured friend to all
that love or learn music,
William Byrd

Reasons Briefly Set Down by th' Auctor to Persuade Everyone to Learn to Sing

1. First, it is a knowledge easely taught and quickly learned where there is a good master and an apt scoler.

2. The exercise of singing is delightful to nature, and good to preserve the health of man.

3. It doth strengthen all parts of the breast, and doth open the pipes.

4. It is a singuler good remedy for a stutting and stammering in the speech.

5. It is the best means to procure a perfect pronunciation and to make a good orator.

6. It is the only way to know where nature hath bestowed the benefit of a good voice, which gift is so rare as there is not one among a thousand that hath it, and in many that excellent gift is lost because they want art to express nature.

7. There is not any music of instruments whatsoever comparable to that which is made of the voices of men where the voices are good and the same well-sorted and ordered.

8. The better the voice is, the meeter it is to honor and serve God therewith, and the voice of man is chiefly to be imployed to that end.

III-19   Jan Pieters Sweelinck to the Burgomasters of Amsterdam

In offering his settings of the Psalms of David to the Burgomasters and
Aldermen of Amsterdam, the famed organist Jan Pieters Sweelinck
(1562-1621) affirms the metaphysical nature of music as justification for its
existence.

                                                        Amsterdam, 30 March, 1603

Your Lordships:

So great is the correspondence between music and the soul that many, seeking
out the essence of the latter, have thought it to be full of harmonious accords, to
be, indeed, a pure harmony. All nature itself, to speak the truth, is nothing but a
perfect music that the Creator causes to resound in the ears of man, to give him
pleasure and to draw him gently to Himself. This we recognize at a glance in the
excellent arrangement, the splendid proportions, and the orderly movements and
revolutions of the celestial bodies. Therefore some have declared that the
Firmament is the original Patron of Music and a true image of the elemental
region, as can be observed in the number of elements and their four primary
qualities and in the wondrous manner in which their opposites are reconciled.

This is the reason why the sages of ancient times, considering that each thing
has the property of turning, moving, and inclining toward and in accordance with
its like, made use of music not only to bring pleasure to the ear, but principally to
move and moderate the emotions of the soul. They appropriated it for their
oracles in order to gently instil yet firmly incorporate their doctrine into our
minds, and thus, having awakened them, could raise them more easily to the
contemplation and admiration of the divine. Orpheus among the pagans and David
among the Hebrews made studies of these matters. The latter, truly inspired by
the spirit of God, composed psalms, which he gave out to the master singers to be
sounded on diverse instruments. His work has been preserved through the
unwavering constancy of divine truth, but the work of these singers is unknown to
us, owing to the ravages of time.

Having cast my eye on so excellent a subject, I set myself the task of reclothing these psalms in another music. It is true that others before me have laboured at this, but as with human faces, there being no two that resemble each other in all respects, so is it with the conceptions and creations of the spirit. Therefore I am disposed to hope that my endeavour will not be rejected by those for whose use and delectation I have brought these psalms to light. Should they meet with your pleasure, I shall take occasion in due time, with God's grace, to bring forth the rest.

Meantime I take the liberty of presenting to Your Lordships these first fruits of my labour, not for the value of what they contain, or the merit of him who offers them, still less in the hope or desire of any emolument or advantage that might come to me. My purpose is partly to lend splendour to this my work by gracing it with the names of Your Lordships, and partly in acknowledgment of the close obligation that binds me to those whom I recognize to be the true fathers of my country, who have favoured me in many ways since the time of my youth and who, being students and amateurs of all the polite arts and skills, have placed me in the post that I have occupied for many years in this city.

I beseech Your Lordships to accept my labour in as good part as it is offered you, with a sincere heart, and in humble devotion.

Your Lordships' most humble and obedient servant,

Jan Sweelinck

III-20   Peter Paul Rubens to Annibale Chieppio

In 1603 several problems faced young Rubens (1577-1640), worrying about the fate of paintings, as his embassy progressed over rough seas and bumpy roads from Mantua to Philip III in Madrid. In addition to the unreasonable demands of a powerful patron, there were the problems of defacement of paintings, lack of time, incompetent collaborators, false attribution of his own works, and the lack of appreciation in Spain of his Italianate style—which style as a Fleming he had acquired with great effort.

Valladolid, 24 May, 1603

To Annibale Chieppio:

Malicious fate is jealous of my too great satisfaction: as usual, it does not fail to sprinkle in some bitterness, sometimes conceiving a way to cause damage which human precaution cannot foresee, still less suspect. Thus the pictures which were packed with all possible care by my own hand, in the presence of my Lord the Duke, then inspected at Alicante, at the demand of the custom officials, and found unharmed, were discovered today, in the house of Signor Hannibal Iberti, to be so damaged and spoiled that I almost despair of being able to restore them. . . . The colors have faded and, through long exposure to extreme dampness, have swollen and flaked off, so that in many places the only remedy is to scrape them off with a knife and lay them on anew.

Such is the true extent of the damage. (Would it were not!) I am in no way exaggerating, in order to praise the restoration later. To this task I shall not fail to apply all my skill, since it has pleased His Most Serene Highness to make me a guardian and bearer of the works of others, without including a brush stroke of my own. I say this not because I feel any resentment, but in reference to the suggestion of Signor Hannibal, who wants me to do several pictures in great haste, with the help of Spanish painters. I agreed to this, but I am not inclined to approve of it, considering the short time we have, as well as the extent of the damage to the ruined pictures; not to mention the incredible incompetence and carelessness of the painters here, whose style (and this is very important) is totally different from mine. God keep me from resembling them in any way! In short, *pergimus pugnantia secum; cornibus adversis componere.* *

Moreover, the matter will never remain secret, because of the gossiping of these same assistants. They will either scorn my additions and retouches, or else take over the work and claim it as all their own, especially when they know it is in the service of the Duke of Lerma, which may easily mean that the paintings are destined for a public gallery. As for me, this matters little, and I willingly forgo this fame. But I am convinced that, by its freshness alone, the work must necessarily be discovered as done here (a thankless trick), whether by the hands of such men, or by mine, or by a mixture of theirs and mine (which I will never tolerate, for I have always guarded against being confused with anyone, however great a man). And I shall be disgraced unduly by an inferior production unworthy of my reputation, which is not unknown here.

Peter Paul Rubens

* We proceed to combine things that are hostile, with horns directed against each other.

III-21   Claudio Monteverdi to Alessandro Striggio

Claudio Monteverdi (1567-1643), responding to a letter from his patron's councillor, dons the cloak of humility in expressing his reservations about setting an inferior libretto.

To Alessandro Striggio [1]

Venice, 9 December, 1616

My Most Illustrious Lord and Patron:

I have received from Signor Carlo de Torri your kind letter and the libretto of the sea-fable *Nozze di Tetide* [*Wedding of Thetys*]. Your Lordship writes that you are sending it to me for me to peruse carefully and then give you my opinion on how it should be set to music to serve at the future marriage of His Most Serene Highness.[2] I desire nothing but to be of the greatest service to His Most Serene Highness; otherwise I would not say in the first reply that I promptly offer to fulfil his commands without objection and that I shall always most obediently honour and respect his wishes. Consequently, if His Most Serene Highness himself approve this libretto, then I would say that the fable is most beautiful and to my taste.

However, since you request my opinion—I shall obey the commands given me with all respect and promptness—understanding that my opinion is of slight importance coming from one who himself is worth little, and who honours all men of talent, in particular this poet whose name I do not know,[3] and the more so since poetry is not my profession, in respectful observance of your commands, I humbly give you my opinion.

First, in general, I say that the music should be mistress of the air and not only of the water. By this I mean that the melodies described in this fable are all heavy and low and cling close to the earth. Thus there would be little opportunity for

1. Librettist for Monteverdi's *Orfeo* and councillor to Duke Ferdinando da Gonzaga of Mantua. Monteverdi had been in the service of the Gonzaga family for over twenty years.
2. Duke Ferdinando da Gonzaga, who was to marry Catherine de' Medici.
3. Scipione Agnelli.

beautiful harmonies, which would be too low, and it would be difficult to hear and to perform them, but I leave this to your most cultivated and discriminating judgment. Because of this defect, instead of one lute there would need to be three, and instead of one harp three, and so on. Instead of a delicate singing voice there would have to be a strong, forced one.

Moreover, in order to express the speech correctly, in my opinion, the melody would have to be supported by brass instruments instead of delicate strings, for it seems to me that the songs of Triton and the other sea gods call for trumpets and cornets, not harps, lutes, and cembali. This is a sea-story and therefore it takes place outside of the city, yet does not Plato write that the lute should be used for the city and the flute for the country *(cithara debet esse in civitate et thibia in agris)?* So either the delicate will not be appropriate or the appropriate will not be delicate.

Then I have studied the list of characters: Winds, Little Loves, Little Zephyrs, Sirens, which would require many soprano˜ voices. Further I note that the Winds—that is, the northern and western Winds—also have to sing. But how, dear sir, can I ever imitate the speech of winds when they do not speak! And in this way how should I ever be able to move the emotions?

Arianna was moving because she was a woman, and Orfeo [4] because he was a man, not a wind. Melodies represent people and not the noises of winds, nor the bleating of sheep, nor the neighing of horses, and they do not imitate the language of winds when this does not exist.

Also the ballets scattered through this libretto lack the proper dance rhythm. The entire fable does not move me at all, and, in accordance with my great ignorance, I do not think it ever will. I do not believe that it proceeds with any naturalness to a suitable ending, and I have great difficulty in understanding it at all. Arianna moved me to a true lament; Orfeo to a prayer; but what kind of music this requires, I cannot possibly imagine. What does Your Lordship wish this music to convey? But I shall always most dutifully and respectfully carry out the commands of His Most Serene Highness, and if it be commanded that I set this libretto to music, I shall do so. Yet considering that there are gods who speak in this piece, I should prefer to hear these gods speak with grace.

Concerning the Sirens, I believe that the three sisters, Signora Adrianna and the others, could sing these roles and compose them as well. Likewise Signor Rasi and Signor D. Francesco their parts. In this we should be following the example of Cardinal Montalto, who wrote a comedy in which each character wrote his own part. Now, if this were a work that developed toward only one ending, as was the case in *Arianna* and *Orfeo,* it would have to be composed by one person; there it

4. *Orfeo,* 1607; *Arianna,* 1608.

was a question of speaking in song, but here it is singing in speech. All the speaking parts are too long, and there are several other considerations.

I beg forgiveness, dear sir, if I have said too much. It is not to find fault, but because I desire to carry out your commands, and if I have to set this to music, Your Lordship will know my way of thinking.

I most humbly and respectfully pay reverence to His Most Serene Highness, and I humbly kiss Your Lordship's hand and pray God for your felicity. I wish you a happy holiday. Your Lordship's most humble and obedient servant,

Claudio Monteverdi

III-22   Heinrich Schütz to Wilhelm Ludwig Moser

The German composer Heinrich Schütz (1585-1672) tactfully ventures an opinion concerning remuneration due Samuel Scheidt for the first two volumes of his *Tablatura Nova.*

30 December, 1624.

Honourable, most learned, and gracious Sir:

Since you desire my personal report and opinions on the music sent you by Samuel Scheidt, Kapellmeister at Halle, I wish to assure you of my constant readiness to serve you. These works (two folio books bound in tawed leather with gilt-edged boards and variegated edges, each book about three fingers thick) are pieces for the organ composed in the Scheidt style and that of the Netherlanders, and they are most pleasing to the ear. The first of these two volumes is dedicated with a special preface to our gracious Lord and Elector.

Further, kind sir, you will probably recall that the said Samuel Scheidt some time ago sent in two other works, the manuscripts of which were nearly lost by one of the boys when I, some time ago, came to pay my respects. But these compositions were not dedicated to our gracious Lord and merely presented to him. They are still in existence, but thus far have not been catalogued since no remuneration has yet been received for them.

In view of this dedication, it is my humble belief that our gracious Lord and

Elector should come to terms with him once and for all and grant him some recompense. I venture the opinion since you, dear sir, chose to request it, that 30 to 35 taler would be sufficient. Or, if our gracious Lord so chooses, I believe that 20 taler together with a portrait of His Grace, since part of the work is dedicated to him, would be in keeping with the generous reputation of our gracious Lord.

Of course it remains my most gracious Lord's pleasure and yours, kind sir, to accept my suggestion or to reject it. Commending you to God's protection, I am,

Your obediant servant,
Heinrich Schütz

CHAPTER 4

SCIENCE AND SUPERSTITION. ASTRONOMY. ASTROLOGY. MEDICINE.

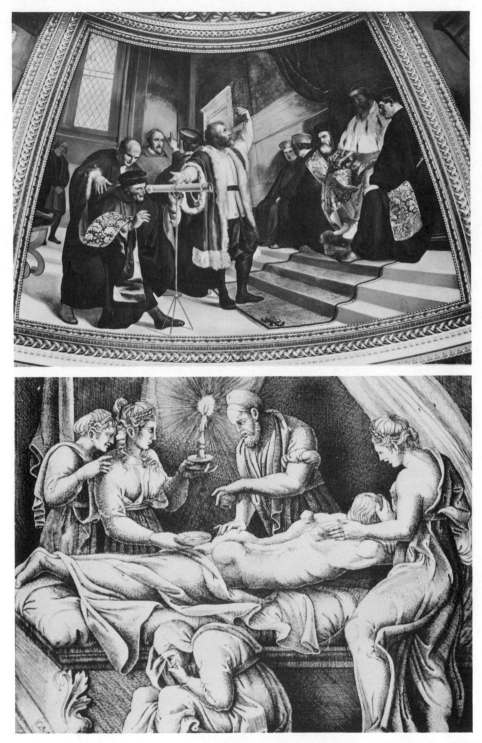

VIII. *Physician Attending Patient* by Giorgio Ghisi

Several basic discoveries in the sciences certify that the Renaissance marked a remarkable saltation for the human mind. The most fascinating and immediately challenging to monarchs, business men, explorers, Church expansionists, and others in addition of course to the scientists, was the confirmation that the earth was indeed a globe. The circumstances leading to this discovery are related in the letters of Chapter VIII below. The even more important discovery, perhaps, first anticipated by the Polish astronomer Nicolaus Copernicus in his "Letter against Werner" (IV-5) and again six years later in his *De revolutionibus orbium coelestium* (1530) was that the geocentric universe proposed by the Alexandrine astronomer Ptolemy (100-170 A.D.) must be rejected before the demonstrable fact that the earth moved around the sun. Although the enlightened Cardinal Nicolaus von Schoenberg supported him and his "new world system" and tried to gain recognition for him in Italy (IV-8), Copernicus was harassed by many. His own bishop even tried to impugn his moral character, impugning incidentally as well the character of the scientist's housemaid (IX-12).

Galileo Galilei supported the theory of Copernicus and tried, by means of his improved telescope which revealed incidentally four satellites around Jupiter and the ring of Saturn, to confirm it in his *Dialogue on the Two Maximum Systems of the World* (1630). The German scientist Kepler had rallied earlier to his cause, sending him one of his own scientific treatises to make him feel less alone (IV-16). Kepler's freedom in Germany made him worry about Galileo's caution, and he urged a militant dissemination of the new truth, asking Galileo, "Would it not be better to pull the rolling wagon to its destination with united effort?" (IV-17). In England Sir Henry Wotton wrote to the Earl of Salisbury that Galileo's discovery of four new "planets" has "overthrown all former astronomy and astrology," with Galileo risking "to be either exceeding famous or exceeding ridiculous" (IV-18). To Thomas Hariot, later to become "the English Galileo," Sir William Lower held that the Italian astronomer's discoveries were more important than those of Magellan. Galileo's work provided a foundation for the discoveries and laws of Kepler and Sir Isaac Newton, working in the freer climate of northern Europe. In August, 1610, Kepler, who had over a decade earlier suggested that Galileo remove his researches to Germany, wrote again to encourage Galileo to "despise the noise that has been created" (IV-19). Yet Kepler realized that the new cosmography was troubling orthodox Christians everywhere, and found it necessary to send an open letter to the bookstores in Italy (the Index of Forbidden Books had been established over half a century) not to hesitate to sell tracts and books expounding the new science.

Kepler's fears were indeed grounded. Politicians and Churchmen alike refused even to examine the evidence Galileo presented (IV-20). The Pope and Cardinal Firenzuola persisted in their attempt to force Galileo to abjure his belief in a heliocentric universe. One of the saddest letters in the history of science is that of Vincenzio Cardinal da Firenzuola, announcing as late as 1633, not long before Galileo's final trial, that the scientist had agreed to recant (IV-22). This recantation saved his life, but he was sentenced to house imprisonment just the same. Even more unfortunate was Giordano Bruno (1548-1600), whose death on the pyre was probably still vivid in Galileo's memory. It was not until the late 1960s that the Roman Church saw fit to exonerate Galileo. *Eppure si muove!*

Galileo also invented the first thermometer, discovered laws of weight, and contributed observations on the pendulum quickly applied to clockmaking.

Comets and novae, still unexplainable among Renaissance scientists, were charted and their durations recorded, as we learn from the letter of Sir Thomas Smith to Francis Walsingham (IV-12). Other sciences made rapid strides. After Arabic numbers were accepted in the late Middle Ages, mathematics and algebra added new concepts (logarithms, plus and minus numbers). The calendar was reformed under Pope Gregory XIII, now providing for leap years. Georg Bauer's *De re metallica* laid the groundwork for metallurgy. Studying the magnet and magnetism, William Gilbert invented the word electricity, shortly after the Flemish chemist Jan van Helmont coined the word gas.

In his famous letter of Gargantua to Pantagruel Rabelais hailed the triumph of the new sciences over the old pseudo-sciences: chemistry over alchemy, astronomy over astrology, mathematical sciences over numerology, etc. Yet the practitioners of the old sciences were still about. In a single letter of Erasmus to Colet (IV-1) the Humanist pokes fun at an alchemist who professes to have discovered the fifth element (quintessence) which turns dross to gold and makes old men young. At the same time Erasmus chides the astrologers for claiming that our destiny and character are determined by the conjuncture of planets at our birth. Yet the Renaissance suspicions of astrology will not prevent Nostradamus from becoming the official astrologer to the King of France (IV-11) and having his prophecies, which he claimed as emanations from God, taken most seriously by people until the twentieth century, when Hitler took him as a guide.

Medicine made considerable progress in physiology and surgery, as the latter practice slowly overcame Church opposition to anatomical dissections. The great Flemish anatomist Andreas Vesalius did his researches at the University of Padua, while the Italians Bartolomeo Eustachio and Gabriello Falloppio immortalised their names by the study of physiology. The Renaissance prepared the way for the discoveries of William Harvey. Rabelais, a pioneer in dissectomy at Montpellier University, excited by the new upsurge of medicine based on solid Greek foundations, worried to André Tiraqueau that a pseudo-medicine still existed, nurtured on Mediaeval prejudice (IV-7).

Physicians were obviously a target of Renaissance satire, satire which spilled over into personal letters. Typical is Aretino's letter to Dionigi Capucci (IV-9). Like Rabelais, Aretino felt that too few doctors had lived up to the ideal of ancient medicine, that "the sum and total of their knowledge of the art of Galen is to give mallow-water in an enema." Stefano Guazzo once wrote to advise a widow not to pay a hundred crowns to a physician who had treated her dead husband. "Why pay so dearly for death, when one can die at no cost?" Guevara, usually so unperturbed, complains to his personal physician that the doctor, like his colleagues, is as inadequate as the diagnoses and nostrums they prescribe (IV-6). Yet even the satirical Aretino does admit that a few physicians, like his own Elias Alfan, were admirable for their competence, sympathy, and bedside manner (IV-10).

Some of the common diseases, as in our own century, resisted all possible remedies. It would appear from the letters that gout and gallstones were rampant in the Renaissance. Erasmus felt that his stone was caused by drinking beer (he preferred wine). Michelangelo found that only the waters of Viterbo could relieve his gallstone, whereas Erasmus had found no cure for this same "fatal" illness (IV-2). The most notorious gout in England was apparently that of Lord Burghley, who received many curious and complicated remedies in the mail, including oil of stag's blood and a distilled waters cure offered to him for the price of 400 or 500 pounds (IV-15).

Epidemics and plagues were common, and memories of the Black Death of 1348 lived on. Of a sweating sickness in England (1517) Sir Thomas More wrote that there was scarcely a family which had not lost one member to it (IV-3). The total deaths recorded on the Plague Bill of 1625 and reported by Joseph Mead (IV-21) were sufficiently terrifying to have everyone from the King down avoiding contagion at all costs. A curious letter of Calvin to Myconius (V-15) charges certain citizens of Geneva with deliberately spreading the plague, smearing doorlocks with a mysterious ointment.

In no century, including our own, has science swept away superstition. King Henri III, as we learn from a 1586 letter of Lucinge, was willing to pay over 24,000 crowns for an alleged unicorn's horn (IV-13). Many letters came out of Austria on the subject of a curious, early *Wienerblut* (1597), a rain of blood which mystified everyone in that charming Danubian capital.

The burning witches' flesh clouded skies in Europe as well as those of New

England. In vain were reasonable voices like that of Cornelius Agrippa calling to city-fathers and Inquisitors to cease this barbaric, ruthless persecution of so-called witches, "contrary to sacerdotal custom, the profession of the (Dominican) rule, the form of laws and canons" (IV-4). The incredible drama of Walpurga Hausmännin of Dillingen was one of the best known of these public murders, illustrating how multiple charges could be concocted against a chosen victim (IV-14). In the Renaissance the devil was still lurking about—a living, lascivious tempter eager to "indulge in fornication" with unwary witches like Walpurga.

IV-1   Desiderius Erasmus to John Colet

In a jocular mood, Desiderius Erasmus (1466?-1536) describes his brief journey from London to Cambridge, using the occasion to ridicule two pseudo-sciences: astrology and alchemy. John Colet (1467?-1519) lectured at Oxford and became Dean of St. Paul's.

Cambridge, 24 August, 1511

If our mishaps, my Colet, can make you laugh, there is cause for abundant laughter. For besides all that happened in London, the servant's horse went dreadfully lame, the carrier having changed the one that Bullock * had sent. Then there was nothing to eat on the whole journey. Next day continual rain until dinner; after dinner thunder, lightning and showers. The horse fell three times on his nose. Bullock has consulted the stars, and says that Jupiter was in an angry mood!

Now I have a fresh gratification. I see before me the footprints of Christian poverty. I have so little hope of any profit, that I understand I shall have to drop here whatever I may be able to tear from my patrons. There is a doctor here from my country who by the aid of the Fifth Essence proposes to work miracles, makes old men young, and brings the dead to life, so that I have some hope of becoming young again, if I can only get a taste of the quintessence. In that case I shall not be altogether sorry to have come here; as for profit, I see no chance of it. What can I

* See Letter V-2.

take from those that are bare, not being a hard-hearted man, nor born under the good graces of Mercury?

Farewell, most excellent preceptor. When we have begun our lecture, I will let you know how the thing answers, and so give you more occasion for laughter.

I shall venture perhaps even to attack your author, Paul. Only look at the boldness of your Erasmus. Farewell again.

Queen's College, Cambridge, St. Bartholomew's day.

IV-2 Desiderius Erasmus to William, Archbishop of Canterbury

Erasmus tells the Archbishop of Canterbury of the disease which has prostrated him, revealing his lack of faith in the medics of his day. Michelangelo, who also suffered from gallstones, once wrote in a letter that he had "more faith in prayers than in doctors."

Cambridge (January, 1513)

Your Erasmus has to face a dangerous conflict with the Stone, the most serious he has had. He has fallen into the hands of doctors and apothecaries, in other words, of butchers and harpies! I am still in labour. The pain is settled in the loins; but it is uncertain, when and what I shall bring forth.

I suspect that I owe this sickness to the beer, which I have drunk for some time for want of wine. These are forsooth the first fruits that we are to gather from this famous war with France!

I have only dictated this letter, and that not without some trouble. Farewell, and be careful of your own health, most excellent Maecenas.

IV-3   Sir Thomas More to Desiderius Erasmus

A letter to Erasmus from Sir Thomas More (1478-1535) bears news of the
plague or "Sweating Sickness" which swept through London, Cambridge
and Oxford, destroying countless lives including that of a mutual friend,
Andrew Ammonius.

19 August, 1517.

The departure of our friend Palgrave having been put off from day to day has
led to your receiving both my letter and those of others much later than I intended
and than you ought to have received them. It seemed suitable, that the same
bearer that brought me your letter should carry back my answer. It has therefore
become necessary to add this to my former communication, so that you may know
the cause of the delay, and at the same time be informed what is taking place
among us. We are in greater distress and danger than ever; deaths are frequent all
around us, almost everybody at Oxford, at Cambridge, and here in London,
having been laid up within the last few days, and very many of our best and most
honoured friends being lost. Among these,—I am distressed to think how it will
distress you,—has been our friend Andrew Ammonius, in whom both good letters
and all good men have suffered a grievous loss. He thought himself protected
against contagion by his temperate habit of life, and attributed it to this, that,
whereas he scarcely met with any person, whose whole family had not been sick,
the malady had not attacked any one of his. This boast he made to me and others
not many hours before his death. For in this Sweating Sickness, as they call it, no
one dies but on the first day. I, with my wife and children, am as yet untouched; the
rest of my family have recovered. I can assure you, that there is less danger upon
a field of battle, than in this town. It is now, I hear, beginning to rage at Calais,
when we are being forced thither ourselves, to undertake a diplomatic mission,—as
if it were not enough to have been living in contagion here without following it
elsewhere. But what is one to do? What our lot brings us must be borne; and I have
composed my mind for every event. Farewell.

IV-4   Cornelius Agrippa to a new Magistrate

The feminist sympathies of Heinrich Cornelius Agrippa von Nettesheim (1486-1535), German physician and theologian, are evident in this letter to a new magistrate urging the removal of the Inquisitor, Nicolas Savin, for having subjected an innocent woman to atrocities because her mother had been burnt as a witch. This cause brought an ecclesiastical condemnation upon Agrippa, and he left Metz for Cologne in 1520.

1519

You have seen lately, most honorable man, from the acts themselves, those impious articles of a most iniquitous information by virtue of which brother Nicolas Savin, of the Dominican convent, Inquisitor of heretics, has fraudulently dragged into his slaughter-house this innocent woman, in spite of God and justice, in spite of law and equity, contrary to Christian conscience, brotherly kindness, contrary to sacerdotal custom, the profession of his rule, the form of laws and canons: and has also, as a wicked man, wickedly and wrongfully exposed her to atrocious and enormous torments; whereby he has earned for himself a name of cruelty that will not die, as the lord official John Leonard, your predecessor now departed, himself testified upon his death-bed: and the lords of the chapter themselves know it with abhorrence. Among those articles of accusation one and the first is, that the mother of the said woman was burnt for witchcraft. I have excepted against this man as impertinent, intrusive, and incompetent to exercise in this case the judicial function; but lest you be led astray by false prophets who claim to be Christ, and are Antichrist, I pray your reverence to bear with a word of help, and only pay attention to a conversation lately held with me upon the position of this article, by the before-named bloodthirsty brother. For he asserted superciliously that the fact was in the highest degree decisive, and enough to warrant torture; and not unreasonably he asserted it according to the knowledge of his sect, which he produced presently out of the depths of the *Malleus Maleficarum* and the principles of peripatetic Theology, saying: "It must be so, because it is the custom with witches, from the very first, to sacrifice their infants to the demons, and besides that" (he said), "commonly, or often, their infants are the result of intercourse with incubi. Thus it happens that in their offspring, as with an hereditary taint, the evil sticks." O egregious sophism! Is it thus that in these days we theologize? Do figments like these move us to the torturing of harmless women? Is there no grace in baptism, no efficacy in the priests bidding: "Depart, unclean spirit, and give place to the Holy Ghost," if, because an impious parent has been sacrificed, the offspring must be given to the devil? Let any one who will, believe in this opinion, that incubi can produce offspring in the flesh. What is the fruit of this impossible position, if it be admitted, unless, according to the heresy of the Faustinians and Donatists, we get a greater evil as result? But to speak as one of the faithful, what matters it if one is the child of an incubus, what hurt is it to have been devoted as an infant to the devil? Are we not all from the nature of our humanity born one mass of sin, malediction, and eternal perdition, children of the devil, children of the Divine wrath, and heirs of damnation, until by the grace of baptism Satan is cast-out, and we are made new creatures in Jesus Christ, from whom none can be separated, except by his own offence. You see now the worth of this position as a plea for judgment, at enmity with law, perilous to receive, scandalous to propound. Farewell, and either avoid or banish this blaspheming brotherkin. Written this morning in the city of Metz.

IV-5   Nicolaus Copernicus to the Reverend Bernard Wapowski

Having been asked by the Reverend Bernard Wapowski, once his fellow student at the University of Cracow, for an opinion of John Werner's treatise entitled *The Motion of the Eighth Sphere,* Nicolaus Copernicus (1473-1543) responded with the following letter (in itself a minor astronomical work), copies of which were circulated for a time and served the same purpose as today's scientific articles and reviews.

Frauenburg, 3 June, 1524

To the Reverend Bernard Wapowski, Cantor and Canon of the Church of Cracow, and Secretary to His Majesty the King of Poland, from Nicolaus Copernicus.*

Some time ago, my dear Bernard, you sent me a little treatise on *The Motion of the Eighth Sphere* written by John Werner of Nuremberg. Your Reverence stated that the work was widely praised and asked me to give you my opinion of it. Had it been really possible for me to praise it with any degree of sincerity, I should have replied with a corresponding degree of pleasure. But I may commend the author's zeal and effort. It was Aristotle's advice that "we should be grateful not only to the philosophers who have spoken well, but also to those who have spoken incorrectly, because to men who desire to follow the right road, it is frequently no small advantage to know the blind alleys." Faultfinding is of little use and scant profit, for it is the mark of a shameless mind to prefer the role of the censorious critic to that of the creative poet. Hence I fear that I may arouse anger if I reprove another while I myself produce nothing better. Accordingly I wished to leave these matters, just as they are, to the attention of others; and I intended to reply to your Reverence substantially along these lines, with a view to a favorable reception of my work. However, I know that it is one thing to snap at a man and attack him, but another thing to set him right and redirect him when he strays, just as it is one thing to praise, and another to flatter and play the fawner. Hence I see no reason why I should not comply with your request or why I should appear to hamper the pursuit and cultivation of these studies, in which you have a conspicuous place. Consequently, lest I seem to condemn the man gratuitously, I shall attempt to show as clearly as possible in what respects he errs regarding the motion of the sphere of the fixed stars and maintains an unsound position. Perhaps my criticism may even contribute not a little to the formation of a better understanding of this subject.

In the first place, then, he went wrong in his calculation of time. He thought that the second year of Antoninus Pius Augustus, in which Claudius Ptolemy drew up the catalogue of the fixed stars as observed by himself, was A.D. 150, when in fact it was A.D. 139. For in the *Great Syntaxis*, Book III, chapter i, Ptolemy says that the autumnal equinox observed 463 years after the death of Alexander the Great fell in the third year of Antoninus. But from the death of Alexander to the birth of Christ there are 323 uniform Egyptian years and 130 days, because the interval between the beginning of the reign of Nabonassar and the birth of Christ

---

* This history-making letter is of such a technical nature as to defy total understanding by the non-scientist, even as the latter gleans from it an admiration for the new Renaissance method. The scientist may consult the detailed annotations in the edition edited by Professor Edward Rosen, translator of the present letter.

is computed as 747 uniform years and 130 days. This computation, I observe, is not questioned, certainly not by our author, as can be seen in his Proposition 22. It is true that according to the Alfonsine Tables there is one additional day. The reason for this discrepancy is that Ptolemy takes noon of the first day of the first Egyptian month Thoth as the starting point of the years reckoned from Nabonassar and Alexander the Great, while Alfonso starts from noon of the last day of the preceding year, just as we compute the years of Christ from noon of the last day of the month December. Now the interval from Nabonassar to the death of Alexander the Great is given by Ptolemy, Book III, chap. viii, as 424 uniform years; and Censorinus, relying on Marcus Varro, agrees with this estimate in his *De die natali,* addressed to Quintus Caerellius. This interval, subtracted from 747 years and 130 days, leaves a remainder of 323 years and 130 days as the period from the death of Alexander to the birth of Christ. Then from the birth of Christ to the aforementioned observation of Ptolemy there are 139 uniform years and 303 days. Therefore it is clear that the autumnal equinox observed by Ptolemy occurred 140 uniform years after the birth of our Lord, on the ninth day of the month Athyr; or 139 Roman years, September 25, the third year of Antoninus.

Again, in the *Great Syntaxis,* Book V, chap. iii, Ptolemy counts 885 years and 203 days from Nabonassar to his observation of the sun and moon in the second year of Antoninus. Therefore 138 uniform years and 73 days must have elapsed since the birth of Christ. Hence the fourteenth day thereafter, that is, the ninth of Pharmuthi, on which Ptolemy observed Basiliscus in Leo, was the 22nd day of February in the 139th Roman year after the birth of Christ. And this was the second year of Antoninus, which our author thinks was A.D. 150. Consequently his error consists of an excess of eleven years.

If anyone is still in doubt and, not satisfied by our previous criticism, desires a further test of this treatise, he should remember that time is the number or measure of the motion of heaven considered as "before" and "after." From this motion we derive the year, month, day, and hour. But the measure and the measured, being related, are mutually interchangeable. Now since Ptolemy based his tables on fresh observations of his own, it is incredible that the tables should contain any sensible error or any departure from the observations that would make the tables inconsistent with the principles on which they rest. Consequently if anyone will take the positions of the sun and moon, which Ptolemy determined by the astrolabe in his examination of Basiliscus, in the second year of Antoninus, on the ninth day of the month Pharmuthi, 5½ hours after noon, and if he will consult Ptolemy's tables for these positions, he will find them, not 149 years after Christ, but 138 years, 88 days, 5½ hours, equal to 885 years after Nabonassar, 218 days, 5½ hours. Thus is laid bare the error which frequently vitiates our author's examination of the motion of the eighth sphere when he mentions time.

The hypothesis in which he expresses his belief that during the four hundred years before Ptolemy the fixed stars moved with equal motion only involves a second error no less important than the first. To clarify this matter and make it more intelligible, attention should be directed, I think, to the propositions stated below. The science of the stars is one of those subjects which we learn in the order opposite to the natural order. For example, in the natural order it is first known that the planets are nearer than the fixed stars to the earth, and then as a consequence that the planets do not twinkle. We, on the contrary, first see that they do not twinkle, and then we know that they are nearer to the earth. In like manner, first we learn that the apparent motions of the planets are unequal, and subsequently we conclude that there are epicycles, eccentrics, or other circles by which the planets are carried unequally. I should therefore like to state that it was necessary for the ancient philosophers, first to mark with the aid of instruments the positions of the planets and the intervals of time, and then with this information as their guide, lest the inquiry into the motion of heaven remain interminable, to work out some definite planetary theory, which they seem to have found when the theory agreed in some harmonious manner with all the observed and noted positions of the planets. The situation is the same with respect to the motion of the eighth sphere. However, by reason of the extreme slowness of this motion, the ancient mathematicians were unable to pass on to us a complete account of it. But if we desire to examine it, we must follow in their footsteps and hold fast to their observations, bequeathed to us like an inheritance. And if anyone on the contrary thinks that the ancients are untrustworthy in this regard, surely the gates of this art are closed to him. Lying before the entrance, he will dream the dreams of the disordered about the motion of the eighth sphere and will receive his deserts for supposing that he must support his own hallucination by defaming the ancients. It is well known that they observed all these phenomena with great care and expert skill, and bequeathed to us many famous and praiseworthy discoveries. Consequently I cannot be persuaded that in noting star-places they erred by ¼° or 1/5° or even 1/6°, as our author believes. But of this I shall say more below.

Another point must not be overlooked. In every celestial motion that involves an inequality, what we want above all is the entire period in which the apparent motion passes through all its variations. For an apparent inequality in a motion is what prevents the whole revolution and the mean motion from being measured by their parts. As Ptolemy and before him Hipparchus of Rhodes, in their investigation of the moon's path, divined with keen insight, in the revolution of an inequality there must be four diametrically opposite points, the points of extreme swiftness and slowness, and, at each end of the perpendicular, the two points of mean uniform motion. These points divide the circle into four parts, so that in the first quadrant the swiftest motion diminishes, in the second the mean diminishes, in the third the slowest increases, and in the fourth the mean increases. By this device they could infer from the observed and examined motions of the moon in what portion of its circle it was at any specified time; and hence, when a similar motion recurred, they knew that a revolution of the inequality had been completed. Ptolemy explained this procedure more fully in the fourth book of the *Great Syntaxis.*

This method should have been adopted also in studying the motion of the eighth sphere. But because it is extremely slow, as I have said, in thousands of years the unequal motion quite clearly has not yet returned upon itself; and we are not permitted to give a final statement forthwith in dealing with a motion that extends beyond many generations of men. Nevertheless it is possible to attain our goal by a reasonable conjecture; and we now have the assistance of some observations, added since Ptolemy, which agree with this explanation. For what has been determined cannot have innumerable explanations; just as, if a circumference is drawn through three given points not on a straight line, we cannot draw another circumference greater or smaller than the one first drawn. But let me postpone this discussion to another occasion in order that I may return to the point where I digressed.

We must now see whether during the four hundred years before Ptolemy the fixed stars indeed moved, as our author says, with equal motion only. But let us not be mistaken in the meaning of terms. I understand by "equal motion," usually called also "mean motion," the motion that is halfway between the slowest and the swiftest. We must not be deceived by the first corollary to the seventh proposition. There he says that the motion of the fixed stars is slower when on his hypothesis the equal motion occurs, while the rest of the motion is more rapid and hence would at no time be slower than the equal motion. I do not know whether he is consistent in this regard when later on he uses the expression "much slower." He derives his measure of the equal motion from the following uniformity: in the period from the earliest observers of the fixed stars, Aristarchus and Timocharis, to Ptolemy, and in equal periods of time, the fixed stars moved equal distances, namely, approximately 1° in a century. This rate is given quite clearly by Ptolemy, and is repeated by our author in his seventh proposition.

But being a great mathematician, he is not aware that at the points of equality, that is, the intersections of the ecliptic of the tenth sphere with the circles of trepidation, as he calls them, the motion of the stars cannot possibly appear more uniform than elsewhere. The contrary is necessarily true: at those times the motion appears to change most, and least when the apparent motion is swiftest or slowest. He should have seen this from his own hypothesis and system and from the tables based on them, especially the last table which he drew up for the revolution of the entire equality or trepidation.

In this table the apparent motion is found to be, according to the preceding calculation, only 49′ for the century following 200 B.C., and 57′ for the next century. During the first century A.D. the stars must have moved about 1°6′, and during the second about 1°15′. Thus in equal periods of time the motions were successively greater by a little less than 1/6°. If you add the motion of the two centuries in either era, the total for the first interval will fall short of 2° by more than 1/5°, while the total for the second will exceed 2° by about ¼°. Thus again in equal times the later motion will exceed the earlier by about 34′, whereas our author had previously reported, trusting in Ptolemy, that the fixed stars moved 1° in a century. On the other hand, by the same law of the circles which he assumed, in the swiftest motion of the eighth sphere it happens that during 400 years a variation of scarcely 1′ is found in the apparent motion, as can be seen in the same table for the years 600-1000 A.D.; and similarly in the slowest motion, from 2060 B.C. for 400 years thereafter. Now the law governing an inequality is that, as was stated above, in one semicircle of trepidation, the one that extends from extreme slowness to extreme swiftness, the apparent motion constantly increases; and in the other semicircle, the one that extends from extreme swiftness to extreme slowness, the motion, previously on the increase, constantly diminishes. The greatest increase and decrease occur at the points of equality, diametrically opposite to each other. Hence in the apparent motion for two continuous equal periods of time equal motions cannot be found, but one is greater or smaller than the other. An exception occurs only at the extremes of swiftness and slowness, where the motions to either side pass through equal arcs in equal times; beginning or ceasing to increase or decrease, they equal each other at those times by undergoing opposite changes.

Therefore it is clear that the motion during the four hundred years before Ptolemy was not at all mean, but rather the slowest. I see no reason why we should suppose any slower motion, for which we have not been able thus far to get any evidence. No observation of the fixed stars made before Timocharis has come down to us, and Ptolemy had none. Since the swiftest motion has already occurred, we are now as a consequence not in the same semicircle with Ptolemy. In our semicircle the motion diminishes, and no small part of it has already occurred.

Hence it should not be surprising that with these assumptions our author could not more nearly approach the recorded observations of the ancients; and that in his opinion they erred by ¼° or 1/5°, or even ½° and more. Yet nowhere does Ptolemy seem to have exercised greater care than in his effort to hand down to us a flawless treatment of the motion of the fixed stars. He could be successful only in that small portion of it from which he had to reconstruct the entire revolution. If an error, however imperceptible, entered that whole vast realm, it might have prodigious effects on the outcome. Therefore he seems to have joined Aristarchus to Timocharis of Alexandria, his contemporary, and Agrippa of Bithynia to Menelaus of Rome; in this way he would have most certain and unquestionable evidence when they agreed with each other, although separated by great distances. It is incredible that such great errors were made by these men or Ptolemy, who could deal with many other more difficult matters and, as the saying goes, put the finishing touches to them.

Finally, our author is nowhere more foolish than in his twenty-second proposition, especially in the corollary thereto. Wishing to praise his own work, he censures Timocharis with regard to two stars, namely, Arista Virginis, and the star which is the most northerly of the three in the brow of Scorpio, on the ground that for the former star Timocharis's calculation fell short, and for the latter was excessive. But here our author commits a childish blunder. For both stars the difference in the distance, as determined by Timocharis and Ptolemy, is the same, namely, $4°20'$ in approximately equal intervals of time; and hence the result of the calculation is practically the same. Yet our author disregards the fact that the addition of $4°7'$ to the place of the star which Timocharis found in $2°$ of Scorpio cannot possibly produce $6°20'$ of Scorpio, the place where Ptolemy found the star. Conversely when the same number is subtracted from $26°40'$, the place of Arista according to Ptolemy, it cannot yield $22°20'$, as it should, but it gives $22°32'$. Thus our author thought that in the one case the computation was deficient by the amount by which in the other case it was excessive, as though this irregularity were inherent in the observations, or as though the road from Athens to Thebes were not the same as the road from Thebes to Athens. Besides, if he had either added or subtracted the number in both cases, as parity of reasoning required, he would have found the two cases identical.

Moreover, between Timocharis and Ptolemy there were in reality not 443 years, but only 432, as I indicated in the beginning. Since the interval is shorter, the difference should be smaller; hence he departs from the observed motion of the stars not merely by $13'$ but by $\frac{1}{3}°$. Thus he imputed his own error to Timocharis, while Ptolemy barely escaped. And while he thinks that their reports are unreliable, what else is left but to distrust his observations?

So much for the motion in longitude of the eighth sphere. From the foregoing remarks it can easily be inferred what we must think about the motion in declination, which our author has complicated with two trepidations, as he calls them, piling a second one upon the first. But since the foundation has now been destroyed, of necessity the superstructure collapses, being weak and incohesive. What finally is my own opinion concerning the motion of the sphere of the fixed stars? Since I intend to set forth my views elsewhere, I have thought it unnecessary and improper to extend this communication further. For it is enough if I satisfy your desire to have my judgment of this work, as you requested. May your Reverence be of sound health and good fortune.

Nicolaus Copernicus

IV-6   Fray Antonio de Guevara to Doctor Melgar, Physician

Fray Antonio (1480-1545), Inquisitor and bishop, accuses one of his physicians of incompetence and makes the point that medical ignorance and useless remedies do more harm than good. His *Familiar Epistles* were published from 1539 to 1545.

Madrid, 27 December, 1525

Very reverend doctor and court physician,

I have received your letter and the prescription it contained. How I spoke to the presiding official about your case, you will learn from my dispatch as well as from your young messenger, so that you will see that whereas you have treated me as a doctor I have treated you as a friend. We shall see which of us treats better, you through your medical treatment or I through my dispatch. Your matter is receiving favorable attention but I still have my gout. I ordered those herbs and roots and, as per your instructions, I got them out, chewed them, and even drank them, and may God grant salvation to your soul if they succeeded in doing anything for my gout. They merely heated up my liver and chilled my stomach. I must confess that you not only failed to diagnose my illness, but even made it worse. The chill in my stomach makes me keep belching, leaving me to conclude that Dr. Melgar never improves. Since my illness is not above the waist, but below the thigh-bone, and I didn't ask you to stir up my humours but to remove my pains, I don't understand why you are punishing my stomach, the chief villain being my ankles.

I spoke to Doctor Soto, nearby here in Toledo, about a muscular lumbago and he had me take two pills of *huego* in my ears. The good it did me was to set all the court laughing and to make my ears ache. I often talked with Dr. Cartagena at Alcalá University and he prepared me a prescription of cow-dung, rat excrement, oat flour, nettle leaves, rosebuds, and fried scorpions which he mixed into a plaster and applied over my muscle. All the profit I got from it was a lack of sleep for three nights and I had to pay the apothecary who made it six *reales*. From now on I disown the medical counsels of Hippocrates, Avicenna, Ficino, Rasis, and Erophilus, if there is found in any of their writings that damned plaster which left me neither sleep nor rest. I not only threw it away. I buried it. For it was hard to tell whether it burned or stank the more.

I remember that in Burgos, in 1521, Doctor Soto treated me for erratic fevers, and had me take so much celery and pearl-barley and drink so much endive-water that I fell into such a loathing that I could no longer eat or even smell. Not long after I went to consult the same Doctor Soto, ailing in Tordesillas, and I saw him eating an orange and drinking a cup of savorous white wine. When his chill left him and he warmed up, I said to him half-marveling and half-scandalized and with a laugh: "Tell me, Doctor, by what law or justice do you cure your chill with Saint Martin wine and my lumbago with cow-dung?" He replied good-humoredly: "Our master Hippocrates ordered all his followers, to avoid his curse, to cure ourselves with wine and our patients with distilled water." Although he was joking, I remember that you told me one day in Madrid that though you took a purge every day you did not know the taste of distilled water. There is nothing in the world which makes me lose my mind, or rather my senses, than the way doctors treat someone, for we see them eager to cure and enemies of effecting cures. Since you write me asking, on the honor of my father Don Beltràn, to tell you what I think of medicine, and what I've read about its origins, I do as you request, although not as others might wish, because it is a topic on which wise physicians fall silent, leaving ignorant doctors to condemn the average man to the devil.

Nothing else, except that Our Lord guard and keep you, and give me the grace to serve Him.

(trans. R. J. C.)

(See also Letter IV-15, on the cure of gout.)

IV-7   François Rabelais to André Tiraqueau

In his writings Rabelais (1494-1553) called upon his fellow-Humanists to renounce the pseudo-sciences of the Middle Ages for the true sciences of the Renaissance: astrology for astronomy, alchemy for chemistry, etc. A pioneer in medicine himself, performing anatomies when the Church still forbade it, he writes to the learned law-scholar of Poitou an eloquent appeal for restoration of "the ancient and legitimate medicine."

Lyon, 3 June, 1532

How comes it about, my learned Tiraqueau, that in this resplendence of our century, when, as if by a singular favor of the gods, we see welcomed in our land all the best disciplines, one still finds here and there men so made that they neither can nor wish to raise their eyes above this thick fog of Gothic times toward the illustrious torch of the sun? Is it because, as is written in Plato, "In every trade many are the ignorant and persons without merit, but rare are men zealous and of great merit"? Is it rather because such is the force of darkness of this sort that those whose eyes are penetrated by this twilight are necessarily hallucinated and blinded, as from an incurable optic inflammation unrelieved by eye-lotions or spectacles? This one might believe from what we read in Aristotle's *Categories:* "The change from being to nothingness is possible; from nothingness to being impossible."

Judging the matter sanely—weighing it, as they say, on the scales of Critolaus—this odyssey of errors seems to me to be born of nothing other than that infamous self-love so strongly condemned by philosophers, which, once it has struck men scarcely aware of what they must wish or fear, ordinarily dulls and fascinates their senses and their souls, so that they see without seeing and understand without understanding. For those whom the ignorant throng regard as being of a certain rank because they take pride in a wisdom which is foreign to them, if you pull off this disguise, this lion's skin, and if you succeed in making the throng recognize finally that the art which has advanced them to their lofty situation is merely appearance, pure illusions and ineptitudes, what else will you appear to have accomplished than make stupid people recognize the obvious? Then those who at first were seated in the pit will with difficulty find a place in the last rows, until they succeed not only in making laugh freedmen and the slaves of whom a few now have the rhinoceros nose, but moving their stomach and bile in indignation, when they shall no longer be able to endure the fact that they had been the dupes of fraud and trickery.

It is the same we have learned about men about to perish in a shipwreck seizing a beam or clothes or a straw at the moment the vessel breaks and founders, clutching it in their hands without thinking of swimming, trusting in it until they are engulfed in the sea. It's the same with these people, our lovable friends, for even if they see the vessel of false science broken and exposed on all sides, they swear by and cling to the books they've been used to since childhood. If you pull the books from their hands, they think you're tugging at their souls.

Thus this science of law of yours has reached the point of an established discipline. Yet there are people from whom you couldn't tear away the antiquated law glosses of the Barbarians. In our business of medicine, getting finer every day, how many expend the effort to arrive at better results? One good thing, however, is that people are perceiving that some men claiming to be doctors, if you look at them closely, are devoid of learning, good faith, and reflection, even full of arrogance, envy, and ordures. They conduct their experiments leaving dead bodies (as Pliny once complained) and they are more dangerous than the disease itself. Now at least those distinguished by their respect for the pure medicine of the classics command the respect of the mighty. If this esteem is to spread further, we need not be surprised to see reduced to beggar's rags those charlatans and adventurers who had undertaken to impoverish the human body from top to bottom. Well, among those in our time who have applied their mind and will to restoring its ancient brilliance to ancient and legitimate medicine, you used to praise with enthusiasm, when I was your neighbor, that Manardi, the able and learned doctor of Ferrara, and you approved his first writings as if they had been edited by Apollo or Aesculapius. That is why, having received recently his last writings from Italy, my great consideration for you has led me to have them printed and published under the auspices of your name. I remember in fact and know how much that medical art which I strive to perfect owes to you who sang the praises of medicine in your illustrious remarks on the municipal laws of Poitou. I beg you urgently not to torment studious minds by making them wait for your observations any longer. Stay well. Greet for me the illustrious bishop of Maillezais, my well-disposed Maecenas, should you visit him, and our dear Hilaire Coguet if he is still there by chance.

F. Rabelais
(trans. R. J. C.)

IV-8   Cardinal Nicolaus von Schoenberg to Nicolaus Copernicus

Nicolaus Copernicus, the Polish astronomer whose heliocentric theory revolutionized planetary astronomy, was sufficiently encouraged by the following letter from Cardinal Nicolaus von Schoenberg, Bishop of Capua, to place it at the beginning of his famous *De Revolutionibus orbium coelestium* in 1543, preceding his dedication to Pope Paul III. It is interesting that in the beginning, some of the Catholic leaders tried to further the work of Copernicus while the Reformation leaders were opposed to him, a situation that soon reversed itself.

Rome, 1 November, 1536

Cardinal Nicolaus von Schoenberg, Bishop of Capua, sends Nicolaus Copernicus his greetings.

A few years ago when I heard everyone constantly speaking of your amazing investigations, I conceived a regard for you, and congratulated our people for their wisdom in spreading your fame. For I had learned that you not only profoundly understood the teachings of the ancient astronomers, but that you had also constructed a new world system. You teach, as I have heard, that the earth is moving, and that the sun occupies the center of the world, and that the eighth heaven, the firmament, remains constant and motionless; and that the moon together with the elements of its sphere between Mars and Venus revolves about the sun in an annual orbit. You have also written explanations of this theory and composed tables of the planetary orbits, that fill everyone with the greatest admiration. Therefore may I earnestly beg you, highly-learned man, if it is not too much trouble, to communicate your discoveries to those desirous of knowledge, and to send me, as soon as possible, the result of your nightly meditations upon the universe, together with the tables and everything else pertinent to this subject.

Dietrich von Rheden has been charged to have everything copied at my expense and to send it to me. If you do me this favor you will learn that I have your fame greatly at heart and am trying to obtain recognition for your work. Farewell!—

(See also Letter IX-12, which shows that not all high prelates held the same respect for Copernicus and his stunning discoveries.)

IV-9   Pietro Aretino to Dionigi Capucci

Pietro Aretino (1492-1556) tries to dissuade Dionigi Capucci from conforming to the medical profession, riddled as it is with ignorance, avarice and instances of malpractice.

Venice, 15 December, 1537

Do not let it upset you, O excellent fellow, that the physicians pick on you. They want you to conform to the canons of their sacrosanct procedure.

Instead say to anyone who wishes to explain to others what you do: "I use syrups instead of medicine. May God pardon the man who invented the latter!"

As far as I am concerned, I compare medicines to the raging of a torrential stream which carries away whole fields and not merely boulders and the trunks of trees. I insist that these villainous concoctions suck out months and years from your vitals, leaving life itself all withered away.

Indeed, if I did not have respect for their high-sounding titles, I would call doctors themselves "the alchemists of the body" since the presumption that intoxicates them stakes an ounce of health against the full measure of two lives, and our ignorant laws decree that they shall not be punished but praised for their homicides. Why the worthy fellows are thrown into utter confusion if they ask a sick man if his bowels have moved, and he answers them: "My lord, yes!" For the sum and total of their knowledge of the art of Galen is to give mallow-water in an enema.

What a sad thing it is to see some poor devil reduced to skin and bones by the diet they have prescribed for him when they don't know either the nature of his disease nor the kind of physique he has! That is why his victims first ask for his physics, then for a word of comfort, then for wax candles, then for the grave.

O wise country folk! You do not have access to these pretended cures. You medicine each other, always doing what seems fitting to do.

How confident are the Latin phrases of these doctors—and then the patient dies! How often do they hold someone to be as good as gone—and yet that very evening he arises from his bed! That is because they haven't got the faintest comprehension that every single case is different.

Moreover what shall we say of their avarice which makes them pound some little fever into pieces so small that it will take a month to cure a man afflicted with one? It is the truth what they declare at Rome. Namely that over and over again some servant is allowed to die because his master tried to save something and keep the "without this, no cure" at home. Do you think that they would have felt the pulse even of St. Francis if he had said that he did not have a penny and would not pay them?

I except, of course, the expert, learned and worthy Messer Jacopo Buonacosa of Ferrara and some others like him.

But to come back to you. I urge your Lordship to persevere in using the same incorruptible distillations with which your famous father—to the overweening glory of Città di Castello—restored so many people.

IV-10   Pietro Aretino to Elias Alfan, Physician

In a moving encomium to Elias Alfan, Aretino hails the Jewish physician as a model worthy of emulation by Christians.

Venice, 16 July, 1542

There is no occasion, O excellent physician, for you to apologize to me because you did not keep your appointment, for the faith that I have in your ability is not circumscribed by any limits of time.

It is enough for me to know that I can always call on you to minister to the needs of any illness to which either myself or any of the numerous staff that lives in my house may fall victim. I say "staff." I don't want to call them servants, for I maintain them with a warmth of affection that makes me seem more like their father than their master.

That I can so call on you, Catarina's malady bears witness. She was restored, not from the sickbed, but from the grave, by God's mercy and by your skill in medicine. Those who had seen her more than dead, and who now behold her hale and hearty, can scarcely believe it.

To be sure, I myself rejoice less in the reputation that you gained in curing her, than in the fact that you restored her to health again, and yet why haven't I the means to reward you for this, as well as thank you? Why can't the words with which I praise you, become gifts which would bring you pleasure? Why cannot those who have the power relieve you from your poverty, look upon you with my regard?

Ricchi, Biondo, Capuccio and Fragemellica *—and I name them first both for their own merits and because of the esteem I have for them—are singing your praises and the high admiration they have for the way you handled such a difficult case. Am I not obliged, then, to see to it that my ink pots consecrate themselves to making your fame eternal?

But even if your skill did not give me reason to do this, I would have to do so anyway, pointing out that although you are a Jew, men could learn how to be a Christian from you. After all, fearing God and loving your neighbor are inherent to your nature. What else does a Christian have to do?

Indeed, I do not know if anyone has ever seen a man who has equalled the loving kindness with which you treated your own kinfolk. Anyone who stood at your side when, with your eager affection, and your doctor's art, and with prayers from your heart, you restored to health her who brought you into the world, would have learned how we should care for, protect, and honor our mothers. I wish everyone who has a wife or daughters would consider the sweet tenderness and the grave integrity with which you enable your own wife to live in seemliness and virtue, and your own children to be well-mannered and good.

But even all that is nothing when compared to the enthusiasm which you showed when, moved by your pious, religious and spiritual zeal, you told me that you wanted to point out to me certain passages in Holy Writ that were not known even to our own theologians. They spoke of the Virgin Mary, and in such manner that no one could ask for anything more. With my eyes filled with so many tears that they are incontinently flooded with them, I beg you to keep your promise to me that from your own lips I should hear these pure words.

But it would be well if the Pope himself should give ear to these holy sayings, and that, in honor of our true religion, he should listen to your inspired voice. He would then have to give thanks on behalf of the church that an inner necessity compelled you to win servants and friends for Christ by citing these passages.

It is His mercy that inspired you to confess His laws—while at the same time you observe your own.

* Four outstanding local physicians.

IV-11   Nostradamus to King Henri II of France

Michel de Nostredame, or Nostradamus (1503-1566), the French astrologer who is still remembered for his prophecies, dedicates the enlarged second edition of his *Centuries,* a book of rhymed prophecies, to Henry II of France. Long after his death, Nostradamus' predictions continued to arouse controversy, but in 1781 they were denounced by the Congregation of the Index (the body set up by the Roman Catholic Church to examine books and manuscripts).

Salon, 27 June, 1558

To the most invincible, very puissant, and most Christian Henry King of France the Second: Michael Nostradamus, his most humble, most obedient servant and subject, wishes victory and happiness.

For that sovereign observation that I had, O most Christian and very victorious King, since that my face, long obscured with cloud, presented itself before the deity of your measureless Majesty, since that in that I have been perpetually dazzled, never failing to honour and worthily revere that day, when first before it, as before a singularly humane majesty, I presented myself. I searched for some occasion by which to manifest good heart and frank courage, by the means of which I might grow into greater knowledge of your serene Majesty. I soon found in effect it was impossible for me to declare it, considering the contrast of the solitariness of my long obnubilation and obscurity, and my being suddenly thrust into brilliancy, and transported into the presence of the sovereign eye of the first monarch of the universe. Likewise I have long hung in doubt as to whom I ought to dedicate these three Centuries, the remainder of my Prophecies amounting now to a thousand. I have long meditated on an act of such audacity. I have at last ventured to address your Majesty, and was not daunted from it as Plutarch, that grave author, relates in the life of Lycurgus, that, seeing the gifts and presents that were made in the way of sacrifice at the temples of the immortal gods in that age, many were staggered at the expense, and dared not approach the temple to present anything.

Notwithstanding this, I saw your royal splendour to be accompanied with an incomparable humanity, and paid my addresses to it, not as to those Kings of Persia whom it was not permissible to approach. But to a very prudent and very wise Prince I have dedicated my nocturnal and prophetic calculations, composed out of a natural instinct, and accompanied by a poetic fervour, rather than according to the strict rules of poetry. Most part, indeed, has been composed and adjusted by astronomical calculation corresponding to the years, months, and weeks, of the regions, countries, and for the most part towns and cities, throughout Europe, Africa, and a part of Asia, which nearest approach [or resemble] each other in all these climates, and this is composed in a natural manner. Possibly some may answer—who, if so, had better blow his nose [that he may see the clearer by it]—that the rhythm is as easy to be understood, as the sense is hard to get at. Therefore, O most gracious King, the bulk of the prophetic quatrains are so rude, that there is no making way through them, nor is there any interpreter of them. Nevertheless, being always anxious to set down the years, towns, and regions cited, where the events are to occur, even from the year 1585, and the year 1606, dating from the present time, which is the 14th of March, 1557.

Then passing far beyond to things which shall happen at the commencement of the seventh millenary, deeply calculated, so far as my astronomic calculus, and other knowledge, has been able to reach, to the time when the adversaries of Jesus Christ and of His Church shall begin to multiply in great force. The whole has been composed and calculated on days and hours of best election and disposition, and with all the accuracy I could attain to at a moment [blessed] "*Minerva libera et non invita,*"[1] my calculations looking forward to events through a space of time to come that nearly equals that of the past even up to the present, and by this they will know in the lapse of time and in all regions what is to happen, all written down thus particularly, immingled with nothing superfluous.

Notwithstanding that some say, "*Quod de futuris non est determinata omnino veritas,*"[2] I will confess, Sire, that I believed myself capable of presage from the natural instinct I inherit of my ancestors, adjusted and regulated by elaborate calculation, and the endeavour to free the soul, mind, and heart from all care, solicitude, and anxiety, by resting and tranquilizing the spirit, which finally has all to be completed and perfected in one respect *tripode oeneo* [by the brazen tripod]. With all this there will be many to attribute to me as mine, things no more mine than nothing. The Almighty alone, who strictly searches the human heart, pious, just, and pitiful, is the true Judge; to Him I pray to defend me from the calumny of

1. "When Minerva was free and favourable."
2. "There can be no truth entirely determined for certain which concerns the future."

wicked men. Such persons, with equal calumny, will bring into question how all your ancient progenitors the Kings of France have cured the evil; how those of other nations have cured the bite of serpents; others have had a certain instinct in the art of divination, and other faculties that would be too long to recount here. Notwithstanding such as cannot be restrained from the exercise of the malignancy of the evil spirit, [there is hope that] by the lapse of time, and after my extinction here on earth, my writings will be more valued than during my lifetime.

However, if I err in calculation of ages, or find myself unable to please all the world, may it please your Imperial Majesty to forgive me, for I protest before God and His saints, that I purpose to insert nothing whatever in writing this present Epistle that shall militate against the true Catholic Faith, whilst consulting the astronomical calculations to the very best of my knowledge. For the stretch of time of our forefathers [*i.e.* the age of the world] which has gone before is such, submitting myself to the direction of the soundest chronologists, that the first man, Adam, was about one thousand two hundred and forty years before Noah, not computing time by Gentile records, such as Varro has committed to writing, but taking simply the Sacred Scriptures for the guide in my astronomic reckonings, to the best of my feeble understanding. After Noah, from him and the universal deluge, about one thousand and fourscore years, came Abraham, who was a sovereign astrologer according to some; he first invented the Chaldaean alphabet. Then came Moses, about five hundred and fifteen or sixteen years later. Between the time of David and Moses five hundred and seventy years elapsed. Then after the time of David and the time of our Saviour and Redeemer, Jesus Christ, born of a pure Virgin, there elapsed (according to some chronographers) one thousand three hundred and fifty years. . . .

I fully confess that all proceeds from God, and for that I return Him thanks, honour, and immortal praise, and have mingled nothing with it of the divination which proceeds *à fato,* but *à Deo, à natura,* [3] and for the most part accompanied with the movement of the celestial courses. Much as, if looking into a burning mirror [we see], as with darkened vision, the great events, sad or portentous, and calamitous occurrences that are about to fall upon the principal worshippers. First upon the temples of God, secondly upon such as have their support from the earth [*i.e.* by the kings], this decadence draweth nigh, with a thousand other calamitous incidents that in the course of time will be known to happen.

For God will take notice of the long barrenness of the great Dame, who afterwards will conceive two principal children. But, she being in great danger, the girl she will give birth to with risk at her age of death in the eighteenth year, and not possible to outlive the thirty-sixth, will leave three males and one female, and

3. Which proceeds from fate, but from God, and nature.

he will have two who never had any of the same father. The three brothers will be so different, though united and agreed, that the three and four parts of Europe will tremble. By the youngest in years will the Christian monarchy be sustained and augmented; heresies spring up and suddenly cast down, the Arabs driven back, kingdoms united, and new laws promulgated. Of the other children the first shall possess the furious crowned Lions, holding their paws upon the bold escutcheon. The second, accompanied by the Latins, shall penetrate so far that a second trembling and furious descent shall be made, descending Mons Jovis [at Barcelona] to mount the Pyrenees, shall not be translated to the antique monarchy, and a third inundation of human blood shall arise, and March for a long while will not be found in Lent. The daughter shall be given for the preservation of the Christian Church, the dominator falling into the Pagan sect of new infidels, and she will have two children, the one fidelity, the other infidelity, by the confirmation of the Catholic Church. The other, who to his great confusion and tardy repentance wished to ruin her, will have three regions over a wide extent of leagues, that is to say, Roumania, Germany, and Spain, which will entail great intricacy of military handling, stretching from the 50th to the 52nd degree of latitude. And they will have to respect the more distant religions of Europe and the north above the 48th degree of latitude, which at first in a vain timidity will tremble, and then the more western, southern, and eastern will tremble. Their power will become such, that what is brought about by union and concord will prove insuperable by warlike conquest. By nature they will be equal, but exceedingly different in faith.

After this the sterile Dame, of greater power than the second, shall be received by two nations, by the first made obstinate by him who had power over all, by the second, and third, that shall extend his forces towards the circuit of the east of Europe; [arrived] there his standards will stop and succumb, but by sea he will run on to Trinacria and the Adriatic with his mirmidons. The Germans will succumb wholly and the Barbaric sect will be disquieted and driven back by the whole of the Latin race. Then shall begin the grand Empire of Antichrist in the Atila and Xerxes, [who is] to descend with innumerable multitudes, so that the coming of the Holy Spirit, issuing from the 48th degree, shall make a transmigration, chasing away the abomination of Antichrist, that made war upon the royal person of the great vicar of Jesus Christ, and against His Church, and reign *per tempus, et in occasione temporis* [for a time, and to the end of time]. This will be preceded by an eclipse of the sun, more obscure and tenebrose than has ever been since the creation of the world, up to the death and passion of Jesus Christ, and from thence till now. There will be in the month of October a grand revolution [translation] made, such that one would think that the librating body of the earth had lost its natural movement in the abyss of perpetual darkness. There will be seen precursive signs in the spring-time, and after extreme changes ensuing, reversal of kingdoms, and great earthquakes [*i.e.* wars]. All this accompanied with the procreations of the New Babylon [Paris], a miserable prostitute big with the abomination of the first holocaust [death of Louis XVI.]. It will only continue for seventy-three years seven months.

Then there will issue from the stock so long time barren, proceeding from the 50th degree, [one] who will renovate the whole Christian Church. A great peace, union, and concord will then spring up between some of the children of races [long] opposed to each other and separated by diverse kingdoms. Such a peace shall be set up, that the instigator and promoter of military faction by means of the diversity of religions, shall dwell attached to the bottom of the abyss, and united to the kingdom of the furious, who shall counterfeit the wise. The countries, towns, cities, and provinces that had forsaken their old customs to free themselves, enthralling themselves more deeply, shall become secretly weary of their liberty, and, true religion lost, shall commence by striking off to the left, to return more than ever to the right.

Then replacing holiness, so long desecrated by their former writings [circulating slanders], afterwards the result will be that the great dog will issue as an irresistible mastiff [Napoleon?] who will destroy everything, even to all that may have been prepared in time past, till the churches will be restored as at first, and the clergy reinstated in their pristine condition; till it lapses again into whoredom and luxury, to commit and perpetrate a thousand crimes. And drawing near to another desolation, then, when she shall be at her highest and sublimest point of dignity, the kings and generals [*mains militaires*] will come up [against her], and her two swords will be taken from her, and nothing will be left her but the semblance of them. [The following paragraph I can make nothing of, so I give it in the words of Garencières [4] and in inverted commas.] "From which by the means of the crookedness that draweth them, the people causing it to go straight, and not willing to submit unto them by the end opposite to the sharp hand that toucheth the ground they shall provoke." Until there shall be born unto the branch a long time sterile, one who shall deliver the French people from the benign slavery that they voluntarily submitted to, putting himself under the protection of Mars, and stripping Jupiter [Napoleon I.] of all his honours and dignities, for the city constituted free and seated in another narrow Mesopotamia. The chief and governor shall be cast from the midst, and set in a place of the air, ignorant of the conspiracy of the conspirators [Fouché, Duc d'Otranto, etc.] with the second Thrasibulus, who for a long time had prepared all this. Then shall the

---

4. Théophile de Garencières was a seventeenth-century interpreter of Nostradamus, several of whose notes occur here within brackets with those of Charles Ward.

impurities and abominations be with great shame set forth and manifested to the darkness of the veiled light, shall cease towards the end of his reign, and the chiefs of the Church shall evince but little of the love of God, whilst many of them shall apostatize from the true faith.

Of the three sects [Lutheran, Catholic, and Mahometan], that which is in the middle, by the action of its own worshippers, will be thrown a little into decadence. The first totally throughout Europe, and the chief part of Africa exterminated by the third, by means of the poor in spirit, who by the madness engendered of libidinous luxury, will commit adultery [*i.e.* apostatize]. The people will pull down the pillar, and chase away the adherents of the legislators, and it shall seem, from the kingdoms weakened by the Orientals, that God the Creator has loosed Satan from the infernal prisons, to make room for the great Dog and Dohan [Gog and Magog],[5] which will make so great and injurious a breach in the Churches, that neither the reds nor the whites, who are without eyes and without hands [meaning the latter Bourbons, "who learn nothing and forget nothing"], cannot judge of the situation, and their power will be taken from them. Then shall commence a persecution of the Church such as never was before. Whilst this is enacting, such a pestilence shall spring up that out of three parts of mankind two shall be removed. To such a length will this proceed that one will neither know nor recognize the fields or houses, and grass will grow in the streets of the cities as high as a man's knees. To the clergy there shall be a total desolation, and the martial men shall usurp what shall come back from the City of the Sun [Rome], and from Malta and the Islands of Hières [off Marseilles], and the great chain of the port shall be opened that takes its name from the marine ox [Bosphorus]. . . .

Had I wished to give to every quatrain its detailed date, it could easily have been done, but it would not have been agreeable to all, and still less to interpret them, Sire, until your Majesty should have fully sanctioned me to do this, in order not to furnish calumniators with an opportunity to injure me. Always reckoning the years since the creation of the world to the birth of Noah as being 1506 years, and from that to the completion of the building of the ark at the period of the universal deluge 600 years elapsed (let them be solar years, or lunar, or mixed), I hold that the Scripture takes them to be solar. At the conclusion of this 600 years, Noah entered the ark to escape the deluge. The deluge was universal over the earth, and lasted one year and two months. From the conclusion of the deluge to the birth of Abraham there elapsed 295 years, and 100 years from that to the birth of Isaac. From Isaac to Jacob 60 years. From the time he went into Egypt until his coming out of it was 130 years, and from the entry of Jacob into Egypt to his exit was 436

5. *Gog and Magog:* the two nations pitted by Satan at the Battle of Armageddon against the Kingdom of God *(Revelations* 20: 8)

years; and from that to the building of the Temple by Solomon in the fortieth year of his reign, makes 480 years. From the building of the Temple to Jesus Christ, according to the supputation of the Hierographs, there passed 490 years. Thus by this calculation that I have made, collecting it out of the sacred writings, there are about 4173 years and eight months less or more. Now, from Jesus Christ, in that there is such a diversity of opinion, I pass it by, and having calculated the present prophecies in accordance with the order of the chain which contains the revolution, and the whole by astronomical rule, together with my own hereditary instinct. After some time, and including in it the period Saturn takes to turn between the 7th of April up to the 25th of August; Jupiter from the 14th of June to the 7th of October; Mars from the 17th of April to the 22nd of June; Venus from the 9th of April to the 22nd of May; Mercury from the 3rd of February to the 24th of the same; afterwards from the 1st of June to the 24th of the same; and from the 25th of September to the 16th of October, Saturn in Capricorn, Jupiter in Aquarius, Mars in Scorpio, Venus in Pisces, Mercury within a month in Capricorn, Aquarius, and Pisces; the moon in Aquarius, the Dragon's head in Libra, the tail in her sign opposite. Following the conjunction of Jupiter to Mercury, with a quadrin aspect of Mars to Mercury, and the head of the Dragon shall be with a conjunction of Sol with Jupiter, the year shall be peaceful without eclipse.

Then will be the commencement [of a period] that will comprehend in itself what will long endure [*i.e.* the vulgar advent of the French Revolution], and in its first year there shall be a great persecution of the Christian Church, fiercer than that in Africa [by the Vandals from 1439 to 1534], and this will burst out [*durera*] the year one thousand seven hundred and ninety-two; they will think it to be a renovation of time. After this the people of Rome will begin to reconstitute themselves [in 1804, when Napoleon is emperor], and to chase away the obscurity of darkness, recovering some share of their ancient brightness, but not without much division and continual changes. Venice after that, in great force and power, shall raise her wings very high, not much short of the force of ancient Rome. At that time great Bysantine sails, associated with the Piedmontese by the help and power of the North, will so restrain them that the two Cretans will not be able to maintain their faith. The arks built by the ancient warriors will accompany them to the waves of Neptune. In the Adriatic there will be such permutations, that what was united will be separated, and that will be reduced to a house which before was a great city, including the Pampotan and Mesopotamia of Europe, to 45, and others to 41, 42, and 47. And in that time and those countries the infernal power will set the power of the adversaries of its law against the Church of Jesus Christ. This will constitute the second Antichrist, which will persecute that Church and its true vicar, by means of the power of the temporal kings, who in their ignorance will be reduced by tongues that will cut more than any sword in the hands of a madman. . . .

After that Antichrist will be the infernal prince. Then at this last epoch, all the kingdoms of Christianity, as well as of the infidel world, will be shaken during the space of twenty-five years, and the wars and battles will be more grievous, and the towns, cities, castles, and all other edifices will be burnt, desolated, and destroyed with much effusion of vestal blood, married women and widows violated, sucking children dashed and broken against the walls of town; and so many evils will be committed by means of Satan, the prince infernal, that nearly all the world will become undone and desolated. Before the events occur certain strange birds [imperial eagles] will cry in the air, *"To-day! to-day!"* and after a given time will disappear [June, 1815]. After this has endured for a certain length of time [twenty-five years he has said before, 1790 to 1815], there will be almost renewed another reign of Saturn, the age of gold [this might be the discovery of California, but for what follows]. God the Creator shall say, hearing the affliction of His people, Satan shall be precipitated and bound in the bottomless abyss, and then shall commence between God and men a universal peace. There he shall abide for the space of a thousand years, and shall turn his greatest force against the power of the Church, and shall then be bound again.

How justly are all these figures adapted by the divine letters to visible celestial things, that is to say, by Saturn, Jupiter, and Mars, and others in conjunction with them, as may be seen more at large by some of the quatrains! I would have calculated it more deeply, and adapted the one to the other; but, seeing, O most serene King, that some who are given to censure will raise a difficulty, I shall take the opportunity to retire my pen and seek my nocturnal repose *"Multa etiam, O Rex potentissime proeclara, et sane in brevi ventura, sed omnia in hâc tuâ Epistola, innectere non possumus, nec volumus, sed ad intellegenda quoedam facta, horrida fata pauca libanda sunt, quamvis tanta sit in omnes tua amplitudo et humanitas homines, deosque pietas, ut solos amplissimo et Christianissimo Regis nomine, et ad quem summa totius religionis auctoritas deferatur dignus esse videare."* [6] But I shall only beseech you, O most clement King, by this your singular and most prudent goodness, to understand rather the desire of my heart, and the sovereign wish I have to obey your most excellent Majesty, ever since my eyes approached so nearly to your solar splendour, than the grandeur of my work can attain to or acquire.

Faciebat Michael Nostradamus.

(See Letter X-16, which shows how men of the Renaissance could ascribe such phenomena as floods to a conjuncture of the planets.)

6. "Many things, O most potent king of all, of the most remarkable kind are shortly to happen, that I neither could nor would interweave them all into this epistle; but in order to comprehend

IV-12   Sir Thomas Smith to Francis Walsingham

On 11 November, 1572, a brilliant star appeared in the Constellation
Cassiopeia and remained visible until March, 1574. The excitement it
created is echoed in the following lines of Sir Thomas Smith (1513-1577),
English scholar and statesman.

Hampton Court, 11 December, 1572

I am sure you have heard of, and I thincke you have seene the new faire Starre,
or Comett, but without beard or taile, which hath appeared here this three weekes,
over the backside of the Chaire of Casseopea, and on the edge of Lactea Via; [1]
bignes is betwixt the bignes of Jupiter and Venus, and keepes, to my appearance,
who have noe Instruments to observe it, and because of this cold weather alsoe
dare not, the precise order of fixed starres. Such an one never have I observed nor
read of. I pray you lett me knowe what your wise men of Paris doe judge upon it.
I knowe they will not thinke that it is the Admiralls soule, [2] as the Romans did of
the comett next appearinge after the murther of Julius Caesar, that it was his
soule. It may be as wee are now speakinge, out a farre of in the North, to see what
revenge shalbe done upon soe much inocent bloud shedd in Fraunce att a marriage
banquett, and rere suppers after it, yet would doe mee good yet to understand
what your Astronomers and Heuen-gazers there doe judge of it.

Yf I were not so much occupied as I am, I would turne over all my ould bookes
but I would saie somewhat of it myself, and guesse the chance even as wiselye as
they, though I would not publish it but to my friends; for follie the more it is kept
in the better.

Methinkes I heare you saye what a mischeefe meanethe hee to write unto mee

---

certain facts, a few horrible destinies must be set down in extract, although your amplitude and
humanity towards all men is so great, and your piety to the gods, and that you alone seem worthy of
the grand title of the most Christian King, and to whom the highest authority in all religion should be
deferred."

1. *Via Lactea* (also in IV-18), Milky Way.

2. Admiral Coligny, the Protestant leader killed during the St. Bartholomew's Day Massacres of
the previous August (see V-19).

of new Starres and Astronomers, and telleth me nothinge of my comeing home. Sir, if I should tell you any thinge hereof *de die et tempore,* I should but guesse as astronomers doe; but this I can tell you, all your frends hath not onelye bin dilligent, but more then importunate to bringe you home; and your wife with teares and lamentacions; and the Queenes Matie seemed to encline and graunt our requests, but when a pinn is sett fast in a hole, till wee have another to thrust that out, and tarry there itselfe, hard it is to gett it out: and you knowe how longe wee bee heere of resolvinge, and how easilye to be altered.

Yours, allwaies to be commaunded,
Tho. Smith.

IV-13   Sieur René de Lucinge to King Henri III

A creation of Greek mythology, the unicorn existed not only in heraldic designs and on tapestries, but in the minds of otherwise rational people. It was only natural that the Duc de Savoie should wish to buy back the giant unicorn horn that Brissac had taken from his grandfather in 1553. The King's intermediary Lucinge set its value at over 24,000 crowns.

Paris, 8 July, 1586

As I gather from the letters of Messer Chaffre, the difficulty Your Highness was having in acquiring the unicorn (horn) came from the fact that You didn't wish to pay cash. This made me resolve to stay on the good side of the man who has the power to sell it and to keep the dialogue going in a guarded way, telling him to put his intentions in writing since we had to come to terms. He gave me a memorandum on what he says is his final price, but Your Highness can beat him down in his asking price and can lengthen the period of payment, and will win out in every way. As for the value of the horn, if Your Highness would give 24,000 crowns, that would be in my opinion a good price. Jaçoy swears to me that he has refused 22,000 crowns from four merchants who wanted to sell pieces of it to make a profit, plus a thousand crowns for the wine of the man who delivered it. As for the matter of the bonus for the man who works out the contract, that depends on Your Highness's wishes. He asks for the premium in Paris, but would be willing to get it in Lyon or as a transfer of his salt-tax.*

Lucinge
(trans. R. J. C.)

IV-14   Fugger Correspondent at Dillingen to the Augsburg Bankers

A Fugger newsletter enumerates the evil practices imputed to Walpurga Hausmännin, a licensed midwife in Dillingen who confessed to witchcraft following torture and was burnt at the stake on September 20, 1587.

September 1587

The herein mentioned, malefic and miserable woman, Walpurga Hausmännin, now imprisoned and in chains, has, upon kindly questioning and also torture, following on persistent and fully justified accusations, confessed her witchcraft and admitted the following. When one-and-thirty years ago, she had become a widow, she cut corn for Hans Schlumperger, of this place, together with his former servant, Bis im Pfarrhof, by name. Him she enticed with lewd speeches and gestures and they convened that they should, on an appointed night, meet in her, Walpurga's, dwelling, there to indulge in lustful intercourse. So when Walpurga in expectation of this, sat awaiting him at night in her chamber, meditating upon evil and fleshly thoughts, it was not the said bondsman who appeared unto her, but the Evil One in the latter's guise and raiment and indulged in fornication with her. Thereupon he presented her with a piece of money, in the semblance of half a thaler, but no one could take it from her, for it was a bad coin and like lead. For this reason she had thrown it away. After the act of fornication she saw and felt the cloven foot of her whoremonger, and that his hand was not natural, but as if made of wood. She was greatly affrighted thereat and called upon the name of Jesus, whereupon the Devil left her and vanished.

     On the ensuing night, the Evil Spirit visited her again in the same shape and

---

* Brissac's contract asked for 30,000 crowns cash or 35,000 in installments, not a bad price for a mythical *objet d'art.*

whored with her. He made her many promises to help her in her poverty and need, wherefore she surrendered herself to him body and soul. Thereafter the Evil One inflicted upon her a scratch below the left shoulder, demanding that she should sell her soul to him with the blood that had flown therefrom. To this end he gave her a quill and, whereas she could not write, the Evil One guided her hand. She believes that nothing offensive was written, for the Evil One only swept with her hand across the paper. This script the Devil took with him and whenever she piously thought of God Almighty, or wished to go to church, the Devil reminded her of it.

Further, the above-mentioned Walpurga confesses that she oft and much rode on a pitchfork by night with her paramour, but not far, on account of her duties. At such devilish trysts she met a big man with a grey beard, who sat in a chair, like a great prince and was richly attired. That was the Great Devil to whom she had once more dedicated and promised herself body and soul. Him she worshipped and before him she knelt, and unto him she rendered other such-like honours. But she pretends not to know with what words and in which fashion she prayed. She only knows that once she heedlessly pronounced the name of Jesus. Then the above-mentioned Great Devil struck her in the face and Walpurga had to disown (which is terrible to relate) God in heaven, the Christian name and belief, the blessed Saints and the Holy Sacraments, also to renounce the heavenly hosts and the whole of Christendom. Thereupon the Great Devil baptized her afresh, naming her Höfelin, but her paramour-devil, Federlin.

At those devilish meetings, she ate, drank and fornicated with her paramour. Because she would not allow him to drag her along everywhere he had beaten her harshly and cruelly. For food she often had a good roast or an innocent child, which was also roasted, or a suckling pig, and red and white wine, but no salt.

Since her surrender to the Devil, she had seemingly oft received the Blessed Sacrament of the true Body and Blood of Jesus Christ, apparently by the mouth, but had not partaken of it, but (which once more is terrible to relate) had always taken it out of her mouth again and delivered it up to Federlin, her paramour. At their nightly gatherings she had oft with her other playfellows trodden under foot the Holy and Blessed Sacrament and the image of the Holy Cross. The said Walpurga states that during such-like frightful and loathsome blasphemies she at times truly did espy drops of blood upon the said Holy Sacrament, whereat she herself was greatly horrified.

At the command and threat of her whoremonger she had oft dishonoured the consecrated font, emptied it before her house or even destroyed the same. This she was made to do only a few days before she was cast into prison, when she was in the parish church from which she took a holy water stoup and carried it home.

Then her devil paramour arrayed in handsome garments encountered her in the little street between the great cloister and the stable of Martin Müller. He desired to take the holy water stoup out of her hand and forced her to hurl it against the wall. She had also been obliged sorely to dishonour the blessed Mother of God, the Holy Virgin Mary, to spit out in front of her and say: "Shame, thou ugly hussy!" Her paramour, Federlin, came to her in many divers places in order to fornicate with her, even in the street by night and while she lay in durance. She confesses, also, that her paramour gave her a salve in a little box with which to injure people and animals, and even the precious fruit of the field.

He also compelled her to do away with and to kill young infants at birth, even before they had been taken to Holy Baptism. This she did, whenever possible. These as follows:

1 and 2. About ten years ago, she had rubbed Anna Hämännin, who dwelt not far from Durstigel, with her salve on the occasion of her first childbirth and also otherwise damaged her so that mother and child remained together and died.

3. Dorothea, the stepdaughter of Christian Wachter, bore her first child ten years before; at its birth she made press on its little brain so that it died. The Devil had specially bidden her destroy the first-born.

4. Ten years ago she had poisoned with her salve the second child of Anna Kromt, who dwelt by the Altheim Gate, so that it died.

5. When, four years ago, the organist's wife was awaiting her confinement, she touched her naked body with her salve whereby the child promptly died and came stillborn.

6. Ten years ago she destroyed and killed at birth the girl child of the wife of the present tollman.

7. Twelve years ago she had killed at birth, with her salve and by strangulation, a girl child of the Pallingerin, who dwelt in a little house near the Danube baths.

8. Three years ago when she was called to a mill to the miller's wife there she had let the child fall into the water and drown.

9. Six years ago she was called to Eislingen to a poor woman who dwelt near the church. She killed the child by pressing on its brain at the time of delivery.

10. Eight or ten years ago she was called to Steinheim to a poor woman who lived on the other side of the river on the left bank. There also she killed the child by a special manipulation.

11. When six years ago, she partook of food with Magdalena Seilerin, called *Kammerschreiberin* (wife of the chamber scribe), she had put a salve in her drink, so that she was delivered prematurely. This child she, Walpurga, secretly buried under the doorway of the said wife of the scribe on the pretext that then she would have no other miscarriage. The same she also did with many others. When she was

questioned under torture for the reasons of this burial, she admitted that it was done in order to cause disunion between two spouses. This her Devil-Paramour had taught her.

12. A child of Stoffel Schmidt she had, four years ago, put to death and after dug out of the grave.

13 and 14. She confessed that, when, eleven years earlier, the spouse of the late Chancellor, Dr. Peuter, lay a long while in travail, she had rubbed a Devil's salve on the placenta, whereby she became so weak that she had to be given Extreme Unction. Three hours later, mother and child remained together and died.

15. She had also rubbed a salve on a beautiful son of the late Chancellor, Jacob by name: this child had lovely fair hair and she had given him a hobby-horse so that he might ride on it till he lost his senses. He died likewise.

16. Eight years ago she gave the rightfully wedded wife of Otto Vischer, when she was big with child, a drink, whereafter the child was born dead.

17-24. She did slay a child of each of the following: George Gopen, Sybilla Turnerin, the wife of Jäglein, Anna Seirin, Girg Gärtner, Klinger, the coppersmith Simon Leberwurst, the groom Hans Durst.

25. A child of the Governor here, Wilhelm Schenk von Stauffenberg, named Werner, she had so infected with her salve that he died within three days.

26 and 27. She had smeared and killed yet two other children of the Governor with her salve.

28 and 29. She had killed a boy child of both Master Niklas Brügelmaier and publican Kunz.

30. Three years ago she had sucked out the blood of publican Kunz's child, a twin, so that it died.

She confesses likewise, that the blood which she sucked from the child, she had to spit out again before the devil, as he had need of it to concoct a salve. She could work the children no harm if they were protected by holy water. But if she herself gave the child holy water, she was able to do it damage, as she had previously passed water into it.

31-43. She confesses that she killed a child of each of the following: Venedigerin, Hefelinin, Landstrasslerin, Fischerin, Eva auf der Bleiche, Weberin, the wife of the town scribe, Kautzin, Mechin, Weinzieherin, Berlerin and Martin Kautzin, but two of the Berlerin.

Only a short time since she had wished to smear with a salve the small boy of Georg Klinger, but she was encountered by people and was not able to achieve this.

She also rubbed the wife of the Governor with a salve, but as she wore a neck ornament with blessed medals on it the salve did not work.

In the foregone winter at eventide she had rubbed the housewife of the town scribe on the arm with her salve, shortly after she suffered great pain and to this day suffers day and night in spite of all the remedies she has tried.

When eight years ago she was helping Michel Klingler to push a cart, and Klingler wanted to lift the shafts with his head, she touched it with her salve. Since then, Klingler is fading away and death is the only thing before him.

To the daughter of Hans Striegel, who is now in the little cloister, she gave a drink in her youth, since when she languishes and is in bad health.

She rubbed with her salve and brought about the death of Lienhart Geilen's three cows, of Bruchbauer's horse, two years ago of Max Petzel's cow, three years ago of Duri Striegel's cow, two years ago of Hans Striegel's cow, of the cow of the Governor's wife, of a cow of Frau Schötterin, and two years ago of a cow of Michel Klingler, on the village green. In short, she confesses that she destroyed a large number of cattle over and above this. A year ago she found bleached linen on the common and rubbed it with her salve, so that the pigs and geese ran over it and perished shortly thereafter. Walpurga confesses further that every year since she has sold herself to the Devil, she has on St. Leonard's Day exhumed at least one or two innocent children. With her Devil-Paramour and other play-fellows she has eaten these and used their hair and their little bones for witchcraft.

She was unable to exhume the other children she had slain at birth, although she attempted it, because they had been baptized before God.

She had used the said little bones to manufacture hail; this she was wont to do once or twice a year. Once this spring, from Siechenhausen, downwards across the fields. She likewise manufactured hail last Whitsun, and when she and others were accused of having held a witches' revel, she had actually held one near the upper gate by the garden of Peter Schmidt. At that time her play-fellows began to quarrel and struck one another, because some wanted to cause it to hail over Dillingen Meadows, others below it. At last the hail was sent over the marsh towards Weissingen, doing great damage. She admits that she would have caused still more and greater evils and damage if the Almighty had not graciously prevented and turned them away.

After all this, the Judges and Jury of the Court of this Town of Dillingen, by virtue of the Imperial and Royal Prerogative and Rights of His Right Reverence, Herr Marquard, Bishop of Augsburg, and Provost of the Cathedral, our most gracious Prince and Lord, at last unanimously gave the verdict that the aforesaid Walpurga Hausmännin be punished and dispatched from life to death by burning at the stake as being a maleficent and well-known witch and sorceress, convicted according to the context of Common Law and the Criminal Code of the Emperor Charles V and the Holy Roman Empire. All her goods and chattels and estate left after her go to the Treasury of our Most High Prince and Lord. The aforesaid Walpurga to be led, seated on a cart, to which she is tied, to the place of her execution, and her body first to be torn five times with red-hot irons. The first time outside the town hall in the left breast and the right arm, the second time at the lower gate in the right breast, the third time at the mill brook outside the hospital gate in the left arm, the fourth time at the place of execution in the left hand. But since for nineteen years she was a licensed and pledged midwife of the city of Dillingen, yet has acted so vilely, her right hand with which she did such knavish tricks is to be cut off at the place of execution. Neither are her ashes after the burning to remain lying on the ground, but are thereafter to be carried to the nearest flowing water and thrown thereinto. Thus a venerable jury have entrusted the executioner of this city with the actual execution and all connected therewith.

IV-15   Henry Bossevyle to Lord Burghley

The advances of Renaissance medicine did not conquer the plague, or even gout. Sir Christopher Hatton sent to Queen Elizabeth a ring "to be worn betwixt the sweet duggs" to ward off the "infectious ayres" of the plague. Lord Burghley's gout was notorious, as were the remedies proposed to him, one offered him by the Earl of Shrewsbury being "oyle of stags blud." Another proposal came from Bossevyle.

Calais, 1592

For further explanacion of my talke had with your Lordship, and that it maye take the better impression, and forasmuche as your Lordship sayde you wolde gladly talke with me therein, I thoughte it necessarye to set downe my mynde in writinge touchinge that and other things which I have to speake of.

Touchinge the substance of the things that go to this cure, the Styll is used, and there are several waters, and severall things spred upon a certayne beast skynne made leather.

Concerninge the applyenge therof, one water muste bathe the place nere unto the payne, leavinge a joynte betwene the place of payne and the place that is bathed, yf conveniently it maye be. Then muste a peece of the sayde lether be cutte conveniente to make a playster, which muste be well moystned in one of the sayde waters, and thereon severall other things spredde, with playster muste be layde upon the place so bathed, there to remayne xij howers, and afterwardes there muste be freshe bathinge and playsters.

For the operacion therof, the paciente shall shortly fynde the humore stirred, blisters or pymples to rise out of the place where the playster is layde, out of which shall yssue the badde humore; some of which blisters wyll drye up, and others wyll unely breake out so longe as any parte of the humore remaynethe.

When all the badde humore is drawne out, they wyll drye up, and the patient shall fynde himself for the present cured, by havinge the use of his joynts as nymble as ever they were which were so afflicted, and afterwardes shall feele no more payne of the goute.

Nowe yf your Lordship beleve not that the goute is to be cured as I a good while did thinke, seinge that no phisician coulde do yt, yet I desire that your Lordship wyll suspende your judgemente, and that one, as sone as maye be, maye be soughte out who hathe the payne of the gowte notablye and which your Lordship by the advyse of your phisicians shall beleve to be so payned, upon whome I wyll applye these medecynes, and nothinge wyll I use which I wyll not in the presens of the patiente apply to my tunge; and when he is cured your Lordship schall se a difference betwene Alcumists and Phisicians, and then your Lordship maye bouldely deale with me. But this proviso I use herein that excepte your Lordship wyll accepte yt as done to your selfe; for I do affirme yt upon my faythe, that besides the laboure and charges of the things that go to the cure of this which maye be so precious as for the quantetye maye come to above CCCC. or v. C pounds, yt hathe coste me more fayre goulde then I thinke was ever geoven in England for a medecyne.

And forasmuche as I can not satisfye my conscience to come to churche, and that yf your Lordship move not presently her Majestie, some one will begge my lyvinge, I do beseeche your Lordship to get it yourselfe. And yf I performe this cure which I doute not to do, I shall be worthye to have it bestowed on me by your Lordship, with other reasonable favors and yf I do it not then your Lordship maye make your gayne of my livinge as you shall thinke good.

Your Lordships ever at commaundment

in all he can,

Henry Bossevyle.

IV-16   Galileo Galilei to Johannes Kepler

The correspondence which follows provides a glimpse of the exchange of ideas between Galileo Galilei (1564-1642), the Italian physicist and astronomer who built the first complete astronomical telescope and was thus able to confirm the heliocentric theory advanced by Copernicus, and Johannes Kepler (1571-1630), a German astronomer who was Tycho Brahe's assistant and successor. In this first letter, Galileo greets Kepler as a confrère in the pursuit of truth.

Padua, 4 August, 1597

Your book, highly learned gentleman, which you sent me through Paulus Amberger, reached me not days ago but only a few hours ago, and as this Paulus just informed me of his return to Germany, I should think myself indeed ungrateful if I should not express to you my thanks by this letter. I thank you especially for having deemed me worthy of such a proof of your friendship. . . . So far I have read only the introduction, but have learned from it in some measure your intentions and congratulate myself on the good fortune of having found such a man as a companion in the exploration of truth. For it is deplorable that there are so few who seek the truth and do not reject a wrong method of philosophizing. But this is not the place to mourn about the misery of our century but to rejoice with you about such beautiful ideas proving the truth. So I add only this promise that I will read your book in peace, for I am certain that I will find the most beautiful things in it. . . . I would certainly dare to approach the public with my ways of thinking if there were more people of your mind. As this is not the case, I shall refrain from doing so. The lack of time and the ardent wish to read your book make it necessary to close, assuring you of my sympathy. I shall always be at your service. Farewell, and do not neglect to give me further good news of yourself.

Yours in sincere friendship,
Galilaeus Galilaeus
Mathematician at the Academy of Padua

IV-17   Johannes Kepler to Galileo Galilei

In his reply, Kepler exhorts Galileo to be unswerving in following his course to its furthest limits and, moreover, suggests that the intellectual climate of Germany might be more hospitable to their common enterprise.

Graz, 13 October, 1597

I received your letter of August 4th on September 1st. It was a double pleasure to me. First, because I became friends with you, the Italian, and second because of the agreement in which we find ourselves concerning Copernican cosmography. As you invite me kindly at the end of your letter to enter into correspondence with you, and I myself feel greatly tempted to do so, I will not let pass the occasion of sending you a letter with the present young nobleman. For I am sure, if your time has allowed it, you have meanwhile obtained a closer knowledge of my book. And so a great desire has taken hold of me, to learn your judgment. For this is my way, to urge all those to whom I have written to express their candid opinion. Believe me, the sharpest criticism of one single understanding man means much more to me than the thoughtless applause of the great masses.

I would, however, have wished that you who have such a keen insight [into everything] would choose another way [to reach your practical aims]. By the strength of your personal example you advise us, in a cleverly veiled manner, to go out of the way of general ignorance and warn us against exposing ourselves to the furious attacks of the scholarly crowd. (In this you are following the lead of Plato and Pythagoras, our true masters.) But after the beginning of a tremendous enterprise has been made in our time, and furthered by so many learned mathematicians, and after the statement that the earth moves can no longer be regarded as something new, would it not be better to pull the rolling wagon to its destination with united effort. . . . For it is not only you Italians who do not believe that they move unless they feel it, but we in Germany, too, in no way make ourselves popular with this idea. Yet there are ways in which we protect ourselves against these difficulties. . . . Be of good cheer, Galileo, and appear in public. If I am not mistaken there are only a few among the distinguished mathematicians of

Europe who would dissociate themselves from us. So great is the power of truth. If Italy seems less suitable for your publication and if you have to expect difficulties there, perhaps Germany will offer us more freedom. But enough of this. Please let me know, at least privately if you do not want to do so publicly, what you have discovered in favor of Copernicus.

Now I want to ask you for an observation; as I possess no instruments I must turn to other people. Do you possess a quadrant which shows minutes and quarterminutes? If so, then, please, observe at about the time of the 19th of December the smallest and the largest altitude of the middle star of the tail in the great dipper. Likewise observe about December 26th both heights of the polar star. Also observe the first star about the 19th of March 1598 in its height at midnight, the second about September 28th, also around midnight. If, as I wish, there could be shown a difference between the two observations of one or another minute or even 10' to 15', this would be proof of something of great importance for all astronomy. If there is no difference shown, however, we shall earn all the same together the fame of having become aware of an important problem hitherto not noticed by anybody. [Fixed star parallax]. . . Farewell and answer me with a very long letter.

IV-18   Sir Henry Wotton to the Earl of Salisbury

Sir Henry Wotton (1568-1639), the English poet and diplomat, heralds the advances in astronomy made by a certain mathematical professor at Padua, destined for either renown or infamy. Curiously, he does not mention Galileo by name.

13 March, 1610

Now touching the occurrences of the present, I send herewith unto his Majesty the strangest piece of news (as I may justly call it) that he hath ever yet received from any part of the world; which is the annexed book (come abroad this very day) of the Mathematical Professor at Padua, who by the help of an optical instrument (which both enlargeth and approximateth the object), invented first in Flanders, and bettered by himself, hath discovered four new planets * rolling about the sphere of Jupiter, besides many other unknown fixed stars; likewise, the true cause of the *Via Lactae,* so long searched; and lastly, that the moon is not spherical, but endued with many prominences, and, which is of all the strangest, illuminated with the solar light by reflection from the body of the earth, as he seemeth to say. So as upon the whole subject he hath first overthrown all former astronomy—for we must have a new sphere to save the appearances—and next all astrology. For the virtue of these new planets must needs vary the judicial part, and why may there not yet be more? These things I have been bold thus to discourse unto your Lordship, whereof here all corners are full. And the author runneth a fortune to be either exceeding famous or exceeding ridiculous. By the next ship your Lordship shall receive from me one of the above-named instruments, as it is bettered by this man.

* i.e., satellites

IV-19   Johannes Kepler to Galileo Galilei

Continuing his encouragment, Kepler professes admiration for his friend's discoveries made possible with the improved telescope, and scorns the ignorance of those who choose to remain in darkness.

Prague, 9 August, 1610

I have received your observations on the Medicean stars * from the Ambassador of his Highness the Grand Duke of Tuscany. You have aroused in me a passionate desire to see your instruments, so that I at last, like you, might enjoy the great performance in the sky. Of the oculars which we have here the best has a tenfold enlargement, the others hardly a threefold; the only one which I have gives a twentyfold enlargement, but the light is very weak. The reason for this is not unknown to me and I see how the intensity could be improved, but one hesitates to spend the money.

. . . In my opinion, no one is entitled to charge a person with having taken over

* *Sidera Medicea,* named for Galileo's former pupil and future employer, Cosimo II, Grand Duke of Tuscany.

another's ideas unless he is able to recognize and . . . understand the new, rare, and beautifully original ideas which the other has pronounced. To me it is an insult . . . if someone wants to praise me because of my reputation in order to slander others. Nothing annoys me more than the praise of such a man; what an outcast of a human being! He fantastically ascribes to me doubts about the value of your discoveries, because I allow everyone his own opinion. What lack of judgment! The considerations of others need not necessarily be in accord with my own. Regarding something as true, I am, nevertheless, able to tolerate others who are not of the same opinion.

. . . O, you wise Pythagoras, who believed that the majesty of philosophy is present in nothing but silence! But now the die is cast. You, my Galileo, have opened the holy of the holiest of the skies. What else can you do but despise the noise which has been created. . . . The crowd takes vengeance on itself by remaining in eternal ignorance in consequence of its contempt for philosophy.

IV-20   Galileo Galilei to Johannes Kepler

Galileo confesses his sense of frustration at having his theories rejected by the foolish masses, unyielding in their refusal to acknowledge material evidence.

Padua, 19 August, 1610

. . . What is to be done now? Shall we follow Democritus or Heraclitus? We will laugh at the extraordinary stupidity of the crowd, my Kepler. What do you say to the main philosophers of our school, who, with the stubbornness of vipers, never wanted to see the planets, the moon or the telescope although I offered them a thousand times to show them the planets and the moon. Really, as some have shut their ears, these have shut their eyes towards the light of truth. This is an awful thing, but it does not astonish me. This sort of person thinks that philosophy is a book like the Aeneid or Odyssey and that one has not to search for truth in the world of nature, but in the comparisons of texts (to use their own words).

Why have I no time to laugh a little longer with you! How you would burst out laughing, my dear Kepler, if you would hear what the greatest philosopher of the "Gymnasium" told the Grand Duke about me when, with logical reasons as if they were magic formulas, he wanted to tear the planets from the heavens and dispute them away till nothing was left of them! But night begins, I cannot continue to chat with you. Farewell, highly learned gentleman, and continue to show your good will toward me.

IV-21   Joseph Mead to Sir Martin Stuteville

Among the three or more great plagues to strike London, one of the worst was that of 1625, as reported by the Cambridge theologian Joseph Mead (1586-1638).

Cambridge, 30 July, 1625

Sir

Hoping to be at Dalham on Monday I shall need write the less. Blessed be God, we are yet well at Cambridge. The Burials at London are, this Week 3583; whereof they bring of the plague 2471: so that there remain 1112 for other diseases; that is, for the Invisible Plague, for so I take near a thousand of that sum to be. You may see by the note I sent you at the commencement how much this Plague, for the time and number, surpasses that of 1603. August is called the month of corruption, which is not yet come. Lord, what will become of the distressed City then! Remember O Lord thy wonted mercies, and take pity upon their Affliction! I send you the Clerks Bill. You shall not need be afraid of it. It hath lain by me these three weeks. I had a sheet of them. This is the last, whereinto I transcribed with mine owne hand the numbers out of the King's Bill at the Bookbinders.

Concerning the former week we are here certainly informed that there died then in Westminster, Stepney, and Lambeth, &c. (places never counted in the Bill) near eight hundred and forty; whereby we may guesse what number is like to have died in the same place this week.

I send you a Corranto,* brought me besides expectation, and almost against my will; but it was well aired and smok't before I received it, as our Lettres all used to be; nor was the Plague then in Paule's Church yard, whence it came.

* gazette, newspaper

'Tis true that the Masters, Fellows, Heads, and Principals, and Students at Oxford are by Letters of the Council commanded away for the better accommodating the Parliament.

One of the King's Guard died of the Plague at Windsor about last Saturday: whereupon the King, being not far thence, returned no more thither as he was purposed.

Yours most ready to be commanded
Joseph Mead.

IV-22   Vincenzio, Cardinal da Firenzuola to His Holiness the Pope and Cardinal
Barberini

By 1633 the Holy Office leveled charges of heresy at Galileo, with the death penalty the most likely outcome. Shortly before the final trial, Cardinal Vincenzio da Firenzuola convinced Galileo to confess to a lesser crime and obtain a lesser sentence. As Firenzuola the following day wrote to the Pope and Cardinal Barberini, Galileo capitulated. The Inquisitors punished him, however, sentencing him to a life of silence and imprisonment in his home in Tuscany.

28 April, 1633

Most Eminent and Reverend Patron:

Yesterday, in accordance with orders from His Holiness, their Eminences of the Holy Congregation took up the case of Galileo, reviewing its state briefly. And having approved what has been done thus far, they then considered various difficulties as to the manner of prosecuting the case, and getting it speedily under way again. In particular, because Galileo denied in his hearing that which is evident in the book he wrote, it would necessarily follow from his negative attitude that there would be greater rigor in the proceedings, and less regard for the delicacies in this business. Finally I proposed a means: that the Holy Congregation grant me power to deal extra-judicially with Galileo to the end of convincing him of his error, and bringing him to the point, when he understood, of confessing it. It appeared at first sight too daring a proposal; there seemed little hope of succeeding by means of reasonable persuasion; but when I mentioned my basis for advancing the idea, they gave me the power. And not to lose time, I went to reason with

Galileo yesterday after luncheon, and after many exchanges between us, I gained my point by the grace of God, for I made him see plainly his error, so that he clearly knew he was in the wrong, and that in his book he had gone too far. This he expressed in heartfelt words, as if he found consolation in the recognition of his error. He agreed to confess it judicially, but he asked me for a little time to make honest *(honestare)* his confession, which I hope will in substance follow the line mentioned. I felt obliged to let you know at once, having told no one else, so that His Holiness and you will be satisfied that in this way the case can be brought to a point where it can proceed without difficulty. The Tribunal will maintain its reputation *(sarà nella sua reputatione),* and may use benignity with the accused. However it turns out, Galileo will recognize the grace accorded him, and all the other satisfactory consequences that are desired will follow. Today I plan to examine him to obtain the confession; and, with it in hand, as I hope, nothing will remain but to interrogate him on intention and permit him his defenses; this done, it will be possible to return him to his house for imprisonment as you mentioned to me.

Your Reverence's servant,
Vincenzio [Maculano] da Firenzuola

CHAPTER 5

RELIGION.
REFORMATION AND
COUNTER-REFORMATION.
THE NEW BIBLES.
CENSORSHIP.
THE INQUISITION.

X. *Ecstasy of Saint Teresa* by Bernini

Humanism was more than a new ideal of learning. It was a cult, capable of rivaling the Church of Rome. The Platonist Marsilio Ficino burned a candle continuously before a bust of Plato. The young group of Pléiade poets, if we believe them, burned a goat to Bacchus in the forest of Arcueil. In Vida's epic poem on the Saviour, the Redeemer is referred to as Heros and his disciples as senators. Other forces menacing the orthodoxy and authority of the Roman Church were the Protestants, the Turkish Muslims, and the Jews—in that order. The Turkish menace, as letters in Chapter VII will show, became almost as great a threat as North European Protestantism. If the Spaniard Loyola came too late to stem Protestantism on the continent (as he effectively did in Asia and South America), other Spaniards removed the Turkish threat to Catholic Europe in 1572 at the Battle of Lepanto (VII-14).

As Protestantism unleashed its questions of and challenges to the Church, critics censured more openly the corruption and intemperance of the Roman clergy, alleging greed, simony, nepotism, pluralism, and moral laxity. It was widely noted in contemporary writing that wealth could buy a cardinal's red hat, and the popes were obviously scions of such wealthy families as the Medici and Della Rovere. Even Emperor Maximilian of Austria dickered, as we read below, to buy his way to the papacy (V-1). An ironic letter of Aretino claims typically that shame, rather than honor, fares well at the papal court. In his correspondence, we find Fray Antonio de Guevara suggesting that priests never be left alone with married women. And John Ap Rice reported that women of dubious status frequented the monasteries in England (V-10).

The Lutheran Revolt took issue on such traditional elements as the cult of saints, idolatry, relics, miracles, confession, Lent, papal infallibility, all the sacraments save two—and of course, indulgences. Alfonso de Valdés wrote to Pietro d'Anghiera a fact which history has subsequently confirmed, that the Reformation erupted over the wholesale selling of indulgences (V-6). The fallacy of the concept of buying and selling indulgences was of course a major *casus belli* with Luther, and he decried to the Elector Albert the common people's being told in sermons that "if they buy these letters of indulgence, their own salvation is assured" (V-3). Another issue was that of divorce, available only to the moneyed and the powerful—to some kings like Henri IV but not to others like Henry VIII, who married the pregnant Anne Boleyn before a homemade annulment to

Catherine could be contrived. To avoid divorce proceedings with Anne, he resorted simply to the axe (IX-8).

The Reformational adherents felt in general that faith and a good conscience did not need to be supported by rituals, nor did an individual require priests as intermediaries with God. Luther felt, as did Staupitz, that repentance involved a true change of attitude rather than reliance on some ritualistic act. Most of all, as he complained to Pope Leo X, the Roman Church forbade that such basic issues be discussed among colleagues at his University of Wittenberg (V-4). This complaint was echoed by the painter Albrecht Dürer, one of many Germans indignant that Luther's works were burned rather than discussed. The point of no return in the relations of Luther with Leo X was reached on 6 September, 1520, when the Augustinian friar suggested that the Pope had become a veritable anti-Christ and idol (V-7). Another evidence of the break with Rome is Zwingli's letter suggesting that it made more sense for the Swiss theologian to consult with Jews than with Roman Catholics on interpretations of certain Biblical texts (V-8).

Whereas previous generations had depended on Churchmen for knowledge and interpretation of Holy Writ, always based on the approved Vulgate, the spread of printing permitted access not only to the Latin text, but to vernacular translations of which the Church disapproved, translations such as those by Luther and Lefèvre d'Etaples. Even with the approval of his own bishop, Erasmus was condemned by many for translating the New Testament into Latin without authorization from a general council (V-2). The great schism of the Church centered on still another major issue, the very nature and form of the universe. As we saw in the previous Chapter, the Biblical scholars and theologians saw the Scripture approving the old Ptolemaic concept of a geocentric universe, despite the evidence of the new telescopes. Even as the Church created a golden legend of martyred Humanists, including Berquin, Aneau, Dolet, and others, it obstinately condemned Copernicus, Galileo (IV-22), Bruno, Campanella, and other scientists. The Protestants, having rejected the concept of excommunication and more alert to new ideas, had little difficulty accepting the heliocentric universe.

Renouncing the formal rites and acts of the Church in favor of a greater reliance on faith, a generation of Evangelists, like the Jesus cults of twentieth-century youth, set to emulating the Christ of the New Testament, making an ethic of humility, humanitarianism, renunciation of worldly goods, simplicity of religious service, and free examination of Scripture. Most believed that the interpretation of Scriptural text undertaken in good conscience by an intelligent man was as valid as the exegeses of a pope, bishop, or council. This would include Erasmus's Latin translation of the New Testament (V-2) or the Geneva Bible translated by the English Protestants in Switzerland. The position taken on free examination of Scripture by Luther and later by Calvin launched the sustained conflict between Protestants and Catholics which was never settled, although in recent times ecumenical conferences of clerics from the two factions have attempted to conciliate their differences.

Rare was the Protestant or Anglican who returned "to the Roman side," as Donne put it. Yet, as we learn from Calvin's letter to Bullinger, Lutherans, Calvinists, Anglicans, and other Reformed sects diverged on many points of doctrine, and a united front was impossible. Calvin even feared that local dissidents in Geneva were spreading the plague against himself (V-15). Calvin, of whom Henry VIII approved and later disapproved, also worried that in the Reformed Church of England "idle gluttons are supported who chant vespers in an unknown tongue," i.e. Latin (V-16). He also railed at the lack of unity in the French Church in London, whose leaders have "stirred up conflicts" against him.

The increasing sense of nationalism in the Renaissance was a factor contributing to the Reformation, and Counter-Reformation as well. Critics of the Roman Church objected to the flow of monies, fees, and gifts to Rome as well as the spiritual domination of an Italian majority in the College of Cardinals. Individual monarchs like Francis I, Henry VIII, and even the converted Henri of Navarre came to grips with Rome over taxation, confiscation of Church property, jurisdictional issues, and canon law. Henry VIII's attempts to force Thomas More, even in the Tower, to acknowledge Henry as spiritual head of the English Church are described in More's letter to his daughter Margaret (V-9). No one more vigorously than Queen Elizabeth, in her tirade against the five Catholic bishops of England (V-17) questioned the Roman Church's claim to be the legitimate guardian of Christianity. Church loyalties determined national alignments and hostilities. Henri of Navarre takes Paris with the help of the Protestant Queen Elizabeth and the opposition of Catholic Spain, only to offend her grievously by converting to Catholicism (VI-20). The anti-papist English fight in the Lowlands—among them Sir Philip Sidney (VII-15)—to keep out the Catholic Spaniards. Even the local wars of the Scottish Highlanders against Queen Elizabeth are motivated largely by religion. So were also the nine religious wars in France, highlighted by the St. Bartholomew's Day massacre (V-19 and V-20).

Renaissance letters reveal the extent to which the Roman hierarchy mobilized its forces to counter-attack. It instituted inquisitional courts and *autos da fé* against Protestants, Jews, heretics (by its own definition), and other opponents, not forgetting scientists. It lit fires to burn the devil out of witches (IV-4), a public entertainment provided also, alas, by Protestant communities. The ruthlessness of the Seville Inquisition's interrogations and punishments of the Englishman Thomas Pery make uncomfortable reading (V-11). (The Spanish Humanist Luis Vives wrote a famous letter to Erasmus in 1534, complaining that in Spain it had become dangerous to speak out and dangerous to keep silent.) It censored the shelves of the booksellers and in 1559 Pope Paul IV established the Index of Forbidden Books, listing those works which offended the Church's morality, questioned its doctrine, or challenged its authority. Even the great musician Monteverdi had to plead for the life of his son Massimiliano, who had read or owned a book on the Index (V-24).

Not all Churchmen during the first half of the sixteenth century were against Humanism. Cardinal Bembo and Erasmus were examples of Christian Humanists, as was Cardinal Grimani, of whom Erasmus has left such a flattering portrait. Erasmus indeed states to Servatius why, although he is at ease with the greatest of Churchmen, he cannot become a priest or monk. Yet the great Christian Humanist Thomas More found his religious scruples leading to a personal disaster (V-9), while the scholar-poet Torquato Tasso was left a schizophrenic by his fears of censure by Annibal Caro or even the Inquisition (II-6).

If the period of the Counter-Reformation left Europe largely split between a Protestant North and a Catholic South—an irony, since the greatest Mediaeval cathedrals were mainly in the Northern zone—the militant Jesuits carried the competition to other areas outside Europe. As suggested above, under Ignatius Loyola (1491-1556) they gained vast areas for Catholicism in Asia, North and South America before the end of the century (VIII-11 and VIII-12). Loyola's letters show an admixture of dedication and discipline with a personal warmth, as well as a determination to triumph over his enemies, detractors, and persecutors, a determination expressed to King John of Portugal (V-14). Despite the repressive decisions of the Council of Trent (1545-63), the Church continued to be a lavish patron of—and sometimes stabilizing influence on—fine arts, literature, music, education, and philosophy. A hard taskmaster sometimes, as we saw from Chapters II and III, but the one great Maecenas of the Renaissance.

A symbolic peace followed the long religious wars in France when the convert Henri IV tried to conciliate both factions and in 1598 issued the Edict of Nantes granting freedom of worship to the Protestants (V-22). This ecumenical spirit did not protect the Jews, however, and we read of their being persecuted in the Prague ghetto at the turn of the century (V-23).

We have not mentioned a parallel defender of the Church whose egregious energy and vision, combined with a remarkable administrative and promotional talent, built up the widespread order of the Barefoot Carmelites. This was the nun Teresa of Avila (V-21).

V-1   Maximilian I to Paul von Liechtenstein

Believing Pope Julius to be on the brink of death, Maximilian I (1459-1519), Holy Roman Emperor, makes elaborate arrangements to buy his way into the papacy.

September 1511

We do not doubt that you still hold in fresh remembrance our notification, given you some time ago, concerning the reasons for which we desired and intended to seek the papacy, if we can achieve it; about which we have thought from time to time. Now we find in our heart, and indeed it is true, that nothing would more honourably, highly, or better become us than to receive the said papal office.

And since now Pope Julius, who just a short time ago was most deathly ill and, as has been reported to you by our court and Tyrolean Chancellor, Cyprian von Seretin, everyone in Rome was of the opinion that he had died, we have therefore decided to pursue our intention as far as possible and have taken actions and steps to attain the papacy; and thereupon we have now suggested the plan to Cardinal Adrian, who for some time, as you know, has been out here in Germany with us. He advises us strongly in favour of it, and believes there will be no difficulty with the cardinals, and on hearing of our plan he wept for joy.

Since, as you yourself may well imagine and realize, the pope may now die, which is wholly to be expected (for he eats little, and what he does eat is nothing but fruit, and he drinks so much more that as a result his life seems precarious), since, as I say, he may die, the bishop of Gurk has been dispatched by us to post to Rome to help us behind the papal throne. But since this matter cannot well be carried through without a notable sum of money which we must place and invest in it, we have decided, to fulfil our aforesaid purpose, and on the agreement and promise of assistance from the cardinal and various other persons, to raise up to three hundred thousand ducats, and to transmit, order, and agree to the same only through the Fugger Bank in Rome. You know, however, that at the present time we do not have the money on hand, and also that it is not in our power to satisfy the said Fugger for this sum of money except by depositing our crown jewels as security. We therefore command with all earnestness that from this hour and most expeditiously you shall inform Fugger of these matters in the most fitting manner (as you well know how to do), secretly, and in consideration of the duty with which he is bound to us as our councillor, and our great concern with them, and that he should thereupon with the greatest and best diligence, to our honour and satisfaction, arrange it that the aforesaid three hundred thousand ducats for this business be deposited in his bank in Rome. He should also make sure that his agents will certainly give out and pay the money to those who are presented to them by our princes and dear reverent Matthias, Bishop of Gurk, and other of our ambassadors whom we shall send to Rome. And you shall agree and promise to give reasonable interest as is mentioned, and for that purpose give him promissory notes from the bank, as is customary.

In return we shall give him as security the four best chests of treasure, including our robes of investiture, those that do not belong to the Empire but to the house of Austria, and which, if we get the papacy, we will no longer need—for if for the greater honour we have ourselves crowned emperor beforehand, we will use the robes of the sainted Duke Charles, which we intend to take with us. And you are to arrange that he shall send immediately to Rome, to the hands of the said Bishop of Gurk, ten thousand ducats in cash or bills of exchange, either on account of the above determined sum or on your promise (for which we will guarantee you), and that for the above mentioned reasons and because of our special reliance on him, he shall not refuse or delay. We therefore will send you, as soon as you gain our wish from Fugger—write to us immediately and quickly, day or night—sufficient instructions, receipts, and other documents to transfer quickly to Fugger the chests and robes mentioned above.

And if Fugger during these negotiations wishes to know how we will again redeem these our treasures and robes, which he will have in his possession, you shall inform and indicate to him that we intend to pay the said sum of three hundred thousand ducats, and in addition we are willing to give him one hundred thousand ducats for his three jewels which we also wish to have from him—although they are not worth the said sum—but still as secret interest on his loan; which then will make a grand total of five hundred and thirty-three thousand florins Rhenish. This sum will be drawn from the imperial aids, which we will get from the estates of the Empire at the next Reichstag; similarly from the future aids of our hereditary principalities and lands, and taxes, and in addition the money which is always sent us annually by our dear brother the King of Spain, and it will all be allocated to the redemption of our treasure. But if all this should not reach the required sum, we shall then, for the rest, transfer a third of all our income from the papacy until it is all paid. Therefore, let him send one of his friends, whoever he pleases, to us at our court. We will make him our treasurer or master of the exchequer to handle our income and also to receive and collect his third part, and we will also use him in other of our affairs. . . .

We add also for your information that our secretary, Johann Colla, wrote us today by a special post that the Orsini, the Colonna, and the Roman populace have wholly decided and determined not to have or to accept any pope who is French or Spanish or who is supported by one of these states.

(It was through the financial backing of the Fuggers that Maximilian's grandson, Charles V, acquired the Imperial Crown. See Letter VI-5.)

V-2   Desiderius Erasmus to Henry Bullock

A great scholar and theologian, Desiderius Erasmus (1466?-1536) proves his right on ethical and logical grounds to publish the New Testament in its original language with a revised Latin translation. Although addressed to Henry Bullock, a Fellow of Queen's College where Erasmus had once been resident, this letter was undoubtedly intended for circulation in the University at Cambridge.

Rochester, August, 1516

I gather from your letter, that mine, which I left with Thomas More in London, had not yet been delivered to you. . . . I am truly glad to hear that the New Testament, as restored by our industry, is approved at Cambridge by the best people; although I have been told by some credible persons that one of the most theological of your colleges, composed of pure Areopagites, has passed a serious resolution that no one shall either by horse, or boat, or cart, or porter bring that volume within the precincts of the college. I beseech you, most learned Bullock, ought one to laugh or weep over such proceedings?

They say it is wrong to attempt such a work unless by the authority of a general council. But I should like to have an answer from them to this question. Was that very version, of which they are so fond, undertaken by the translator under the authority of a general council, or was it first published, and afterwards approved by the judgment of the Fathers? I believe it was written first, and approved afterwards; and the same may take place with respect to my edition, though that is a thing I neither solicit nor expect. But I have conceded too much; it is more probable that the received version crept into use, and only gained strength by the progress of time. For if it had been approved and promulgated by the public judgment of a council, it would have been in universal use. As it is, one text is cited by Ambrose, another by Augustine, another by Hilary, and another by Jerome. Indeed the copies now in use do not agree. So that, if they think the Christian religion is upset if there is any variation in any part of the book, we were already subject to that risk, though we may have been sleeping through it.

But, say they, the received version is used by the Fathers in their synods. But it remains to be proved that the passages cited in the acts of councils differ from our emendation; while it must be remembered that most of the proceedings of councils were conducted in Greek. And finally it may well be that passages originally cited in another form have been changed by some copyist to our present version, as we constantly find has been done in the Commentaries of Jerome and Ambrose. About twenty years ago the Missal and Book of Hours were being printed at Paris according to the usage of the Church of Treves; but the printer, who had but a smattering of learning, when he found there were many discrepancies, corrected everything according to our usual version, as he himself confessed to me, thinking he was doing a fine thing! Again, I do not think it absurd to suppose that an error may pass unnoticed by a general council, especially in matters not necessary to salvation. It is enough that what is enacted in the synod itself cannot be censured. Finally, why are we more alarmed at a various reading in the Sacred Books than we are at a various interpretation? Surely there is equal danger in both cases. And we constantly find that the explanations given are not only different but conflicting.

Again, let them clear up, if they can, this dilemma. Do they allow any change to be made in the sacred text, or absolutely none at all? If any, why not first examine whether a change is rightly made or not? If none, what will they do with those passages where the existence of an error is too manifest to be concealed? Will they desire to follow the example of the priest who, having been used to say *mumpsimus* for twenty years, refused to change his practice when told that he ought to read *sumpsimus?*

Suppose I had explained all the Sacred Books in a Paraphrase, so that they might, without injury to the sense, be read with less stumbling and be more easily apprehended, would your friends bring me to book for this? Juvencus, who ventured to turn the Gospel history into verse, gained some praise by his work. And who calls to account that great divine, Aegidius Delphus, who embraced almost all the Scriptures in a poem? The Psalms are sung every day in church according to the old edition; and yet there is Jerome's recension, and also his translation after the Hebrew original. The former is read in choirs, the latter in schools or at home; and the one does not interfere with the other. Indeed Felix Pratensis has lately issued a new translation of the whole Psalter, differing considerably from all the former ones, and who has raised any outcry against him? My friend, Jacques Lefèvre of Etaples,* had already done for St. Paul what I have done for the whole New Testament; and why are some people disturbed on this occasion, as if nothing of the kind had happened before? Do they intend to refuse to me alone a liberty they allow to everyone else? Lefèvre, however, has ventured much further than I. He has set up his own translation in opposition to the old, and that in Paris, the queen of all the universities. I, professing only to be a reviser, either correct or explain a few passages. In saying this, I have no intention of casting any reflection upon Lefèvre, who by his high reputation has long raised himself above reflection; I wish only to make it manifest, how unfair it is, when a thing has been constantly done by a number of people without any blame, to reproach me for doing it, as if it were something unprecedented.

What have the Aristotelians lost, since Argyropulos, Leonardus Aretinus, and Theodorus Gaza brought out a new edition? Will it be held that their version ought to be suppressed or abolished, to save those earlier professors of Aristotelian philosophy from the appearance of having been ignorant of some particulars? Or is William Cop prevented from translating the books of Galen and Hippocrates by the fear of letting the world know that former physicians have put a false interpretation on many passages?

But it will be said that what is expedient in human science is a serious danger, if applied to the Sacred Books in all parts and by anyone who pleases. Now in the first place I do not change all parts, for there is only a question about a few passages, the main substance remaining unaltered. Neither do I quite think that I am to be regarded, with reference to this matter, as one of the ordinary crowd. I show how in some places Hilary has been mistaken. So of Augustine, and Thomas Aquinas. And this I do, as it ought to be done, reverently and without contumely, so that, if they were themselves alive, they would thank me, whatever I might be, for setting them right in such a way. They were men of the highest worth, but they were men. Let my opponents prove that they were right, and refute me by argument, and I shall be greatly obliged to them.

But they think it beneath them to descend to these small details of grammarians. For so they call those who have learned Good Letters, thinking the name of grammarian a severe reproach, as if it were a credit to a theologian not to know grammar. It is true that the mere knowledge of grammar does not make a

---

* A protégé of King Francis I. Jacques Lefèvre d'Etaples published the first complete translation of the Bible into French.

theologian; still less does ignorance of it; and certainly some scholarship conduces to a knowledge of theology, while the want of it impedes such knowledge. Indeed it cannot be denied that Jerome, Ambrose, and Augustine, on whose authority our theological system mainly rests, belonged to the class of grammarians. For at that time Aristotle had not yet been received in the theological schools, and the Philosophy which is now in use there was not yet born. But a modest man will not object to be set right by anyone. "Though he be blind that shows the way, you still may pay him some regard," as Flaccus says.

Again, those who make the whole question depend not on judgment but on authority cannot find any great defect in my case. It was provided in the late Lateran Council that a book, before it is published, shall be approved by the Ordinary or his delegates. Now our book was both written and published with the knowledge and approbation of the bishop of the place, and that no common bishop, but one who, not to speak of the reverence due to his age or of the dignity of his birth, is distinguished by a singular integrity of life and no common learning. Indeed he not only approved my work but made me every possible offer, if I had been willing to remain with him; and when I left, pursued me with such kind offices and with so much munificence that I am ashamed to recall the circumstances. Not content with this, he wrote of his own accord to the Archbishop of Canterbury, both commending me in most honourable terms and thanking him on my behalf. So that, if my labour has not been approved by a synod, it has at any rate been approved according to the ordinance of a synod. And the person approving is of such authority that he alone may well stand in the place of many; while his vote ought to have all the more weight, as it was not obtained by any solicitation or obsequious attentions, but was spontaneously offered and almost forced upon me. And if the authority of a single person is wanting in weight, the bishop's judgment has been backed by two professors of theology, who are at the head of that profession. One of these is Louis Bère, a man so practised in the theological arena as to have earned the first place at Paris among the doctors of that faculty. He disapproved our work so much that he offered to share with me all his fortune, which is most ample; and has spontaneously put at my disposal one of the two prebends which he holds. The other is Wolfgang [Capito], who on account of his distinguished theological knowledge has been chosen one of the Chapter of Basel Cathedral, where he fills the office of public preacher, a man who, besides other accomplishments, is pre-eminently skilled in three tongues, Greek, Latin, and Hebrew, and finally is a person of so much integrity and piety that I have never seen anything more stainless. These were the witnesses to the publication of my book, in whose judgment the bishop upon the gravest matter would not hesitate to confide, if he was not certain of his own.

Neither indeed have any other theologians condemned our work. Only some have lamented that they did not learn Greek when they were boys, and that for them the book has come into the world too late. . . .

We sent last winter one volume to [Pope] Leo, to whom it is dedicated, and if it has been delivered, I do not doubt that he will requite our vigils with the highest rewards.

What is it, then, that these people find deficient in me? I have not been the first to take this matter in hand; I have not done it without consideration; and I have followed the rule of the synod. If anyone is influenced by learning, my work is approved by the most learned; if by virtue, it is approved by the most upright; if by authority, it is approved by bishops, by archbishops, by the pope himself. Nevertheless I do not desire to obtain any advantage from their support, if it be found that I have solicited the favour of any of them. Whatever support is given, has been given to the cause, and not to the man.

Are your friends perhaps afraid that, if students are attracted to these subjects, their schools will be emptied? Let them take these facts into consideration. About thirty years ago nothing was taught at Cambridge but Alexander, the *Parva Logicalia,* as they are called, those old "dictates" of Aristotle, and questions from Scotus. In process of time Good Letters were introduced; the study of Mathematics was added, and a new or at least a renovated Aristotle. Then came some acquaintance with Greek, and with many authors, whose very names were unknown to the best scholars of a former time. Now I ask, what has been the result to the university? It has become so flourishing that it may vie with the first schools of the age, and possesses men compared with whom those old teachers appear mere shadows of theologians. This is not denied by the senior men, where you find any of a candid character. They congratulate others on their good fortune, and lament their own infelicity.

Are your friends displeased that in future the Gospels and Apostolic Epistles will be read by more persons and with more attention? Are they grieved to see even this portion of time devoted to studies, on which all our time would be well bestowed? And would they prefer that our whole life should be consumed in the useless subtleties of "Questions"? Is it not well to recall such divines to the original sources?

I have a sure presentiment that posterity will form a more candid judgment of my lucubrations, such as they are; though I have no cause to complain even of my own age. It has rated me higher—I do not say than I ask, but than I either deserve or can justify.

I approve of your having adopted the practice of public preaching, and congratulate you on your success, especially as you teach Christ in simplicity, without any display of the subtleties of men. . . . Farewell, most learned Bullock.

V-3   Martin Luther to the Elector Albert of Mainz

By 24 the archbishop of both Magdeburg and Mainz, the Elector Albert (of Mainz) needed 20,000 guilders to pay for the dispensation to hold two archbishoprics simultaneously. Pope Leo X consented to his selling indulgences to raise money, provided the papacy received one of every two guilders collected. Luther (1483-1546), a monk under Albert's jurisdiction, attacked the orthodoxy of indulgences as well as their morality, adding a vague threat to launch a campaign against them among the people. Albert merely sent a formal report on Luther's letter to Rome.

Wittenberg, 31 October, 1517

To the Most Reverend Father in Christ, the most Illustrious Lord, Baron Albert, Archbishop and Primate of the Churches of Magdeburg and Mainz, Marquis of Brandenburg, etc., my own Superior and Pastor in Christ, held in all due honour and respect, most gracious.

Jesus [1]

May God give you all the grace and mercy that exist, most reverend Father in Christ, and most illustrious Prince. Pardon me, if I, a man of no standing, should yet have the temerity to think of writing to your Sublime Excellency. The Lord Jesus is my witness that I am well aware that I am of mean condition and no consequence; and I have therefore long deferred doing what I am now making bold to do. Above all else, I am urged by my duty of loyalty to you, a duty which I acknowledge I owe you, my most Reverend Father in Christ. Perhaps then, your Excellency will deign to look on me who am but dust, and, of your episcopal clemency, give heed to my request.

Papal indulgences for building St. Peter's are being carried round under the

---

1. It was Luther's almost invariable custom to invoke the name of Jesus before settling down to write. The name was given a full line to itself and was set out distinctly, and apart from the rest.

authority of your most distinguished self. The purpose of the protest I am now making is not concerned with the substance of the message which the preachers proclaim so loudly; for I have not myself actually heard them; but I do deplore the very mistaken impressions which the common people have gained, and which are universally current among the masses. For example, the poor souls believe that if they buy these letters of indulgence, their own salvation is assured. Again, that souls are liberated from purgatory at the very moment that contributions are cast into the chest. Further, that these indulgences are of so effective a grace that there is no sin too great to be wiped out by them, even if, as they say, *per impossible,* it consisted in having violated the mother of God. Again, that these indulgences free a man from all punishment and guilt. God have mercy on us! That is how those committed to your care, good Father, are taught to regard death. It will be very hard for you to render your account for them all, and it will grow still harder. That is why I have not been able to keep silence any longer about these things. For no man is assured of salvation by a gift, be it conferred by a bishop, since such an assurance is not given even by the infused grace of God; rather the Apostle bids us always to work out our salvation in fear and trembling, and, we read, "the righteous shall scarcely be saved." Moreover, so narrow is the way that leads to life that the Lord, speaking through the prophets Amos and Zechariah, calls those who shall be saved "brands plucked from the burning." Indeed the Lord points everywhere to the difficulty of being saved. Why then do the preachers utter those falsehoods, and give promises of pardons, and make the people feel safe and unafraid? At no time do indulgences give anything advantageous to the salvation or sanctity of the soul; at best they only do away with the external punishments, which it has hitherto been the custom to impose according to canon law.

Moreover, works of piety and love are infinitely preferable to indulgences. Yet it is not of these that they preach with great pomp and authority; rather, they pass these works over in silence, in order to proclaim the indulgences. Nevertheless, the prime and sole duty of all bishops is to teach the people the gospel and the love of Christ. Christ nowhere commands the preaching of indulgences, but He insistently commands that the gospel should be preached. Then what a dreadful thing it is, and how great the peril of a bishop, who says nothing about the gospel, but readily allows indulgences to be noised abroad among his people in preference to the gospel! Will not Christ say to him, "You are straining at a gnat and swallowing a camel"? [2]

In addition, there is this fact, Most Reverend Father in the Lord, that an "Instruction" to the sub-commissioners has been issued in your name, Reverend Father, but surely without the knowledge and consent of your Fatherly

2. *Matt.* 23:24

Reverence. This "Instruction" declares that one of the chief graces of these indulgences is God's incalculable gift, whereby a man is reconciled to God, and all the pains of purgatory are abolished; also, that there is no need for contrite hearts on the part of those who pay for souls to be redeemed from purgatory, or who buy the tickets of indulgence.

What am I to do, best of primates and most illustrious of princes, except pray your Most Fatherly Reverence in the name of Jesus Christ to deign to give your paternal attention to this matter, and totally withdraw those summary instructions altogether, and order the indulgence preachers to adopt another style of preaching. Otherwise, it may happen that someone will arise, publish his own summary instructions, and confute those preachers and the present instructions. This will bring your Most Illustrious Sublimity into the greatest disrepute, an event which I should heartily detest; yet I fear that it will happen unless appropriate steps are taken immediately.

I beg your Most Illustrious Grace to accept my humble and dutiful respects in the manner of a prince and a bishop: with the utmost clemency, since I put them forward in good faith, and I am entirely devoted to your Most Fatherly Reverence; and because I am also a member of your flock. May the Lord Jesus guard your Most Fatherly Reverence for ever. Amen.

Wittenberg, 1517. Eve of All Saints. If it please your Fatherly Reverence, you may glance at the theses of mine enclosed herewith, and see how dubious is the question of indulgences, although these people are broadcasting them as if it were most indubitable.

Your unworthy son,
Martin Luther,
Augustinian, Doctor of Sacred Theology.

V-4   Martin Luther to Pope Leo X

By May 1518 the widespread attacks on Martin Luther's ideas on confession, the sale of indulgences, free examination of Scripture, etc. had branded him a heretic to many. Concerned, he wrote to Pope Leo X (1475-1521) requesting support for his freedom to discuss these issues and to protest that his theses were being attacked without being examined.

May, 1518

To the most blessed father Leo X *pontifex maximus,* Friar Martin Luther, Augustinian, wishes eternal welfare.

Holy Father, the worst of reports are in circulation about my own self. I understand that even certain friends of mine have seriously defamed my reputation, and put me in bad odour with you and those around you. I am made out to be one who is undermining the authority and power of the keys and the supreme bishop. Consequently I have been called heretic, apostate, infidel, and 600 other ignominious names. I am horrified and astounded by what I hear and see. Nevertheless, my confidence remains unshaken on account of the fact that I have kept an innocent and peaceful conscience. Moreover, my foes are saying nothing new, even when those whose own consciences are very uneasy, have thrown at me, even in this district, the kind of epithets that would suit themselves. They have tried to impose their own monstrosities on me, and to make their own baseness shine and look splendid in contrast with what they call my shame. But you will deign to hear the truth of the matter from me, though I am but a child and ignorant of courtly language.

The Indulgences of the Apostolic Jubilee have been preached among us quite recently. Matters have already gone to such a length that the preachers have come to think they possessed every licence, owing to the authority attaching to your name; they have even openly dared to teach very impious heresies. This has caused the most serious scandal, and brought derision on the church's authority. They act as if the decretal, *de abusionibus quaestorum,*[1] in no way applied to them. Nor have the preachers been satisfied with spreading this poison of theirs orally, for they have published pamphlets and distributed them among the masses. I will pass over the insatiable and unheard-of avarice with which almost every word they utter positively reeks; but, in these pamphlets, they put forward the same impious heresies as they preach. They put them forward and enjoin them in such a way that priests in confessional are bound by oath to teach them to the people, word for word and most insistently. I am speaking the truth, and none can deny it. The pamphlets are there and cannot be disowned. They sold so well, and the people were carried away so completely by false hopes, that, as the prophet says, "they tore the flesh from the people's bones." Meanwhile the preachers themselves enjoyed the richest and most comfortable fare.

They allayed scandal by one means only, viz.: the honour in which your name is held, the threat of the stake, and the shame of being called heretic. It is unbelievable how prone the preachers are to utter threats, even when they are aware that it is only their own nonsensical notions that are really in question; as if

---

1. Dealing with the method of collecting funds for the church.

this kind of preaching were the way to allay scandal, and not rather to cause schisms and seditions by their very arrogance!

In spite of all, however, tales began to spread in the taverns about the greed of the priests, and other things derogatory to the keys and the Supreme Pontiff, as witness common talk everywhere hereabouts. I confess that I myself was on fire out of zeal for Christ, as it seemed to me, or out of the hotheadedness of youth, as you may think. Yet I did not think that it was my place to make a public protest. Therefore I gave a private warning to certain prelates of the church. I was heeded by some, laughed at by more, and regarded askance by others. The honour in which your name was held, and the threat of ecclesiastical censure, prevailed upon them to do nothing. Then, when no other course was open, I thought it right to show at least a modicum of opposition to the preachers; I therefore called their doctrines into question, and proposed a public debate. I therefore published a list of theses, and invited only the more scholarly to a discussion with me, if they so wished. This should be obvious, even to my adversaries, from the preface to those very theses.

That is the fire which, they complain, has set the whole world alight. Perhaps, they are indignant with me becaase, as a teacher of theology by your own Apostolic authority, I have the right to conduct public debates. This is customary in all universities and the whole church. I have the right, not only to debate indulgences, but also God's power, His forgiveness, and His mercy, which are incomparably greater matters. Yet I am not greatly disturbed that they should envy my having been granted this privilege by the authority of your Holiness. Unfortunately, I cannot avoid accusing them of far more serious matters, viz.: that they mix up irrelevant notions of Aristotle's with matters theological, and put forward purely nonsensical arguments contrary to, and beyond, the terms of reference which they have received.

I am at a loss, indeed, to know why it is fated that these particular theses of mine and no others, whether of mine or of any other teachers, should have spread throughout almost the entire country. They were made public at the university of Wittenberg, and intended only for this university. They were made public in such a manner that it seems incredible that all and sundry could understand them. They are theses; they are neither teachings nor doctrines; as is customary, they are cast in obscure and ambiguous language. If I could have foreseen what would happen, I should certainly have done my part to see that they were more fully intelligible.

As things are, what am I to do? I cannot recall them; and yet I see that I have inflamed against myself an astonishing amount of ill-will once they were published and sold among the masses. I am unwilling to stand or fall by the mere voice of popular opinion with its dangers and differences, especially as I am not a learned man, but a person of dull wits and poor scholarship. In these flourishing times, with the skill in letters and learning that now prevails, it would be easy to corner even Cicero, although in his own time he was held in no mean public esteem. But I am constrained to speak by necessity, though I must croak like a crow among blackbirds.

Thus, in order to mollify adversaries and meet the wishes of many friends, I am sending herewith these all too inadequate explanations of my theses. I am sending them, too, Holy Father, in order that I may be the safer by having your approval as my defence, and your shadow as a protection. By these means, all who so desire will understand that I am simply seeking to maintain the authority of the church and only wanting to add to the respect for the Keys. At the same time also, all mankind will understand how sinful and false it has been when my adversaries have spoken about me in disgraceful terms. If I had been of the sort they try to make me out; and if, on the contrary, I had not done everything strictly in accordance with the regulations for public disputations, that Most Illustrious Prince, Frederick Duke of Saxony, Imperial Elector, etc., would not possibly have suffered me to be a nuisance in his university. He himself holds Catholic and Apostolic truth too dear. Nor would the keen and learned men of this university have borne with me. But I have been able to do what has been done because these men, very loyal to your court as they are, do not fear the outcome even although the prince and the university risk being involved openly in the same opprobrium as I myself. Wherefore, Holy Father, I fling myself prostrate at the feet of your Holiness with all that I am and all that I have. Revive, kill, call, recall, approve, reprove, as it pleases you. I shall acknowledge your voice as the voice of the Christ who is enthroned in you, and who speaks through you. If I merit death, I shall not refuse to die. For the earth is the Lord's and the fullness thereof.[2] He is blessed for ever. Amen, and may He have you for ever in His keeping.

V-5   Albrecht Dürer to Georg Spalatin

Albrecht Dürer (1471-1528), the most important German Renaissance painter, makes known his desire to draw a portrait of the admired Martin Luther in this letter to Georg Spalatin, Chaplain to Duke Friedrich "the Wise," Elector of Saxony. It was due to Spalatin's influence that Duke

2. Ps. 24:1

Friedrich refused to implement the papal bull against Luther in 1520 and later had him conveyed to Wartburg Castle for his protection.

Nürnberg, Early 1520

Most worthy and dear Master, I have already sent you my thanks in the short letter, for then I had only read your brief note. It was not till afterwards, when the bag in which the little book was wrapped was turned inside out, that I for the first time found the real letter in it, and learnt that it was my most gracious Lord himself who sent me Luther's little book. So I pray your worthiness to convey most emphatically my humble thanks to his Electoral Grace, and in all humility to beseech his Electoral Grace to take the praiseworthy Dr. Martin Luther under his protection for the sake of Christian truth. For that is of more importance to us than all the power and riches of this world; because all things pass away with time, Truth alone endures for ever.

God helping me, if ever I meet Dr Martin Luther, I intend to draw a careful portrait of him from the life and to engrave it on copper, for a lasting remembrance of a Christian man who helped me out of great distress. And I beg your worthiness to send me for my money anything new that Dr Martin may write.

As to Spengler's "Apology for Luther," about which you write, I must tell you that no more copies are in stock; but it is being reprinted at Augsburg, and I will send you some copies as soon as they are ready. But you must know that, though the book was printed here, it is condemned in the pulpit as heretical and meet to be burnt, and the man who published it anonymously is abused and defamed. It is reported that Dr Eck wanted to burn it in public at Ingolstadt, as was done to Dr Reuchlin's book.

With this letter I send for my most gracious lord three impressions of a copper-plate of my most gracious lord of Mainz, which I engraved at his request. I sent the copper-plate with 200 impressions as a present to his Electoral Grace, and he graciously sent me in return 200 florins in gold and 20 ells of damask for a coat. I joyfully and thankfully accepted them, especially as I was in want of them at that time.

His Imperial Majesty also, of praiseworthy memory, who died too soon for me, had graciously made provision for me, because of the great and long-continued labour, pains, and care, which I spent in his service. But now the Council will no longer pay me the 100 florins, which I was to have received every year of my life from the town taxes, and which was yearly paid to me during his Majesty's life-time. So I am to be deprived of it in my old age and to see the long time, trouble, and labour all lost which I spent for his Imperial Majesty. As I am losing my sight and freedom of hand my affairs do not look well. I don't care to withhold this from you, kind and trusted Sir.

If my gracious lord remembers his debt to me of the stag-horns, may I ask your Worship to keep him in mind of them, so that I may get a fine pair. I shall make two candlesticks of them.

I send you here two little prints of the Cross from a plate engraved in gold. One is for your Worship. Give my service to Hirschfeld and Albrecht Waldner. Now, your Worship, commend me faithfully to my most gracious lord, the Elector.

Your willing Albrecht Dürer

V-6   Alfonso de Valdés to Pietro Martire d'Anghiera

Sometimes called the Spanish precursor of the Reformation, Alfonso de Valdés (1490-1532) was, like his correspondent Erasmus, a critic of Rome who remained within the Church. A disciple, or at least a friend of Pietro d'Anghiera, he reveals to d'Anghiera his fear that Lutheranism will divide Europe irrevocably.

Brussels, 31st August, 1520

That which you would fain learn from me, as to the origin and progress of the Lutheran sect, which has recently sprung up among the Germans, I am now about to write to you, if without elegance, at least with accuracy, relating things conscientiously, as I have heard them from persons worthy of credit.

I think you are already aware that Pope Julius II had begun to erect, in the city of Rome, a temple dedicated to the Prince of the Apostles, at incredible expense, and exceeding in the vastness of its proportions all similar structures, with good reason thinking it indecorous that the Prince of the Apostles should be meanly lodged, particularly since men, from religious motives, repair thither from all parts of the world. And this greatest and most magnanimous of men would have finished the mighty work had he not been taken off by death during the process of its erection.[1]

1. This immense and costly mausoleum, never completed, is the subject of Letter III-11, in which Michelangelo complains of having sacrificed to it his youth and manhood.

Leo X succeeded him, who, not having adequate funds to defray the large outlay, sent throughout Christendom the amplest absolutions, or pardons, commonly called indulgences, for those who should contribute offerings for the erection of the temple; he thought that by such means he should clear an immense sum of money, getting it especially from the Germans, whose veneration for the Church of Rome was singularly loyal. But as there is nothing firm and stable in human affairs—nothing that is not destroyed either by the damage brought by time or by the malice of men—so it is a fact that these indulgences have brought it to pass that Germany, which surpasses in religion every other Christian nation, may now actually see itself left behind by them all.

For as a certain Dominican was preaching in Wittenberg, a city in Saxony, and urging the people to purchase these pontifical indulgences, from which this friar himself netted no mean profits, an Augustinian monk, of the name of Martin Luther, and the author of this tragedy, came forward, possibly moved by envy of the Dominican, and published certain printed propositions, in which he affirmed that the Dominican attributed to his indulgences effects much greater than the Roman pontiff either did or could concede. The Dominican, having read the propositions, was inflamed with wrath against the Augustinian, and the dispute between the monks was exasperated both by injurious expressions and by arguments—the one defending his sermon, and the other defending his propositions; so that the Augustinian, with the characteristic audacity of the wicked, began to disparage the papal indulgences, and to say that they had been devised, not for the welfare of the Christian body, but to satisfy sacerdotal avarice; and from this point the monk proceeded to discuss the powers of the Roman pontiff.

Here you have the first scene of this tragedy, which we owe to monkish animosity. For since the Augustinian envies the Dominican, and the Dominican, in his turn, the Augustinian, and both of them the Franciscan, what else shall we expect but the gravest dissensions? And now let us come to scene the second.

Frederick, the Duke of Saxony, and Albert, the Cardinal Archbishop of Mainz, were, as Electors, colleagues in the election of Roman emperors; the former, who was not on the best of terms with the latter, had heard that Albert made much money by these indulgences, the prelate and the pope having agreed to share the money thus obtained between them. In the meanwhile the duke, who sought an opportunity to deprive the archbishop of these gains, did not let slip that presented by an audacious monk, who, ready for any bad action, had stood forward to declare war against the pontifical indulgences. Accordingly, the duke seized upon all the money in the hands of the so-called commissaries, which had been collected in his duchy, saying that "he intended to appoint a man, one of his subjects, in Rome, to present that money to the fabric of St. Peter, who should, at the same time, see to the proper expenditure of the other sums which had been collected for that purpose in other parts of Germany." But the pontiff, on whom it devolves to guard the liberties of the Church, and not to permit profane princes to intermeddle in things solely within the province of the Roman pontiff, warned the duke once and again, both by letters couched in the most affectionate terms, and by nuncios specially sent to Germany, that he should not act so injuriously to the apostolic seat, but should refund the confiscated moneys, which the duke obstinately refused to do; whereupon the pontiff, going to the other extreme, declared him excommunicated.

Then the Augustinian, having gained the duke's favour, assured him, with great hardihood, that such a sentence was invalid, because iniquitous, for the Roman pontiff could excommunicate no one unjustly; and he began, through printed circulars, which were spread with facility and rapidity throughout all Germany, to publish many and grave things against the Roman pontiff and the Romanists. Luther, moreover, exhorted the Duke of Saxony not to be driven, by dread of the papal anathema, from the determination he had once formed. Furthermore, he declared that the temper of the Germans was getting irritated by long contemplation of the worse than profane habits of the Romanists, and that they had secretly begun to devise how to loosen and shake off the yoke of the Roman pontiff, which was accomplished when Luther's writings were first published, and received with general admiration and applause. Then the Germans, showing their contempt for the Romanists, evinced at the same time their intense desire, and they demanded it too, that there should be convened a general council of all Christians, in which, those things being condemned, against which Luther had written, better order might be established in the Church. Would to God that this had been realized! In the meanwhile the pontiff obstinately guards his rights and fears lest Christians should hold a meeting; for (to speak freely) his particular interests, which might possibly be endangered by a general council, weigh more with him than the welfare of Christendom. He is also anxious to have Luther's writings suppressed without discussion, and has sent a Legate *a latere* to Maximilian, to procure, amongst other things, that silence be imposed on Luther by the emperor's authority and that of the whole Roman empire.

They then convened a general diet, an Imperial parliament, at Augsburg, a celebrated city of Germany, where Luther appeared, having been summoned by an Imperial decree, and where he defended his writings with great power; whereupon Cajetan [2] had to enter upon the arena. Cajetan—for such was the legate's name—alleged that "a monk ought not to have a hearing, who had written so many blasphemies against the Roman pontiff." And the Estates of the Empire, in their turn, declared "that it was an iniquitous thing to condemn a man unheard,

2. See Letter V-7, note 4.

or without having previously convinced him and compelled him to retract those very writings which he declared himself ready to defend. That if this Cajetan (a man, as you know, profoundly versed in polemics) could convince Luther, they were ready (both the emperor and the Estates of the Empire) to pass sentence on him." Thus Cajetan, seeing that he should make no progress unless he combatted Luther face to face, which he had attempted once but came off unsuccessfully, departed, leaving the affair unsettled. Luther was dismissed with greater glory than that with which he had been received—with a victor's joy. Alas! that human relations are so prone to ill: relying upon the Duke of Saxony's protection, he wrote and published, with fresh vigour, new dogmas opposed to the apostolic institutions.

The pope, seeing that he could, neither by caresses nor by warnings, cause the deserved punishment to be imposed upon the blasphemous monk, in order that he might not diffuse the poison which he scattered on every side with impunity, and that all might flee the man declared a heretic and schismatic, launched a most severe bull, as they call it, against Luther and Luther's partisans.

Luther, much more irritated than dismayed by this proceeding (oh, shame!), proclaimed the pontiff himself a heretic and schismatic, and issued a pamphlet, entitled *De captivitate babylonica ecclesiae (The Babylonian Captivity of the Church)*, in which—Eternal God!—he combats the decrees and statutes of councils and popes, and with what artifices! In it he affirms that John Huss was iniquitously condemned by the Council of Constance, and that he, Luther, would defend as orthodox all those propositions of his which had been condemned. And not content with this, he publicly burned all the books on Roman law that he could find in Wittenberg, saying that "they perverted and contaminated the Christian religion, and that for this reason they ought to be destroyed."

The report of these events, spread throughout all Germany, excites to such an extent the minds of the Germans against the apostolic seat that if the prudence and piety of the pontiff, or the good star of our emperor, in conjunction with a general council, do not come to the relief of these evils, I fear, and I do very much fear, that this evil will spread so widely as to be absolutely incurable. It has appeared to me to be my duty to describe these things, writing them here on the spot, and I hope by so doing to gratify you. Farewell.

V-7   Martin Luther to Pope Leo X

The bull Pope Leo issued in June 1520, ordering the burning of Luther's writings and demanding that he publicly recant on pain of excommunication, was met by the publication of new reforming manifestoes. Urged by the peacemaker Carl von Miltitz to try to conciliate His Holiness, Luther complied by sending the pontiff his third pamphlet, *A Treatise on Christian Liberty,* along with the following letter, hardly a note of apology.

Wittenberg, 6 September, 1520

JESUS.

To Leo the Tenth, Pope at Rome: Martin Luther wishes thee salvation in Christ Jesus our Lord. Amen.

In the midst of the monsters of this age with whom I am now for the third year waging war, I am compelled at times to look up also to thee, Leo, most blessed Father, and to think of thee; nay, since thou art now and again regarded as the sole cause of my warfare, I cannot but think of thee always. And although the causeless raging of thy godless flatterers against me has compelled me to appeal from thy See to a future council, despite those most empty decrees of thy predecessors Pius and Julius, who with a foolish tyranny forbade such an appeal, yet I have never so estranged my mind from thy Blessedness as not with all my heart to wish thee and thy See every blessing, for which I have, as much as lay in me, besought God with earnest prayers. It is true, I have made bold almost to despise and to triumph over those who have tried to frighten me with the majesty of thy name and authority. But there is one thing which I cannot despise, and that is my excuse for writing once more to thy Blessedness. I understand that I am accused of great rashness, and that this rashness is said to be my great fault, in which, they say, I have not spared even thy person.

For my part, I will openly confess that I know I have only spoken good and honorable things of thee whenever I have made mention of thy name. And if I had done otherwise, I myself could by no means approve of it, but would entirely approve the judgment others have formed of me, and do nothing more gladly than recant such rashness and impiety on my part. I have called thee a Daniel in Babylon, and every one who reads knows with what zeal I defended thy notable innocence against thy defamer, Sylvester.[1] Indeed, thy reputation and the fame of thy blameless life, sung as they are throughout the world by the writings of so many great men, are too well known and too high to be assailed in any way by any one man, however great he may be. I am not so foolish as to attack him whom every one praises: it has rather been, and always will be, my endeavor not to attack even those whom public report decries; for I take no pleasure in the crimes of any man, since I am conscious enough of the great beam in my own eye, nor could I be he that should cast the first stone at the adulteress.

I have indeed sharply inveighed against ungodly teachings in general, and I have not been slow to bite my adversaries, not because of their immorality, but because of their ungodliness. And of this I repent so little that I have determined to persevere in that fervent zeal, and to despise the judgment of men, following the example of Christ, Who in His zeal called His adversaries a generation of vipers, blind, hypocrites, children of the devil. And Paul arraigned the sorcerer as a child of the devil full of all subtilty and mischief, and brands others as dogs, deceivers and adulterers. If you will allow those delicate ears to judge, nothing would be more biting and more unrestrained than Paul. Who is more biting than the prophets? Nowadays, it is true, our ears are made so delicate by the mad crowds of flatterers that as soon as we meet with a disapproving voice we cry out that we are bitten, and when we cannot ward off the truth with any other pretext we put it to flight by ascribing it to a fierce temper, impatience and shamelessness. What is the good of salt if it does not bite? Or of the edge of the sword if it does not kill? Cursed be he that doeth the work of the Lord deceitfully.

Wherefore, most excellent Leo, I pray thee, after I have by this letter vindicated myself, give me a hearing, and believe that I have never thought evil of thy person, but that I am a man who would wish thee all good things eternally, and that I have no quarrel with any man concerning his morality, but only concerning the Word of truth. In all things else I will yield to any man whatsoever: to give up or to deny the Word I have neither the power nor the will. If any man thinks otherwise of me, or has understood my words differently, he does not think aright, nor has he understood what I have really said.

But thy See, which is called the Roman Curia, and of which neither thou nor any man can deny that it is more corrupt than any Babylon or Sodom ever was, and

1. Sylvester Prierias.

which is, as far as I can see, characterized by a totally depraved, hopeless and notorious wickedness—that See I have truly despised, and I have been incensed to think that in thy name and under the guise of the Roman Church the people of Christ are mocked. And so I have resisted and will resist that See, as long as the spirit of faith shall live in me. Not that I shall strive after the impossible or hope that by my lone efforts anything will be accomplished in that most disordered Babylon, where the rage of so many sycophants is turned against me; but I acknowledge myself a debtor to my brethren, whom it is my duty to warn, that fewer of them may be destroyed by the plagues of Rome, or at least that their destruction may be less cruel.

For, as thou well knowest, these many years there has flowed forth from Rome, like a flood covering the world, nothing but a laying waste of men's bodies and souls and possessions, and the worst possible examples of the worst possible things. For all this is clearer than the day to all men, and the Roman Church, once the most holy of all, has become the most licentious den of thieves, the most shameless of all brothels, the kingdom of sin, death and hell; so that even Antichrist himself, should he come, could think of nothing to add to its wickedness.

Meanwhile thou, Leo, sittest as a lamb in the midst of wolves, like Daniel in the midst of the lions, and, with Ezekiel, thou dwellest among scorpions. What canst thou do single-handed, against these monsters? Join to thyself three or four thoroughly learned and thoroughly good cardinals: what are even these among so many? You would all be poisoned before you could undertake to make a single decree to help matters. There is no hope for the Roman Curia: the wrath of God is come upon it to the end; it hates councils, it fears a reformation, it cannot reduce the raging of its wickedness, and is meriting the praise bestowed upon its mother, of whom it is written, "We have cured Babylon, but she is not healed: let us forsake her." It was thy duty, indeed, and that of thy cardinals, to remedy these evils, but that gout of theirs mocks the healing hand, and neither chariot nor horse heeds the guiding rein. Moved by such sympathy for thee, I have always grieved, most excellent Leo, that thou hast been made pope in these times, for thou wert worthy of better days. The Roman Curia has not deserved to have thee or men like thee, but rather Satan himself; and in truth it is he more than thou who rules in that Babylon.

O would that thou mightest lay aside what thy most mischievous enemies boast of as thy glory, and wert living on some small priestly income of thine own, or on thy family inheritance! To glory in that glory none are worthy save the Iscariots, the sons of perdition. For what dost thou accomplish in the Curia, my dear Leo? Only this: the more criminal and abominable a man is, the more successfully will he use thy name and authority to destroy the wealth and the souls of men, to increase crime, to suppress faith and truth and the whole Church of God. O truly, most unhappy Leo, thou sittest on a most dangerous throne; for I tell thee the truth, because I wish thee well. If Bernard pitied his Pope Eugene [2] at a time when the Roman See, although even then most corrupt, yet ruled with better prospects, why should not we lament who have for three hundred years had so great an increase of corruption and worthlessness? Is it not true that under yon vast expanse of heaven there is nothing more corrupt, more pestilential, more hateful than the Roman Curia? It surpasses the godlessness of the Turks beyond all comparison, so that in truth, whereas it was once a gate of heaven, it is now an open mouth of hell, and such a mouth as, because of the wrath of God, cannot be shut; there is only one thing that we can try to do, as I have said: perchance we may be able to call back a few from that yawning chasm of Rome and so save them.

Now thou seest, my Father Leo, how and why I have so violently attacked that pestilential See: for so far have I been from raging against thy person that I even hoped I might gain thy favor and save thee, if I should make a strong and sharp assault upon that prison, nay that hell of thine. For thou and thy salvation and the salvation of many others with thee will be served by every thing that men of ability can contribute to the confusion of this wicked Curia. They do thy work, who bring evil upon it; they glorify Christ, who in every way curse it. In short, they are Christians who are not Romans.

To go yet farther, I never intended to inveigh against the Roman Curia, or to raise any controversy concerning it. For when I saw that all efforts to save it were hopeless, I despised it and gave it a bill of divorcement and said to it, "He that is filthy, let him be filthy still, and he that is unclean, let him be unclean still." Then I gave myself to the quiet and peaceful study of holy Scripture, that I might thus be of benefit to my brethren about me. When I had made some progress in these studies, Satan opened his eyes and filled his servant John Eck,[3] a notable enemy of Christ, with an insatiable lust for glory, and thereby stirred him up to drag me at unawares into a disputation, laying hold on me by one little word about the primacy of the Roman Church which I had incidentally let fall. Then that boasting braggart, frothing and gnashing his teeth, declared that he would venture all for the glory of God and the honor of the holy Apostolic See, and, puffed up with the hope of misusing thy power, he looked forward with perfect confidence to a victory over me. He sought not so much to establish the primacy of Peter as his own leadership among the theologians of our time; and to that end he thought it no small help if he should triumph over Luther. When that debate ended unhappily

2. Pope Eugene III, 1145-1153, for whom Bernard of Clairvaux wrote a devotional book, De consideratione, in which he rehearsed the duties and the dangers of the pope.

3. John Maier, born in Eck an der Günz, and generally known as John Eck; an ambitious theologian, who first attacked his professor in Freiburg, then Erasmus' Annotations to the New Testament, and next wrote against Luther's XCV Theses. He was the opponent of Luther and Carlstadt at the Leipzig Disputation (1519), to which Luther here refers.

for the sophist, an incredible madness overcame the man: for he feels that he alone must bear the blame of all that I have brought forth to the shame of Rome.

But permit me, I pray thee, most excellent Leo, this once to plead my cause and to make charges against thy real enemies. Thou knowest, I believe, what dealings thy legate, Cardinal of St. Sixtus,[4] an unwise and unfortunate, or rather, unfaithful man, had with me. When, because of reverence for thy name, I had put myself and all my case in his hand, he did not try to establish peace, although with a single word he could easily have done so, since I at that time promised to keep silent and to end the controversy, if my opponents were ordered to do the same. But as he was a man who sought glory, and was not content with that agreement, he began to justify my opponents, to give them full freedom and to order me to recant, a thing not included in his instructions. When the matter was in a fair way, his untimely arbitrariness brought it into a far worse condition. Therefore, for what followed later Luther is not to blame; all the blame is Cajetan's, who did not suffer me to keep silent and to rest, as I then most earnestly asked him to do. What more should I have done?

Next came Carl Miltitz,[5] also a nuncio of thy Blessedness, who after great and varied efforts and constant going to and fro, although he omitted nothing that might help to restore that status of the question which Cajetan had rashly and haughtily disturbed, at last with the help of the most illustrious prince, Frederick the Elector, barely managed to arrange several private conferences with me. Again I yielded to your name, I was prepared to keep silent, and even accepted as arbiter either the archbishop of Treves or the bishop of Naumburg. So matters were arranged. But while this plan was being followed with good prospects of success, lo, that other and greater enemy of thine, Eck, broke in with the Leipzig Disputation which he had undertaken against Dr. Carlstadt. When a new question concerning the primacy of the pope was raised, he suddenly turned his weapons against me and quite overthrew that counsel of peace. Meanwhile Carl Miltitz waited: a disputation was held, judges were selected; but here also no decision was reached, and no wonder: through the lies, the tricks, the wiles of Eck everything was stirred up, aggravated and confounded worse than ever, so that whatever decision might have been reached, a greater conflagration would have resulted.

4. Jacopo de Vio, born in Gaeta, Italy, in 1469, died in 1534. The name Cajetan he derived from his birthplace, the Latin name of which is Cajeta. In the Dominican Order he was known as Thomas, so that his writings are published under the title, Thomae de Vio Cajetani opera. He was made cardinal-presbyter with the title of S. Sisto in 1517, and in the following year was sent as papal legate to the Diet of Augsburg. Here he met and examined Luther, but accomplished nothing because he insisted that Luther must recant.

5. Carl von Miltitz was educated at Cologne, was prebendary at Mainz, Trier and Meissen, and later went to Rome, where he acted as agent for Frederick, Elector of Saxony, and Duke George the Bearded. After the endeavours of Cardinal Cajetan to silence Luther had failed, Miltitz appeared to be the person most suited to bring the negotiations to a successful ending.

For he sought glory, not the truth. Here also I left nothing undone that I ought to have done.[6]

I admit that on this occasion no small amount of corrupt Roman practices came to light, but whatever wrong was done was the fault of Eck, who undertook a task beyond his strength, and, while he strove madly for his own glory, revealed the shame of Rome to all the world. He is thy enemy, my dear Leo, or rather the enemy of thy Curia. From the example of this one man thou canst learn that there is no enemy more injurious than a flatterer. For what did he accomplish with his flattery but an evil which no king could have accomplished? To-day the name of the Roman Curia is a stench throughout the world, and papal authority languishes, ignorance that was once held in honor is evil spoken of; and of all this we should have heard nothing if Eck had not upset the counsel of peace planned by Carl and myself, as he himself now clearly sees, and is angry, too late and to no purpose, that my books were published. This he should have thought of when, like a horse that whinnies on the picket-line, he was madly seeking only his own glory, and sought only his own gain through thee at the greatest peril to thee. The vainglorious man thought that I would stop and keep silent at the terror of thy name; for I do not believe that he trusted entirely to his talents and learning. Now, when he sees that I have more courage than that and have not been silenced, he repents him too late of his rashness and understands that there is One in heaven who resists the proud and humbles the haughty, if indeed he does understand it at last.

Since we gained nothing by this disputation except that we brought greater confusion to the cause of Rome, Carl Miltitz made a third attempt; he came to the fathers of the Augustinian Order assembled in their chapter, and asked counsel in settling the controversy which had now grown most confused and dangerous. Since, by the favor of God, they had no hope of being able to proceed against me with violence, some of the most famous of their number were sent to me, and asked me at least to show honor to the person of thy Blessedness, and in a humble letter to plead as my excuse thy innocence and mine; they said that the affair was not yet in the most desperate state if of his innate goodness Leo the Tenth would take a hand in it. As I have always both offered and desired peace that I might devote myself to quieter and more useful studies, and have stormed with so great fury merely for the purpose of overwhelming by volume and violence of words, no less than of intellect, those whom I knew to be very unequal foes: I not only gladly ceased, but also with joy and thankfulness considered it a most welcome kindness to me if our hope could be fulfilled.

So I come, most blessed Father, and, prostrate before thee, I pray, if it be possible do thou interpose and hold in check those flatterers, who are the enemies

6. The German reads: "Thus I always did what was required of me, and neglected nothing which it was my duty to do."

of peace while they pretend to keep peace. But that I will recant, most blessed Father, let no one imagine, unless he prefer to involve the whole question in greater turmoil. Furthermore, I will accept no rules for the interpretation of the Word of God, since the Word of God, which teaches the liberty of all things else, dare not be bound. Grant me these two points, and there is nothing that I could not or would not most gladly do or endure. I hate disputations; I will draw out no one; but then I do not wish others to draw me out; if they do, as Christ is my Teacher, I will not be speechless. For, when once this controversy has been cited before thee and settled, thy Blessedness will be able with a small and easy word to silence both parties and command them to keep the peace, and that is what I have always wished to hear.

Do not listen, therefore, my dear Leo, to those sirens who make thee out to be no mere man but a demigod, so that thou mayest command and require what thou wilt. It will not be done in that fashion, and thou wilt not succeed. Thou art a servant of servants,[7] and beyond all other men in a most pitiable and most dangerous position. Be not deceived by those who pretend that thou art lord of the world and allow no one to be a Christian unless he accept thy authority; who prate that thou hast power over heaven, hell and purgatory. These are thy enemies and seek thy soul to destroy it; as Isaiah says, "O my people, they that call thee blessed, the same deceive thee." They err who exalt thee above a council and above the Church universal. They err who ascribe to thee alone the right of interpreting Scripture; for under cover of thy name they seek to establish all their own wickedness in the Church, and alas! through them Satan has already made much headway under thy predecessors. In short, believe none who exalt thee, believe those who humble thee. For this is the judgment of God; "He hath put down the mighty from their seat, and hath exalted the humble." See, how unlike His successors is Christ, although they all would be His vicars. And I fear that most of them have indeed been too literally His vicars. For a vicar is a vicar only when his lord is absent. And if the pope rules while Christ is absent and does not dwell in his heart, what else is he but a vicar of Christ? But what is such a Church except a mass of people without Christ? And what is such a vicar else than antichrist and an idol? How much more correctly did the Apostles call themselves servants of the present Christ, and not vicars of an absent Christ!

Perhaps I am impudent, in that I seem to instruct so great, so exalted a personage, from whom we ought all to learn, and from whom, as those plagues of thine boast, the thrones of judges receive their decisions. But I am following the example of St. Bernard in his book De consideratione ad Eugenium, a book every pope should have by heart. For what I am doing I do not from an eagerness to

7. This was the usual title of the pope, with which the bull of excommunication opened: Leo Episcopus Servus Servorum Dei.

teach, but as an evidence of that pure and faithful solicitude which constrains us to have regard for the things of our neighbors even when they are safe, and does not permit us to consider their dignity or lack of dignity, since it is intent only upon the danger they run or the advantage they may gain. For when I know that thy Blessedness is driven and tossed about at Rome, that is, that far out at sea thou art threatened on all sides with endless dangers, and art laboring hard in that miserable plight, so that thou dost need even the slightest help of the least of thy brethren, I do not think it is absurd of me, if for the time I forget thy high office and do what brotherly love demands. I have no desire to flatter in so serious and dangerous a matter, but if men do not understand that I am thy friend and thy most humble subject, there is One that understandeth and judgeth.

Finally, that I may not approach thee empty-handed, blessed Father, I bring with me this little treatise [8] published under thy name as an omen of peace and of good hope. From this book thou mayest judge with what studies I would prefer to be more profitably engaged, as I could be if your godless flatterers would permit me, and had hitherto permitted me. It is a small thing if thou regard its bulk, but, unless I am deceived, it is the whole of Christian living in brief form, if thou wilt grasp its meaning. I am a poor man, and have no other gift to offer, and thou hast no need to be made rich by any other than a spiritual gift. With this I commend myself to thy Fatherhood and Blessedness. May the Lord Jesus preserve thee forever. Amen.

V-8   Ulrich Zwingli to the Christian Community

Addressing the Christian public on the subject of his enemies' accusations, Ulrich Zwingli (1484-1531), the most influential figure in the Swiss Reformation, clarifies his association with the Jew, Moses of Winterthur, and cites the ecclesiastical authority of Hebrews on the Old Testament.

25 June, 1524

Now, dear brothers, you shall know that certain monks, supported by certain prominent people, are saying that we have learned at Zurich all our knowledge of

8. This treatise did not help; four months later Leo excommunicated Luther.

the Divine Word from the Jews; we would be little concerned with the gossiping of this or that person, were it not that thereby the Word of God they hope to bring into disrepute—the Word of God which above all things must remain undisturbed. Therefore I mention it, since this report is considered everywhere as truth.

It has been said that the Jew, Moses of Winterthur, has openly boasted that he comes to us and teaches us, and that we have repeatedly gone to him in secret, and that I have received him through a third person. I have received from him in response to my letter, the following reply, written on his own initiative:

"Therefore, my dear sir, I wish to tell you that the report which has been spread concerning me, and also has been referred to you, is untrue; such words never came forth from my lips; moreover, I would like very much to see the person, whoever he may be, who uttered this thing concerning me; I will convince him that I have never spoken thus, for it contains not an iota of truth, to which God in heaven can testify."

Thus speaks the Jew. It is true that a short time ago in the presence of more than ten learned and pious men of Zurich, I had converse with him concerning certain prophecies in the Old Testament; but all concerning their error, that they are in misery, since they refuse to accept the Lord Jesus Christ. Moreover, he has come to Zurich twice to attend our Hebrew lessons (lezgen), not however, to teach, but to listen, and to hear whether we can make correct use of the Hebrew writings; afterwards he admitted to us, we can use Hebrew correctly, and wished that he could treat it in such a way.

In addition, to such slanderers who misuse their ignorance in these things, it may be said: Do you not know that in your own laws (Di. xi), it is fixed that one should go to the Hebrews (man zu den Hebraeerern loufen soelle), if one encounters anything doubtful in the Old Testament. But you run to the heathens; and the word of Aristotle is more important to you than the word of God and of His Son Jesus Christ; for you modify the word of Christ according to his words and understanding. There is just as much to complain of in your case as in the case of the stubborn Jews, for God's word means little among you. ("Doct ist mit inen als vil ze handeln als mit den verstopften Juden; denn gottes wort gilt wenig by inen.")

V-9   Sir Thomas More to his daughter Margaret Roper

Almost on the eve of his death, the King's Councillors made the trip to
More's cell in the Tower of London in a final attempt to make him
acknowledge Henry VIII as the head of the Church of England. The
tremendous courage and integrity of More (1478-1535) were never more
apparent than in this summary of the session written to his daughter.

Tower of London
3 June 1535

Our Lord bless you and all yours.

Forasmuch, dearly beloved daughter, as it is likely that you either have heard or
shortly shall hear that the Council was here this day, and that I was before them, I
have thought it necessary to send you word how the matter standeth. And verily to
be short I perceive little difference between this time and the lst, for as far as I can
see the whole purpose is either to drive me to say precisely the one way, or else
precisely the other.

Here sat my Lord of Canterbury, my Lord Chancellor, my Lord of Suffolk, my
Lord of Wiltshire, and Master Secretary. And after my coming, Master Secretary
made rehearsal [1] in what wise he had reported unto the King's Highness, what had
been said by his Grace's Concil to me, and what had been answered by me to them
at mine other being before them last. Which thing his Mastership rehearsed in
good faith very well, as I knowledged [2] and confessed and heartily thanked him
therefor. Whereupon he added thereunto that the King's Highness was nothing
content nor satisfied with mine answer, but thought that by my demeanor [3] I had
been occasion [4] of much grudge [5] and harm in the realm, and that I had an
obstinate mind and an evil toward him and that my duty was, being his subject, and
so he had sent them now in his name upon my allegiance to command me, to make

1. related
2. acknowledged.
3. conduct.
4. cause.
5. injurious influence.

a plain and terminate [6] answer whether I thought the statute lawful or not and that I should either knowledge and confess it lawful that his Highness should be Supreme Head of the Church of England or else to utter plainly my malignity. [7]

Whereto I answered that I had no malignity and therefore I could none utter. And as to the matter I coul none other answer make than I had before made, which answer his Mastership had there rehearsed. Very heavy [8] I was that the King's Highness should have any such opinion of me. Howbeit if there were one that had informed his Highness many evil things of me that were untrue, to which his Highness for the time gave credence, [9] I would be very sorry that he should have that opinion of me the space of one day. Howbeit if I were sure that other should come on the morrow by whom his Grace should know the truth of mine innocency, I should in the meanwhile comfort myself with consideration of that. And in like wise now though it be great heaviness [10] to me that his Highness have such opinion of me for the while, yet have I no remedy to help it, but only to comfort myself with this consideration that I know very well that the time shall come, when God shall declare my truth toward his Grace before him and all the world. And whereas it might haply [11] seem to be but small cause of comfort because I might take harm here first in the meanwhile, I thanked God that my case was such in this matter through the clearness of mine own conscience that though I might have pain I could not have harm, for a man may in such case leese [12] his head and have no harm. For I was very sure that I had no corrupt [13] affection, but that I had always from the beginning truly used myself to looking first upon God and next upon the King according to the lesson that his Highness taught me at my first coming to his noble service, the most virtuous lesson that ever prince taught his servant; whose Highness to have of me such opinion is my great heaviness, but I have no mean [14] as I said to help it, but only comfort myself in the meantime with the hope of that joyful day in which my truth towards him shall well be known. And in this matter further I could not go nor other answer thereto I could not make.

To this it was said by my Lord Chancellor and Master Secretary both that the King might by his laws compel me to make a plain answer thereto, either the one way or the other.

Whereunto I answered I would not dispute [15] the King's authority, what his

6. final.
7. deep-rooted ill will.
8. weighed down with sorrow.
9. accepted as true.
10. sorrow.
11. perhaps.
12. lose.
13. evil.
14. means, opportunity.
15. contest.

Highness might do in such case, but I said that verily under correction it seemed to me somewhat hard. For if it so were that my conscience gave me against the statutes (wherein how my mind giveth me I make no declaration), then I nothing doing nor nothing saying against the statute, it were a very hard thing to compel me to say either precisely with it against my conscience to the loss of my soul, or precisely against it to the destruction of my body.

To this Master Secretary said that I had ere this when I was Chancellor examined heretics and thieves and other malefactors and gave me a great praise above my deserving in that behalf. And he said that I then, as he thought and at the leastwise Bishops did use to examine heretics, whether they believed the Pope to be head of the Church and used to compel them to make a precise answer thereto. And why should not then the King, sith [16] it is a law made here that his Grace is Head of the Church, here compel men to answer precisely to the law here as they did then concerning the Pope.

I answered and said that I protested that I intended not to defend any part or stand in contention,[17] but I said there was a difference between those two cases because that at that time as well here as elsewhere through the corps [18] of Christendom the Pope's power was recognized for an undoubted thing which seemeth not like a thing agreed in this realm and the contrary taken for truth in other realms, whereunto Master Secretary answered that they were as well burned for the denying of that as they be beheaded for denying of this, and therefore as good reason to compel them to make precise answer to the one as to the other.

Whereto I answered that sith in this case a man is not by a law of one realm so bound in his conscience, where there is a law of the whole corps of Christendom to the contrary in matter touching belief, as he is by a law of the whole corps though there hap to be made in some place a law local [19] to the contrary, the reasonableness or the unreasonableness in binding a man to precise answer standeth not in the respect or difference between heading [20] or burning, but because of the difference in charge of conscience, the difference standeth between heading and hell.

Much was there answered unto this both by Master Secretary and my Lord Chancellor over [21] long to rehearse. And in conclusion they offered me an oath by which I should be sworn to make true answer to such things as should be asked me on the King's behalf, concerning the King's own person.

16. since.
17. strife, dispute.
18. body.
19. local law.
20. beheading.
21. too.

Whereto I answered that verily I never purposed to swear any book oath [22] more while I lived. Then they said that was very obstinate if I would refuse that, for every man doth it in the Star Chamber [23] and everywhere. I said that was true but I had not so little foresight but that I might well conjecture what should be part of my interrogatory [24] and as good it was to refuse it at the first, as afterward.

Whereto my Lord Chancellor answered that he thought I guessed truth, for I should see them and so they were showed me and they were but twain. [25] The first whether I had seen the statute. The other whether I believed that it were a lawful made interrogatory [26] or not. Whereupon I refused the oath and said further by mouth that the first I had before confessed, and to the second I would make none answer.

Which was the end of the communication and I was thereupon sent away. In the communication before it was said that it was marveled that I stack so much in my conscience while at the uttermost I was not sure therein. Whereto I said that I was very sure that mine own conscience so informed as it is by such diligence as I have so long taken therein may stand with mine own salvation. I meddle not with the conscience of them that think otherwise, every man *suo domino stat et cadit*. I am no man's judge. It was also said unto me that if I had as lief be out of the world as in it, as I had there said, why did I not speak even out plain against the statute. It appeared well I was not content to die though I said so. Whereto I answered as the truth is, that I have not been a man of such holy living as I might be bold to offer myself to death, lest God for my presumption might suffer me to fall, and therefore I put not myself forward, but draw back. Howbeit if God draw me to it himself, then trust I in his great mercy, that he shall not fail to give me grace and strength.

In conclusion Master Secretary said that he liked me this day much worse than he did the last time, for then he said he pitied me much and now he thought that I meant not well, but God and I know both that I mean well and so I pray God do by me.

I pray you be you and mine other friends of good cheer whatsoever fall of me, and take no thought for me but pray for me as I do and shall do for you and all them.

Your tender loving father,

Thomas More, Kg.

22. oath of special solemnity, on a book (the Bible).
23. judicial sittings of the King's Council, meeting in the Star Chamber at Westminster, usually for criminal jurisdiction.
24. questioning, interrogation.
25. two.
26. question formally put to an accused person; the 1557 *Works* print "statute."

V-10   John Ap Rice to Thomas Lord Cromwell

Having broken with the Church of Rome, Henry VIII set out to abolish the many monasteries in England through investigative commissioners. Their reports, as was to be expected, were so incriminating that Henry's task was made easier. Typical was the following letter from John Ap Rice to Thomas Cromwell, chief administrative aid to the King, after an inspection of the great monastic house at Bury St. Edmunds. A scion of the Ap Rhys family, prominent since the twelfth century in South Wales, the correspondent was apparently a son of Thomas Ap Rice (1449-1525) who helped Henry VII gain the throne.

5 November 1538

Please it your mastership: Forasmuch as I suppose you shall have suit made unto you touching Bury ere we return, I thought convenient to advise you of our proceedings there, and also of the comports [1] of the same. As for the abbot, we found nothing suspect as touching his living, but it was detected that he lay much forth in his granges, that he delighted much in playing at dice and cards, and therein spent much money, and in building for his pleasure. He did not preach openly. Also that he converted divers farms [2] into copyholds, whereof poor men doth complain. Also he seemeth to be addict to the maintaining of such superstitious ceremonies as hath been used heretofore.

As touching the convent, [3] we could get little or no reports among them, although we did use much diligence in our examination, and thereby, with some other arguments gathered of their examinations, I firmly believe and suppose that they had confedered and compacted before our coming that they should disclose nothing. And yet it is confessed and proved that there was here such frequence of women coming and resorting to this monastery as to no place more. Amongst the relics we found much vanity and superstition, as the coals that St. Lawrence was toasted withal, the paring of St. Edmund's nails, St. Thomas of Canterbury's

1. behaviour
2. rents
3. i.e. monastery

pen-knife and his boots, and divers skulls for the headache, pieces of the holy cross able to make a whole cross of, other relics for rain and certain other superstitious usages, for avoiding of weeds growing in corn, with such other. Here depart of them that be under age upon an eight,[4] and of them that be above age upon a five would depart if they might, and they be of the best sort in the house, and of best learning and judgment. The whole number of the convent before we came was sixty, saving one, beside three that were at Oxford. Of Ely I have written to your mastership by my fellow, Richard a Lee. And thus Almighty God have you in his tuition. From Bury, 5 November.

Your servant most bounden,
John Ap Rice

V-11 Thomas Pery to Mr. Ralph Vane

The following letter from prison, necessarily abridged, is remarkable as the transcript of an Inquisitional interrogation resulting in the imprisonment of an English resident in Spain. When Henry VIII attacked Catholicism, closed the monasteries, and sold the church bells, Thomas Pery was called before the Triana *auto da fè* and ordered to swear that Henry was a heretic. Pery refused. Henry's rejection of Catherine of Aragon also rankled the Spaniards, as we read below. For his principles Pery was finally condemned as a heretic by the frightening judge Pero Diez.

Seville, 1539

. . . Also the xxvij daye of the same monthe the Inquisitor cawllyde me agayne, and sayde unto me here hath byne dywars [1] lernyd men, and hathe seyne yowre prosses, and saythe for asmyche as the wyttnes doythe prowe in the depossycyone [2] that yowe spayke the wordes whiche ye hawe denyde, theye sayeing that yowe muste neydes confes hit and that yowe dyde belewe hit in yowre harte; to the which I answeryde and sayde that yf the wyttnes dothe depowys any otherwyse then I hawe confessyde, they hawe the more to answere fore afore Gode, for I sayde no notherwise, and so he sent me awaye; and within a nower

4. *upon an eight,* about eight
1. divers.
2. deposition.

after he sent for me agayne, and axkyd me yf I hade remembryde my selffe, I sayeing that I had no other thinge to remembre me of but that I hade confessyde; then he sayeing that ye ar senttensyde to torment for cawse ye wyll not tell the trwthe; "Sir, I have towlde yowe the truthe and ye wyll not belewe me."

Than he commayndyd the Alcaylde to hawe me into the prysson of torments, wher althinges was preparyde for me, and strypyde me fowrthe of my clowthis as nakyde as ever I was bowrne, and then the porter browghte me a payer of lynnen breches and then cam in the Jwge and his strywano,[3] and he sette hym downe in a chayer within the prysson, haweinge a kwsshing[4] óf tapstery worke under hys feytte, and then I knelyde downe apone my knewyes holdinge up my handes to hym, dessyring hym to be goode unto me and to do me jwstys, he sayeing unto me confes yow the trwthe and we axke no more. I answeryd and sayde I hawe confes the trwthe and ye wyll not belewe me, therapone the porter and another tooke me be the armes and cawsyde me for to set downe apone the syde of the bwrryco[5] and browght the wone of my armes over the other, and caste a rope v. tymis abowtte them bothe, and so drewe the sayde rope withall ther myght.

I thynking they wold a plockyde[6] the fleshe from the bownys, and cryed apone the sayde Jwge to showe me mercy, sayeing to hym yowe saye thys is a howsse of mercy but hit is more lycke a howsse of morder then of mercy; wherapone he comandyd me to be layde apone the bwrryco and at the yend therof ther was a nerthen pane whiche myghte holde iij or iiij gallones of watter, and in hit a tocke[7] of fyne cotten contayenyng iij yardes longe or more, whiche I showlde a recewyde into my boddy by dropys of watter in at my mowthe, whiche is a greweus[8] payne, and to be bownde with ropys to the sayde bwrryco, and when I sawe so lyttyll mercy in hym I axkyde hym what he wolde that I showlde do, he sayeinge I wolde ye showlde tell the trwthe; I have sayd the trwthe and ye wyll not belewe me, I mwste saye as yow saye or elles ye are dysposyd for to morther me; he sayeing "no morther but jwstys"; and so I confeste that I sayde hit and thowght hit and so he cawssyde hit to be wrytten, and so went hys waye, and I was onelowesyde[9] agayne.

The xxix[th] daye of the same monthe I was cawllyde agayne befowre the sayd Jwge Pero Diez, and he cawssyde me to be sworne of the holly Awangeleste and exemenyde me be the vertue of the sayde othe, and cawssyde the nottary to rede all thinge that passyde in the pressone of tormente whether hit was trew or no. I

3. Escribano, *Span.* a notary.
4. cushion.
5. burrucho, the wooden horse?
6. have plucked.
7. tuck.
8. grievous.
9. unloosed.

sayeing God knowythe all trwthe; he sayeinge to me, was hit not trwthe; yf hit were not, ye mwste go thyther agayne. Then I sayde "Ye Ser, hit ys trewe." Then afterwarde I dessyeryng [10] hym for the onor of Gode to gewe me good consell that I maye sawe [11] my sowlle, to the intent that I wolde prowe his mynde, he sayeing to me that he wolde gewe me good consell, sayeing unto me "Brother ye shall understonde that abowyt x or xij yere agowe yowr Kyng wrytte agaynste Lwtther that greyt erytycke, and no crystyan Kinge so myche as he; and nowe he is the gretteste erytycke in the worlde; and if we hade hym heyere we wolde borne hym; all the world showlde not sawe hym. I sayeinge so, I besyche yowr worship to showe me what pennyones [12] he hathe he sayeinge that he ys a wery tyrante, and a man qwyller, and he kepythe no jwstys but doythe all thinges of hys owne ryall power. And spendithe hys tyme in all vysshwsnes, [13] and in howntyng and halkynge; and more, he hathe absentyde hymselff frome the holly mother chyrche of Rome and from the Popys attoryte for cawsse the Pope gewye a senttanes with Qwyne Katterin to be hys lawefwll wyffe; which he wolde not upserwe [14] nor keype but toke another and lewyde [15] with hyr in a vowetery; and within shorte space after he cawssyd hir heyde to be stroken of; sayeing unto me that I knewe wherfore, and that I knewe that all thys was trwe: to the whiche I answeryd and sayde that I knewe hys Grace of a good Crystyan, and that he dyd nothinge in hys Reyme but with consell of hys nobull conssell, and be the order of jwstys; and when the Qwyne was heyddyd I was not in the Reyme, I knewe nothing of hit; and so he sent me in agayne.

The viijth daye of Februarii I was cawllyde owyte of the presson by the Alkaldy, and he strocke of my yerones and hade me fowrthe into the courte of the Castyll, wher I was bade kneyll downe apone my kneysse befor ten prystys; and in my company Johne Robyns, Harry Hollande, Robarte Morgante, and Willam Alcot, and so we were assoyllyde, sayeinge the sawme of "Messerery" [16] ower us, and dysplyde us with a fagget stycke and so commandyd us to stande up apone a rowe be the wallys syde bare hedyde in owr cottes; and the porter of the castyll browght for ewery man a nabet [17] of sent Benettes, of yellowe canwas with two rede crossys a pece, whiche he caste over owr heydys apone owr backys, whiche abett [17] myghte be halfe a yarde deype and every wone of us a candyll of waxe in

10. desiring.
11. save.
12. opinions, reasons.
13. viciousness.
14. observe.
15. lived.
16. Psalm li.
17. habit.

owr handys; and so we were caryde fowrthe of the Castyll into the streytte, wher the pressyssyon [18] taryid for us with the nomber of iij or iiij thowssande pepwll; for the daye afore they cawssyde the trompettys with dronscellettys [19] to go abowit the Cyte, that sowche a nalt showlde be downe the nexte daye; so we followyde the Crosse, and apone ewery syde of us went a man, and so we went to a parysshe chyrche cawllyde sent Annes in Tryana, and in the boddy of the chyrche ther was a skafolde mayde which we were set apone, and ther reymaynd the hye masse tyme, and a sermonte was mayde bye a awstyne [20] fryer wone of the fathers of the sayde inkyzystyon. [21]

And the aserte of thys sermonte was declaring that we hade aryde innessentlye [22] for cawse we knewe not the scrypture, and, after he hade downe, ther cam into the pwlpytte a nottary of the inkyzytyone, and openly declaryde every manes sentaunes; the seycte of my sentaunes was that theye condemnyde my boddy to do that opyn pennanns for cawsse I hade sayde that the Kyng of Ynglande was a goode Crystyan, he beinge an erytycke; and sayeinge that I sayde that the Kyng petting downe of Monesterys, and taycking awaye the Belles, and that he was Pope within his Reyme, I dyd saye and belewe hit to be well downe; the sayd nottary declaryng that hit was erezy and agaynst owr hollye Mother Chyrche.

And also he declaryde that theye hade condemnyde my boddy to the prysson of Perpetwe, ther to remayne vj monthys, and not to departte owte of it withowtte the sayde a bett [23] apone my backe; ewery Sonedaye to go to Sent Salwadorys, and ther to heyer hye masse and a sermone; also he declaryde that theye hade sentensyde all my goodes to be loste, the wone halfe to the emperowrys mageste, and the other halfe to the howsse of the holly inkyzyscyon; and so I was caryde with pressesshyon agayne to the castell of Tryana, wher I dyd remayne tyll thre of the clocke at afternowne whiche was apone Shrowe sonedaye, [24] and then we were cawllyd in before docter Pero Diez, he sayeinge unto us we have usyde yowe as a loweinge mother dowythe use hir chylde, for yf she lowe hym she wyll chastyse hym, and so hathe owr holly Mother Chyrche ussyde yowe; but if yowe affende agayne in never so lyttell a thing, ther ys no remedy but you mwste be bowrnde; [25] and so he comandyde us to be caryde from the castyll of Tryana to the prysson of Perpetwe wher I do remayne, abyddinge the mercy of the Lorde; and myght dye

18. procession.
19. Dromslades, a species of Drum.
20. Augustinian.
21. Inquisition.
22. erred innocently.
23. habit.
24. Shrove Sunday.
25. burnt.

for fawyt [26] of comfort yf hit were not of the goodnes of Mr. Haryson, Johne Fylde, with dywers other of owr nassyon whiche dothe helpe us of cheryte; for theye hawe not lefte me wone blancke [27] nor it garment to my backe, Gode amende them.

Be me

Thomas Pery.

To his ryghte worshipefull Rayffe Vane gentyllman belonginge to my Lorde Prewe Sealle dwellinge in Hadleye besyds Twnebryche in Kente this be dd.

V-12   John Calvin to Heinrich Bullinger

John Calvin (1509-1564), the Genevan religious reformer, believed that the Reformation was not founding something new but, rather, purifying the Church. Along with other Swiss theologians, he broke with the Lutherans over a dispute regarding interpretation of the Eucharist. In this letter to Heinrich Bullinger, the successor of Ulrich Zwingli at Zurich, he makes an appeal on behalf of the Waldenses, a Christian sect of dissenters originating in the 12th century and adopting Calvinist doctrines in the 16th century. Noting that Luther has vehemently attacked Bullinger, Calvin nevertheless recognizes his remarkable gifts and suggests that the Protestant cause be strengthened by presenting a united front.

Geneva, 25th November 1544

You will receive from this brother who has delivered to you my letter, a crown-piece and two silver testons; for this, if I remember correctly, was the amount that remained. Excuse me, I pray you, for not having sent it sooner. As for the reason why this brother has been sent to you, by those of Neuchatel, he will himself tell you. There is, in my opinion, no difficulty, or very little, indeed, if any, in the case. But the perverseness and importunity of one individual, compels them to be troublesome both to you and to ourselves. They have in their meeting a man belonging to that class of doctors, from which, hitherto, not a single good man has

26. fault.
27. blanket.

ever yet come forth, one who has never ceased from time to time to pester them with some troublesome affair or another. There are two causes which urge him on in this course. For he seems born to contradict, and because he is not so very highly esteemed by others as he rates himself, it is after this fashion that he takes his revenge. Had he been in our Church, he would easily have been restrained. For we had a means of breaking him in quite ready at hand. But where he is, he has the Prince's deputy by whom he is countenanced. For it is thus, that men of this sort of pretension secure and fortify themselves with defences, so as to work mischief with impunity. That you would, all of you, do of your own accord what I am now about to ask, I am well aware. Nevertheless, I would entreat of you, that in so sacred a cause you may reach forth a helping hand to the brethren; that is, that you would support them by your authority, and train them by a right method that they may bridle up that Ishmael. This much have I written, not because it might be supposed to be needful, but rather to please our brother.

There is another affair, besides, in which I wish very specially to implore your aid. There are brethren in Provence, for whom you are aware, that we have always taken much pains. Nor were they any way undeserving that we should do so; for they are a people so harmless, and withal so piously disposed, that their peace and safety ought to be the peculiar care of all good men. It is now three years bypast, since they were so far advanced as to have presented to the Parliament of Aix a confession of faith, pure and simple as we could have set it forth ourselves. And besides, that you may not suppose that such a step was taken from some sudden impulse, which might immediately have evaporated, whenever they have been called to account concerning it they have constantly stood firm to their profession. In the meantime, however, they were cruelly harassed. After they had been exposed for some time to the savage tyranny of their enemies, they obtained at length of the King that he would appoint a commission, who might hear evidence and report truly upon the whole case. The King commissioned two persons, whose duty was to make inquiry; he wished to take the entire cognizance of the cause to himself, and so to pronounce an award. The tenor of the commission was, that the persons who were to be sent were to inquire particularly, and take special knowledge concerning their doctrine and morals, both in public and private. This the brethren have no dread or anxiety about. For they have so conducted themselves toward all around them as to have an unexceptionable testimony to their sterling worth, even from their adversaries.[1] As for their doctrine, they are about to present their confession of faith, clear and sincere, to the King as he has required, which document comprises, and that distinctly, far more points than can

1. William du Bellay, in his quality of lieutenant of the King at Turin, charged with the duty of making a report to Francis I, renders a very striking homage to the piety and purity of the Waldenses.

be alleged against them. At this present time, both the bishops, the royal officers, and even the parliament itself, are striving with all their might to set aside the royal commission; if it be quashed, they will then be exposed to the fury of lions and wolves, that they may spend their rage upon them. Indeed, their adversaries are mainly desirous that they may have full license to discharge all their fury upon these wretched people. If the commission be received and acted upon, even in that event they will not have escaped the danger. For in three small towns,[2] and in very many of the villages, they profess the pure doctrine of the Evangel. In one little town they have thoroughly cleansed the parish church from all its defilements, and there they celebrate the Supper and Baptism in the same manner as we do. The more immediately the danger is impending over them on either side, they are all the more on that account to be succoured by us; in this their wonderful stedfastness, especially, to which should we be found wanting, we would be chargeable with the basest cowardice. You must also take into account that it is not their cause alone which is here concerned; but either a way will be opened by their destruction to the cruel persecution of the godly throughout the whole kingdom, or, according to this method, he will assault and break up the Evangel. What can we do, therefore, but strain every nerve that these godly brethren may not, through our short-coming in duty, become the victims of such cruelty, and that the door may not for a long time be shut against Christ? I have desired beforehand to warn you of the likelihood of this coming to pass, that if sooner or later they fly to you, you may have inclined the hearts of all your friends to render them all the help they can. One or other of these two things will have to be done, either the King must be sought unto, that he may allow them to enjoy the benefit which has been already granted, or his anger must be appeased, if it shall have begun to wax hot against them.

I hear that Luther has at length broken forth in fierce invective, not so much against you as against the whole of us. On the present occasion, I dare scarce venture to ask you to keep silence, because it is neither just that innocent persons should thus be harassed, nor that they should be denied the opportunity of clearing themselves; neither, on the other hand, is it easy to determine whether it would be prudent for them to do so. But of this I do earnestly desire to put you in mind, in the first place, that you would consider how eminent a man Luther is, and the excellent endowments wherewith he is gifted, with what strength of mind and resolute constancy, with how great skill, with what efficiency and power of doctrinal statement, he hath hitherto devoted his whole energy to overthrow the reign of Antichrist, and at the same time to diffuse far and near the doctrine of salvation. Often have I been wont to declare, that even although he were to call me

2. Cabrières, Mérindol, et Lourmarin, in the present department of Vaucluse.

a devil, I should still not the less hold him in such honour that I must acknowledge him to be an illustrious servant of God. But while he is endued with rare and excellent virtues, he labours at the same time under serious faults. Would that he had rather studied to curb this restless, uneasy temperament which is so apt to boil over in every direction. I wish, moreover, that he had always bestowed the fruits of that vehemence of natural temperament upon the enemies of the truth, and that he had not flashed his lightning sometimes also upon the servants of the Lord. Would that he had been more observant and careful in the acknowledgment of his own vices. Flatterers have done him much mischief, since he is naturally too prone to be over-indulgent to himself. It is our part, however, so to reprove whatsoever evil qualities may beset him as that we may make some allowance for him at the same time on the score of these remarkable endowments with which he has been gifted. This, therefore, I would beseech you to consider first of all, along with your colleagues, that you have to do with a most distinguished servant of Christ, to whom we are all of us largely indebted. That, besides, you will do yourselves no good by quarrelling, except that you may afford some sport to the wicked, so that they may triumph not so much over us as over the Evangel. If they see us rending each other asunder, they then give full credit to what we say, but when with one consent and with one voice we preach Christ, they avail themselves unwarrantably of our inherent weakness to cast reproach upon our faith. I wish, therefore, that you would consider and reflect on these things rather than on what Luther has deserved by his violence; lest that may happen to you which Paul threatens, that by biting and devouring one another, ye be consumed one of another. Even should he have provoked us, we ought rather to decline the contest than to increase the wound by the general shipwreck of the Church. Adieu, my much honoured brother in the Lord, and my very dear friend. Salute reverently in my name all the brethren in the ministry. May the Lord preserve you, and more and more increase His own gifts in you. My colleagues very kindly salute you.

V-13 Saint Ignatius Loyola to a Man Who Was Tempted

Saint Ignatius Loyola (1491-1556), the Spanish soldier and ecclesiastic who founded the Society of Jesus, was looked on by Protestant leaders as one of their principal opponents. In addition to vows of poverty and chastity, the

Society was bound by a special vow of obedience to the Pope which Saint Ignatius called "the cause and principal foundation" of his order. Canonized in 1622 by Pope Gregory XV, the saint was declared patron of all spiritual retreats as recently as 1922 and his teachings survive today in the lives of over 30,000 Jesuits, scattered throughout the world.

The unknown recipient of the following letter apparently wished to dissociate himself from the Society in Padua while still remaining in the house, or else return to his homeland. Saint Ignatius instead advises him to take lodging in Padua and devote himself to attaining strength in mind and spirit.

Rome, 28 November, 1544

JHUS

May the perfect grace and love of Christ our Lord always be our protection and support.

I could not at all fail in the affection my heart feels for you, and so I will briefly answer your letter and that of Master Lainez, as God grants me understanding.

First, with regard to your going back home and living there, I do not think that anything could be worse for you. Because, as past experience proves, it is the last thing you should think of, as I have explained at length in other letters.

Second, I do not think that I could approve of your remaining in the house with Ours, nor can I feel satisfied that it would be a good thing; partly because you would not find the fruit you are looking for and which you have every right to expect, and partly because of the disappointment both Ours and you would feel at their inability to help you in body and soul as they desire. All things considered, I always thought that it would be safer in our Lord and better for all concerned if you took lodging apart from Ours in Padua, with some good companions, paying what you would expect to pay at home, and try that out for a year. You should go to confession frequently and have a talk with some of Ours several times a week. For the rest, you could attend several lectures, but with the purpose rather of strengthening and clearing your mind than of acquiring academic learning for the sake of others. See that your associations are pleasant and take some innocent recreation that will leave the soul unsullied, for it is better to keep the soul unsullied than to be made lord of all creation. By means of these interior consolations and the spiritual relish they will give you, you will attain to that peace and repose of conscience, and then, as your strength of body and soul allows, you can better give yourself to study for the sake of others and be sure of better results. But above all, I beg of you for the love and reverence of God our Lord to remember the past and to reflect not lightly but seriously that the earth is only earth.

May God in His infinite and perfect goodness be pleased to give us His perfect grace, so that we may know His most holy will and entirely fulfill it.

V-14   Saint Ignatius Loyola to John III, King of Portugal

Determined that the false accusations voiced against him and his companions in Rome should not create further difficulties in Portugal, Saint Ignatius writes with utmost candor to King John III. In a dramatic narration of his sufferings at the hands of persecutors in Alcalá, Salamanca, Paris, Venice and Rome, the saint affirms his innocence and his willingness to undergo even greater trials for the glory of Christ.

Rome, 15 March, 1545

IHS

May the perfect grace and everlasting love of Christ our Lord come and abide with your highness. Amen.

From more than a few tokens and indications I am convinced, our Lord knows, that, if certain experiences of mine have not already come to the ears of your highness, they soon will. They concern our Lord more than they do me; may His be the glory forever. I could desire always to glory in them, not for myself but for our Creator and Lord, and as we are under such obligations to your Christian highness, I thought that I should acquaint you with them sooner or later, even though briefly.

On my return from Jerusalem my superiors in Alcalá de Henares subjected me to three different trials. I was arrested and kept in custody for forty-two days. The same thing took place in Salamanca, where I was not only confined to jail but also put into chains for twenty-two days. I underwent another trial at Paris, where I was pursuing my studies. In all these five trials and two imprisonments, by God's grace I never wished to have, nor did I have, any other advocate or attorney than

God, in whom, by His favor and grace, I have placed all my confidence for the present as well as for the future. Seven years after the first trial in Paris another was held in the same university, another in Venice, and the last in Rome, which involved the whole Society. In the three trials last mentioned, because of my connection with others of the Society, which is your highness' even more than it is ours, we wanted to let justice have its course to prevent God's being offended by the defamation of its members. It happened, when the final sentence was passed, that there were present in Rome three persons who in the quality of judges had heard the indictment against me, one at Alcalá, one at Paris, and the other at Venice. In all these eight trials, by God's grace and mercy alone, not a single proposition, not a syllable even of mine, was condemned. Nor was I punished or banished for any more serious charge.

And if your highness wishes to know why there was so much indignant investigation of my case, you should be advised that there was never any question of being involved with schismatics or Lutherans or Illuminati, for I never knew any of them or had anything to do with them. The reason, particularly in Spain, was that I, being without education, should venture to speak at such length on spiritual subjects. People were surprised at this. The fact is—and our Lord, who is my Creator and judge, will be my witness—that not for all the power and wealth under heaven could I wish not to have gone through this experience. It is my desire to have as much and ever more to suffer in the future for the greater glory of His Divine Majesty.

If, therefore, some report of these happenings should reach your highness, I am sure that, with the perfect grace and gentleness which His Divine Majesty has bestowed on your highness for His greater service and praise, your highness will take time to recognize His graces and will be able to distinguish what is good from what is bad, to your own advantage. You will understand that, the more we desire to succeed, apart from offense on the part of our neighbor, in clothing ourselves with the livery of Christ our Lord which is woven out of insult, false witness, and every other kind of injustice, the more we shall advance in spirit and earn those spiritual riches with which, if we are leading spiritual lives, our souls desire to be adorned.

In view of the great desire which Ours have here of seeing Master Simon and because of the need we have of taking thought in matters which touch the Society closely, we humbly beg your highness, for God's glory, graciously and affectionately to give the permission, which his holiness has already given. I have the greatest confidence that his coming here together with the others from whom we expect such help will be for the service of His Divine Majesty and of your highness, to whom the Society belongs more than it does to us.

I pray that her majesty will consider this letter as addressed to herself, and to her kindness and prayers I humbly commend myself in our Lord, begging that He in His infinite goodness will give us His perfect grace to know His most holy will and perfectly to fulfill it.

V-15   John Calvin to Oswald Myconius

Calvin relates the discovery of a heinous conspiracy for spreading the plague throughout Geneva. This letter serves to remind us that the Calvinists in Geneva also instituted their own inquisitorial trials and their own Index of Forbidden Books.

Geneva, 27th March 1545

Accept my best thanks for your communication about what you had heard concerning the Emperor and the Imperial Diet;[1] with regard to your opening my letter by mistake, I do not forgive you for that, since you have been no way to blame. The Lord is sorely trying us in this quarter.[2] A conspiracy of men and women has lately been discovered, who, for the space of three years, had spread the plague through the city, by what mischievous device I know not. After fifteen women have been burnt; some men have even been punished more severely; some have committed suicide in prison; and while twenty-five are still kept prisoners;—the conspirators do not cease, notwithstanding, to smear the door-locks of the dwelling-houses with their poisonous ointment. You see in the midst of what perils we are tossed about. The Lord hath hitherto preserved our dwelling, though it has more than once been attempted. It is well that we know ourselves to be under His care.—Adieu, most accomplished Sir, and my much respected brother.

This nobleman, who is not unknown to you, will explain the great straits and difficulties with which at present our brethren of Provence are oppressed.[3] Because I am aware that, as one might expect, you have their welfare at heart, I only ask that when the time for assisting them shall arrive you will be ready

1. The Imperial Diet was then met at Worms. The Roman prelates were preparing for the celebration of the approaching Council by a life of gaiety and dissipation.
2. The plague had then broken out afresh and was raging at Geneva.
3. See also Calvin's letter to Bullinger (V-12).

prepared, as we hitherto always found you. But, in the first instance, as seemed right, I have stated the case to Bucer, that he may consider maturely whether any seasonable or likely access will be practicable to the King. Salute particularly your wife and friends.—Yours,

John Calvin.

V-16   John Calvin to Archbishop Thomas Cranmer of Canterbury

In a letter to the first Protestant Archbishop of Canterbury, Thomas Cranmer, Calvin urges him to assume aggressive leadership in reforming the Church in England by purging it of papal corruptions. Cranmer's devotion to Protestantism resulted in his eventual execution under the Catholic Mary Tudor.

(July 1552.)

Seeing that, at the present time, that which is most of all to be desired is least likely to be attained, viz., that an assembly of the most eminent men of learning, from all the various Churches which have embraced the pure doctrine of the Gospel, after having discussed separately the controverted topics of the day, might transmit to posterity, out of the pure Word of God, a true and distinct confession; I nevertheless highly commend the plan which you, reverend Sir, have adopted, to make the English frame for themselves, without delay, a religious constitution, lest, by matters remaining longer in an unsettled state, or not being sufficiently adjusted, the minds of the common people should be confirmed in their suspense. And it is the duty of all in your country, who have any influence, to direct their energies with united zeal toward this object, so that your duties may still be special. You see what such a position as yours demands, or rather what God may legitimately require of you in consideration of the nature of the office which He has imposed on you. Supreme authority is vested in you—an authority which your high rank entitles you to, not more than the previously entertained opinion regarding your wisdom and integrity. The eyes of many are fixed upon you, either to second your exertions, or to imitate your lukewarmness. And sincerely do I desire that, under your leadership, they may be advanced to such an extent during the next three years, that the difficulties and contests of the present time, caused by the removing of the grossest superstition, shall have ceased to exist. I, for my part, acknowledge that our cause has made no little progress during the short period the Gospel has flourished in England. But if you reflect on what yet remains to be done, and how very remiss you have been in many matters, you will discover that you have no reason to advance towards the goal with less rapidity, even although the most of the course has, as it were, been gone over; for I need not inform you that I, as it were, take note of your assiduity, lest, after having escaped danger, you should become self-indulgent. But to speak freely, I greatly fear, and this fear is abiding, that so many autumns will be spent in procrastinating, that by and by the cold of a perpetual winter will set in. You are now somewhat advanced in years, and this ought to stimulate you to increased exertions, so as to save yourself the regret of having been consciously dilatory, and that you may not leave the world while matters remain in so disordered a condition. I say matters are still in a disorganized state, for external religious abuses have been corrected in such a way as to leave remaining innumerable young shoots, which are constantly sprouting forth. In fact, I am informed that such a mass of Papal corruptions remain, as not only to hide, but almost to extinguish the pure worship of God. Meanwhile the life of the whole ecclesiastical order is all but extinct, or at least is not sufficiently vigorous: take, for example, the preaching of doctrine. Assuredly pure and undefiled religion will never flourish, until the Churches shall have been at greater pains to secure suitable pastors, and such as shall conscientiously discharge the duties of teaching. Satan, indeed, opposes his secret wiles to the accomplishment of this. I understand that there is still one shameful obstacle, viz., that the revenues of the Church have been plundered; truly an insufferable evil. But iniquitous as this is, there appears to me to be another vice of equal magnitude, viz., that out of the public revenues of the Church, idle gluttons are supported who chant vespers in an unknown tongue.* I shall say nothing farther on this point, except that it is inconsistent for you to approve of such mockery, and it is openly incompatible with the proper arrangements of the Church; besides, it is in itself exceedingly ridiculous. I do not doubt, however, but that these considerations will immediately occur to your own mind, and will be suggested to you by that most upright man Peter Martyr, whose counsel I am exceedingly glad to know you enjoy. Difficulties so numerous and so trying as those against which you are contending, appear to me a sufficient excuse for the exhortations I have offered.—Adieu, most distinguished and esteemed Primate. May the Lord long preserve you in safety; may He fill you more and more with the Spirit of wisdom and fortitude, and bless your labours! Amen.

John Calvin.

* Latin

V-17   Queen Elizabeth to five Catholic Bishops of England

Five Catholic bishops, newly deprived of their sees for denying the legitimacy of the Church of England, wrote to the Queen (1533-1603) condemning as schismatic and heretical any church outside "the ancient Catholic faith, which hath been long since planted within this realm by the motherly care of the Church of Rome." The Queen in her reply attacks their premises as historically incorrect.

Greenwich, 6 December 1559.

E.R. Sirs,

As to your entreaty for us to listen to you, we waive it: yet do return you this our answer. Our realm and subjects have been long wanderers, walking astray, whilst they were under the tuition of Romish pastors, who advised them to own a wolf for their head (in lieu of a careful shepherd), whose inventions, heresies, and schisms be so numerous, that the flock of Christ have fed on poisonous shrubs for want of wholesome pastures. And whereas you hit us and our subjects in the teeth, that the Romish Church first planted the Catholic faith within our realms, the records and chronicles of our realms testify the contrary; and your own Romish idolatry maketh you liars: witness the ancient monument of Gildas;[1] unto which both foreign and domestic have gone in pilgrimage there to offer. This author testifieth Joseph of Arimathea to be the first preacher of the word of God within our realms. Long after that, when Austin [2] came from Rome, this our realm had bishops and priests therein, as is well known to the wise and learned of our realm by woeful experience, how your church entered therein by blood; they being martyrs for Christ, and put to death, because they denied Rome's usurped authority.

As for our father being withdrawn from the supremacy of Rome by schismatical

1. Ecclesiastic who wrote late in 6th century a history of the conquest and destruction of Britain, *De excidio et conquestu Britanniae.*

2. St. Augustine.

and heretical counsels and advisers; who, we pray, advised him more, or flattered him, than you, good Mr. Hethe, when you were bishop of Rochester? And than you, Mr. Boner, when you were archdeacon? And you, Mr. Turberville? Nay further, who was more an adviser of our father, than your great Stephen Gardiner, [3] when he lived? Are not ye then those schismatics and heretics? If so, suspend your evil censures. Recollect, was it our sister's conscience made her so averse to our father's and brother's actions, as to undo what they had perfected? Or was it not you, or such like advisers, that dissuaded her, and stirred her up against us and other of the subjects?

And whereas you would frighten us, by telling how Emperors, Kings, and Princes have owned the Bishop of Rome's authority; it was contrary in the beginning. For our Saviour Christ paid His tribute unto Caesar, as the chief superior; which shows your Romish supremacy is usurped.

As touching the excommunication of St. Athanasius by Liberius and that Council, and how the Emperor consented thereunto; consider the heresies that at that time had crept into the church of Rome, and how courageously Athanasius withstood them, and how he got the victory. Do ye not acknowledge his creed to this day? Dare any of you say he is a schismatic? Surely ye be not so audacious. Therefore as ye acknowledge his creed, it shows he was no schismatic. If Athanasius withstood Rome for her then heresies, then others may safely separate themselves from your church, and not be schismatics.

We give you warning, that for the future we hear no more of this kind, lest you provoke us to execute those penalties enacted for the punishing of our resisters: which out of our clemency we have forborne.

V-18   Fugger Correspondent in Seville to Augsburg Bankers

A Fugger correspondent in Seville reports on the wholesale burning of "heretics."

---

3. Bishop of Winchester and chancellor of England, Gardiner was the major exponent of conservatism in the first generation of the English Reformation.

Seville, the 13th day of May 1569.

The *auto da fé* * of which I have already written took place here to-day. Seventy persons were brought forth, of which have been burned two Burgundians, one Frenchman and one Dutchman. The others were for the most part Spanish rabble of poor mien, namely blasphemers of the name of God, and such as had been married twice or more. There were also among them such as did not hold fornication as sin. Likewise were there some of Jewish and Mohammedan faith.

V-19   Fugger Correspondent in Amsterdam to the Augsburg Bankers

A Fugger correspondent writes from Amsterdam describing the savage St. Bartholomew's Day slaughter of Protestants in France. Reformational historians set the number of casualties as high as 70,000, while Catholic historians estimate the deaths at 2,000. The first victim was Admiral Coligny.

From Amsterdam, the 30th day of August 1572.

Of the extraordinary happenings which took place in Paris a few days ago, Your Honour, without doubt, will already have heard through other channels. If not, then be it made known to you that the Admiral of France was on his way on horseback to court on the 22nd day of this month. As he was reading a letter in the street, a musket was fired at him from a window. He was but hit in the arm, yet stood in danger of his life. Whereupon it is said that the King evinced great zeal to probe into this matter. With this the Admiral did not rest content, but is reported to have said, he well knew who was behind this, and would take revenge, were he to shed royal blood. So when the King's brother, the Duke of Anjou, and the Guises and others heard of this, they decided to make the first move and speedily to dispose of the whole matter. On the night of the 23rd day of this month they broke into the Admiral's house, murdered him in his bed, and then threw him out of the window. The same day they did likewise unto all his kin, upon whom they could lay their hands. It is said that thirty people were thus murdered, among them the most noble of his following, and also Monsieur de La Rochefoucauld, the

* *Auto da fé* (Port), ritual of the Faith (Church)

Marquis de Retz, the King's bastard brother, and others. This has been likened unto Sicilian Vespers, by which the Huguenots and the Gueux of this country had their wings well trimmed. The Admiral has reaped just payment. We hear that the Prince and his retinue are being watchful that no such fate befall them. Truly, potentates do not permit themselves to be trifled with, and whosoever is so blind that he cannot see this learns it later to his sorrow. Since the Admiral, as has been reported, has now been put out of the way, it is to be supposed that all his scheming plots and secrets will be brought to the light of day. This may in time cause great uproar, as it is more than probable that many a one at present regarded as harmless was party to this game.

(Repercussions of Admiral Coligny's death were widespread in England. See Letter IV-12).

V-20   Queen Elizabeth to Sir Francis Walsingham, Ambassador to France

Every Protestant community or country in Europe was shocked by the St. Bartholomew's Day Massacres of French Protestants, 23 August, 1572. The widespread slaughter distressed the Queen especially, since she was entertaining the thought of marrying the Duke of Anjou, brother to the King of France. It seemed to her that the event humiliated and demeaned herself.

Reading, 28 September, 1572

De la Mothe, the French Ambassador, on Monday the 22d of this month having asked audience came to the Court at Reading, and there had large communication with us; the which seemed to us at that time the more strange, because we had heard before of the daily murdering of those of the Religion there in France, at Paris and at Orleans, as also at Lyons and Rouen, and divers other places and cities of that Realm, all the which was said to be done by the King's appointment and commandment. Whereupon, when we had heard what he could say unto us, he heard us so reply at the time, as we did think he found himself unable to satisfy us, and nevertheless we told him, that we would be further advised for our answer, which we should have within three or four days, whereupon communicating this negotiation, with our Council, upon their French tongue an answer as appeareth by this here enclosed, which is the copy of that which we delivered to Mirasius to interpret in French to the said de la Mothe as our full answer and resolution at the time, with the which, as Mirasius reporteth, de la Mothe seemed very well content and satisfied, in the which yet you may perceive that divers things are left to be further ascertained unto us by you.

Wherefore you shall do well with convenient speed to demand audience of the King, and there to declare, both to him and to the Queen Mother, what hath passed betwixt his Ambassador and us, and upon that point we did at that time stand. And you may say, as touching any worthy punishment executed upon his own subjects, we have not to deal therein, but if they have worthily suffered, we are sorry for their evil doings. But yet the King to destroy and utterly root out of his Realm all those of that Religion that we profess, and to desire us in marriage for his brother, must needs seem unto us at the first a thing very repugnant, and contrary to itself, specially having confirmed that liberty in them of the Religion by an Edict of his, perpetual and irrevocable; of the which to whom the liberty was granted, if any were partakers of any evil conspiracies against him, surely a great part of them must needs be ignorant, and ignorant of any evil fact or thought against him, especially women and innocent children, who, we do understand, are not yet spared. And therefore if that Religion of itself be so odious unto him that he thinks he must root out all the professors of it, how should we think his brother a fit husband for us, or how should we think that the love may grow, continue and increase betwixt his brother and us, which ought to be betwixt the husband and the wife.

You had in our former letters unto you things that we required you to decipher by all means that you could, especially, whether the King himself is inclined and bent to all these cruelties and the rooting out of true Religion, or whether he be but [   ] and overruled, to the which article hitherto you have not answered, and yet these things might give great light unto us, how to direct our action in the conferences and talks with his Ambassador.

And we would have you to be earnest in that matter of Strozzi, praying him frankly and roundly to declare unto us, what he meaneth, with that great army of ships and men of war, which hath been kept of long time close and undiscovered, to which intent or to what place it should be bent. You may say we have the more occasion to desire to know his meaning and dealing herein because of late they of Strozzi's company there hath spoiled divers of our merchants, some of their artillery and victual, and other of their goods and merchandises, as was accustomed betwixt the two Realms in times past, the which kind of dealing is very much contrary to the amity and to such things as by his Ambassador is propounded unto us; wherefore as we do go roundly and plainly to work with him to show flatly that which we do think or doubt upon, so do we pray him, with the same flatness and roundness to deal with us, for it is the way and means to make the continuance of amity and also the increase, and may induce us the sooner to come for a further resolution of such things as be required of us.

The Vidame of Chartres of whom we have great compassion is come into this Realm, at whose humble and lamentable suit, we have been content to write this letter to my brother the French King, in his favour, which you shall deliver, with as good words as you may to the French King, and require his answer.

If this our letter do chance to come to you in Paris or in the way coming from Paris towards England, after you have obtained licence of the King to come away by favour of our letters, which we wrote unto him, yet, if you be not too far on the way, or very near the sea coast, we would you should return in post otherwise to the Court to hear a direct answer of the King to these our letters, except that great and unfeigned danger of yourself do move you to keep on journey. In which case you shall commit the doing of this passage and receiving of answer to your secretary, whom you shall leave behind, so that he be a man able to do this charge.

V-21   Saint Teresa of Avila to Doña Inés Nieto

So many girls wished to enter the Carmelite order of Barefoot Nuns that their families or relatives were willing to pay an appropriate dowry. With all the good will in the world, Saint Teresa (1515-1582) could not admit a candidate for the marriage to Christ without a dowry being offered.

Valladolid, 28 December, 1574

JHS

May the grace of the Holy Spirit be with Your Mercy. Although I have not written you before now, Your Mercy may be certain that I do not forget you in my prayers to Our Lord and that I have derived contentment from your welfare. May it please Our Lord that you enjoy many years in His service. For I have hopes that His Majesty will in no way impede Your Mercy in this design, even though there may be hindrances.

All those things that people call boons in this miserable life are just that. Thus he will appreciate very much that Your Mercy for the past years has dedicated yourself to God, according to every thing its true worth, and, as will come about very soon, make manifest his esteem.

Lady Isabel de Córdoba has been negotiating for many days with the prioress of this nunnery in Valladolid, whom she considers a true servant of God, and thus I found a way to speak with her. She tells me she is a close relative of Lord Albornoz, which was the reason for my desiring her to enter here; although, since this building is not yet completed, having been founded by Lady de Mendoza, it is necessary to contribute charity for her to be accepted here. As she told me that Lord de Albornoz had promised her financial assistance to become a nun, I told her that Your Mercy's greatest wish was that she belong to his nunnery. Still, although I should wish it otherwise, she could not be admitted, either through Doña María or through the nuns. For the number of nuns is so small and so many aspire to be nuns, and, as I say, are in need, it would be an affront to them if the prioress did not choose those who can help them financially. I have heard that the Albornoz family have property, but of such a nature that they declare they cannot sell it. When we hit upon a solution, even if it is to take a lesser dowry than is taken from other novitiates, I shall do what I can. For I wish, certainly, to serve Your Mercy and Lady Albornoz, as is my duty, and I commend myself to their orisons. Although a humble person, I shall in my prayers beseech what Your Mercy commands.

May God repay Your Mercy for the painting. Our Lord owes this to me. I beg Your Mercy to keep it well guarded until I ask for it, which will be when I have more permanent quarters in some cloister than I have now, in order to enjoy it. Let Your Mercy thank me only by not forgetting me in your orisons. Let the Lord God give Your Mercy all the spiritual wealth which I beg for you. Amen. Today is the Day of the Innocents.

The unworthy servant of Your Mercy,
Teresa de Jesús, Carmelita

(trans. R. J. C.)

(See also Letter IX-23 on the financial arrangements undertaken by Lope de Vega in getting his daughter into a convent.)

V-22   The Fugger correspondent in Lyon to the Augsburg Bankers

The Fugger correspondent in Lyon dispatches news of the decree issued by
Henri IV, granting restricted religious and civil liberties to Huguenots. The
Edict of Nantes, incidentally, was revoked in 1685 by Louis XIV.

Lyons, the 21st day of March 1599.
Fresh letters from Paris of the 15th of this month report that the Edict about
religious peace was published in Parliament on the morning of the 25th of
February. On the same afternoon the King's sister started on her journey to
Lorraine, but on the way stopped to visit His Majesty at Saint-Germain. The
Edict has, however, not yet been published in the city, as it appears that once more
something has happened to prevent this.

V-23   The Fugger Correspondent in Prague to the Augsburg Bankers

A Fugger newsletter from Prague describes ruthless measures taken in
confiscating the estate of a deceased Jew.

From Prague, the 5th day of April 1601.
A short time ago there died here the Jew Meisel. Notwithstanding that he had left
His Imperial Majesty ten thousand florins, and much cash also to the Hospital for
poor Christians and Jews, His Imperial Majesty on the following Saturday, viz. the
Sabbath of the Jews, ordered Herr von Sternberg, at that time President of the

Bohemian Chamber, to enter the Jew's house forcibly and to seize everything there was. The widow of Meisel handed this over willingly, for she had already set aside and hidden the best part of the treasure. That which was taken away came to forty-five thousand florins in cash, besides all manner of other things, such as silver plate, promissory notes, jewels, clothes and all kinds of coins. After this, however, the President, against whom the Jewess and the sons of the two brothers of Meisel had raised a strong protest to the privy councillors, was not satisfied with all this money and booty, and no doubt at the command of His Majesty, once more broke into the house at night. The son of one of the brothers was taken prisoner, secretly led away and tortured in such guise that he confessed to the executioners, as a result of which the following substance was handed to the Bohemian Chamber:

80,000	ordinary single ducats of 2 florins apiece make	160,000 florins.
5,000	pure golden Portugalese of 20 florins apiece make	100,000 florins.
15,000	pure golden Rosenobles of 4 florins	61,250 florins.
	5 kreuzer apiece make	
30,000	turnip ducats of 2 florins apiece, make	60,000 florins.
10,000	Styrian ducats of 2 florins apiece make	20,000 florins.
60,000	silver thalers of 7 kreuzer apiece make	70,000 florins.
Together with the above-mentioned		45,000 florins.
Make altogether		516,250 florins.

V-24   Claudio Monteverdi to Alessandro Striggio

The first great operatic composer, Claudio Monteverdi (1567-1643), begs the Councillor at Mantua to intercede on behalf of his son Massimiliano, a young physician whom the Inquisition had arrested for allegedly owning or having read a book proscribed by the Church. To his father's intense relief, Massimiliano was eventually released.

Venice, 8 July 1628

. . . I understand from your most gracious letter that you went in person to speak to the Most Reverend Father Inquisitor, a favour so extreme that it makes me blush, and that he replied to Your Excellency that Massimiliano will be set free after only two days in prison. I suspect, Your Excellency, and forgive me if I speak so frankly, in face of your so great confidence, I suspect, and my son also suspects, that it may come to the rack or that it may come to some more than ordinary fine, or to some prison sentence of far, far more than two days; if they wish to examine him in everything he has ever thought or done, and even should their suspicions prove completely groundless, nevertheless the dread that fills his mind appals him greatly, and believe me, Your Excellency, scarce a day goes by but he weeps and laments over this persistent thought. The Most Reverend Father has written to me; if therefore he has this good intention, and has enquired into my son's life during six months in prison why does he not vouchsafe to relieve him from this tribulation and me likewise, and leave him to practise medicine to his and my satisfaction, and if need be that he pay twenty or twenty-five ducats as a token of punishment, and vow that he will never more read things vain and impertinent, let that be done also, since I know for certain that in any case he will never do so again, and I would pay the money willingly. Dear my Lord, if it were possible to obtain the favour of which I speak, I beg you with all my heart and soul to do me that favour that I may receive it, and I assure you that it will give life both to the boy and to me, for truly I feel my affection tormented by this thought; console me, I beseech you, if it be at all possible, for I can never receive a greater boon, the goods of this world are most dear to me, but much dearer are peace of mind and my own honour; forgive me, I beseech you, for thus troubling you while with heartfelt affection I make my most humble reverence and kiss your hand. . . .

CHAPTER 6

GOVERNMENT AND POLITICS.
LIFE AT COURT.
THE NOBILITY.

XI. *Queen Elizabeth I* (artist unknown)

XII. *Las Meninas* by Velasquez

As suggested earlier, the Renaissance witnessed a widespread rise of nationalism which undermined both the feudal system and the concept of a Holy Roman Empire. Nationalism breeds wars, and the many Renaissance letters treating of the rampant warfare are well represented in Chapter VII below. The strong new monarchs of the West and North of Europe found it difficult to pay allegiance to a pope in Italy, to say nothing of the vast sums of money sent as a national tithe. The monarchs found it equally galling to have the pope interfere with their personal lives, their marriages and divorces (IX-4). The most strong-willed and God-anointed was the tyrannical Czar Ivan the Terrible (VI-12).

Two expanding monarchies kept the Renaissance in a turmoil, that of the Sultan Suleiman and that of Charles V of Spain, whose motto was *semper plus ultra*. This great king ruled at one point from the Lowlands to the Danube, trying to preserve these areas from the taint of Protestantism. At one startled moment, he found that he had extended himself so far that he was in danger of being "captured in bed" (VI-10). One reason for his success was the support of Jacob Fugger, the great international banker of Augsburg (VI-5), whom Charles V however was slow to repay. ("You will order that the money which I have paid out, together with the interest upon it, shall be reckoned up and paid, without further delay.") Charles V was unable to break the threat of the Turk during his lifetime, and indeed Henry VIII slyly chided him for killing Christians instead of Turks (VII-8). Nevertheless it was his natural son John of Austria who directed the great defeat of the Turkish navy at Lepanto in 1571 (VII-14). Charles's most constant antagonist was Francis I, whom his forces captured at Pavia in Italy, that disunited country invaded by French and Spanish armies, Turkish ships (VII-10), German landsknechts, and Swiss mercenaries. Charles's chivalrous treatment of his royal captive illustrates that courtliness was indeed an ideal of the Renaissance (VII-5). If Charles's political maneuverings and alliances earned him the satire of Henry VIII, Francis I had his sharp critic in Aretino, the "scourge of princes" (VI-7), who chided him rightly for aligning himself with the Turks: "My Lord, you have thrust the Ottoman sword into the heart of Christendom."

Just as Aretino presumed to lecture Francis I on the ideals he must live up to, so did Erasmus advise Henry VIII on the just ruler: "Kings become wise by wise companionship, etc." Reading these blueprints of the ideal king, including the

longer tracts on the subject by Saavedra Faxardo and others, one understands the
shocked reaction which followed publication of Machiavelli's *Prince.*

Just or not, the Renaissance monarch could rightly fear assassination, violence,
or revolt. The mere suspicion of disloyalty was punished by death or
imprisonment, as Raleigh learned (VI-21). Both Henri III and Henri IV were
assassinated, even though the former could not believe that God would reserve
such an end for him: "Within a few days He will give me both my former health
and victory over my enemies" (VI-17). Within a few days he was buried at Senlis,
and his assassin Jacques Clément was a hero (VI-18). Alessandro de' Medici was
assassinated by his cousin Lorenzaccio, who then wrote a little book justifying
tyrannicide and comparing himself to Brutus. Indeed, discussions of tyrannicide
and the guilt of Brutus were many in the Renaissance, spilling over into the
theater with Shakespeare and into art with the famous bust of Michelangelo. In
fact, although Michelangelo was politically prudent, avoiding conversations about
politics (VI-3), in his published dialogues with Donato Giannotti he reluctantly
concludes that Dante was wrong to assign Brutus to deepest hell. Whether Henri
IV's conversion to Catholicism led indirectly to his assassination, the conversion
was a shocking blow to Queen Elizabeth, as she reminded him (VI-20).

Renaissance monarchs kept a close surveillance of their enemies, real or
potential. Thomas More (V-9), Cardinal Wolsey (IX-4), Francis Bacon (VI-22),
Sir Walter Raleigh and Thomas Wyatt (IX-9), lived to see how the slightest
offense to a prince was repayable by prison or death. Monarchs were aware of
their divine right (Dieu et mon droict) and Queen Elizabeth, victimized and even
imprisoned during her unhappy youth, shows through her letters *(passim)* an
imperious will capable of crushing the strongest opponent. Her cat and mouse
game with Mary Stuart, a game with the greatest of stakes, she was destined to win
(VI-16). A series of contemporary letters below report consecutively Mary's
passion for Bothwell (IX-17), who had intrigued against her murdered husband
Lord Darnley, Mary's eager advice to Babington on how they might capture the
crown of England ("all your forces shall be simultaneously in the field to receive
me") (VI-14), Queen Elizabeth's final warning to her rival pretender (VI-15), and
finally the pathetic letter on her beheading ("When the executioner held up the
head, it fell in disarray so that it could be seen that her hair was quite grey and had
been closely cropped") (VI-16).

Courtliness and court life are the subject of an interesting corpus of letters. Just
as Castiglione had, in his *Book of the Courtier,* enumerated the qualities which make
up the ideal gentleman—to be followed by many courtesy books in France and
England—so did Fray Antonio de Guevara leave us a mini-description of the ideal
knight or captain (VII-4), addressed to the Marquis of Pescara. Ironically, three
courtly knights of great fame fought in vain the Franco-Spanish campaigns of

1524-1525: King Francis I, the Knight Bayard, "without fear and without reproach," and the Duke of Alençon. Pescara emerged with ever greater honors, although dying shortly thereafter.

Many a letter-writer of the Renaissance, familiar with the artificial codes of court life, took up his pen to damn it. An unexpected example came from the learned Cornelius Agrippa, disillusioned with court hypocrisy and servility after being dismissed as physician to the Queen Mother of France in 1526. He lists ironically "the rules I have prescribed for myself if ever I am tempted to return to the court service." The haughtiness of the newly-ennobled was especially irritating (VI-11). Aretino, comfortably and indeed scandalously ensconced in his large house in Venice (X-10), was able to "feel like a pope and act like an emperor" without having to flatter or be obsequious to anyone. Perhaps the best-known English condemnation of court life is Thomas Wyatt's splendid verse-satire on his decision to flee the court sent to John Poins in 1536: "Rather than to live thrall, under the awe / Of lordly looks, wrapped within my cloak" (VI-8). In Spain Fray Antonio de Guevara wrote to console the Abbot of Monserrat that monastery life was far more desirable than an existence at court. The courtier's constant exposure to the king's whims and unpredictable favor were all too well known to Francis Bacon under James I: "I was toward you but a bucket and cistern, to draw forth and conserve, whereas yourself was the fountain" (VI-22). To conclude on a happier note, Erasmus admitted to Faustus Andrelinus that from a bookworm he had suddenly become a courtier "of some practice," and that court life in England wasn't all bad, especially when one benefited from the ladies' fragrant kisses (VI-2).

Renaissance letters reveal habits of astute diplomacy, gracious protocol, and professions of honest principle. Kings are "brothers" or "cousins" when they address one another. Yet this decorous comportment applied more easily on land than on sea, where an honor code seemed to be lacking. Slave traders plied the Atlantic, Turks kidnapped victims on the high seas, Spaniards and English buccaneers sank ships and sacked coastal towns of the New World (VIII-13), and Mediterranean ports like Cadiz suffered continual harassment (VII-16). Charles Somerset, later a respected diplomat, was to King Manoel of Portugal the most unprincipled of pirates, as we learn from the moral lecture on honor at sea which Manoel sent to Henry VII of England (VI-1). It would be a long time before marine law would bring justice and safety to the seas.

The widespread expansion of diplomatic relations emerges, of course, from Renaissance letters. Elizabeth Regina sent envoys to Abyssinia, Morocco, Russia, and other new areas to counteract the expansionist policies of the Turk and the Spaniard. Her emissary Edmund Hogan wrote a letter depicting the Sultan of Morocco as an ingratiating double-dealer able to handle the rival European powers (VI-13). Elizabeth had no scruples about forbidding publishers to publish anything referring to the czarist tyrannies of her new Russian allies (VI-19). Political suppression of the rights of such colonial peoples as the Safi Arabs and the Mexican Aztecs will appear in letters of the following Chapters, as will the policies of the European powers regarding the special problem of Turkish political ambitions.

VI-1   King Manoel I of Portugal to King Henry VII of England

Relying on the assumption that sovereigns bear responsibility for the conduct of their subjects, Manoel I (1469-1521), King of Portugal, calls upon Henry VII of England to put an end to acts of piracy committed by the general of the English fleet.

1495

Many various things happen to men in a lifetime when they least expect them. Some are minor, others are major, and others most important indeed. Nevertheless, major events cannot justify forgetting the minor things, the more so when everyone is not trying to offend, but to avoid offending, and to keep and defend his rights. During recent years, Charles Somerset, general of Your Highness's fleet, against our agreements and friendship, boarded off the English coast a Portuguese ship and plundered it of the goods and merchandise it was carrying and took from my vassal Alfonso de Palma of Lisbon in this seizure a value of one hundred and twenty-two *milreis*. For indemnity I went twice to Your Highness with letters of our King Dom João, my predecessor, and it profited him so little that when he sought to recover what had been taken from him, he squandered in the effort another abundance of wealth. Thus I who am accustomed to order my men never to do offense to anyone, suffer deeply when others do offense to them. I beseech Your Highness that you put an end to this practice, ordering everyone restore to each his own (as you promised when you ordered me to have restored his goods to Thomas Somita[?], which I afterward ordered done) for it is not fitting for those who hold office or royal charge to be pirates rather than gentlemen. And the prince who never punishes his men, often incites them to such behavior. As for my friendship and affection for Your Highness and for the good will which I bear Your vassals, Your Highness will learn more fully through my ambassadors.

(trans. R.J.C.)

(See also Letter VII-16, showing that Francis Drake kept up the piratical behavior of Charles Somerset.)

VI-2   Desiderius Erasmus to Faustus Andrelinus

Desiderius Erasmus (1466?-1536) basks in the hospitality of the English court, submitting with particular delight to the kisses of English ladies.

England, 1499

Heavens, what do I hear? Is our Scopus really turned all at once from poet to soldier, and handling deadly weapons instead of books? . . .

We too have made progress in England. The Erasmus you once knew is now become almost a sportsman, no bad rider, a courtier of some practice, bows with politeness, smiles with grace, and all this in spite of himself. If you are wise, you too will fly over here. Why should a man with a nose like yours grow to old age with nothing but French filth about him? But you will say, your gout detains you. The devil take your gout, if he will only leave *you!* Nevertheless, did you but know the blessings of Britain, you would clap wings to your feet, and run hither; and if the gout stopped you, would wish yourself a Daedalus.

To take one attraction out of many; there are nymphs here with divine features, so gentle and kind, that you may well prefer them to your Camenae. Besides, there is a fashion which cannot be commended enough. Wherever you go, you are received on all hands with kisses; when you take leave, you are dismissed with kisses. If you go back, your salutes are returned to you. When a visit is paid, the first act of hospitality is a kiss, and when guests depart, the same entertainment is repeated; wherever a meeting takes place there is kissing in abundance; in fact whatever way you turn, you are never without it. Oh Faustus, if you had once tasted how sweet and fragrant those kisses are, you would indeed wish to be a traveller, not for ten years, like Solon, but for your whole life, in England.

The rest of my story we will laugh over together, for I hope to see you before long. Farewell.

VI-3   Michelangelo Buonarroti to his father Lodovico

When his father writes that the artist was reportedly speaking out against the Medici, Michelangelo (1475-1564) becomes concerned for his family back in Florence and for himself. The Sack of Prato, carried out by the Imperial troops to reinstate the Medici in Florence (August-September, 1512), shocked everyone, but Michelangelo denies having spoken out.

Rome (October, 1512)

Dearest Father,—In your last letter you tell me to be careful not to keep money in the house and not to carry any about with me; also that I am reported in Florence as having spoken against the Medici.

As to the money, all I have lies in Balducci's bank, and I keep none of it either in the house nor upon my person, except such sums as are necessary from day to day. With regard to the Medici, I have never uttered a single word against them except in the general terms in which everybody talks—as, for instance, after the sack of Prato. I think that even the very stones would have spoken of it, had they been able. There have been many other things said since then, to which, when I heard them, I have always replied: "If they are really doing these things, they are doing wrong." Not that I believed the reports, and God grant they be not true. About a month ago someone who pretended to be my friend criticized their actions very adversely. I rebuked him, saying that those who spoke in such a way did wrong, and that he was not to mention the subject to me again. However, I should like Buonarroto to find out quietly where the man in question heard that I had spoken against the Medici, so that I may endeavor to trace the origin of the rumor, and find out whether it came from someone professing to be my friend. I shall then be upon my guard. I have nothing more to add. . . .

VI-4   Desiderius Erasmus to King Henry VIII of England

Having returned in 1517 from a brief sojourn in England where he was cordially received by both Henry VIII and Cardinal Wolsey, Erasmus was eager to cement his relations with these two, especially since, as the following letter intimates, the King may have promised a generous provision should Erasmus enter his service. Accordingly, the Dutch Humanist dispatched a handsome volume to each, accompanied by a politic note.

Antwerp, 9 September, 1517

Illustrious King, among your numberless truly royal and heroic endowments,— by which you not only recall the merits of your admirable parent, Henry, the Seventh of that name, but even surpass them,—various admirers may choose different subjects for praise. For myself, I regard them all with respect; but what chiefly commands my approbation is this, that whereas, being gifted with an extraordinary clearness of mind, you have no lack of wisdom yourself, you still delight in familiar converse with men of prudence and learning, and most of all with those who do not know how to flatter. It is as though you had somewhere read that verse of Sophocles,—and indeed I do not doubt you have read it,

Σοφοὶ τύραννοι τῶν σοφῶν συνουσίᾳ,

Kings become wise by wise companionship.

Another chief merit is this, that among so many affairs in which your kingdom, and indeed the whole world, is concerned, you scarcely let a day pass but you bestow some time upon reading, and delight in converse with those ancient sages, who are anything but flatterers; while you choose especially those books, from which you may rise a better and a wiser man, and more useful to your country. Thus you are far from agreeing with persons who think that princes of the highest rank ought, of all things, to keep clear of serious or philosophic study, and that, if books are taken in hand at all, nothing should be read but amusing stories scarcely good enough for women, or mere incitements to folly and vice. The two conceptions of wisdom and of sovereignty are thus assumed to be diametrically opposed to each other; whereas they are so closely connected, that, if you take away one from the other, you leave nothing but the mere title of Sovereign, like the cenotaphs, which display on the outside the names and pedigrees of the dead, the inside being empty.

Moreover, as an intelligent and pious prince is wise, vigilant, and provident for the whole community, being one that is transacting, not his own business, but that of the public, so is it right, that every man should endeavour to the utmost of his power to help him in his cares and anxieties; and the wider his empire, the more need has he of this kind of service. A sovereign is an exceptional being among mortals, an image of the Deity; and yet he is a man. For my own part, since it is only out of my small stock of literature that I can make any payment of this duty to kings,—I did some time ago turn from Greek into Latin Plutarch's little work upon the means of distinguishing a Flatterer from a Friend, and dedicated it to your Majesty by the mediation of the Cardinal, who in the government of your realm fills the same part to you as Theseus did to Hercules, or Achates to Aeneas. But being suddenly drawn at that time into the hurricane of war by a sort of fatal storm, which then fell upon all Christendom, you had no leisure,—I may well suppose,—to give any attention to literature, when the business in hand could only be conducted with the sword. I now therefore send again to your Highness the same book, though it has been since communicated to the world and is now printed for the third time; and I send it with interest, having attached to it the Panegyrical Eulogy of Philip, king of Castile, whose memory I know you keep sacred, as one whom, when you were yourself a boy, you loved as an elder brother, and whom your excellent father had adopted as a son.

To these I have added the Institution of a Prince, an offering which I made not long since to Charles the King Catholic, when he was newly initiated into sovereignty. Not that he stood in need of our admonitions; but, as in a great storm, the steersman, however skilful he may be, is contented to receive a warning from any quarter; so a Sovereign, destined to rule so many kingdoms, ought not to spurn any advice that is proffered in a serious spirit, while he is resolved to follow that, which of all the plans proposed he may judge to be best. But what estuary will you anywhere find, that has such disturbing currents as the tumults that arise in extensive empires? Or who ever saw at sea such fearful tempests, as those hurricanes of human affairs, which we have witnessed in these last few years? And still more dangerous storms appear to be impending, if things are not set in order by the wisdom and piety of Princes. As a last consideration, having been raised to the rank of Councillor, I thought it right to respond at once to my appointment by this act of duty, and not merely to give my opinion in particular cases, but to show to a Prince of no ordinary character, but still a boy, some of the sources, as it were, from which all counsels flow.

That your Majesty stands in need of any such admonitions, is so far from being the case, that one who studies your likeness with due attention might well compose after the model before him the portrait of a perfect sovereign. I have sent the book nevertheless, because I knew that in any case it would not be disagreeable to you to be reminded of two kings, who have been most dear to you. Moreover, these precepts, provided they are sound, will come with an added recommendation to all kings or kings' sons, if they are aware that they have not been disapproved by the most intelligent, the most unspoiled, and the most successful of all living monarchs. As a last consideration, I shall at any rate escape the blame of ingratitude, if I do not cease to bear witness with all the pains I can to the interest which your Majesty has been pleased to take in me. What indeed do I not owe you, having been so often distinguished by the testimony of your voice, and having been invited, I may add, when lately with you, to enter your service upon such generous terms,—and that without solicitation, and with a condescension truly royal,—when I think it in itself no small distinction that so insignificant a person is approved, recognized and loved by so great a Sovereign?

May Jesus Christ, Best and Greatest, Prince of Princes, long keep your Majesty in safety and happiness.

Antwerp, the morrow of the Nativity of the Blessed Virgin.

VI-5   Jacob Fugger to Emperor Charles V of Spain

The powerful Augsburg banker Jacob Fugger (1459-1525) demands repayment of an enormous debt owed by His Imperial Majesty Charles V, reminding the mighty ruler that his election in 1519 could by no means have been accomplished without Fugger money. (Jacob had personally provided 544,000 florins out of total election expenses of 852,000.)

Augsburg, 1523

His Most Serene, All-Powerful Roman Emperor, and Most Gracious Lord!
Your Royal Majesty is undoubtedly well aware of the extent to which I and my
nephews have always been inclined to serve the House of Austria, and in all
submissiveness to promote its welfare and its rise. For that reason, we co-operated
with the former Emperor Maximilian, Your Imperial Majesty's forefather, and, in
loyal subjection to His Majesty, to secure the Imperial Crown for Your Imperial
Majesty, pledged ourselves to several princes, who placed their confidence and
trust in me as perhaps in no one else. We also, when Your Imperial Majesty's
appointed delegates were treating for the completion of the above-mentioned
undertaking, furnished a considerable sum of money which was secured, not from
me and my nephews alone, but from some of my good friends at heavy cost, so that
the excellent nobles achieved success to the great honor and well-being of Your
Imperial Majesty.

It is also well known that Your Majesty without me might not have acquired the
Imperial Crown, as I can attest with the written statement of all the delegates of
Your Imperial Majesty. And in all this I have looked not to my own profit. For if
I had withdrawn my support from the House of Austria, and transferred it to
France, I should have won large profit and much money, which were at that time
offered to me. But what disadvantage would have risen thereby for the House of
Austria, Your Imperial Majesty with your deep comprehension may well
conceive.

Taking all this into consideration, my respectful request to Your Imperial
Majesty is that you will graciously recognize my faithful, humble service,
dedicated to the greater well-being of Your Imperial Majesty, and that you will
order that the money which I have paid out, together with the interest upon it,
shall be reckoned up and paid, without further delay. In order to deserve that from
Your Imperial Majesty, I pledge myself to be faithful in all humility, and I hereby
commend myself as faithful at all times to Your Imperial Majesty.

Your Imperial Majesty's most humble servant
Jacob Fugger

VI-6   Cornelius Agrippa to a Friend

Following his dismissal as physician to the Queen-mother of France, Cornelius Agrippa (1486-1535) draws up a stingingly ironic code of behavior for the model courtier.

1526

Hear what rules I have prescribed for myself, if ever I am tempted to return to the court service: to make myself a proper courtier, I will flatter egregiously, be sparing of faith, profuse of speech, ambiguous in counsel, like the oracles of old; but I will pursue gain, and prefer my own advantage above all things: I will cultivate no friendship save for money's sake; I will be wise to myself, praise no man except through cunning, decry any man you please. I will thrust forth whom I can, that I may take what he is forced to leave, will place myself on half a dozen seats, and despise every one who offers me his hospitality but not his money, as a barren tree. I will have faith in no man's word, in no man's friendship; I will take all things ill and brood on vengeance; the Prince only I will watch and worship, but him I will flatter, I will agree with, I will infest, only through fear or greed of my own gain. You may admire me for that I have become so good a courtier only now, when I am liberated from the court. . . . The astrological judgments, as I before told you, I have not finished, and will not finish, until the Queen has replied to my letter, and herself required them of me. . . . But I should like you to tell me who my evil genius is by whom the Queen's mind is possessed, to the obliteration of her good will, so recently expressed towards me: because I ought to cast him out by some religious exorcism, or appease him by some magical sacrifice, or fortify myself against him with barbarous names of the gods and cabalistic pentacles. . . .

VI-7   Pietro Aretino to King Francis I of France

Pietro Aretino (1492-1556) advises King Francis I not to accept Turkish aid in reinforcing his position against Emperor Charles V, warning him that such a maneuver will inevitably backfire. Francis had engaged in a long series of wars with Charles, the most famous conflict being the Battle of Pavia in 1525 (see Letter VII-5) and for the last two wars (1536-38 and 1542-44) he allied himself with the Protestant princes in Germany as well as with the Turks, who were threatening Hungary.

Venice, 1536

Although I know full well that in the opinion of the world it is not seemly to write a person of royal estate upon a matter of such moment without being requested to, yet since the commandments of God forbid deception and in Christ's republic there are no differences of rank, I dare to appeal to you once again, and in the same frame of mind as when I wrote my last letter.

In that epistle I doubted—and as a Christian I grieved that I could not do so—that I could address you by that title of "Most Christian," of which you once were worthy. Now I lament—and, as your servant, I regret this—that I can call you neither King of France nor Francis, for one cannot truthfully be called either King or Free (which last is what Francis and France mean) if he goes about begging the aid of those barbarians who are both enemies of his race and rebels against his God.

My lord—for so I still name you—you have thrust the Ottoman sword into the heart of Christendom, and by doing this you have gravely wounded the glory of your hitherto unconquered excellence. Moreover—and with little or no harm to him—you have but strengthened the cause of that Caesar, whom you hold to be your enemy. For where will you find a Christian prince who—either from zeal for our religion, or because he fears Turkish arms—does not gird himself, or at least turn his sympathies, against you, now that you have chosen such an ally?

Look at the wise king of England. Although for a long time, he was estranged from both the Pope and the Emperor, no sooner did he realize that Turkish fury was directed against the West, than he turned his pious and his truly Christian arms against you. Those others, who, for one reason or another, have not yet done the same, either will do so shortly, or else—and it is of some weight—will long for, and will pray to God for your ruin. For they will be afraid that their own ruin would follow shortly if—but God will not permit this—the arms of Caesar should go down in defeat.

And do you believe for a moment, Sire, that if the strength of the infidel were greater he would keep faith to this pact of brotherhood and alliance which has brought you such dishonor? O my Lords examine the reasons which have led the Turk to give you his protection against Caesar. Believe me, if the arms of Caesar were less potent than yours, he who is now on your side would array his might against you, for he knows that he cannot—and this is his objective—defeat you both at the same time, and so he hopes to defeat you separately, using your arms to help him.

For remember, Sire, that Amurath—one of this tyrant's greatest ancestors— never could have invaded Europe to its ultimate woe, if the men of Trebizond had not summoned him in their misfortune, just as this sultan is now called by you. Remember the Roman Republic. Even though it was the sworn enemy of barbarian ways, the true friend of keeping faith, and rich in honorable examples, it would never have become the master of Capua, if the men of that city had not called it in to their assistance. When Jugurtha quarreled with his vassals, the same Romans were called in by the weaker party, and thus the empire was enlarged. To humble Philip, the Greek people gave the Romans a similar chance to grow greater. And how also—even in our own times—did unhappy Milan fall into the power of Charles? By those very arms which they put into his hands!

All of these things happened between pagan and pagan, or between Christian and Christian, and yet you think, O Sire, that you can have confidence in the leader of the enemies of your religion. Do you imagine that he does not know how much treasure and what lavish blood your predecessors poured out against the Mahomettans? That he does not know that if the Christian armies were united under your right royal leadership, he would see the standard, and the unconquerable gonfalon of Christ before him, and that you would be the leader and the guide of Turkish ruin? Do you believe that he does not know that it is neither lack of Christian faith—for so great a sin is not entertained by royal mind—nor the affection that you have for him who is its enemy, that binds you to his cause, but only your contempt for Caesar that moves you to such action?

Cast aside then, O Sire, break and cut to pieces this treacherous so-called brotherhood—that is if you want to be called a Christian. For we cannot all be brothers in Christ together, if you at the same time are the brother of Christ's most potent enemy.

But even if—and I do not want to believe it—neither zeal for our religion, respect for God the All Highest, nor alarm that you and all Christians may taste disaster together makes you draw back, at least let that honor which is prized even by pagans, barbarians, and infidels, have some weight in your royal mind. Surely, you do not want the blame that will come to you for not fitting your action to your words. You call yourself "Most Christian" but you act like the worst enemy of Christ.

You would perhaps like to make answer that these men are your mercenaries, that they are not bound to you by any alliance, that they serve you only because they are paid by you. Take heed, O Sire, lest you be the one to introduce so wicked a practice among Christian princes, and believe me, too, that the Ottoman armies have no need of your gold.

But even if it were true, think of the reproaches you will earn. In the days of the great Camillus, France burst through the Roman walls with sword and fire, and on the Capitol itself made the sacred shrines of that unconquerable people quake with fear. When Laelius Emilius and Caius Statius were consuls, her name alone sent terror through all of Italy, and made us arm 80,000 horsemen and 70,000 footsoldiers. In the days of old, France overran Asia and won such victories that she left behind the name of Gallogrecia. That name endures even today. And in more modern times, under Charlemagne, she won renown and gave proof of her valor in Spain and Germany and against the Saracens. Yes, I tell you, France has gained a thousand victories, earned a thousand triumphs throughout the world. Yet you would be willing to have her bow the knee and seek the succor of those who are her enemies and the enemies of her God. You would have her hope that under the leadership of a greedy corsair, of a vile and infamous pirate, her armed forces would conquer!

Yet France is still the same France that she was in her better days. The same sky shines down on her. She is watered by the same streams. Yet with different desires and with none of the same strength, she is obedient to your slightest nod. Whence comes this change? What is the cause of her great contumacy? With sorrow and yet respectfully, I am obliged to tell you in part.

Believe me, Sire, if you had esteemed brave and strong hearts as you do vile adulation, it would never have come to pass. If your court had valued the sweat of soldiers as it does soft perfumes, it would never have happened. If the perspiration that drips from you, the fatigues that you endure, and the treasure that you squander in hunts, dances and splendid banquets, had been bestowed and lavished upon worthy undertakings and valorous endeavors, you would not have any need for Turks or Moors!

Once upon a time, in the France of old, tippling and high-living was held in such scorn that not only were they unknown among you, but even your merchants were forbidden to indulge in them when they went into foreign lands. But in our day—though I shame to say it—not he who runs a good course with his lance, not the expert swordsman, not the valiant heart, is the one who is admired in that land, but rather he who guzzles the most wine.

The wise Romans decreed that women should kiss their kinfolk. This was to ensure their abstinence, for if wine—which brings so many evils—were smelled upon their breath, they were punished. But in your country, not only their kin, but whoever else wants to, is permitted to kiss the women, so that those who do not reek of the grape may be punished. For the women are no more continent than the men.

Yet even though idleness and unmanly living have brought your kingdom to this pass, do not decide to medicine it with a greater evil. For believe me, Sire, neither the conquest of Milan, nor for that matter of all the rest of Italy, would honor you with as much honor, as you will merit condemnation for the crime of seeking shameful aid from Turks and Moors. Moreover, I am convinced that even with their aid, it would be difficult if not impossible to accomplish this end, for where before you had only Caesar as foe, you would then have—as I said above—not only Caesar, but all others who love Christ, and the hearts of your servants and vassals and even God for an adversary. In fact, I feel certain that God has already turned His wrath against you, since He has allowed you to be beyond all decent bounds, and not see what the whole world sees.

I wish that I could write to you with that restraint which is due to your rank and to your past merits, but our nature makes us far more conscious of a shabby present than of an excellent past, and for that reason I lament your crime of today rather than rejoice at the good deeds you once did—all the more so since the error you persist in, is by all people held to be so great that neither your old-time piety and religion nor that of Charlemagne and all your other forebears can atone for it.

Moreover, if it is a kingly envy that so pricks at your soul that it cannot endure the greatness and the superiority of Caesar, let your calm wisdom rule you for a while, and then decide which is the more dangerous to you, Caesar's lofty and sterling qualities, or the haughtiness and boundless barbarity of the Turk. And remember that it is an ancient and an honorable custom to give crowns and kingdoms to those who most deserve them.

Therefore, either do not lament Caesar's greatness or act with such judgment that you are his equal or superior. And because subjects model their ways after their lord, strive to set your court and all your kingdom the same example of continence, justice and piety that Caesar does. Like Caesar, take up your honorable sword for Christ. Even now, fighting the Turks and Moors, he makes his breast a shield to fend off these rebels against God. And if anyone tells you that he does not do this for the sake of our faith—that he does it to help his brother, or for fame, or for some other earthly reason—answer them that only God can see into our hearts, and that no matter what the end his work was done for, it is still worthy of eternal glory.

Such then, O Sire, be your own undertakings that you need envy no one, and such be your people that they are not mendicants for dire and infidel aid. In God's name, rise up against the venomous serpent. Do not permit Turkish scorn to be seen parading through your cities and palaces and through the holy temples of Christ. Do not let it stain with its profane eyes the clear sanctity of our rites. Remember that to the ravening of this brindled beast, your blood will taste as sweet as Caesar's if ever he can consummate his barbarian contempt. Not only because of today's shame, but for fear of future harm, drive him from you. He is not your help, but your destruction. He is not your ally, but your foe. He is not your brother, but your adversary.

The Christian princes urge you to do this, for they fear the Turkish despot. So do the common people who fear being enslaved by barbarian cruelty. So do all poor women, who fear to see their own honor and that of their daughters smirched by Turkish lust. So, in fine, Sire, does that Christ Who lifted you up to divine honors and Who shed his very Christian blood for you.

When you have done that, you will pardon me for my fault of being your rash yet faithful servant just as readily as I hope you will soon ask God to pardon you for your own sin. And if what people are saying reaches royal ears as it does those of ordinary men, you will not blame me for having written you. You will blame me for waiting so long.

VI-8   Sir Thomas Wyatt to John Poins

Banished from court to his father's place in Kent, Sir Thomas Wyatt (1503-1542) satirizes the courtier's life in this verse epistle to his close friend, John Poins. The poet was twice arrested by Henry VIII, first in May 1536, in connection with adultery charges against Anne Boleyn (Wyatt's first cousin), and again in January 1541, when he was accused of treason. On both occasions, he returned to full royal favor.

(1536)

Mine own John Poins, since ye delight to know
The cause why that homeward I me draw,
And flee the press of courts, whereso they go,
Rather than to live thrall, under the awe
Of lordly looks, wrapped within my cloak,
To will and lust learning to set a law;
It is not for because I scorn and mock
The power of them to whom Fortune hath lent
Charge over us, of right to strike the stroke.
But true it is that I have always meant   10
Less to esteem them than the common sort,
Of outward things that judge in their intent
Without regard what doth inward resort.
I grant sometime that of glory the fire
Doth touch my heart; me list not to report
Blame by honor, and honor to desire.
But how may I this honor now attain
That cannot dye the color black a liar?
My Poins, I cannot frame me tune to feign,
To cloak the truth, for praise without desert,   20
Of them that list all vice for to retain.
I cannot honor them that sets their part
With Venus and Bacchus all their life long;
Nor hold my peace of them, although I smart.
I cannot crouch nor kneel to do so great a wrong,
To worship them like God on earth alone,
That are as wolves these sely [1] lambs among.
I cannot with my words complain and moan
Nor suffer naught, nor smart without complaint,
Nor turn the word that from my mouth is gone;   30
I cannot speak and look like a saint,
Use wiles for wit, or make deceit a pleasure;
And call craft counsel, for profit still to paint;
I cannot wrest the law to fill the coffer,
With innocent blood to feed myself fat,
And do most hurt where most help I offer.
I am not he that can allow the state

1. blessed

Of high Caesar, and damn Cato to die,
That with his death did scape out of the gate
From Caesar's hands, if Livy do not lie,   40
And would not live where liberty was lost,
So did his heart the common weal apply.
I am not he, such eloquence to boast
To make the crow in singing as the swan,
Nor call the lion of coward beasts the most,
That cannot take a mouse as the cat can;
And he that dieth of hunger of the gold,
Call him Alexander, and say that Pan
Passeth Apollo in music manifold;
Praise Sir Thopas [2] for a noble tale,   50
And scorn the story that the Knight told;
Praise him for counsel that is drunk of ale;
Grin when he laugheth that beareth all the sway,
Frown when he frowneth, and groan when he is pale;
On others' lust to hang both night and day,—
None of these points would ever frame in me;
My wit is naught: I cannot learn the way;
And much the less of things that greater be
That asken help of colors of device
To join the mean with each extremity.   60
With nearest virtue to cloak alway the vice,
And as to purpose, likewise it shall fall
To press the virtue that it may not rise;
As drunkenness, good fellowship to call;
The friendly foe, with his double face,
Say he is gentle and courteous therewithal;
And say that favel [3] hath a goodly grace
In eloquence; and cruelty to name
Zeal of justice, and change in time and place;
And he that suff'reth offense without blame,   70
Call him pitiful, and him true and plain
That raileth reckless to every man's shame,
Say he is rude that cannot lie and feign,
The lecher a lover, and tyranny

2. Chaucer (as Sir Thopas) tells a wretchedly bad, unfinished tale in *Canterbury Tales* in contrast to the fine courtly Knight's Tale.
   3. flattery

To be the right of a prince's reign.
I cannot, I: no, no, it will not be.
This is the cause that I could never yet
Hang on their sleeves, that weigh, as thou mayst see,
A chip of chance more than a pound of wit.
This maketh me at home to hunt and hawk,   80
And in foul weather at my book to sit,
In frost and snow then with my bow to stalk.
No man doth mark whereso I ride or go.
In lusty leas at liberty I walk,
And of these news I feel nor weal nor woe,
Save that a clog [4] doth hang yet at my heel.
No force for that, for it is ordered so
That I may leap both hedge and dike full well;
I am not now in France, to judge the wine,
With sav'ry sauce those delicates to feel;   90
Nor yet in Spain, where one must him incline,
Rather than to be, outwardly to seem.
I meddle not with wits that be so fine;
Nor Flanders' cheer letteth not [5] my sight to deem
Of black and white, nor taketh my wit away
With beastliness, they beasts do so esteem.
Nor am I not where Christ is given in prey
For money, poison and treason—at Rome
A common practice, used night and day.
But here I am in Kent and Christendom,   100
Among the Muses, where I read and rhyme;
Where, if thou list, my Poins, for to come,
Thou shalt be judge how I do spend my time.

(See also Letter IX-9, dating from this same period, in which Wyatt, instead of "hanging day and night on other's lust," tells Henry VIII forthrightly of a sexual adventure he had experienced with Anne Boleyn.)

4. Wyatt had lost the trust of Henry VIII
5. prevents

VI-9   Pietro Aretino to Giovanni Agnello

Aretino pens a scathing indictment of life at court to Giovanni Agnello, brother of the Mantuan ambassador to Venice.

Venice, 26 November, 1537

My lord Benedetto who is the ducal ambassador and your brother, asked me yesterday how I was and what I was doing—and for no other reason than to tell you, who, because you love me, had expressed a desire to know. Let me reply that I keep well, and am doing excellently. Furthermore, it is not only I, who am able to be hale when many another *could* not, and to do deeds that many another *would* not, who can feel like a pope and act like an emperor. The sorriest wretch there is can do the same if he lives in this city and away from courts.

I have never been in Heaven as far as I know, so I cannot imagine whether its blessings are worth it, but I do know that if you die of hunger you are playing a jest upon the world. So you had better stay away from their Inferno!

Courts, ah? Courts eh? Well, for my part I would be happier to be a gondolier here than a gentlemen of the bedchamber there. Hopes yonder! Little favors there! But any real reward, some other day!

Have a look at just one poor old servitor. He stands on his feet, done to death by the cold or burned up by the heat. Where is the fire to warm him, or the water to refresh him? If he falls ill, what room, what stable, or even what charity ward will have a place for him? Then there is the rain, the snow, and the mud. Don't they murder him when he rides for his master upon the latter's business? But where are there any clean clothes into which to change? Is there even a nod of acknowledgement for all that he has done?

It burns me up to see men grown hoary-bearded before their time serving young lads—to see their hair turned white prematurely as they squander their youth waiting upon tables, standing in entrance halls, and cleaning privies.

"You can have my share of courts!" cried a certain good and learned man. He had been hounded to the gallows because he would not commit some piece of pimpery.

It is better for the belly to dine on bread and jests than to try to feast on the smell of fine viands on a silver platter. You cannot assuage the gnawing of your hunger with one chestnut or one walnut either before or after dinner.

No, there is no suffering like that of a courtier who is weary and has nowhere to sit down, who is hungry and may not eat, and who is overcome by sleep and yet must stay awake, and there is no happiness like mine, who can sit down when I am worn out, eat when I am hungry and sleep when sleep assails me. All my hours are my own.

I don't know what we ought to say about the cringing state of mind of those who think that the right to tumble onto an untidy heap of straw is ample reward for all the servitude and loyalty there is, but I, for my part, glory in my wants, since I do not have to take off my cap to any Durante or Ambrogio.[1]

Think it over then. Don't you agree that I keep well, and do even better?

Yet my happiness would be even greater if your lordship would only make constant use of my abode. I can think of no practice that would please me better. Then when we talked together or dined together or with Titian, I would not need to say "your reverence" to the whole College of Cardinals, and not even to Chieti.[2]

The days seem years to me that his Excellency, your prince, has kept you away from me at the court of His Imperial Majesty in Spain. I like lordly and noble philosophers as you are and as the worthy Gianiacopo Bardellone was, and not rag-and-tatters ones who spend all the time trying to make themselves appear something.

VI-10   Emperor Charles V of Spain to his brother Ferdinand

Charles V's political manipulations after defeating the Protestant Prince at Mühlberg were strangely incautious. Replacing the imprisoned Elector of Saxony by Maurice, a young relative of the Elector in whom he trusted blindly, the great Emperor (1500-1558) found himself suddenly trapped with a small escort in Innsbruck. Maurice headed in his direction with an army.

He who has conquered so much of Europe wonders which way to flee.

1. Two courtiers, chamberlain and secretary, of Pope Paul III.
2. Ironic reference to the new Order of Theatine Monks, founded at Chieti in 1524.

Innsbruck, 4 April, 1552

Seeing that the Duke Maurice has put off his journey to meet you, and since I am informed of a certainty that he is in person at Augsburgh, and knowing well how little I myself am in any posture of defence here in this fine country, and if I linger much longer here that I stand a chance of finding myself some morning taken in my bed, I have been resolving on my departure . . .* But where to go? The road to Italy is not so safe, but that many difficulties are there before me . . . Were I indeed to go thither, destitute as I now am of troops, I should find myself in every place without authority. I see no safety in passing through the Venetian states; and more than that, supposing I were allowed to pass, I should arrive in a province in no securer state for me than this . . . Besides I should find myself among soldiers under no restraint; and most licencious, discontented at not having received their pay at the time appointed, and among people in despair at the bad treatment they apprehend. . . . And if I take my departure before those who are now at Augsburgh commence their march in this direction, you may well imagine the dilemma in which I may perchance find myself; and if they approach this place by forced marches, a couple of days gained before I am off, I must hasten my retreat according to the rapidity of their advance in a way little suited to the care requisite for my infirmities. . . . In abandoning Germany, I cannot see what I may find myself compelled to, having none to declare in my favour, and so many with power in their hands against me. . . . And where to go, neither having money, nor means of obtaining it. . . . It is also much to be apprehended that the Turkish fleet with that of France would oppose the passage of my galleys, were I to embark for Spain . . . You may well conceive what an honourable adventure this might prove, and what a pleasant end I should come to in these my declining days. Besides I hold it for certain, that half of Italy would be in a state of revolt; and our Low Countries fall a prey to France. . . . I am well aware, whatever I determine on, if it succeeds, will be placed to the account of good fortune; if it fails, the fault will be mine. . . . Finding myself in such extremities, recommending myself to God, I would rather be set down as an old fool, than allow myself to be undone in my old age, without attempting all I can to prevent it, aye and more. If I am to choose between a great disgrace and a great danger, I will take the part of danger . . . And therefore I have determined to set off this night for Flanders, where at present I have the most troops . . . And there I shall not be far from Germany.

(Charles fled shortly to the village of Villach in Carinthia until the Peace of Passau, favorable to the Protestants.)

* . . . All ellipses herein reproduced from actual manuscript.

VI-11   Sertorio Quattromani to his nephew Francesco della Valle

Sertorio Quattromani (1541-1607) reproaches his nephew Francesco, recently ennobled, for becoming a snob and disowning his uncle. From Cosenza, Quattromani achieved a distinguished career in Naples as a philologist specializing in the classical and Provençal languages.

Rome, 18 April 1563

Is it my fault you have been made a Baron? For this must I lose your kinship and friendship? Well then, shall fortune's blessings have the power to break the tie that binds us? As for myself, I can't believe it. Signor Cesare Sersale writes me that you have become insufferably arrogant and that you offer a thousand lies to all those who presume to say I am your uncle; why can't you imagine that a poor man such as I, can be the uncle of a Baron such as you? And he tells me many other things that make me believe this and worse. You will tell me not to believe Signor Cesare because he is joking, and he's writing you these things to make you angry with me. What a lot of excuses! I likewise see the signs, because since the purchase of Ferolito I've had no letter from you. For goodness' sake, don't rely so much on worldly aggrandizements because they are fleeting and unsubstantial. Devote yourself entirely to study and behave in such a way that people say you lend grace to wealth rather than wealth lending grace to you. You have a teacher so wise and learned, he could make men of letters from stones; and your talent is so admirable that I promise myself great things will come of it; wherefore I don't need to say a great deal to convince you. So I beg you that to begin with, you remember me and write me a few little letters in your own hand which would give me great comfort. Stay well. Answer me in Latin because I want to show the letter to Bishop Severino, who is staying in the house of Signor Cardinal d'Aragona, and is very much my friend and master, and commends himself everlastingly to your noble father.

    M. Lattantio Crasso is writing you a letter that has neither head nor tail, neither sense nor purpose. Answer him for the sake of courtesy and let him understand that if he knows how to write out of turn through nature, you know how to do it through art.

(trans. L.L.)

VI-12   Czar Ivan the Terrible to Prince Kurbsky

In the Middle Ages the theocratic emperors took for granted their divine right to rule. In the nationalist kingdoms of the Renaissance few rulers claimed this divine authority with the zeal of Ivan IV, "The Terrible" (1529-1584).The desertion of Prince Andrey Kurbsky, a general of Muscovy, to the Polish-Lithuanian forces in April, 1564, thus prompted the following outburst (here, much reduced) from the anointed Orthodox tyrant whom Soviet autarchs have exalted to a symbol of Russian unity. Note how Ivan turns to the Bible to enrich his invective. In Ivan's use, "Christian" means only Orthodox, leaving out Catholic and Protestant alike.

The Orthodox City of Moscow, 5 July 7072 (1564)
    The autocracy of this Russian kingdom of veritable Orthodoxy, by the will of God, [has its] beginning from the great tsar Vladimir, who enlightened the whole Russian land with holy baptism, and [was maintained by] the great tsar Vladimir Monomach, who received the supreme honour from the Greeks, and the brave and great sovereign, Alexander Nevsky, who won a victory over the godless Germans,[1] and the great and praiseworthy sovereign, Dimitry, who beyond the Don won a mighty victory over the godless sons of Hagar,[2] [and autocracy was handed down] even to the avenger of evils, our grandfather, the Grand Prince Ivan, and to the acquirer of immemorially hereditary lands, our father of blessed memory, the great sovereign, Vasily—and [autocracy] has come down even to us, the humble sceptre-bearer of the Russian kingdom. And we praise [God] for his great mercy bestowed upon us, in that he has not hitherto allowed our right hand

1. In 1242 Alexander Nevsky defeated the knights of the Teutonic Order on the ice of Lake Peipus.
2. The "Sons of Hagar," or "Ishmaelites," was the common Russian appellation for all Mohammedans, more particularly for the Tatars. In 1380 Dimitry Donskoy defeated the khan of the Golden Horde, Mamai, on the field of Kulikovo.

to become stained with the blood of our own race; for we have not seized the kingdom from anyone, but, by the grace of God and with the blessing of our forefathers and fathers, as we were born to rule, so have we grown up and ascended the throne by the bidding of God, and with the blessing of our parents have we taken what is our own, and we have not seized what belongs to others; [From the ruler] of this Orthodox true Christian autocracy, which has power over many dominions, a command [should be sent to you]; but this is our Christian and humble answer to him who was formerly boyar and adviser and voevoda of our autocratic state and of the true Christian Orthodox faith, but who is now the perjurer of the holy and life-giving Cross of the Lord and the destroyer of Christianity, the servant of those enemies of Christianity who have apostatized from the worship of the divine icons and trampled on all the sacred commandments and destroyed the holy temples and befouled and trampled on the sacred vessels and images. . . .

You, however, for the sake of your body have destroyed the soul and for the sake of short-lived fame have scorned imperishable glory, and having raged against man, you have risen against God. Consider, wretch, from what heights and into what depths you have descended in body and soul! On you have come to pass the words: "from him . . . shall be taken away even that which he hath." [3] Is this then your piety, that you have destroyed yourself because of your self-love and not for the sake of God? Those who live there [i.e. in your new fatherland] and those who have understanding can understand your evil poison, how, desiring short-lived glory and wealth, and not in order to escape from death, you have done this deed. If you are just and pious as you say, why did you fear a guiltless death, which is no death but gain? [4] In the end you will die anyhow! If you did fear a false death sentence against you owing to the villainous lying of your friends, the servants of Satan, then is your [*plur.*] treacherous intention clear from the beginning up to now. Why did you despise even the apostle Paul? For he said: "Let every soul be subject unto the higher powers. For there is no power ordained that is not of God. . . . Whosoever, therefore, resisteth the power, resisteth the ordinance of God." [5] Think on this and reflect, that he who resists power, resists God; and who resists God is called an apostate, which is the worst sin. And these words were said concerning all power, even when power is obtained by blood and strife. But consider what I said above, that I did not take my kingdom by rape; if you then resist [such] power, all the more so do you resist God. . . .

Your epistle has been received and clearly understood. And since you have put adder's poison under your lips,[6] [your epistle] was filled, according to your

3. Matt. xxv. 29.
4. Cf. Phil. i. 21.
5. Almost literally from Romes. xiii. 1-2.
6. Cf. Ps. cxl. 3.

understanding, with honey and the honeycomb [7] and yet is found to be bitterer than wormwood, according to the prophet who says: "their words were softer than oil, yet were they drawn swords." [8] Are you thus accustomed, being a Christian, so to serve a Christian sovereign? And is this then the fitting honour to pay to a master given by God, that you should belch forth poison in a devilish manner? . . . You, blinded by your evil ways, cannot see the truth. How, thinking that you will stand at the throne of the Almighty and serve for ever with the angels, and how, having deemed yourselves worthy to slaughter the Sacrificial Lamb for the salvation of the world,—how, when you have trampled under foot all these things with your devilish advisers, could you bring so many torments on us with your evil designs? And therefore, in view of your having in devilish manner shattered piety since the days of my youth, and in view of your having seized and appropriated the power handed down to me by God from our forefathers—is this then the sign of a "leprous conscience" to hold my kingdom in my hand and not to let my servants rule? And is it contrary to reason not to wish to be possessed and ruled by my own servants? And is this "illustrious Orthodoxy"—to be ruled over and ordered about by my own servants?

(On the "tirannycall state of the Russe government" under later Czar Fedor, see VI–19 below.)

VI-13   Edmund Hogan to Queen Elizabeth

When Queen Elizabeth sought to extend her sphere of influence into Morocco, her commercial agent found the Sultan of Morocco well aware of the rivalry between Anglican England and Catholic Spain. The Arab tactfully agreed to favor English interests in all ways. Morocco (Safi) had been free of Portuguese occupation since 1541 (See Letter VIII-4).

11 June, 1577

Maye it please your Majestie to be advertised that after your Highnes Lettres beeinge derecktid unto the Kinge of Barbere, with your Majesties Commission

7. Cf. Ps. xix. 10.
8. Ps. lv. 21.

signid, delyverid unto me, I preparid myselfe for theese partis, imbarking at Portesmothe, the vj[th] daye of Maye, and the . . . of the same monthe aryved on this coste of Barbere, at a porte of the Kinges cawlid Saphia. I remanid a boorde shipp in the Rode, and wrott lettres to Marocus, wheare the Kinge keepes his Coorte. At the ende of v. dayes, the Kinge beinge informyd of my arivall, sente sartayne captaynes with soldiers and Englishe marchauntes to me for to sap-hecundit [1] me upp to his Coorte, declaringe that he greatley rejoysed at the Letter from your Majestie. So as the first of June I cam to his City of Marocus, and upon the third by his order mett me all the Christean marchauntes; and neere to the Citty, some of his souldiors; whome declarid it was the Kings pleasur to honnor your Majestie all he coolde devise, and thearfore I thoughte it good I shoolde cum to his presence. So to his pallace I was broughte, and to the presence of the Kinge settinge in his chare of estate, and his Cownsallors, beeinge as well Moores as Christeans, standinge abowte hym. I dutifulley delyverid your Ma[ties] lettres and declarid my message in Spanishe, which allbeit he well undarstoode, and cawsid one to make relation what I said in the Arrabik language that the Moores mighte undarstande the same. And after, the Kinge geving greate thankes to your Majestie declarid that he with his Contre and all thinges thearin, shoolde be at your Majesties commandemente, regarding his honnor and law. I aunswearyd your Majestie reservid the same, as by yowr Highnis lettres he shoolde parceave. Theareuppon, I being conducktid to my lodginge, beeing appoyntyd of purpose with necessaries accordinglye, the same nighte he sente for me to the Coorte, where as he held late conferance with me, declaringe that the Kinge of Spayne had sente to hym for lycence that he myghte send an Embassador heather [2] with request that his Honnor woolde not gyve audyence to anie [3] that mighte cum from yowr Majestie, which leycence he had grauntid, butt (sayd the Kinge) when he comethe he shall see that I make more accompte of you, comynge from the Queen's Majestie of England, then of anne from Spayne; ffor I will use hym after the use of some placis in Chrystendome, to tarre [4] twentie dayes before I speake with hym, for that that the Kynge cannott govarne his owne Cuntrie, but ys govarnid by the Pope and Inquesityon, which religion hee doothe holley myslieke of.[5] Fyndinge hym to be a very earnist pr . . . . ante of good religion and lyvinge, and well experementyd [6] as well in the Olde Testamente as New, bearinge greate affecktyon to Gods trew relygion used in yowr Highnes Realme, I fynde hym agreeable to doo good to yowr marchants more then to anie other natyon: and not

1. safeconduct
2. hither
3. any
4. tarry
5. wholly dislike
6. experienced

to urge anie demawnde of yowr Majestie that maye tend to your dishonnor or breache of leage [7] with other Christian Princes, whear as appartanithe [8] to my duty I specialley regarde. He is not yett all in quiett within his cuntre, for the Blacke Kinge keepythe in the Mowntaynes, beeinge of small force. Thus praing to the Lorde for the presarvatyon of yowr Majesties Royall estate and honnor longe to govarne. From Marrocus in Barberia, the xj[th] of June, Anno Dom. 1577.

Your Ma[ties] moste humble sarvaunte,
Edmond Hogan

VI-14   Mary Stuart to Anthony Babington

Mary Stuart, Queen of Scots (1542-1587) was beheaded for her continual conspiring since 1569 with Catholic leaders like Anthony Babington and with Catholic rulers abroad to dethrone Queen Elizabeth. A letter to Babington in mid-year 1586 reveals her concern over the deteriorating Catholic situation and her eagerness to assume the throne herself.

July, 1586.

Trusty and well-beloved: According to the zeal and entire affection which I have known in you in the common cause of the religion and of my own in particular, I have ever based my hope upon you as a chief and most worthy instrument to be employed in both causes. . . . I cannot but praise, for divers great and important reasons, too long to recite here, your desire to hinder in time the plans of our enemies who seek to destroy our religion in this realm, and ruin all of us together. For long ago I pointed out to the other foreign Catholic princes, and experience has proved me right, that the longer we delayed intervening from both sides the greater advantage we give to our opponents to prevail against the said princes, as they have done against the King of Spain; and meanwhile the Catholics here, exposed to all kinds of persecution and cruelty, steadily grow less in numbers, power and means. . . .

Everything being prepared, and the forces, as well within as without, being ready, then you must set the six gentlemen to work and give order that their design being accomplished, I may be in some way got away from here and that all

7. fealty
8. appertaineth

your forces shall be simultaneously in the field to receive me while we await foreign assistance, which must then be brought up with all speed. Now as no certain day can be appointed for the performance of the said gentlemen's enterprise, I desire there to be always near them, or at least at court, four brave men well horsed to advertize speedily the success of their design, as soon as it is done, to those appointed to get me away from hence, so as to be able to get here before my keeper * is informed of the said execution. . . .

This plan seems to me the most suitable for this enterprise, so as to carry it out with care for our own safety. To move on this side before we are sure of good foreign help would simply be to risk to no purpose falling into the same miserable fortune as others who have formerly undertaken in this way. . . .

(Mary Stuart's willfulness and passionate nature are clearly revealed in Letter IX-17.)

VI-15   Queen Elizabeth to Mary Stuart, Queen of Scots

Having already occupied in her lifetime the throne of France and that of Scotland, Mary Stuart coveted the English crown and plotted long to win it. When finally she was put on trial for treason, she received from Elizabeth (1533-1603) the following blunt message, in French.

October 1586.

You have in various ways and manners attempted to take my life and to bring my kingdom to destruction by bloodshed. I have never proceeded so harshly against you, but have, on the contrary, protected and maintained you like myself. These treasons will be proved to you and all made manifest. Yet it is my will, that you answer the nobles and peers of the kingdom as if I were myself present. I therefore require, charge, and command that you make answer for I have been well informed of your arrogance.

Act plainly without reserve, and you will sooner be able to obtain favour of me.

Elizabeth.

* The keeper is Sir Amias Paulet, later to be a commissioner at Mary's trial.

VI-16   Emanuel Tomascon to an unknown Fugger Correspondent

The plot of Babington and Mary Stuart to assassinate the English Queen having been uncovered, Mary was brought to trial and convicted, but it was more than three months before Elizabeth could bring herself to sign the death warrant. Mary's courage and noble demeanor in the hour of her execution, attested by the following Fugger account, have made her long remembered as a sublimely tragic heroine.

February 1587

After there had been revealed to the Queen of England, Elizabeth, several plots, hatched at the instigation of the Pope and the heads of the neighbouring states, enemies of the Crown of England, the said Queen found that she had not only to fear for her throne, but also for her life. She then realized that their aim was to release the Queen Mary of Scotland from her durance and to establish her as the next heir, although she was a Catholic and had been detained in prison in England for many years. In this prison she was persecuted for a long time by the Parliament and the States of the Scottish Kingdom, in order that she might be condemned to death, for she had murdered a king, and had set fire to a house with gunpowder, because she was in love with Bothwell, a Scottish baron. Thereupon she abdicated in favour of her son James, the present King of Scotland. But when she again escaped from prison, she assembled troops, so as to rob the said son of his crown. However, she was put to flight and returned again to England. In spite of these charges Queen Elizabeth yet desired to spare her life, not wishing to be her judge, on account of her being such a near blood relation.

But as the Scottish Queen now presumed to covet the Crown of England, the English Queen could not let her go free and scathless, because her life, her country and religion were imperilled. Also she did not wish to create any suspicion in the minds of the Scots. Although the Scottish Queen was kept in such lax and pleasurable confinement that she could even go hunting and enjoy all the pleasures of the chase, she, nevertheless, did not rest content with the pastimes that were allowed to her. She tried many and various devices to become free again, namely through encompassing the death of the Queen of England. To this end she enticed many persons of the nobility, among them the Duke of Norfolk, as well as other earls and gentlemen, so that the Queen of England was to have lost her life at her Court in the previous summer. On that account the above-named lords met a miserable end. Also England was to have been attacked by foreign troops, the Scottish Queen set upon the thrones of Scotland and England, and the Romish faith established in both kingdoms. All of this the Queen of England gathered from various informants, and the Queen of Scotland was proved guilty in the presence of the nobility, the knighthood and the officials.

It was discussed in Parliament and by the States, how the person of the Queen and the religion of the country could be guarded in future against such dangers. As, however, the Scottish Queen was a close blood relation, her life was to be spared. Since also she was not in the free enjoyment of her liberty and rights, a sentence of death would make a rare and amazing departure.

Thereupon Parliament decided thus:—the life of the Scottish Queen would mean the death of the English Queen and the ruin and destruction of England and of her religion. Therefore it is admitted that she, the Scottish Queen, has to be put to death. Shortly thereafter, a conspiracy was discovered against the person of Her Majesty, wherein her ambassador and others of her retinue were involved. Thereupon, latterly, the Queen of England has resolved to abolish the cause of such evil and of the above-mentioned danger, although she agreed to the execution with but a heavy heart: She therefore dispatched several persons to carry out the sentence upon the Queen of Scotland. The officials who received this command hastened forward the execution, but this against the repeated injunction of the English Queen. Because of this, the secretary of Her Majesty, Davison, was thrown into the Tower and several others fell into disgrace.

And the execution therefore took place in this wise:

At the command of the Queen of England (through the secretary, Beale) the Earls of Shrewsbury and Kent, who were at the time in the neighbourhood of the castle of Fotheringhay, together with other gentlemen, knights and noble persons, with Sir Amias Paulet and Sir Drury, who had order to guard the Queen of Scotland, had on the previous day, namely the 17th day of February, made known to the imprisoned Queen the will of Her Majesty of England. Thereupon she made reply that she was prepared and had long awaited this. She inquired when the execution would take place. Although this was left to her own choice, she asked that it might take place at once, on the very next day, namely on the 18th day of February of the new calendar, on a Wednesday. She besought God's help thereto. At the same time as this notification there were laid before the Queen various apologies, namely that the kingdom of England and its Queen had been compelled to make such a decision.

Hence on the 18th day of February, at 7 o'clock of the morning, the afore-mentioned earls, knights and noblemen forgathered in the castle of Fotheringhay. Two followers were allocated to each knight, but only one to the others present, so that about eighty to a hundred persons entered the castle, beside the guard and the officials of the court.

There, in the large hall, in front of the fireplace, in which burnt a great fire, a dais had been set up, which was twelve feet wide and eight feet high. It was completely covered with black cloth, and thereon stood a chair with a cushion. As now all was ready, and the gentlemen had collected there between the hours of eight and nine, a message was sent to the imprisoned Queen that the gentlemen had come on the errand of which she had been forewarned in the afternoon of yesterday, and wished to know whether she were ready.

The messenger, however, found the door of her chamber locked and bolted. All her people were with her in the chamber. When the gentlemen heard this, they sent a messenger once more commanding him to knock at the door, should he not find it open and to deliver the former message.

But he found the door unlocked. He sent one of the Queen's servants to her in order to acquaint her with his command. The servant brought answer that the Queen was not yet ready. After half an hour, the gentlemen sent to her once more, and thereto she made answer that she would be ready in half an hour.

After this time the chief official went to the Queen. He found her on her knees with her ladies-in-waiting, praying, and told her that her time was now come. Thereupon she stood up and said that she was ready. She was led between two men of her retinue into the antechamber. There she found all her people assembled. She exhorted them all to fear God and to live in humility of spirit. She took leave of them all, kissed the women and held out her hand to the men to kiss. She begged them not to grieve on her account but to be of good cheer and to pray for her. Then she was led to the stairway. There all the gentlemen advanced from the hall towards her, and the Earl of Shrewsbury said to the sorrowing Queen: "Madame, we are here to carry out the behest of our most gracious Queen of England, which was communicated unto you yesterday." The warrant and sentence the Earl of Kent held in his hand. The Great Seal of the Crown of England was thereon. Then the Queen replied that she would as lief die as live any longer. As she turned round she perceived her most distinguished servitor, Melville, and said to him: "My faithful servant Melville, though thou art a Protestant and I a Catholic, there is nevertheless but one Christendom and I am thy Queen, born and anointed, of the lineage of Henry VII. And so I adjure thee before God that thou give this command to my son: I beg him to serve God, and the Catholic Church, and to rule and keep his country in peace and to submit (as I have done) to no other Master, although I had the right good will to unite the kingdoms of this island. I renounce this, may he do likewise, and do not let him put overmuch trust in the presumption of the world. Let him trust God and then he will be blessed by Him. Let him speak no evil of the Queen of England, and thou, Melville, art my witness that I die like a true Scotswoman, Frenchwoman and Catholic, which belief has ever been mine." These words and such like did she repeat.

Thereupon Melville made answer: "Most venerable and most august Princess, as I have been at all times your Majesty's faithful servant, so will I now with the help of God, faithfully and honestly transmit to the King, your Son, your Majesty's words and message."

Thereupon she turned to the above-mentioned gentlemen and desired to have her priest with her on the dais, so that he might bear witness for her to the King of France and in other places, that she had died righteously and a good Catholic. To this the gentlemen made reply that it had been ordained otherwise.

She then demanded that her servants might remain with her. This was refused, in order to curb her impatience and to free her mind from certain superstitions. Nevertheless five of her servants and two tiring-women were permitted to come to her, because she complained that she was being poorly served. She promised that she would cause no hindrance, either by cries or by tears. Further she demanded for her servants and her maids liberty to depart, with good escort, and free of cost to their own countries without let or hindrance. This the gentlemen promised her. Also that they should be permitted to retain everything that the Queen of Scotland had presented to them. But she repeated once more: "I desire that this take place." Thereupon she was led by two servants of the Governor to the dais. There she seated herself upon a chair, for she could stand but with difficulty. The two earls seated themselves beside her. Then the Secretary Beale read the warrant and the sentence of execution in an over loud voice.

The gown in which the Queen was attired was of exquisite black velvet, which she had likewise worn when she appeared before the gentlemen. In her hand she held a small cross of wood or of ivory with the picture of Christ thereon, and a book. On her neck hung a golden crucifix, and from her girdle a rosary.

Near her stood a doctor of theology, Dean of Peterborough, who, at the command of the gentlemen spoke words of Christian comfort to her, exhorting her to die as a Christian with a repentant heart. She at once interrupted him and begged him to keep his peace, for she was fully prepared for death The Dean answered that he had been commanded to speak the truth to her. But she said for the second time: "I will not listen to you, Mr. Dean. You have naught to do with me. You disturb me." Thereupon he was bidden to be silent by the gentlemen.

The Earl of Kent said to her: "Madame, I am grieved on your account to hear of this superstition from you and to see that which is in your hand." She said it was seemly that she should hold the figure of Christ in her hand thereby to think of

Him. Thereupon he answered that she must have Christ in her heart, and further said that though she made demur in paying heed to the mercies vouchsafed to her by God All-Highest, they would nevertheless plead for her with God Almighty, that He would forgive her sins and receive her into His Kingdom. Thereto the Queen made reply: "Pray, then will I also pray." Then the aforesaid Doctor fell on his knees on the steps of the dais and read in an over loud voice a fervent and godly prayer for her, most suitable to such an occasion, also for the Queen of England and the welfare of the Kingdom. All those standing round repeated the prayer. But as long as it lasted the Queen was praying in Latin and fairly audibly, holding the crucifix in her hand.

When this prayer was now ended on both sides, the executioner knelt in front of the Queen. Him she forgave his deed, as also all those who lusted after her blood, or desired her death. She further forgave all and sundry and craved from God that He might also forgive her own trespasses. Thereafter she fell on her knees in ardent supplication and besought the remission of her sins. She said that she trusted to be saved through the death of Christ and His Blood and that she was ready to have her own blood spilt at His feet, wherefore she held His picture and the crucifix in her hands. Further she prayed for a happy, long and prosperous reign for the Queen of England, for the prosperity of the British Isles, for the afflicted Christian Church and the end of all misery. She also prayed for her son, the King of Scots, for his upright and honourable Government and of his conversion to the Catholic Faith. At the last she prayed that all the saints in heaven might intercede for her on this day, and that God of His great goodness might avert great plagues from this Island, forgive her her sins and receive her soul into His heavenly hand.

Thereupon she stood up and prepared herself for death. She doffed her jewels and her gown, with the help of two women. When the executioner wished to assist her, she said to him that it was not her wont to be disrobed in the presence of such a crowd, nor with the help of such handmaidens. She herself took off her robe and pushed it down as far as the waist. The bodice of the underskirt was cut low and tied together at the back. She hastened to undo this.

Thereafter she kissed her ladies, commended them to God, and because one of them was weeping too loudly, she said to her: "Have I not told you that you should not weep? Be comforted." To her she gave her hand, and bade her leave the dais. When she was thus prepared, she turned to her servitors, who were kneeling not far off, blessed them and made them all witnesses that she died a Catholic and begged them to pray for her. Afterwards she fell on her knees with great courage, did not change colour, and likewise gave no sign of fear. One of her tirewomen bound a kerchief before her eyes. As she knelt down she repeated the 70th Psalm: *"In te, Domine, speravi. . . ."* When she had said this to the end, she, full of courage, bent down with her body and laid her head on the block, exclaiming: *"In manuas tuas, Domine, commendo spiritum meum."* Then one of the executioners held down her hands, and the other cut off her head with two strokes of the chopper. Thus ended her life.

The executioner took the head and showed it to the people, who cried: "God spare our Queen of England!"

When the executioner held up the head, it fell in disarray so that it could be seen that her hair was quite grey and had been closely cropped.

Her raiment and other belongings were by command taken from the executioner, but he was promised their equivalent in money. Everything that had been sprinkled with her blood, also the garments of the executioner and other objects, were promptly taken away and washed. The planks of the dais, the black cloth and all else were thrown into the fire, at once, so that no superstitious practices could be carried on therewith.

Her body was carried out, embalmed and made ready for burial. Where this will take place is as yet unknown. Her servants and courtiers were instructed to abide there until her remains had been honourably laid to rest. She was four-and-forty years of age, and was the most beautiful princess of her time.

She had as first spouse, Francis II, King of France, after him Henry Stuart, the son of the Earl of Lennox, her cousin, a truly handsome young man, by whom she had issue, James VI King of Scotland. But after she had caused Henry Stuart to be murdered, she took in marriage the Earl of Bothwell, who was imprisoned in Denmark, lost his senses and there died.

After this execution had taken place, the portals of the castle remained shut, until Henry Talbot, son of the Earl of Shrewsbury, had been dispatched to the English Court. When, the other day, he brought the tidings to London, the citizens of this town lit bonfires on all sides and rang the bells, because they were rid of the danger in which they had lived so long. It looks as if the populace believed that a new era had begun in which they hope that all will remain at peace.

Described by Emanuel Tomascon, who was present at the happenings.

(On the report is a note in old handwriting: From a Calvinist source.)

VI-17   Henri III to Duplessis

His reign undermined by the continuing French wars of religion, and members of the Holy League, formed to protect Catholic interests, arguing for his deposition, Henri III (1551-1589) was compelled to ally himself with Henri of Navarre and together they laid siege to Paris. However, on the morning of August 1, 1589, he was stabbed in the abdomen by Jacques Clément, a fanatical Jacobin friar who had gained admittance to his chamber.

   Believing the wound not to be fatal, Henri dictates the following message:

(1 August 1589)

   Monsignor Duplessis, after my enemies employed all the worthiest stratagems of their crime and treachery in order to reach the objective of their betrayal, this morning a young Jacobin was admitted by my procurator general in order to give me (so he said) some letters from Monsieur de Harlay, first speaker in my court of assembly, my very good and very faithful servant, held for this reason prisoner in Paris, and to tell me something on his behalf. He was ushered into my chamber at my command; and when I was still alone, having no one present but Monsieur de Bellegarde, first gentleman of my chamber, and my procurator general, after having presented me with the false letters and pretending to have something secret to tell me, I had the two aforementioned persons withdraw; and then this wretch stabbed me, thinking indeed he would kill me; but God who takes care of His own and who did not intend to allow, by the reverence I bear those who are consecrated to His service, His very humble servant to lose his life, saved it through His grace and thwarted his damnable design, making the knife slide in such a way that nothing will come of it, if He so pleases, and that within a few days He will give me both my former health and victory over my enemies.

Henry

P.S. I beg you to notify quickly the noblemen and neighboring towns of the above so that the reports that my enemies circulate do not bring any harm to my service.

(trans. L.L.)

(Henri III died in the early hours of August 2, after acknowledging Henri of Navarre as his successor.)

VI-18   The Fugger correspondent in Rome to the Augsburg Bankers

A correspondent in Rome records the accession to the French throne of Henri IV, who was to restore order and prosperity to France and become one of the most popular figures in her history.

Rome, the 2nd day of September 1589. From France confirmation is received of the fact that the King of Navarre has adopted the large coat of arms of France. He causes himself to be publicly acclaimed and styled King of France. The body of the young murdered King Henry he had buried in Senlis.

In all parish churches of Paris obsequies have been celebrated for Jacques Clément, who murdered the King. It is thought that the Paris people wish to erect a statue in eternal memory of him as the liberator of his country.

VI-19   The Company of Eastland Merchants to Sir William Cecil

Having returned from a diplomatic mission to Russia, Dr. Giles Fletcher proceeded to write a treatise, *Of the Russe Commonwealth,* exposing the country's despotic and unjust system of government. However, the Company of Eastland Merchants, fearful that their trade with Russia might suffer by the book's publication, vigorously protested to Sir William Cecil and, despite its dedication to Queen Elizabeth, the work was quickly suppressed.

(1591)

To the right Honorable S[r] William Cecell, Knight, Lord High Treasurer of England.

The Companie of Merchauntes tradinge Muskovia havinge bene manie waies preiudiced by the errors w[ch] have bene committed by her Mat[es] subjectes imploied by the Companie in those partes, in givinge offence or some smale color of offence to the government of the state of the Countrie of Russia, doe greatelie feare that a Booke latelie sett out by Mr. Doctor Fletcher, dedicated to her Ma[tie], intituled the Russe Commonwealth, will turne the Companie to some great displeasure with the Russe Empero[r], and endaunger boeth theire people and goodes nowe remayninge there, except some good order be taken by your Lordships honorable consideration for the callinge in of all the bookes that are printed, and some cowrse holden therein signifyinge her Ma[tes] dislike of the publishinge of the same. In w[ch] Booke (besides the discowrse of the discription of the Countrie,) the militarie government and forces thereof, the Empero[rs] revenue, and howe yt ryseth (w[ch] is offensive to the Russe that anie man should looke into), the person of the Empero[r] his father, his Brother, & the L: Boris Fedorow[ch] the protector, and generallie the nature of the people, are towched in soe harde tearmes, as that the Companie doubt [1] the revenge thereof will light on theire people, and goodes remayning in Russia; and vtterlie overthrowe the trade for ever. Out of w[ch] booke for your Lordship's readines there is hereunder noted certen places offensive, whereof the whole discowrse is full.

In the epistle dedicatorie of the booke he tearmeth the Russe government a strange face of a tirannycall state.

The intollerable exactions of the Emperor vppon his subjectes maketh them carelesse to laye vp anie thinge, for that yf they have ought, yt causeth them to be spoiled not onlie of theire goodes, but of their lives.

In shewinge the likelihoode of the ende of the whole race of the Empero[r] concluded in one, two, or some fewe of the bloud, he saieth there is noe hope of yssue in the Empero[r] by the constitution of his bodie, and the barenes of his wief.

He noteth there the death of the Empero[rs] elder brother, murthered by his father in his furie, whose death was the murtheringe of the olde Empero[r] by extreame greefe.

He noteth what practisinge there hath bene, by such as aspire the succession, to

1. suspect

distroye the younger brother of the Empero[r] that is yet livinge, beinge about sixe yeares olde, wherein he seemeth to ayme at Boris Fedorow[ch].[2]

He noteth in that younge infant an inclination to crueltie resemblinge his father, in delighte of bloude, for that he beinge but sixe yeares olde taketh pleasure to looke into the bleedinge throtes of beastes that are killed, and to beate geese and hens w[th] a staffe untill they dye.

The Russe government is plaine tirannycall, and exceadeth all just measure, w[th]out regard of nobilitie or people, gevinge to the nobilitie a kinde of vnjuste and unmeasured libertie to exact on the baser sorte of people.

If the late Empero[r] in his progresse had mett a man whose person or face he had not liked, or yf he looked vppon him, he would commaunde his heade to be stricken of and to be cast before hime.

The practise of the Godonoes to extinguishe the bloud Royall, who seeke to cut of or keapt downe the best of the nobilitie.

That yt is to be merveled howe the nobilitie and people will suffer themseives to be brought vnder suche oppression and slaverie.

That the desperate state of thinges at home maketh the people to wishe for some forrein invasion.

That Boris Godonoe and the Empresse kindred accompt all that commeth to the Empero[rs] treasurie theire owne.

Divers grosse practises of the Empero[r] to drawe the wealth of the land into his treasurie, w[ch] he concludeth to be straunge kinde of extortions, but that yt agreeth wth the qualitie of the Empero[r], and the miserable subjection of the poore countrie.

Theire onlie lawe is theire speakinge lawe, that is the pleasure of the Prince and Magistrates, which sheweth the miserable condition of the people; against whose injustice and extreame oppression they had neede to be armed with manie good Lawes.

The practise of the Godones against the Empero[rs] brother to prove him not legittimate, and to turne awaie the peoples likinge from him as next successor.

The discription of the Emperour, viz. meane of stature, lowe and grosse, sallowe of complexion, enclyninge to dropsey, hawcke nosed, unsteadie in his pase by reason of the weaknes of his lymes,[3] heavie and vnactive, commonlie smilinge almost to a laughter; for quallitie simple and slowe-witted; but verie gentle and of an easie nature, quiet, mercifull, &c.

It is to be doubted whether is greater the Crueltie or the Intemperauncie that is vsed in the Countrie; it is so foull that is not be named. The whole Countrie

---

2. Elizabeth will nevertheless consider a marriage of convenience between their two families proposed by Czar Boris Godunov in 1598 (Letter IX-21).

3. limbs

overfloweth with the synne of that kinde, and noe mervell as havinge no lawe to restrayne whoredomes, adulteries, and like vncleanes of lief.

From the greatest to the smallest, except some fewe that will scarcelie be founde, the Russe nether beleeveth anie thinge that an other man speaketh nor speaketh anie thinge himself worthie to be beleaved.

(The suppression of this book by the counselors of Queen Elizabeth may be better explained by Letter VIII-10, which clarifies the Queen's commercial open door policy with Russia.)

VI-20   Queen Elizabeth to Henri IV of Navarre, King of France

When the Protestant Henri of Navarre sought to capture Paris and the crown of France, Elizabeth aided him with money and troops under the Earl of Essex. To end the bloody religious wars in France, Henri decided that "Paris is worth a mass" and became a Catholic convert. Elizabeth could hardly believe this seeming betrayal, and worried about both Henri's immortal soul and her financial investment in him.

July 1593.

Ah what griefs, what regret, what groanings I feel in my soul at the sound of such news as Morlains has recounted. My God, is it possible that any earthly respect should efface that terror wherewith Divine fear threatens us? Can we reasonably even expect a good issue from an act so iniquitous? He who has for many years preserved you by His hand, can you imagine that He allows you to go alone in the greatest need? Ah, it is dangerous to do ill that good may come of it. Yet I hope that sounder inspiration shall come to you. In the meantime I shall not cease to set you in the foremost rank of my devotions that the hands of Esau undo not the blessing of Jacob. And where you promise me all friendship and faith, I confess that I have dearly merited it, and of that I shall not repent, provided that you will not change your father: otherwise I shall be to you but a bastard sister, or at least not of the same father. For I shall prefer always the natural to the adopted, as God best knows, Who guides you to the right way of the best feeling. Your very assured sister, if it be after the old manner; with the new, I have nothing to do.

E.R.

(Elizabeth Regina's anger at the French Catholics, whom Henri IV had conciliated, is clear from Letter V-20 to Walsingham on the St. Bartholomew's Day massacres.)

VI-21   Dean Robert Tounson to Sir John Isham

Sir Walter Raleigh's disastrous expedition to Guiana led to a charge of his conspiring with Spain, and he was eventually beheaded on 29 October, 1618, in Westminster. To many he remained an innocent victim, and his comportment on the scaffold was admired by all. We learn from the letter below that tobacco, which he apparently introduced to his countrymen, was a solace to him during his last hours.

Westminst. Coll., 9 November, 1618

Sir,

The last weeke was a busy weeke with me, and the weeke afore that, was more. I would gladly have writt unto you, but could find no time: yet I hope yow had the relation of sir Walter Rawleigh's death; for so I gave order, that it should be brought unto yow. I was commaunded by the lords of the counsayle to be with him, both in prison and att his death, and so sett downe the manner of his death as nere as I could: there be other reports of itt, but that which yow have from me is trew: one Craford, who was sometimes Mr. Rodeknight's pupil, hath penned it pretily, and meaneth to putt itt to the presse, and came to me about it, but I heare not that it is come forth. The summe of that, which he spake att his death, yow have I suppose, already: when he never made mention of his offence for which he dyed, namely his former treason; but only desired to cleare himself of new imputations, there mentioned: privately he told me in prison, that he was charged to have broken the peace with Spaine, but he putt that, he sayd, out of the count of his offences: saving that he heard, the king was displeased att it; for how could he breake peace with him, who within these 4 yeares, as he sayd, tooke diverse of his men, and bound them backe to backe and drowned them; and for burning the towne, he sayd, it stood upon the king's owne ground, and therefore he did no wrong in that. He was the most fearlesse of death that ever was knowen; and the most resolute and confident, yet with reverence and conscience. When I begann to incourage him against the feare of death, he seemed to make so light of itt, that I wondered att him, and when I told him, that the deare servants of God, in better causes than his, had shrunke backe and trembled a litle, he denyed not, but yet gave God thankes, he never feared death, and much lesse then, for it was but an opinion and imagination, and the manner of death though to others might seeme greevous, yet he had rather dye so then of a burning fever: with much more to that purpose, with such confidence and cheerfullnesse, that I was faine to divert my speach another way, and wished him not to flatter himselfe, for this extraordinary boldnesse, I was afrayd, came from some false ground: if it sprong from the assurance he had of the love and favour of God, of the hope of his salvation by Christ, and his owne innocency, as he pleaded, I sayd he was an happy man, but if it were out of an humour of vainglory or carelessnesse or contempt of death, or senslessnesse of his owne estate, he were much to be lamented &c. For I told him, that heathen men had sett as litle by their lives as he could doe, and seemed to dye as bravely. He answered, that he was perswaded, that no man, that knew God and feared him, could dye with cheerfullnesse and courage, except he were assured of the love and favour of God unto him; that other men might make shewes outwardly, but they felt no joy within: with much more to that effect, very christianly, so that he satisfyed me then, as I thinke he did all his spectators att his death. After he had received the communion in the morning, he was very cheerfull and merry, and hoped to perswade the world, that he dyed an innocent man, as he sayd; thereat, I told him, that he should doe well to advise what he sayd, men in these dayes did not dye in that sort innocent, and his pleading innocency was an oblique taxing of the justice of the realme upon him. He confessed justice had bene done, and by course of law, he must dye, but yet, I should give him leave, he sayd, to stand upon his innocency in the fact; and he thought, both the king, and all that heard his aunsweres, thought verily he was innocent for that matter. I then pressed him, to call to mind what he had done formerly, and though perhaps in that particular, for which he was condemned, he was cleare, yet for some other matter, it might be, he was guilty; and now the hand of God had found him out, and therefore he should acknowledge the justice of God in itt, though att the hands of men he had but hard measure: and here I putt him in mind of the death of my lord of Essex, how it was generally reported, that he was a great instrument of his death, which if his hert did charge him with, he should hertily repent, and aske God forgivenesse: to which he made aunswere, as is in the former relation, and sayd moreover, that my lord of Essex was fetcht of by a trick, which he privately told me of. He was very cheerefull that morning he dyed, eate his breakefast hertily, and tooke tobacco, and made no more of his death, then if he had bene to take a journey, and left a great impression in the minds of those that beheld him, in so much that sir Lewise Stukely and the French man grow very odious. This was the newes a weeke since: but now it is blowen over, and he allmost forgotten.

The king and prince, thankes be to God, are very well. The queene is still at Hampton-court, and crazy they say. Yow will remember me kindly to my lady and your mother, and if yow have any imploiment for me here, yow shall find me allwayes

Att your service
Robert Tounson.

(See Letter VIII-13 for the principal charge leading to Raleigh's execution, and for a clarification of his sense of guiltlessness.)

VI-22   Francis Bacon to King James I of England

Sentenced to the Tower for having accepted bribes while serving as Lord Chancellor, Francis Bacon (1561-1626), one of the wisest philosophers of his age, forms a piteous appeal for clemency to James I. Whether the King received this letter or not, Bacon was released after a few days of imprisonment and later pardoned, but never allowed to return to Parliament.

London Tower, 1622.

To the King,—

It may please your most excellent Majesty, in the midst of my misery, which is rather assuaged by remembrance than by hope, my chiefest worldly comfort is to think, that, since the time I had the first vote of the Commons House of Parliament for Commissioner of the Union, until the time that I was, by this last

Parliament, chosen by both Houses for their messenger to your Majesty in the petition of religion (which two were my first and last services), I was evermore so happy as to have my poor services graciously accepted by your Majesty, and likewise not to have had any of them miscarry in my hands; neither of which points I can anywise take to myself, but ascribe the former to your Majesty's goodness, and the latter to your prudent directions, which I was ever careful to have and keep. For, as I have often said to your Majesty, I was towards you but as a bucket and cistern, to draw forth and conserve, whereas yourself was the fountain. Unto this comfort of nineteen years' prosperity, there succeeded a comfort even in my greatest adversity, somewhat of the same nature, which is that, in those offences wherewith I was charged, there was not any one that had special relation to your Majesty, or any your particular commandments. For as towards Almighty God there are offences against the first and second table, and yet all against God; so with the servants of kings, there are offences more immediate against the sovereign, although all offences against law are also against the king. Unto which comfort there is added this circumstance, that as my faults were not against your Majesty, otherwise than as all faults are; so my fall was not your Majesty's act, otherwise than as all acts of justice are yours. This I write not to insinuate with your Majesty, but as a most humble appeal to your Majesty's gracious remembrance, how honest and direct you have ever found me in your service, whereby I have an assured belief that there is in your Majesty's own princely thoughts a great deal of serenity and clearness towards me, your Majesty's now prostrate and cast-down servant.

Neither, my most gracious sovereign, do I, by this mention of my former services, lay claim to your princely graces and bounty, though the privilege of calamity doth bear that form of petition. I know well, had they been much more, they had been but by bounden duty: nay, I must also confess, that they were, from time to time, far above my merit, over and super-rewarded by your Majesty's benefits, which you heaped upon me. Your Majesty was and is that master to me that raised and advanced me nine times, thrice in dignity, and six times in offices. The places were indeed the painfullest of all your services; but then they had both honour and profits; and the then profits might have maintained my now honours, if I had been wise; neither was your Majesty's immediate liberality wanting towards me in some gifts, if I may hold them. All this I do most thankfully acknowledge; and do herewith conclude, that for anything arising from myself to move your eye of pity towards me, there is much more in my present misery than in my past services; save that the same, your Majesty's goodness, that may give relief to the one, may give value to the other.

And indeed, if it may please your Majesty, this theme of my misery is so plentiful as it need not be coupled with anything else. I have been somebody by your Majesty's singular and undeserved favour, even the prime officer of your kingdom. Your Majesty's arm hath often been laid over mine in council when you presided at the table; so near was I! I have borne your Majesty's image in metal, much more in my heart. I was never, in nineteen years' service, chidden by your Majesty; but, contrariwise, often overjoyed when your Majesty would sometimes say, I was a good husband for you, though none for myself; sometimes, that I had a way to deal in business *fauvibus modis,* which was the way which was most according to your own heart; and other most gracious speeches of affection and trust, which I feed on to this day. But why should I speak of these things which are now vanished but only the better to express my downfall?

For now it is thus with me: I am a year and a half old in misery; though, I must ever acknowledge, not without some mixture of your Majesty's grace and mercy. For I do not think it possible that any one, whom you once loved, should be totally miserable. Mine own means, through my own improvidence, are poor and weak, little better than my father left me. The poor things that I have had from your Majesty are either in question or at courtesy. My dignities remain marks of your past favour, but burdens of my present fortune. The poor remnants which I had of my former fortunes, in plate or jewels, I have spread upon poor men unto whom I owed, scarce leaving myself a convenient subsistence; so as to conclude, I must pour out my misery before your Majesty, so far as to say, *Si tu deferis, perimus.*

But as I can offer to your Majesty's compassion little arising from myself to move you, except it be my extreme misery, which I have truly opened; so looking up to your Majesty's own self, I should think I committed Cain's fault if I should despair. Your Majesty is a king, whose heart is as inscrutable for secret motions of goodness as for depth of wisdom. You are, Creator-like, factive, not destructive; you are the prince in whom hath ever been noted an aversion against anything that savoured of an hard heart; as on the other side, your princely eye was wont to meet with any motion that was made on the relieving part. Therefore, as one that hath had the happiness to know your Majesty near-hand, I have, most gracious sovereign, faith enough for a miracle, and much more for a grace, that your Majesty will not suffer your poor creature to be utterly defaced, nor blot that name quite out of your book, upon which your sacred hand hath been so oft for the giving him new ornaments and additions.

Unto this degree of compassion, I hope God (of whose mercy toward me, both in my prosperity and adversity, I have had the great testimonies and pledges, though mine own manifold and wretched unthankfulness might have averted them) will dispose your princely heart, already prepared to all piety you shall do for me. And as all commiserable persons (especially such as find their hearts void of all malice) are apt to think that all men pity them, so I assure myself that the lords of your council, who, out of their wisdom and nobleness, cannot but be sensible of human events, will, in this way which I go, for the relief of my estate, further and advance your Majesty's goodness towards me; for there is, as I conceive, a kind of fraternity between great men that are, and those that have been, being but the several tenses of one verb. Nay, I do further presume, that both Houses of Parliament will love their justice the better if it end not in my ruin; for I have been often told, by many of my lords, as it were in the way of excusing the severity of the sentence, that they knew they left me in good hands. And your Majesty knoweth well I have been all my life long acceptable to those assemblies; not by flattery, but by moderation, and by honest expressing of a desire to have things go fairly and well.

But if it may please your Majesty (for saints I shall give them reverence, but no adoration; my address is to your Majesty, the fountain of goodness), your Majesty shall, by the grace of God, not feel that in gift, which I shall extremely feel in help; for my desires are moderate, and my courses measured to a life orderly and reserved, hoping still to do your Majesty honour in my way; only I most humbly beseech your Majesty to give me leave to conclude with these words, which necessity speaketh. Help me, dear sovereign, lord and master, and pity so far, as that I, that have borne a bag, be not now in my age forced, in effect, to bear a wallet; nor that I, that desire to live to study, may not be driven to study to live. I most humbly crave pardon of a long letter, after a long silence. God of heaven ever bless, preserve, and prosper your Majesty. Your Majesty's poor ancient servant and beadsman,

Fr. Bacon.

CHAPTER 7

WARFARE

XIV. *The Surrender of Breda* by Velásquez

For all its scientific and cultural attainments, the Renaissance was overridden by the familiar horseman of the Apocalypse, War. The subject dominated much of the correspondence. As Erasmus complained, "I wonder what it is that drives—I will not say Christians, but men—to such a degree of madness as to rush with so much pains, so much cost, so much risk, to the destruction of one another" (VII-3). As in any age, the pretexts for war were varied. Rising nationalisms, religious fanaticism, and even parochialisms spawned wars. The nationalisms of such giants as Turkey and Spain generated centrifugal force *(semper plus ultra,* as stated earlier, being the motto of Charles V). After Spain had gained the right to half of the newly-discovered and undiscovered world by a papal decision, not to mention the Lowlands and the Rhineland, Spain's and Turkey's collision course met on land along the Danube and on sea at the Battle of Lepanto (VII-14). Personal ambitions led to warfare as did such personal rivalries as that between Francis I and Charles V. The residue of feudalism led to clashes of arms like the Peasant's Revolt in Germany. Parochialism led to wars between the city-states of Italy, reinforced by foreign mercenaries, which Machiavelli deplored. Colonialism led to wars, crowned by atrocities in distant lands like India or South and Central America (VIII-13). Or in North Africa, where the Safim were compelled to petition the King of Portugal for relief (VIII-4). Nations were driven to war to maintain a balance of power or create cordons sanitaires, such as the difficult campaign of the English to exclude the Spaniards from the Netherlands (VII-15) or Spain's occupation of the Rhineland.

Christianity did not split in twain at this time without a plethora of wars, one of the most savage being the aforementioned struggle between Anglican England and Catholic Spain for control of the Lowlands, a "sore war" in which Sidney anticipated his imminent death (VII-15). France during the sixteenth century was torn by nine religious wars, or nine stages of one religious war, leading to such violence as the Saint Bartholomew's Day massacre (V-19). No region suffered more, as Montaigne reports, than the Southwest (VII-12). Troops, especially mercenaries, often got out of hand, and killed or sacked even the "friendly" local populations (VII-13). Religious motivations strengthened political pretexts for beating the tocsin of war. Thus, when Henri IV of Navarre prepared to assume the crown in Paris, Anglican Albion aided him while Catholic Spain maneuvered to prevent his seizure of Paris (VI-18). Similarly, the Ottoman Turk's seizure of

Constantinople was viewed by Cardinal Bessarion not only as a growing political danger, but as the threat of an infidel religion without ethics: "They have made camps of the Churches of God" (VII-1). Religion was also a motivation of the Swedish wars leading to the deposition of King Sigismund III.

The threat of the Ottoman Empire was a major theme of Renaissance letters. While viewing Luther as a major threat during the first half of the century, letter writers decried Suleiman and his successors throughout the entire Cinquecento (VII-6). Not without reason, of course. The ambitions and *hubris* of Sultan Suleiman ("his air was by no means gracious") were dutifully noted by Ogier Ghiselin (VII-11). A realization of an inevitable confrontation, comparable to that later generated by Napoleon and by Hitler, swept over Europe as far west as Portugal. In Venice, whence so many Crusaders had embarked against Constantinople, the Doge of Venice was moved by a secular hatred (VII-1). There was a feeling of mixed terror and disbelief when the Turks first sailed into an Italian port (VII-10) less than thirty kilometers from Rome. Men were chilled by the possibility of fighting Turks, whose savagery lived up to its reputation. Men worried about their wives' behavior under the stress of war, and the pope began to plan curbs on wives' activities during this ancient test invented by Mars.

The Turks, meanwhile, took advantage of their domination of the Mediterranean even outdoing the British buccaneers by their piracy, seizure of vessels, and surprise raids on ports. Being captured by Turks and surviving to tell of it was an experience to write about to friends and relatives. It was only with the slaughter of the Hungarian army, described by Ferdinand of Austria in his letter to the Archbishop of Cologne (VII-6), that the Turkish threat reached full dimensions. After all, man's natural propensity to flee the threat of war is illustrated in the letters of Michelangelo. It was shortly after the rout of the Hungarian army that Machiavelli, the specialist on war, complained to Bartolomeo Cavalcanti of the disastrous military strategies of Clement VII (VII-7), and shortly after that defeat that Henry VIII in 1529 chided Charles V on doing nothing about the Turks' arrival in Austria, wondering why Charles "should not go to its rescue instead of making war on Christians" (VII-8). A severe setback to Turkish expansionism on land, comparable to their earlier marine defeat at Lepanto, was dealt them at Prague in 1588. The battle of Lepanto was probably the more decisive in its destruction of the Turkish fleet: "One hundred Turkish galleys are captured, sixty have been sent to the bottom" (VII-14).

As victors of Lepanto, the Spaniards were encouraged to sail on England with their Invincible Armada. King Philip II decided to offer its command to the Duke of Medina Sidonia, who had helped pursue Drake after Cádiz. The Duke's refusal, not accepted, left the monarch surprised (VII-17). A rather late Fugger letter from the port of Hamburg details the disastrous end of the Armada (VII-19). Meanwhile a prudent Queen Elizabeth, fearful that Catholic Spanish soldiers, washed ashore on the beaches of Scotland, might be helped by the Catholic Scots, warned James VI not to give aid and comfort to the enemy (VII-18).

Land warfare, like coastal defence, required experts in fortification. Fortunately Renaissance architects were trained on Vitruvius, whose manual included instruction on military architecture and engineering. Michelangelo designed the bastions of Florence against the invading Spaniards in 1529, declaring his superiority in this area over Sangallo and Leonardo. Yet he was a fugitive at heart ("life is more precious than worldly goods") and fled Florence before returning to undertake its defence. Milan, on the invasion route from France or from Spain, had great need of architects and engineers to construct defences, and Leonardo da Vinci wrote to Duke Lodovico Sforza his willingness to "acquaint Your Excellency with certain of my secrets" (VII-2).

With its emphasis on courtliness and gentility, the Renaissance insisted that a humanistic training had to be rounded out by the arts of war for, as Rabelais put it, the defence of one's homeland. This same dedication to courtliness and nobility encouraged the claim that wars bring out the best in man. It is true that the capture and detention of Francis I after Pavia were a ritual of courtliness, with Emperor Charles V assuring his kingly captive that he would "maintain throughout this matter our own honor without sullying yours" (VII-5). Thus letters were common about such noble heroes as Giovanni de' Medici, whose courageous death in battle ranked him with such other military commanders as the French knight Bayard, *sans peur et sans reproche,* the Marquis of Pescara (VII-4), and Sir Walter Raleigh. The desire to be a Protestant hero led to such derring-do as Drake's seizure of Cadiz, "burning the monastery and the altars and pictures in the churches," (VII-16) somewhat devaluating the concept of chivalry. Just as Castiglione defined the ideal Renaissance gentleman in *The Book of the Courtier,* so did Fray Antonio de Guevara write a letter on the ideal captain addressed to—no remarkable coincidence—his distant relative the Marquis of Pescara (VII-4).

The current of antimilitarism so necessary for the eventual survival of a society was to be expected in the Renaissance. We have already quoted Erasmus's pacificism in the first paragraph of this Introduction. Rabelais's satire of the ridiculous pretexts and comic vicissitudes of war was enjoyed by even the warriors themselves, including Francis I. As always the best attack on militarism was satire and spoof. As expected the satirist Aretino penned his protest against the life of a soldier ("soldiers, like bread, end up mouldy and worthless") (VII-9). Yet Renaissance man, like his descendants today, read the condemnations of war and waited in vain for peace.

VII-1   Cardinal Bessarion to Doge Francesco Foscari of Venice

Cardinal John Bessarion (c. 1400-1472), the Byzantine humanist and theologian who had favored a union between the Byzantine and western churches, bemoans the fall of Constantinople to Turkish infidels and exhorts Francesco Foscari, Doge of Venice, to unite with other Christian princes in averting the possibility of an Ottoman invasion in Italy.

13 July, 1453

Most illustrious and excellent prince, I have put off until this day commending to your highness my unhappy and wretched city of Constantinople. This I have done partly because I was restrained by a certain provincial modesty, lest in asking something for her advantage and welfare, I should seem to seek my own profit; I have also held back because, of its own accord, your renowned Senate, as it has been most merciful to all those who are suffering, had prepared so much aid and assistance that all doubtless might think it sufficient, indeed more than enough, to save this city, to hold back the barbarians from the walls, to contain the attack of a most cruel enemy. Would that it might have been brought to bear at the proper time! Would that we had not been deprived of hope and deceived in our judgment; but truly it was not through any negligence on your part, of which, in so great a crisis, there was never a shadow.

But it so happened, because of the proximity of the enemy and the unfavourable season of the year, and by the will of the fates, that while your fleet was in midcourse, while in hope of victory fresh forces were being brought against the enemy, the barbarians conquered the city [May 29, 1453]. This city which was most heavily protected by its situation, its walls and supplies and by all manner of defence, this city which, it was hoped, would be able to withstand a total siege for an entire year, the barbarians stormed and overthrew. A thing terrible to relate, and to be deplored by all who have in them any spark of humanity, and especially by Christians.

Wretched me! I cannot write this without the most profound sorrow. A city which was so flourishing, with such a great empire, so many illustrious men, such very famous and ancient families, so prosperous, the head of all Greece, the splendour and glory of the East, the school of the best arts, the refuge of all good things, has been captured, despoiled, ravaged, and completely sacked by the most inhuman barbarians and the most savage enemies of the Christian faith, by the fiercest of wild beasts.

The public treasure has been consumed, private wealth has been destroyed, the temples have been stripped of gold, silver, jewels, the relics of the saints, and other most precious ornaments. Men have been butchered like cattle, women abducted, virgins ravished, and children snatched from the arms of their parents. If any survived so great a slaughter, they have been enslaved in chains so that they might be ransomed for a price, or subjected to every kind of torture, or reduced to the most humiliating servitude. The sanctuaries and shrines of the saints have been defiled by curses, scourgings, bloodshed, and all kinds of shameful acts. They have made camps of the churches of God, and have exposed the sacred things of God in their camps. O unhappy, O wretched, and so swift and manifold a transformation of a city! If anyone reads this, ignorant of what has been done, he will not believe that these things have happened.

But I do not wish to lament the calamities of my fatherland to you, to whom these things are perhaps better known than to me, and especially lest I should seem to reopen your wound, whom the fates decreed should share our miseries. So many Venetian citizens and most noble gentlemen were besieged in that city, so many men of patrician rank. Would that they have experienced better fortune than ours, and may return unharmed to their native city. Certainly it is to be feared that, tossed in the same tempest, they may have perished in the same way.

To me, however, has been given the opportunity freely to implore aid, not for my fatherland, not for the good of my city, but for the safety of all, for the honor of Christians. On this occasion I could explain in great detail how much danger threatens Italy, not to mention other lands, if the violent assaults of the most ferocious barbarians are not checked. But I am not sure that these arguments are not better known to your Senate than to me. And this letter hastens to its close. I say but this one thing briefly. One of two things must happen; either your Highness, together with other Christian princes, must curb and crush the violence, not to say madness, of the barbarian, in these very beginnings, not only to safeguard yourselves and your own, but also in order to take the offensive against the enemy; or the barbarian, when he has shortly become master in what remains of Greece, which is now still subject to our rule, and in all our islands and also in Pannonia and Illyricum, may bring Italian affairs to a most dangerous crisis.

There is no one who may not hope, however, that Christian princes will take the offensive the more readily, seeing that there are such important reasons, so grave, so serious, so urgent. They would act for the common good, for the

Christian religion, and for the glory of Christ, especially if they were summoned by your Highness and your Senate, whose authority is very great.

Therefore I exhort you, renowned and most illustrious prince, and I entreat, beseech, and implore you, with what prayers I can, that, when Italian affairs have finally been settled, and those wars ended in which Christian princes have attacked each other, you will direct your attention to greater matters and behold the enemy raging on the boundaries of Christian territories and destroying everything savagely.

Why do you think the barbarian has burst forth with such great insolence? Doubtless because he has learned that Christian princes, waging wars against each other, have stained their hands with the blood of their own people, have defiled their arms with the blood of Christians. These things make the enemy bold; relying on them, he has lately assaulted the chief city of Greece, and has conquered, ravaged, and destroyed it. But if he should learn that, with our own hostilities resolved, united and harmonious as Christian princes should be, we would rise up to defend the Christian religion, believe me, he would not only refrain form invading foreign lands, but would withdraw to that place within his own territories which is most favorable for defence.

Rise up then, renowned prince, and when the mutual animosities of Christians have been extinguished (and this will be easy for you, who are exceedingly influential in authority and wisdom), awaken, awaken at once, and arouse their peaceful and tranquil spirits. Exhort them, challenge them, induce them to join you, before the enemy takes the Peloponnesus, in dedicating themselves to avenging the violence of the barbarian, to destroying the enemy of the Christian faith, to recovering that city which formerly belonged to your republic, and which would be yours again once victory had been achieved. Nothing you could do would be more profitable for your empire, more advantageous for Italy, and for the whole commonwealth of Christians; nothing more acceptable to the immortal God; nothing more glorious for your own fame. If your highness knows anything that my smallness can contribute to this task, either by calming the spirits of our people or by exhorting them to wage war on the barbarians, I shall spare no labour, no care or solicitude.

VII-2   Leonardo da Vinci to the Duke of Milan

Having quit his native Florence at the age of thirty, Leonardo da Vinci (1452-1519), recognized by posterity as a "universal genius," applies to Lodovico Sforza, Duke of Milan, for employment as a military architect.

(1482?)

Having, most illustrious lord, seen and considered the experiments of all those who pose as masters in the art of inventing instruments of war, and finding that their inventions differ in no way from those in common use, I am emboldened, without prejudice to anyone, to solicit an appointment of acquainting your Excellency with certain of my secrets.

1. I can construct bridges which are very light and strong and very portable, with which to pursue and defeat the enemy; and others more solid, which resist fire or assault, yet are easily removed and placed in position; and I can also burn and destroy those of the enemy.

2. In case of a siege I can cut off water from the trenches and make pontoons and scaling ladders and other similar contrivances.

3. If by reason of the elevation or the strength of its position a place cannot be bombarded, I can demolish every fortress if its foundations have not been set on stone.

4. I can also make a kind of cannon which is light and easy of transport, with which to hurl small stones like hail, and of which the smoke causes great terror to the enemy, so that they suffer heavy loss and confusion.

5. I can noiselessly construct to any prescribed point subterranean passages either straight or winding, passing if necessary underneath trenches or a river.

6. I can make armoured wagons carrying artillery, which shall break through the most serried ranks of the enemy, and so open a safe passage for his infantry.

7. If occasion should arise, I can construct cannon and mortars and light ordnance in shape both ornamental and useful and different from those in common use.

8. When it is impossible to use cannon I can supply in their stead catapults,

mangonels, *trabocchi*, and other instruments of admirable efficiency not in general use— In short, as the occasion requires I can supply infinite means of attack and defense.

9. And if the fight should take place upon the sea I can construct many engines most suitable either for attack or defense and ships which can resist the fire of the heaviest cannon, and powders or weapons.

10. In time of peace, I believe that I can give you as complete satisfaction as anyone else in the construction of buildings both public and private, and in conducting water from one place to another.

I can further execute sculpture in marble, bronze or clay, also in painting I can do as much as anyone else, whoever he may be.

Moreover, I would undertake the commission of the bronze horse, which shall endue with immortal glory and eternal honour the auspicious memory of your father * and of the illustrious house of Sforza.——

And if any of the aforesaid things should seem to anyone impossible or impracticable, I offer myself as ready to make trial of them in your park or in whatever place shall please your Excellency, to whom I commend myself with all possible humility.

VII-3   Desiderius Erasmus to Antony of Bergen, Abbot of St. Bertin

In an impassioned defense of peace addressed to the Abbot of St. Bertin but doubtless intended for a wider audience, Desiderius Erasmus (1466?-1536) cites the incalculable destruction wrought by war and intimates the feasibility of international arbitration.

London, 14 March, 1514

Most honorable Father, I heard by the report of the Bishop of Durham and of Andreas Ammonius, the King's Secretary, of your interest in me and of your truly fatherly love, and am all the more impatient to be restored to my country, if only such a fortune be provided for us by our Prince as will suffice to maintain our

* See Letter III-1.

leisure. Not that I dislike England, or am discontented with my patrons. I have a great number of friends here, and many of the bishops show me no ordinary favour. Indeed the Archbishop of Canterbury treats me with so much kindness and affection, that if he were my brother or my father, he could not deal more lovingly with me. By his gift I have a considerable pension from a benefice which I resigned, and this second Maecenas adds an equal amount out of his own purse. Further assistance is provided by the generosity of noblemen, and this would be much greater if I cared to press my claims. But preparations for war are quickly changing the genius of the Island. Prices are rising every day, and liberality is decreasing. It is only natural, that men so frequently taxed should be sparing in their gifts. And not long ago, in consequence of the scarcity of wine, I was nearly killed by Stone, contracted out of the wretched liquor that I was forced to drink.* Moreover, while every island is in some degree a place of banishment, we are now confined more closely than ever by war, insomuch that it is difficult even to get a letter sent out. And I see that some great disturbances are arising, the issues of which are uncertain. I trust it may please God mercifully to allay this tempest in the Christian world.

I often wonder what thing it is that drives, I will not say Christians, but men, to such a degree of madness as to rush with so much pains, so much cost, so much risk, to the destruction of one another. For what are we doing all our lives but making war? The brute beasts do not all engage in war, but only some wild kinds; and those do not fight among themselves, but with animals of a different species. They fight too with their natural arms, and not like us with machines, upon which we expend an ingenuity worthy of devils.

For us, who glory in the name of Christ, of a master who taught and exhibited nothing but gentleness, who are members of one body, and are one flesh, quickened by the same spirit, fed by the same sacraments, attached to the same Head, called to the same immortality, hoping for that highest communion, that as Christ and the Father are one so we may be one with him,—can anything in the world be of so great concern, as to provoke us to war, a thing so calamitous and so hateful, that even when it is most righteous, no truly good man can approve it. Think, I beseech you, who are those employed in it. Cut-throats, gamblers, whoremongers, the meanest hireling soldiers, to whom a little gain is dearer than life,—these are your best warriors, when what they once did at their peril, they do now for gain and with applause. This scum of mankind must be received into your fields and into your cities, in order that you may wage war; in fact you make yourself a slave to them in your anxiety to be revenged on others.

Consider too how many crimes are committed under pretext of war, when as

* See Letter IV-2 on Erasmus' gallstone.

they say, In the midst of arms, laws are silent; how many thefts, how many acts of sacrilege, how many rapes, how many other abuses which one is ashamed even to name; and this moral contagion cannot but last for many years, even when the war is over. And if you count the cost, you will see how, even if you conquer, you lose much more than you gain. What kingdom can you set against the lives and blood of so many thousand men? And yet the greatest amount of the mischief affects those who have no part in the fighting. The advantages of peace reach everybody; while in war for the most part even the conqueror weeps; and it is followed by such a train of calamities, that there is good reason in the fiction of poets, that War comes to us from Hell and is sent by the Furies. I say nothing of the revolutions of states, which cannot take place without the most disastrous results.

If the desire of glory tempts us to War,—that is no true glory which is mainly sought by wrongful acts. It is much more glorious to found, than to overthrow, states; but in these days it is the people, that builds and maintains cities, and the folly of princes that destroys them. If gain is our object, no war has ended so happily, as not to have brought more evil than good to those engaged in it; and no sovereign damages his enemy in war without first doing a great deal of mischief to his own subjects. And finally, when we see human affairs always changing and confused, like the ebb and flow of Euripus, what is the use of such great efforts to raise an empire, which must presently by some revolution pass to others? With how much blood was the Roman empire raised, and how soon did it begin to fall!

But you will say, that the rights of sovereigns must be maintained. It is not for me to speak unadvisedly about the acts of princes. I only know this, that *summum jus,*—extreme right, is often *summa injuria,*—extreme wrong; there are princes who first decide what they want, and then look out for a title with which to cloak their proceedings. And in such great changes of human affairs, among so many treaties that have been made and abandoned, who, I ask you, need lack a title?

But suppose there is a real dispute, to whom some sovereignty belongs, where is the need of bloodshed? It is not a question concerning a nation's welfare, but only whether it is bound to call this or that personage its sovereign. There are Popes, there are Bishops, there are wise and honorable men, by whom such small matters may be settled, without sowing the seeds of war upon war, and throwing things divine and human alike into confusion. It is the proper function of the Roman Pontiff, of the Cardinals, of Bishops, and of Abbots to compose the quarrels of Christian Princes, to exert their authority in this field, and show how far the reverence of their office prevails. Julius, a pope not universally admired, had power enough to raise this tempest of war. Will not Leo, a learned, honest and pious pontiff, be able to calm it?

We should also remember, that men, and especially Christian men, are free agents; and after they have long prospered under a certain sovereign and still acknowledge his sovereignty, why should everything be upset by a revolution? Long consent creates a sovereign even among heathen nations, much more among Christians, to whom sovereignty is a service, not a lordship, so that, if a part of his subjects are taken away, he should be regarded not as injured, but relieved from part of his burden.

But suppose, you will say, the other side refuses to yield to the decision of good men; in that case what would you have me do? In the first place, if you are a true Christian, I would have you bear and forbear, disregarding that right of yours, whatever it may be. And in the next place, if you are only a wise man, pray calculate what the vindication of your right will cost you. If the cost is excessive,—and it will surely be so, when you assert it by arms,—do not then insist upon your title, perhaps unfounded after all, at the cost of so much misery to mankind, of so many killed, so many orphans, so many tears. What do you suppose the Turks think, when they hear that Christian princes are raging with so much fury against each other, and that only for the title of sovereignty? Italy is now delivered from the French, and what has been the effect of so much bloodshed, but that where a Frenchman was in office before, someone else is in office now? And the country flourished better before than it does now!

If there are any rights which admit of being defended by war, they are rights of a grosser kind, which savour of a Christianity already becoming degenerate and burdened with the wealth of this world; and I know not whether I should sanction such wars; though I see that war is sometimes not disapproved by pious authors, when for the maintenance of the faith, the peace of Christendom is defended against the invasion of barbarians. But why should we dwell on these few human authorities, rather than on those many sayings of Christ, of the Apostles, and of the orthodox and most approved Fathers on the subject of peace and the tolerance of evils. What policy is there, that may not in some way be defended, especially when the persons, who have the conduct of affairs, are those whose very crimes are praised by many for the sake of flattery, while no one dares to find fault with their errors? But in the meantime it is not unknown, what are the sighs and longings and prayers of reasonable men. But if you look a little closely, you will find that it is generally the private interests of princes that give occasion to war. And I would ask you, do you think it consistent with humanity, that the world should be at any moment disturbed by war, when this or that sovereign has some cause of complaint against another, or perhaps pretends to have one.

We may wish the best event, but can only wish. For my own part, whatever fortune I have is in England, but I would willingly resign it all, on condition that a Christian peace might be established between Christian sovereigns. This object will be no little promoted by your authority, which has much influence with prince Charles, and very much with Maximilian, while it is favorably regarded by the

English nobility. I have no doubt you have already found, what heavy losses occur in war-time even through the acts of friends. You will therefore be attending to your own interest, if you endeavour to bring this war to an end.

I shall hasten to your embrace, as soon as I can fly hence. Meantime farewell, most reverend Father. My best wishes to Doctor Ghisbert and Antony Lutzenburg.

VII-4   Fray Antonio de Guevara to the Marquis of Pescara

One of the most aristocratic of the fighting knights of the Renaissance—and a relative of Fray Antonio (1480-1545)—the Marquis was known as a model of chivalry in France, Spain, and his native Italy. He practised the knightly virtues extolled in the following letter right up to the battle of Pavia, the following year, where his brilliant military strategy defeated the French army.

19 August, 1524

Being with Caesar in Madrid on 22 May, they gave me your letter dated 30 January, and God is my witness that when I saw and read it, I should have preferred it to be 30 January than the date of the blockade of Marseilles, if not even of the conquest of the Holy See, for if you were conquering Asia, and not France, your campaign would be more famous and sublime, and even more acceptable to God. Livy writes that Marcellus and Quintus Fabius carried on a great competition between themselves, on the subject of military consulships, because good Marcellus did not wish to be a military captain of an unjustifiable war and Quintus Fabius wouldn't agree to fight in a war that wasn't perilous. The Romans took much vainglory in that century which produced these two valiant princes. But in the end they esteemed Marcellus more for being just than Quintus Fabius for his daring.

The Romans were never so badly treated or resisted in Africa or Asia than they were in the siege of Numancia, * less because of the savage defense of the populace than because the Romans had no justification for their warring and the

* Scipio Aemilianus besieged the Spaniards of Numantia. After a heroic resistance, they surrendered in 133 B. C., completing Rome's control of Spain. Cervantes wrote a popular drama on this event.

Numantines had every reason to defend themselves. The successful Emperor Trajan never undertook a war without just cause. The King of Pontus, Mithridates, wrote to the consul Silla, when they were warring, as follows: "I marvel that thou, Consul Silla, undertakest war on a foreign soil like mine, since we have neither offended nor know each other." Silla replied to these words: "I am indifferent about carrying on war far from Rome, Mithridates, since Rome was always lucky in war . . . I trust that the gods will favor my sense of what is just over your great fortune." Emperor Augustus used to say often that wars, if just, had to be commended by gods, accepted by princes, justified by philosophers, and carried out by captains.

I write this, Lord Marquis, so that if your war were in Jerusalem, we should hold it to be just. Being rather around Marseilles, we still hold it to be scrupulous. "Cor regis in manu dei est," says the Holy Scripture. This being so, who can solve the riddle of whether the King may be offending God, his heart being in God's hand? One thing seems clear. We see nothing other than Christians warring and the Moors living in peace and prospering. Nor do I understand what we see every day, that God in his secret wisdom lets the churches honoring him be destroyed and leveled, while the mosques which offend him remain entire and free.

You, my Lord, are a good Christian knight, my close kinsman and special friend. These things make me to be sensitive to your travails and sorry for your perils. I refer to your bodily, not spiritual travail, for the honorable captain values only lightly his life. I speak of peril to your soul only, for among Christians there is no war so justified that one may not be scrupulous about the soul. In this matter, Sire, you see that I wish to save you, not delude you, rather telling you my feelings that you may afterwards do as you must. The obligation of a captain general, my Lord, is to avoid unjust damage, punish blasphemers, protect the innocent, chastise the insolent, reward the armies, defend cities, avoid plunder, and keep faith even with your enemies. Keep in mind, Lord Marquis, that the time will come when you must give an accounting to God as well as the king, not only for your deeds but your decisions. Don Juan de Guevara was your grandfather and my uncle, one of the knights who helped King Alonso take the Kingdom of Naples. For this he was named Great Seneschal of the Kingdom. Remember this, my Lord, and work to leave such fame to your descendants as your ancestors left to you.

(trans. R.J.C.)

VII-5   Emperor Charles V of Spain to Charles de Lannoy, Viceroy of Naples

What does one do with one of Europe's greatest Kings after capturing him
in battle? The many courtesies extended by Emperor Charles V (1500-
1558) of Spain, absentee-victor of the Battle of Pavia, to the captive
Francis I of France illustrate the gallantry and courtliness for which the
Renaissance was famous.

                                                        Toledo, 20 June, 1525

Tres cher et Feal!
We have received your letters from Villa Franca of the 10th of this month, and
have seen the instructions you have given to Manuel Malversin, the contents of
which have given us great satisfaction, as well as the arrangements you have made
for the removal of the King of France. With regard to the desire you express to
know our good pleasure respecting the place, where his person may be securely
deposited, as well as the time of your own coming to us, and how the fleet you have
brought, for which we have to remit ten thousand ducats, should be disposed of,
we have to answer,
    First as to the person of the King of France; it is our desire that he should be
well treated, and even better, if it be possible, than he has already been,—provided
always that he is well secured; and for this purpose three places have been named
to us, which are said to be very suitable. The one is Patina near Valencia, another
Chinchilla in Castile, for which it would be necessary to disembark at Carthagena,
and the third Mora, which is a considerable distance from you and not more
than five leagues hence. It appears to us that the said Patina, being situated in an
agreeable part of the country, and being the nearest point to Saulo or to any port
in Catalonia where you might disembark, would be the best and most secure place
we could fix on for the King, always, be it understood, with a good guard about
him, as usual, and as you know to be necessary. At the same time, if any other place
should appear to you more likely to keep his person in greater safety, and not
liable to inconvenience, you are at liberty to determine on this point as you think
best, with this condition, that a sea port must not be fixed on, which might be

dangerous. As to your coming to us, it is the thing which we have always most desired were it possible, and now that there is so good an opportunity we the more desire it, when you may be sure you will be more than welcome, and not only give us pleasure, but render us service. The sooner you come the better, as you will see by the dispatch which we believe Figueroa, who left us two days ago, will have already brought you, in which we inform you of many important things touching the affairs of Italy, that inasmuch as new circumstances require new counsels, it is our intention so with you to advise, conclude and resolve, as may best promote our service.

After which it will be necessary with all diligence to make known our resolves to those in Italy, who ought to be acquainted with them, that no time may be lost in the execution of whatever, as has been intimated, shall in your presence and with your advice be determined on. As every thing therefore must remain in suspence till your arrival, we have dispatched a special courier to M. de Bourbon, begging him to await where he at present is the further communication of our intentions, and another also to the Marquis of Pescara, requiring him not to abate in his endeavours to fulfil the charge which you committed to him, holding out a good hope that his services will not be unrequited. Whether you think good to accompany the said King of France to Patina, or to whatever place he may be conducted, or to come incontinently to us, leaving the aforesaid charge to Alarcon, we commit to your own discretion; begging you not to forget that your presence here is most desirable, and to take care, that the King and his attendants should have no lack of horses on his journey, that he may be sensible of the interest we take in his progress, and of our earnest desire that his treatment in all respects may be good and honorable. We write to our cousin the Marquis of Brandenburgh now being at Valencia, that he should pay the King a visit on our part, and see that horses be provided. This letter will be intrusted to your care, and you will read it.—Write also yourself to the said Marquis, giving him your instructions as to what he should do and say, and among them, that he make his visit handsomely accompanied, as he well knows how.

As to what is to be done with our said fleet which you have brought, it is my wish on this subject also to consult with you in person, and to have your opinion and advice. It is our desire that before you take your leave of the King of France you should endeavour, if possible, that, besides what he has already accorded, in case it should prove not desirable that his Galleys should return to Genoa, the rest of the French fleet should abstain from making war or causing damage to any of our vassals or servants during the term of fifteen days after the arrival of our fleet on the coasts of Spain. You might indeed prolong this term to two months or less after the expiration of the fifteen days, but for this it would be necessary to take the precaution of sufficient security, and also that the six galleys of the King of

France should remain with ours, as you have been at the charge of their equipment. With regard to the ten thousand ducats which you have thought necessary for the said fleet, we have incontinently ordered them to be forthcoming, and will transmit them as soon as possible without fail.

For the rest, we have no doubt, but you will take care to make the King of France satisfied with the proposed movement to the said Patina, telling him of the honorable treatment he may expect, and of our good intentions towards an universal peace and his consequent enlargement, maintaining throughout this matter our own honor without sullying his, and preserving the good opinion of the friends of both. You may further assure him in the most courteous terms, that his present removal is only until we have time to come to a good resolution and conclusion of the whole matter. We write thus, because we think it proper that you should spare no pains to make him satisfied, and to keep him cheerful, that he may not take in ill part, or as unkind treatment, his being placed in the Castle of Patina, where his person, I repeat, must be kept in perfect security.

Instead of your Maitre d'Hotel, who has been taken ill on the road, we send Colin Bajonier; and we have now nothing further to say, until we hear from you, which we much desire; and for this purpose you can send back the said Colin, or some other person as soon as possible, and inform us of what you have done, in the aforesaid matters, and when we may expect you here.

(Contrast this gracious letter, composed shortly after the triumph of Pavia, with the desperate epistle of the Emperor trapped in Innsbruck, VI-10.)

VII-6   Ferdinand of Austria to Hermann Archbishop of Cologne

A series of letters from Ludwig of Hungary to Henry VIII between 1521 and mid-1526 warn that the Turk Suleiman plans to march up the Danube Valley to Hungary and that a coalition must be found to stop him. Europe did not unite. On 29 August, 1526, the superior Turkish forces destroyed King Ludwig and his army at Mohatz. The day following the victory the Turks beheaded 1500 Hungarian prisoners. The Turk was unopposed and on the march to Vienna, a threat to Western Europe until the Battle of Lepanto in 1571. The widespread terror of the Tyrant Turk is expressed here by Ferdinand I of Austria (1503-1564).

Innsbruck, 7 September, 1526

Unto the right reverend Prince my Lord Herman, Archbishop of Cologne, Lord High Chancellor of the Holy Roman Empire through Italy, Elector and Duke of Westphalia and Engern, Our singular good friend.

Right reverend Elector, in the most friendly wise we greet you well, signifying unto you, with sad and heavy heart, that yesterday at our arrival here, a post has reached us from our Lower Austrian dominions, by which we have received communication that the hereditary enemy of our holy Christian faith, the Tyrant Turk, is bruited to have beaten and conquered our dear Lord and brother-in-law the King of Hungary with his royal army. But of the place where such battle was fought, and likewise touching the fate of the King's Grace we have not yet received advertisement. Howbeit we look hourly forward to other tidings: God grant they shall be gladder than the first. This we signify to your good Grace from singular high confidence, trusting you and other Christian hearts will have especial friendly compassion with his said Grace and us, and will mind the Turk's exploit and victory so far, that, if the said Turk should further pursue his victorious career this autumn or winter, or in the spring, and boldly invade our Lower Austrian dominions, your good Grace, together with other Electors, Princes, and States of the Empire, will not forsake the King's Grace and ourselves, but grant their princely succour. The like are ourselves in a readiness, with good heart and mind to do according to the best of our power, if necessity, as we no wise wish, should require it. For to behold your good Grace's honour and weal, and to preserve the same in constant integrity, is a right particular pleasure to Us. Given at Inspruck, on the 7th day Septembris, A.D. 1526.

Postscripta. We have received another despatch, the which we grieve to say containeth, that the Battle chanced on the nine and twentieth of August last passed, and was lost by his Grace of Hungary; neither is it yet known if the King's Grace is still alive or killed. Wherefore the realm of Hungary, together with our Austrian dominions are brought into great jeopardy; and what terrour and ruin will fall to Christendom thereby, your good Grace's wisdom doth right well understand. We therefore beseech you most seriously to call this to mind, and in likewise not omit to send Us the succour aforesaid, and specially divers arquebuss-masters, such as may from time to time be required.

By your Grace's loving friend,
Ferdinand

VII-7   Niccolò Machiavelli to Bartolomeo Cavalcanti

It is interesting to note that in his pessimistic analysis of the unsuccessful
military policies of Pope Clement VII, Machiavelli (1469-1527) is very
concerned about the "ruin of Hungary" described in the preceding letter.
Does he sense that the following May the Spanish army and German
mercenaries will sack papal Rome with unmitigated fury, leaving it
plundered and plagueridden?

Florence (?), November 1526 [1]

Dearest Bartolomeo:

The reason why the Pope started this war before the King of France sent his
soldiers into Italy and took action in Spain according to his agreement, and before
all the Swiss arrived, was his hope in the people of Milan, and his belief that six
thousand Swiss, whom the Venetians and the Pope had sent on learning of the first
rebellions in Milan, would be so prompt that they would arrive at the same time as
the Venetians arrived with their army. Besides, he believed that the King's
soldiers, if they were not so prompt, would at least be early enough to aid in
carrying through the undertaking. To these hopes was joined the needs of the
Castle,[2] which was showing that it required aid. All these things, then, made the
Pope hasten, and with such hope that we believed this war would end in fifteen
days; this hope was increased by the capture of Lodi. The armies of the Venetians
and of the Pope did unite, then; but of the presuppositions above, two of the most
important were lacking, because the Swiss did not come, and the people of Milan
were of no value. Hence, when we appeared before Milan, the people did not stir,
and not having the Swiss, we did not have courage to stay there, and retired to
Marignano, and did not return to Milan until five thousand Swiss had come. Their
coming, as earlier it would have been useful, was harmful, because it gave us
courage to return to Milan in order to relieve the Castle, and it was not relieved,
and we committed ourselves to remaining there, because, the first retirement
having been shameful, nobody advised the second.

---

1. The reference to All Saints' Day near the end of the letter puts its date after October 31, 1526.
The Spanish fleet, mentioned just before as not yet arrived, reached Naples on December 1.
2. Of Milan.

This caused the attempt on Cremona to be made with part of the infantry and not with all, as it would have been made if on the loss of the Castle we had been at Marignano. For these reasons, then, and also since we expected it to be easy, we carried on the affair of Cremona weakly. This was contrary to a rule of mine that says it is not a wise plan to risk all one's fortune but not all one's forces. They believed, because of the fortress, that four thousand soldiers would be enough to capture her. This attack, because it was weak, made Cremona more difficult, because those forces did not assail, but did point out, the weak places; as a result those inside did not lose them but strengthened them. Furthermore, they settled their courage to the defense; hence, although later the Duke of Urbino went there, and there were fourteen thousand soldiers round about, they were not enough; while if he had been there early with the whole army—able at one time to make several attacks—of necessity they would have taken her in six days, and perhaps this campaign would have been won, because we would have had the prestige of the capture, along with a very large army. Because, since thirteen thousand Swiss came, either Milan or Genoa, or perhaps both of them, would have been mastered. And the enemy would have had no recourse; the troubles at Rome would not have occurred; the reinforcements, which have not yet come, would not have been in time. And we have spent fifty days hoping for Milan, and the capture of Cremona is brought about late, when all our affairs have gone to ruin.

We have then on our side lost this war twice; once when we went to Milan and did not stay there; the second time when we sent and did not go to Cremona. The reason for the first was the timidity of the Duke; of the second, the vanity of us all, because, feeling disgraced by the first retreat, nobody dared advise the second. The Duke could do badly against the will of all; against the will of all he could not do well. These are the errors that have taken victory away from us; I say *taken it away* through our not having conquered early; because we might have deferred but not lost the campaign, if our bad arrangements had not been added. These also have been two; the first is that the Pope has not raised money in times when he could with reputation have done so, and in the ways used by other popes. The other is that he remained in Rome in such a condition that he could be captured like a baby—something that has snarled this skein up in such a way that Christ could not straighten it out, because the Pope has taken his soldiers from the field, and Messer Francesco is still in the field, and today the Duke of Urbino must have arrived there. Many leaders, of many opinions, are left, but all ambitious and unbearable, and, lacking anybody who knows how to assuage their factions and keep them united, they will be a chorus of dogs.[3] From this results a confusion in our doings that is very great, and already Lord Giovanni does not intend to remain

3. Cf. the quarrelsome leaders of *Prince* 26.

there, and I believe that today he will leave. These bad arrangements were all corrected by the eagerness and effort of Messer Francesco. Besides this, if money has been coming sparingly from Rome, now it will fail entirely. So I see little order in our houses, and if God does not aid us to the south, as he has done to the north, we have few resources left.

Because, as, with the ruin of Hungary, he impeded aid from Germany for the northerners, so he will need to impede aid from Spain with the ruin of the fleet; hence we need to have Juno go to beseech Aeolus for us and promise him *la Contessa* and all the ladies in Florence,[4] so that he will give full freedom to the winds in our favor. And without doubt, if it were not for the Turk, I believe the Spanish would have come to celebrate All Saints' Day with us.

I, having seen the Castle lost, and observed how the Spaniards have established themselves in three or four of those cities and made themselves sure of the people, judged that this war was going to be long, and through its length dangerous. Because I know with what difficulty cities are taken when there is somebody inside who means to defend them, and that a province is taken in a day, but a city requires months and years to take, as is shown by many ancient narratives, and in modern times by Rhodes and Hungary. For that reason I wrote to Francesco Vettori that I believed we could not support this undertaking, except to bring about that the King of France should take Milan (we should give him that state), or possibly as a diversion through which we would leave the frontiers of these states guarded, so that the Spanish could not make progress. The Pope then with all his forces should attack the Kingdom, which I believe could be taken before one of these cities here. Because there would be neither obstinate defenders nor peoples conquered [5] . . . , such as a man would like. Besides this, the war would feed itself, because in addition to the assistance he could have from the cities, he would have tribute, and the richness of the country, not ravaged, would make assistance more lasting. Also the Pope without new expense would live securely in Rome, and we would see which the Emperor estimated higher, Lombardy or the Kingdom. And if this is not done, I look on the war as lost, because its length is sure, and in length dangers can be reckoned as certain, either through lack of money or through other accidents such as those that have come up. And it has seemed to me a strange plan to wear ourselves out in the field, and that the enemy should be at ease in the city, and that, when at last his reinforcements came, finding us worn out, he should ruin us like the Admiral and the King.

Niccolò Machiavelli.

(The contents of this letter are to be juxtaposed to the political and military analyses found in Machiavelli's *Prince* [see Letter II-3].)

4. *Aeneid* 1.65ff.
5. Something is lacking from the manuscript.

VII-8   Ambassador Chapuys to Emperor Charles V

Although Charles V of Spain hailed Henry VIII as "most dear brother" before Parliamentary dissolution of Henry's marriage with his aunt Catherine of Aragon, their conflicting personalities, ambitions, and religious views prevented a real compatibility. In the following letter of Chapuys, the Spanish Ambassador to London (who becomes Capucius in Shakespeare's drama *Henry VIII*, IV, ii), we find the Tudor King unwilling to cooperate in Charles's wars and even sarcastic about Charles's preference for Christians over Turks as his antagonists.

London, 25 October 1529

Sire! on the evening of the ensuing day, which was the 22nd, my Secretary returned with letters from the King informing me that he was leaving Winesor (Windsor) for his palace at Grennevys (Greenwich) where he would be on Saturday, but that as he should not arrive till late, I had better not repair thither till the next day. Accordingly, about 8 o'clock on the following morning (Sunday) I arrived at the said Greenwich, and on getting out of the boat found a very civil gentleman, M. Poller, accompanied by two others with their servants, who had been sent on the part of the King to attend and conduct me to the palace. On entering the second gate of the Court, I found Monseigneur the Bishop of London ready for the same purpose and charge, who led me to the antechamber of the King where the greatest part of the Court was assembled, and where I was received by the two Dukes, and the Archbishop of Canterbury. Here whilst waiting for the King, who was about to attend Mass, I remained in conversation with these seigneurs. . . .

Sire! immediately after Mass the King coming up to me resumed the same subject, asking me if I thought it were possible that he could be backward in such a proceeding? I then laid before him more expressly and more particularly the great necessity there was to resist without further delay this formidable enemy the Turk, which would appear most pressing from extracts of letters which the king of Hungary had addressed to Your Majesty, as well as from the tenor of those which Madame had been pleased to write to me. I told him that I had reason to fear also that the Pope's expected arrival at Bologna on the 5th of this month, would scarcely admit of his ambassadors who were to set out and travel at their ease, being in time for the conference; and therefore it might be expedient I observed, were he to send another power by post to the Ambassadors already with his Holiness, that they might treat on all the subjects in question, should the case require it. He told me that he had given the Ambassadors sent to your Majesty especial charge to expedite their journey, and that he would repeat his injunctions on this point. With regard to Your Majesty's expectations from him in this war with the Turk, it was right, he said, to be clearly understood, that he could only do little, but that he was ready to do all in his power.

I was unwilling to let this observation on the smallness of his ability pass without remarking, that it could not be inconsiderable as to men, and certainly was very far from being so as to money, with which, it was well known he was provided at least as well as any Prince in Christendom. Were it indeed otherwise, I added, since he was absolute as the Pope, in his dominions, and had moreover such an abundance of rich ecclesiastics, he could hardly plead a want of wealth. He would not be wanting, he rejoined, to assist and promote the enterprize in view as far as the object appeared to him to require his exertions; but Your Majesty, he strongly intimated, as the principal in the affair, the greatest personage, and the most powerful, ought to be the conductor and leader of the way to others, and the more effectually to accomplish this, ought without delay to make peace with the potentates of Italy. He said that all the success you could gain there, would not add one jot to your greatness or your power, and the more Your Majesty could abstain from wasting means in that quarter which might be employed on a much greater and fitter object elsewhere, the more would it redound to Your Majesty's honour, praise and reputation in the face of all the world. It was not, he said, out of any favour or affection towards the Italian powers, to whom he was bound by no tie or obligation, but out of a sense of duty to Your Majesty, that he made this remark, for whose exaltation and glory he was always anxious. Not that he presumed to offer advice to Your Majesty, he continued, who was not only provided with a store of faithful counsellors, but who was yourself greatly distinguished for your prudence. Your Majesty, I assured him, had never ceased to use your best efforts for bringing about a safe peace, union and tranquillity in Italy, and that this was one of the motives of the present journey, as I had before observed. I told him that the parties with whom you had to deal were so difficult to bring to reason, having always some reserved point in their proposals, that caution in proceeding with them was, so to speak, no less necessary than with the Turks, and consequently that their very offers of amity were not immediately to be acceded to, much to the discomfiture of Your Majesty; as might be seen in the case of the Duke Francisco Sforza.

"But come," said the King interrupting me, "what are they about, with this poor Duke? What harm can he do?" I told him according to the tenor of the letter Your Majesty was pleased to write, how it was intended to treat with him. "Perhaps," said he, "You may be wishing to refer his case to Arbitrators whom he may have reason to think not the most impartial." It was impossible, I replied, for any Judges to be more fair than those who had been named, and that nothing could be more gracious and advantageous to the Duke, than the terms proposed, which had been rendered the more so, out of consideration to the Pope, and to himself, who had on this and former occasions interceded with your Majesty in favour of the said Duke. The King said, that his motive in so doing was no other than to bring about an universal peace; and that as to the Pope he was bound to it by their Holy League, in which he had himself been made, he knew not how and certainly not with his own consent, a party concerned. With regard to another point the cession of Pavia and Alessandria; those towns, he allowed, might be given up to your Majesty, as far as you were personally responsible for such a charge; but to be handed over to your own people was a different thing, as in your absence it would appear there was but little safety and security, judging from what had lately occurred at Sienna, which place, notwithstanding its devotion to Your Majesty had been entered and plundered by some of Your troops under the Prince himself. The King, when he perceived that I did not give credit to such an assertion which bore so little appearance of truth or probability, continued more stoutly to confirm it, declaring that he had received letters to this express effect from his ambassadors. "As far as relates to Pavia," I observed, "that is out of the reach of any dispute, for it has been already given up." He demanded two or three times whether I knew this of a certainty; I had not, I replied, received any letters from your Majesty to this effect, but I had heard it from a friend who was not in the habit of transgressing the truth, and I was the more disposed to credit his account from a particular circumstance he at the same time mentioned, namely the capture of the Count de Gayaz, and his subsequent escape. "I have also heard," said the King, "that it had been given up, and was afterwards retaken; but," he continued "I would make one observation, and this I should wish to remain between ourselves; I think it a very great shame, the Turk being in Austria, the true patrimony of the Emperor, that he should not go to its rescue instead of making war upon Christians." . . .

VII-9   Pietro Aretino to Ambrogio degli Eusebii

Pietro Aretino (1492-1556) deflates the aspirations of a would-be *miles gloriosus,* Ambrogio degli Eusebii, and takes a hard look at the lot of a soldier.

Venice, 28 November, 1537

You are a large fool, Messer Ambrogio, for it was only a few days ago that I had to knock out of your head your unholy notion to take a wife, and I now have to line up my arguments to cure you of your idea of becoming a soldier. Isn't it a known truth that soldiers, like bread, end up mouldy and worthless—even though someone might reply to this: "What would you do without one and the other in times of famine or of war?"

It seems to me that you are crazy even to think of enlisting, and stark mad if you actually sign the roster, for the soldier's life is so much like that of the courtier that they might well be called twin sisters. They are both hand-maidens of the desperate, and step-daughters of swinish Fortune. Indeed, the camp and the court should always be spoken of in the same breath, for in one you find want, envy and old age, and end up in the poor house, while in the other you earn wounds, a prison camp and starvation.

I confess that you can hear high-sounding chatter about the former if you sit at table where they revel in the idea of going to Rome or to Mirandola. At the end of the meal, some fellow with ambition in his soul, takes himself thither in imagination.

"I'd like to get ready my habits, my steed and my servant," he rambles on "and go to the household of the Pope or of the Reverend So-and-So. I am a good musician, have some learning, and I love the chase."

I am all for talking this fantastic kind of balderdash. It makes a man a Trojan here in his own mind. But I say a pox on turning words to action. If you do, you will wear out your clothes, your servant and your palfry in two months. Your patron will become your enemy as will paradise itself if you should ever get there.

In the same way, the man who fulminates with martial fury, makes a bestial fool of himself. Talking big of what you said and did when you served France, giving yourself a thousand foot soldiers and two hundred men in armor, you invest castles, burn villages take prisoners and amass treasure. But if you want to caracole on your steed a couple of times under the window of your doxy, you can do it just as bravely if you stay at home.

For a "hip, hip, hurrah, boys!" in front of some rustic lout's chicken yard, you will go without bread for supper for at least ten weeks. For a bundle of rags—which is all your booty amounts to—and for the dungeon in which you will end up whenever God wills it, you will be rewarded by coming home limping on a cane, and by selling your vineyard so as to keep out of the hands of the loan-sharks.

This is my answer to your tall talk about the insignia and the medals and the collars you have seen worn, forsooth, by those who came back from Piedmont: *"If you had seen those who did not come back, if you had seen those who could not keep a groat, you would feel as great pity for them as we all feel for those wretches who go to, and then cannot escape, the knaveries of the court.*

Come now, change your mind. You can write a sonnet much better than you could go through a drill. So keep on having a good time at my expense. For few people ever get their clutches on the tickets that win the big prizes in the lottery.

In conclusion, the money that you get from soldiering lasts about as long as that won by gamblers, or as the revenues of churchmen. I know all about this. I have seen Cardinals' nephews squander the fortunes left them, and so die in poverty. And I, whom you see before you, have kept the pay of soldiers safe for them. It would have been a sad day for them if I had not.

Put all of that into your head, and then go and buckle on your tin armor.

My Lord Giovanni de' Medici once said upon a similar occasion: "They babble that I am a valiant man, but that has never kept me from being poor!"

VII-10   Claudio Tolomei to Giovanni Francesco Bini

Claudio Tolomei (1492-1555) recreates for Giovanni Francesco Bini the mood of panic unleashed in Rome upon the arrival of the Turkish fleet in Ostia, led by the Greek-born corsair Khair ed-Din Barbarossa. Tolomei, a Sienese critic, was also a writer of sonnets and an orator who was nominated ambassador to France.

30 June, 1543

To Giovanni Francesco Bini,

You are having a good time because you are there in a safe place, but we, poor people, have here the Turks at Ostia and at Porto. This is not gossip. The fleet of Barbarossa is made up of one hundred and twenty galleys, thirty-five other vessels, and four huge ships. All of Rome is in a panic today, the day of Saint Peter. It seems that Barbarossa calculated expressly to do honor or reverence to this saint, because I understand that our apostles are still being venerated among the Turks. I believe that if it were not for a letter which was written by Captain Polino, three quarters of Rome would be crowding the streets into the country. Even so, more than a thousand persons have been seeking a more secure place. Captain Polino has let it be known that there should be no doubts, since the Great Turk has commanded expressly to Barbarossa not to annoy the lands of the Pope. Here is a new religion of which we were not aware. I send you a copy of the letter in order that you may see better for yourself the honor that Sultan Suleiman accords to the Holy Seat.

Begin then to be of a better state of mind, for perhaps that prophecy will be fulfilled which holds that he will become a Christian. He certainly is so well disposed toward the interests of Christians that he would wish to handle all those things by himself if he could. We shall wait and see what Karadim Bey will do and I shall follow this letter with another tomorrow.

This morning, while we are at the end of the month, it became known that Barbarossa has taken sail toward Civitavecchia where it is assumed that he will do no more harm. Nor will he demand anything but some provisions, paying for them honestly, as has been done in all the other places. I really believe that when he comes across the Sienese, he will do an about-face, and if he is able to do them harm, he will do it without conscience. The Virgin Mother of God has saved us from greater perils, and we hope still that she will preserve us from this one. Last evening all of Rome was topsy-turvy, but I think that once the voyage of Barbarossa is understood, those who have fled with a pallor on their cheeks will return blushing somewhat.

If I don't write of anything else, you will pardon me. For when the sun suddenly appears, all the other stars disappear. Thus, when one is reasoning about Barbarossa all the other trivial daily events are overshadowed. Be happy and give another glance at my earlier letters. Knight Gandolfo has returned from the spas quite recovered, and sends greetings to you.

Claudio Tolomei
(trans. R. J. C.)

VII-11   Ogier Ghiselin de Busbecq to a Friend

Having been dispatched to Constantinople in the service of Ferdinand of Austria (whose claim to the Hungarian throne was disputed by Suleiman the Magnificent), Ogier Ghiselin de Busbecq (1522-1592), the Flemish diplomat and writer, pens his much-admired observations on the Turks. On his second visit to the Sultan's court, he was imprisoned, but finally succeeded in drawing up peace terms which were ratified upon his return to Vienna.

1555-1562

I undertook, when we parted, to give you a full account of my journey to Constantinople, and this promise I now hope to discharge with interest; for I will give you also an account of an expedition to Amasia, which is by far the rarer treat of the two.

To an old friend like yourself I shall write very freely, and I am sure you will enjoy some pleasant passages which befell me on my way; and as to the disagreeables which are inseparable from a journey so long and so difficult, do not give them a thought, for I assure you that, though they annoyed me at the time, that very annoyance, now they are past and gone, only adds to my pleasure in recalling them.

You will remember that, after my return home from England, where I attended the marriage of King Philip and Queen Mary, in the train of Don Pedro Lasso, whom my most gracious master, Ferdinand King of the Romans, had deputed to represent him at the wedding, I received from the last-mentioned sovereign a summons to undertake this journey. . . .

At Buda I made my first acquaintance with the janizaries; this is the name by which the Turks call the infantry of the royal guard. The Turkish state has twelve thousand of these troops when the corps is at its full strength. They are scattered through every part of the empire, either to garrison the forts against the enemy, or to protect the Christians and Jews from the violence of the mob. There is no district with any considerable amount of population, no borough or city, which has not a detachment of janizaries to protect the Christians, Jews, and other helpless people from outrage and wrong.

A garrison of janizaries is always stationed in the citadel of Buda. The dress of these men consists of a robe reaching down to the ankles, while, to cover their heads, they employ a cowl, which, by their account, was originally a cloak sleeve, part of which contains the head, while the remainder hangs down and flaps against the neck. On their forehead is placed a silvergilt cone of considerable height, studded with stones of no great value.

These janizaries generally came to me in pairs. When they were admitted to my dining room they first made a bow, and then came quickly up to me, all but running, and touched my dress or hand, as if they intended to kiss it. After this they would thrust into my hand a nosegay of the hyacinth or narcissus; then they would run back to the door almost as quickly as they came, taking care not to turn their backs, for this, according to their code, would be a serious breach of etiquette. After reaching the door, they would stand respectfully with their arms crossed, and their eyes bent on the ground, looking more like monks than warriors. On receiving a few small coins (which was what they wanted) they bowed again, thanked me in loud tones, and went off blessing me for my kindness. To tell you the truth, if I had not been told beforehand that they were janizaries, I should, without hesitation, have taken them for members of some order of Turkish monks, or brethren of some Moslem college. Yet these are the famous janizaries, whose approach inspires terror everywhere.

During my stay at Buda a good many Turks were drawn to my table by the attraction of my wine, a luxury in which they have not many opportunities of indulging. The effect of this enforced abstinence is to make them so eager for drink that they swill themselves with it whenever they get the chance. I asked them to make a night of it, but at last I got tired of the game, left the table, and retired to my bedroom. On this my Turkish guests made a move to go, and great was their grief as they reflected that they were not yet dead drunk, and could still use their legs. Presently they sent a servant to request that I would allow them access to my stock of wine and lend them some silver cups. With my permission, they said, they would like to continue their drinking bout through the night; they were not particular where they sat; any odd corner would do for them. Well, I ordered them to be furnished with as much wine as they could drink, and also with the cups they asked for. Being thus supplied, the fellows never left off drinking until they were one and all stretched on the floor in the last stage of intoxication.

To drink wine is considered a great sin among the Turks, especially in the case of persons advanced in life: when younger people indulge in it the offence is considered more venial. Inasmuch, however, as they think that they will have to pay the same penalty after death whether they drink much or little, if they taste one drop of wine they must needs indulge in a regular debauch; their notion being that, inasmuch as they have already incurred the penalty, appointed for such sin in another world, it will be an advantage to them to have their sin out, and get dead drunk, since it will cost them as much in either case. These are their ideas about drinking, and they have some other notions which are still more ridiculous. I saw an old gentleman at Constantinople who, before taking up his cup, shouted as loud as he could. I asked my friends the reason, and they told me he was shouting to warn his soul to stow itself away in some odd corner of his body, or to leave it altogether, lest it should be defiled by the wine he was about to drink, and have hereafter to answer for the offence which the worthy man meant to indulge in. . . .

I must now return to my subject. A messenger was despatched to Suleiman, with a letter announcing my arrival. During the interval, while we were waiting for his answer, I had an opportunity of seeing Constantinople at my leisure. My chief wish was to visit the Church of St. Sophia; to which, however, I only obtained admission as a special favour, as the Turks think that their temples are profaned by the entrance of a Christian. It is a grand and massive building, well worth visiting. There is a huge central cupola, or dome, lighted only from a circular opening at the top. Almost all the Turkish mosques are built after the pattern of St. Sophia. Some say it was formerly much bigger, and that there were several buildings in connection with it, covering a great extent of ground, which were pulled down many years ago, the shrine in the middle of the church alone being left standing. . . .

If I had not visited the Black Sea, when I had an opportunity of sailing thither, I should have deserved to be blamed for my laziness, since the ancients held it to be quite as great an exploit to have visited the Black Sea as to have sailed to Corinth. Well, we had a delightful voyage, and I was allowed to enter some of the royal kiosks. On the folding doors of one of these palaces I saw a picture of the famous battle between Selim and Ismael King of the Persians, executed in masterly style, in tesselated work. I saw also a great many pleasure grounds belonging to the Sultan, situated in the most charming valleys. Their loveliness was almost entirely the work of nature; to art they owed little or nothing. What a fairyland! What a landscape for waking a poet's fancy! What a retreat for a scholar to retire to! I do declare that, as I said just now, these spots seem to grieve and ask for Christian help and Christian care once more; and still truer are these words of Constantinople, or rather of the whole of Greece. That land was once most prosperous; today it is subject to an unnatural bondage. It seems as if the country, which in ancient times discovered the fine arts and every liberal science, were demanding back that civilization which it gave to us, and were adjuring us, by the claim of a common faith, to be its champion against savage barbarism. But it is all in vain. The princes of Christendom have other objects in view; and, after all, the

Greeks are not under heavier bondage to the Turks than we are to our own vices—luxury, intemperance, sloth, lust, pride, ambition, avarice, hatred, envy, malice. By these our souls are so weighed down and buried that they cannot look up to heaven, or entertain one glorious thought, or contemplate one noble deed. The ties of a common faith and the duty we owe our brethren ought to have drawn us to their assistance, even though glory and honour had no charm for our dull hearts; at any rate, self-interest, which is the first thing men think of nowadays, should have made us anxious to rescue lands so fair, with all their great resources and advantages, from the hand of the barbarian, that we might hold them in his stead. At present we are seeking across the wide seas the Indies and Antipodes. And why? It is because in those lands there are simple, guileless creatures from whom rich booty may be torn without the cost of a single wound. *For these expeditions religion supplies the pretext and gold the motive.*

This was not the fashion with our ancestors. They scorned to place themselves on the level of a trader by seeking those lands where gold was most plentiful, but deemed that land most desirable which gave them the best opportunity of proving their valour and performing their duty. They, too, had their toil; they, too, had their dangers; they, too, had their distant expeditions; but honour was the prize they sought, not profit. When they came home from their wars, they came home not richer in *wealth,* but richer in *renown.*

These words are for your private ear, for perhaps some may hold it foul wrong for a man to suggest that the moral tone of the present day leaves aught to be desired. However that may be, I see that the arrows are being sharpened for our destruction; and I fear it will turn out that if we *will* not fight for glory, we shall be *compelled* to fight for existence. . . .

On our arrival at Amasia we were taken to call on Achmet Pasha (the chief vizier) and the other pashas—for the Sultan himself [Suleiman the Magnificent] was not then in the town—and commenced our negotiations with them touching the business entrusted to us by King Ferdinand. The pashas, on their part, apparently wishing to avoid any semblance of being prejudiced with regard to these questions, did not offer any strong opposition to the views we expressed, and told us that the whole matter depended on the Sultan's pleasure. On his arrival we were admitted to an audience; but the manner and spirit in which he listened to our address, our arguments, and our message were by no means favourable.

The Sultan was seated on a very low ottoman, not more than a foot from the ground, which was covered with a quantity of costly rugs and cushions of exquisite workmanship; near him lay his bow and arrows. His air, as I said, was by no means gracious, and his face wore a stern, though dignified, expression.

On entering we were separately conducted into the royal presence by the chamberlains, who grasped our arms. This has been the Turkish fashion of admitting people to the sovereign ever since a Croat, in order to avenge the death of his master, Marcus, Despot of Servia, asked Amurath for an audience, and took advantage of it to slay him. After having gone through a pretence of kissing his hand, we were conducted backwards to the wall opposite his seat, care being taken that we should never turn our backs on him. The Sultan then listened to what I had to say; but the language I held was not at all to his taste, for the demands of his Majesty [Ferdinand] breathed a spirit of independence and dignity, which was by no means acceptable to one who deemed that his wish was law; and so he made no answer beyond saying in a tetchy way, *"Giusel, giusel,"* i.e., well, well. After this we were dismissed to our quarters.

The Sultan's hall was crowded with people, among whom were several officers of high rank. Besides these there were all the troopers of the Imperial Guard, Spahis, Ghourebas, Ouloufedgis, and a large force of janizaries; but there was not in all that great assembly a single man who owed his position to aught save his valour and his merit. No distinction is attached to birth among the Turks; the deference to be paid to a man is measured by the position he holds in public service. There is no fighting for precedence; a man's place is marked out by the duties he discharges. In making his appointments the Sultan pays no regard to any pretensions on the score of wealth or rank, nor does he take into consideration recommendations or popularity; he considers each case on its own merits, and examines carefully into the character, ability, and disposition of the man whose promotion is in question. It is by merit that men rise in the service, a system which ensures that posts should only be assigned to the competent. Each man in Turkey carries in his own hand his ancestry and his position in life, which he may make or mar as he will. Those who receive the highest offices from the Sultan are for the most part the sons of shepherds or herdsmen, and so far from being ashamed of their parentage, they actually glory in it, and consider it a matter of boasting that they owe nothing to the accident of birth; for they do not believe that high qualities are either natural or hereditary, nor do they think that they can be handed down from father to son, but that they are partly the gift of God, and partly the result of good training, great industry, and unwearied zeal; arguing that high qualities do not descend from a father to his son or heir any more than a talent for music, mathematics, or the like; and that the mind does not derive its origin from the father, so that the son should necessarily be like the father in character, but emanates from heaven, and is thence infused into the human body. Among the Turks, therefore, honours, high posts, and judgeships are the rewards of great ability and good service. If a man be dishonest, or lazy, or careless, he remains at the bottom of the ladder, an object of contempt; for such qualities there are no honours in Turkey!

This is the reason that they are successful in their undertakings, that they lord it over others, and are daily extending the bounds of their empire. These are not our ideas; with us there is no opening left for merit; birth is the standard for everything; the prestige of birth is the sole key to advancement in the public service. But on this head I shall perhaps have more to say to you in another place, and you must consider what I have said as strictly private.

For the nonce, take your stand by my side, and look at the sea of turbaned heads, each wrapped in twisted folds of the whitest silk; look at those marvellously handsome dresses of every kind and every colour; time would fail me to tell how all around is glittering with gold, with silver, with purple, with silk, and with velvet; words cannot convey an adequate idea of that strange and wondrous sight: it was the most beautiful spectacle I ever saw. . . .

From this you will see that it is the patience, self-denial, and thrift of the Turkish soldier that enable him to face the most trying circumstances, and come safely out of the dangers that surround him. What a contrast to our men! Christian soldiers on a campaign refuse to put up with their ordinary food, and call for thrushes, becaficos, and such-like dainty dishes! If these are not supplied they grow mutinous and work their own ruin; and, if they are supplied, they are ruined all the same. For each man is his own worst enemy, and has no foe more deadly than his own intemperance, which is sure to kill him, if the enemy be not quick. It makes me shudder to think of what the result of a struggle between such different systems must be; one of us must prevail and the other be destroyed; at any rate we cannot both exist in safety. On their side is the vast wealth of their empire, unimpaired resources, experience and practice in arms, a veteran soldiery, an uninterrupted series of victories, readiness to endure hardships, union, order, discipline, thrift, and watchfulness. On ours are found an empty exchequer, luxurious habits, exhausted resources, broken spirits, a raw and insubordinate soldiery, and greedy generals; there is no regard for discipline, licence runs riot, the men indulge in drunkenness and debauchery, and, worst of all, the enemy are accustomed to victory, we, to defeat. Can we doubt what the result must be? The only obstacle is Persia, whose position on his rear forces the invader to take precautions. The fear of Persia gives us a respite, but it is only for a time. When he has secured himself in that quarter, he will fall upon us with all the resources of the East. How ill prepared we are to meet such an attack it is not for me to say. . . .

But my letter is too long already; expect to see me in person very shortly; if anything remains to be told, it shall be kept for our meeting. But mind you invite men of worth and learning to meet me, so that pleasant company and profitable conversation may serve to rub off the remains of the rust I have contracted during my long sojourn among the Turks. Farewell.

VII-12   Michel de Montaigne to Messire Antoine Duprat, Provost of Paris

Montaigne's native region of France, the Southwest around Bordeaux, strongly favored "the religion" (Protestantism) and thus suffered severely during France's nine wars of religion. A skeptic and marginal Catholic, Montaigne (1533-1592) suffered with them. He who defined philosophers as those who have learned how to die found painful this endless violence and death.

24 August, 1562

In my last letter, sir, I told you about the troubles that ravaged Agenais and Périgord, where our mutual friend Memy,[1] taken prisoner, was brought to Bordeaux and had his head cut off. Today I want to tell you that the people of Nérac, having, through the indiscretion of a young captain of their town, lost between a hundred and six-score men in a skirmish against some troops of Monluc,[2] withdrew into Béarn with their ministers, not without great danger to their lives, about the fifteenth day of July, at which time the people of Casteljaloux surrendered, and the minister of that place was put to death. The people of Marmande, Saint-Macaire, and Bazas [3] also fled, but not without cruel loss, for immediately the château of Duras was pillaged and that of Monségur was forced, a little stronghold where there were two ensigns and a great number of people of the religion.

There every kind of cruelty and violence was practiced, on the first day of August, without regard for quality, sex, or age. Monluc violated the daughter of the minister, who was killed with the others. I have the extreme sorrow to tell you that involved in this massacre was your relative, the wife of Gaspard Duprat, and two of her children. She was a noble woman, whom I have been in a position to see often when I went into those parts, and at whose house I was always assured of

1. The Protestant governor of Castillon.
2. Blaise de Monluc was a Catholic general and historian, about sixty at this time.
3. Nérac, Casteljaloux, Marmande, Saint-Macaire, Duras, Monségur, and Bazas were Protestant towns not far from Bordeaux.

finding good hospitality. In fine, I say no more to you about it today, for this account gives me pain and sorrow.

Whereupon, I pray God to have you in his holy care.

Your servant and good friend,

Montaigne

(These massacres of Protestants in Southwest France preceded by a decade the wholesale slaughter of their co-religionists on St. Bartholomew's Day, August, 1572, recorded in Letters V-19 and V-20.)

VII-13   The future King Henri III to the Count of Santa-Fiore

Professional soldiers and mercenaries like the Swiss Landsknechts and German Reiters were often so poorly paid that they lived on pillaging, robbing, and holding captives for ransom (as they did at Pavia). As the future Henri III (1551-1589) reported from the field, their lack of discipline and their predatory habits made their presence a menace even in friendly territory.

Camp of Allassac, 3 July, 1569

Count My Lord,

Being advised that several Italian gentlemen and soldiers under your charge, although they are in a friendly territory and are well fed and housed, persist in carrying off and pillaging the cattle, horses, and furnishings of the poor people—afterward marketing and selling them—I am obliged to send you this letter. Although I know that such insolent acts are not committed with your knowledge and consent, I must point out that if they continue, they will ruin everything and cut the throats of the subjects of the King, my lord and brother, and destroy his realm instead of preserving it. Moreover other objectionable things are happening, namely, that with this pillaging, the French, Italian, and German *reiters* come to blows and kill one another for this booty, a pernicious and dangerous thing to happen.

For this reason I beg you to issue an immediate order that such behavior come to a halt. To implement this have the order spread aloud by foot and horseback among all your troops, forbidding, on pain of death, that anything be taken but needed food, without pillaging cattle, horses, and furnishings, or rifling from one another and picking quarrels with the French and the *reiters,* under pain of being hanged on the battlefield. I am writing also to all the colonels, *reiters,* and French captains to give a similar order to their regiments. I am publishing moreover a ban and general alarm throughout the entire army, so that these insubordinate acts cease immediately, as I expect you to do in turn among all your troops. Praying God, sire Count, to keep you in His holy and worthy care. Your good friend

Henry

(trans. R. J. C.)

VII-14   The Fugger Correspondent with the Christian Armada to the Augsburg Bankers

A Fugger correspondent sends tidings of the naval victory of allied Christian forces under the command of Don John of Austria over the Turks, at Lepanto on October 7, 1571. The allies captured 117 galleys as well as thousands of men, and sank or burned approximately 50 galleys; they lost 12 galleys and had about 8,000 wounded, Miguel de Cervantes among them. This first great victory over a Turkish fleet, the last engagement with oar-propelled vessels, was commemorated the following year when Pope Pius V established the feast of Our Lady of Victory.

8 October, 1571

As soon as the Christian Armada arrived at 6 o'clock in the evening in the little channel of Cephalonia, it was at once espied by the crafty Turkish Armada, which lay in the Gulf of Lepanto. This is not to be wondered at, for the pirate Caragoggia offered the Turkish commander to inspect the Christian Armada and to count its ships, which he achieved with such skill that he suffered no damage thereby. Perhaps he was over hasty in this or prevented by some unknown cause from giving the correct number of our galleys. Thereupon, the wind being very favourable, the Turkish Commander began preparations for battle with great joy, and took on board twelve thousand men over and above the soldiery he had in the Armada. Thus, thanks to divine Providence and Fate, he robbed himself of an advantage, contrary to all usage of sea warfare. Don Juan of Austria also set sail with his Armada and sent ahead several galleys to inspect the enemy. Moreover, he sent forth six galleons from the harbour. These reported that the Turkish Armada was already nearing, and not far from Cephalonia. Thereupon Don Juan attired himself in a light suit of armour and boarded a small ship, called a frigate. Holding a crucifix in his hand, he visited one galley after the other, appointing to each its proper place in the battle and exhorting the crew to fight valiantly against the arch-enemy of the Christian Faith. Not he, but Christ, who had died for us upon the Cross, was the Father of all, and the Patron of this Armada, and he hoped that they would find help and sustenance in His mercy. Thereupon the whole soldiery sent forth great shouts of jubilation and forthwith placed themselves in battle formation. Whereafter the above mentioned Don Juan of Austria again entered his galley and went out to meet the Turkish Armada. Then the sea became quite still and the galleasses, which had sailed ahead, opened with heavy fire which brought great damage and terror to the Turks, causing them to cry: "Maom, Maom!" which means in their language "Big ships, big ships with big cannon!" Thus the Turkish Armada, which had been sailing ship to ship in half-moon formation, fell into disorder and was split into three parts. The first and largest part attacked the left wing of the Christian Armada, the second the centre and the third the right wing, which was led by Don Andrea Doria, who had lost almost all his fighters on ten of his galleys at the outset of the fight, although they had put up a most valiant and brave defence. It would have fared ill with him had not several galleys from the centre squadron come to his rescue, which help instilled fresh courage into his men, so that they forced the enemy again to withdraw. The left wing also put up a brave and gallant fight, but it also would have been in a sorry plight had not the rear, led by the Marques de Santa Cruz, come to relieve it, attacking the enemy in such fashion that the scales of victory turned completely in our favour. There also sprang up a wind to our assistance. In the smoke of battle Uluch Ali escaped. It is unknown whether he has fled to Africa or to the Gulf of Lepanto. Of forty of the principal galleys, of which we captured twenty-nine, one only was he able to save. Our general, Don Juan of Austria— whose achievements I should have reported first of all—rammed with his galley that of the Turkish commander, finally captured it, cut off the head of the Turkish Pasha with his own hand and placed it at the end of a spear of his own galley. The galley of Don Vittorio Colonna was attacked by two Turkish ones, fore and amidships, but he defended himself valiantly and was finally rescued, and thus was victorious. The Venetian Chief, Venier by name, who is seventy years of age, appeared, clad in light armour, on his own galley, at the head of all and fought right valiantly alongside his men, so that he captured Ali Pasha and his vessel. Don Barbarigo also carried himself like a true knight in this battle. An arrow pierced his right eye and he died in great pain and greatly to the sorrow of those near to him.

In this battle Don Quirin and Don Andrea Doria, Don Ascanio della Corina, Signor Fabio Serbelon, Don Pompeo Colonna, Don Prospero Colonna and Orsini with their attendant knights, Spaniards and Italians both, fought with such bravery that it cannot be fittingly recounted in so scant a space. The battle began on the 7th day of this month, two hours after daybreak, and within five hours the Christians had achieved victory with the help of the Lord. Almost all the Turkish nobles and nearly eighteen thousand men were killed, ten thousand taken prisoner, and fifteen thousand Christians, who had been slaves on the Turkish galleys, were set free. These latter caused the Turks much harm when the battle began. On several galleys there were also found a large number of Sultanas and Zechines and on Caragoggia's galley a beautiful young woman, a Christian. She was daintily and richly attired and her neck adorned with large pearls and other precious stones and jewels. She offered to buy her release with 60,000 ducats.

As far as can be gathered in all haste, on our side twenty Venetian noblemen and several thousand men lost their lives. One hundred Turkish galleys are captured, sixty have been sent to the bottom. Plans are being concerted to take the greatest advantage from this victory and to pursue Uluch Ali, who has made his escape. Through God's special grace the generals and colonels are all of one mind and well satisfied with each other.

Praise and glory be to God Almighty and His Blessed Mother in all Eternity. Amen.

VII-15   Sir Philip Sidney to Sir Francis Walsingham, his Father-in-Law

Shortly before losing his life in the battle outside Zutphen, Sir Philip Sidney (1554-1586), considered by some an idealized type of the soldier-poet, recounts to his father-in-law the difficulties besetting him while campaigning in support of the Low Countries in their struggle against Spain.

Utrecht, 24 March, 1586

Right Honourable,—

I receive divers letters from you, full of the discomfort which I see, and am sorry to see, that you daily meet with at home; and I think, such is the good will it pleaseth you to bear me, that my part of the trouble is something that troubles you. But, I beseech you, let it not. I had before cast my count of danger, want, and disgrace; and, before God, sir, it is true in my heart, the love of the cause doth so far over-balance them all, that, with God's grace, they shall never make me weary of my resolution. If her Majesty were the fountain, I would fear, considering what I daily find, that we should wax dry; but she is but a means whom God useth; and I know not whether I am deceived, but I am faithfully persuaded that if she should withdraw herself, other springs would rise to help this action; for methinks, I see the great work indeed in hand against the abusers of the world, wherein it is no greater fault to have confidence in man's power, than it is too hastily to despair of God's work. I think a wise and constant man ought never to grieve while he doth play, as a man may say, his own part truly, though others be out; but if himself leave his hold because other mariners will be idle, he will hardly forgive himself his own fault. For me, I cannot promise of my own course, because I know there is a higher power that must uphold me, or else I shall fall; but certainly I trust I shall not by other men's wants be drawn from myself. Therefore, good sir, to whom for my particular I am more bound than to all men besides, be not troubled with my troubles, for I have seen the worst, in my judgment, beforehand, and worse than that cannot be.

If the Queen pay not her soldiers she must lose her garrisons. There is no doubt thereof. But no man living shall be able to say the fault is in me. What relief I can do them, I will. I will spare no danger if the occasion serves. I am sure no creature shall be able to lay justice to my charge; and for further doubts, truly I stand not upon them. I have written by Adams to the Council plainly, and therefore let them determine.

It hath been a costly beginning unto me, this war, by reason I had nothing proportioned unto it; my servants inexperienced, and myself every way unfurnished; but hereafter, if the war continue, I shall pass much better through with it. For Bergen-ap-Zoom, I delighted in it, I confess, because it was near the enemy; but especially having a fair house in it, and an excellent air, I destined it for my wife; but finding how you deal there, and that ill payment in my absence thence might bring forth some mischief, and considering how apt the Queen is to interpret everything to my disadvantage, I have resigned it to my Lord Willoughby, my very friend, and indeed a valiant and frank gentleman, and fit for that place; therefore I pray you know that so much of my regality is fallen. I understand I am called very ambitious and proud at home, but certainly if they knew my heart they would not altogether so judge me.

I wrote to you a letter by Will, my Lord of Leicester's jesting player, enclosed in a letter to my wife, and I never had answer thereof. It contained something to my Lord of Leicester, and counsel that some way might be taken to stay my lady there. I since, divers times, have writ to know whether you had received them, but you never answered me that point. I since find that the knave delivered the letters to my Lady Leicester, but whether she sent them to you, or no, I know not, but earnestly desire to do, because I doubt there is more interpreted thereof. Mr Erington is with me at Flushing, and therefore I think myself at the more rest, having a man of his reputation; but I assure you, sir, in good earnest, I find Burlas another manner of man than he is taken for, or I expected. I would to God, Bourne had obtained his suit. He is earnest but somewhat discomposed with the consideration of his estate. Turner is good for nothing, and worse for the sound of the sackbuts.

We shall have a sore war upon us this summer, wherein if appointment had been kept, and these disgraces forborne, which have greatly weakened us, we had been victorious. I can say no more at this time, but pray for your long and happy life. At Utrecht, this 24th of March, 1586.

Your humble son,
Philip Sidney.

I know not what to say to my wife's coming till you resolve better; for, if you run a strange course, I may take such an one here as will not be fit for any one of the feminine gender. I pray you make much of Nicholas Grey. I have been vilely deceived for armours for horsemen; if you could spare me any out of your armoury I will send them you back as soon as my own be finished. There was never so good a father found a more troublesome son. Send Sir William Pelham, good sir, and let him have clerk's place, for we need no clerks, and it is most necessary to have such an one in the council.

VII-16   The Fugger correspondent in Madrid to the Augsburg Bankers

A Fugger newsletter from Madrid reports the surprise raids of Sir Francis Drake, the most famous of Elizabethan seamen and the first Englishman to circumnavigate the world. The exploit at Cadiz, undertaken to thwart preparations of the Spanish Armada, became known as "singeing the King of Spain's beard."

Madrid, 30, May, 1587.

On the 24th inst. they wrote from Cadiz how Francis Drake, the English pirate, made a surprise landing there with forty-eight ships great and small, not all warships. He pillaged and stripped about fourteen ships laden with all sorts of merchandise and lying in the roads, and stayed there for some days. Those ships which he could not take with him he afterwards burnt or sank. Thereupon the chief citizens with women and property fled to Seville and elsewhere, although the King at once sent five hundred men to the fort as garrison, together with some galleys. On the 25th inst. news again came from His Serene Highness the Cardinal Archduke Albert of Austria to the effect that this Drake, after sailing away from Cadiz, first proceeded to Cape St. Vincent and remained there ten days with his fleet, and after the 15th went to the province of Algarvia situated in Portugal, not far from the town of Lagos. There he landed some two thousand men and drew them up in order of battle, as though the enemy were in sight and forced to fight him. With his troops he advanced in battle order to within half a mile of the town of Lagos, whereupon the citizens in great haste ran up on the walls, and the Governor made a sally with three hundred horse. On this Drake slowly retired. Now, although the Governor pursued the marauders with his troopers, neither side attacked or harmed the other. On the following day, that is the 16th, Drake landed again with some troops and appeared before a fortress named Sagres, situated near the town of Lagos. He took it after two assaults, as he had brought with him scaling ladders and other apparatus for attack. Although one hundred and fifty Portuguese soldiers were in the fortress, they offered no resistance. Drake burnt the fortress with the monastery and the altars and pictures in the church. The monks fled to safety. Then he came to two castles, from which the garrisons had likewise fled. These also he burnt down and razed. All the cannons, armour and weapons, as also all the wood which he found there, he carried off to his ships. On the 18th he arrived with his fleet off the port of Lisbon, and on the morning of the 19th he passed between the two harbour forts. And although Don Alonzo de Bazan, brother of the Marquis de Santa Cruz, sailed out with the seven galleasses which he commands at Lisbon, he began to skirmish with his cannon, and the firing and skirmishing lasted till six o'clock in the evening. But the firing of the big guns from the enemy's ships was so severe that the galleasses were ultimately forced to retire, without producing any effect on the English. When the English fleet had also withdrawn a little way in its turn, a few soldiers were sent out to prevent the English from landing. But early on the 20th inst. the English fleet left the river and went out to sea, in what direction is unknown. Thus far the Lisbon letters of May 25. His Sacred Majesty of Spain has slept long enough, and from pride, preoccupation or parsimony has paid no attention to such visitors. But now he has been roused afresh and must hurriedly protect himself with money and troops. The Marquis de Santa Cruz is already arming, and money and troops are being sent him in great haste. He is to sail from Lisbon as soon as possible with thirty-two well-armed galleasses and pursue the enemy. As news has been received that Don Antonio of Portugal is to sail from England with another fleet, and it is likewise impossible to know whether he too will not come to Portugal and join Drake and whether one of the fleets or even both may not again make for India, His Sacred Majesty has ordered the Duke of Medina Sidonia * to sail out as quickly as possible and pursue the enemy with 32 galleys which are already fitted, and 32 big warships also which are being prepared. With the utmost despatch His Majesty is sending money to Seville in Andalusia and to Biscay, where some large ships are likewise being constructed for war, and to all places where it is required. Troops are being raised all over Spain. Recently also fifteen hundred soldiers, all trusty Spaniards, arrived in Cartagena from Sicily. Another two thousand are expected from Italy. It is said too that men are to be transferred from Germany to Italy as garrisons in place of those who have been brought to Spain.

There is moreover some fear that the Portuguese might have an understanding with Drake or Don Antonio. Now what will happen over all this time will show. A large sum of money was recently sent for the King from here to Barcelona through some Genoese and Messrs. Fugger of this city. It should have gone to Italy and the Netherlands, but whether much of it will reach the Netherlands and the unhappy troops there we shall hear shortly.

* For Duke of Medina Sidonia, see the following letter.

P.S.—Just this moment His Majesty is sending a Knight of Malta, who is a famous Italian architect, with some workmen to Cadiz, to pull down the old fortress and build up a new one.

(As recorded in Letters VI-1 and VIII-13, the British code of fair play did not always need to apply to the piratical navigators under the British flag.)

VII-17   The Duke of Medina Sidonia to King Philip II

Ordered by Philip II to take over the command of the Spanish Armada from the Marquis of Santa Cruz, Don Alonso Perez de Guzman, Duke of Medina Sidonia (d. 1619) warns the King of his total unsuitability for such an undertaking.

16 February 1588

I humbly thank his Majesty for having thought of me for so great a task, and I wish I possessed the talents and strength necessary for it. But, Sir, I have not health for the sea, for I know by the small experience that I have had afloat that I soon become seasick. . . . The force is so great, and the undertaking so important, that it would not be right for a person like myself, possessing no experience of seafaring or of war, to take charge of it. . . . I possess neither aptitude, ability, health or fortune. . . . For me to take charge of the Armada afresh, without the slightest knowledge of it, of the persons who are taking part in it, of the objects in view, of the intelligence from England . . . would be simply groping in the dark, even if I had experience, seeing that I should have suddenly and without preparation to enter a new career. So, Sir, you will see that my reasons for declining are so strong and convincing in his Majesty's own interests, that I cannot attempt a task of which I have no doubt I should give a bad account . . . for I do not understand it, know nothing about it, have no health for the sea, and no money to spend upon it.

(Notwithstanding this negative self-appraisal—which history has confirmed—Philip promptly signed his official appointment as Commander-in Chief.)

VII-18   Queen Elizabeth to James VI, King of Scotland

The victory over the Invincible Armada of Spain in the late summer of 1588 was a blow to the constant Spanish threat against England and the Lowlands. After a week of combat, the Spanish ships were caught in a gale which destroyed many of them and drove the remaining ones northward toward Scotland. Already exulting in her triumph, Queen Elizabeth (1533-1603) quickly warned the young Scottish Catholic King not to unite with the Spanish survivors.

                                                              August 1588.
Now may appear, my dear Brother, how malice conjoined with might strivest to make a shameful end to a villainous beginning, for, by God's singular favour, having their fleet well beaten in our Narrow Seas, and pressing with all violence, to achieve some watering place, to continue their pretended invasion, the winds have carried them to your coasts, where I doubt not they shall receive small succour and less welcome; unless those Lords that, so traitors like, would belie their own Prince, and promise another King relief in your name, be suffered to live at liberty, to dishonour you, peril you, and advance some other (which God forbid you suffer them live to do). Therefore I send you this gentleman, a rare young man and a wise, to declare unto you my full opinion in this great cause, as one that never will abuse you to serve my own turn; nor will you do aught that myself would not perform if I were in your place. You may assure youself that, for my part, I doubt no whit but that all this tyrannical, proud and brainsick attempt will be the beginning, though not the end, of the ruin of that King, that, most unkingly, even in the midst of treating peace, begins this wrongful war. He hath procured my greatest glory that meant my sorest wrack, and hath so dimmed the light of his sunshine, that who hath a will to obtain shame, let them keep his forces company. But for all this, for your self sake, let not the friends of Spain be suffered to yield them force; for though I fear not in the end the sequel, yet if, by leaving them unhelped, you may increase the English hearts unto you, you shall not do the

worst deed for your behalf; for if aught should be done, your excuse will play the *boiteux;* * if you make not sure work with the likely men to do it. Look well unto it, I beseech you.

The necessity of this matter makes my scribbling the more speedy, hoping that you will measure my good affection with the right balance of my actions, which to you shall be ever such as I have professed, not doubting of the reciproque of your behalf, according as my last messenger unto you hath at large signified, for the which I render you a million of grateful thanks together, for the last general prohibition to your subjects not to foster nor aid our general foe, of which I doubt not the observation if the ringleaders be safe in your hands; as knoweth God, Who ever have you in His blessed keeping, with many happy years of reign.

Your most assured loving sister and cousin,
Elizabeth R.

VII-19   The Fugger Correspondent in England to the Augsburg Bankers

The final destruction of the Armada sent by Philip II of Spain, leader of Catholic Europe, against Protestant England is depicted in the following Fugger report. The Armada's defeat, significant as the first gun duel between fleets propelled exclusively by sail, may have saved the Reformation, and it demonstrated to England that her naval strength would determine her greatness in the future.

Received 19 November, 1588

The Armada of the King of Spain set sail from Portugal with one hundred and thirty-five ships, to wit: four galleasses from Naples, four galleons from Portugal, ten vessels with victuals, fourteen Venetian ships, among them several galleons. The remainder was made up of other large and small craft. The Armada arrived in Corunna on the 5th day of July, from whence it intended to sail for Flanders, there to join forces with the Duke of Parma and invade England. At that time the English Armada was in Plymouth Port.

* play the *boiteux:* be limp and unconvincing.

After they had been under sail from Corunna eight days they arrived in Ostend and thereupon lay south of the shores of England, where for four or five days they had various skirmishes with the English Armada. On that occasion the English took two ships. On one of these there was Don Pedro di Mendoza, whom they took prisoner and so to England. Storms south of England caused them the loss of four Portuguese galleons which remained stranded on the French coast. They then proceeded and cast anchor off Calais, since they could no longer get as far as Dunkirk. They wished to wait for the Duke of Parma in Calais, but he sent word that he could not be ready under eight days. Thereupon the admiral sent reply that he would again set sail for Spain. Meanwhile the English sent forth against the Spanish Armada several burning ships, so that they were forced to cut their moorings and to retire hastily. Each ship left two anchors behind and four of the largest galleasses were stranded and wrecked off Calais. The following day at eight o'clock, the two Armadas had a further encounter, heavily bombarding each other for eight hours. In this battle the Spanish lost four ships, namely two Portuguese galleasses, a vessel from Biscay and one other. All four went to the bottom of the sea. Three large Venetian craft remained behind off the coast of Flanders and were in great peril of going under. The inhabitants of Flushing took two of these ships, and the third was shipwrecked. One of them had on board the Colonel commanding the garrison of Seville. According to the prisoners' report the Spaniards lost four thousand men in the battle off Calais, amongst them the Commander-in-Chief of the cavalry at Naples and Seville. The Spaniards are said to have left one hundred and twenty ships, although others could count only one hundred and ten. The big galleon, which the Duke of Florence had sent, was not to be seen anywhere after the battle.

Hereafter the Armada made off and was pursued by the English for five days as far as Scotland. When they counted their men there they found that they had already lost eight thousand, most of whom had been killed or died of disease. From thence they set sail for Ireland without taking provisions on board. Off Ireland they lost two ships, the *San Sebastian* and the *San Mathias,* which had four hundred and fifty-six men on board. Lacking fresh water, the fleet threw many horses and mules overboard off Ireland. When they sailed away from Ireland, the Commander-in-Chief, the Duke of Medina Sidonia, ordered each one of his captains to set his course for Corunna or the first Spanish port. They thus sailed together throughout ten days. Then the storm separated the Duke of Medina Sidonia with twenty-seven of his ships from them and no one knew where they had gone.* The last time the Armada was assembled it counted no more than

* The medallion struck by Queen Elizabeth to commemorate the victory thanked Providence for the assistance of the stormy and shifting gales.

seventy-eight ships. Of the big galleasses not one was left. Two of the Duke of Medina Sidonia's ships ran ashore. Only two or three of the men were saved. They say that the Chief Admiral had left on board only five-and-twenty more barrels of wine, but little bread and no water. His masts had been so weakened by firing that he could not carry full canvas. The Duke had three English pilots on board ship. On the 10th day of September a further large ship of five hundred tons, *Maria della Rosa,* ran ashore off Ireland. On it were the Colonel Michael Oquendo, commander of part of this fleet, and also the Prince of Ascoli, the bastard son of the King of Spain, twenty-eight years of age. There were besides these ten noblemen, seven captains and five hundred soldiers. They all perished excepting one pilot who saved himself on a plank. He says that the King's bastard son came on board this ship off Calais. The vessel carried fifty cannon and twenty-five other metal pieces, as well as 15,000 ducats and silver reals and much gold. The same day two big vessels put eight hundred and fifty men ashore in Ireland, seven hundred of whom died, and the remainder were taken prisoner. The vessels were cast ashore. On the 12th day of September another big ship was wrecked. Thirteen noblemen were taken prisoner and four hundred men reached land. From yet another ship seventy-eight bodies were washed ashore. From a further wrecked vessel three noblemen, a bishop and seventy-nine mercenaries were taken prisoner. The others perished. On the 17th day of September two large vessels, the *St. Joaquim* and the *St. Martin,* sank. The admiral was de Ricaldo, and his ship was almost the largest in the whole fleet. There were on it eight hundred soldiers, sixty Portuguese and forty Biscay fishermen. They had starved for almost four days.

Finally another galleon of four hundred and fifty tons was wrecked with an Italian margrave and the old Naples and Seville garrison. On it were also Don Alonzo de Layba, Mestre de Campo of the Cavalry in Milan. On the 18th day of September there arrived news from Ireland that very many bodies had been washed ashore.

CHAPTER 8

TRAVEL. EXPLORATION. COLONIES. FOREIGN TRADE AND PEOPLES.

XV. *Christopher Columbus* by Sebastiano del Piombo

XVI. *Americo Vespucci Greeting Allegorical Figure of America* by Giovanni Stradano

Eager to clarify his notions on the physical universe, man of the Renaissance felt compelled to travel and explore. Inspired by a series of beliefs rooted in racial memory—an Ultima Thule, a Northwest passage, a mid-ocean continent of Atlantis, a Vinland found by Norsemen, and especially by the staggering conception of a round world which might be circumnavigated—he sailed past the Pillars of Hercules to the most remote places. The Spaniards took possession of the Canary Islands in the fourteenth century and the Portuguese moved into the Azores. In 1487 Bartolomeo Díaz sailed round the Cape of Storms, later renamed Cape of Good Hope. Since Arab and Turk blocked the water and land routes to Asia, Vasco da Gama followed this new eastward route in 1498 to initiate trade with the East. Also accepting the radical notion that the earth might be a sphere, Columbus crossed the Atlantic in 1492 seeking new trade routes with the East. When he landed in the Bahamas (VIII-1), realizing that he was not in Japan or Cathay, he urged the early conversion to Christianity of the natives. It was after Cabot's discovery of North America in 1497 and Cabral's discovery of Brazil in 1500 that the Portuguese navigator Ferdinand Magellan, though killed by natives in the Philippines, demonstrated posthumously that three years of sailing (1519-1522) could get one around the world.

With this increase of navigation undertaken by the rivals Spain and Portugal, the Pope decided that it would be only fair to draw a line down the mid-Atlantic and deed all lands east of it to Portugal and west to Spain, splitting between them the lands beyond the Pillars of Hercules. It was thus with reason that a disillusioned old Columbus reminded ungrateful members of the Spanish court, "I have placed under Spain's sovereignty more land than there is in Africa and Europe" (VIII-2).

We learn from letters that Magellan's voyage, with its disastrous episodes in the Pacific, was not launched under auspicious circumstances. The Portuguese were vexed that their compatriot was to undertake under the Spanish flag such an historic voyage. A letter from Alvaro da Costa, ambassador to Spain, shows how persistent were the attempts to dissuade King Charles I from subsidizing this enterprise. Magellan himself, in a desperate letter of 24 October, 1518, reports how officials in the port of Seville insulted and molested him, even chasing crewmen from his vessel (VIII-6). As late as July, 1519, the agents of King Manoel of Portugal were doing everything in their power to frustrate Magellan's plans, charging him with a lack of patriotism and stressing the perils of such a voyage (VIII-7).

Thus, the letters of three great navigators, like the earlier letters we have read of the writers, artists, and musicians, show misunderstanding and discouragement by their patrons: Columbus, a better navigator than administrator; Magellan, harassed by Manoel and underprovisioned by Charles I; Sir Walter Raleigh, blamed by King James I on his return from Guiana for cruelties and indiscretions committed by disloyal men under his command (VIII-13).

Four letter-writers who plied the coasts of North and South America were Vespucci, Balboa, Cortés, and Verrazzano. The Florentine Americo Vespucci, giving his name to the new continents, found people back home incredulous about the Indians he described, questioning for example why they were not black like the Africans, since both lived in the same latitudes (VIII-3). Nuñez be Balboa showed indisputably in his letters that the chief goal of the explorers and their backers was less scientific than financial—the search for and discovery of El Dorado, the land where even utensils were made of gold—and that they were willing to subject the Indians to tortures in their search for it (VIII-5). Balboa's letter below contains the first reference to the Pacific Ocean ("the other sea"), so calm that the natives sailed it easily. Hernán Cortés was another conquistador participating in the gold rush. One of the most informative letters of the Renaissance is his description of the highly-organized daily and commercial life in Tenochtitlan, the modern Mexico City (VIII-8). This letter, whose details helped Diego Rivera paint his murals of Tenochtitlan, affords a remarkable portrait of the Aztec chieftain Montezuma, abased to the point of apologizing for the fact that his people worshipped idols. Shortly later (1524) the Italian Giovanni 'da Verrazzano sends King Francis I his relation of voyaging along the North American coast (VIII-9), including a description of Indians in the general area of New York City, which was to be called Angoulême in honor of his patron.

That the thirst for gold shared by Spanish and Portuguese navigators—and the English buccaneers who plundered them—was sated is clear from Philip Sidney's letter of 1580 to his brother Robert and from such Fugger letters as VIII-11. The material benefits of the explorations were thus numerous and apparent. Thanks to the influx of precious metals and stones and to the increased commerce with Asia and the New World, the quality of living rose markedly. New financial resources became available for a saltation of the arts and sciences, for the founding of schools and academies, for the printing and purchase of books—in sum, for the consolidation of the Humanistic and scientific Renaissance.

A Fugger letter from East India shows that by 1590, the merchant marines of Portugal, England, and even Turkey were setting up enclaves in Asia, later to be augmented by the French *comptoirs* (VIII-11). Queen Elizabeth's merchant fleet had opened up a trade route to Russia by 1582, and she was confident enough of its safety to ship a vast amount of gold bullion through the Baltic (VIII-10). The expansion of trade was accompanied by missionaries of the Society of Jesus. A remarkable testimony from Japan in 1590 (VIII-12) records that "several members of the nobility have become Christians and vie with their subjects in Christian zeal."

Even as courageous men circled the globe, an abundance of other letters attest that the simplest of trips on land and sea offered lesser men risks and inconveniences, whether crossing the Mediterranean, the Tyrol, or making a horseback trip from London to Cambridge (IV-1). *Quot homines tot audaciae.*

VIII-1   Christopher Columbus to Gabriel Sanchez

Having crossed the Atlantic and come ashore on the Bahama Islands, Christopher Columbus (1451-1506) gives a candid account of his experiences in the land he believed at first to be Japan or China, assuring his correspondent, King Ferdinand's treasurer, of his intention to Christianize the natives. According to tradition, in this and three subsequent voyages Columbus was seeking the westward route to the fabulous islands of Asia.

Lisbon, 14 March, 1493

Because my undertakings have attained success, I know that it will be pleasing to you: these I have determined to relate, so that you may be made acquainted with everything done and discovered in this our voyage. On the thirty-third day after I departed from Cadiz, I came to the Indian sea, where I found many islands inhabited by men without number, of all which I took possession for our most fortunate king, with proclaiming heralds and flying standards, no one objecting.

To the first of these I gave the name of the blessed Saviour,[1] on whose aid relying I had reached this as well as the other islands. But the Indians called it

1. In Spanish, San Salvador, one of the Bahama Islands. It has been variously identified with Grand Turk, Cat, Watling, Mariguana, Samana, and Acklin islands. Watling's Island seems to have much in its favor.

Guanahany. I also called each one of the others by a new name. For I ordered one island to be called Santa Maria of the Conception,[2] another Fernandina,[3] another Isabella,[4] another Juana,[5] and so on with the rest.

As soon as we had arrived at that island which I have just now said was called Juana, I proceeded along its coast towards the west for some distance; I found it so large and without perceptible end, that I believed it to be not an island, but the continental country of Cathay;[6] seeing, however, no towns or cities situated on the seacoast, but only some villages and rude farms, with whose inhabitants I was unable to converse, because as soon as they saw us they took flight.

I proceeded farther, thinking that I would discover some city or large residences. At length, perceiving that we had gone far enough, that nothing new appeared, and that this way was leading us to the north, which I wished to avoid, because it was winter on the land, and it was my intention to go to the south, moreover the winds were becoming violent, I therefore determined that no other plans were practicable, and so, going back, I returned to a certain bay that I had noticed, from which I sent two of our men to the land, that they might find out whether there was a king in this country, or any cities. These men traveled for three days, and they found people and houses without number, but they were small and without any government, therefore they returned. . . .

This island is surrounded by many very safe and wide harbors, not excelled by any others that I have ever seen. Many great and salubrious rivers flow through it. There are also many very high mountains there. All these islands are very beautiful, and distinguished by various qualities; they are accessible, and full of a great variety of trees stretching up to the stars; the leaves of which I believe are never shed, for I saw them as green and flourishing as they are usually in Spain in the month of May; some of them were blossoming, some were bearing fruit, some were in other conditions; each one was thriving in its own way. The nightingale and various other birds without number were singing, in the month of November, when I was exploring them.

There are besides in the said island Juana seven or eight kinds of palm trees, which far excel ours in height and beauty, just as all the other trees, herbs, and fruits do. There are also excellent pine trees, vast plains and meadows, a variety of birds, a variety of honey, and a variety of metals, excepting iron. In the one which was called Hispana, as we said above, there are great and beautiful mountains, vast

2. Perhaps Crooked Island or, according to others, North Caico.
3. Identified by some with Long Island; by others with Little Inagua.
4. Identified variously with Fortune Island and Great Inagua.
5. The island of Cuba.
6. China.

fields, groves, fertile plains, very suitable for planting and cultivating, and for the building of houses.

The convenience of the harbors in this island, and the remarkable number of rivers contributing to the healthfulness of man, exceed belief, unless one has seen them. The trees, pasturage, and fruits of this island differ greatly from those of Juana. This Hispana, moreover, abounds in different kinds of spices, in gold, and in metals.

On this island, indeed, and on all others which I have seen, and of which I have knowledge, the inhabitants of both sexes go always naked, just as they came into the world, except some of the women, who use a covering of a leaf or some foliage, or a cotton cloth, which they make themselves for that purpose.

All these people lack, as I said above, every kind of iron; they are also without weapons, which indeed are unknown; nor are they competent to use them, not on account of deformity of body, for they are well formed, but because they are timid and full of fear. They carry for weapons, however, reeds baked in the sun, on the lower ends of which they fasten some shafts of dried wood rubbed down to a point; and indeed they do not venture to use these always; for it frequently happened when I sent two or three of my men to some of the villages, that they might speak with the natives, a compact troop of the Indians would march out, and as soon as they saw our men approaching, they would quickly take flight, children being pushed aside by their fathers, and fathers by their children. And this was not because any hurt or injury had been inflicted on any one of them, for to every one whom I visited and with whom I was able to converse, I distributed whatever I had, cloth and many other things, no return being made to me; but they are by nature fearful and timid.

Yet when they perceive that they are safe, putting aside all fear, they are of simple manners and trustworthy, and very liberal with everything they have, refusing no one who asks for anything they may possess, and even themselves inviting us to ask for things. They show greater love for all others than for themselves; they give valuable things for trifles, being satisfied even with a very small return, or with nothing; however, I forbade that things so small and of no value should be given to them, such as pieces of plate, dishes and glass, likewise keys and shoestraps; although if they were able to obtain these, it seemed to them like getting the most beautiful jewels in the world. . . .

In all these islands there is no difference in the appearance of the people, nor in the manners and language, but all understand each other mutually; a fact that is very important for the end which I suppose to be earnestly desired by our most illustrious king, that is, their conversion to the holy religion of Christ, to which in truth, as far as I can perceive, they are very ready and favorably inclined. . . .

In all these islands, as I have understood, each man is content with only one wife, except the princes or kings, who are permitted to have twenty. The women appear to work more than the men. I was not able to find out surely whether they have individual property, for I saw that one man had the duty of distributing to the others, especially refreshments, food, and things of that kind. . . .

Truly great and wonderful is this, and not corresponding to our merits, but to the holy Christian religion, and to the piety and religion of our sovereigns, because what the human understanding could not attain, that the divine will has granted to human efforts. For God is wont to listen to his servants who love his precepts, even in impossibilities, as has happened to us on the present occasion, who have attained that which hitherto mortal men have never reached.

For if anyone has written or said anything about these islands, it was all with obscurities and conjectures; no one claims that he had seen them; from which they seemed like fables. Therefore let the king and queen, the princes and their most fortunate kingdoms, and all other countries of Christendom give thanks to our Lord and Saviour Jesus Christ, who has bestowed upon us so great a victory and gift. Let religious processions be solemnized; let sacred festivals be given; let the churches be covered with festive garlands. Let Christ rejoice on earth, as he rejoices in heaven, when he foresees coming to salvation so many souls of people hitherto lost. Let us be glad also, as well on account of the exaltation of our faith, as on account of the increase of our temporal affairs, of which not only Spain, but universal Christendom will be partaker. These things that have been done are thus briefly related. Farewell. Lisbon, the day before the ides of March.

Christopher Columbus, admiral of the Ocean fleet

VIII-2   Christopher Columbus to Certain Gentlemen of the Spanish Court

A great admiral but poor colonial administrator, Columbus returned from his third expedition in chains, having been arrested by Francisco de Bobadilla whom Ferdinand and Isabella had appointed governor of Hispaniola. Totally disillusioned, he makes a pathetic attempt to engage the sympathies of certain gentlemen of the Spanish court, possibly the members of the powerful Council of Castile.

Cadiz, November/December, 1500

It is now seventeen years since I came to serve these princes with the Enterprise of the Indies; they made me pass eight of them in discussion, and at the end rejected it as a thing of jest. None the less I persisted therein. . . .

Over there, I have placed under their sovereignty more land than there is in Africa and Europe, and more than seventeen hundred islands, without counting Hispaniola. . . . In seven years I, by the divine will, made that conquest. At a time when I was entitled to expect rewards and retirement, I was incontinently arrested and sent home loaded with chains, to my great dishonor and with slight service to their Highnesses.

The accusation was brought out of malice, on the basis of charges made by civilians who had revolted and wished to take possession of the land. And he who did it had the order to remain as governor if the testimony was grave. By whom and where would this be considered just? I have lost in this enterprise my youth, my proper share in these things, and my honor; but my deeds will not be judged outside Castille. . . .

I beg your graces, with the zeal of faithful Christians in whom their Highnesses have confidence, to read all my papers, and to consider how I who came from so far to serve these princes, . . . now at the end of my days have been despoiled of my honor and my property without cause, wherein is neither justice nor mercy.

VIII-3   Americo Vespucci to a Florentine friend *

When Americo Vespucci's voyage along the South American coast first revealed to Europe that the New World was indeed a vast continental land mass, skeptics challenged his veracity on two points especially: the fact that natives on the same latitude as Africans would not have black skin or that those natives, if the climate were cooler, would go about naked. In the following letter, Vespucci (1451-1512) "justifies himself against the malevolent."

* The recipient may have been Zenobio Acciaiuoli or Giorgio Vespucci.

As I have already said, the people of that land go naked. That is based on natural reasons, and because I saw too many of them to count. . . . As the philosopher says "custom changes nature."

I have made three voyages. . . . I have seen some 2,000 leagues of coastland and over 5,000 [of?] islands, a great many of them inhabited. I found the mainland to be full of innumerable people, and I never saw one of them clothed, or even with their private parts covered, much or little. Both men and women.

As for the opinion I have expressed that the people of that region are white and not black, and especially those who inhabit the torrid zone, I have this to say, with all respect to the philosophers. It is not necessary that all the men dwelling in the torrid zone be black because of nature and scorched blood, as are the Ethiopians and the greater part of the people who inhabit the region of Ethiopia. As I said before, I have sailed through all the parallels from Morocco to the end of Ethiopia, and have reached a point 32° south of the Line. I have been in many parts of Africa and Ethiopia, at Cape Catim, Cape Anghila, Zanaga, Cape Verde, Rio Grande, Sierra Leone, lying 7° on the equator. I have seen and spoken with countless people there, and they are all black in color, more so in certain areas than in others. And even if such knowledge lies within the province of the philosophers, I shall not refrain from expressing my opinion, be it well or ill received. I hold that the main reason is the compression of the air and the nature of the land, because all the land of Ethiopia is very sparsely populated, and there is a lack of fresh water, little rainfall, and the soil is very sandy and scorched by the heat of the sun. There are vast sandy deserts and very few woods or forests, and the prevailing winds in that region are the levanter and the sirocco, both hot. Also nature has turned blackness into habit, and we see this in our own country: Negroes engender Negroes, and if a white man has offspring with a Negress, the child will be brown—that is to say, less black than the mother and less white than the father. Or inversely. Which indicates that nature and habit are more powerful factors than the compression of the air and the land. For this reason I deduce that as the land and air I have discovered in the same position as the aforesaid land of Africa and Ethiopia, or, to put it more clearly, between the same parallels, is much pleasanter and more temperate, and of better compression, for that reason the people are white, though verging on tawny, because, as I say, in that region the air is more temperate than in Ethiopia; and the land is much more agreeable and abounds in fresh water, and the dew falls there nearly every day. The winds are southerly and westerly, so that the heat there is not so great as in Ethiopia. For that reason the trees there are always green and covered with foliage. These are the facts. Anyone who does not believe them can go there and see for himself, as I did. . . .

VIII-4   The Moors of Safi, Morocco, to King Dom Manoel of Portugal

Portugal's occupation of Morocco was one of the first phases of a colonialism which quickly extended to South America and Asia. However, it was easier for a dissatisfied nearby colony, like the city of Safi, to demand withdrawal of a colonial governor and get action from the King, who promptly withdrew the unscrupulous Diego de Azambuja. The Portuguese occupation lasted from 1501 to 1541.

Safi, 3 August, 1508

To the King of Kings, Dom Manoel, from Your Servants who kiss your hand and the earth under your feet:

The Moors, dwellers in Your city of Safi and Cabila de la Grega and Aduquela, who thus kiss your hands, and our leaders Sidi Cayde Gias, Sidi Celacem, Aben Mafamede, Ben Abrahim, and others we name not, are dedicated to your service and obeisance.

We remain in this Your city only through the confidence we have in God and Your lofty estate, whereas this captain of yours Diego de Azambuja has no desire to listen to the population of this city, but rather a desire to expel and depopulate. By force and by sword he insists that we obey and love Aleximen, who is to judge and command us. We surely cannot have good feelings toward your evil and treasonable leader, so malicious and so deceitful that he commits treason, hiding it from Your Majesty, against your man Bentafufa loyal to the Portuguese crown. Bentafufa cast out the thieves who were senselessly robbing and killing the inhabitants. For this reason we cannot bear to look upon the face of Diego de Azambuja. If we found ourselves with him inside Paradise, we would surely leave even though we were without sin. We therefore beg and request of God and Your great virtues that you provide and look after us, that we may live in our homes and in Your realm in repose, that we may never find better dwellings than our own.

Thus, Lord, if You wish to populate our city with Moors, send Bentafufa back to us, and if you wish to settle Christians here, the city is Yours and in Your hands.* If it be said that we Moors of Safi wish Bentafufa back only to rise with him against Christians, Lord, we love that man only for his virtues, his honesty, goodness, and good will, and for his disinterested kindness to all. From what we know of him, he would die to keep his word and bond, and if Your Highness decreed something, he would support it to the death. As for us, Lord, we are in your power and hands, and we speak to you as to our true liege lord. We bow to kiss Your hands and commend ourselves to the counsel of Your Highness and Your captains and alcaldes.

On the third of August 913 Years after the birth of Mohammed.

(trans. R. J. C.)

VIII-5   Vasco Nuñez de Balboa to King Ferdinand

More than any other, Balboa's letter illustrates the driving lust for gold, for discovery of the El Dorado where everything used or worn is of gold. The lust was shared by navigators and kings alike. (Visitors to the Gold Museum in Bogotá will realize that El Dorado was not entirely a myth.) Even students on leaving the university joined the search—as Balboa (1475-1517) bitterly complains. This historical letter, somewhat abridged here, contains the first mention in writing of the Pacific Ocean, which Balboa was the first European to see "upon a peak in Darién" (to set Keats straight).

Santa Maria del Antigua, Province of Darién, Gulf of Uraba, 20 January, 1513
Most Christian and Most Mighty Lord:
  Some days past I wrote to Your Royal Majesty by a caravel which came to this Town making known to Your Most Royal Highness all the things that happened in these parts: likewise I wrote by a brigantine which set out from this Town for the island Española to make known to the Admiral how we were in very urgent need; and now God has supplied us with two ships loaded with provisions with which we were relieved, and it has been the cause of this land remaining settled; for we were in such great extremity that if the help had delayed much, when it

* King Manoel returned Bentafufa to Morocco and promoted him to Alcalde of Duquela.

might come it would not be necessary, because it would not find any one to succor on account of the famine; for by reason of the great necessity we have had, there would be lacking the three hundred men that we find here, whom I have ruled; those from Huraba of Alonso de Ojeda, and those from Veragua of Diego de Niquesa, who with much labor I have united the one to the other, as Your Royal Majesty will see in another letter that I am writing to Your Most Royal Highness making report of everything that has passed here. . . .

Most puissant Lord, that which I with great industry and much labor by good fortune have discovered is this:—

In this province of Darién are found many very rich mines, there is gold in much quantity: twenty rivers have been explored, and thirty which contain gold issue from a ridge of mountains which is about two leagues from this Town, running toward the region of the south: the gold-bearing rivers flow within two leagues of this Town toward the south: this mountain turns down by this coast toward the west: from this Town to the west along this mountain no river with gold has been found: I believe that they exist.

Going up this great river of San Juan as far as thirty leagues, upon the right hand is a province which is called Abanumaqué, which has very great distribution of gold: I have very certain news that in it are rivers very rich with gold: I know it from a son of the Cacique of that province that I have here, and from other Indians here, men and women, whom I have captured from that land.

Going up this great river [Atrato] thirty leagues, on the left hand enters a very large and beautiful river, and two days journey up this river is a Cacique who is called *Davaive* [or Davaibe]: he is a very great Lord of a very large territory thickly settled with people. He has gold in great quantity in his house, and so much that for one who does not know the things of this land it will be quite dubious to believe:

I know this from sure information, that from the house of this Cacique de Vaive comes all the gold that goes out through this gulf [Urabá] and all that the Caciques of these districts possess. It is reported that they have many gold pieces of strange form, and very large. Many Indians who have seen it tell me that this Cacique de Vaive has certain baskets of gold which require a man to carry one of them on the back: this Cacique collects this gold in the way that he does, because he is distant from the mountain.

Two days' march from there is a very beautiful country in which is a very evil Carib people, they eat as many men as they can get: this people is without a Lord and they have no one to obey, they are warlike and each one lives for himself alone. These people are Lords of the mines, and these mines according to the news I have, are the richest in the world: these mines are in a province which has a mountain that appears to be the highest in the world, I believe that never has been seen another of such great height. It rises toward the Urabá side of this gulf somewhat within the land, which may be twenty leagues from the sea. This mountain goes its way running to the territory of the south; rising from the level ground it continues to increase in height until it is so high that it is covered with the clouds; two years that we are here the top of it has not been seen except two times, because continually it is hidden by the heavens. From the highest summit the mountain turns to decline until it becomes covered with woods and thickets, and from there fall some mountainous ridges without any forest, terminating in a more level country, the most beautiful in the world, close to this Cacique de Daive.

The very rich mines are in this point of this land turning toward the place of the rising sun, whose rays fall on the mines: it is two days' travel from this Cacique Davaibe to these rich mines. The method of collecting this gold is without any labor, in two ways; the one is that they wait for the streams to rise in the ravines, and when the floods pass they become dry and the gold remains exposed, washed down from the gullies in the mountain side in very large grains: the Indians indicate that they are of the size of oranges and like the fist, and according to their signs there are pieces in the form of flat plates.

The other method to gather gold is to wait until the vegetation on the mountains becomes dry and set it on fire, and after it is burnt they go and search for the gold in the most likely places on the mountain, and they collect it in great quantity and in very beautiful grains: these Indians who pick up the gold carry it in grains as they find it to this Cacique Davaibe to be melted, and they barter it with him. He gives them in exchange Indian boys and young men to eat and Indian girls to serve their wives; these they do not eat. He gives them pigs [peccaries], of which there are many in this region and quantities of fish and cotton clothing and salt. He gives them gold pieces worked as they wish them: only with this Cacique Davaibe do those Indians carry on this trade, because there is no place elsewhere.

This Cacique Davaibe has a large smelter for gold in his house: he keeps one hundred men continually working the gold: I know all this for a certainty, for wherever I go I never hear otherwise; I have sought to know it of many Caciques and Indians and also from the neighbors of this Cacique Davaibe, the same as from those of other parts; I find all to be true, because I have learned it in many ways and methods, giving to some torture, to others things from Spain, and from others through affection.

I have certain information that fifty leagues up the river of S. Juan there are very rich mines on the one side and the other of the river: the manner that this river has to be navigated is in canoes of the Indians, because it makes many small and narrow arms concealed with groves of trees, and one cannot enter through there except in canoes of about three or four palms in width. . . .

The natives who live up this great river are bad and warlike: much cleverness is required in dealing with them: I have news of many other things which I do not certify until I know them more fully: I believe I shall know them by the help of God. . . .

One day's journey from this Cacique Pocorosa are some mountains the most beautiful that have been seen in these parts; they are very clear mountains without any thicket, save some groves along the streams which descend from the mountains. In those mountains are certain Caciques who have great quantity of gold in their houses: they say that all those Caciques keep their gold in the *barbacoas* like corn, because they have so much gold that they do not care to hold it in baskets: they say that all the rivers of those mountains contain gold and that there are very fat grains in much quantity. The Indian manner of collecting the gold is by seizing the nuggets when they see them in the water and casting them in their baskets: they also gather it in the ravines after they are dry; and in order that Your Most Royal Highness may be more completely informed of the things of those parts, I am sending to you a branded Indian from that region who has collected it many times: Your Most Royal Highness should not take this as a laughing matter, for in truth I am well assured of it by many principal Indians and Caciques.

They say that the Indians of the other coast are very sociable and polite: they tell me that the other sea is very good to navigate in canoes, for it is continually smooth and never rough like the sea on their side, according to what the Indians say: I believe that in that sea are many islands where are many rich pearls in abundance, and that the Caciques have baskets full of them, as well as have all the Indians, men and women, generally.

This river runs from this Cacique Comogre to the other sea, and before arriving there it forms three arms, and each one of them empties by itself into the other sea: they say that by the arm which enters toward the west come the canoes with pearls to the house of Cacique Comogre to trade: they say that through the arm that enters toward the East come the canoes with gold from all sides, which is an incredible thing and without any comparison.

Since our Lord has made you the Master of such a great land where so much treasure is, it must not be cast in oblivion, for if Your Most Royal Highness is pleased to give and send me men, I dare venture, therefore, through the goodness of our Lord, to discover very eminent things, and where one can obtain so much gold and enough riches with which to be able to conquer a large part of the world. . . .

Most mighty Lord, one favor I want to entreat Your Highness to do me, for it conduces much to your service, and it is that Your Highness command that no Bachelor of Law nor any other thing, unless it should be of medicine, may pass to these parts of the mainland under a heavy penalty that Your Highness order to provide for it, for no *Bachiller* comes here who is not a devil, and they lead the life of devils, and not only are they bad, but they even contrive and possess methods how to bring about a thousand lawsuits and villainies: this will advance much the service of Your Highness, because the country is new.

Most potent Lord, by a brigantine that we sent from here on which went Juan de Quicedo and Rodrigo de Colmenares, I forwarded to Your Highness 500 *pesos de oro* in most beautiful grains from the mines, and for the reason that the navigation is somewhat dangerous for small vessels, I now send to Your Highness with Sebastián del Campo 370 *pesos de oro* from the mines: more would be sent if it were not because it could not be gathered while the ships were here. In everything that I have said, I beseech Your Highness to provide what most will promote his service.

May our Lord prosper the life and most Royal estate of Your Highness with increase of many more Kingdoms and Lordships to his Holy service, and which in these parts may be discovered, and all come to the hands of Your Highness as Your most Royal Highness desires, for there are more riches here than in all the world.

The creature and creation of Your Highness, who kisses your most Royal hands and feet.

Vasco Núñez de Valboa

VIII-6 Ferdinand Magellan to King Charles I of Spain

Ferdinand Magellan (1480?-1521), the Portuguese navigator who was first to circumnavigate the globe, faced strong opposition from his country when he proposed an expedition to reach the Spice Islands by the western route, and thus, like Columbus a quarter century before, he entered the service of Spain. In a letter to his elected sovereign Charles I, Magellan gives a forthright account of an outrage instigated by the King of Portugal's factor in Seville, requesting punishment for the principal offenders and security against future acts of violence.

Seville, 24 October, 1518

My Lofty and Powerful Lord,

I have written to Your Highness by a commercial courier despatched the fifteenth of October. In it I gave you an account of everything I had done with this fleet, at the same time requesting Your Highness to have money provided which was lacking to the amount of 160 ducats without which it could not be completed . . . At the same time I requested Your Highness to provide thirty ducats for goods we have to carry, still lacking us. And because, Sire, I see that such a small quantity would not be enough to fill our ships with [traded] spices—and it would be a great loss to sail back empty—Your Highness must graciously supply us with a greater quantity of goods or arrange that the traders of your realms should send them, offering a certain quantity of their cargoes which Your Highness will determine, since our eventual gain, God willing, may be twenty to one, speaking literally. I should like in this enterprise for the total profit to be Your Highness's. Without possessing the merchandise with which we may load the aforementioned ships, I have written to Your Highness and to the Bishop of Burgos, that the situation may be widely known, and I write it here again that no one may reproach me, and with this and what I have already written, I am satisfying my obligation to You.

Similarly I requested Your Highness to have treasury officials provide funds for artillery, arms, and powder, things which it was agreed You would supply. Kindly supply us with these monies if they have not been sent, that we may serve You better.

I also wrote Your Highness, Sire, how little favor and assistance I was receiving from Your Assistant and his lieutenants, as from the other persons who manage your affairs, I having great need of him. In helping he would be merely doing his duty as well as his duty to me. And since what he has offered me is something less than what is needed, I sent my last letter for no other purpose than to tell you what is going on. Friday the twenty-second of October I was to bring a vessel to shore, and since high tide was very early in the morning, I rose at three o'clock to make sure the tackle and rigging were ready. When it was time for the crew to work I ordered them to fly four flags of my coats of arms on the capstans where it is customary to place the Captain's arms, with Your Excellency's coat of arms topmost along with the Trinity, the baptismal symbol of the ship. That of the Portuguese Factor * was to fly with them. But they had not brought it since it was not yet finished. Busy with hoisting anchor, I didn't take notice. But many of the people working on board stopped to look, as though at something which was unusual in this city. And as this world has no lack of invidious people, they began to grumble and talk. I had apparently given an evil order, putting my coats of arms

* This Factor was the Portuguese commissioner in Seville.

on the capstans. They were saying this without my hearing, until some came to tell me, followed by an Admiral of the Sea escorted by a lieutenant, son of Pedro de Nalcázar. The Admiral told the men to take down the arms and destroy them. I was then informed of the matter and I went to where he stood. I explained that the arms were not those of the King of Portugal, but rather my own, and that I was a vassal of Your Highness. I started back to my duties, but he was not satisfied. When I was leaving him, he insisted that his order be carried out, but Dr. Matienzo who was standing there did not consent. He then came up to me warning that I should be wise to take them down. I replied that I preferred them in their place, and since a knight of the King of Portugal [Sebastian Alvarez] was there present, it would be an offense to do otherwise. A knight who had been sent by that King to negotiate with me to return to Portugal or undertake some other profitable business. The Admiral recognized the affront to me he was committing.

Meanwhile the Governor of the port went to the Admiral's lieutenant and told him to bring down the flags. The latter, without further counsel or anyone with whom to consult, came up the steps shouting to people to seize the Portuguese Captain who was flying the flags of the King of Portugal, and coming up to me, asked, "Where are the flags? Why had I flown them on the capstans?"

I replied that I was giving him no reasons, nor did I desire to. He summoned constables seize me, laying hold of me, shouting for them to arrest my men as well. A few wished to show their intention to harm us rather than to help us fulfill our duty to Your Highness. At this point, Dr. Matienzo [the chief official of India House] arrived and saw the unreasonable behavior displayed toward me and my men, laid hold of the Admiral's lieutenant and urged him in Your Highness's name to do nothing so contrary to your service. The lieutenant's men seized Dr. Matienzo in turn and placed drawn swords against his head, frightening away crewmen and workers who had been paid. Aware now of the disappearing crew and the peril to the ship, I gave in to the Admiral's lieutenant and the others, only to restore order and to render service to your absent Highness.

Seeing that without me the ship could not be sailed, the Doctor took charge of me to ensure my safety. I asked one of the two lieutenants and even the major Governor of the Duke of Medina Sidonia not to leave the ship and to grant me their assistance and favor. But they, having seen that my men were without arms and some in stocks, took leave without assisting me. This is the sum and substance of what happened.

It seems to me, Sire, very unlike Your Excellency to allow such ill treatment to men leaving their kingdom and nationality to come and serve You through such a distinguished enterprise as the one to which Rui Faleiro and I are offering ourselves. I humbly beseech Your Highness to order me in this matter what may best serve Your interests and I shall willingly abide by Your orders. For the insult directed at me was not directed at Fernando de Magellan, but at the Captain of Your Highness, and those who committed it, less Your servants than I, for they serve You only through words. I serve you through my person, property, and life at your disposition, valuing more fulfilling my word than promises offered me from Portugal. I and my companion, who left Portugal under less auspicious circumstances, recognize Your good will, and with this letter urge You to make provision that we shall be well treated and Yourself well served. Let not those go unpunished who acted wrongly, because the result of their disconcerting actions was to stab one of Your Highnesses's pilots as he was working, to seize my men, and to disarm them. Let Your Highness send some one to institute an inquiry into what happened.

May our Lord grant Your Highness and Realm increase for many years.

Fernando de Magallanes

(trans. R. J. C)

VIII-7   Sebastian Alvarez to King Manoel of Portugal

When the initial attempts of the Portuguese to frustrate Magellan's venture were unavailing, Sebastian Alvarez, King Manoel's unscrupulous representative in Seville, was told to step up opposition to the project in any way he could. His report to the King which follows provides an insight into some of the difficulties Magellan had to overcome.

Seville, 18 July 1519

. . . Seeing the affair begun, and that it was a convenient season for me to say what your Highness commanded, I went to Magellan's house, where I found him filling baskets and chests with preserved victuals and other things. I pressed him, pretending that, as I found him thus engaged, it seemed to me that his evil design was settled, and since this would be the last word I should have with him, I desired to bring back to his memory how many times, as a good Portuguese and his friend, I had spoken to him, dissuading him from the great mistake he was committing. And after asking pardon of him, lest he should be offended at what I was about to say, I reminded him how many times I had spoken to him, and how well he had always replied to me, and that from his replies I always hoped that in the end he would not go, to the so great injury of your Highness. And what I always told him was, that the path he had chosen was beset with as many dangers as the wheel of Saint Catherine, and that he ought to leave it and take that which led to Coimbra, and return to his native land and to the favour of your Highness, at whose hands he would always receive benefits. In our conversation I brought before him all the dangers I could think of, and the mistakes he was making. He said to me that now, as an honourable man, he could only follow the path he had chosen. I replied that unduly to gain honour, and to gain it with infamy, was neither wisdom nor honour, but rather lack of wisdom and honour, for he might be sure that the chief Castilians of this city in speaking of him held him for a low person and of no breeding, since, to the dis-service of his true king and lord, he embarked in such an undertaking, and so much the more since it was set going, arranged, and petitioned for by him. And he might be certain that he was considered as a traitor, engaging himself thus in opposition to your Highness's country. Here he replied to me that he saw the mistake he made, but that he hoped to observe your Highness's service, and by his voyage to be of assistance to you. I told him that whoever should praise him for such an expression of opinion did not understand it; for unless he touched your Highness's possessions how was he to discover what he said? Besides, it was a great injury to the revenues of your Highness, which would affect the whole kingdom and every class of people, and it was a far more virtuous thought that inspired him when he told me that if your Highness ordered him to return to Portugal that he would do it without further guarantee of reward, and that when you granted none to him, there was Serradossa, and seven yards of grey cloth, and some gall-nut beads open to him.[1] So then it seemed to me that his heart was true as far as his honour and conscience were concerned. Our conversation was so long of duration that I cannot write it.

At this juncture, sire, he began to give me a sign, saying that I should tell him more; that this did not come from me and that, if your Highness commanded me, that I should tell him so, and also the reward that you would grant him. I told him that I was not a person of such weight that your Highness would employ me for such a purpose, but that I said it to him as I had on many other occasions. Here he wished to pay me a compliment, saying that if what I had begun with him was carried on without the interference of others, your Highness would be served, but that Nuño Ribeiro had told him one thing, which meant nothing, and João Mendez another, which bound him to nothing, and he told me the favours they offered him on the part of your Highness. He then bewailed himself greatly, and said he was much concerned about it all, but that he knew nothing which could

1. Magellan's irony is the more amusing from the fact that it is utterly lost upon Alvarez, who takes literally his alternative of a hermit's life.

justify his leaving a king who had shown him such favour. I told him that it would be a more certain matter, and attended with a truer honour, to do what he ought to do, and not to lose his reputation and the favours your Highness would grant him. And if he weighed his coming from Portugal (which was for a hundred reals more or less of *moradia* that your Highness did not grant him, in order not to break your laws), and that there had arrived two sets of orders at variance with his own, which he had at the hands of the King, Don Carlos, he would see whether this insult did not outbalance it—to go and do what it was his duty to do, rather than to remain here for that for which he came.

He was greatly astonished at my knowing so much, and then he told me the truth, and how the messenger had left—all of which I already knew. And he told me that certainly there was no reason why he should abandon the undertaking, unless they failed to fulfil anything in the terms of the agreement; but that first he must see what your Highness would do. I said to him, what more did he desire to see than the orders!—and Ruy Faleiro, who said openly that he was not going to follow his lantern,[2] and that he would navigate to the south, or he would not sail with the fleet; and that he (Magellan) thought he was going as admiral, whereas I knew that others were being sent in opposition to him, of whom he would know nothing, except at a time when it would be too late to save his honour.[3] (And I told him) that he should pay no heed to the honey that the Bishop of Burgos put to his lips, and that now was the time for him to choose his path, and that he should give me a letter to your Highness and that I, out of affection for him, would go to your Highness and plead his cause, because I had no instruction from your Highness concerning such business, and only said what I thought I had often said before. He told me that he would say nothing to me until he had seen the answer that the messenger brought, and with this our conversation finished. I will watch the interests of your Highness to the utmost of my power.

. . . I spoke to Ruy Faleiro twice, but he replied nothing to me, save "how could he do such a thing against the King, his lord, who conferred such benefits upon him"; and to all that I said to him he gave me no other answer. It seems to me that he is like a man affected in his reason, and that this his familiar has taken away whatever wisdom he possessed. I think that if Fernão de Magalhães were removed that Ruy Faleiro would follow what Magalhães did. . . .

The route which it is reported they are to take is direct to Cape Frio, leaving Brazil on the right, until they pass the boundary-line, and thence to sail W. and W.N.W. direct to Maluco, which land of Maluco I have seen laid down on the globe and chart which Fernando de Reynell made here, the which was not finished when his father came here for him, and his father finished the whole and marked

2. The *capitana* or flag-ship always carried the *farol* or lantern.
3. From this the previous plotting of the mutiny is evident.

these lands of Maluco, and on this pattern are constructed all the charts which Diogo Ribeiro makes. And he makes all the compasses, quadrants, and globes, but does not sail with the fleet; nor does he desire anything more than to gain his living by his skill.

From this Cape Frio to the islands of Maluco by this route there are no lands laid down in the charts they take. May God the Almighty grant that they make a voyage like that of the Cortereals,[4] and that your Highness may remain at rest, and ever be envied—as your Highness is—by all princes.

VIII-8   Don Hernando Cortés to Emperor Charles V of Spain

After the explorer Cortés (1485-1547) had apparently convinced the powerful and gallant Aztec emperor Moctezuma to accept allegiance to the crown of Spain, exchanging many presents and compliments with him, he despatched to Spain a remarkably detailed letter in describing life in Tenochtitlan, later to become Mexican City. Within a month of his arrival, Cortés began to profane the Aztec gods, as we read below.

Segura de la Frontera, Mexico, 30 October 1520
Most high, Mighty and Catholic Prince, Invincible Emperor and our Sovereign Liege:

I am desirous that your Majesty should know of matters concerning this land, which is so great and marvelous that, as I wrote in my former letter, your Majesty may well call himself Emperor of it with no less reason and title than he now does of Germany. . . .

The great city of Tenochtitlan is built in the midst of this salt lake, and it is two leagues from the heart of the city to any point on the mainland. Four causeways lead to it, all made by hand and some twelve feet wide. The city itself is as large as Seville or Córdova. The principal streets are very broad and straight, the majority of them being of beaten earth, but a few and at least half the smaller thoroughfares are waterways along which they pass in their canoes. Moreover, even the principal streets have openings at regular distances so that the water can freely pass from

4. J. V. Corte-Real explored Greenland in 1472-73 and Gaspar Corte-Real was, John Cabot, a co-discoverer of Newfoundland (1500).

one to another, and these openings which are very broad are spanned by great bridges of huge beams, very stoutly put together, so firm indeed that over many of them ten horsemen can ride at once. Seeing that if the natives intended any treachery against us they would have every opportunity from the way in which the city is built, for by removing the bridges from the entrances and exits they could leave us to die of hunger with no possibility of getting to the mainland, I immediately set to work as soon as we entered the city on the building of four brigs, and in a short space of time had them finished, so that we could ship three hundred men and the horses to the mainland whenever we so desired.

The city has many open squares in which markets are continuously held and the general business of buying and selling proceeds. One square in particular is twice as big as that of Salamanca and completely surrounded by arcades where there are daily more than sixty thousand folk buying and selling. Every kind of merchandise such as may be met with in every land is for sale there, whether of food and victuals, or ornaments of gold and silver, or lead, brass, copper, tin, precious stones, bones, shells, snails and feathers; limestone for building is likewise sold there, stone both rough and polished, bricks burnt and unburnt, wood of all kinds and in all stages of preparation. There is a street of game where they sell all manner of birds that are to be found in their country, including hens, partridges, quails, wild duck, fly-catchers, widgeon, turtle doves, pigeons, little birds in round nests made of grass, parrots, owls, eagles, vulcans, sparrow-hawks and kestrels; and of some of these birds of prey they sell the skins complete with feathers, head, bill and claws. They also sell rabbits, hares, deer and small dogs which they breed especially for eating. There is a street of herb-sellers where there are all manner of roots and medicinal plants that are found in the land. There are houses as it were of apothecaries where they sell medicines made from these herbs, both for drinking and for use as ointments and salves. There are barbers' shops where you may have your hair washed and cut. There are other shops where you may obtain food and drink. There are street porters such as we have in Spain to carry packages. There is a great quantity of wood, charcoal, braziers made of clay and mats of all sorts, some for beds and others more finely woven for seats, still others for furnishing halls and private apartments. All kinds of vegetables may be found there, in particular onions, leeks, garlic, cresses, watercress, borage, sorrel, artichokes, and golden thistles. There are many different sorts of fruits including cherries and plums very similar to those found in Spain. They sell honey obtained from bees, as also the honeycomb and that obtained from maize plants which are as sweet as sugar canes; they also obtain honey from plants which are known both here and in other parts as *maguey,* which is preferable to grape juice; from *maguey* in addition they make both sugar and a kind of wine, which are sold in their markets. All kinds of cotton thread in various colours may be bought in skeins, very much in the same way as in the great silk exchange of Granada, except that the quantities are far less. They have colours for painting of as good quality as any in Spain, and of as pure shades as may be found anywhere. There are leathers of deer both skinned and in their natural state, and either bleached or dyed in various colours. A great deal of chinaware is sold of very good quality and including earthen jars of all sizes for holding liquids, pitchers, pots, tiles and an infinite variety of earthenware all made of very special clay and almost all decorated and painted in some way. Maize is sold both as grain and in the form of bread and is vastly superior both in the size of the ear and in taste to that of all the other islands or the mainland. Pasties made from game and fish pies may be seen on sale, and there are large quantities of fresh and salt water fish both in their natural state and cooked ready for eating. Eggs from fowls, geese and all the other birds I have described may be had, and likewise omelettes ready made. There is nothing to be found in all the land which is not sold in these markets, for over and above what I have mentioned there are so many and such various other things that on account of their very number and the fact that I do not know their names, I cannot now detail them. Each kind of merchandise is sold in its own particular street and no other kind may be sold there: this rule is very well enforced. All is sold by number and measure, but up till now no weighing by balance has been observed. A very fine building in the great square serves as a kind of audience chamber where ten or a dozen persons are always seated, as judges, who deliberate on all cases arising in the market and pass sentence on evildoers. In the square itself there are officials who continually walk amongst the people inspecting goods exposed for sale and the measures by which they are sold, and on certain occasions I have seen them destroy measures which were false.

There are a very large number of mosques or dwelling places for their idols throughout the various districts of this great city, all fine buildings, in the chief of which their priests live continuously, so that in addition to the actual temples containing idols there are sumptuous lodgings. These pagan priests are all dressed in black and go habitually with their hair uncut; they do not even comb it from the day they enter the order to that on which they leave. Chief men's sons, both nobles and distinguished citizens, enter these orders at the age of six or seven and only leave when they are of an age to marry, and this occurs more frequently to the first-born who will inherit their father's estates than to others. They are denied all access to women, and no woman is ever allowed to enter one of the religious houses. Certain foods they abstain from and more so at certain periods of the year than at others. Among these temples there is one chief one in particular whose size and magnificence no human tongue could describe. For it is so big that within the lofty wall which entirely circles it one could set a town of fifteen thousand inhabitants.

Immediately inside this wall and throughout its entire length are some admirable buildings containing large halls and corridors where the priests who live in this temple are housed. There are forty towers at the least, all of stout construction and very lofty, the largest of which has fifty steps leading up to its base: this chief one is indeed higher than the great church of Seville. The workmanship both in wood and stone could not be bettered anywhere, for all the stonework within the actual temples where they keep their idols is cut into ornamental borders of flowers, birds, fishes and the like, or trellis-work, and the woodwork is likewise all in relief highly decorated with monsters of very various device. The towers all serve as burying places for their nobles, and the little temples which they contain are all dedicated to a different idol to whom they pay their devotions.

There are three large halls in the great mosque where the principal idols are to be found, all of immense size and height and richly decorated with sculptured figures both in wood and stone, and within these halls are other smaller temples branching off from them and entered by doors so small that no daylight ever reaches them. Certain of the priests but not all are permitted to enter, and within are the great heads and figures of idols, although as I have said there are also many outside. The greatest of these idols and those in which they placed most faith and trust I ordered to be dragged from their places and flung down the stairs, which done I had the temples which they occupy cleansed for they were full of the blood of human victims who had been sacrificed,* and placed in them the image of Our Lady and other saints, all of which made no small impression upon Muteczuma and the inhabitants. They at first remonstrated with me, for should it be known, they said, by the people of the country they would rise against me, believing as they did that to these idols were due all temporal goods, and that should they allow them to be ill used they would be wroth against them and would give them nothing, denying them the fruits of the earth, and thus the people would die of starvation. I instructed them by my interpreters how mistaken they were in putting their trust in idols made by their own hands from unclean things, and that they must know that there was but one God, Lord of all, Who created the sky, the earth and all things, Who made both them and ourselves, Who was without beginning and immortal, Whom alone they had to adore and to believe in, and not in any created thing whatsoever: I told them moreover all things else that I knew of touching this matter in order to lead them from their idolatry and bring them to the knowledge of Our Lord: and all, especially Muteczuma, replied that they had already told me that they were not natives of this land but had come to it long time since, and that therefore they were well prepared to believe that they had erred

* The two sun gods of the Aztecs, Huitzilopochtli and Tezcatlipoca, demanded the sacrifice of human victims.

somewhat from the true faith during the long time since they had left their native land, and I as more lately come would know more surely the things that it was right for them to hold and believe than they themselves: and that hence if I would instruct them they would do whatever I declared to be best. Upon this Muteczuma and many of the chief men of the city went with me to remove the idols, cleanse the chapels, and place images of the saints therein, and all with cheerful faces. I forbade them moreover to make human sacrifice to the idols as was their wont, because besides being an abomination in the sight of God it is prohibited by your Majesty's laws which declare that he who kills shall be killed. From this time henceforth they departed from it, and during the whole time that I was in the city not a single living soul was known to be killed and sacrificed.

The images of the idols in which these people believed are many times greater than the body of a large man. They are made from pulp of all the cereals and greenstuffs which they eat, mixed and pounded together. This mass they moisten with blood from the hearts of human beings which they tear from their breasts while still alive, and thus make sufficient quantity of the pulp to mould into their huge statues: and after the idols have been set up still they offer them more living hearts which they sacrifice in like manner and anoint their faces with the blood. Each department of human affairs has its particular idol after the manner of the ancients who thus honoured their gods: so that there is one idol from whom they beg success in war, another for crops, and so on for all their needs.

The city contains many large and fine houses, and for this reason. All the nobles of the land owing allegiance to Muteczuma have their houses in the city and reside there for a certain portion of the year; and in addition there are a large number of rich citizens who likewise have very fine houses. All possess in addition to large and elegant apartments very delightful flower gardens of every kind, both on the ground level as on the upper storeys.

Along one of the causeways connecting this great city with the mainland two pipes are constructed of masonry, each two paces broad and about as high as a man, one of which conveys a stream of water very clear and fresh and about the thickness of a man's body right to the centre of the city, which all can use for drinking and other purposes. The other pipe which is empty is used when it is desired to clean the former. Moreover, on coming to the breaks in the causeway spanned by bridges under which the salt water flows through, the fresh water flows into a kind of trough as thick as an ox which occupies the whole width of the bridge, and thus the whole city is served. The water is sold from canoes in all the streets, the manner of their taking it from the pipes being in this wise: the canoes place themselves under the bridges where the troughs are to be found, and from above the canoes are filled by men who are especially paid for this work.

At all the entrances to the city and at those parts where canoes are unloaded, which is where the greater amount of provisions enters the city, certain huts have been built, where there are official guards to exact so much on everything that enters. I know not whether this goes to the lord or to the city itself, and have not yet been able to ascertain, but I think that it is to the ruler, since in the markets of several other towns we have seen such a tax exacted on behalf of the ruler. Every day in all the markets and public places of the city there are a number of workmen and masters of all manner of crafts waiting to be hired by the day. The people of this city are nicer in their dress and manners than those of any other city or province, for since Muteczuma always holds his residence here and his vassals visit the city for lengthy periods, greater culture and politeness of manners in all things has been encouraged.

Finally, to avoid prolixity in telling all the wonders of this city, I will simply say that the manner of living among the people is very similar to that in Spain, and considering that this is a barbarous nation shut off from a knowledge of the true God or communication with enlightened nations, one may well marvel at the orderliness and good government which is everywhere maintained.

VIII-9   Captain John da Verrazzano to His Most Serene Majesty the King of France

It is now established that Verrazzano (1485?-1528) first explored the North American coast as far south as Georgia. We excerpt from his famous 1524 letter to King Francis I his description of the mouth of the Hudson and the site of New York City (40° 47′) and the neighboring coastline. His description of the Indian tribes and their customs has an authentic ring, obviously documented by his logs.

Dieppe, Normandie, 8 July, 1524

. . . After proceeding one hundred leagues, we found a very pleasant situation among some steep hills, through which a very large river, deep at its mouth, forced its way to the sea; from the sea to the estuary of the river, any ship heavily laden might pass, with the help of the tide, which rises eight feet. But as we were riding at anchor in a good berth, we would not venture up in our vessel, without a knowledge of the mouth; therefore we took the boat, and entering the river, we found the country on its banks well peopled, the inhabitants not differing much from the others, being dressed out with feathers of birds of various colours. They came towards us with evident delight, raising loud shouts of admiration, and showing us where we could most securely land with our boat. We passed up this river, about half a league, when we found it formed a most beautiful lake three leagues in circuit, upon which they were rowing thirty or more of their small boats, from one shore to the other, filled with multitudes who came to see us. All of a sudden, as is wont to happen to navigators, a violent contrary wind blew in from the sea, and forced us to return to our ship, greatly regretting to leave this region which seemed so commodious and delightful, and which we supposed must also contain great riches, as the hills showed many indications of minerals. Weighing anchor, we sailed *eighty* (ottanta) leagues towards the east, as the coast stretched in that direction, and always in sight of it; at length we discovered an island of a triangular form, about ten leagues from the mainland, in size about equal to the island of Rhodes, having many hills covered with trees, and well peopled judging from the great number of fires which we saw all around its shores; we gave it the name of your Majesty's illustrious mother.*

We did not land there, as the weather was unfavourable, but proceeded to another place, fifteen leagues distant from the island, where we found a very excellent harbour. Before entering it, we saw about twenty small boats full of people, who came about our ship, uttering many cries of astonishment, but they would not approach nearer than within fifty paces; stopping, they looked at the structure of our ship, our persons and dress, afterwards they all raised a loud shout together, signifying that they were pleased. By imitating their signs, we inspired them in some measure with confidence, so that they came near enough for us to toss to them some little bells and glasses, and many toys, which they took and looked at, laughing, and then came on board without fear. Among them were two kings more beautiful in form and stature than can possibly be described; one was about forty years old, the other about twenty-four, and they were dressed in the following manner: The oldest had a deer's skin around his body, artificially wrought in damask figures, his head was without covering, his hair was tied back in various knots; around his neck he wore a large chain ornamented with many stones of different colours. The young man was similar in his general appearance. This is the finest looking tribe, and the handsomest in their costumes, that we have found in our voyage. They exceed us in size, and they are of a very fair complexion (?); some of them incline more to a bronze, and others to a tawny colour; their faces are sharp, their hair long and black, upon the adorning of which they bestow great

---

* Louise de Savoie and the King were of the Angoulême dynasty, and Verrazzano intended the New York City area to be called Angoulême.

pains; their eyes are black and sharp, their expression mild and pleasant, greatly resembling the antique. I say nothing to your Majesty of the other parts of the body, which are all in good proportion, and such as belong to well-formed men. Their women are of the same form and beauty, very graceful, of fine countenances and pleasing appearance in manners and modesty; they wear no clothing except a deer skin, ornamented like those worn by the men; some wear very rich lynx skins upon their arms, and various ornaments upon their heads, composed of braids of hair, which also hang down upon their breasts on each side. Others wear different ornaments, such as the women of Egypt and Syria use. The older and the married people, both men and women, wear many ornaments in their ears, hanging down in the oriental manner. We saw upon them several pieces of wrought copper, which is more esteemed by them than gold, as this is not valued on account of its colour, but is considered by them as the most ordinary of the metals—yellow being the colour especially disliked by them; azure and red are those in highest estimation with them. Of those things which we gave them, they prized most highly the bells, azure crystals, and other toys to hang in their ears and about their necks; they do not value or care to have silk or gold stuffs, or other kinds of cloth, nor implements of steel or iron. When we showed them our arms, they expressed no admiration, and only asked how they were made; the same was the case with the looking-glasses, which they returned to us, smiling, as soon as they had looked at them. They are very generous, giving away whatever they have. We formed a great friendship with them, and one day we entered into the port with our ship, having before rode at the distance of a league from the shore, as the weather was adverse. They came off to the ship with a number of their little boats, with their faces painted in divers colours, showing us real signs of joy, bringing us of their provisions, and signifying to us where we could best ride in safety with our ship; and keeping with us until we had cast anchor. We remained among them fifteen days, to provide ourselves with many things of which we were in want, during which time they came every day to see our ship, bringing with them their wives of whom they were very careful; for, although they came on board themselves, and remained a long while, they made their wives stay in the boats, nor could we ever get them on board by any entreaties or any presents we could make them. One of the two kings often came with his queen and many attendants, to see us for his amusement; but he always stopped at the distance of about two hundred paces and sent a boat to inform us of his intended visit, saying they would come and see our ship—this was done for safety, and as soon as they had an answer from us they came off, and remained awhile to look around; but on hearing the annoying cries of the sailors, the king sent the queen, with her attendants, in a very light boat, to wait, near an island a quarter of a league distant from us, while he remained a long time on board, talking with us by signs, and expressing his fanciful notions about every thing in the ship, and asking the use of all. After imitating our modes of salutation, and tasting our food, he courteously took leave of us. Sometimes, when our men staid two or three days on a small island, near the ship, for their various necessities, as sailors are wont to do, he came with seven or eight of his attendants, to enquire about our movements, often asking us if we intended to remain there long, and offering us every thing at his command, and then he would shoot with his bow, and run up and down with his people, making great sport for us. We often went five or six leagues into the interior, and found the country as pleasant as is possible to conceive, adapted to cultivation of every kind, whether of corn, wine or oil; there are open plains twenty-five or thirty leagues in extent, entirely free from trees or other hinderances, and of so great fertility, that whatever is sown there will yield an excellent crop. On entering the woods, we observed that they might all be traversed by an army ever so numerous; the trees of which they were composed, were oaks, cypresses, and others, unknown in Europe. We found, also, apples, plumbs, filberts, and many other fruits, but all of a different kind from ours. The animals, which are in great numbers, as stags, deer, lynxes, and many other species, are taken by snares, and by bows, the latter being their chief implement; their arrows are wrought with great beauty, and for the heads of them, they use emery, jasper, hard marble, and other sharp stones, in the place of iron. They also use the same kind of sharp stones in cutting down trees, and with them they construct their boats of single logs, hollowed out with admirable skill, and sufficiently commodious to contain ten or twelve persons; their oars are short, and broad at the end, and are managed in rowing by force of the arms alone, with perfect security, and as nimbly as they choose. We saw their dwellings, which are of a circular form, of about ten or twelve paces in circumference, made of logs split in halves, without any regularity of architecture, and covered with roofs of straw, nicely put on, which protect them from wind and rain. There is no doubt that they would build stately edifices if they had workmen as skilful as ours, for the whole sea-coast abounds in shining stones, crystals, and alabaster, and for the same reason it has ports and retreats for animals. They change their habitations from place to place as circumstances of situation and season may require; this is easily done, as they have only to take with them their mats, and they have other houses prepared at once. The father and the whole family dwell together in one house in great numbers; in some we saw twenty-five or thirty persons. Their food is pulse, as with the other tribes, which is here better than elsewhere, and more carefully cultivated; in the time of sowing they are governed by the moon, the sprouting of grain, and many other ancient usages. They live by hunting and fishing, and they are long-lived. If they fall sick, they cure themselves without medicine, by the heat of the fire, and their death at last comes from extreme old age. We judge them to be very affectionate and charitable towards their relatives—making loud lamentations in their adversity, and in their misery calling to mind all their good fortune. At their departure out of life, their relations mutually join in weeping, mingled with singing, for a long while. This is all that we could learn of them. This region is situated in the parallel of Rome, being 41° 40' of north latitude, but much colder from accidental circumstances, and not by nature. . . .

VIII-10   Queen Elizabeth to Captains on the High Seas between England and Russia

To open up trade with Muscovy, Elizabeth (1533-1603) sent eight ships to Russia laden with English products and a thousand pounds for purchase of Russian goods. Piracy and enforced tribute on the high seas being rampant—and the English captains were some of the worst offenders— Elizabeth promises that any interference will be direly punished.

London, 20 May 1582

Whereas our Merchaunts Adventurers trading into the countrees of Moscovia, have, at this present, almoost in a redines eight good shippes, fraighted with clothes and other Englishe commodities, to make saile from our port of London toward Sainct Nicholas and other portes of Russia, We lett you witt that for certen consideracōns us speciallye moving, We have licenced, and by these presents doe licence the bearers hereof in the name of the sayd marchaunts to cary and transport with them out of this our realme towards the said Sainct Nicholas, and other ports of Russia, the quantetye of one thowsand pound waight in bullion. Wherefore we will and commaund you to suffer the sayd bearer of theis our lettres quietlie to passe by you with the sayd one thousand pound waight of bullion for the purpos aforesayd without any your staie, lett, or molestacōn, as ye tender our pleasure and will aunswere for the contrarye at your perils. And theas our lettres shalbe your sufficient warraunt and discharge in this behalfe. Given under our signet, at our manour of Grenewich, the twentieth daie of May, 1582, in the fower and twentieth yeare of our raigne.

To all Maiours, Sherifs, Bailiffs, Constables, Customers, Comptrollers,

Searchers, and all other our Officers, Ministers, and Subjects to whom it shall appertayne in this case and to everye of them.

(As we have seen from Letter VI-19, Elizabeth's new program of trade with Russia led to censorship of books criticizing the despotic government of the czars.)

VIII-11   The Fugger Correspondent in East India to the Augsburg Bankers

A Fugger newsletter from East India bears witness to the invasion of parts of southern Asia by Portuguese, Turkish and English merchant marines. Piracy and cannibalism accompanied the establishment of trade with Asia and the Spice Islands.

13 January, 1590

When the last ships set sail in the year 1589, the following exploits of war took place. The Armada, which Manuel Continho and his brother Thomas de Sansa had dispatched to the coast of Melindo on the 19th day of January 1589, numbered five galleys and fifteen other ships. They carried twelve hundred Portuguese. When, after heavy storms, there arrived within sight the Estrecho de Moqua, they noticed that four Turkish galleys had landed on the coast of Melindo near a place called Mombassa. On this island the Turks had built a fortress for their protection, not suspecting the coming of the Portuguese. The latter went ashore, and near on three hundred thousand natives banded themselves together in order to proceed to the island at low tide and to eat the people living there, which they had also done now and again on the mainland. For this reason the Turks had removed the cannon from the galleys for their protection, not apprehending any danger from the open sea. But the Portuguese Armada intervened, captured the Turkish galleys without resistance, and thereupon landed. When the Turks saw this they sought to take refuge on the mainland, but they were cruelly handled and eaten by the wild natives. Some of the Turks surrendered to the Portuguese, preferring captivity to being devoured by the cannibals. Thus the Portuguese took prisoner several Turks and Arab Moors.

The Portuguese general ordered the King of Mombassa, who owes allegiance to the King of Portugal, to be decapitated, because he had granted the Turks asylum in his territory. The fortress erected by the Turks was razed to the ground and the island pillaged. Then the Portuguese left the field clear to the Simbas, who killed and ate the people before the eyes of the Armada, so that within five days not a living creature was there left on the island. When they had cleared everything and had nothing more to eat, they again went to the mainland. They thereupon set out northward for the land of John, the Priest.[1] Those of the Armada relate that the Simbas are well equipped with sharp arrows and eat all the men they can lay their hands on, and their wives they lead away with them alive. But they do not suffer a sick person among them. As soon as one falls sick, they kill and eat him. The Portuguese report that the natives were six hundred thousand strong when they set out upon their quest. Once they reach a place they do not leave it as long as they can find a man to eat, after which they depart. Victory fell to our Armada because the Simbas had caused so much trouble to the Turks that it was an easy matter to capture the galleys, which were taken into Goa on the 16th day of March.

Letters were sent with the ships from Santa Cruz to Portugal last January that two of our galleys and twelve galleots fought bravely with the blacks near Goa. The galleots withdrew into a harbour twelve miles from Goa, whither the Governor dispatched a fleet. This fleet conquered the coast and drove the natives inland.

The fortress which our Armada destroyed in Malacca has been built up anew by the people there. The Governor, however, with three hundred Portuguese, once more drove the people away and tore down the building. All the ports of Malacca are of great importance, for it is thither the ships come to take in cargoes of pepper and other condiments and freight. It would be well to conquer the island of Sumatra. With four to six thousand Portuguese it would be possible to prevent all navigation to Moqua. The money, however, is lacking. Last year an English ship entered the Sunda Straits and took in a load of pepper. The captain had brought with him a letter and a present to the Bishop there, but the latter accepted neither. When the English made their way back towards England round the Cape of Good Hope they sailed forth with two more ships and took their course through the Estrecho de Moqua, where one of the ships was wrecked. With the other two they proceeded to New Spain and Mexico where they pillaged and took whatever they could lay their hands upon. From thence they sailed to the Philippines, where they loaded all manner of wares from China. One ship then sailed home, and another to the Sunda Straits to fetch a cargo of pepper. Navigation from New Spain to China has become an ordinary occurrence. Ships arrive there daily. Last

1. Prester John was a legendary king-priest whose realm was variously assigned to Ethopia or the Far East.

year Don Juan de Gona sailed to Mexico, but when our Governor learnt of this he sent a galleot to fight him, for it would be India's ruin if he were allowed free passage. For there is a convention between the King of Portugal and the King of Spain according to which the Spaniards are not allowed to sail to the Philippines.[2] By this the King, our Lord, vowed he would abide when he took possession of Portugal.

The Jesuits daily convert people in Japan to the Christian Faith. They have entire mastery of this island.[3]

The Moors of Ceylon have taken a Christian for their king. He is the cousin of the last King. He asks for two hundred monks who are to baptize his subjects.

VIII-12   Brother Aegidius Matta to the General of his Order

The following Fugger report is actually part of a letter written by a Jesuit priest, Aegidius Matta, to the General of his Order, in which he details the startling achievements of Christian missionaries in Japan and cherishes hopes of a widespread conversion. The Portuguese first sailed to Japan in 1543. In 1549 Francis Xavier arrived at Kyushu for a two-year stay during which he converted 1000 natives.

25 July 1590

King Sapume, hitherto the most embittered enemy of the Christian Faith, demands that one of our brethren, who have come hither from the Spanish Philippines, be sent to Kangoxima, the most important harbour of his whole kingdom (whence I am writing), in order to hear confessions, preach and instruct his subjects. He also wishes that we found a settlement in the aforesaid port. He first did greatly insist upon this, but now has agreed to defer the matter till the arrival of the Father Inspector.

P. Caspar Celius, Vice-Provincial for Japan, who has lived the life of a saint and died immaculate, was taken to his grave in solemn state. This was marked not only by the numerous attendance of our Fathers, who chanced at this time to be present here, but by the presence of many Thomus-Christians who followed the funeral to

2. In a papal bull of 1493, Alexander VI granted to Spain all new territories west, and to Portugal all east, of a longitudinal line 270 miles west of the Azores. Obviously the bull was duly revised.

3. On the Christianizing of Japan, see the following letter.

Arima, where he was buried. His successor is Pater Gometius, who, despite his delicate health, is held in no less esteem than the departed. Concerning the position of Christianity in Japan, it is to be reported that three years have now passed since our Order was banished from this country.* But by the protection of God we have met with no hindrance as the result of this banishment. Also the number of Christians in spite of this has not decreased, but, on the contrary, increased at a quicker rate than at the time when the Tyrant pretended to favour our doings. Several members of the nobility have become Christians and vie with their subjects in Christian zeal. D. Augustinus, a Christian, a vassal of the Tyrant, himself converted the Prince of Gotti to the Faith. It is of no mean advantage to the state of Christendom, that the islands upon which the said Christians are living, are situate far from the trading route of the Chinese. For this reason, also, all those who instruct in the Faith are removed far from the danger of a rebellion.

Nevertheless in towns which are in closer proximity to the Chinese such as Arima and Omura, the secrets of our Faith have been taught at all times openly and fearlessly and that with great success. In proof whereof there is the multitude of those who received the Blessed Sacrament. Apart from this, many crucifixes have been erected at various places, and frequented by servants of the Tyrant, without their being mutilated or pulled down. There are not many persons either who would easily consent to denounce us to the Tyrant, for they do not wish to cause him any annoyance, since he prefers to avoid trouble where he can. He likewise has the habit of passing things over in silence—although they be well known to him—when they appear to be vexatious.

The penalty of banishment is not so severely carried out in the case of the Japanese as it occasionally is elsewhere. It is therefore less strange, that we, though we be banished, yet continue our work with little hindrance. For all things that follow appear to the Japanese as banishment: the deprivation of the sight of that Mighty One, who has expelled us, and the avoidance of places that are greatly frequented, and the exhibition of grief and mourning in demeanour and attire, and a life fashioned on that of the Bonzes.

But now I revert again to the progress which Christianity has made here. One Ethnicus, or First Lord, of the name of Taikosama, a most violent enemy of Christianity, has not been able to hinder the spread of the Faith in his territory. Churches and crucifixes have been erected and all the inhabitants of a not unimportant town were baptized by me. A church was also built in many places—not only in those of great importance—and crosses were erected although the full time does not seem as yet at hand. Moreover a large number of those who have so far besieged our Port of Kangoxima now demand to be baptized. Further, also several Ethnici, who have been held prisoners by the Christians at various

* In 1587 the general-emperor Hideyoshi ordered the Jesuit and Franciscan missionaries to leave Japan, but the order was not enforced.

places, are also admitted to Holy Baptism, so that once the Tyrant Taikosama has been vanquished, we cherish the great hope—please God—that all those persons will adopt the Christian Faith. Our Ethnici here can scarcely recover from their wonderment at perceiving how little, if at all, we, who have been banished by the order of the Tyrant, allow ourselves to be frightened by his ordinances. Even three of the Thomi Ethnici extol our innocence, because, although all counsel us to do so, we cannot be prevailed upon to travel to China, leaving one or the other behind, in order to escape the present persecution.

They say it seems as though we were being detained by Providence, likewise as if we were endeavouring through our safety to demonstrate the might of God, Whose messengers we claim to be, as against the power of His enemies. As is men's custom they have taken this into their heads and firmly believe that we draw our strength from the enemies of Taikosama, so that our banishment from Japan may be rendered the more difficult. The Tyrant will imagine the same, when he hears that we are still in Japan.

We take credit to ourselves for hoping for the best. In the seminaries, which were instituted by Gregory XIII in Japan, a multitude of helpers grows day by day. This will be of the greatest importance for the growth of the Faith when Christianity is once more tolerated in these islands.

VIII-13   Sir Walter Raleigh to King James I

James I had already placed Raleigh (1552?-1618) in the Tower for thirteen years, on a trumped-up charge of treason. Released in 1616, Raleigh led an expedition to Guiana, promising to bring back gold without provoking Spain now finally at peace with England. On the contrary, his lieutenant Keymis attacked and burned the Spanish-garrisoned town of San Tomás while Raleigh suffered from a tropical fever in Trinidad. Raleigh's son was killed during this assault. Goaded by the Spanish, James I arrested him again on his return and Raleigh was sentenced to death.

1618

May it please your most excellent Majesty.

If in my journey outward-bound I had my men murdered at the islands, and yet spared to take revenge; if I did discharge some Spanish barks taken without spoil;

if I forbore all parts of the Spanish Indies, wherein I might have taken twenty of their towns on the sea coasts, and did only follow the enterprise I undertook for Guiana; where, without any directions from me, a Spanish village was burnt, which was new set up within three miles of the mine: by your majesty's favour, I find no reason why the Spanish ambassador should complain of me. If it were lawful for the Spaniards to murder twenty-six Englishmen, tying them back to back, and then cutting their throats, when they had traded with them a whole month, and came to them on the land without so much as one sword amongst them all; and that it may not be lawful to your majesty's subjects, being charged first by them, to repel force by force; we may justly say, O miserable English!

If Parker and Metham took Campeachy and other places in the Honduras, seated in the heart of the Spanish Indies, burnt towns, and killed the Spaniards, and had nothing said unto them at their return; and myself forbore to look into the Indies, because I would not offend, I may as justly say, O miserable Ralegh!

If I have spent my poor estate, lost my son, suffered by sickness and otherwise a world of miseries; if I have resisted with the manifest hazard of my life the robberies and spoils with which my companions would have made me rich; if when I was poor I could have made myself rich; if when I had gotten my liberty, which all men and nature herself do much prize, I voluntary lost it; if when I was master of my life I rendered it again; if I might elsewhere have sold my ship and goods, and put five or six thousand pounds in my purse, and yet brought them into England; I beseech your majesty to believe, that all this I have done, because it should not be said to your majesty, that your majesty had given liberty and trust to a man, whose end was but the recovery of his liberty, and who had betrayed your majesty's trust.

My mutineers told me, that if I returned for England I should be undone; but I believed in your majesty's goodness more than in all their arguments. Sure I am, that I am the first who, being free and able to enrich myself, have yet embraced poverty and peril. And as sure I am, that my example shall make me the last. But your majesty's wisdom and goodness I have made my judges, who have ever been, and shall ever remain,

Your majesty's most humble vassal,
Walter Ralegh.

(See Letter VI-21 on the courageous demeanor of Raleigh at his execution.)

CHAPTER 9

LOVE, SACRED AND PROFANE. MARRIAGE AND FAMILY. STATUS OF WOMEN.

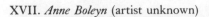

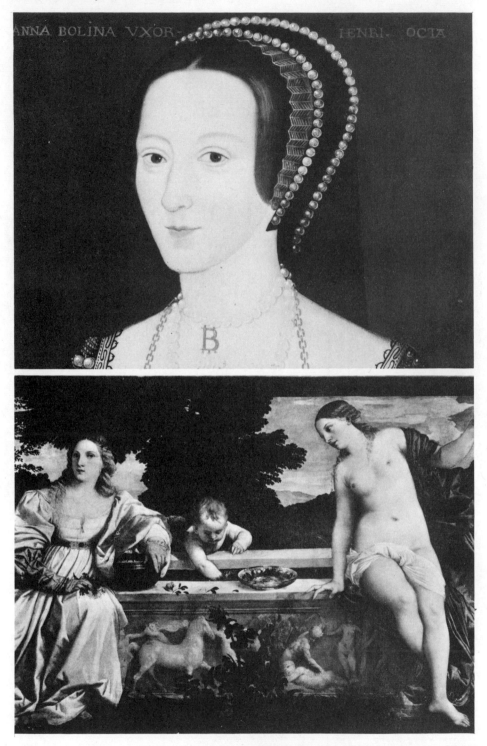

XVIII. *Sacred and Profane Love* by Titian

The greatest theme of Renaissance poetry was love, as if the poets, ever mindful of their Greco-Roman models, were echoing Anacreon's admission that his lyre always returned to thoughts of love. The great Greek myths of lovers, such as Venus and Adonis (II-10), reappeared in pastorals, romances, and narrative poetry. Two major influences on thought and literature, Ficinian neo-Platonism and Petrarchism, gave form and variety to the expression of love. As the mediaeval morality waned, sensual love was given a boost by being so often paired with divine love, *amor bueno,* a comparison exquisitely depicted in Titian's *Sacred and Profane Love.* With love the dominant topic of so many literary forms, it is small wonder that the correspondents of the Renaissance dwelt on it so often. It did not take Platonism or Petrarchism of course to make realists like Machiavelli enthuse over a new love for "a creature so gracious, so delicate, so noble that I cannot praise her or love her so much that she would not deserve more" (IX-1).

Canon law, which continued operative throughout the century even in those countries invaded by Protestantism, was explicit about love. The only permitted sexual love was conjugal. Anything less was adultery, and many free-thinking couples were burned at the stake (V-18). Divorce was unthinkable, although Henri IV, having decided that "Paris was worth a mass" (VI-20), could order his cardinals to find excuses to permit him a divorce. Still, free love was spreading, despite such dubious birth control as the use of silk kerchiefs, and even kings and clergymen had bastards—some of these offspring, like Erasmus, to become luminaries. Both Mary Stuart (IX-17) and Elizabeth Regina were thought to have had children outside marital bonds.

The popes, wrote Erasmus, worried about the continence of wives, especially those with husbands away from home. They were to wear no silk, gold, or jewels, nor drink wine. A letter of Fray Antonio de Guevara even told priests to stay away from wives with absent husbands, lest they end up behaving like Lothario in Cervantes's *Curioso impertinente.* Churchmen also worried about maids working in the homes of older men, even if that employer were the greatest scientist of the Renaissance (IX-12).

Canon law exerted its influence on continuity of the family, emphasizing large families. Although Montaigne noted that the more sophisticated males of Paris were declaring around 1570 that one should seduce women, but not marry them

(IX-18), we may suppose that most Frenchmen, under social and religious pressures, adhered to the "old manner" of monogamy, as Montaigne put it. The steady population growth indicated that blissful conjugality was exercising its mandate.

Families kept the wraps on their unwed daughters. Getting the young girls married before disaster struck was a theme of both epistles and literature. Unmarried girls were to stay home away from temptation, and a letter of Cardinal Bembo shows him depositing his daughter, like a day-student, in a convent. Indeed, he even forbade his long-suffering daughter Elena to play the monochord: "Playing is for vain and frivolous women. I want you to be the most serious, chaste, and virtuous woman alive" (IX-13). The solution of placing girls permanently in nunneries was decried by Rabelais as the caging of birds. Yet, without a system of schools for the education of women, Renaissance families often caged their daughters this way, provided they paid for entry with a dowry (V-21). The manner by which this dowry had to be negotiated is explained in Lope de Vega's dunning letter to the Duke of Sessa (IX-23).

If an unwed girl became pregnant, the usual thing was to arrange a wedding promptly. Illegitimacy was subject to gossip of course, but the stigma was lessened when the father was known. That Erasmus was the natural son of a priest, Gerard de Gouda, left all doors open to him. The natural son of Emperor Charles V proved a revered international hero after Lepanto.

The object of wedlock was always to marry into a "good" family, implying either a good genealogical table or at least a comfortable inheritance. Yet even if Michelangelo insisted to his nephew that the Buonarroti were "citizens descended from noble lineage," specifically from the Counts of Canossa, he warned the young man to marry the girl and not the dowry (IX-16). The family was important, he cautioned, for whenever a girl "without a family" associated with courtiers, she became a whore. The arranged marriage of suitability *(convenance)* was common, especially among the noble classes. Such a union for a son was proposed in a letter from Czar Boris Godunov to Queen Elizabeth, a political proposal which becomes amusing when the Czar asks specifically if the English ward is related to her father or her mother Anne Boleyn (IX-21).

An unequal marriage was that of John Donne with the young daughter of the aristocratic Sir George More, Chancellor of the Garter, etc. Donne's letter of apprisal to his new father-in-law rightly predicted More's anger and vindictiveness (IX-22). Marriage without parental consent was not only an explosive issue in the Renaissance—Rabelais fulminated against it and Shakespeare illustrated its dangers in *Romeo and Juliet*—but was one of the abuses which the Reformation found in the system of the confessional and autonomy of individual priests. Donne was punished for thus challenging parental authority over a minor.

Platonic love was not necessarily based on pederasty or homophilia, but much pederasty went on in its name. Like heterosexual love, it could be sacred or profane. The expression of Platonic love in the sonnets of Shakespeare or the poetry and prose of Michelangelo to Tommaso Cavalieri encourages the modern reader to assume a chaste relationship, even when the sculptor distills the most ingenuous declarations of love (IX-5). On the other hand, the skeptical Aretino who chided Michelangelo on the latter's relations with Cavalieri and with the young Gherardo Perini (III-13), apparently a model, holds the scornful view that Platonists are effeminates whose sexual debility makes them what they are, scarcely capable of "one volley a year" (IX-14).

Antifeminism, a legacy of the Middle Ages, remained curiously alive in the Renaissance, with witch-burning the most scandalous evidence of it (IV-4 and IV-14). Few misogynists were so explicit as Doctor Rondibilis in Rabelais, defining women as "the excrement of nature," or Rabelais himself, declaring the female pudenda the most cheap and available material for rebuilding the walls of Paris. In his letter to the eternal playboy, Mosén Rubín, Fray Antonio de Guevara views affairs with women as a source of everlasting annoyances (IX-3). The same Erasmus who in an unguarded moment had enthused over the perfumed kisses of the court ladies in England (VI-2), rejoiced in a letter to Robert Fisher over his single-blessedness, whether the result of accident or choice. Aretino complained that one has to pay for love the price of sleepless nights and disdainful days, and that women require more patience than Job's (IX-10), granting that it is less a mistake to take an expendable mistress than a wife. He believed in making love at least forty times a month, even in maturity: "An old man in love is like a youth without the youth's wildness and folly" (IX-14). To accomplish this goal he deigned the company of mistresses and whores, especially his favorite call-girl Angela Zaffetta (IX-11). His concupiscence and sophisticated standards did not however extend his taste and activities to include transvestites, male or female (IX-15).

In this period when the archetypal male chauvinist, Don Juan Tenorio, was born, it is hard to pick the most conspicuous exploiter of women. The most highborn of the Don Juans, outpointing his "cousins" Francis I and Henri IV, was surely Henry VIII. Various letters follow the course of his relations with Anne Boleyn. A letter from the Spanish ambassador to London relates early the pressures of Anne on Henry to divorce Catherine of Aragon (IX-4). A subsequent letter of Henry anticipates their next tryst and the pleasure of kissing her "pritty duckys" (IX-6). The tragic aftermath is sounded in Anne's letter from the Tower still protesting her fervence of love and loyalty and entertaining a fading hope that she will not undergo the axe (IX-8). An unexpected postscript to these letters is that of Thomas Wyatt, specifying to King Henry that he too had played with the duckys in question (IX-9). Elizabeth, the daughter of this tragic union, inherited Henry's sexual chauvinism, and when she dropped a would-be husband or lover like Essex, Leicester, or the Duke of Anjou (IX-19), her words carried the brittle crack of a whip.

We have proposed Henri IV of France, whose love affairs won him the admiring title of the *vert galant,* as contender for the title of male chauvinist. A study of his abundant love letters shows a Latin temperament busily at work. "I kiss your hands a million times" frequently closes them. For the benefit of apprentices in this art, we enclose a typical letter to his great love Gabrielle d'Estrées, who had mastered the art of keeping him guessing (IX-20). Gossip around the courts being what it was, Gabrielle was aware that when Henri was campaigning in the field, he liked to stagger his ladies one at a time every couple of days, as his letters make clear.

Although a select few in the Renaissance carried their orgies to epic proportions, as when Alexander VI and Lucrezia Borgia spent a night sharing fifty Roman whores, such memorable feats were discreetly omitted from letters. Similarly, incest in high circles was not divulged in writing, leaving us wishing for more details on the Cenci scandal. One exception is a careless letter from Marguerite de Navarre to her brother Francis I which the latter neglected to burn (IX-2).

It is to the honor of the Renaissance that during the last phase of what was called *la querelle des femmes* there were more books upholding or idealizing women than continuing the threadbare attacks on them. Many of the great ladies appearing in the present volume—Vittoria Colonna, Marguerite de Navarre, Teresa of Avila, Beatrice Sforza, and of course Elizabeth Regina—did much to elevate the status of their sex.

IX-1   Niccolò Machiavelli to Francesco Vettori

Niccolò Machiavelli (1469-1527) describes his passion for an unnamed mistress. Francesco Vettori was ambassador to the Pope, appointed by the Medici government.

Florence, 3 August, 1514

You, my friend, have with many accounts of your love at Rome kept me all rejoicing, and you have removed from my mind countless worries, through my reading and thinking of your pleasures and your angers, because one is not good without the other. And truly Fortune has brought me to a place where I can render you just recompense for it, because being at my farm I have encountered a creature so gracious, so delicate, so noble, both by nature and environment, that I cannot praise her so much or love her so much that she would not deserve more. I ought to tell you, as you did me, the beginning of this love, with what nets he took me, where he spread them, of what sort they were; and you would see that they were nets of gold, spread among flowers, woven by Venus, so pleasant and easy that though a villainous heart might have broken them, nonetheless I did not wish to, and for a bit I enjoyed myself in them, until the tender threads became hard and secured with knots beyond untying.

And you should not believe that Love, in order to take me, has used ordinary methods, because knowing that they would not have been enough for him, he used extraordinary ones, of which I knew nothing, and from which I could not protect myself. May it be enough for you that, already near fifty years, neither do these suns harm me, nor do rough roads tire me, nor the dark hours of the night frighten me. Everything to me seems level, and to all her desires, even though unlike mine and opposed to what mine ought to be, I adapt myself. And though I seem to have entered into great labor, nevertheless I feel in it such sweetness, both through what the face so wonderful and soft brings me, and also through having laid aside the memory of all my troubles, that for anything in the world, being able to free myself, I would not wish it. I have abandoned, then, the thoughts of affairs that are great and serious; I do not any more take delight in reading ancient things or in discussing modern ones; they all are turned into soft conversations, for which I thank Venus and all Cyprus.* So if it occurs to you to write anything about the lady, write it, and of the other things talk with those who estimate them higher and understand them better, because I never have found in them anything but harm, and in these of love always good and pleasure. Farewell.

Your Niccolò Machiavelli.

---

* Cyprus or Cytherea was the island of Aphrodite.

IX-2   Marguerite of Navarre to her brother King Francis I of France

The tenacious rumor that Marguerite de Navarre (1492-1549) had an incestuous relationship with her brother, King Francis, is supported by this desperate appeal that he allow her on some false pretext to visit him. Since she was married to the Duke of Alençon at the time, her brother cut off the signature from this letter and possibly burned others as requested.

1521

To the King, my Sovereign Lord,

Sire, what it pleased you to write me—that in subsequent letters you would tell me that I want to know—has sustained me and moreover allowed me to hope that you would not wish to abandon your straight road to flee those who, as the governor of their fortune, wish to see you, even if for bad or worse. Let my intention be forbidden if you will never again need the frank and longtime servitude which I have borne and bear to Your fortunate and kind Grace. And if the total imperfection of a hundred thousand faults makes you disdain my obeisance, at least, Sire, do me the honour and goodness as not to increase my lamentable misery by demanding experience for defeat, there where you know that without your assistance is only helplessness; as a token I am sending you will testify, requesting you simply for the ending of my misfortunes and the beginning of a new year that you kindly be for me just a fraction of what you are infinitely to me, and always remain in my thoughts.

Awaiting the good fortune of being able to see you and speak with you, Sire, my anxiety over this constrains me humbly to beg you—unless this be a bore to you—to give answer through the bearer, and I shall leave here forthwith, feigning some occasion or other. There is no wretched weather or painful highway which will not be converted for me into a most pleasant and agreeable relaxation if you will oblige me so much—too much, to you—and even more so if you will please bury my letters in the fire and my words in silence. Otherwise you would render

Worse than death my sorrowful life,
Living with my only hope in you,
The knowledge of which brings me assurance
Without my ever mistrusting you.
And if my hand supplicates too feebly,
Your kindness will excuse its ignorance,
    Worse than dead. . .

Your very humble and very obedient
more than subject and servant.

(trans. R. J. C.)

IX-3   Fray Antonio de Guevara to Mosén Rubín

The sexagenarian playboy Mosén Rubín, who has for decades recited to Fray Antonio (1480-1545) his triumphs and trials with the fair sex, is here reminded by the churchman that Rubín is now too old for such pursuits and that the latter should give up his new young mistress.

3 March, 1527

Magnificent Lord and veteran innamorato,

On reading and rereading your letter, I recalled that it was from my old neighbor Mosén Rubín, the innamorato. I remember that once when we were playing chess in my inn you were willing to give away your queen to me, but I don't remember that you ever let me even see your mistress . . . And I remember that when we were in Játiva, I advised and even persuaded you to abandon to the devil those mistresses you recall, because they were annoying, dangerous, and expensive. I remember that once when we were in Algeciras, you said to me between sighs and tears you couldn't drive them from your mind or heart, and I had once again to swear and forswear that they were not loves able to agree with or suit you. I remember that when we met by chance in Torres Torres I asked you how those loves had turned out, you answered me that it had been only with great sorrow and travail, since you had escaped them stabbed, bored, ridiculed, defamed, and even robbed.

In this present letter you write me that you are in love once again, and since I spoke truthfully to you about the early love affairs, I shall write you my frank opinion about this new one, certain that I shall be able to stay your blood and bind your wounds. I wish that you were asking me, Mosén Rubín, about some other subject, for speaking frankly, you are no longer of an age to be chasing after loves nor is it my business to be writing you about them. My habit, my profession, my authority, and my charge make it fitting for you to ask for confession rather than for remedies for love. In truth, love should not be seeking us out and offering itself, for you are old and I am a churchman. Believe me, my Lord, you may be sure that these are not loves, but pains; not happiness, but unfulfillable desires; not diversion, but confusion. This is always true when the lover has neither youth nor freedom nor liberality . . .

I should like to know why a man over sixty like yourself, plagued with mange and gout, wishes to take a young and beautiful mistress who will keep busier robbing you than bestowing her favors. Why do you wish a mistress when the only way you will be able to serve her is to tie her ribbons and shoo flies from her? . . . Why do you wish a mistress who will never darken your door unless you keep giving her money, to whom you won't dare deny whatever she asks for, or complain of the annoyances she causes you? A mistress who will run your household in any mad way she pleases, who will praise you only to get favors from you, before whom you will have to seem gay even when your gout is raging with pain, who will have wasted your fortune before revealing her true self, whom you will shower with gifts only to have her finally leave you.

If you wish to fall in love in these conditions, good luck to you—and you will need a lot of luck—because at your age and weakness, it would be better to have a male companion to pass your time with than a mistress who will only molest you.

No more, except to hope that God may preserve thee from an evil mistress, and cure you of your gout.

(trans. R. J. C.)

IX-4   Ambassador Chapuys to the Emperor Charles V

From a code-letter of the Spanish Ambassador to the Emperor (see VII-8) we learn of the pressures exerted by Anne Boleyn and her relatives the Duke and Duchess of Norfolk to discredit her enemy Cardinal Wolsey and to force the amorous Henry VIII to divorce Catherine of Aragon, the Emperor's aunt. Given the impossible task of obtaining an annulment from an unwilling Pope, Wolsey's downfall was inevitable. He died of illness while being led to the Tower just two days after the following letter was written. Thomas More had already succeeded him as Chancellor.

London, 27 November, 1530

Sire, within the last few days a present of poultry has been sent to the Queen by the Duchess of Norfolk, and with it an orange, in which was enclosed a letter from Gregory Cassal * which I deem proper to send to your Majesty. The Queen thinks, that the Duchess sent her this present of her own accord, and out of the love she bears her, but I fear it was done with the knowledge of her husband; at all events this seems to open a way for the Queen to communicate secretly with her more easily.

Eight days ago the King ordered the Cardinal to be brought here; on hearing which, the said Cardinal abstained from food for several days. It is said that he hoped rather to end his life in this manner than in a more ignominious and dishonourable one, of which he had some fears; and in consequence of this abstinence he has been taken ill on the road, and is not yet arrived. They say also, that a lodging is prepared for him in the Tower, in the same part that the Duke of Buckingham occupied; many reasons are assigned for his arrest, but they are all mere conjectures.

A gentleman told me, that a short time ago, the King was complaining to his Council of something that had not been done according to his wish, and exclaimed

---

* Gregory Cassal, one of Henry's VIII's ministers at the papal court. Henry VIII and Catherine were at this time pressing their own views of a divorce or annulment upon the Pope. Catherine's were obviously opposed to either course.

in great wrath, that the Cardinal was a very different man from any of *them*, for conducting all things properly; and having repeated the same twice over, he left them in displeasure. Since this time the Duke, *the Lady*, [Ann], and the Father have never ceased plotting against the said Cardinal, and the lady especially, who has wept and lamented over her lost time and honour, and threatened the King that she would go away. They say the King has had enough to do to quiet her, and even though he entreated her most affectionately, and with tears in his eyes, not to leave him, nothing would satisfy her but the arrest of the Cardinal. The pretext given out, was, that he had written to Rome to be reinstated in his possessions, and to France for support and credit, that he was beginning to resume his former splendid habits of living and that he was trying to corrupt the people. Now, however, they have got the physician of the said Cardinal into their hands, and have discovered what they looked for.

The said physician, ever since the second day of his coming here, has been, and still is, treated as a prince in the house of the Duke of Norfolk, which clearly shews that he has been singing to the right tune.

Johan Jocquin would not say a word about it to the Pope's Nuncio who interrogated him very closely, but he told the Venetian Ambassador, that by the Doctor's own confession the Cardinal had solicited the Pope to excommunicate the King, and to lay an interdict on the Kingdom if the King did not dismiss the lady from court, and treat the Queen with proper respect. By this means he hoped, it is said, to cause a rising throughout the country against the Government, and in the confusion to seize upon the management of affairs again himself.

IX-5   Michelangelo Buonarroti to Tommaso Cavalieri

The artist felt a great Platonic love for the aristocratic young Tommaso Cavalieri, for whom he executed several allegorical sketches on the theme of love. Michelangelo (1475-1564) drew up three versions of the following letter sent to Cavalieri on New Year's Day, 1533.

Without due consideration, Messer Tomao, my very dear Lord, I was moved to write to your Lordship, not by way of answer to any letter received from you, but being myself the first to make advances, as though I felt bound to cross a little stream with dry feet, or a ford made manifest by paucity of water. But now that I have left the shore, instead of the trifling water I expected, the ocean with its towering waves appears before me, so that, if it were possible, in order to avoid drowning, I should gladly retrace my steps to the dry land whence I started. Still, as I am here, I will e'en make of my heart a rock, and proceed further; and if I shall not display the art of sailing on the sea of your powerful genius, that genius itself will excuse me, nor will be disdainful of my inferiority in parts, nor desire from me that which I do not possess, inasmuch as he who is unique in all things can have peers in none. Therefore your Lordship, the light of our century without paragon upon this world, is unable to be satisfied with the productions of other men, having no match or equal to yourself. And if, peradventure, something of mine, such as I hope and promise to perform, give pleasure to your mind, I shall esteem it more fortunate than excellent; and should I ever be sure of pleasing your Lordship, as is said, in any particular, I will devote the present time and all my future to your service; indeed, it will grieve me much that I cannot regain the past, in order to devote a longer space to you than the future only will allow, seeing I am now too old. I have no more to say. Read the heart and not the letter, because "the pen toils after man's good will in vain."

I have to make excuses for expressing in my first letter a marvelous astonishment at your rare genius; and thus I do so, having recognized the error I was in; for it is much the same to wonder at God's working miracles as to wonder at Rome's producing divine men. Of this the universe confirms us in our faith.

It would be permissible to give the name of the things a man presents, to him who receives them; but proper sense of what is fitting prevents its being done in this letter.

(As illustrated by Aretino's letter, III-13, contemporaries failed to understand the chaste nature of the artist's love for young Cavalieri, who married while remaining a dear friend of Michelangelo whose eyes he closed in death.)

IX-6   King Henry VIII of England to Anne Boleyn

Anne Boleyn (1507-1536) was not a beauty, but her fascination was such
that Henry VIII (1491-1547) was willing to wrench his kingdom from papal
authority in order to obtain a divorce from Catherine of Aragon in 1533 and
marry Anne. Evidence of the King's ardor is apparent in the following letter.

(1533)

Myne awne Sweetheart, this shall be to advertise you of the great ellingness [1] that
I find here since your departing, for I ensure you, me thinketh the Tyme longer
since your departing now last than I was wont to do a whole Fortnight; I think
your Kindness and my Fervence of Love causeth it, for otherwise I wolde not
thought it possible, that for so little a while it should have grieved me, but now that
I am comeing toward you, me thinketh my Pains by half released, and also I am
right well comforted, insomuch that my Book maketh substantially for my Matter,
in writing whereof I have spent above IIII Hours this Day, which caused me now
write the shorter Letter to you at this Tyme, because of some Payne in my Head,
wishing my self (specially an Evening) in my Sweethearts Armes whose pritty
Duckys [2] I trust shortly to kysse. Writne with the Hand of him that was, is, and
shall be yours by his will,

H.R.

1. tedium
2. breasts

IX-7   Sir Thomas More to his Daughter Margaret

While imprisoned in the Tower for having upheld the Roman Catholic Church in defiance of Henry VIII, Sir Thomas More (1478-1535) scribbled the following note "wyth a cole" to his daughter Margaret Roper. He was beheaded on July 7, 1535, and canonized four hundred years later.

1535.

Myne own good doughter,—

Our Lorde be thanked I am in good helthe of bodye, and in good quiet of minde: and of all worldly thynges I no more desyer than I have. I beseche hym make you all mery in the hope of heuven. And such thynges as I somewhat longed to talke with you all, concerning the worlde to come, our Lorde put theim into your myndes, as I truste he dothe and better to by hys holy spirite: who blesse you and preserve you all. Written wyth a cole by your tender loving father, who in hys pore prayers forgetteth none of you all, nor your babes, nor your nurses, nor your good husbandes, nor your good husbandes' shrewde wyves, nor your fathers shrewde wyfe neither, nor our other frendes. And thus fare ye hartely well for lacke of paper.

Thomas More, Knight.

(See also Letter V-9 for further evidences of the stoicism of Sir Thomas More.)

IX-8   Queen Anne Boleyn to King Henry VIII

Sentenced unjustly to the Tower in 1536, while her husband prepared to wed Jane Seymour, Anne Boleyn made a desperate appeal to Henry's conscience. The following entreaty was of no avail—"Queen Anne Lack-Head," as she ruefully dubbed herself, was executed—but ultimately she had her revenge: her daughter became Queen Elizabeth of England.

6 May, 1536

Sir, Your Grace's Displeasure, and my Imprisonment, are Things so strange unto me, as what to Write, or what to Excuse, I am altogether ignorant. Whereas you send unto me (willing me to confess a Truth, and to obtain your Favour) by such an one whom you know to be mine ancient professed Enemy; I no sooner received this Message by him, than I rightly conceived your Meaning; and if, as you say, confessing a Truth indeed may procure my safety, I shall with all Willingness and Duty perform your Command.

But let not your Grace ever imagine that your poor Wife will ever be brought to acknowledge a Fault, where not so much as a Thought thereof proceeded. And to speak a truth, never Prince had Wife more Loyal in all Duty, and in all true Affection, than you have ever found in *Anne Boleyn,* with which Name and Place I could willingly have contented my self, if God, and your Grace's Pleasure had been so pleased. Neither did I at any time so far forget my self in my Exaltation, or received Queenship, but that I always looked for such an Alteration as now I find; for the ground of my Preferment being on no surer Foundation than your Grace's Fancy, the least Alteration, I knew, was fit and sufficient to draw that Fancy to some other Subject. You have chosen me, from a low Estate, to be your Queen and Companion, far beyond my Desert or Desire. If then you found me worthy of such Honour, Good your Grace let not any light Fancy, or bad Councel of mine Enemies, withdraw your Princely Favour from me; neither let that Stain, that unworthy Stain of a Disloyal Heart towards your good Grace, ever cast so foul a Blot on your most Dutiful Wife, and the Infant Princess your Daughter:

Try me good King, but let me have a Lawful Trial, and let not my sworn

Enemies sit as my Accusers and Judges; yea, let me receive an open Trial, for my Truth shall fear no open shame; then shall you see, either mine Innocency cleared, your Suspicion and Conscience satisfied, the Ignominy and Slander of the World stopped, or my Guilt openly declared. So that whatsoever God or you may determine of me, your Grace may be freed from an open Censure; and mine Offence being so lawfully proved, your Grace is at liberty, both before God and Man, not only to execute worthy Punishment on me as an unlawful Wife, but to follow your Affection already settled on that Party, for whose sake I am now as I am, whose Name I could some good while since have pointed unto: Your Grace being not ignorant of my Suspicion therein.

But if you have already determined of me, and that not only my Death, but an Infamous Slander must bring you the enjoying of your desired Happiness; then I desire of God, that he will pardon your great Sin therein, and likewise mine Enemies, the Instruments thereof; and that he will not call you to a strict Account for your unprincely and cruel usage of me, at his General Judgment-Seat, where both you and my self must shortly appear, and in whose Judgment, I doubt not, (whatsoever the World may think of me) mine Innocence shall be openly known, and sufficiently cleared.

My last and only Request shall be, That my self may only bear the Burthen of your Grace's Displeasure, and that it may not touch the Innocent Souls of those poor Gentlemen, who (as I understand) are likewise in strait Imprisonment for my sake. If ever I have found favour in your Sight; if ever the Name of *Anne Boleyn* hath been pleasing in your Ears, then let me obtain this Request; and I will so leave to trouble your Grace any further, with mine earnest Prayers to the Trinity to have your Grace in his good keeping, and to direct you in all your Actions. From my doleful Prison in the *Tower,* this 6th of *May.*

Your most Loyal and ever Faithful Wife,
Ann Boleyn

IX-9   Thomas Wyatt to King Henry VIII

Although Thomas Wyatt (1503-1542) was a personal friend of Henry VIII, he had been an intimate of Anne Boleyn before Henry's infatuation with her. Unlike the other lovers of Anne with whom he was arrested in 1536, he was not executed. From prison he allegedly wrote the following letter to which his biographer Kenneth Muir attributes "some basis in fact."

London, 1536

Your Majesty knows that before you married Queen Anne Boleyn you said to me: "Wyatt, I wish to marry Anne Boleyn; what do you think about it?" And I told your Majesty that you should not do it, and you asked me why, and I said she was a bad woman. Your Majesty, in wrath, ordered me not to appear before you for two years. You refused to ask me my reasons, and since I could not then tell you by word of mouth, I shall do so now in writing. It happened that one day when the Lady Anne's father and mother were in the court eight miles from Greenwich, where, as everybody knows, they had taken up residence, that night I took horse and went there. I arrived when Anne Boleyn was in bed, and went up to her chamber. When she saw me she said: "Lord! Master Wyatt, what are you doing here at such a late hour?" I replied: "Lady, this heart of mine, which is so tormented, has been yours for so long that for love of you it has brought me here into your presence, thinking to receive consolation from the one who for so long has caused it such suffering." And I went up to her as she lay in bed and kissed her, and she lay still and said nothing. I touched her breasts, and she lay still, and even when I took liberties lower down she likewise said nothing. I began to undress, but before I had finished I heard a great stamping above her bedchamber, and straightway the lady got up and put on a skirt and climbed a staircase which was behind her bed. I waited for her more than an hour, and when she came down she would not let me approach her. I believe that the same thing happened to me as to a gentleman in Italy who, like me, was madly in love with a lady and, as fortune would have it, found himself in the same situation. The lady heard a stamping, got up, and went upstairs. That gentleman was more prudent than I was, for shortly after the lady had gone up, he followed her, and found her lying with a groom. And I believe that this happened to me on that occasion, and if I had been as prudent, I should have seen what she did. And I tell your Majesty that within a week I had my way with her, and if your Majesty, when you banished me, had permitted me to speak, I should have told you what I now write.

IX-10   Pietro Aretino to Ambrogio degli Eusebii

In a declaration of unrestrained misogyny, Pietro Aretino (1492-1556) warns Ambrogio degli Eusebii, a minor poet and one of his secretaries, to avoid marriage at all costs.

Venice, 1 June, 1537

I thought, my son, that I was teaching you the art of poetry, but I find that I was staking your efforts to put on a ball and chain. I believed that I was going to hear your verses, but I was treated to a lover's lament.

Come, come! You would make less of a mistake if you get yourself a mistress than you would if you took a wife. I assure you that I am very sorry for you. If a man falls in love and is not rich, he is headed for every kind of calamity.

But all this comes from not taking my advice. I warned you to resist the first assaults of love. It is a frenzy that begins by making you satisfy your lustful desires and ends with your repenting the pleasures you had. As for marrying, the lucky fellow is the one who says that he is going to marry and not the one who really does.

Do you know who ought to take wives? Those who wish to be taught how to be more patient than Job. For if a man can put up with a wife's falseness in his own house, he has learned how to bear insults when he is abroad, and is indeed king of long suffering.

If your wife-to-be is as beautiful as you say she is, you will have a hard time to be sure of her. If she is a scarecrow, you must want to make yourself a slave of repentance. And the more you boast that she has virtue enough the more you cast doubts upon your own sense, for, as all women know, music, songs and letters are the key you need to unlock the gates of their chastity. They do not regard marriage as necessary to this or even holy.

But when they are rewarded with children, they want the solace of a sacrament. But why should you dishonor the revered name of father by wishing to be one when you are still a graceless son?

The worst thing about marriage is the ease and security that you will bring your wife, but which she can not bring you. Indeed your carefree bed will become a slave to arguments and a charity ward for quarrels.

So show that you have at last grown up—unless you wish to be a callow youth forever. Leave the heavy burden of a wife to those who have the shoulders of an Atlas. Leave her nagging to the ears of tradesmen. Leave her notions to someone who knows how to beat her or can put up with them. Gather the laurel branches of honor—don't hang yourself from them as a man does when women are untrue to him. Come and go from your own house without having to say: "To whom am I handing her over now, and with whom will I find her when I get back?" Come and go without having to grind your teeth in jealousy. Be able to appear in church and in the piazzas without fear of that whispering which follows every husband of every wife that ever lived. And if you must have a son and heir, beget him on some other man's wife.

You may feel remorse because this is adultery. Then do the most you can to make your son legitimate with kindness and with virtue. For every kind thing you do and every virtuous one removes some of the stigma from his birth, and makes men forget his mother's sin.

But when the day comes when continence has mastered all your lusts, then I will really praise your sense and urge you to take comfort in Poetry. You are already in debt to her for she gave you a name before you deserved to be famous. Love her and embrace her. If you do not you will betray your own fame which is already beginning to grow wings. Are you not ashamed, then, even to think of losing your eternal glory for the sensual pleasures of Woman, whose beauty only lasts a day?

IX-11   Pietro Aretino to Angela Zaffetta

Aretino pays tribute to Angela Zaffetta, once the mistress of Cardinal Ippolito de' Medici, an honorable whore whose virtues place her far above all others of her profession.

Venice, 15 December, 1537

Even though Rumor, pretending that she really knows something, has gone about Italy spreading the report that in your person and by your doings, Love has done me wrong, the truth is that I have always held your favor to be a fine thing since there is no fraud in anything which you do.

Indeed, I give you the palm among all those of your kind there ever were. More than anyone else you know how to put the mask of decency upon the face of lust, gaining by your wisdom and discretion both riches and praise.

You do not use your wiles—which are the essence of a harlot's trade—to betray men, but rather with such skill that he who spends his money on you, swears he is the gainer. It would not be possible to describe the charms with which you win new friends, nor the means you employ to draw to your house those who are doubtful and hesitate between a *yes* and a *no*. It would be difficult even to imagine the effort you make to keep the affection of those who have become your servants.

You distribute so well your kisses, your caresses, your laughter and your bed sharings that no one ever hears anyone quarrel nor curse at you nor complain. Modest in your demands, you take what is given you without trying to appropriate what is not. Your anger only comes at the right time, yet you are not anxious to become known as "the mistress of flatteries," nor, either, to keep people dancing on a string. You hold in contempt all those who study the devices of Nanna and of Pippa.*

You are not suspicious when there is no need to be suspicious, thus making people jealous who never even thought of it. You do not pull woes and consolations from your pocket, nor, pretending that you are in love, do you die and come to life again whenever you wish.

You do not rowel the flanks of gullible suitors with the spurs of your serving maids whom you have taught to swear that you do not eat, drink, sleep or find any peace on their account, and whom you make assert that you had come near to hanging yourself because your lover visited another lady. By God no, you are not one of those who are always ready with tears, and who, when they do weep, mingle their weeping with certain little sighs and sobs which come all too easily from the heart, the while they scratch their heads and bite their fingers with an "Alas! So be it!" in a hoarse and scarce-heard voice. Nor do you busy yourself with keeping those who want to go, while sending off the ones who long to stay. There is no place in your soul for such niggling deceits.

Your womanly wisdom moves, rather, in a royal manner, nor is feminine gossip to your taste, nor do you gather around you frivolous ladies and conceited men. Those who deal honorably rejoice in your gentle beauty which makes you shine in a most rare fashion. Your hopes remain unshaken that you will attain a position in which you can triumph over the things which you must do.

Lying, envy, and slander—once again the innate characteristics of a harlot—do not keep your mind and your tongue in a constant turmoil. You caress virtue and adore the virtuous. This is something which is usually a stranger to the habits and the nature of those who, for a price, yield to the desires of others.

And so I give myself to your ladyship, feeling that your ladyship is worthy.

IX-12   Nicolaus Copernicus to Bishop Dantiscus of Ermland

For daring to suggest that the sun, not the earth, was the center of the universe, Nicolaus Copernicus (1473-1543) came under fire from the Catholic church whose harassment began with an unusual demand from

---

* In Aretino's volume called *Sei Giornate,* three dialogues transcribe the whore Nanna's counsels to Pippa on the profession of prostitution, on the ways men trick women, and the art of pandering.

Bishop Dantiscus of Ermland: for his own moral salvation, the elderly astronomer (who was also a canon of Frauenberg) was told to dismiss his young lady housekeeper, Anna Schillings. After the order had been given a second time, Copernicus formed a submissive reply. Contrast this tormentor of Copernicus with the enlightened prelate of Letter IV-8.

2 December, 1538

Highly Reverend etc. etc.

The admonition of Your Reverence is fatherly enough, and more than fatherly, as I admit; and I read its contents with all my heart. I have by no means forgotten your previous remonstrance which Your Reverence at first had sent out in general terms: I wanted to do what I was ordered; and although it was not easy to find a closely related and honest person, I nevertheless resolved to put an end to the thing at fasting time. In order that Your Reverence will not imagine that I am looking for pretexts for postponement, I have limited the term to one month; verily it could not be shorter as Your Reverence yourself can readily understand. For I wish to the measure of my strength to prevent that I become an offense to good morals, and even less so to Your Reverence, who deserves that he be revered, respected and above all beloved by me; to which I devote myself with all my talents.

Your Reverence's
most obedient
Nicolaus Copernicus.

IX-13   Cardinal Bembo to his Daughter Elena

Cardinal Pietro Bembo (1470-1547) counsels his daughter Elena that a modest young lady should not aspire to study a musical instrument.

10 December 1541

I am pleased you are well, as you write me, and that your brother is applying himself diligently to his studies, all of which will redound to his honor and profit.

As for the favor you ask of me, that I agree to your learning to play the monochord: I would have you understand something which perhaps at your tender age you can't be expected to know: that playing is a thing for vain and frivolous women. And I want you to be the most serious or the most chaste and virtuous woman alive.* Besides, if you should learn to play poorly, your playing would bring you little pleasure and not a little shame. You won't succeed in playing well unless you spend ten or twelve years practicing, without ever thinking of anything else. You can consider for yourself all this before you, without my telling you. So, don't think any more about it, and try to be humble, good, wise and obedient; and don't let yourself be carried away by these desires; oppose them instead with a firm mind, and if your girlfriends want you to learn to play in order to give them pleasure, tell them that you don't wish to afford them an opportunity to laugh at the expense of your shame. And be satisfied to practice reading and sewing; if you can perform these two skills well, you will have accomplished not a little.

Thank those ladies for the prayers they are offering for me: for this I am much obliged to them. Stay well and greet Lucia.

(trans. L.L.)

IX-14   Pietro Aretino to Gianbattista Fossa

In a paean to his own virility, Aretino celebrates the "Gather Ye Rosebuds" philosophy as a means of cheating time.

December, 1547

Worthy Signor Gianbattista, Titian, who is as much our brother as we are his, told you the truth when he told you that I was living the gay life no differently than I would have if even now the locks of my beard sprouted from my chin black, just as they grow from my temples pure white. I live this way because it seems to me that so living I take a revenge upon time by making a jest of his years in the same way that I revenge myself upon Fortune by despising her lavish gifts.

I am aware that philosophical bigwigs will call me mad for this. They will swear that I lack the decorum of gravity which spits round, and of the prudence which speaks slowly. If they do, tell them they have it wrong. There is not a pedagogue

---

* It is well known that Bembo courted—without success—the notorious Lucrezia Borgia, to whom he dedicated *Gli Asolani*.

who would say out of the corner of his mouth that I was shallow and trivial just because he saw me make a show of all the lively conduct which my vigorous nature permits me. There is not one who would call me a stupid clown for making light of the world since I always do so with due fear of God.

I grant you that the young should always spend their time having a good look at life, and that the old should think about the salvation of their souls. But beyond that the latter should not have any more dealings with staid deportment than I do. For do not gaffers who laugh at their age, teach the young to give up some of the harlotries of youth?

For my part, it seems that every hour I spend in youthful escapades, lifts ten hundredweight from the burden of my years until my shoulders scarcely feel the weight of their so bestial load. Indeed, I am still struggling to conjure up a figure of speech that can be used to describe the way I feel when a servant girl of twenty-five carats presses me to her thighs. By our faith, when I but see one of these wild creatures, all milk and vermilion, my senses, my spirits, my very vitals revive. Reviving, they live again. Living again, they are aroused. And aroused, they leap into flame just like a log of wood, which has not entirely burned out, does, when that blowing mechanism begins to fan it with its breeze. When I have done my business, I am like a tree which somebody has cut down for firewood so that he can warm himself, and then sees it burst out into leaves and buds.

I do not deny that there are Platonic steers who in their decrepitude scarce can afford the luxury of one small volley a year, but if I did not draw a bow at this handmaiden or that at least forty times a month, I would hold myself to be all washed out. I swear to you by the holy symbol of the blessed etc. that even as I write these words, here comes one of them, and then two, in such manner, that by the body of unafraid Cupid, I must stop now, and not until I have left them, can I return to you.

But to get back to what I am talking about. After I had consummated matrimony with one of these ladies, she said to me: "Get away with you! Would you trust an old man yourself? What kind of a joke did you make in your comedy when you said that old men are the eunuchs of time? What a hard matter this is! What a solid piece of news! You would do better to think about death."

And I to her: "Light of my life, an old man's thinking about dying is the horse upon which Death rides posthaste to take him the sooner to his grave, but not thinking about it is the tribute which the years pay to the days of their living."

That is why neither after breakfast, nor before dinner, nor at any hour, do I turn away from one of them. I am able to do this because of the health which I have gotten by the grace of God and as a gift from nature. What youth is there who cannot be called old if he is ailing? What old man cannot be called young when he is well?

I forgot to say this to you. If a single black hair among all those which hang down makes your face seem ten years younger, how many years will a carefree fancy erase?

The unique painter whom I mentioned above, grieved greatly when to my good health I attributed my ability to do that thing. For in his case, neither stomach nor loins nor kidneys nor gout nor erysipelas nor any other ailment has ever wronged him, but only that which without ever rising from its seat, always sits down again. If that ever happened to me, the nurse who gives milk to the daughter which was born to me only a few days ago, would not have come to me for the money I owe her. I will get me gone forever if others are not born to me too.

No, I will not give up following pleasure because of my age, for an old man in love is like a youth without the youth's wildness and folly.

In conclusion, let me say this. I, who never hated any man when I was young, can not keep from loving any woman now that I am old.

IX-15　Pietro Aretino to La Zufolina

The sexual ambiguities of La Zufolina, "My Lady Chatterbox," a courtesan who once had an affair with Alessandro de' Medici, alternately repel and attract Aretino.

March, 1548

Twice my good fortune has sent your fair person into that house which is mine and others—the first time as a woman dressed like a man and the next time, as a man dressed like a woman. You are a man when you are chanced on from behind and a woman when seen from in front. I say this because *extra muros* you bemerde the world with your *billet-doux*, but within you drench the heavens as from a hot furnace. Now please understand me right-side-up even if I say everything upside-down. Your showing yourself sometimes visibly and sometimes invisibly has made me neglect the intellect of my tongue for the fantasy of my pen.

Certain it is that nature has so compounded you of both sexes that in one moment you show yourself a male and in the next a female. Indeed, Duke Alessandro did not wish to sleep with you for any other reason than to find out if you were a hermaphrodite in reality or merely in jest. For look you, you talk like a fair lady and act like a pageboy. Anybody who did know you would think that you were now the rider and now the steed—i.e. now a nymph and now a shepherd; that is, now active and now passive.

What more can I say? Even the clothes which you wear upon your back, and which you are always changing, leave it an open question whether my she-chatterbox is really a he-chatterbox, or whether my he-chatterbox is really a she-one. Meanwhile, even Dukes and Duchesses are diverted by the entertainment of that very salty, very spicy prattle of yours. Vaporishly it escapes from your lips. Your conversation is like pine-nut tartlets, like honey on the comb, like marchpane, to those who find it amusing. Neither Florence nor Ferrara would want you to be a housecat, who are a sly fox amid the hens and roosters.

Old Time is the fellow who rusts, wears out, consumes, devours, corrupts, ruins, unhinges, foreshortens, breaks, lops away, cuts short, unmakes, spoils and slaughters everything, but he would not dare get into a contest with you. In proof of this, try to recall the very visage, the very face, the very appearance which you had ten years ago! You have them still today!

Away with wrinkles! Get thee away from me, catarrh! Leave rheumy eye to those wish them! And haven't I the right to say this to you? Last night I dreamt I did that thing with you, I hung you on the hook, I drove an auger through your ladle with such a comedy of sport, with such a farce of japery, with such an eclogue of titillations that there is not a lustful priest, lewd friar or concupiscent nun who would not have exchanged the love notes of their youth for the conjugation of your old age with mine.

But our dreams would make us stand before the world like very fools if we were willing to exchange our real pleasures for empty visions. Come what may, we must all stand before the gates of Hell, and it will add little or subtract little whether we have worked the treadle more or less. So come up and see me, and let us give ourselves over to it. And if anyone dies, let him die!

But if it please you to ride the post to France first, and then to come to me, make certain that the steed you ride upon does not know that you are a filly. Otherwise you will not come back to my arms a virgin.

Now up and off, dear sister, and hie you to the queen. You will have good fortune and a pleasant voyage. For since Her Majesty is a Florentine, she will send you back to Pistoia, your native city, content. It is only what the sharp-witted genius, the facetious cleverness and the aristocratic good-breeding which have been bestowed upon you by the air of Tuscany will deserve.

IX-16   Michelangelo Buonarroti to his Nephew Lionardo Buonarroti

Michelangelo, who once admitted that he had wife enough in his art, wanted to see his grandnephew safely married off in order to perpetuate the line of the Buonarroti.

1 February 1549

Lionardo, I sent you in my last a memorandum on several marriageable girls that was sent me from up there, I believe from some marriage broker, who cannot help but be a man of little judgment, for I having been stuck here in Rome for sixteen or seventeen years, he should have considered what little news I have of the families in Florence.

Wherefore I tell you, if you wish to take a wife, not to rely upon me, for I cannot give you the best counsel; but I can at least tell you not to go after money, but only after goodness and a good reputation.

I believe that there are likely in Florence many noble and poor families, and that it would be a bounty to marry into them, even if there weren't a dowry for you; nor would you have to contend with family pride. You have need of a girl who will stay at your side and whom you can command, and who doesn't want to parade about, taking in banquets and marriages every day. Because wherever there is a court, it's an easy thing to become a whore, and especially those girls without a family. And you will excuse my adding that it might be well for you to enter the nobility, for it is well known that we are ancient Florentine citizens and just as noble as any other house. Have trust in God and pray that He will arrange for your needs; and I shall be obliged if, when you have found something that seems fitting to you and before you unite in marriage, you keep me informed.

IX-17   Queen Mary Stuart to the Earl of Bothwell

The collection of letters and verses allegedly written by Mary Stuart (1542-1587) to James Hepburn, earl of Bothwell, was used to implicate the queen in the murder of her second husband, Lord Darnley. Called the "Casket Letters" because they were kept in a silver box, they betray Mary's infatuation for Bothwell whom she married on May 15, 1567, an event which proved disastrous to both.

Mary's pregnancy is intimated in the letter of reproach which follows.

(1567)

Alas, my Lord, why do you allow so unworthy a person to make you distrust something which is wholly yours? I am angry. You promised that you would decide everything and that you would send word each day to tell me how to proceed. You have done nothing. I gave you good warning to be very careful of your faithless brother-in-law. He came to me, without showing in any way that he came from you, and said that you had charged him to write to you what I might wish to say to you, and when and where I could go to you, and what you might decide to do with him. And thereupon he preached at me, saying that it was a mad enterprise and that for my honour I could never marry you inasmuch as, being yourself already married, you carried me away, and that his relatives would never allow of it, and that the Lords would deny what they once said. In a word, he was utterly against us. I told him that since I had gone so far, and unless you yourself were to draw back, no argument and not even death itself could make me retract my promise. As for the place, you must forgive me if I say that you are very casual about meeting me. Choose the place yourself, and let me know. Meanwhile I am not at all at my ease, because it is now too late, and it never occurred to me that you did not think of such a possibility earlier.* If you have not changed your mind during my absence any more than I have, you would not now be trying to make your mind up. Well, there is nothing amiss on my side: and seeing that your negligence puts

* Mary is said to have had a daughter by Bothwell, and the child is said to have gone into a nunnery.

both of us in danger from a false brother-in-law, if things do not go right, I will never stir from this spot. I send this bearer to you because I dare not trust your brother with this letter nor do I rely on his discretion. He [the bearer] will tell you about me, and do try to imagine how little I benefit by having such uncertain news. I would I were dead. For I see everything is going wrong. You promised me a very different state of affairs, but absence has great power over you—who have two strings to your bow. Make haste to send me an answer so that I may not lose heart, and do not consult with your brother about our plan, for he has spoken of it and is altogether opposed to it. God give you a good night.

IX-18   Michel de Montaigne to his Wife "Mademoiselle de Montaigne"

The essayist Michel de Montaigne (1533-1592) writes from Paris reassuring his wife that their marriage is firmly rooted in established tradition, despite currently fashionable attitudes disdaining matrimony.

Paris, 10 September, 1570

Milady, you well understand that it is not the tactic of a gallant man, by the rules of these times, to court and caress you still. For they say that an astute man can easily take a woman, but that to wed her is reserved for stupid fellows. Let people talk. For my part I cling to the simple fashions of old times, which I still bear under my skin. And in truth the new ways cost so dear up to this hour and this state (and I wouldn't swear that we haven't reached the final bid) that in every way I'm renouncing the game. Let us live, milady, you and I, in the old French manner.

Well, you may remember how the late Monsieur de la Boétie, my dear brother and inseparable companion, gave me on his deathbed his papers and his books, which have been since the favorite furnishings of mine. I cannot stingily hoard them all myself, nor do I deserve to be the only one to use them. For this reason I have chosen to share them with my friends. Since no friend of mine is more deprived of them than you, I am sending you the letter of consolation which Plutarch sent to his wife, translated by La Boétie into French, grieving that fortune has made this present so appropriate for you and that, having as only child a long awaited daughter, after four years of our marriage, you had to lose her in the second year of her life. But I leave to Plutarch the task of consoling you and to advise you on what is expected of you in the situation, begging you to believe him out of love for me. For Plutarch will uncover my sentiments, and the things to be said under the circumstances, much better than I could do myself. Upon which, milady, I commend myself to your good graces and pray that God will keep looking after you.

Your worthy husband,
Michel de Montaigne
(trans. R. J. C.)

IX-19   Queen Elizabeth to Duke François of Anjou

Of all the suitors for her hand considered by Queen Elizabeth (1533-1603), the one who came closest to marrying her was the Duke of Anjou, brother of the King of France. Although the difference of their religions was an impediment, especially after the Saint Bartholomew's Day massacres in France, political maneuverings and suspicions dragged out the courtship interminably. Finally wearying of the whole protracted business and observing the little influence François held over his brother, Elizabeth dropped him irrevocably in the following letter, composed in French.

10 September, 1583

Monsieur,

After a long expectation of receiving some news of you and your affairs, Monsieur de Reaux came to visit me from you, bearing only letters quite full of affection and assurance of its continuance for ever, for which I return you an infinity of thanks, since I have heard of the care which you take for fear of some ill impression that I might conceive of your actions. And then he spoke to me in a way that seemed very strange, as desiring to know what will be the help that we shall give for the preservation of the Low Countries; telling me that you are assured by the King that he will aid you as well as I. My God, Monsieur, what? are you not mad to believe that the means of keeping our friends is always to weaken them? Whoever has given you the advice has thought to make a blemish on our friendship or to break it altogether; in order by the same means to accomplish their designs and bring you to their desire. Do you not remember, Monsieur, against how many friends I have to prepare? Must I look unto those afar off as much as I neglect the nearest? Is the King, your brother, so weak a prince that he cannot defend you without another neighbour who has enough on her back, or so weakened that he must open a way to his enemies? You will not consider me so unworthy of reigning that I may not fortify myself, forsooth, with the sinews of war while awaiting too much courtesy from those who seek my ruin. I am astonished at the King, your brother, who has given me the precedence in fortifying you in such great need, having commenced before him, and seeing that he does not lack better means with less inconvenience. Pardon me, I beg you, if I tell you that this answer is quite clear, that he would not do anything, thinking that I should have little reason for not giving. So much so that if the King will not speak, and will not do much more than before, such an enterprise will break very soon, and if he be not for himself, I think that such is his determination. There is my opinion. As to you, Monsieur, I think that you are so surrounded with contrary persuasions and such differing humours, doubting so much, and assuring yourself of nothing that you know not where conveniently to turn, as you have reason good enough. Would to God that I were clever enough in wisdom to give you counsel, the best and most assured counsel, and that I had the understanding as I have the will. Then rather I would bear it to you than send it. I hope among other things that you will remember that he is very worthy of tripping who enters a net: do not only take advice; be ruthless; that is enough. I hear to my great regret that the King, the Queen Mother, indeed you yourself, put on me the fault which I have never committed, it always having depended on the King to perfect that of which I cannot make more mention, except to beg you to do me so much justice as to purge me, even by the opinion of your very ministers who know my innocence. For I cannot endure such a wrong, that they bite at and lament my affection for you. I appeal to the King's Ambassador, to Monsieur la Motte, Marchaumont, and Baqueville, how that God will not permit such an agreement, if I cease not ever to love, honour and esteem you, like the dog who being often beaten returns to his master. God keep you from painted counsel, and permit you to follow those who respect you more than themselves.

IX-20   King Henri IV to Gabrielle d'Estrées

Surpassing even the amorous exploits of King Francis I of France, King Henri IV (1553-1610) kept a bevy of mistresses near at hand even during his military campaigns. The *vert galant* (lusty rake) was stirred most deeply by the famous Gabrielle d'Estrées, an expert in the game of love who realized that to outwit her rivals and hold the King's love she must keep the upper hand, playing other men against him.

(Late) December, 1594

There is nothing which keeps my suspicions alive or can increase them more than the way you are acting in my regard. Since it pleases you to command me to dispel them entirely, I shall try. But you will not take it ill if, baring my soul, I tell you how they may best be dispelled. For the few accusations which I made fairly openly against you, you pretended not to hear them at all. At least, I judged so from your responses. That is why yesterday I began my letter with: There is no worse deafness than one which doesn't want to hear. To begin, my dear mistress, I shall protest before you that what I consider the offenses of which I have been victim are not the result of any bitterness that remains in my soul, feeling too happy over the pains you have gone to to content me, but of a desire to show you my justifiable reasons to suspect you.

You know how offended I was on arriving in your presence at the trip of my rival. The power your eyes held over mine spared you half of my complaints. You satisfy my mouth, but not my heart, as it appeared. But if I had known then what I later learned at Saint Denis about the aforementioned trip, I'd have refused to see you and have broken with you on the spot. I should rather burn my hand lest it write it and should rather cut out my tongue than have it say it ever to anyone but you.

After seeing you, do you know what you have done to me? All things considered, judge what I am to expect if you do not banish the cause of my state. What assurance can you give me about what you have done? What oath can you swear that you have not broken already twice? You must give me facts.

You suspect the reasons behind my suspicions and are not offended by the perfidies and infidelities of other men. The disparity is too great. You tell me that you'll keep the promises made to me when we last met. Just as the Old Testament was annulled by the coming of our Saviour, so have our promises been by the letter you wrote to Compiègne.

Let's have no more talk about "I shall" do this and that. You must say "I am doing." Make the decision, mistress mine, to have only one servitor. It is in you to change me, to make me devoted. You would do me wrong to suppose that anything or anyone could serve you with such love as mine. No one can equal my fidelity. If I have committed some indiscretion, of what follies isn't jealousy capable! It's your decision. No mistress ever made me jealous before. That's why there was never a more discreet man than I. In fearing the armies of the League, Feuillemorte made it clear that he was neither in love, nor loyal to me.

I am so eager to see you that I'd give four years of my life to get there as fast as this letter, which I finish by kissing your hands a million times. Alas, you do not esteem me worthy of sending me your portrait!

(trans. R. J. C.)

IX-21   Czar Boris Godunov to Queen Elizabeth of England

The politically arranged marriage flourished in the Renaissance, with its insistence on "blood" and virginity. When the Czar Boris (ca. 1551-1605) wishes to marry off a son to a "pure mayden" of eleven years, he insists upon knowing whether the girl is descended from Henry VIII or the less reputable Anne Boleyn if related to the Queen. The *mariage de convenance* or of *raison* was widespread in bourgeois as well as noble circles.

Moscow, April, 1598

Through the tender mercie of God wherby the daie spring from on high doth guyde our feete into the way of Peace, the God in Trinitie we praise for his mercie.

From the great Lord, King, and great Duke Burrys Phedeorowich, of all Russia only upholder, of Volodemio, Mosco, Novogorode, King of Cazan and Astrachan,

Lord of Volsko, and great Duke of Smolensko, Otver, Vghery, Pernie, Veatskey, Bolgharie, and other Regions, great Duke allso of Novogorod in the lowe Contries, Chernico, Razan, Pelotsko, Rostoveskey, Yearoslauley, Belozera, and of Leyuffland, of Vdorskey, Condinsko, and Commander of all the Contrie of Syberia and of the North parts, and Lord over the Contrey of Verskey, Grusmiskey, and King over the Contrey of Kabordinskey, Chereaske, duke over the Countrey of Igorskey, and Ruler over many other kingdoms and dominions, our dere and loving Sister, greeting,

To the right high and wourthie prynce our deare and loving sister Elizabeth, by the grace of God, Queene of England, France [*sic*] and Ireland, and of many other Countries.

Your Matie our loving sister hath sent unto us your princely and kynde Lettres, professing your sisterly love and affections towards us, which we have diligently perused and readd, and doe most kindlie conceave therof.

And concerning the argument of your princely Lettres, it cannot but geve us an extraordinary contentment; wee fynding therin your Ma^ts love and affection towards us and our Children, carefully endevoring the matching and bestowinge of them in your owne lyne and race. By which your Letters your highnes made knowne unto us that, amongst others, you have made choise of a yong Ladie, being a pure mayden, nobly descended by father and mother, adorned with graces and extraordinary guifts of nature, about eleven yeres of age, of whom you made an offer unto us, that yf it be the pleasure of God to encline the harts of the twoe yonge coople to like one of the other, all circumstances shalbe accommodated on your part, and that your princely desire is to knitt more and more, if it can be, soe mutuall bonds of frendshipp, as that no practize of others envie should have power to weaken or blemysh the same.

Of which Ladie, and others, your Matie intended to send and represent unto us as many livelie Images as absence could affourd by a gentleman well qualified, and well trusted by you, who should frely and perticulerly deale with us in all things necessary for an affaire of this importance: wisshing us to suspend from embracing any other course in that kinde, till we have heard what your Embassador (whom you purpose to sende) could saie in the matter.

But your Matie hath therein not perticulerlie written unto us (of that wourthie ladie) what she is; whether shee be of your Highnes blood, discended of your Royall race; by your father or mother; or from some other Archduke or Duke; whereof we are desirous to be resolved. Upon consideracon of which your Maties most kynde Lettres, wee great Kinge and great Duke Burris Phederowich of all Russia doe acknowledg our self much beholding unto yow, that yow our loving sister are pleased to make unto us so loving and free an offer in this kynde, wherein it cannot be unknowne unto your Matie that we have byn moved and formerly dealt withall by divers other great princes who have sent unto us with earnest entreatie to match with our children. And in respect of our Conceipt of your Maties good affection towardes us, we doe rather and more willingly enclyne to your princely offer, than to the offer of any other great Prince what soever.

And to that end, our desire is, that You our loving Sister would be pleased before you doe send your Embassador, to lett us knowe howe this Ladie (purposed by your Matie to be offred unto us in maryage) standeth allied to your Matie or otherwise from what Duke or Archduke she is descended: upon notice whereof we shall apply ourself to resolve of the matter. And in the meane tyme we will suspende the embracing any other course in this busynes; expecting with all expedition to be satisfied fullie by your Matie herein. Written in our princely Pallaice in the Cittie of Moskoe in the yeare since the beginning of the World 7111. and in the moneth of Aprill.*

IX-22 John Donne to Sir George More

Following his elopement with Anne More in 1601, John Donne (1573-1631) pens a conciliatory letter to her father, Sir George More, Chancellor of the Garter and Lieutenant of the Tower of London. Through his clandestine marriage, Donne not only lost his post as secretary to Sir Thomas Egerton, Lord Keeper of the Great Seal (and Anne's uncle), but was imprisoned for the offense of marrying a minor without her guardians' consent. Sir George More finally became reconciled to his son-in-law in the autumn of 1608.

2 February, 1602

Sir,

If a very respective feare of your displeasure, and a doubt that my Lord whom I know owt of your worthiness to love you much, would be so compassionate with you as to add his anger to yours, did not so much increase my sicknes as that I cannot stir, I had taken the boldnes to have donne the office of this letter by wayting upon you myself to have given you truthe and clearnes of this matter

* April, 1598

between your daughter and me, and to show you plainly the limits of our fault, by which I know your wisdome will proportion the punishment. So long since as her being at York House this had foundacion, and so much then of promise and contract built upon it withowt violence to conscience might not be shaken. At her lyeing in town this last Parliament, I found meanes to see her twice or thrice. We both knew the obligacions that lay upon us, and we adventured equally, and about three weeks before Christmas we married. And as at the doinge, there were not usd above fyve persons, of which I protest to you by my salvation, there was not one that had any dependence or relation to you, so in all the passage of it did I forbear to use any suche person, who by furtheringe of it might violate any trust or duty towards you. The reasons why I did not foreacquaint you with it (to deale with the same plainnes that I have usd) were these. I knew my present estate lesse than fitt for her, I knew (yet I knew not why) that I stood not right in your opinion. I knew that to have given any intimacion of it had been to impossibilitate the whole matter. And then having these honest purposes in our harts, and those fetters in our consciences, me thinks we should be pardoned, if our fault be but this, that wee did not, by fore-revealinge of it, consent to our hindrance and torment. Sir, I acknowledge my fault to be so great, as I dare scarse offer any other prayer to you in mine own behalf than this, to beleeve this truthe, that I neyther had dishonest end nor meanes. But for her whom I tender much more than my fortunes or lyfe (els I woould I might neyther joy in this lyfe, nor enjoy the next), I humbly beg of you that she may not to her danger feele the terror of your sodaine anger. I know this letter shall find you full of passion; but I know no passion can alter your reason and wisdome, to which I adventure to commend these particulers; that it is irremediably donne; that if you incense my Lord you destroy her and me; that it is easye to give us happines, and that my endevors and industrie, if it please you to prosper them, may soone make me somewhat worthyer of her. If any take the advantage of your displeasure against me, and fill you with ill thoughts of me, my comfort is, that you know that fayth and thanks are due to them onely, that speak when theyr informacions might do good; which now it cannot work towards any party. For my excuse I can say nothing, except I knew what were sayd to you. Sir, I have truly told you this matter, and I humbly beseeche you so to deale in it as the persuasions of Nature, Reason, Wisdome, and Christianity shall inform you; and to accept the vowes of one whom you may now rayse or scatter, which are that as my love is directed unchangeably upon her, so all my labors shall concur to her contentment, and to show my humble obedience to your self.

Yours in all duty and humblenes,
J. Donne.

IX-23   Lope de Vega to the Duke of Sessa

When Marcela, Lope de Vega's daughter, entered a Trinitarian Order, it was necessary to find a dowry to facilitate this marriage to Christ. The letter of Lope (1562 1635) to his patron, the Duke of Sessa, affords interesting details on the financial aspects of this serious decision.

Madrid, November or early December, 1621

Duke my Lord,

I wish not to stress to Your Excellency, Lord, the years I have served You, but rather my desire to serve You, so that on this occasion You may favor and assist me as such a generous friend and satisfy my desires as an appreciative one.

My daughter Marcela has announced to me with tears the great desire she has always had to devote herself to God. It is such a true desire that, as if to shed all worldly concerns, she wishes to be barefoot.

I have been discussing this matter with the Trinitarian Nuns, and they, commiting her to the Lord, are accepting her. You know that I am so poor that if You had not succoured me, I should not be alive today: blame it on Fortune or on my ignorance. I cannot give them what they ask if You do not assist and favor me with the thousand ducats I have promised. I should not have dared to beg You to guarantee them, without His Majesty being grateful to You for this patronage, which will entail on Your behalf prayers and sacrifices.

The matter has been set for Easter or later, and the nuns out of affection for both of us are satisfied with this dowry. As for the bridal costume and the tips, and the rest, which will amount to three thousand *reales,* I intend to take care of these. Would to God I could afford the whole business, to relieve Your Excellency from this concern, since You have so many. It must be put in writing the day she enters who will be her guarantor for the period of one year. If Your Excellency, My Lord, grants me this favor, You can do it in two stages, set down among Your pensions, or however You please, so that from the year 1622 to 1623 she will be provided for and she will serve as a chaplain to You for the rest of Your

Excellency's life and to my Lord the Count. She will certainly be capable of it, this girl who offers God her sixteen years, neither ugly nor imprudent ones, and offers herself to so much barefoot penitence, whereas the girls these days are inclined toward other comforts. Alberto of Avila will discuss this in person with Your Excellency, for I dare not, loath to obligate You with my presence to something which may not please You. Alberto will think up the wording and prevent the disappointment which so often results from one's being asked to do a favor.

For this, Most Excellent Lord, I shall celebrate all my life the name, greatness, piety, and valor of Your Excellency, son of such illustrious lineage and blood. And God will repay You this charity given a gentleman and a motherless girl with a long life and increase of estate which is in His power and which we all desire.

Your Excellency's henchman,
Lope de Vega Carpio

(See also Letter V-21, in which Saint Teresa explains why girls entering nunneries must provide dowries, even though the sum may be negotiable.)

(trans. R. J. C.)

CHAPTER 10

DAILY LIFE.

DOMESTIC CONCERNS.

TOWN VS. COUNTRY.

PASTIMES. MONEY.

XIX. *Pietro Aretino* by Titian

XX. *Concert Champêtre* by Giorgione

Personal letters concern themselves by nature with the routine of daily living, its satisfactions and its concerns. Our most basic concern is where we are to live out our lives. The decline of feudal society had left Europe with many growing, attractive towns, with improvements in plumbing, lighting, and roads unknown to the Middle Ages. Job opportunities and commerce created a comfortable middle class. As to be expected, the regional capitals seemed the most exciting and the most affluent. Girolamo Lippomano, the Venetian ambassador to Paris, is impressed by the conveniences, wealth, and architecture of Paris, but he seems especially impressed by the *cordon bleu* quality of Parisian gastronomy (X-14). Aretino was the greatest booster of Venice, with its astonishing Byzantine and baroque qualities, and in various letters compared Venetian sunsets to great paintings for the benefit of Titian (III-12) and enthused to his landlord on "the heavenly site on which your house stands," finding Venice superior to anything offered by Rome: "For in one you see the insolence of fortune strutting up and down, and in the other you see the grave march of rule and dominion. It is a strange thing to see the confusion of the papal court, but a beautiful sight to see the unity of purpose in this republic." Albrecht Dürer found the population of Venice an interesting combination of knaves and "men of sense and knowledge, men of much noble sentiment and honest virtue" hospitable to foreigners (III-2).

Many Renaissance travelers, and Montaigne was one of the most enthusiastic, found life in German towns comfortable and affluent. Another enthusiast was an unidentified British envoy to Emperor Charles V, writing to the Duke of Norfolk (X-6). The *bequem* and *gemütlich* qualities of German life even today, with its feather pillows and eiderdown bolsters, deeply impressed the envoy. One's choice of town was often none other that that where one had spent happy years of youth. Thus, Roger Ascham, after "having some experience of life at home and abroad," hoped to spend his mature life in Cambridge (I-12).

Renaissance letters also list the towns in which one would not choose to live, towns which find themselves in battle areas, forced to support monarchs and mercenaries who brutalize them and confiscate their belongings (VII-13), towns plundered either by Turks or such pirates as Drake (VII-10 and VII-16) etc., towns like Seville where one might be arraigned by the Inquisition on unfounded or improvised charges (V-11 and V-18), towns like Bologna and Rome, where unruly students become a public menace (I-11 and I-15).

Like the two mice of Horace debating whether it is better to live in the city or the country, this question was debated in Renaissance letters. Sir Thomas More found the simple virtues of country life most laudable, but urged his friend Colet to return to the city, where the best physicians are found (X-3). Tommaso Spica preferred life in Rome to that in the hick town of Gubbio: "I used to get more enjoyment in a single hour going for a walk through Rome with you," he wrote to his friend Atanagi, "or tarrying in one of those bookstores at Campo di Fiore playing chess with Palatino, than I would have here in an entire epoch seeing trees, grass, mountains and rocks and hearing the sounds of cuckoos, crickets and owls" (X-18). One remembers Michelangelo's letter complaining of a brother "who walks behind oxen" and urging that he come live in Florence. Yet the advocates of country living filled their letters with the joys of *la vie champêtre*. Prominent among these were Camillo Massari depicting to Matteo Bruno the salubrious daily life offered by Macerata and the charming Beatrice Sforza praising to Isabella d'Este the temperate climate and daily routine at Villanova (X-2). Aretino's letter to Simon Bianco would imply that even while living in the Venetian area one can "return to the honest ways of nature" and a simplicity of daily living (X-12). Nor should one forget Niccolò Machiavelli's pleasant routine on his farm outside Florence which served as background for his long nights writing *The Prince* (II-3).

One reads in the letters a similar debate on whether summer or winter life is preferable. This controversy led Aretino to one of his most famous double-metaphors: "God's truth, indeed, winter seems to me an abbot who floats downstream in comfortable ease, taking just a little too much pleasure in eating and sleeping and doing that other thing. But summer is a rich and noble harlot, who, drenched with cheap perfume, throws herself down disgusted and does nothing but drink and drink again" (X-9).

One's contentedness within the home varied with the efficiency and behavior of one's servants. If Beatrice Sforza is delighted with Villanova, it is because her large retinue of servants will include even musicians, grooms, and boys to beat the bushes and stir the herons up into the air. Yet every middle-class family seemed to be able to afford a maid, often mentioned in Renaissance epistles. One memorable servant is mentioned by Aretino, the one who "split the head of Giannozzo Pandolfini while he was raging with fever by playing on a rebec day and night" (X-12). It was this same letter which recalled a certain bishop at death's door who was not sure of being exempt from hell, but said to his confessor, "I don't mind about Satan at all, unless he has serving men in his house."

Erasmus could be amused by the bickering of landladies and maids, even though it hampered his writing schedule, and he found it natural to take the part of the underdog. As is well known, the brassy servant, male or female, was a stock character from Renaissance comedy through the theater of Molière, usually shrewder than his master. One who disapproved of this theatrical convention was Aretino. "In everything I have written about comedy, I have always criticized those authors who put witty sayings into the mouths of menials." However, writing to Coccio (X-17) he admits how many times his own servant girls surprised and amused him with their shrewd observations and concludes, "I saw that it was not without reason that they put servants on the stage and make them talk the way they do."

Money problems, the bane of the householder, inform the letters. City-living, as Lippomano observed about Paris, was more expensive than rural life. When things got tight, one could borrow money from bankers or money-lenders. The old Scholastic scruples against money-lending were breaking down, especially under pressures of the mercantile and industrial centers where Protestantism was taking root. Changing attitudes on usury were one of the less-publicized issues splitting the Church in twain. It is in a letter of John Calvin that we find the new Reformed opinion that it is ethical and moral to charge interest on loans (X-15) under normal business conditions. Shortly Francis Bacon will support this view in the *Essays,* specifying a charge of 7% for loans without real property as security or 6% with such security.

With the rise of the great commercial bankers, the Fuggers, Gondi, and Medici, princes and popes found them a convenience (VI-5 and V-1), but suspicion of banks remained great among the masses. One should try to borrow money elsewhere, as Michelangelo wrote to his father Lodovico, "so that we may avoid taking the money from the bank." The great artist was typical of his rustic origins at Caprese and Settignano in warning that "all banks are fraudulent," that one must not deposit money in them, and that they cannot be trusted. Again, it is Michelangelo speaking for his generation, who rails against any modest tax imposed by the commune of Florence: "We have paid taxes in Florence for three hundred years . . . And still I have to pay. Everything will be stripped from me!" (X-4).

If a fool and his money are soon to be parted, two ways to accomplish this were money-lending and gambling. Charity being a Christian virtue, the lending of money could be so clothed, whether it is Jacob Fugger lending money to Charles V or Shakespeare lending money to his fellow-townsman Richard Quiney (X-20). Although assured by Quiney that "you will neither lose credit nor money by me," one wonders whether Shakespeare, like the master banker of Augsburg, had in the end to goad for repayment. As for gambling, with the old concept of Providence giving way to the alternate concepts of fate, fortune, and chance (despite objections by the papal curia), this practice became more popular. Along with dice, cards, tarot, and betting on sporting events, the lottery emerged. One of the memorable parodies of the lottery, which leaves foolish participants with purses "empty as pricked bladders," was written by Aretino to Giovan Manenti (X-11).

At the end of the fifteenth century the English public had a peculiar type of money problem found in their correspondence. Irish coins which circulated in England resembled exactly their English counterparts, but were of a lesser alloy and therefore value. To remedy this disparity to the advantage of his subjects, Richard III ordered his Keeper of the Seal to mint coins clearly differentiated from those of Ireland (X-1).

Money was obviously a greater problem to the gypsies than to anyone else. The incursions of the nomadic gypsies, a parasitic group, irritated all the hardworking tradesmen and farmers of Western Europe. Their begging, singing, dancing, palm-reading, and fortune-telling by cards failed to make them a living, which was replaced by poaching, rustling, kidnapping, and (as even Cervantes admits) thievery. The nations of Western Europe tried to expel them during the Renaissance. A letter of Thomas Cromwell details the harsh order of banishment issued by Henry VIII, reinforced by capital punishment (X-13). In view of the difficulties of mass exodus of an indigent people, it is to be supposed that many were hanged.

Another problem of concern to the wealthy and middle classes especially was inefficiency of the mails. Thomas Cromwell was again brought into the situation, as we learn from the letter of Bryan Tuke (X-8), but the contents of the letter lead us to suppose that England's pony express was probably more advanced than the mail transportation in other countries.

If such an affluent world as our present one is experiencing fuel shortages and energy crises, one is not surprised to learn from the Duke of Suffolk's letter to Cardinal Wolsey that Newcastle and the other coal-mining localities were not producing enough for the basic needs of even their surrounding towns (X-5).

Three sports recommended in the courtesy manuals of the Renaissance were dueling, jousting, and wrestling. Dueling was practised by noblemen as a feudal privilege. Campaigns against this privilege were launched by the new monarchs, trying to replace feudal by national loyalties, and we gather from Sir Francis Cottington's letter to Northampton that the campaigns were rather successful (X-21). For it appears that swordsmen who wished to settle a grudge or a challenge were traveling abroad for their duels, outside the monarch's jurisdiction. New laws and penalties were required to prevent this evasion, and Lord Northampton looked to the rigorous laws on dueling in Spain to draw up appropriate legislation. As for wrestling and fisticuffs, these sports were classless, being practised down the social scale from Kings Francis I and Henry VIII (the French King toppled Henry) to frisky schoolboys. William Godolphin's letter to

Cromwell indicates that King Henry was eager to set up a national wrestling team (X-7).

Along with the household concerns and afflictions attributable to man himself—wars, poverty, and the like—which are regretted in these letters from the Renaissance, there are mentions of plagues (IV-21), incurable diseases (IV-3), and other ills beyond man's control which we cynically call acts of God. Niccolò Martelli's letter to the Countess of Bagno attributes the ravaging 1547 flood at Florence to astrological causes, more specifically the conjuncture of Mars and Saturn (X-16). Onorio Belli seeks a more specific scientific cause when writing to Alfonso Ragona of the 1584 earthquake at Canea, attributing it to the excessive heat and resulting aridity of that year (X-19). Even as the new scientists were struggling to achieve recognition and acceptance, the laymen themselves were groping for better explanations of natural phenomena than those of Mediaeval pseudo-science or of theology.

X-1   King Richard III to the Keeper of the Privy Seal

Irish coins circulating in England during Richard III's reign looked like those minted in England, but were lacking in both weight and alloy. Thus the King (1452-1485) ordered Letters of Commission to be prepared changing the outward appearance of Irish coins. This, to prevent loss and inconvenience to his English subjects.

18 July 1483

By the King.

Right trusty and welbeloued We grete you wele, and woll and charge you that under oure Priue Seale being in your warde ye make our Lettres in forme following. Forsomuche as We doubt not but afore this tyme ye have herd and understande of the gret clamor grugge[1] and complainte which our liege people of this our Roy^me have made of and upon the coigne of silver made in our lande of Irland for discoording both in weight, allay, and in forme the coigne of sylver of this our Roy^me. And the which for lak of expresse difference that shuld have be

1. grudge

graved upon the same hath be ignorantly received here within this our Roy^me in stede of suche substanciall coigne as is by good auctorite coigned within the same to the universall losse and hurt of all thoo to whose hands it hath comin in wey of payment. Which inconvenience by subtill and crafty meanes of coveties persones aswele bringeng out of this our Roy^me sylver bullion in gret quantete to our Mynte of Irland as ther forging and streking the same unto the sam deceavable prynte daily encreseth more and more and is like to bring this our Roy^me by processe of tyme to extreme poverte and desolacion, enlesse that then [2] other due provision be had therupon in all hast. We therfore woll and charge you and everie of you as to him it shall or may apperteigne [3] in the straytest wise that incontynent upon the rescept of thise our lettres ye see and provide that on either side of every pece of sylver to be coigned herafter within our said land of Irland ther be prynted and set in the mydill [4] thereof a clere and expresse difference fro that sylver that is coigned here within this our Royalme, that is to say on the one side the Armes of England and on the other side iij. Crownes; damnyng [5] and utterly distroying all the stamps and Irons as touching the graving that is in them wherwith the sylver Coignes of that our lande hath hiderto be made and stryken at any place or tyme, Revoking also and utterly setting aside all maner power of Coyning in any place within the same our land, except our Cite of Dyvelyn and our Cite of Waterforde upon payne of forfaitur of all that shall happen to be coigned elleswhere within our said land or otherwise then [6] is afore expressed unto the tyme We have otherwise ordeigned in this behalue. And that ye certifie us and our Counsaill by writing from you in all spede possible how ye shall have put you in devor touching the premisses.[7] Not failling herin as ye love and tendre the honnor wele and profite of us and of all our subgetts. Youen the xviij^th day of Juyll the first yere of our Reigne.

X-2   Beatrice Sforza to Isabella d'Este

During her short lifetime, the gifted Beatrice Sforza (1475-1497), teen-age wife of Lodovico il Moro, regent and later duke of Milan, patronized the leading Italian artists and writers of the day, though she exercised less

2. than
3. appertain
4. middle
5. damaging
6. than
7. how you shall undertake to carry out these conditions

influence politically than her sister Isabella d'Este who, as Francesco Gonzaga's wife, guided the policies of Mantua for more than thirty years. In the letter that follows, Beatrice exults in the country pleasures of life at Villanova.

Villanova, 18 March 1491

. . . I am presently here at Villanova where, on account of the good country life and fresh air, which can only be compared to that of the month of May, so lovely and temperate is it, I go horseback riding every day with the dogs and falcons, and never do my lord and I return home without having experienced boundless delights in hunting herons and river birds. For brevity's sake I won't tell you more than this, because the number of hares that leap out from every corner is so great that sometimes we don't know which way to turn to enjoy the sight, since the human eye is not capable of seeing all that appeals to our desire and that the country affords with its animals. Still, I shant neglect to tell you that every day the illustrious Messer Galeazzo and I, with a few others of these courtiers, take pleasure in playing croquet after dinner; and frequently we invite and desire the presence of Your Ladyship to whom I make this address not to diminish the pleasure she will have when she is here, warned in advance of everything she can expect, but because she knows that I am well and dearly cherished by the aforementioned lord my husband, and that no diversion or joy could delight me if not confided to Your Ladyship, advising her that I have had a garlic field planted so that when she is here, Your Ladyship can avail herself of all the garlic sauce her heart desires.

(trans. L.L.)

X-3   Sir Thomas More to John Colet

A clear preference for city life is found in the following amiable letter of Thomas More (1478-1535), who apparently found Oxford about as far out in the country as he cared to travel.

London
23 October (1504)

Thomas More to his John Colet, greeting.

As I was walking in the law courts the other day, unbusy where everybody else was busy, I met your servant. I was delighted to see him, both because he has always been dear to me, and especially because I thought he would not have come without you. But when I heard from him not only that you had not returned, but that you would not return for a long time, I cannot tell you from what rejoicing I was cast into what dejection. For what could be more grievous to me than to be deprived of your most pleasant companionship, whose prudent advice I enjoyed, by whose most delightful intimacy I was refreshed, by whose powerful sermons I was stirred, by whose example and life I was guided, in fine, in whose very countenance and nod I was accustomed to find pleasure? And so when encompassed by these defenses I felt myself strengthened; now that I am deprived of them I seem to languish and grow feeble. By following your footsteps I had escaped almost from the very gates of hell, and now, driven by some force and necessity, I am falling back again into gruesome darkness. I am like Eurydice, except that she was lost because Orpheus looked back at her, but I am sinking because you do not look back at me.

For in the city what is there to move one to live well? but rather, when a man is straining in his own power to climb the steep path of virtue, it turns him back by a thousand devices and sucks him back by its thousand enticements. Wherever you betake yourself, on one side nothing but feigned love and the honeyed poisons of smooth flatterers resound; on the other, fierce hatreds, quarrels, the din of the forum murmur against you. Wherever you turn your eyes, what else will you see but confectioners, fishmongers, butchers, cooks, poulterers, fishermen, fowlers, who supply the materials for gluttony and the world and the world's lord, the devil? Nay even houses block out from us I know not how large a measure of the light, and do not permit us to see the heavens. And the round horizon does not limit the air but the lofty roofs. I really cannot blame you if you are not yet tired of the country where you live among simple people, unversed in the deceits of the city; wherever you cast your eyes, the smiling face of the earth greets you, the sweet fresh air invigorates you, the very sight of the heavens charms you. There you see nothing but the generous gifts of nature and the traces of our primeval innocence.

But yet I do not wish you to be so captivated by these delights as to be unwilling to fly back to us as soon as possible. For if the inconveniences of the city so displease you, your country parish of Stepney (of which you should have no less care) will afford you hardly less advantages than where you now dwell, whence you can sometimes turn aside, as to an inn, to the city (where there is so much that needs your service). For in the country, where men are of themselves either almost innocent, or at least not ensnared in great sins, the services of any physician can be useful. But in the city because of the great numbers that congregate there, and because of their long-standing habits of vice, any physician will have come in vain unless he be the most skillful. Certainly there come from time to time into the pulpit at St. Paul's preachers who promise health, but although they seem to have spoken very eloquently, their life is in such sharp contrast to their words that they irritate rather than soothe. For they cannot bring men to believe that though they are themselves obviously in direst need of the physician's help, they are yet fit to be entrusted with the cure of other men's ailments. And thus when men see that their diseases are being prescribed for by physicians who are themselves covered with ulcers, they immediately become indignant and obstinate. But if (as observers of human nature assert), he is the best physician in whom the patient has the greatest confidence, who can doubt that you are the one who can do most for the cure of all in the city? Their readiness to allow you to treat their wounds, their trust, their obedience, you have yourself proved in the past, and now the universal desire and anticipation of you proclaim it all again.

Come then, my dear Colet, for Stepney's sake, which mourns your long absence as children their mother's; for the sake of your native place which should be no less dear to you than are your parents. Finally (though this will be a weak force for your return), let regard for me, who am entirely devoted to you and hang anxiously upon your coming, move you.

Meanwhile, I shall pass my time with Grocin, Linacre, and our dear friend Lily, the first as you know the sole guide of my life (in your absence), the second my master in learning, the third the dearest partner of my endeavors. Farewell, and love me ever as now. London, 23 October.

X-4   Michelangelo Buonarroti to his Family

The universal plague of taxes existed in the Renaissance and with his sensitivity about money, Michelangelo (1475-1564) suffered more from them than most.

July, 1524

Yesterday I ran into someone who told me that I was going to have to pay, or else by the end of this month I'd fall into punishments. I didn't believe that there were other punishments than those of hell, or an income tax of two ducats if I were the draper of a silk craft or a gold beater, and I lent the rest at usury. We have paid taxes in Florence for three hundred years: once at least I could have been a bailiff of the Judges and Notaries' Guild. And still I have to pay! Everything will be stripped from me, and I'll have to come back down there to Rome. If my affairs were settled, I'd have sold something and bought credits at the Bank which might have paid my taxes, and I could then stay in Florence.

X-5   Charles Brandon, Duke of Suffolk, to Cardinal Wolsey

Fuel shortages and the energy crisis were not new to the sixteenth century. For one thing, in the 1520s there was too little carrying of coals from Newcastle, especially in the direction of Suffolk and Norfolk. Charles Brandon (ca. 1484-1545) was an effective spokesman for these counties as a courtier and close friend of Henry VIII.

25 September (1526)

Pleas it your Grace to be aduertised that this berer, deputie for the costs [1] of Suff. and Norff. and other Counties of this Realme, hath byn with me with the supplicacōn and peticion of th'enhabitaunts of the said coostes, purporting the great losses and enpouerisshement [2] that may ensue vnto the Kings subjects by reason of the derthe of Cooles callid New Castell cooles, which Peticōn after my poer mynd is entended much for a cōmyn weale, for I am enformyd the coostes here in thees parties ar grevously enpouerysshed by reison of skantines [3] of the said ffewell [4] of coles. Wherfor' I besech yoᵣ Grace to be good lord herin and to

1. coasts
2. impoverishment
3. scantness
4. fuel

putt your helping hand for the reformacōn of the same, the rather for my sake. From Henhamhall the xxv. day of Septembre.

by youres assured
Charlys Suffolke.

To my Lorde Cardinall is Grace.

X-6   Unnamed English Ambassador to the Duke of Norfolk

This anonymous account of the *gemütlich* and prosperous towns of Germany (to be echoed by Montaigne) is a testimony as well of German thoroughness and efficiency. It also provides early evidence of German modifications of Roman ritual during the spread of Lutheranism.

Nuremberg, 1530

I have promysid to the King to write to your Grace the ordre of things in the towne of Nurenberg, specially concerning the fayth, but first I will reherce [1] some other townes as they laye in oure waye. The Citie of Wormes, for the more part, and allmoste the hole, is possessid with Lutherians and Jewes, the residue is indifferent to be shortly the one or the other; trouthe it is that the Busshop kepith well his name of Episcopus which is in Englissh an overseer, and is in the case that overseers of testamentes be in England, for he shall have leve to looke so that he meddle not, yet some tyme men callyth hym overseene, that is drunke, whan he neither knowith what he doeth, nor what he owght to doe. The Citie of Spire, as I here saye, kepith yet their faith well, except some saye there be many do err in taking to largely this article *Sanctorum Communionem* which hath inducid more charitie than may stonde with honestie. One thing I markid, suche as were lovers, divers of them hadd theire paramors sitting with theim in a draye which was drawen with a horse trapped with bells, and the lovers, whipping theim, causid theim to trott and to draw theim thurghoute everie strete, making agrete noyse with their bells; the women sate with theire heddes discoverid, [2] saving a chaplet or

1. rehearse, review
2. uncovered

crounet wrought with nedil [3] wark. I hadd forgoten to tell that there were grete hornes sett on the horsis heddis. I suppose it was the tryumphe of Venus, or of the Devil, or of bothe. All townes ensuing be rather wars [4] than better. But I passe theim over at this time.

Touching Nurenberg, it is the moste propre towne and best ordred publike weale that ever I beheld. There is in it so moche people that I mervaylid how the towne mowght contayne them, beside theim which folowid the Emperor; and notwithstanding, there was of all vitaile [5] more abundance than I could see in any place, all thoughe the contrey adjoyning of his nature is very barrayn. I appoyntid to lodge in an Inne, but for Laurence Staber the Kinges servaunt came to me, desyring me to take his house, whereunto I browght with me the Frenche Ambassador, where we were well entertayned, and that night the Senate sent to us thirty galons of wyne, twenty pikes, thirty carpes, a hundrid dasis, with sondry confectiones; the residue of oure chier [6] I will kepe in store untill I speke with your Grace, which I pray God may be shortly. Allthough fish was sent to us, yet universally and openly thurghout the towne men did eate flessh. Allthowgh I hadd a chapleyne, yet could not I be suffrid to have him to sing Mass, but was constrayned to here their Mass which is but one in a Churche, and that is celebrate in forme folowing. The Preest in vestmentes after oure manner, singith everi thing in Latine, as we use, omitting suffrages. The Epistel he readith in Latin. In the meane time the sub Deacon goeth into the pulpite and readeth to the people the Epistle in their vulgare [7]; after thei peruse other thinges as our prestes doo. Than the Preeste redith softly the Gospell in Latine. In the meane space the deacon goeth into the pulpite and readith aloude the Gospell in the Almaigne [8] tung. M[r] Cranmere [9] sayith it was shewid to him that in the Epistles and Gospels thei kept not the ordre that we doo, but doo peruse every daye one chapitre of the New Testament. Afterwards the prest and the quere [10] doo sing the *Credo* as we doo; the secretes and preface they omitt, and the preest singith with a high voyce the wordes of the consecration; and after the Levation the Deacon torneth to the people, telling to them in Almaigne tung alonge process how thei shold prepare theim selfes to the communion of the flessh and blode of Christ; and than may

3. needle
4. worse
5. victuals
6. feast, banqueting
7. vernacular
8. German
9. Thomas Cranmer who, before becoming Archbishop of Canterbury (see Letter V-16), served as a leading member of an embassy to Germany.
10. choir

every man come that listith, withoute going to any Confession. But I, lest I sholde be partner of their Communyon, departid than; and the Ambassador of Fraunce fo[llowed] which causid all the people in the Churche to wonder at us, [as though] we hadd ben gretter heretikes than thei. One thing liked me well (to shew your Grace freely my hart). All the preestes hadd wyves; and thei were the fayrist women of the towne, &c. To saye the trouth all women of this contray be gentill of spirit, as men report. The day after our coming the Senate sent gentilmen to shew us their provision of harneis, ordinance, and corne. I suppose there was in our sight thre thousand pieces of complete harneys for horsemen; the residue we saw not for spending of tyme; of gunnes grete and small it required half a daye to numbre them; arkbusshes [11] and crossebowes, I thowght theim innumerable. The provision of grayn I am aferd to reherse it for jeoperding my credence. [12] I saw twelve houses of grete length, every house having twelve floures, on every one corne thurghoute, the thickness of three feete. Some of the Senate shewed me that thei hadd sufficient to kepe fifty thousand men abundantly for one yere. Moche of it have layen long and yet is it goode, as it shall appier by an example that I have now sent to your Grace of rye, which was layde in there 190 yeres passid, whereof there remaynith yet above v^c. quarters. I doubtid moche to report this to your Grace, but that I trustid your Grace wold take it in stede of tidinges, and not suppose me to be the author. Considering that moche strange report may bring me in suspicion of lying with some men, which hath conceyvid wrong opinion of me. And here an ende of my poure lettre, which I besieche your Grace to take in goode part with my harty service. And our Lord mayntayne you in honor with long lif.

X-7   Sir William Godolphin to Thomas Lord Cromwell

Sir Thomas Elyot's *Governour* proposes wrestling as a "profytable" art to be learned by courtiers. Indeed, at the 1520 meeting between Francis I and Henry VIII in France, the two monarchs, after watching their best wrestlers fight it out, set down their flagons and indulged in a royal match themselves. Honors went to the French king. Aware that Henry was always on the

11. harquebuses
11. risking disbelief

lookout for top wrestlers, Godolphin here promises to send him two. Sir William was a scion of the ancient Godolphin family of Cornwall.

14 June, 1532

My devty [1] with dev [2] reuerens yn my most vmbyll [3] wysse don, plesyzth hyt yowr Maysterschyppe [4] to onderstond that I recevyd yowr gentyll and lovyng Letter to me derectyd, datyd the ffurste day of June, by yowr seruant Herry; the tenor ther off was to have ij. proper ffelowes for the fett of wrastelyng.[5] I have send to yowr Maysterschyppe ij. off my hovsold [6] seruants, whyche yowr seruant Herry dyd very well know that yn thes partes thay wer takyn ffor the beste and the suryst ffor that ffett. Yowr Maysterschyppe may truste them ffor ther truthe, I wilbe bound yn as moche as I am worthe. Ther Ynglysse ys not perffett. I coud not macke no fferder [7] serche to try any better then thes, the tyme was so schorte, as yowr seruaunt Herry can aserten yow [8]; but in contenent a pone the syzth off yowr letter y causyd wrastelyng gamys to be mad, to the entent I wolde have the beste. Yff hyt wolde plesse yow to avertes the Kyngys good Grace, yff he commaunde me by hys letter or oder wysse [9] to serve hym yn thys jernay, I wilbrynge with me vj. or viij[th]. Ther schalbe no better off ther bygnes [10] come owte off that partes, and at my comyng uppe yowr Maysterscyppe schalle see them all tryyd by ffor any man see them doo any ffett; and yff ye lyck [11] any off them better then thys ij. ye schalhave yowr plesar yn thys and yn all that ever I can doo whylle I leve, God wyllyng, how ever have yow yn hys blessyd keppyng with longe lyffe and prosperyte. Wrytyn at my powr howsse, the xiiij[th] day off June.

Yowrs to hys lytyll power
Will'm Godolphyn.

1. duty
2. due
3. humble
4. Lordship
5. feat of wrestling
6. household
7. further
8. assure
9. otherwise
10. of their size
11. like

X-8   Bryan Tuke to Thomas Lord Cromwell

One of the most universal concerns of daily life is an inefficient postal service. We learn from Bryan Tuke that the state of England's mails in 1533 incensed the King. By 1538 Tuke held three offices: Master of the Posts, Clerk of the Signet, and Treasurer of the Chamber.

17 August, 1533

Right worshipful Sir, in my best maner I recōmende me unto you. By your lettres of the xijth of this moneth, I perceyve that there is grete defaulte in conveyance of Lettres, and special men ordeyned to be sent in post, and that the Kings pleasure is that Posts be better appointed and laide [1] in all places most expedient, with comaundment to alot wushippes,[2] in al places, on payn of life, to be in suche redynes and to make suche provision of horses at al tymes as no tract,[3] or losse of tyme, be had in that behalf.

Sir, it may like you to understande the Kings Grace hathe no moo[4] ordinary posts, ne of many days hathe had, but bitwene London and Calais, and they in no wags save the post of London in xij[d]. and Calais iiij[d]. by day; but riding by the jorney: whereof most parte passe not ij. in a moneth. And sens Octobre last the posts northeward every on at xij[d]. by day. Thise in wags be bounde but to on horse, whiche is inough for that wags; albe it som of them have moo. I never used other ordre but to charge the towneshippes to lay and appoint suche a post as they wol answer for; and Butler, the Kings messenger for thise northeward, was sent, when I laide them, to see them sufficient. And surely the Postes northeward, in tyme past, have ben the most delegent of al other. Wherfore, supposing by my conjecture that the default is there, I incontinently sent thorough them a writing, sharpe inough, shewing their defaults, the Kings high displeaser, and the daunger. I also wrote al the towneships that way semblably,[5] towching obeyng of placards

1. situated
2. magistrates
3. delay
4. more
5. similarly

and other writings sent for provision of post horses. Nowe, Sir, if the default be ellis where [6] where posts lye, I, upon knowlege had from you, wol put to it the best remedy I can: but if in any other wayes like ordre shalbe taken, I pray you advertise me; ffor, Sir, ye knowe wel that except the hakney horses bitwene Gravesende and Dovor, there is no suche usual conveyance in post for men in this realme, as is in the accustumed places of France and other parties. Ne [7] men can kepe horses in redynes withoute som way to bere the charges; but when placards be sent for suche cause, the constables many tymes be fayn [8] to take horses oute of plowes and carts, wherin can be no extreme diligence.[9] This I write lest the tract shulde be imputed there it is not; but, Sir, not taking upon me to excuse the Posts I wol advertise you that I have knowen in tymes past folks whiche for their own thanke have dated their Lettres a day or ij. or more bifore they wer writen, and the Conveyers have had the blame. As to Posts betwene London and the Corte, there be nowe but ij. wherof the on is a good robust felowe, and was wont to be diligent, evil intreated many tymes; he and other posts, by the herbigeors,[10] for lak of horserome or horsmete, withoute whiche diligence can not be. The other hathe ben the most payneful felowe in nyzt [11] and day that I have knowen amongs the messengers. If he nowe slak he shalbe changed, as reason is; he sueth to the Kings Grace for som smal living for his olde service, having never had ordinary wages til nowe, a moneth or litle more, this posts wages. It may please you to advertise me in whiche of them ij. ye fynde default, and he shal be changed. I wrote unto my lorde of Northumberlande to write on the bak of his pacquetts the houre and day of the depeche,[12] and so I did to other, but it is seldome observed. I wol also desire you to remember that many tymes happen ij. depeches in a day on way, and somtyme moo, and that, often seasons, happen countre posts; [13] that is to ride bothe northeward and southewarde. This is moche for on horse or on man. My lorde of Northumberlande hathe sent a post, my Lorde Dacres an other in the nek of hym, they of Berwike a iij.ᵈ, and somtyme Sir George Lawson, aparte, an other, and in the same tyme depeches from hens [14] northewarde. Nowe I have advertised you of the premysses, it may please you I may knowe the Kings further pleaser, and I shall according to my most bounden duetye diligently obeye the same by Godds grace who preserve you. At my poore house, the xvij[th] day of August, 1533.

Al at your commaundment,

Brian Tuke.

6. elsewhere
7. No
8. inclined
9. rapidity
10. graziers
11. night
12. despatch
13. round-trip service
14. hence

X-9   Pietro Aretino to Agostino Ricchi

In contrasting the qualities of two lively seasons, Pietro Aretino
(1492-1556) argues persuasively for the merits of winter over summer.

Venice, 10 July, 1537

If knowledge and learning, my son, were as important as living well, I would
implore you to go on with your appointed studies. But since living well comes first,
I beg you instead to hie you hither. For here you need not torment your mind
about the devilish subtleties of Aristotle. Here your one occupation will be to
keep yourself sane while the frenzy of this heat wave endures which is so trying to
our patience and our poor frames.

As far as I am concerned, I would much rather see the snow falling from the sky
than to be scorched by the so-called balmy breezes. God's truth, indeed, winter
seems to me an abbot who floats downstream in comfortable ease, taking just a
little too much pleasure in eating and sleeping and doing that other thing. But
summer is a rich and noble harlot, who, drenched with cheap perfume, throws
herself down disgusted and does nothing but drink and drink again. Nor are the
iced wines and flower-decked rooms, with whatever man-made breezes and dishes
of galantined meat that June or July can imagine, worth the crust of buttered
bread which you eat before the fire in December or January, tossing off several
glasses of wine, the while, turning the spit, you steal a piece of roast pork
therefrom, and do not trouble yourself about your mouth and your fingers, both of
which are burned during the theft.

At night—this is in winter—you climb into a bed which a warming pan has
already made ready for you, and there you embrace your companion, or better
still, all huddled up and under the covers, you take comfort in the pervasive heat.
The rain and the thunder and fury of the north wind only keep you firm in your
resolve not to get up until day.

In contrast, who can put up with the cruel torturing of fleas, bed-bugs,
mosquitoes, and flies? Especially when they are added to the other unpleas-
antnesses of summer? You lie stark naked upon your pallet, and your rogue
of a serving man has a good laugh as he hears you fussing and fretting. But he runs

off as soon as he thinks you have closed your eyes. You wake up in the midst of the first good sleep you have had. You begin to sweat again. You drink and pant and toss this way and that. You wish that it were possible to flee from yourself and to get out of your own body. So great is the unpleasantness of the suffocating heat that it almost makes you die even as it drenches you.

Indeed, if it were not for your craving for melons, those pimps of the appetite, which almost overpowers you, and makes you long for the days when they are in season, you would cry a pox on the hot weather just as ragged beggars cry a pox on the cold. But there are many who like the summer just because of its plentiful fruit. They praise the artichokes, the cherries, the figs, the peaches, and the grapes as if the truffles, the olives, and the chard of winter were not worth them all.

Over and above that, there is better conversation around a roaring fire than there is under the shadow of a handsome beech tree, for under the beech tree you need a thousand harlot tricks to whet your appetite. You must have the song of birds, the murmur of the water, the sighing of the breezes, the freshness of the grass and other such trifles. But you only need four well-seasoned logs to provide all that is necessary for a conversation of four or five hours, with chestnuts on a platter and a jug of wine between your knees.

Yes, we should love winter, for it is the spring of genius. But, to return to our own affairs, I tell you again that you should hie yourself hither. For our Messer Niccolo Franco,[1] that best and most learned of youths, has found himself his own room where he can lie off and take his ease and he has summoned to it a thousand gay young blades.

I have nothing more to say to you, except that you must deign to commend me to Signor Sperone [2] and to Ferraguto.[3]

X-10   Pietro Aretino to Domenico Bolani

To his landlord, Domenico Bolani, Aretino recounts the gratifications afforded by his home on the Grand Canal.

1. Secretary of Aretino later hanged for writing satires against Pope Paul IV.

2. Sperone Speroni, a learned playwright and philologist who died the year this letter was written.

3. Ferraguto di Lazzara, a close friend who "supposedly twice saved Aretino's life from assassins in Rome" (Chubb).

Venice, 27 October, 1537

It seems to me, honored sir, that I would commit the sin of ingratitude, if I did not repay with praises some part of the debt which I owe to the heavenly site on which your house stands. I now dwell in that house with more happiness than I have ever had in my life.

For it is so placed that neither above it nor below it, neither if it were here nor there, could you find the slightest improvement. As a result, I am almost as afraid to begin upon its merits as I would be to begin upon those of the Emperor.

Certainly its builder chose for it the high honor of the finest place upon the Grand Canal, and since that canal is the patriarch of all others, and since Venice is the Lady Pope of all cities, I can truthfully say that I enjoy both the finest highway and the most jocund view in all the world.

I never look out of my windows at the hour when the merchants foregather that I do not see a thousand persons and as many gondolas. On my right hand, are the meat markets and the fish markets. On my left hand are the Bridge and the warehouses of the German Merchants. In the middle, is the Rialto, that gathering place of busy men.

There are grapes in the barges, game and game birds in the shops, and vegetables laid out upon the pavement. Nor do I have to long for streams rippling through the meadows when every morning I can gaze upon waters that are covered with every sort of different thing, each one in its own season.

What a ball I have when I watch those who bring great quantities of fruit and vegetables passing them ashore to those who carry them to the booths set up for them! All is animated confusion, except perhaps aboard the twenty to twenty-five sailboats laden with melons. Moored side by side, they make a sort of island, and then the crowd surges aboard them sniffing and weighing to find out whether the cargo was of high quality or not.

Of the good wives, seated proudly in their gondolas and gleaming in silk and gold and jewels, I will not speak. I do not wish to advertise their pomp and circumstance. But I will say that I cracked my jaws laughing at the hoots, whistles, and catcalls which the gondoliers hurled at those who had themselves rowed about by servants without scarlet breeches.

And who would not have guffawed until he wet himself if he had seen a boatload of Germans who had just reeled out of a tavern capsize into the cold waters of the canal? That is what Giulio Camillo[1] and I did. Giulio is the good fellow who pleasantly remarked that the land entry to my house is like the terrible name that I have earned for myself by spewing forth the truth. That is because it is dark, badly designed, and has a broken-down stairway. But he then added that anyone who came to know me, would find that my disinterested, straightforward

---

1. A learned polyglot and classicist from Friuli.

and innate friendship gave you the same tranquil contentment that you found in passing through its portico and coming out upon the balcony above.

Nothing is lacking which might delight my eyes. For, look you, on one side I am able to gaze on the orange trees that gild the base of the Palazzo de'Camerlinghi and on the other on the little canal and on the bridge of San Giovanni Crisostomo, nor does the winter sun ever deign to rise and shine without first sending word to my bedroom, to my study, to my chambers and my great hall.

Yet more even than by that, am I pleased by the distinction of my neighbors. For just across the piazza dwells His Eloquent and Honorable Magnificence, Maffeo Lioni.[2] It was his genius that instilled learning, science and good manners into the fine intellects of Girolamo, Piero and Luigi, his most admirable sons. There too dwells Angela Sirena, life and inspiration of my studies, and the magnifico Francesco Mocinigo who is always giving splendid feasts to knights and gentlemen. Next door is the worthy Messer Giambattista Spinelli whose paternal dwelling place sheltered my friends, the Cavorlini—may God pardon Fortune for the wrongs done to them by Fate! Nor do I consider the least of my blessings the dear and pleasant propinquity of Monna Jacopa.

In short, if I could nourish my touch and other senses as I can my sight, the room which I praise would be paradise, since in it I can satisfy myself with all the pleasures which these loved objects give it.

And I must not forget either the great foreign and Venetian lords who are continually passing me as I stand at my door, nor the pride which lifts me up to heaven when I see the *Bucentaur* plying hither and thither, nor the regattas, nor the festivals which are always being celebrated in the canal which I look down on like a lord. And what too of the lights? After dusk they seem like stars which have been scattered upon those very places where they sell what we need for our feastings and our banquets? And what of the music? What of the harmonies that sooth my ears all night long?

I could far more easily express the profound judgement which you have in things literary and in the affairs of state than I could come to the end of the delights I see before me. And I assure you that if any genius breathes in the trifles which I have written, it comes not from the light and not from the shade, not from the violet nor from the verdant, but from the inspiration which is given me by them from the airy happiness of this your mansion.

May God grant that I live out in it in health and vigor those years which a man of good deeds ought to have!

(See also Letter III-12 on Aretino's enthusiasm for the scenic charms of Venice.)

2. Of these assorted neighbors, the one outstanding figure was Maffeo Lioni, a statesman of promise who was unseated and exiled for selling classified information to the King of France.

X-11   Pietro Aretino to Giovan Manenti

Aretino ridicules the victims of Giovan Manenti's lottery in Venice, lured into gambling away their entire possessions by those "gypsy sisters" Hope and Luck.

                                       Venice, 3 December, 1537

My good friend, when I heard the curses of sixty thousand persons rained upon you—those sixty thousand who were as good as hung, drawn and quartered when they lost their hope of winning in the lottery—I boiled over in your defense into my most vigorous language. In the end, I had silenced some of those wrong-headed fellows who were insisting that you were the inventor of gambling. I can assure you that I defended you against their ill-will far better than a bushel basket of scimitars would have.

For actually this new mania is the invention of Luck, who is a tomfool, and Hope, who has a whore's morals. These two take a fiendish pleasure in setting up a thousand gallows so that the swindled can first deny God, and then hang themselves. They are like gypsy sisters at the fair of Folingo or Lanciano, who dupe one man, and show up as a ninny the next who comes along. Hope leads the gullible forward, and Luck hauls them back again. They both say they are trying to be helpful. They are. Their victims still have their purses, but they are empty as pricked bladders.

I say the deuce with Hope, the deuce with Luck. If we knew we would not find these two bitches in Satan's home, everybody would be happy enough to go there. They are a cogging, cheating pair, and when they have cut the weasand of some worthy fellow, they go into ecstasies just as peasants do when they munch buttered bread. But wait a minute! Is this Lottery of yours a man or woman? For my part I think he is hermaprodite, since we speak both of Messer Chance and Lady Luck.

Anyway, the mountebank who manages its affairs * must be the stoutest-hearted rogue in Italy, since he ruins such a mort of men at one fell swoop. He makes whores fall in love with his gambling device, while the rabble and the artisans hang

---

* The professional gambler Manenti.

at his tail. Yes, as soon as he set up his booth in the piazza, twelve thousand devotees come packing to it. The Ark of the Covenant, Noah's Ark, the Temple of Solomon, and the Synagogues disgorge, while up come whole cohorts of priests, and hierarchies of friars, followed by a mob of bankrupts and half desperate men.

When they are assembled, the sly fellow stands there, looking like an innocent body who has just gathered a basket of snails by lanthorn light, and is beside himself with astonishment to see them stick their horns out. Then he sets out his miserly prizes: his cups, rings, collars and small change. After that, with almost lustful relish, he starts to banter with the crowd of idle good-for-nothings who have come up to see the show.

Sometimes he almost splits with inward laughter, as, for example, when some man or other gives him a look out of the corner of his eye, heaves two heartfelt sighs, and then says to himself: "Why not? Maybe this time?"

Another wishful thinker puts out his hand. He imagines that he has won a ring or a chain. He can see himself placing it on his finger or around his neck.

The rest paw at the beakers and the basins. They are theirs already—or at least so they fondly believe.

Here is a man who lays down all his ducats, while a second pledges his possessions, and a third his houses. I see the press of people swarming forward in a kind of frenzy. They trample on and suffocate each other in their surge to buy the tickets.

And what language they use! It is the ugliest, most villainous, silliest, wittiest, dirtiest and most diabolic in the world. They take words from the Psalms, Gospels, Epistles and Calendar of the Saints! Whole verses and half verses! I could write about it till the Day of Judgment damns them all. But it is all merely lady-talk to those who want to throw away their money.

The tragic thing is that men without a *soldo* have their heads turned by it. I don't know how many sell the very beds they lie on just to buy two tickets.

A widow speaks to the village priest. He wears only a ragged robe.

"Take this chaplet," she says, "and say the Mass of St. Gregory for my poor benighted soul!"

"To the devil with masses!" answers his reverence. "It won't be long now before I can defecate on the burned-down candles!"

Then he gives two little dogtrots to show what he thinks of the Church, and explains to the worthy lady that the three *lire* he has invested in the lottery will keep him for the rest of his life.

A country bumpkin comes up. He always wanted to see a scene like this, and when he learns that six *marcelli* can win something, he sells his rough cloak to get them. As far as he is concerned, the winnings are as good as his already.

"I'll never touch a spade again," cries he. "Not even the one Christ used when he was a gardener!"

I myself once had a groom who served me for a long time, and he was all swollen with pride because he had acquired three of the bits of paper which they use in these affairs. When I cursed because I didn't have a coin, he said to me: "Don't give up hope, master. I am not the kind who will let you down!"

How many housewives spend all their allowance in this business? How many harlots have squandered all they have earned in the weary treadmill of their trade? How many servants have lost their Sunday-go-to-meeting clothes? I tell you it would be a good thing for all those who are going to get rich in the lottery if they never drew a number, for as long as the prizes belong to nobody, everyone has gained one, and at that time the air around the place is sweet as Araby the Blest because so many gardens have been planted there by those two gardeners, Hope and Luck.

By God, it would be a comedy that would make the whole world die laughing if I should ever write a book about the thoughts that arise when the six thousand zechins of the lottery are about to be distributed. One man is going to refurnish his chambers. Another will buy embroidered tapestries. Another will buy prancing steeds. A fourth man will put his money in the bank. A fifth man has doweries for his daughters. The last one will invest in a farm.

The groom that I spoke of above writes to his father that he is going to buy a palace with its gardens from a man who wants money to win with, and that he doesn't care whether he pays a hundred more or less for it. Everybody is happy except those who have sold the winning tickets and kept the losing ones.

"Go away and don't bother to hang yourself!" cries a fellow who just sold a lucky number and kept—as the pedants say—"the white leaves blow away."

And how does everybody feel at the moment when the longed-for drawing is made? They throng about the stand which is very high and is so well-appointed that you would think that Master Gambling had just taken a wife, or Dame Fortune was about to get married. The gambler's assistant has already plunged his hand into one of the urns. It is well-filled with tickets. Everybody's heart is in his throat, and they are all eyes and all ears as they gaze upon the fellow. He laughs merrily and then in a loud voice, he first reads the number, and then calls out: "White!"

But a prize is no sooner handed out than a thousand simpletons cease their babble and their faces fall, and when the grand prize has been awarded, Hope shouts "It's all over with!" and then decamps, leaving them in the same frame of mind that an army is left when a lily-livered general surrenders it. Indeed, anyone who has seen one of these mobs disperse knows what the household of Pope Leo was like when it returned weeping from his funeral. They had to live on the gifts they had picked up during the forty days grace they had before the papacy was given over to misers.

So I tell you that he is a wise man who, amid all these mad doings which they still permit to go on, is proud that he has played for, locked up, and used the money won by the last tickets he will ever buy in this fine business.

In the meantime, those who insist that Fortune has stripped them naked and are as angry as if she had taken their lives away, mouth their imprecations at your Lordship. And if it were not for the friends who defend you from their wrath just as I have, you would be worse off than those who are in despair after the winners have been listed and their names are not among the lucky ones.

X-12   Pietro Aretino to Simon Bianco

Aretino lauds the simple mode of living adopted by his friend Simon Bianco, a Tuscan sculptor and resident of Venice.

Venice, 25 June, 1538

To me, who would not change my state for half a dukedom, has come a thousand times the strange whim that I would like to be you. This is not because I know you to be a handsome fellow, an excellent sculptor, and a very loyal friend. It is rather because you have found out how to live in the world without being a part of it, and being in it and yet not being a part of it, you can laugh both at those who are better off and those who are worse off than you are.

You certainly conduct yourself in a happy-go-lucky way. You shun company when you are at home and seek it when you go abroad, so that in one person you are both a lonely hermit and a man of affairs. Indeed, what happiness, what beatitude, yea even what glory will be his, who knows how to, and who can, and who is willing to follow your example? Woe's me! I waste my money and wear out my spirit by being a slave to the foolish demands of my servants!

But what a pleasant world is that of those who return to the honest ways of nature, of those who observe her modest laws in a sober manner, of those who content themselves with minding their own business, who don't want to leave it to dumb animals to be the only ones to show this common sense.

Take your own case. You return at evening to your humble shack. It is just large enough for the kind of life you have chosen. You don't have to worry about a grumbling wife who would nag just as much if you came home early as if you came home late. If your coals banked with ashes have not burned out, you can light your candles with a quarter of a sulphur taper. If they have, you can call to your neighbor. She will hand you a faggot through her window or pass you a red-hot charcoal on a platter. After that, tossing a bundle of sticks upon the hearth, you can sit like an unbreeched friar in front of the roaring blaze. Humming a snatch of song, you can lounge there until you feel hungry. Then, turning your kidneys toward the fireplace, you can start in with the appetite of a fisherman on the salad you have dressed or the sausages you have grilled. You can lift up your wine keg, and drink out of the bunghole without worrying about the faces that some whorish maidservant or some brigand of a man servant may be making behind your back. Then you can turn toward the fire and study your own shadow. Sitting when you sit and rising when you rise, it pays humble reverence to Your Lordship who is whiling away his time by exchanging gossip with the cat or reading about the frenzied doings of other people.

When sleep assails you, all you need to do is to say "pleasant dreams" or "good night" to yourself, and then climb into bed. You have made it with your own hands and scarcely bother about clean linen twice a month. You say an *avemaria* and a *paternoster* and make the sign of the cross, and no other prayers are needed since he who has no servants has no sins. You put your head down upon a feather bolster. It would take a monstrous big thunderstorm to awaken you.

In the morning you get up, and rejoicing in your happy skill, you wait until two slices of bacon or a small omelet or some roast pork bids you to be seated. Then having lifted up your drinking glass, shaken off your tablecloth, and replaced it on a table which is always set and is always presided over by a generous firkin of wine which fills you with delight whenever you look at it, you eat to live and do not live to eat.

After breakfast you go out—at whatever time suits your convenience—and with a few *soldi* furnish yourself with liver and lights or a sheepshead all ready to be soaked in pungent sauces. You buy a small mess of fish, or some eggs which have just been brought in fresh from the farm. You honor Easter and its solemn festivities with fat capons and little broilers. You pay tribute to All Saints' Day with its goose. Nor do you ever return to that inn of yours without a radish in your hands and mixed greens in your scarf. And you go singing as you do this.

In summer, you come back with plums, or with ten figs, two clusters of muscatels and a bunch of grapes, or you even take a chance and buy a small melon, bright in luster and slender of stem though heavy in weight. You take it home with you. Then, since you always like cold water to glint upon the table, you plunge your fat water jug into the well bucket and thrusting your nose and a knife into the said melon and finding it juicy and sweet, you have a feast worthy of the Pope. You swallow two slices of it at one mouthful, and flavor penetrates your very bones. Thereupon you cry: "The deuce with courts! They give you nothing but dry meat or stale cheese to eat. It is madness to live any other kind of life than this!" Yet you know that only a lout makes his gullet a paradise for foods and his belly a valise for viands.

I can assure you that I get sleepy myself when I think of your after-dinner nap. I can see you nodding in armchair. With your head on your shoulders, you doze peacefully. You leave cares behind you for almost twenty minutes.

Then you get up, make a bundle of your dirty linen, and give it to the woman who fills your lamp for you and lays your fire, nor do you curse her and go from street to street complaining of the soap and wood she uses up while she is washing and bleaching your laundry.

"To be sure, I spend a penny! Nevertheless you have to send it to a wash-erwoman."

But someone might say, as I celebrate your solitary way of life:

"What provision does he make for sickness and other misfortunes?"

You leave that to the goodness of God and to the will of Christ, whose mercy forsakes no one. His grace keeps you in good health while you tire yourself out with a fine piece of marble, carving it into heads as excellent as those the Cinami sent to the King of France. And if a longing for high living assails you, you answer it by plying your chisel and mallet, and if it still tempts you, if you still cannot attain it, you remind yourself not that "he who has hands has riches" but rather "wherever there is even the smallest coin, there is confusion." And that even the cricket can enjoy himself if he indulges in the whim of taking short hops from the Rialto without even giving a thought to the peace treaty that was made at Nice and the council that was not called at Vicenza.

And now let us pass from your joys to my troubles which are so infinite in number that they almost seem like the lottery tickets of Manenti. I will not speak of my good name being crucified, nor of my being swindled in my accounts, nor robbed when I spend money, nor having my strongboxes rifled (this would be folly), but rather how cruelly my Ambrogio slaughtered me.* I hope that is the last trick he ever plays. I am convinced that he was only persuaded to do it by inflated opinion of themselves that people always have when a little talent makes them arrogant. They think that they are more worthy to command than obey. It is true that I seem to have had revenge on him, for I saddled him with the punishment of a wife. I only wish that I could make him have two of them. Then he would run back and forward all day from Purgatory to Hell and from Hell to Purgatory.

But to go back to the matter of servants, a certain bishop, who was the most hapless of priests, knew what he was talking about. When he was at death's door, he turned to a friar who was tormenting him by asking him to think about his soul.

* This refers to the time Ambrogio collected 600 crowns for Aretino from the King of France and then lost them gambling with Cardinal Gaddi.

"I don't mind about Satan at all," he said, "unless he has serving men in his house."

Giannozzo Pandolfini once vowed that if he got well from his illness, he would then kill himself just so that he need never have another servant. He had one who, among other ways of plaguing him, split his head while he was raging with fever by playing on a rebec day and night.

So you are thrice blessed who never have to have a servant and when you need one are both your own servant and your own master.

X-13   Thomas Lord Cromwell to the Earl of Chester

Although Cervantes's famous tale of the gypsies depicted them as gay, musical people (with some thievery thrown in), most Renaissance peoples viewed their nomadic incursions as a plague. They were expelled from France in 1560, from Spain in 1591. England cast them out even earlier, as we see below, weary of their widespread violence, robbery, deception, falsehoods, felonies, and treasons. Thomas Lord Cromwell (1485?-1540) handled the situation with his usual efficiency.

5 December, 1538

After my right hartie commendations. Whereas the Kings Maiestie, about a twelfmoneth past, gave a pardonne to a company of lewde [1] personnes within this realme calling themselves Gipcyans, for a most shamfull and detestable murder commytted amongs them, with a speceall proviso inserted by their owne consents, that onles they shuld all avoyde this his Graces realme by a certeyn daye long sythens expired, yt shuld be lawfull to all his Graces offycers to hang them in all places of his realme, where they myght be apprehended, without any further examynacion or tryal after forme of the lawe, as in their letter patents of the said pardon is expressed. His Grace, hering tell that they doo yet lynger here within his realme, not avoyding the same according to his commaundement and their owne promes, and that albeit his poore subjectes be dayly spoyled, robbed, and deceyved by them, yet his Highnes officers and Ministres lytle regarding their dieuties towards his Majestye, do permyt them to lynger and loyter in all partys, and to

1. ignorant, unlearned.

exercise all their falshods, felonyes, and treasons unpunished, hathe commaunded me to sygnifye unto youe, and the Shires next adjoynying, whether any of the sayd personnes calling themselfes Egipcyans, or that hathe heretofore called themselfes Egipcyans, shall fortune to enter or travayle in the same. And in cace youe shall here or knowe of any suche, be they men or women, that ye shall compell them to depart to the next porte of the See to the place where they shalbe taken, and eyther wythout delaye uppon the first wynde that may conveye them into any parte of beyond the Sees, to take shipping and to passe in to owtward partyes, or if they shall in any wise breke that commaundement, without any tract [2] to see them executed according to the Kings Hieghnes sayd Lettres patents remaynyng of Recorde in his Chauncery which, with these, shalbe your discharge in that behaulf: not fayling t'accomplishe the tenor hereof with all effect and diligence, without sparing uppon any Commyssion, Licence, or Placarde that they may shewe or aledge for themselfes to the contrary, as ye tender his Graces pleasor which also ys that youe shall gyve notyce to all the Justices of Peax in that Countye where youe resyde, and the Shires adjoynant, that they may accomplishe the tenor hereof accordingly. Thus fare ye hertely wel; From the Neate the vth day of December the xxix[th] yer of his Ma[ties] most noble Regne

Yo[r] louyng ffreend
Thomas Crumwell.

X-14   Girolamo Lippomano to the Doge of Venice (?)

Girolamo Lippomano, Venetian ambassador to the French capital, observes that Paris in the sixteenth century—as always—eats well.

n.d. (1540?)

Paris has an abundance of everything that could be desired; wares from all countries abound there: provisions are brought there by way of the Seine from Normandy, Auvergne, Burgundy, Champagne and Picardy. Therefore, though the population is numerous, nothing is lacking: everything seems to fall from heaven. The price of foodstuffs there, however, is a bit high, to tell the truth,

---

2. stay, hesitation.

because the French spend for nothing else as willingly as for eating and for what they call setting a sumptuous table. That is why butchers, dealers of meats and roasts, peddlers, pastry-cooks, inn-keepers and restaurateurs are found in such vast quantities that it actually creates confusion. There is no street, however inconspicuous, that does not have its share of them. Do you wish to buy livestock at the market, or else meat? You can do it at any time in any place. Do you wish your foods all prepared, cooked or raw? The roasters and pastry-chefs in less than an hour will organize a dinner for you, a supper for ten, twenty or a hundred people: the roast-meat dealer provides you with the meat, the pastry-chef the pastes, pies, first course and desserts; the cook gives you jellies, sauces and seasonings. This art is so advanced in Paris that there are inn-keepers at whose establishments you can dine for any price; for a *teston,** for two, for a crown, for four, for ten, for twenty even per person, if you so desire. But, for twenty crowns, you will be given, I hope, a tureen of heavenly porridge or roast phoenix, in short, the greatest delicacies in the world. The princes and the king himself go there sometimes (as Duke Lodovico of Milan was wont to do, when he was alive). . . .

(trans. L.L.)

X-15   John Calvin to his friend Sachinus

Protestantism grew quickly in the industrial and commercial areas of Northern Europe, which needed money for their capitalistic development and were willing to borrow it at a modest rate. The first prominent theologian to attack the traditional Catholic condemnation of usury was Calvin (1509-1564). He felt that an interest rate of 5% was ethical, and urged observance of the Golden Rule in all transactions. Thus, interest should never be charged against the poor.

1545

While I have had no experience myself, I have learned from the example of others how dangerous it is to give an answer to the question on which you ask my

---

* *teston:* coins newly minted in 1513 and carrying a head, hence the name; of slight value.

advice. For if we wholly condemn usury, we impose greater fetters on the conscience than God himself. Yet if we permit it in the least, many under this pretext will take an unbridled liberty which can then be held in bounds by no restriction. If I were writing to you alone, I should have no fear, for I know well your prudence and restraint: but since you are asking for another, I fear that he may gather a little more permission from my words than I wish. However, since I have no doubt that you will act with discretion according to the nature of the man and the circumstances, I will tell you how the matter seems to me.

In the first place, by no testimony of the Scriptures is usury wholly condemned. For the meaning of the saying of Christ, commonly thought to be very clear, i.e., "Lend, hoping for nothing again" (Luke 6:35) has been perverted. As elsewhere in speaking of the sumptuous feasts and ambitious social rivalry of the rich he commands rather that they invite in the blind, the lame and the poor from the streets who cannot make a like return, so here, wishing to curb abuses in lending, he directs us to loan chiefly to those from whom there is no hope of receiving anything. . . . The words of Christ mean that he commends serving the poor rather than the rich. Thus we do not find all usury forbidden.

The law of Moses (Deut. 23:19) was political, and should not influence us beyond what justice and philanthropy will bear. It could be wished that all usury, and even the name, were banished from the earth. But since this is impossible, it is necessary to concede to the common good.

We have passages in the Prophets and Psalms in which the Holy Spirit inveighs against usury. Thus a city is described as wicked because usury is found in its market-place and streets. (Ps. 55:11) But as the Hebrew word here means *fraud* in general, the passage can be otherwise interpreted. Even if we grant that the prophet speaks explicitly of usury, it is not surprising that among the great evils of his time he should mention it, for with an improper use of usury, cruelty and many evil deceptions are often joined. . . .

It is said in praise of a holy and God-fearing man that "he putteth not out his money to usury." * Indeed, it is a very rare thing for a man to be honest and at the same time a usurer. The prophet Ezekiel (Ezek. 22:12) goes even further, for in enumerating the crimes which enflamed the wrath of the Lord against the Jews, he uses two Hebrew words, Nesec and Tarbit: one of which means *usury* and is derived from a root meaning to *consume,* while the second signifies an *increase* or *addition,* doubtless because each man contriving to further his own gain takes or rather extorts it at his neighbor's loss. . . .

Now it is said that today, too, usury should be forbidden on the same grounds as among the Jews, since there is a bond of brotherhood among us. To this I reply,

* Psalms, 15:5.

that in the civil state there is some difference; for the situation in which the Lord had placed the Jews, and many other circumstances, made it easy for them to engage in business among themselves without usury. Our relationship is not at all the same. Therefore I do not consider that usury is wholly forbidden among us, except it be repugnant to justice and charity.

The reasoning of Saint Ambrose and of Chrysostom, that money does not beget money, is in my judgment too superficial. What does the sea beget? What does the land? I receive income from the rental of a house. Is it because the money grows there? The earth produces things from which money is made, and the use of a house can be bought for money. And is not money more fruitful in trade than in any other form of possession one can mention? Is it lawful to let a farm, requiring a payment in return, and unlawful to receive any profit from the use of money? . . .

How do merchants derive their profit? By their industry, you will say. Certainly if money is shut up in a strong-box, it will be barren—a child can see that. But whoever asks a loan of me does not intend to keep this money idle and gain nothing. The profit is not in the money itself, but in the return that comes from its use. It is necessary then to draw the conclusion that while such subtle distinctions appear on the surface to have some weight, they vanish on closer scrutiny, for they have no substance. *I therefore conclude that usury must be judged, not by any particular passage of Scripture, but simply by the rules of equity.*

X-16   Niccolò Martelli to the Countess of Bagno

Niccolò Martelli (1498-1555) was a business man-poet influenced by Luigi Alamanni, the Latin poet, and by Aretino. He was a founder of the Academy of the Umidi. The belief in astrology so widely held even in the enlightened Renaissance (see Chapter IV) leads Martelli to ascribe a flood of the Arno River to the conjunction of Mars and Saturn.

Florence, 10 October 1547

The violent conjunction of Mars and Saturn this year (so say these astrologers after the fact) has caused the occurrence among mortals of terrible and diverse calamities. Among these—not just because they alleged so, but because it must have been true—the death of both Henry King of England and Francis I of France. Then there followed the awful occurrence in Piacenza of the harsh death of Pier Luigi da Farnese, the son of a pope, an event much more memorable for the historians than a simple writer of letters, and so I quickly pass over it. Along with these there came about in our own Tuscany on the thirteenth day of August, when the world should have been scorched with heat, cloudbursts lasting three days and nights, gushing rains to the disaster of all. The sun did not even dare to peer out of his cherished hostel. As a result, the tributaries of the Mugello poured such a quantity of water into the magnificent and turbulent Arno that the Arno, rising up by itself lofty and proud, advanced its banks right into the beautiful city of Florence. And if this swelling of the river had not occurred at two o'clock in the afternoon, there would not have been such multitude of people who perished in the sea of Pharaoh, so many were the bodies a prey of its pitiless, ruinous action.

You could see utensils, pots, beds, earthenware that families out in the country collect all come floating down. And the cute little children and matrons with their children at their breast were a pity to behold. Some of them were dragged down afloat by their tresses wound around trunks and bramble bushes. Others came floating down the river just as the waves disposed of them, prey to the freedom of whoever wanted to see them.

Oils, wheat, grains, which the poor people drowned trying to fish out of the water. It was pitiful! Not merely content with this, as they became city-borne, the waves of the rollicking, overflowing Arno entered with its swollen pressures the loggias and downstairs rooms, making prey of so many goods that it seemed that the Arno should have been assuaged. Timbers of walnut and furniture encrusted with gold, similar pompous beds made by fathers and ancestors for the ancient nobility of the household were the first despoiled furnishings to flow out of their ordained places. And the draperies and costly clothing, lined with very rich furs and other soft materials which had been placed in the downstairs closets as a security against the heat, it was necessary to throw them away after they had been coated and corrupted by the slime. And there was no way that anyone could save himself from loss or take provision against it, since the Arno arrived so impetuously that it did not hesitate to strike the side and the rialto of the ducal palace of His Illustrious Excellency. Persons just let their belongings become prey to the river, knowing no other way to make their escape themselves. Slime accumulated within the houses and spread out onto the streets. So much of it remained inside that three huge thresholds would not have sufficed for it to ooze out and leave the inside dry. And thus, Illustrious Lady, was this nice overflow that harmed everyone, ruined bridges, spoiled palaces, and especially in the countryside, where the olives were spoiled by too much rain and mist, the grapes and the vines deprived of their accustomed support by oaks and elms have reduced the profit of the farmer's harvest. There is an infinity of other damages which, not to be tedious, I shall spare you. Have compassion on me, pardon and command me, as your good servant. May the Lord God keep you happy and content in His grace.

(trans. R.J.C.)

X-17   Pietro Aretino to Francesco Coccio

Reversing himself on a long-held opinion, Aretino admits to the poet Francesco Coccio that ordinary domestic servants are frequently wellsprings of wisdom and wit.

Venice, April 1548

Who could ever have believed that two of my maids would make me understand something that no learned man has ever been able to show me?

In everything I have ever written about comedy, I have always criticized those authors who put witty sayings into the mouths of menials. It seemed to me that they had badly observed what comported with a servant's character.

But Monsignor Montluc,* not long ago French ambassador here, a literary man and one well informed about the way things really are, spoke in defense of the ancient comedies, with which he was very familiar. He insisted that there was nothing to marvel at in the fact that people of this sort spewed forth so many words of wisdom, since it was entirely possible that once they had not only been free, but likewise educated. He added that in the hands of the Turk was many a slave whose lineage was noble and whose wits had gone to school.

Once and for all I should have agreed with this statement, for fortune has done many a deed far more evil than forcing a noble spirit to wash dishes and carry pitchers of water. But in these days when you no longer hear hirelings prate about tasty foods and perfect jugs of wine, I persisted in my opinion, until lo and behold,

* Jean de Monluc, Bishop of Valence, served from 1542 as French Ambassador to Venice. He was the brother of the more famous Blaise de Monluc accused of gross cruelty by Montaigne in Letter VII-12.

Lucietta and Maddalena, the first abbess of my kitchen, and the second lady governor of my bedchamber, set me right.

The former, when a basket filled with soiled clothes was upset on her, cried to the other who had carelessly overturned it:

"Discretion is the better part of valor."

The latter said not a word, but stood with her elbow on her knee, and with weary hand under the left side of her chin. The sinister look on her ugly mug made her seem more like a cat that had gone wild than a crafty servant.

I said to her:

"Why do you keep silent?"

"Because," she said, *"you* can't write down saying nothing."

But then, starting to talk to me, her tongue unloosened so many shrewd sayings that I saw that it was not without reason that they put servants on the stage and make them talk the way they do. For they have learned to remember everything good and everything bad which they have ever heard people say.

And so I beg pardon of their memory as many times as I have blamed them wrongly for that for which I now praise them rightly.

X-18   Tommaso Spica to Dionigi Atanagi

Tommaso Spica confesses that he finds country life disagreeable and explains his preference for Rome.

Gubbio, 3 June 1549

These lands of yours, my dear and honored Messer Dionigi, are beautiful indeed, and I certainly believe that searching the Apennines on every side, one could not find there a place like this, which would be beautiful in Latium and delightful in the ancient countryside, especially not among mountains as rugged as these: and were they as good for tilling, they could serve the need for an earthly paradise; but the ground is very barren and very dry so that the peasants around here have to draft the water, as do certain birds whose name I don't remember. But I had my fill of all its beauty at the outset, and I should gladly reside, for instance, at Rome for this reason: if I rise from bed in the morning, looking about I truly see a beautiful and most delightful land; if I return there at mid-day, I again find the same thing; and thus it strikes me also in the evening, and at such other times that I come back and look, so that all my days seem to be of a single cast. Wherefore you can consider how amusing this must be for someone who wishes to see new things.

I used to get more enjoyment in a single hour going for a walk through Rome with you or tarrying in one of those bookstores at Campo di Fiore playing chess with Palatino, than I would have here in an entire epoch seeing trees, grass, mountains and rocks and hearing the sounds of cuckoos, crickets and owls. I have to cater, willy nilly, to my own pleasures. I had therefore at least better arrange my life so as not to remain forever out of step, whence these lines. And this shall be, if you would have me share in some of your beautiful poetry, or that of others, keeping me happy with your letters. Which favor I beg of you with all my might, so that in this way my stay will be less boring for me. Since I arrived here I have had no mind for writing verse, much less for studying, so that if I don't change direction, I suspect I will lead the life of a lazybones.

Commend me to Signor Claudio Tolomeo,* my very solicitous lord, when you see him, and our other mutual friends, Messer Cinthio and Messer Angelo Clavarij. And you, as I've said, deign to write to me and to keep me always in your good graces as I greatly desire. And may Our Lord keep you from harm.

(trans. L.L.)

X-19   Onorio Belli to Alfonso Ragona of Vicenza

From Canea or Khania on the Island of Crete Onorio Belli (died after 1597) describes a widespread earthquake of 1584 which devastated communities on that and neighboring islands. Belli, a distinguished botanist from Vicenza, won fame among Renaissance scientists for his book on plants in Crete and Egypt.

Canea, 22 January, 1585

At five o'clock in the afternoon, last November 11, on a Sunday, the entire Island of Crete and roundabout experienced a horrible earthquake. I have wished

* See Letter VII-10.

to describe it to Your Lordship as best I can. If sometimes you have heard it said that earthquakes can drive men out of their minds, do not smile at the idea. For whoever does not experience fear before such an event must be totally deprived of his senses, the more so if one finds himself at home, as I was that day, writing a letter to Venice. The sky was serene and clear and the sea calm, when one heard a thunderous noise, as though fifteen or twenty carriages were racing over a rocky road. With this came a vibration in the air and a rumbling of the earth and a crashing of houses (accompanied and mixed with stucco, dust, and smoke issuing from the ruins of the fallen walls), and I cannot find any other name for it except hell breaking loose. The land was shaking, the sea was boiling, buildings were crumbling, and the walls and beams and roofs fell with such a roar that who has not seen the spectacle with his own eyes or heard it with his own ears cannot understand of what a diabolical harmony it was composed.

If this misfortune had overcome us at night or in the late evening, it would have killed an infinity of people, but thank God, few are dead. The Franks had just finished attending mass, but the Greeks were still in church. Everyone swore that the vaults of the church had opened up and that they could see the heavens through the fissures, which opened to the width of a foot and then fell closed again. Many churches have suffered damage. The Church of St. Francis is full of crevices, and people swear that they saw its belltower sway over three times and touch the Church of Santa Clara across the street. And yet St. Francis didn't really suffer damage except for a twisted chimney. The tower of Saint Nicolas of the Dominican Friars is loftier and for many years had been threatening to collapse. Yet it was unharmed. The tower with the clock over the city square is smashed to bits. Buildings with fallen walls are swaying perilously. Curiously the newest and most noble homes have suffered the most, while the humble and old ones came off best. Three galleys in the port, along with other boats, were almost engulfed.

The same evils and even greater ones were visited upon the towns of Rettimo and Candia and all over the island of Crete. Even up the archipelago and throughout all the islands the earthquake did much damage, especially at Milo, where some boats from Rhodes fifty or more miles out at sea were said to be sinking. To sum up, every year we feel an earthquake, but in comparison with this one, they're just conversation pieces. When the fury died down, the Greeks marched with Crosses inside and outside the city. There were boys, old men, women, girls together shouting *"Kyrie eleison, Kyrie eleison!"* with great devotion. One felt pity for them. At that moment concord reigned and long-standing enmities disappeared. One sensed a universal fear at the ire of God. Next day the Franks joined the Greeks in processions and everyone fasted for three days. Everyone went to confession and communion, although the Franks show less contrition than the Greeks. Even the peasants, who rarely go to church or mass, abstained and marched from farm to farm. Even the Jews fasted for three days. Many prodigies and miracles happened. I must tell you one. A young man on the shore was sucked in by a tidal wave which scorched all of his limbs severely, like boiling water. He suffered but did not die. The cause of this earthquake, I believe, was the frightful drouth of the autumn and early winter. November was hotter than August. This month, January, is hotter than it would be in March. Already, up to the sixth of November we were without rain. People here were in panic, for up to that time they had not planted yet—an unusual thing in this climate. It finally rained a few times and they have started planting. Yet if this dry spell continues, people here will die of hunger. There is a lack of everything here. Grain is worth six liras a measure, the double of other years. Meat is not to be found. The animals have died of hunger because of the drouth and lack of pasturage. Normally, when it rains in October, there is enough grass for pasturage all winter. This year every meadow is bare and scorched, with only little patches of grass breaking out of the soil. Coming to an end, I kiss your hands.

O. Belli

(trans. R.J.C.)

X-20   Richard Quiney to William Shakespeare

When young Richard Quiney found himself strapped in London, both his father and relative Abraham Sturley explained to him how he might extract thirty pounds from the newly-famous Will Shakespeare offering land as security. Wrote Sturley as early as 24 January, 1598, "We think it a fair mark for him to shoot at and not impossible to hit." A letter from Sturley to Richard Quiney dated in November implies that Shakespeare was willing to help his fellow Cantabrigian, whose son Thomas was in 1616 to marry Shakespeare's youngest daughter Judith.

25 October, 1598

Loveinge Contreyman, I am bolde of yowe as of a ffrende, craveinge yowre helpe with xxx[11] vppon Mr Bushells & my securytee or Mr Myttons with me. M^r

Rosswell is nott come to London as yeate & I have especiall cawse. Yowe shall ffrende me muche in helpeinge me out of all the debettes I owe in London, I thancke god, & muche quiet my mynde which wolde nott be indebeted. I am nowe towardes the Cowrte in hope of answer for the dispatche of my Buysenes. Yowe shall neither loase creddytt nor monney by me, the Lorde wyllinge, & nowe butt perswade yowre selfe soe as I hope & yowe shall nott need to feare butt with all hartie thanckefullenes I will holde my tyme & content yowre ffrende, & yf we Bargaine farther yowe shalbe the paiemaster yowre self. My tyme biddes me hasten to an ende & soe I committ thys (to) yowre care & hope of yowre helpe. I feare I shall nott be backe thys night ffrom the Cowrte. Haste. The Lorde be with yowe & with vs all Amen. ffrom the Bell in Carter Lane the 25 October 1598. Yowres in all kyndenes Ryc. Quyney. [*Addressed*] H(aste) To my Loveinge good ffrend & contreymann M^r W^m. Shackespere deliver thees. [*Seal*] On a bend three trefoils slipped.

X-21   Sir Francis Cottington to Lord Northampton

Although Renaissance courtesy books recommended training in dueling, the kings of the sixteenth and seventeenth centuries tried to outlaw it. With their new national states taking shape, they sought to reduce the feudal privileges of lords who still ruled in the smaller provinces or duchies or who still held feudal titles. When, in the summer of 1613, Edward Lord Bruce of Kinlos and Sir Edward Sackville retired to the Lowlands to fight their bloody duel, the Crown decided that duels staged abroad must be prohibited as well as those fought at home. Sir Francis Cottington (1579-1652) reports here on restrictions imposed by the Spanish Crown.

12 November, 1613

My Good Lord
According to your Lordship's commaundment I was yesterday with the Spanish Embassador, who having understood myn errant and your Lordships pleasure seemed very desirous to give your Lordship satisfaction, and soe fell into a long discourse of the rigorous Lawes (well) practised in Spaine for restrayning and punishing of Challenges and Combates, much to the same effect as I have alredy

delyvered unto your Lordship; only he added that yf in his Masters domynions such jentlemen and noblemen as thes now spoken of, had withdrawn themselves into forraine parts with intention there to have performed a Duella, theyr lands and goods had been immediatly seased, and all thos (as theyr friends, servants, or others,) who had any notice of theyr going, been strictly imprisoned and punished for nott reveling yt, for that theyr lawes doo punish the concealers of a quarrell grown between two Jentlemen (though in a different measure) as well as the parties themselves. As touching the two poynts wherin your Lordship desires to be satisfied; to the first he says, that whosoever shall in Spaine make a chalenge, eyther by word or writing, and after forme yt in forraine partes, shall at his returne be punished with death though he hurt not his adversary, yea and allthough the challenge be allso made wher the combat ys fought; and he who ys the defendant incurrs the same danger yf he aunswer the challenge.

Touching the quallitie of evyll and reprochfull words, he sayes, yt ys ordinaryly left to the judgement and understanding of the Lords, or the tribunall before whom the complaynt ys made; but if any quarrell be lyke to grow through words or otherwayes, both the parties are immediately imprisoned (but not wher all theyr frends and gallants shall visite them and animate them), and none to speake with them but theyr chargable keepers, and have put in seurties to a great valew nott to offend each other.

Yf any of base qualyty shall use disgracefull wordes unto a Jentleman, he is punished by whipping and sent to the Gallics.

What with the strictness of the Lawes in Spaine and the punctual executing of them, the perpetuall disgrace that quarrelling Jentlemen doe fall into with theyr King, and above all the excommunion of the Pope, amongst the subjects of the King of Spaine a quarrell (or at leaste a combate) ys never heard of. I wyll hartely pray for your Lordships good success in soe noble and Christian a busyness as his Majestie hath now imposed on you, and for your long life and health for the comfort of us all.

Your Lordships most dutifull Servant
Fra. Cottington.

London this Sunday
The 12th of Novemb. 1613.

INDEX OF PERSONS

ACKNOWLEDGEMENTS

The editors express thanks to the following copyright holders whose interest and generosity in granting the following permissions encouraged us in the preparation of this anthology:

To Chilton Book Company, Radnor, Penn., for Text III-8, translated by Piero Weiss in his *Letters of Composers through Six Centuries,* 1967. To Columbia University Press, for Text IV-5, translated by Professor Edward Rosen in his *Three Copernican Treatises;* 1939; third edition, Octagon Books, a Division of Farrar Straus and Giroux, 1971. To Columbia University Press, for Text V-8, translated by Louis Israel Newman, in his *Jewish Influence upon Christian Reform Movements,* 1925. To Doubleday & Company, Inc., for Text IV-4 and Text VI-6, translated by Henry Morley, in *A Renaissance Treasury,* edited by Hiram Haydn. Copyright 1953 Hiram Haydn. To Dover Publications, Inc., 180 Varick Street, New York City, for Text II-8, translated by A. M. Nagler, in his *Source Book in Theatrical History,* 1959. To Duke University Press for Text II-3, Text VII-7, and Text IX-1 by Machiavelli, translated by Professor Allan H. Gilbert in his *The Letters of Machiavelli,* 1961. To Mr. Hermann Kesten for Texts I-3, IV-8 and IX-12, translated by Mr. Kesten in his *Copernicus and His World,* Roy Publishers, 1945. To Alfred A. Knopf, Inc., for Text VIII-3, translated by Harriet de Onís, in *Amerigo and the New World,* by Germán Arciniegas, 1955.

To Little, Brown, Publishers, for Text VIII-2, translated by Samuel Eliot Morison in his *Admiral of the Ocean Sea,* 1942. To Liverpool University Press, for Text IX-9, in *Life and Letters of Sir Thomas Wyatt,* by Kenneth Muir, 1963. To Loyola University Press, Chicago, for Text V-13 and Text V-14, translated by William J. Young, S. J., in his *Letters of Saint Ignatius Loyola,* 1959. To Oxford University Press, for Text II-16, in *The Complete Works of Ben Jonson,* edited by C. H. Herford and P. and E. Simpson, vol. I, 1925. To G. P. Putnam's Sons, for Texts IV-14, V-18, V-19, V-22, V-23, VI-16, VI-18, VII-14, VII-16, VII-19, VIII-11, VIII-12, edited by George T. Mathews in his *News and Rumor in Renaissance Europe: The Fugger Letters,* copyright 1959. To Fleming H. Revell Company, Old Tappan, New Jersey, for Text VIII-5, translated by Charles L. G. Anderson in his *Life and Letters of Vasco Nuñez de Balboa,* 1941. To Charles Scribner's Sons for Text IV-11, translated by Charles Ward in his *Oracles of Nostradamus,* revised edition copyright 1940 by Charles Scribner's Sons. To Simon & Schuster, Inc., for Text VII-2 and Text VIII-1, by Leonardo da Vinci and Christopher Columbus, in *A Treasury of the World's Great Letters,* edited by M. Lincoln Schuster, 1940; copyright renewed by Publisher Simon and Schuster, Inc., 1968. To Thames and Hudson, Publishers, London, for Text V-24, translated by Hans Gál in his *The Musicians' World,* 1965. Additional corroborating permission was granted by Arco Publishing Company, New York City. To the Viking Press, Inc., for Text I-4, translated by Mary Martin McLaughlin, in *The Portable Renaissance Reader,* edited by James Bruce Ross and Mary Martin McLaughlin, copyright 1953 by the Viking Press. To the Viking Press, Inc., for Text V-1, translated by H. F. Schwartz, in *The Portable Renaissance Reader,* edited by James Bruce Ross and Mary Martin McLaughlin, copyright 1953 by The Viking Press, Inc. To the Viking Press, Inc., for Text VII-1, translated by Mary Martin McLaughlin, in *The Portable Renaissance Reader,* edited by James Bruce Ross and Mary Martin McLaughlin, copyright 1953 by the Viking Press.

To Archon Books, published by Shoestring Press, for the translations from *The Letters of Pietro Aretino,* by Thomas Caldecot Chubb, 1967. To Victor Gollancz, Ltd., London, for Text I-10, translated by Ernest Boyd in his *Rabelais,* 1929. To Dr. Elizabeth Gilmore (Mrs. John B.) Holt, for Text I-6, from *A Documentary History of Art,* vol. I: Middle Ages to Renaissance, 1957. To Kegan Paul & Co., London, for Text VII-11, from *The Life and Letters of Ogier Ghiselin de Busbeq,* by C. T. Forster, London, 1881. To Cambridge University Press, for Text VI-12, from *The Correspondence between Prince A. M. Kurbsky and Tsar Ivan IV of Russia,* edited by J. L. I. Fennell, Cambridge, 1955. To E. P. Dutton for Text II-2 from J. Cartwright, *Baldassare Castiglione, His Life and Letters,* New York, 1908. To the Philosophical Library, Inc., for Texts III-2, III-3, and V-5, from the *Writings of Albrecht Dürer,* translated by William M. Conway, New York, 1958. To Philosophical Library, for Texas IV-16, IV-17, IV-20, and IV-19, from *Johannes Kepler: Life and Letters,* by Carola Baumgardt, 1952. To McGraw-Hill Book Co., New York, for Text IV-22, translated by Stillman Drake from the Italian biography *Galileo Galilei,* by Ludovico Geymonat, 1965. To the Lutterworth Press, for Texas V-3 and V-4, from *Reformational Writings of Martin Luther,* translated by Bertram Lee Wolfe, London, 1952—. Finally, to Longmans Green, for the many letters of Eramus, translated and edited by Francis Morgan Nichols in *The Epistles of Erasmus,* London, 1901-1918.